DESIGNING WITH OBJECTS

T0314535

DESIGNING WITH OBJECTS

Object-Oriented Design Patterns Explained with Stories from Harry Potter

AVINASH C. KAK
Purdue University

Published by John Wiley & Sons, Inc., Hoboken, New Jersey
Published simultaneously in Canada

For general information on our other products and services or for technical support, please contact our Customer Care Department within the United States at (800) 762-2974, outside the United States at (317) 572-3993 or fax (317) 572-4002.

Wiley also publishes its books in a variety of electronic formats. Some content that appears in print may not be available in electronic formats. For more information about Wiley products, visit our web site at www.wiley.com.

Library of Congress Cataloging-in-Publication Data:

Kak, Avinash C.
  Designing with objects : object-oriented design patterns explained with stories from Harry Potter /
  Avinash C. Kak.
    pages   cm
  Includes index.
  ISBN 978-1-118-58120-9 (paperback)
1. Object-oriented programming (Computer science)   2. Rowling, J. K.–Themes, motives.
3. Rowling, J. K.–Characters.   4. Potter, Harry (Fictitious character)   I. Title.
  QA76.64.K3548 2014
  005.1′17–dc23
                                                                    2014007132

10 9 8 7 6 5 4 3 2 1

CONTENTS

PREFACE   xiv

ACKNOWLEDGMENTS   xix

1   Why Learn Design Patterns and Why Do So with Help from Harry Potter?   **1**

1.1   The OO Design Patterns "Bible" by GoF   2
1.2   But What Has Harry Potter Got to Do with OO Design Patterns?   4
1.3   Is Familiarity with Harry Potter a Requirement for Understanding This Book?   6
1.4   How the Pattern Explanations are Organized   7
1.5   The Terminology of Object-Oriented Programming   7
1.6   The UML Notation Used in the Class Diagrams   12
    1.6.1   Association as a Relationship Between Classes   14
    1.6.2   Aggregation and Composition as Relationships Between Classes   15
    1.6.3   Representing Attributes   16
    1.6.4   Representing Operations   17

I   CREATIONAL PATTERNS   **19**

2   Abstract Factory   **21**

2.1   The Concept of a Factory in Software   21
2.2   Intent and Applicability   22
2.3   Introduction to the Abstract Factory Pattern   22
2.4   The Abstract Factory Pattern in Real-World Applications   23
2.5   Harry Potter Story Used to Illustrate the Abstract Factory Pattern   23
2.6   A Top Level View of the Pattern Demonstration   25

2.7   The Abstract Class Factory   27
2.8   The Helper Class FactoryStore   27
2.9   The Abstract Class Enchanted   30
2.10   The Concrete Classes for Magical Objects   31
2.11   The Concrete Factory Classes   32
2.12   The Client Class Diagon AlleyRetailer   34
2.13   Playing with the Code   36

3 Builder   **38**

3.1   Building Complex Objects   38
3.2   Intent and Applicability   39
3.3   Introduction to the Builder Pattern   39
3.4   The Builder Pattern in Real-World Applications   41
3.5   Harry Potter Story Used to Illustrate the Builder Pattern   42
3.6   A Top-Level View of the Pattern Demonstration   43
3.7   The Abstract Class PotionMaker   45
3.8   The Concrete Extensions of PotionMaker   46
3.9   The Director Class   52
3.10   The Potion Class   54
3.11   The Ingredient Class   55
3.12   The PotionMakingFeasibilityViolation Class   55
3.13   The Client Class   55
3.14   Playing with the Code   56

4 Factory Method   **59**

4.1   Revisiting the Concept of a Factory in Software   59
4.2   Intent and Applicability   60
4.3   Introduction to the Factory Method Pattern   60
4.4   The Factory Method Pattern in Real-World Applications   61
4.5   Harry Potter Story Used to Illustrate the Factory Method Pattern   62
4.6   A Top Level View of the Pattern Demonstration   63
4.7   The Enchanted Class Hierarchy   65
4.8   The ArtifactFactory Class Hierarchy and the Factory
       Methods Contained Therein   68
4.9   The Client Class   70
4.10   Playing with the Code   71

5 Prototype   **73**

5.1   Why Not Make New Objects by Copying Old Objects?   73
5.2   Intent and Applicability   74
5.3   Introduction to the Prototype Pattern   74
5.4   The Prototype Pattern in Real-World Applications   77
5.5   Harry Potter Story Used to Illustrate The Prototype Pattern   78
5.6   A Top Level View of the Pattern Demonstration   79
5.7   The Dragon Class   81
5.8   The PrototypeManagerAndDuplicator Class   84

5.9   The DragonAficionado Class   87
5.10   The UnknownDragonException Class   88
5.11   Playing with the Code   88

6   Singleton   **90**

6.1   Singular Objects   90
6.2   Intent and Applicability   90
6.3   Introduction to the Singleton Pattern   91
6.4   The Singleton Pattern in Real-World Applications   91
6.5   Harry Potter Story Used to Illustrate the Singleton Pattern   92
6.6   A Top Level View of the Pattern Demonstration   92
6.7   The MinisterForMagic Class   93
6.8   The TestSingleton Class   94
6.9   Variations on the Singleton Pattern   95
6.10   Playing with the Code   97

II   STRUCTURAL PATTERNS   **99**

7   Adapter   **101**

7.1   Getting Things to Work Together   101
7.2   Intent and Applicability   102
7.3   Introduction to the Adapter Pattern   102
7.4   The Adapter Pattern in Real-World Applications   103
7.5   Harry Potter Story Used to Illustrate the Adapter Pattern   104
7.6   A Top Level View of the Pattern Demonstration   104
7.7   The Target Interface: TeachingDADA   106
7.8   The TeacherForDADA Class   107
7.9   The AdapterForSafeTeaching Class   108
7.10   The Client Class SchoolOfMagic   110
7.11   Object Adapter   111
7.12   Pluggable Adapter   113
7.13   Playing with the Code   119

8   Bridge   **122**

8.1   Concepts and Their Implementation   122
8.2   Intent and Applicability   123
8.3   Introduction to the Bridge Pattern   123
8.4   The Bridge Pattern in Real-World Applications   126
8.5   Harry Potter Story Used to Illustrate the Bridge Pattern   127
8.6   A Top Level View of the Pattern Demonstration   130
8.7   The Humanoid Class   130
8.8   The Dementor, Goblin, and HouseElf Classes   132
8.9   The Humanoid_Imp Class   134
8.10   Implementation Classes for the Dementor, Goblin,
       and HouseElf Classes   137

8.11	The Client Class MinistryOfMagic	139
8.12	Playing with the Code	140

9   Composite — **142**

9.1	Relationships That Loop Back	142
9.2	Intent and Applicability	143
9.3	Introduction to the Composite Pattern	144
9.4	The Composite Pattern in Real-World Applications	145
9.5	Harry Potter Story Used to Illustrate the Composite Pattern	146
9.6	A Top Level View of the Pattern Demonstration	147
9.7	The WizardTraits Interface	148
9.8	The Wizard Class	149
9.9	The Auror Class	152
9.10	The Obliviator Class	153
9.11	The DepartmentHead Class	155
9.12	The Minister for Magic Class	156
9.13	The Client Class Test	158
9.14	Playing with the Code	159

10 Decorator — **161**

10.1	Onion as a Metaphor	161
10.2	Intent and Applicability	162
10.3	Introduction to the Decorator Pattern	162
10.4	The Decorator Pattern in Real-World Applications	164
10.5	Harry Potter Story Used to Illustrate the Decorator Pattern	165
10.6	A Top Level View of the Pattern Demonstration	168
10.7	The CoreMessageDeliveryClass Class	170
10.8	The Decorator Classes	170
10.9	The Client Class Test	172
10.10	Playing with the Code	173

11 Facade — **175**

11.1	Hiding Complexity	175
11.2	Intent and Applicability	175
11.3	Introduction to the Facade Pattern	176
11.4	The Facade Pattern in Real-World Applications	177
11.5	Harry Potter Story Used to Illustrate the Facade Pattern	177
11.6	A Top Level View of the Pattern Demonstration	179
11.7	The Abstract Root Class Facade	181
11.8	The Network Class	183
11.9	The Node, Link, and Path Classes	193
11.10	The Three Concrete Facade Classes	198
11.11	Testing the Demonstration Code	203
11.12	Playing with the Code	207

12 Flyweight **212**

12.1 The Idea of Customized Duplications 212
12.2 Intent and Applicability 213
12.3 Introduction to the Flyweight Pattern 213
12.4 The Flyweight Pattern in Real-World Applications 214
12.5 Harry Potter Story Used to Illustrate the Flyweight Pattern 214
12.6 A Top Level View of the Pattern Demonstration 215
12.7 The HeadMasterPortrait Class 218
12.8 The FlyweightImageStore Class 218
12.9 The ImageManager Class 219
12.10 The PortraitBorderChoices Class 225
12.11 The ImageNotAvailableException Class 226
12.12 The PortraitMakerAssignment Class 226
12.13 Playing with the Code 228
12.14 Acknowledgment 229

13 Proxy **230**

13.1 Is It Always Necessary to Have the Real Thing? 230
13.2 Intent and Applicability 230
13.3 Introduction to the Proxy Pattern 231
13.4 The Proxy Pattern in Real-World Applications 232
13.5 Harry Potter Story Used to Illustrate the Proxy Pattern 233
13.6 A Top Level View of the Pattern Demonstration 235
13.7 The Abstract Class Wizard 235
13.8 The DarkWizardTraits Interface 237
13.9 The DarkWizard Class 238
13.10 The DarkLord Class 242
13.11 The ClientClass Class 245
13.12 Playing with the Code 246

III BEHAVIORAL PATTERNS **249**

14 Chain of Responsibility **253**

14.1 Passing the Buck 253
14.2 Intent and Applicability 254
14.3 Introduction to the Chain of Responsibility Pattern 254
14.4 The Chain of Responsibility Pattern in Real-World Applications 255
14.5 Harry Potter Story Used to Illustrate the Chain
     of Responsibility Pattern 256
14.6 A Top Level View of the Pattern Demonstration 258
14.7 The Interface Class Violations 260
14.8 The Abstract Class Adjudicator 261
14.9 The Player Class 263
14.10 The Classes with the Authority to Resolve Violations 265
14.11 Testing the Code 268
14.12 Playing with the Code 269

15 Command   **272**

    15.1   Actions Versus the Actors   272
    15.2   Intent and Applicability   273
    15.3   Introduction to the Command Pattern   274
    15.4   The Command Pattern in Real-World Applications   274
    15.5   Harry Potter Story Used to Illustrate the Command Pattern   276
    15.6   A Top Level View of the Pattern Demonstration   277
    15.7   The Command Interface   279
    15.8   The MyPlaces Interface   279
    15.9   The ProtectHarryPotter Class   279
    15.10 The Wizard Class   282
    15.11 The Squib Class   284
    15.12 The Invoker Class   285
    15.13 The UnableToProtectHarryPotterException Class   286
    15.14 The Client Class   286
    15.15 Playing with the Code   288

16 Interpreter   **290**

    16.1   Parsing versus Interpretation   290
    16.2   Intent and Applicability   292
    16.3   Introduction to the Interpreter Pattern   292
    16.4   The Interpreter Pattern in Real-World Applications   293
    16.5   Harry Potter Story Used to Illustrate the Interpreter Pattern   294
    16.6   A Parser Front-End for the Interpreter Pattern   296
    16.7   A Top Level View of the Pattern Demonstration   304
    16.8   The Driver Class   307
    16.9   The Interpreter_Sentence Class   310
    16.10 The Worker Classes for Interpretation   312
    16.11 The Utility Class ShowSyntaxTree   315
    16.12 Playing with the Code   316

17 Iterator   **321**

    17.1   Storing Object Collections and Interacting with Them   321
    17.2   Intent and Applicability   323
    17.3   Introduction to the Iterator Pattern   323
    17.4   The Iterator Pattern in Real-World Applications   324
    17.5   Harry Potter Story Used to Illustrate the Iterator Pattern   325
    17.6   A Top Level View of the Pattern Demonstration   326
    17.7   A Utility Interface for Demonstrating the Iterator Pattern   328
    17.8   The Iterator Interface   330
    17.9   The Fresher Class   330
    17.10 The SortingHat Class   334
    17.11 The MagicCollection Interface   344
    17.12 The MagicList and MagicSet Classes   344
    17.13 The Class Range   349

17.14 Playing with the Code   349
17.15 Credits   352

18 Mediator   353

18.1   The Role of Mediation in Collaborative Problem Solving   353
18.2   Intent and Applicability   354
18.3   Introduction to the Mediator Pattern   354
18.4   The Mediator Pattern in Real-World Applications   355
18.5   Harry Potter Story Used to Illustrate the Mediator Pattern 357
18.6   A Top Level View of the Pattern Demonstration   357
18.7   The Abstract Class Mediator   359
18.8   The Interface TrialElements   360
18.9   The MinistryOfMagicTrialMediator Class   361
18.10 The Witness Class   366
18.11 The Trial Interface   367
18.12 The HarryPotterTrial Class   367
18.13 Playing with the Code   369

19 Memento   371

19.1   Recalling the Past   371
19.2   Intent and Applicability   372
19.3   Introduction to the Memento Pattern   372
19.4   The Memento Pattern in Real-World Applications   374
19.5   Harry Potter Story Used to Illustrate the Memento Pattern 374
19.6   A Top Level View of the Pattern Demonstration   377
19.7   The HogwartsHappening Class and The Inner
       Memento Class   378
19.8   The Client Class   380
19.9   Playing with the Code   384

20 Observer   386

20.1   Subscription-Based Broadcasting   386
20.2   Intent and Applicability   387
20.3   Introduction to the Observer Pattern   387
20.4   The Observer Pattern in Real-World Applications   388
20.5   Harry Potter Story Used to Illustrate the Observer Pattern 389
20.6   A Top Level View of the Pattern Demonstration   391
20.7   The Observer Interface   391
20.8   The Observable Interface   393
20.9   The DarkLord Class   393
20.10 The DeathEater Class   396
20.11 The GodProcess Class   399
20.12 Playing with the Code   401

21 State   **405**

21.1   Contextual Dependence of Behaviors   405
21.2   Intent and Applicability   406
21.3   Introduction to the State Pattern   406
21.4   The State Pattern in Real-World Applications   406
21.5   Harry Potter Story Used to Illustrate the State Pattern   407
21.6   A Top Level View of the Pattern Demonstration   408
21.7   The DADA_State Interface   410
21.8   The Year-by-Year Implementation Classes for the State   411
21.9   The TeachingDADA Class   417
21.10 The Hogwarts Class   418
21.11 Playing with the Code   419

22 Strategy   **421**

22.1   Strategies in the Pursuit of Goals   421
22.2   Intent and Applicability   422
22.3   Introduction to the Strategy Pattern   422
22.4   The Strategy Pattern in Real-World Applications   423
22.5   Harry Potter Story Used to Illustrate the Strategy Pattern   424
22.6   A Top Level View of the Pattern Demonstration   425
22.7   The Abstract Root Class for Strategies: StrategyAbstractRoot   428
22.8   The Concrete Strategy Classes   429
22.9   The Champion Class   432
22.10 The SecondTaskManager Class   434
22.11 Playing with the Code   436

23 Template Method   **437**

23.1   Customizable Recipes   437
23.2   Intent and Applicability   438
23.3   Introduction to the Template Method Pattern   438
23.4   The Template Method Pattern in Real-World Applications   440
23.5   Harry Potter Story Used to Illustrate the Template
       Method Pattern   441
23.6   A Top Level View of the Pattern Demonstration   442
23.7   The Abstract Root of Narrative Generation Classes   444
23.8   Concrete Classes for Narrative Generation   445
23.9   The Executable Class   449
23.10 Playing with the Code   450

24 Visitor   **453**

24.1   Hooks, Good and Evil   453
24.2   Intent and Applicability   454
24.3   Introduction to the Visitor Pattern   454
24.4   The Visitor Pattern in Real-World Applications   457
24.5   Harry Potter Story Used to Illustrate the Visitor Pattern   457

24.6   A Top Level View of the Pattern Demonstration   459
24.7   The Visitor Interface   460
24.8   Two Concrete Implementations of the Visitor Interface   462
24.9   A Re-Implementation of the Wizard Hierarchy of the
       Composite Pattern   463
24.10 The Executable Class Client   469
24.11 Playing with the Code   470

REFERENCES   **473**

INDEX   **474**

PREFACE

Readers who have been following the progress of my Objects Trilogy project will be pleased to see this third and final book of the Trilogy — even if it is almost two years behind schedule.

As to the cause for the delay, the primary culprit was finding the right medium for explaining the design patterns. When I first announced my Objects Trilogy project several years back, my plan, as stated then, was to explain the patterns through famous short stories of the world. By famous I meant classic and universal — the sort that would not need to be re-told when used for explaining the patterns. These would be the stories by Hans Christian Anderson, the Brothers Grimm, and their counterparts from around the world. But, unfortunately, when I started mapping the patterns onto the stories, it became increasingly clear that such stories did not possess the level of complexity that was needed for the patterns. That's when I turned to Harry Potter.

I should also mention that, at the beginning of this book project, Harry Potter was the farthest thing from my mind. Not that I was unaware of the worldwide phenomenon that Harry Potter had become. After all, who could have missed media reports like the mile-long lines of kids and parents waiting for the stores to open with the release of each new Harry Potter book. But to me, having grown up with time-honored and celebrated short stories of the sort mentioned above, it seemed unnecessary to have to wade though a very long story (seven books) in order to explore its possibilities for explaining the design patterns.

However, after realizing the limitations of traditional folklore and fairy tales for this project, I turned to Harry Potter with a greater seriousness of purpose. As I started reading the series, I was completely blown away not only by the story-telling powers of J. K. Rowling, but also by the delightful complexity of the subnarratives within the overall multi-volume story. As I wended my way though successive Harry Potter books, every once in a while I'd have an "Aha!" moment when I encountered a segment of the story that

appeared to have the complexity I was looking for.[1] Despite numerous such moments, it still took multiple readings of the series — besides conversations with family and friends and, especially, the children of family and friends who had devoured Harry Potter many times over — before I had any confidence in using a particular part of the story for explaining a pattern.

I would not be surprised if the initial reaction of a reader to my use of Harry Potter for explaining the patterns would be something like: "Where is the need for using a literary medium of any sort for such explanations?" Such readers are likely to add: "If the current explanations of the patterns are not satisfactory, why not base any further explanations on real-world examples as opposed to stories from a magical world?" I am going to address these questions next.

In addition to the seminal book "*Design Patterns — Elements of Reusable Object-Oriented Software*" by Erich Gamma, Richard Helm, Ralph Johnson, and John Vlissides that first introduced the patterns to the programming world, there now exist virtually hundreds of explanations of these patterns in various books and on the internet. I maintain that the large quantity of this material has not made it any easier to understand many of the more difficult patterns. Rather, the more difficult patterns continue to be as opaque today as they were at the time of their first presentation by Gamma et al. And the fact that they were quite difficult to understand even through the original explanations provided by Gamma et al. can be inferred from the following comment in the Preface of their book: "*A word of warning and encouragement: Don't worry if you don't understand this book completely on the first reading. We didn't understand it all on the first writing!*"

Let me now address the issue of using real-world examples to improve upon the current stock of explanations of the patterns. Note that for a large majority of the explanations that are currently out there, the authors have indeed tried to use real-world examples. But these explanations do not work well for various reasons. The main reason, probably, is that the typical space constraints prevent the authors from fully presenting a real-world application.[2] As such, what a reader gets is a highly abbreviated version of some real-world example that is often difficult to appreciate from the standpoint of its relevance to the pattern. Additionally, a reader may have zero interest in the real-world application being used by an author. If for whatever reason a reader cannot connect with the so-called real-world examples, why not use examples from a familiar literary work in the hope that the reader would find those easier to relate to.

Based on my own experience with the teaching of object-oriented (OO) design patterns, I have observed that when a student tries to grasp the software abstraction in a pattern

---

[1] I vividly remember the first "Aha!" moment that occurred when I was reading about the Sorting Hat in the first Harry Potter book. As anyone who has had any exposure to serious programming knows, sorting by a computer has occupied some of the best minds in computer science over the years. We now have all kinds of algorithms with different tradeoffs between the time it takes to sort a list and the memory required to do so. So, while I was reading about the Sorting Hat, I wondered how a sorting algorithm in the world of muggles would take into account the constraints that the Sorting Hat had to work with — placing equal number of students in each of the four houses while factoring in the student preferences and their aptitudes — and produce perfectly sorted results in constant time. While sorting in and of itself is not the focus of any of the patterns, I have used the Sorting Hat story in one of the pattern explanations in this book.

[2] This is not to imply that our problems with the teaching and learning of the object-oriented design patterns would disappear if we could use fully developed real-world examples for explaining them. In most cases, doing full justice to the presentation of any serious real-world example is likely to overwhelm the role of a pattern in the example.

through an instructor's highly abbreviated presentation of some real-world application that fails to motivate, what you get is an immediate disconnect between the student and the instructor. And if it should happen that a pattern explanation is based on an application that the instructor is not familiar with, the student is likely to receive a presentation that lacks clarity and conviction.

I believe it's due to a lack of any explanatory material *that can hold the attention of the students and that, at the same time, lends itself to teaching without placing a large burden on the instructors* that the OO patterns, despite their great importance, are taught mostly in a piecemeal fashion. In most cases, a software engineering instructor teaches just a half dozen patterns that he/she is comfortable with. It's rarely the case that all of the patterns are taught in any concerted fashion.

I must emphasize that not all patterns are difficult to understand. In fact, several that deal with object creation are downright easy and can be comprehended immediately with the simplest of explanations. But those patterns that involve fairly complex run-time inter-actions between different objects can require significant effort before they begin to sink in. It is these more complex patterns that Gamma et al. were surely referring to in the quote from their preface that I showed earlier. The goal of my book is to make it easier to understand these patterns in particular with the help of stories drawn from Harry Potter.

It is possible that some of you are thinking that Harry Potter is already passé — since it is not as constantly in the news as it used to be — so I might be hitching my wagon to a fading star for explaining the patterns. Yes, it does appear that the extremely intense media hype that surrounded Harry Potter for several years has passed. But that's because nothing lasts forever in the media, and that applies as much to themes that are merely ephemeral as it does to themes that are timeless. I still see a lot of young peo-ple reading and enjoying Harry Potter. My sense is that Harry Potter is as timeless as, say, Dr. Seuss. Neither receives much media attention any longer, but both continue to be widely enjoyed around the world.

I am obviously under no illusion that all readers who have had difficulty understanding the more complex patterns with the currently available crop of explanations will suddenly have "Aha!" moments when they read my Harry Potter-based explanations for the same. I am also reasonably certain I'll be at the receiving end of brickbats for melding the serious subject of OO design with the airy material of Harry Potter. Nonetheless, at the very least, this book will demonstrate that it is possible to construct explanatory analogies for OO design patterns using themes that we resonate to emotionally (through our fantasies or otherwise). Even if this book only encouraged other authors to write books in the future that use unconventional analogies — analogies that we can relate to on the basis of our shared human experiences — for explaining ideas that are generally considered to be complex and dry, I'd be satisfied.

That brings me to the subject of the Harry Potter stories I have used in this book. If you have read the series, you probably have your own favorite stories. As to what those might be is likely to depend on several factors, including possibly your educational background and cultural perspectives. However, if you are of a scientific bent of mind, it is difficult for me to imagine that the stories related to the following magical objects did not leave indelible impressions on your mind: the Sorting Hat for placing each year's fresh crop of admittees in the four Hogwarts houses; the Remembrall as a memory aid; the Time-Turner for time travel; the Howlers for conveying emotions in the strongest possible sense; the Floo network for quick travel around London; the Death Mark for instantaneous signaling; and several others. What these stories convey is not too far from our own fantasies that are

borne partly of our scientific exuberance and partly from our desires to cope with everyday life and all its frustrations. I have used several of these stories in the explanations of the patterns in this book.

With regard to the organization of the book, it consists of three parts: the first is devoted to Creational Patterns, the second to Structural Patterns, and the last to Behavioral Patterns. Within each part, each chapter is devoted to a single pattern. The explanation of a pattern begins with the key idea that the pattern is based on — I have tried to express the key idea in as general a manner as possible through its relationship to our everyday experiences. The key-idea section is followed by an "Intent and Applicability" section that should mirror the pattern's intent and applicability as annunciated by GoF.

The rest of the chapter on a pattern starts with a section that mentions the better known real-world problems solved by the pattern. That is followed by a section that reviews the Harry Potter story used for explaining the pattern. I have tried to write this part in such a way that even a reader who has not previously read Harry Potter will see a more-or-less complete account that can serve as a "medium" for demonstrating the pattern in the rest of the chapter. It remains to be seen as to what extent I have succeeded in that endeavor. Subsequent sections in a chapter first present a top-level view of the pattern demonstration with the help of an overall class diagram, followed by sections that present the Java classes used in the demonstration. Each chapter ends in the section "Playing with the Code" that first shows what the reader can expect to see by executing the demonstration code, and then talks about how the reader can himself/herself extend the code further for gaining additional insights into the pattern.

All of the code shown in this book is available for download at `https://engineering.purdue.edu/kak/designingwithobjects/`. At this time, all of this code is in Java. If time permits, the website will also include implementations in other languages at some point in the future. If I discover any errors after the book is in print — or if I receive from the readers any reports to that effect — they will be posted in an erratum at the same website. I'd certainly love to hear from the readers regarding any typos, errors, etc., in this book, and suggestions for improvements in future versions of the book.

It is my hope that this book will be received just as well as the first two books of the Objects Trilogy. The first, "Programming with Objects," has been adopted as a text in a number of universities. The second, "Scripting with Objects," is gaining traction as a text and as a reference, although it is more likely to be used as the latter. This book, "Designing with Objects," in addition to possibly serving as a text or a reference for courses in advanced programming, is also meant to be used simply for personal enjoyment.

West Lafayette, Indiana   AVINASH C. KAK

ACKNOWLEDGMENTS

I would like to thank my erstwhile editor George Telecki at John Wiley for getting the ball rolling on this book project. Considering the rather unusual nature of this undertaking, it took an editor like George with a large technological worldview to appreciate the merits of such a book.

I also owe many thanks to Kari Capone and Brett Kurzman, both editors at John Wiley. Kari took over for George and then handed the project over to Brett who saw it to completion.

Many thanks go to Malena de la Fuente for our many Harry Potter conversations. Malena has devoured Harry Potter many times over and done so in two different languages—English and French. For several of the patterns, it was not immediately clear to me which Harry Potter episode would serve as the best medium for constructing an explanation. The conversations with Malena were often helpful in choosing the best episode.

Final cleanup of the manuscript was much helped by Sriram Karthik Badam, a rare individual with a deep knowledge of both Harry Potter and Java programming. He spotted several typographical errors and made several useful suggestions for improving the code used for explaining the patterns.

I also wish to thank the developers of ArgoUML, the open-source UML diagramming tool that I used for creating the class diagrams shown in this book.

Finally, and most importantly, I wish to express my deepest thanks to Stacey Smythe for being the source of not only the most important things in life that make us human, but also for being the first to suggest that I look at Harry Potter for constructing pattern explanations. I cannot think of a greater joy than to share life with someone whose values so reflect my own.

A.C.K.

1

WHY LEARN DESIGN PATTERNS AND WHY DO SO WITH HELP FROM HARRY POTTER?

Design, in general, involves complex mental processes, most of them poorly understood. However, it is commonly believed that all design entails using previously learned patterns at some level of detail. One can certainly assume that the designers who are celebrated for their work use patterns at a fairly low level of detail. A musical genius like Mozart probably used any previously learned patterns for only the most basic of the sound effects he wanted to create. On the other hand, it would be safe to say that the lesser composers of his time (or, for that matter, of any time) have probably borrowed significantly from the harmonies and the rhythms created by the geniuses.

Whereas the need for the content to be original in the artistic and the literary domains necessitates that the use of existing patterns be kept to a minimum in a new design, exactly the opposite is true for the case of software. In software design, although the need to be original and creative is important in dealing with hitherto unseen problems, of greater importance are the correctness and the robustness of the software produced.

If a new problem in software design is similar to one seen previously (and for which a correct software solution is already known to exist), the previously developed solution is preferred over what would otherwise be a new and creative way of solving the new problem. Using a previously known trusted solution to the problem can only increase the confidence that others place in your software.

And, should it happen that you are dealing with a large complex problem that does not lend itself to any single previously known solution strategy, you'd be expected to be creative in decomposing the problem into subproblems that can be solved with previously known trusted solutions.

In general, when you decompose a large problem, the subproblems that result are likely to be of varying levels of difficulty and detail. It is even possible that your overall decomposition will be hierarchical in which the smallest of the problems can be solved by using the well-known programming idioms in the language you are using for your software development. And, yes, those programming idioms can also be called patterns. However, we will not concern ourselves with such low-level design issues in this book.

On the other hand, this book is about the trusted solutions for what may loosely be referred to as the mid-level problems you are likely to encounter in creating a software

Designing with Objects: Object-Oriented Design Patterns Explained with Stories from Harry Potter,
First Edition. Avinash C. Kak.
© 2015 John Wiley & Sons, Inc. Published 2015 by John Wiley & Sons, Inc.

solution for a large problem. In particular, we will focus on the mid-level problems that can be solved by the twenty-three patterns first proposed by four authors who are now affectionately referred to as the Gang of Four (GoF). The book in which these patterns first appeared is now commonly referred to as the "Bible" of the object-oriented (OO) design patterns. The next section is devoted to this book and its contents.

1.1   THE OO DESIGN PATTERNS "BIBLE" BY GoF

The patterns movement in the software community was started by the much celebrated book "*Design Patterns — Elements of Reusable Object-Oriented Software*" by Erich Gamma, Richard Helm, Ralph Johnson, and John Vlissides [1]. Drawing from their collective experience with object-oriented programming, the authors succeeded in crystallizing out twenty-three design patterns that have become, as is now universally acknowledged, the building blocks of much modern object-oriented software. As mentioned in the previous section, these authors are known as the Gang of Four (GoF) and the book frequently referred to as the "OO Patterns Book by GoF."

What is amazing about the GoF book, and also what makes the book timeless, is not only the large variety of programming problems that can be solved by its twenty-three patterns, but also the fact that the authors had the foresight to recognize a host of basic issues in object-oriented design that are likely to endure for all time. To grasp the reality of the moment and to abstract from it new fundamental understandings that can serve us for a long time into the future is no small feat.

Central to most GoF patterns is the interplay between the following four tenets of good object-oriented programming: (1) Programming to the public interfaces declared at the roots of class hierarchies, as opposed to calling directly the methods defined in the implementations of those interfaces. (2) Choosing composition over inheritance if a purely inheritance-based implementation is likely to result in an unmanageable number of classes as you try to figure out the best way to create representations for all the different variants of a generic object. (3) Again choosing composition over inheritance when the flexibility made possible by the former in how the objects relate to one another is more important than the representational efficiency provided by the latter. (4) Exploiting function overriding for runtime adaptation of the behavior of a class to the implementations provided by its subclasses.

Here we will briefly review the intuitive underpinnings of the tenets listed above: When the users of a class hierarchy make sure that their own code calls only the public methods declared in the root interface of the hierarchy, folks whose business it is to provide and maintain the implementation code in the hierarchy acquire the freedom to change that code as long as the interface declarations remain unchanged.

Regarding the second tenet, even though inheritance is enshrined as a cornerstone of object-oriented programming, using it without thought may result in class hierarchies that are much too large. If you try to create a subclass for capturing every small variation from a generic class, you could end up with too many subclasses. Why not take care of the small variations through composition, that is, by endowing your generic class with additional instance variables for the extra degrees of freedom that would allow you to create a larger variety of instances from the class? Since the objects constructed from a class definition are "composed" of the values given to the instance variables — these values may themselves be class type objects — you can see why we use the word "composition" to describe this alternative to inheritance.

Favoring composition over inheritance, as in the third tenet, also makes sense in situations where there is a need to maintain programming flexibility with regard to how the different types of objects relate to one another. Although inheritance makes for efficient representational frameworks (since the common attributes declared in the general classes do not need to be repeated in the specialized classes), the resulting inter-object relationships once created become hardcoded in the code base.

The intuition behind using function overriding for runtime customization of the behavior of a class, as mentioned in the fourth tenet, is just as straightforward. When you put function overriding to use, the code you write for the methods — especially when methods call other supporting methods defined in the same class — becomes much more efficient from the standpoint of being able to represent a *range* of behaviors. The specific behavior you elicit at runtime can then be customized by overriding the supporting methods in the subclasses.

Getting back to the subject of the twenty-three patterns in the GoF book, those patterns were placed by GoF in the following three categories: (1) Creational, (2) Structural, and (3) Behavioral. And, for finer differentiation, each pattern was given a mnemonic name that captures the essence of what that pattern is about.

The Creational Patterns examine issues in designing classes and the methods to construct instances from those classes from the standpoint of a number of considerations that frequently arise in object-oriented programming. Consider, for example, one of the aforementioned tenets of good object-oriented programming: The users of object-oriented software should only program to the interfaces of the class hierarchies. Keeping in mind this tenet, here is an example of a question addressed by the Creational Patterns: Say we have two class hierarchies, one in which we model the domain knowledge and the other in which we have code that, using indirection, can spit out instances of the classes in the first hierarchy. Can we still have the clients of this software adhere to the above mentioned tenet of good object-oriented programming? The Creational Patterns also recognize that calling willy-nilly the constructor of a class can be a dangerous thing to do if the instances to be produced require special computational resources. Included in the lessons that these patterns teach us is how to design a class so that it gives us some control over the instances created from the class — control in the sense of how many of the instances are allowed to exist at the same time.

The Structural Patterns are also about designing classes and constructing instances from the classes, but now the representational issues related to class design are more complex. As a case in point, let's say that the basic representation for a problem domain as captured by a single class must be enriched with arbitrary combinations of certain embellishments. What is the best way to create an overall representation that would allow for efficient production of the instances while incorporating the embellishments in them? Another representational question important to the Structural Patterns is how to design a class hierarchy when the problem domain calls for instantiating large objects that are made up of smaller objects, with all the objects (including the large objects) being of the same fundamental type. The Structural Patterns are also concerned about how to write a new class that must simultaneously adapt itself to the behavior of an old class while providing new services to a client of the old class, about creating different usage views of a complex system of classes for different categories of users, and so on.

The Behavioral Patterns are about eliciting useful runtime behaviors from a set of classes working together. These behaviors are dynamic, in the sense that how a class (or a group of classes working together) responds to a runtime condition (which may be created by user input or by a change in the state of one of the objects) will, in general, depend on the

states of all other objects relevant to the condition. A major consequence of this is that the flow of execution for how the classes interact at runtime cannot be predicted in advance — unlike what is the case with the Creational and the Structural Patterns. Dynamic effects exhibited by the Behavioral Patterns include synthesizing at runtime a large behavior from more elementary behaviors provided by support classes, regulating the interaction among a set of classes so that it conforms to a protocol selected at runtime, rolling back the state of an object to what it was at an earlier time, and so on.

1.2   BUT WHAT HAS HARRY POTTER GOT TO DO WITH OO DESIGN PATTERNS?

Although some of the twenty-three design patterns are straightforward and can be understood easily, several require multiple readings from the GoF book before the ideas sink in. And, even after multiple readings, it is not until you have yourself programmed a pattern that you can claim to have fully understood what the GoF authors have tried to convey. The following quote from the preface to the GoF book is perhaps the best indicator of the complexity of several of the patterns:

> "A word of warning and encouragement: Don't worry if you don't understand this book completely on the first reading. *We didn't understand it all on the first writing!*"

The italics are by the author of this book.[1]

It is the complexity of the more difficult patterns that has served as a motivation for what you will find in the rest this book: An attempt to demystify the patterns by explaining them through the stories in Harry Potter. Thanks to the story-telling genius of J. K. Rowling, the richness of how the various characters interact in Harry Potter can be put to use to explain even the most complex object interactions in the OO patterns. The rest of the chapters in this book do exactly that.

A reader who has not read the GoF book might ask as to what mode of explanation was used by the authors of that book for the original presentation of the patterns. Or even, what sorts of explanations have been used in the other books on OO design patterns that have been published since the GoF book. In a majority of the explanations that the reader will see in the existing literature, the authors have attempted to use "real-world" problems in object-oriented software development to both motivate the reader to learn the patterns and to demonstrate their inner workings. But, unfortunately, in practically all cases, the typical space constraints of a book prevent a full airing out of the "real-world" problems.

Therefore, what a reader actually sees for a pattern explanation in practically all other books are just skeletal versions of some real-world problems. For most readers, it is not so easy to relate to the pattern explanations based on those highly abbreviated accounts of the original real-world problems — unless they themselves happen to be working in those problem domains. Let's put it this way: Are we to really believe that someone who spends all his/her time writing code for financial applications would understand all of the nuances

---

[1] This self-effacing statement by the GoF was also a reflection of their personality that placed a higher value on learning and exploring than on hubris and hype. And that, in turn, brings to mind the quote "Knowledge begins with humility — with wonder and with appreciation for what you don't know. The more you learn, the more you see how much you want and need to learn," that was made by the Bryn Mawr College President Katharine McBride in 1964.

associated with a pattern that is explained with the help of a highly abbreviated version of a problem in text format conversion or in computer-aided design?

This disconnection that a reader experiences with a pattern explanation that is based on a brief made-up version of a real-world problem often becomes even more pronounced for a young student who must simultaneously straddle two worlds: the world in which he/she is still trying to come to terms with the fundamental notions of encapsulation, inheritance, concurrency, polymorphism, and so on, and the real world used for pattern explanations.

So if skeletal versions of the so-called real-world problems are not the best medium for explaining the patterns, how about constructing pattern explanations with generic-sounding names for the classes, for their attributes, and for their methods? For example, for class names, we could use letters like A, B, C, etc., and for method names we could use `fooA()`, `barA()`, `bazA()`, `footB()`, etc. Subsequently, we could describe through method calls what it is that an object constructed from one class does to an object constructed from another class and weave these interactions into a narrative that explains the pattern. The main problem with this approach is that as the number of classes and the number of interactions between the classes increases, it becomes difficult to remember the roles assigned to the different classes and the behaviors programmed into their methods.

One could, of course, give more meaningful names to the classes and their methods, names that are evocative of their purpose. But that frequently leads to either absurd names or absurdly long names. For example, suppose you write an explanation for a pattern that shows how you can adapt a new class to an old class. You could try to refer to the old class as `OldClass` and the new class as `NewClass`. Let's now say your explanation requires you to name multiple such old and new classes with different roles. As an attempt at using "meaningful" names, you could try `OldClassForRoleM`, `NewClassForRoleN`, etc., with the suffixes `RoleM` and `RoleN` replaced by the names of the actual roles of the classes. As you can see, as you increase the number of classes, your explanation will sound boring, clumsy, and dry.

Figures 1.1 and 1.2 are meant to convey the difference in the quality of the explanations that can be created from a class diagram that uses arid symbolic names like

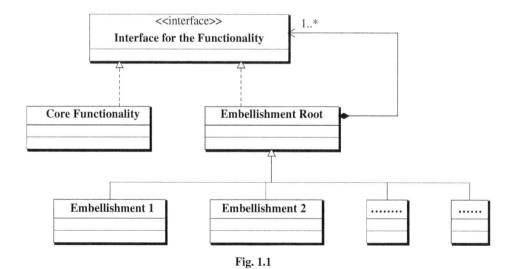

Fig. 1.1

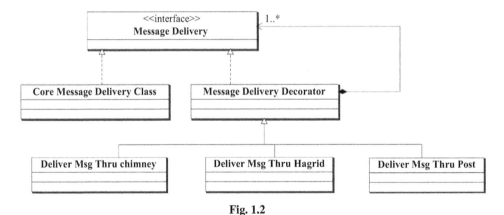

Fig. 1.2

Core Functionality, Embellishment Root, etc., and a class diagram that uses easier-to-relate-to names such as Message Delivery, Deliver Msg Thru Chimney, Deliver Msg Thru Hagrid, and so on. As the reader will see in Chapter 10, both of these class diagrams can be used to explain the notion of recursive nesting of class embellishments in the Decorator pattern. Figure 1.1 uses boring generic names, whereas Figure 1.2 uses names that are evocative of a hilarious snippet from the first Harry Potter book in which Mr. Dursley does everything in his power to keep the admission letter sent by Hogwarts from reaching Harry. This connection between Figure 1.2 and a most delightful episode related to Harry Potter makes the Decorator pattern both easier to understand and easier to remember. As a measure of Figure 1.2 possessing greater explanatory power over the more generic depiction in Figure 1.1, the former figure, with its richly evocative class names, along with just a couple of words about what the Decorator pattern is all about, is likely to cause a reader to immediately experience an aha moment with regard to understanding the core idea of the pattern.

1.3 IS FAMILIARITY WITH HARRY POTTER A REQUIREMENT FOR UNDERSTANDING THIS BOOK?

Although the book is written for a reader who is already familiar with Harry Potter, that does not imply that the explanations presented would be inaccessible to someone who has not read those books. Starting with the next chapter, every chapter includes a section titled "Harry Potter Story Used to Illustrate the XYZ Pattern" that, while intended primarily for a Harry Potter fan to recall the ideas used in the explanation of that pattern, should nevertheless be understandable to others as a "brief story" in its own right. If a reader who has no desire to read Harry Potter before launching into this book would be indulgent enough to accept this section as a standalone account that is either related to some magical objects or that is about an interaction between certain characters — although by no means an account written in the same compelling style as by J. K. Rowling — he/she should be able to use that account to understand the rest of the explanation of the pattern.

1.4   HOW THE PATTERN EXPLANATIONS ARE ORGANIZED

Each pattern is presented in a separate chapter, and each chapter consists of the following sections:

- An introduction to the key thought in the pattern.
- The intent and the applicability of the pattern.
- A general introduction to the pattern.
- A section that describes which part of the Harry Potter story was used for explaining the pattern. The title of this section is always "Harry Potter Story Used to Illustrate the XYZ Pattern" for the pattern XYZ.
- A section titled "A Top Level View of the Pattern Demonstration" that presents the overall class diagram and the related explanations for the pattern in question. The explanation of the pattern in this section is an extension of the narrative in the preceding "Harry Potter Story" section.
- The "Top Level View" section is followed by multiple sections, each devoted to explaining one class, although, and in some cases, a single section may present multiple classes that are closely related.
- Each chapter ends in a section named "Playing with the Code" that first describes how to compile and execute the Java code presented for the pattern and then talks about how a reader may extend the demonstration code in order to gain additional insights into the pattern.

1.5   THE TERMINOLOGY OF OBJECT-ORIENTED PROGRAMMING

It is possible that a casual reader skipping through the book — especially a reader with minimal prior exposure to object-oriented programming — would be bewildered by some of the terminology used for describing how objects are created and manipulated in software, how they interact with one another, how the clients interact with them, and so on. The terminology definitions shown below are meant for such a reader especially, the idea being that it might help the reader grasp at a high level, if not in detail, the explanations of the patterns in this book.[2]

The definitions shown below are specifically for the case of object-oriented programming in Java — since that is the language used in the code for demonstrating the patterns. Note, however, most of the definitions are language agnostic and apply to object-oriented programming in general.

The words that appear italicized in the definitions are also defined in the Terminology that follows.

abstract class: To add to the entry shown for *class*, a class is abstract if it is not possible to construct *instances* from that class. Abstract classes play a very important role in object-oriented programming by serving as interfaces for class hierarchies (although,

---

[2]The "definitions" shown have been excerpted from Chapter 3 of Programming with Objects [2].

more commonly, you'd use Java interfaces for that purpose if you are programming in Java) and as "mix-in" classes to lend specialized behaviors to other classes. They can also be of great help in building a *class hierarchy* incrementally. In Java, a class becomes abstract when it is explicitly declared to be so.

abstract method: To add to the entry for *method*, a method can be declared *abstract* if its header includes the keyword abstract. When a method is declared abstract, it does not come with any implementation code. You declare a method abstract in a class because you expect the subclasses of that class to provide the implementation code for the method. A class remains abstract as long it has any abstract methods.

access control modifiers: Each member of a class, whether it is a variable or a method, has associated with it an access control property that for Java is one of *private, public, protected*, and *package*.

The *public* members of a class can be directly accessed anywhere in the source code. Additionally, the public members of a class are inherited by the subclasses.

On the other hand, the *private* members of a class are accessible only within that class. Although the private members of a class are inherited by its subclasses, they cannot be directly accessed in the subclasses.

The access control modifier *protected* is used for a variable or a method in a class if we wish for that member of the class to be visible in only the subclasses of the class across all packages. A protected member acts like a public member within the same package.

When no access control modifier is mentioned for a class member in Java, that implies *package* access control for that member. Such members behave like public members within the same package but private with respect to the code in all other packages.

attribute: See the entry for *instance variable*.

base class: See the entry for *inheritance*.

child class: See the entry for *inheritance*.

class: At a high level of conceptualization, a *class* can be thought of as a category or a type. We may think of "User" as a class and a specific user would then be an *instance* of (or an *object* constructed from) this class. The following constitutes a definition of the class User in Java:

```
class User {
    private String name;
    private int age;
}
```

class hierarchy: See the entry for *inheritance*.

class method: See the entry for *method*.

class variable: First read the entry for *instance variable*. In addition to *instance variables*, we may endow a class with one or more *class variables*. Whereas an instance variable is given values on a per-instance basis, the value of a class variable is global with respect to all instances constructed from a class. Class variables are frequently referred to as *static variables*. In Java, a class variable is declared by using

the keyword `static`, as in the class definition below that declares a class with two instance variables and one class variable:

```
class SavingsAccount {
    private String name;
    private int age;
    public static double interestRate;
    // ....
}
```

concrete class: A class that is not *abstract* is informally referred to as a *concrete class.*

constructor: A class is generally provided with a *constructor* whose job is to create instances from the class. A constructor sets aside the memory needed for the instance and in that memory sets the values of the instance variables according to the arguments supplied to the constructor (or, in the absence of arguments, by the default values if those are known). Shown below is another definition of the `User` class. What you see in the lines labeled "(A)" through "(D)" is the constructor for the class.

```
class User {
    private String name;
    private int age;

    public User(String str, int yy) {          //(A)
        name = str;                             //(B)
        age = yy;                               //(C)
    }                                           //(D)
}
```

In general, a class is allowed to have any number of constructors. When a class has multiple constructors, they differ with respect to the number of parameters and the parameter types. The compiler uses *overload resolution* to figure out which constructor to invoke for a given constructor call.

derived class: See the entry for *inheritance.*

extended class: See the entry for *inheritance.*

final: See the entries for *inheritance*, *instance variable*, and *overriding.*

implements: First read the entry for *interface.* A class that provides implementation code for the methods declared in an interface is said to *implement* that interface.

inheritance: Earlier we defined *class* as a category. A subcategory of a more general category can also be defined as a class — in the form of a *subclass* of the more general class. The subclass *inherits* some or all of the attributes and the methods defined for the class that corresponds to the more general category.

Since, in general, a class may be extended into multiple *subclasses*, each such subclass further extended into even more specialized *subclasses*, and so on, we can end up with what is known as a *class hierarchy.*

A subclass is also commonly referred to as a *derived class*, an *extended class*, or a *child class.* And the more general class is commonly referred to as the *base class* or the *superclass.*

The syntax used in Java for defining a subclass is illustrated by the following example:

```
class User {
    private String name;
    private int age;
    public User(String str, int yy) { name = str; age = yy; }
}
```

```
class StudentUser extends User {                          //(A)
    private String schoolEnrolled;
    public StudentUser( String nam, int y, String sch ) {
        super(nam, y);                                    //(B)
        schoolEnrolled = sch;
    }
}
```

where `StudentUser` is a subclass of `User`. Note the Java keyword `extends` in line (A). Also note how the *constructor* definition for the subclass calls on the constructor of the *base class* in line (B) through the keyword `super` for the construction of the base-class slice of the subclass object. With class–subclass definitions as shown above, an instance of type `StudentUser` can act like an instance of type `User`. That is, we can construct an instance of type `StudentUser` and assign it to a variable of type `User`. The fact that a subclass-type object can act like a superclass type is referred to as *polymorphism*. Also note that a class declared *final* cannot have subclasses.

instance: Given a class, you may construct a specific *instance* of that class by calling its *constructor*. An *instance* created by a constructor is also frequently referred to as an *object*.

instance method: See the entry for *method*.

instance variable: In the definition of the `User` class in the entries for *class*, *constructor*, and *inheritance*, we refer to `name` and `age` as the *instance variables* of the class. In general, we expect the values of such variables to vary from one instance to another. Again, in general, the value assigned to an *instance variable* can be changed, unless the variable is declared to be *final*, in which case it can only be assigned to once. An *instance variable* may also be given a default value in the class definition.

   An *instance variable* is also referred to as *data member*[3] and *attribute*. The UML notation that is described briefly in the next section specifically uses *attribute* when referring to *instance variables*.

instantiation: The word *instantiation* means constructing an *instance* of a class.

interface: A Java *interface* is an *abstract class* that, in its most common usage, declares a set of methods by only mentioning their *signatures*. A Java *interface* must not include any implementation code. Here is an example of an interface from the Java Collections Framework:

```
interface Collection {
    public boolean add( Object a );
    public boolean remove( Object a );
    // other methods
}
```

---

[3] It's the latter usage, meaning *data member*, that you will find in [2] when referring to the instance variables of a class.

Interfaces in Java are also used for grouping together related constants. When a class inherits from such an interface, the constants appear as if locally defined in the class. Such constants are treated implicitly as `static` and `final`.

method: A class is commonly endowed with behaviors through functions that are normally invoked on the instances constructed from the class. Such functions are most commonly referred to as methods. The definition of `print()` in the `User` class shown below is an example:

```
class User {
    private String firstname;
    private String lastname;
    public User(String str, int yy) { name = str; age = yy; }
    public void print() {
        System.out.print( firstname + " " + lastname );
    }
}
```

Note that when an *instance* is created, the methods in a class are bound to the instance at run time. That is referred to as "dynamic binding" — unless the method is declared to be *static*, in which case it is bound at compile time to the class itself. It's for that reason that a method such as `print()` shown above is also referred to as an *instance method*. A *static method*, on the other hand, is also referred to as a *class method*.

object: First see the entry for *instance*. The term *object* with the lowercase 'o' is not to be confused with *Object* with the uppercase 'O' in Java. Whereas the former can refer to any instance created by calling the constructor of a class, the latter is the name of the superclass of all classes in Java. Therefore, all objects in Java are of type *Object*. Every Java class, user defined or otherwise, inherits implicitly from the root class *Object*.

overloading: Overloading a method name or a constructor name means being able to use the same name with a different number and/or types of parameters. When a class has overloaded constructor or method names, it is the compiler's job to determine which of the constructors or the methods to invoke for a given call. The compiler does this by using what is known as the *overload resolution algorithm*.

overload resolution: See the entry for *overloading*.

overriding: A *subclass* can provide an override implementation for a method defined in the base class. Subsequently, if this method is invoked on a variable whose type is that of the base class but that is actually pointing to an object of type subclass, it is the subclass definition for the method that will be used. A *method* that is declared to be *final* in a base class cannot be overridden in a subclass of the base class.

package: See the entry for *access control modifiers*. *Package* may also refer to a "Java package" that groups together related classes and defines a namespace for them. For example, the basic classes of Java that are made available automatically in a user program are in the `java.lang` package. In general, if you need to use a class from a package, either you must import the package in your program or you must use the fully qualified name for the class.

polymorphism: See the entry for *inheritance*.

private: See the entry for *access control modifiers*.

protected: See the entry for *access control modifiers.*

public: See the entry for *access control modifiers.*

signature: By the *signature* of a method we mean the return type, followed by the name of the method, followed by a list of the data types in its parameter list.[4]

static: See the entries for *class variable* and *class method.*

static method: See the entry for *method.*

subclass: See the entry for *inheritance.*

superclass: See the entry for *inheritance.*

The object-oriented programming terminology listed above is by no means complete. We have only defined the terms that occur most frequently in the rest of the book. Obviously, only a book devoted to just OO, such as Programming with Objects [2], can do full justice to all of the terminology of object-oriented programming.

1.6 THE UML NOTATION USED IN THE CLASS DIAGRAMS

The diagrams used in this book for explaining the patterns are mostly class diagrams that are based on the UML conventions for constructing such diagrams.[5]

In UML, a class is represented by a rectangular box that in its most detailed representation is divided into three parts vertically. The name of the class is written in the uppermost partition of the box, followed by its instance and static variables (referred to as *attributes* in UML) in the middle partition, followed by its methods (called *operations* in UML) in the lowest partition. The name of the class is shown in bold for a concrete class and in italics for an abstract class. Figure 1.3 shows an example of this representation for a class named Employee.

In its most common usage, a class diagram shows two relationships between different classes: *generalization* and *association.* A superclass is considered to be a generalization of its subclasses. By the same token, a subclass is considered to be a specialization of its superclass. For example, the class diagram of Figure 1.4 shows with an arrowed solid line the class Employee as a superclass, and therefore a generalization, of the class Manager. Note that the generalization arrow, with a closed triangle arrowhead, points to the superclass. In Figure 1.4, the class Manager would be considered to be a specialization of the class Employee. An association, on the other hand, is depicted with a solid line between two

---

[4]In some languages, the return type may not be considered to be a part of the signature. Another word that is used for the signature of a method is *header.* The header of a method always includes its return type.

[5]UML stands for Unified Modeling Language. It was promulgated by the Object Management Group (OMG), a not-for-profit organization founded by the leading software corporations of the world. UML is a visual language that allows one to create different types of graphical representations of software. These visual representations, in the form of various types of diagrams, greatly facilitate the conceptualization and dissemination of object-oriented designs, especially because the diagrams only need to be drawn with the level of detail that is required for explaining how the classes are meant to be used. The main repository of all information related to UML can be found at [3]. If all that a reader wants is a level of familiarity with UML that would be sufficient to understand the diagrams in this book, he/she is only going to need the information presented in Chapter 14 of [2]. The most relevant sections from that source are reproduced here for the convenience of the reader.

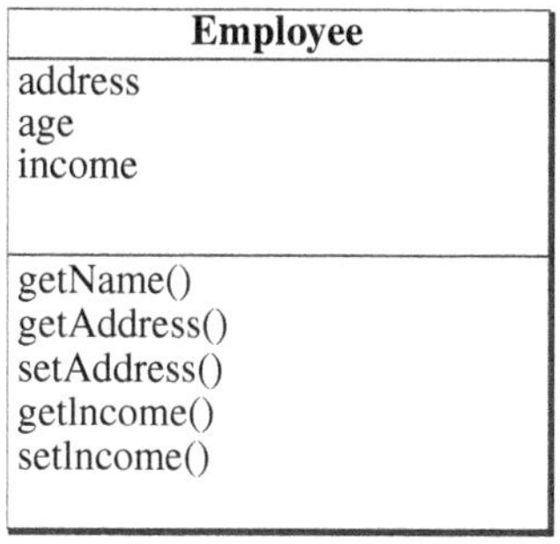

Employee
address age income
getName() getAddress() setAddress() getIncome() setIncome()

Fig. 1.3

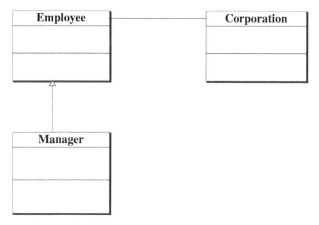

Fig. 1.4

classes, as between Employee and Corporation in the figure. You show an association link between two classes if the objects constructed from one class use in some capacity — say as instance variables — the objects constructed from the other class.

Other types of relationships between classes that can be depicted in a class diagram are *aggregation* and *composition*. The next two subsections discuss in greater detail the depiction of associations, aggregations, and generalizations in class diagrams.

We placed only the names of the classes in the boxes in the class diagram of Figure 1.4. In general, how much detail one shows for a class depends on the perspective used in drawing the diagram. A class diagram may be drawn using three different perspectives: (i) *conceptual*, (ii) *specification*, and (iii) *implementation*.

At the conceptual level, for each class you include only the bare minimum information needed to convey an overall sense of the main concepts of a problem domain. This is the diagram you are likely to draw when you are just getting started with the design of an OO program. However, even after you have fully developed an OO system, a conceptual level diagram can be useful for communicating to others a coarse-level description of the system. At the specification level, you want to show the interfaces of each class. At this level you'd want to make explicit the class responsibilities, as embodied in the

public operations for each class. At the implementation level, you want to show more precisely how a class was (or needs to be) implemented in code. Now you'd include the private
and the protected attributes and operations as well.

In the OO literature, one also commonly sees mention of IsA and HasA relationships
between classes. The former represents a generalization-specialization relationship and the
latter an association, an aggregation, or a composition. The name IsA is supposed to capture
relationships such as

```
A Manager IsAn Employee
A CorporateCustomer IsA Customer
```

In such statements, what comes after IsA is a generalization or a super-type of what comes
before. On the other hand, statements like

```
An Order HasA Customer
An Orchestra HasA Player
A Window HasA Slider
```

express containment, in the form of an association, an aggregation, or a composition.

1.6.1 Association as a Relationship Between Classes

The class diagram of Figure 1.4 showed an association to display the conceptual link
between an object of type `Employee` and an object of type `Corporation`. An example
of a more elaborate representation of such an association is shown in Figure 1.5.

In the example depicted, an `Employee` has an instance variable called `employedBy` of
type `Corporation`; this instance variable is shown as a label at the head of the arrowed
association link from `Employee` to `Corporation`. We can talk about the label `employedBy`
as the *role* played by a `Corporation` in an instance of type `Employee`. The arrowhead
on the association link from `Employee` to `Corporation` is referred to as the *navigability* arrow. The arrow tells us which of the two objects implements the association. In the
example shown, the association with the rolename `employedBy` is implemented in the
`Employee` class and therefore "belongs" to instances of type `Employee`. The label '`0..1`'
at the `Corporation` end of the association is referred to as the *multiplicity* of the association, which specifies *how many* instances of type `Corporation` in the role `employedBy`
may associate with a single instance of type `Employee`. The multiplicity of '`0..1`' means
that an `Employee` is employed by no more than one `Corporation`.

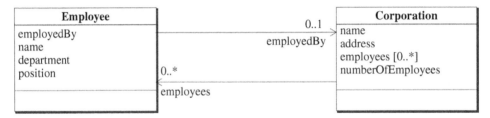

Fig. 1.5

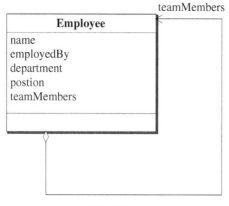

Fig. 1.6

About the association link that goes from `Corporation` to `Employee` in Figure 1.5, the navigability arrow points toward the latter, and the rolename label is `employees` with the multiplicity symbol '`0..*`'. The multiplicity of '`0..*`' means that any number of employees, including zero, is allowed in an instance constructed from `Corporation`. If there was a legal requirement that a corporation possess at least one employee, with no constraints on the upper limit, the multiplicity label associated with the rolename `employees` would change to '`1..*`'. As you might have guessed already, the symbol '`*`' in a multiplicity label means *an indefinite number*.

The two association links in Figure 1.5 could also be shown as a single line between the two classes. If we were to do so for our example, the line would show navigability arrows, rolenames, and multiplicity symbols at both ends. An association with no navigability arrows is considered bidirectional.

Figure 1.5 is an example of a binary association between two different classes. A binary association is also allowed to connect a class to itself, in which case the association is called *reflexive*. Figure 1.6 shows an example of a reflexive association. The next subsection talks about the role of the diamond that you see at the base of the association link in Figure 1.6.

1.6.2 Aggregation and Composition as Relationships Between Classes

The objects connected through an association may or may not exist independently of each other, and it is useful to differentiate between the two cases in a class diagram, especially when an association is a link between a "whole" and its "parts."

When there exist lifetime dependencies between the whole and its parts — in the sense that the parts exist solely for the benefit of the whole — we refer to the relationship between the whole and the parts as a *composition*. That is, we consider the whole to be a composite of its parts. Such an association is depicted with a filled diamond at its base. Even though such a relation can also be depicted as a straightforward association with appropriate navigability arrows and multiplicities, showing it as composition draws attention to the lifetime dependencies between the composite and its parts.

Consider the example in Figure 1.7 where we have used filled diamonds to show a `Window` composite. Obviously, the "parts" that form the composite, such as sliders, scrollbars, and so on, will cease to exist when a `Window` is closed.

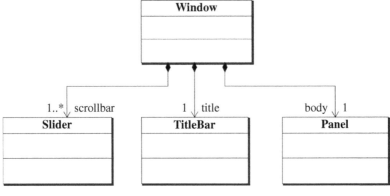

Fig. 1.7

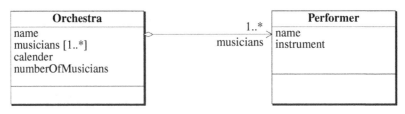

Fig. 1.8

When you have a whole–parts relationship in which the parts can exist independently of the whole, you have an *aggregation*. In the aggregation depicted in Figure 1.8, the performers would continue to exist even after the Orchestra object has ceased to do so. An aggregation is depicted with a hollow diamond at one end of the association link, the end that is an aggregate of the objects at the other. Although this type of a relationship could also be displayed as a straightforward association with appropriate navigability arrows and multiplicities, the concept of an aggregation is supposed to capture the fact that even though an orchestra is the sum total of its performers, the performers would continue to exist even if the orchestra ceased to do so.

1.6.3   Representing Attributes

As mentioned earlier, the attributes of a class — which could either be instance variables or static variables — are shown in the middle partition of the box that represents a class. The UML convention for displaying an attribute is as follows:

```
visibility  name [N] : type =  initialValue {property-string}
            ---------------
```

where the visibility is one of

```
+ for  public visibility

# for protected visibility

- for private visibility
```

although the keywords *public, protected*, and *private* can also be used directly. The absence of a visibility marker indicates only that the visibility is not shown (not that it is undefined or public) because, say, its depiction is not important to use intended for the class diagram.

In the UML notation for displaying the attributes, the name of the attribute goes where you see the string `name`. The symbol N inside square brackets denotes the multiplicity allowed for the attribute. The convention for expressing multiplicity is the same as for an association. For example, if an attribute is allowed to take one or more values, the multiplicity symbol N would be replaced by '`1..*`'. The absence of multiplicity designation means that exactly one value is allowed for the attribute.

A language-dependent specification of the implementation type of the attribute goes where you see the string `type`. The string `initialValue` is a language-dependent expression for the default value of the attribute for a newly created instance of the class, and `property-string` is a string for expressing those traits of the attribute that are not captured by the rest of the syntax. For example, for an attribute that is read-only (such as an attribute that is declared to be `final` in Java), the `property-string` would be set to `frozen`.

The underscore, shown under `name` and `type`, if used, signifies that the attribute has class scope, which means the same thing that it is static or one per class, as opposed to one per instance. Except for the `name`, all other elements of the syntax specification are optional.

1.6.4 Representing Operations

The third partition from the top, when it exists, of a class box shows its *operations*, meaning the methods defined for the class. When a class is drawn at the specification level, only the public operations of the class are displayed. However, at the implementation level, you'd also want to show the private and the protected operations. The full UML syntax for an operation is

```
visibility name (parameter-list) : return-type {property-string}
               -----------------------------------
```

where *visibility* and *name* mean the same as for the case of attributes. The *parameter-list* is a comma-separated list of the formal parameters for the operation, each specified using the syntax

```
kind name : type = defaultValue
```

where `kind` can be *in, out,* or *inout,* where *in* is for a parameter that passes a value to the operation, *out* is for a parameter that fetches a value from the operation, and *inout* for a parameter that can play both roles. The symbols `name`, `type`, and `defaultValue` serve their usual roles.

Regarding the syntax for an operation, the symbol `return-type` is an implementation-dependent language type of the value returned by the operation. The `property-string` can be used to express such traits as whether an operation is abstract, which is the case when only the header of the method is a part of the class definition and no implementation code is provided. Finally, operations that have class scope — meaning that they are static — are underlined as shown.

It is useful to make a distinction between two types of operations: *query* and *modifier.* A query operation simply tries to get the value of some class attribute without changing the state of the object. On the other hand, a modifier operation will change the state of the object. Informally, these two types of operations are also referred to as the *getter* and the *setter* methods of a class, respectively.

PART I

CREATIONAL PATTERNS

The Creational Patterns show us how to write code for a class, or for a hierarchy of classes, so that the clients can adhere to the tenets of good object-oriented programming (as described in Chapter 1) when creating instances from the classes.

In particular, we want our class definitions to make it easy for the clients to create instances by programming to just the interfaces. Additionally, when our classes are complex, the code written by the clients is more likely to be bug-free if we can somehow hide that complexity in the means we make available for instance production. There is also much to be said for making the interfaces uniform with respect to all the classes in a hierarchy. And, occasionally, we need to exercise control over the number of instances constructed from a class. The Creational Patterns show us how these and other similar goals can be met in object-oriented software.

In what follows, we list the five Creational Patterns that are presented in Part I of the book:

Abstract Factory: The Abstract Factory pattern shows us how to efficiently organize the production of a family of related objects through a family of related factory classes so that a client would need to program to just two interfaces, one for each family, for constructing all objects.

Builder: The Builder pattern is about constructing complex objects that are composed of several parts and whose construction may involve algorithmic steps that impose constraints on how the parts come together in the objects. The goal here is to insulate the clients from much of the complexity associated with the classes.

Factory Method: When factory methods are used for object construction and we find ourselves dealing with a hierarchy of classes, we are faced with the problem of how to best create a uniform interface for all the factory methods involved. It is this problem that is solved by the Factory Method pattern. By the way, there can be many practical reasons for routing calls to constructors through methods known as the factory methods. We will review those in Chapter 4.

Designing with Objects: Object-Oriented Design Patterns Explained with Stories from Harry Potter, First Edition. Avinash C. Kak.

Prototype: The Prototype pattern is useful when the instance variables in a class can take on only a small number of discrete values. Each set of discrete values for the instance variables can be thought of as constituting a prototype. By "pre-manufacturing" the prototypes and storing them away somewhere, all instance creation subsequently can reduce to supplying a clone of one of the prototypes. This pattern is particularly useful when creating a new instance by cloning is cheaper than doing the same through a constructor call.

Singleton: The Singleton pattern is useful if there exist practical constraints on how many instances of a class are allowed to exist at any given time. In typical uses of this pattern, a class allows only one instance to be created. Any subsequent requests for an instance return a copy of the same instance that was created for the first such request.

2

ABSTRACT FACTORY

2.1 THE CONCEPT OF A FACTORY IN SOFTWARE

Factories are, as everyone knows, where you make products. Factories in software systems serve the same purpose — as makers of new software objects. Hearing this, a reader familiar with object-oriented programming might ask: Aren't the constructors in class definitions supposed to take care of object construction? Why introduce yet another mechanism for constructing objects when the notion of a constructor has served us so well?

To understand the distinction between object construction by a constructor in a class definition and by a factory, think of the latter as the outsourcing of the task. Despite the bad press that outsourcing has received in recent years, there are indeed situations when outsourcing can be advantageous for all parties involved. It creates a larger separation between the code where object specifications are laid out and the code where the objects are used. If you think of the designers, the producers, and the consumers of the objects as constituting some sort of a chain, the larger the separation between the two ends of the chain, the greater the freedom each end has to alter its code without affecting the code at the other end.

Outsourcing as a metaphor for understanding the notion of a factory in software works well provided one keeps in mind the following limitation of the metaphor: Whereas in most examples of actual outsourcing, the details concerning how the products are actually manufactured are delegated to the 'outsourcee' organization, in software development, on the other hand, the ultimate responsibility for how to construct an instance from a class remains vested in the class itself. In all cases, with or without there being a factory, a class must provide a constructor that allows an instance of the class to be created. *When a factory is deployed, it serves merely as an intermediary that decides on behalf of the clients when and how to call the constructor.*

The "when and how" of calling a constructor, as made possible by a factory, can be very important in situations when a class is in high demand; when the production of instances requires special computational resources; when there exist practical constraints on the number of instances that are allowed to exist at any given time; when a class must work in

Designing with Objects: Object-Oriented Design Patterns Explained with Stories from Harry Potter, First Edition. Avinash C. Kak.

collaboration with other classes for instance production; and so on. Additionally, having a factory as an intermediary between the vendor of a class and the clients of that software also gives the vendor greater freedom to upgrade the implementation code for the class as long as its interface used by the factory remains unchanged.

There are two related patterns in GoF that deal with factories: The Abstract Factory and the Factory Method. The basic notion of a factory in the software context as introduced above applies to both these patterns in equal measure. As for the difference between the two, the Abstract Factory deals with creating a family of related instances from a family of associated factories under the condition that the clients of the software would only need to program to two interfaces, one for the object classes and the other for the factories. This is the pattern that is the focus of what we present in the rest of this chapter. The Factory Method pattern, on the other hand, as you will see in Chapter 4, is more concerned with creating instances with method calls (that, in turn, call the constructors) and establishing a uniform interface for such method calls for a hierarchy of classes.

2.2   INTENT AND APPLICABILITY

The intent of the Abstract Factory pattern is to make it possible for a client to construct a family of related objects by programming to a small number of interfaces, typically just two: one at the root of the class hierarchy that describes the objects and the other at the root of a hierarchy of factory classes.

You should consider using this pattern when:

- the different possible customizations of all the objects can be characterized by common themes (you may think of each theme as standing for a family of closely related objects);
- all the related objects that belong to the same theme can be produced by the same factory class;
- all factory classes that are required for the different possible themes can be manipulated through a common factory interface.

2.3   INTRODUCTION TO THE ABSTRACT FACTORY PATTERN

As mentioned in Section 2.1, the main focus of the Abstract Factory is on the creation of *families of closely related objects*. A classic example of "families of closely related objects" — an example that can be found in virtually every presentation of this pattern — is a GUI (Graphical User Interface) platform that is equipped with the means to produce user interfaces with different kinds of looks and feel. A GUI platform gives us windows, buttons, scroll bars, and other widgets with a characteristic look-and-feel or with a small set of look-and-feel effects from which a user can choose one. We can think of the widgets for each look-and-feel as being closely related and therefore as belonging to a single family. Programming the front-end to such a library according to the Abstract Factory pattern makes it more efficient to create the widgets for any desired look-and-feel.

Organizing all of the widgets required for a given look-and-feel into a single family is just one way to use this pattern for GUI applications. An alternative way of conceptualizing

families of objects that is more convenient in some cases is to consider, say, all of the GUI buttons for the different look-and-feel effects as constituting a family, all of the scrollbars for the different look-and-feel effects as another family, and so on. A separate factory would be designated for each such family. The goal of the Abstract Factory pattern would now be to facilitate the production of the desired objects from the respective factories under the condition *that all the factories be manipulated purely through the abstract interface at the root of the factory hierarchy of classes.*

Regardless of how the objects are organized into families, the important design lesson that this pattern teaches us is how a client of the software can use just a small number of interfaces, typically only two, with one interface serving as the root for a factory class hierarchy and the other serving as the root for the class hierarchy describing the objects to be created, in order to interact with the entire object creation software.

2.4   THE ABSTRACT FACTORY PATTERN IN REAL-WORLD APPLICATIONS

For exactly the same reasons as stated in the previous section, this pattern is used by the software vendors who create similar-in-functionality yet unique-in-appearance web-based GUIs for commercial enterprises engaged in e-commerce. Each such enterprise would want its customer-facing front-end to be unique. Yet, all such front-ends must do very similar things: provide a search widget that allows the customers to search for a product; provide a product-browsing widget; provide a "shopping cart" widget; provide a widget that elicits shipping information from the customer; and so on. In their generic form, all of the widgets needed for an e-commerce site can be considered to constitute a family of widgets.

For creating the factories for the production of these widgets, a software vendor is likely to design a root factory interface that can then be implemented by a concrete class for the customization needed for the look-and-feel for a particular e-commerce client. You can think of the root factory interface as defining a generic factory.

Utilizing the concrete factory class created specifically for an e-commerce client, the client would only need to call the methods in the root interfaces of the widget hierarchy and the factory hierarchy in order to produce the different GUI components that have the desired background/foreground colors, shapes, layouts, etc. The client would not need to know the precise details of what classes work together for the look-and-feel for the client's web-based business portal.

2.5   HARRY POTTER STORY USED TO ILLUSTRATE THE ABSTRACT FACTORY PATTERN

Consider the case when we want our factories to produce the following three types of magical objects: MagicWands, Broomsticks, and Owls. Let's also say that each of the three wizarding schools, Beauxbatons, Durmstrang, and Hogwarts, would like for these objects to be customized for its own students, with the customization consisting of imprinting the school crest on the objects. For example, when a magic wand is supplied to a Hogwarts student, it must show the school crest for Hogwarts near one end of the wand. As for the owls, the school crests are emblazoned on them near their rear ends.

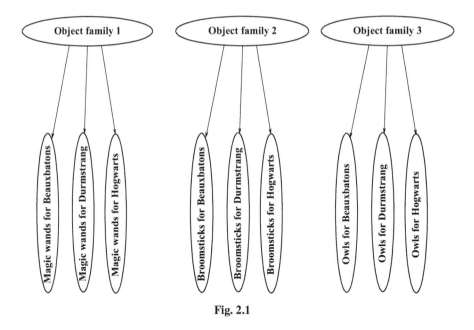

Fig. 2.1

We may think of each object type, along with its school specific customizations, as defining a single object family. The resulting three *families of objects* can then be visualized as in Figure 2.1.

With regard to the production of these objects, we can set up a factory called `MagicWandFactory` to produce the family of magic wands, a factory called `Broom stickFactory` to produce the family of broomsticks, and an owl emporium called `OwlEmporium` to breed the family of owls. Each factory would be unique in the sense that what it produces would be different from what the other factories produce. However, assuming that the factories are run by the same business enterprise, one would expect them to share certain higher-level attributes related to how the customers interact with them, how the inventories are maintained and replenished, and so on. These sorts of commonalities between the factories can be established by having them all implement the same interface that would be defined in the root class of a factory hierarchy as shown in Figure 2.2. With such a factory hierarchy in place, a client (such as a retailer on the Diagon Alley) will be able to interact with all three factories through the interface defined in the abstract `Factory` class shown in the figure.

Let's now talk about the objects to be created by the factories. Remember, the Abstract Factory pattern is about the creation of objects that are related in some fashion, since only such objects would lend themselves to being manipulated through a common interface. So what do broomsticks, magic wands, and owls have in common in the world of magic? From the standpoint of our demonstration here, what they have in common is that they are all enchanted. Therefore, we can consider all of these objects as belonging to the class hierarchy shown in Figure 2.3.

In order to demonstrate the pattern, we are going to need a customer for placing orders with the factories. For that we will use a class called `DiagonAlleyRetailer`. This class will represent a retailer on Diagon Alley in London. This street, generally hidden from

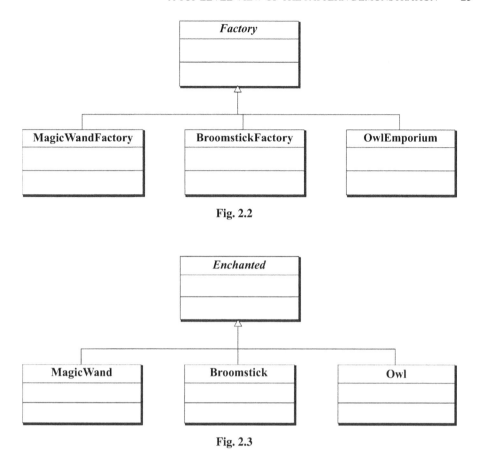

Fig. 2.2

Fig. 2.3

the muggles, that is, from folks who are not wizards or witches, is the main hub for wizard commerce in London. The students who attend schools like Hogwarts shop at Diagon Alley for their school supplies at the beginning of each school year.

2.6   A TOP LEVEL VIEW OF THE PATTERN DEMONSTRATION

The class diagram in Figure 2.4 is a top-level view of our demonstration of the Abstract Factory pattern. The only executable class in the code, `DiagonAlleyRetailer`, is a client of two class hierarchies, one headed by the root class `Enchanted` and the other headed by the root class `Factory`. The former root class serves as the interface for the magical-object classes and the latter does the same for the factory classes.

As the class diagram shows, the client class `DiagonAlleyRetailer` manipulates both class hierarchies through just the interfaces defined in the two root classes, `Enchanted` and `Factory`. Manipulation here means that the methods called in the implementation code for the client class are just those that are declared in the `Factory` and the `Enchanted` interfaces. That is what will be demonstrated through the code in the rest of the sections in this chapter. The class diagram also shows that the factory root interface declares the

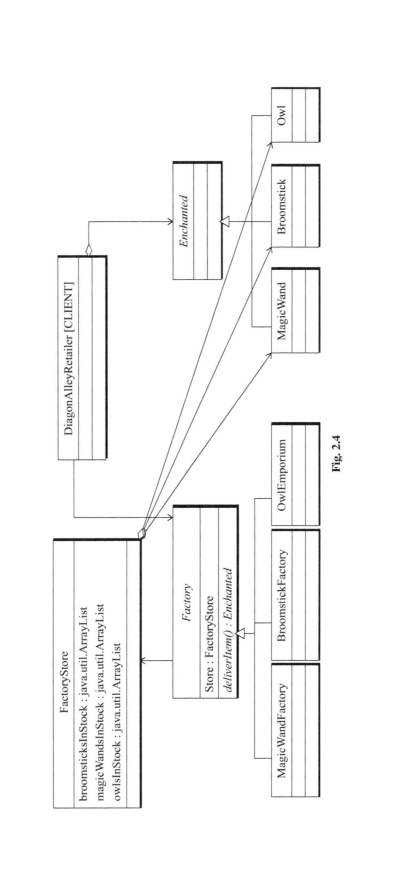

Fig. 2.4

method `deliverItem()`. A Diagon Alley retailer's interaction with the factories consists of making calls to this method.

Our demonstration code also uses a helper class named `FactoryStore`, as shown in the class diagram. If a Diagon Alley retailer wants to order, say, magic wands for a Hogwarts student, the retailer would use the `Factory` interface method `deliverItem()` to place the order with the `MagicWand` factory. However, unbeknownst to the retailer, the order would actually be processed by `FactoryStore`. It is only when the `FactoryStore` inventory runs out of its supply of magic wands, that the actual factory responsible for the production of wands would be asked to replenish the stock in the store.

The rest of this chapter presents the code for our demonstration of Abstract Factory. We start with the abstract `Factory` class.

2.7   THE ABSTRACT CLASS Factory

This is the root for the factory class hierarchy in our demonstration. Aside from declaring the method `deliverItem()` that must be implemented by all the concrete factory classes that descend from this root, this class also instantiates the `FactoryStore` class. A reference to the store is held by the `protected` variable `store`. This way, the store becomes accessible in all of the concrete factory classes that extend `Factory`.

```
public abstract class Factory {

    protected FactoryStore store;

    public Factory( String schoolName ) {
        store = FactoryStore.makeFactoryStore(schoolName);
    }

    abstract Enchanted deliverItem();
}
```

2.8   THE HELPER CLASS FactoryStore

We now describe the helper class `FactoryStore` whose purpose is to serve as a "buffer" between the Diagon Alley retailers and the factories — a fact that is hidden from the retailers. In other words, the use of the store we describe in this section is a detail that is completely internal to the operation of the factory hierarchy and is not known to the clients. Remember, a Diagon Alley retailer is a client of just the two class hierarchies, the magical-object hierarchy and the factory hierarchy in our demonstration of the Abstract Factory pattern.

As to how the store is actually used, when a retailer orders magical objects from a factory, the first thing the factory does is to send the order to the store. The store manages its inventories by ordering N magical objects at a time from the factories. This is done separately for each magical object and for each school-specific customization of the magical objects. When the inventory runs out for any school-specific magical object, the

store automatically places a request for a fresh order consisting of N items of that object with the appropriate factory. As long as the magical object in the order received from a retailer is in stock, the store goes ahead and fulfills the order without bothering the factories.

In the definition of the `FactoryStore` class shown below, the instance variable `forWhichSchool` is meant for the school-specific customization of the magical objects ordered. The static variable N determines the batch size for the manufacture of each magical object by any of the concrete factory classes. With N set to 2, for example, for any given school, the `MagicWand` factory will be asked to produce exactly two magic wands at a time. Only when both of the wands have been ordered by the customers (that is, only when the `FactoryStore` has supplied both of the magic wands it receives at a time from the `MagicWandFactory`), the `FactoryStore` instance will order two more.

An instance variable like `broomsticksDeliveredFromNewStock` keeps track of how many items of a given kind have already been ordered. When that number reaches the value specified by N for any item category, the corresponding factory invokes its `replenishBroomstickStock()` method to manufacture another batch of the item. The factory then calls on the store's `acquireMoreBroomsticksFromFactory()` method to acquire the new batch of items. The initialization methods with names like `initializeBroomstickStock()` are called by the individual factories to initialize variables like `broomsticksDeliveredFromNewStock` when, for these method and variable names, a fresh batch of broomsticks is ordered upon the exhaustion of the previous order.

The predicates like `checkBroomstickStockIsEmpty()` are also called by the individual factories to check if the previously constructed batch of magical objects is sold out. Finally, there are the three `deliverXXXX` methods for delivering the items, one at a time, from the factory store to the individual factories when they receive requests for such items from a Diagon Alley retailer. As you would expect, when a factory discovers that the store's inventory of items constructed previously is empty, it replenishes the stock in the store by constructing a fresh batch. You will see this logic in the concrete factory classes.

The `FactoryStore` class has been implemented using the Singleton pattern you will see in Chapter 6. That is because we want only one factory store to service all of the retailers. The Singleton pattern is implemented by making the constructor private, as you see in the code shown below, and also by making available a method like `makeFactoryStore()` for acquiring a reference to the one and only one factory store that is allowed to come into existence.

```
import java.util.*;

public class FactoryStore {

    private static FactoryStore theStore;

    private String forWhichSchool;
    private static final int N = 2;
    private int broomsticksDeliveredFromNewStock;
    private int magicWandsDeliveredFromNewStock;
    private int owlsDeliveredFromNewStock;

    private ArrayList<Broomstick> broomsticksInStock =
```

```
                                             new ArrayList<Broomstick>();
private ArrayList<MagicWand> magicWandsInStock =
                                     new ArrayList<MagicWand>();
private ArrayList<Owl>  owlsInStock = new ArrayList<Owl>();

private FactoryStore( String forWhichSchool ) {
    this.forWhichSchool = forWhichSchool;
    broomsticksDeliveredFromNewStock =
                            magicWandsDeliveredFromNewStock  =
                            owlsDeliveredFromNewStock = 0;
    for ( int i = 0; i < N; i++ ) {
        broomsticksInStock.add( new Broomstick( forWhichSchool ));
        magicWandsInStock.add( new MagicWand( forWhichSchool ));
        owlsInStock.add( new Owl( forWhichSchool ));
    }
}

public static FactoryStore makeFactoryStore(String forWhichSchool) {
    if (theStore == null) {
        theStore = new FactoryStore(forWhichSchool);
    }
    return theStore;
}

public int batchSize() { return N; }
public String forWhichSchool() { return forWhichSchool; }
public void acquireMoreBroomsticksFromFactory(
                             ArrayList<Broomstick> freshStock) {
    broomsticksInStock = freshStock;
}
public void initializeBroomstickStock() {
    broomsticksDeliveredFromNewStock = 0;
}
public void acquireMoreMagicWandsFromFactory(
                               ArrayList<MagicWand> freshStock) {
    magicWandsInStock = freshStock;
}
public void initializeMagicWandStock() {
    magicWandsDeliveredFromNewStock = 0;
}
public void acquireMoreOwlsFromEmporium(ArrayList<Owl> freshStock) {
    owlsInStock = freshStock;
}
public void initializeOwlStock() {
    owlsDeliveredFromNewStock = 0;
}
public boolean checkBroomstickStockIsEmpty() {
    return broomsticksDeliveredFromNewStock == N ? true : false;
}
public boolean checkMagicWandStockIsEmpty() {
    return magicWandsDeliveredFromNewStock == N ? true : false;
}
```

```
    public boolean checkOwlStockIsEmpty() {
        return owlsDeliveredFromNewStock == N ? true : false;
    }
    public Broomstick deliverOneBroomstickToClient() {
        return broomsticksInStock.get(broomsticksDeliveredFromNewStock++);
    }
    public MagicWand deliverOneMagicWandToClient() {
        return magicWandsInStock.get(magicWandsDeliveredFromNewStock++);
    }
    public Owl deliverOneOwlToClient() {
        return owlsInStock.get(owlsDeliveredFromNewStock++);
    }
}
```

2.9   THE ABSTRACT CLASS Enchanted

The abstract class Enchanted is the root of the magical-objects class hierarchy. All concrete magical-object classes must extend this class. The class defines the attributes common to all magical objects that are made by the factories.

In the definition of the class shown below, the instance variables idNum, schoolID, and itemType are meant for the customization of magical objects for the three different schools. Note that we do not try to achieve school-specific customization by further derivation from the concrete classes MagicWand, Broomstick, and Owl that will be derived from the root class Enchanted. This keeps the magical-object hierarchies simple and makes for a simpler interface in the root class. This approach to customization suffices for us since the customization requirement is simple — we only need to include the name of the school in the description of the instances constructed from the enchanted object classes. However, for more complex customizations, it may become necessary to derive customized classes from the concrete classes in the next section.

The school specific customization, in the form of a label, is automatically generated by the toString() method in the class definition shown below. The label for a magical object includes the name of the school for which the object was made along with a unique numerical identifier, a serial number really, for tracking purposes. The serial number is supplied by the instance variable idNum.

The serial numbers are kept track of separately for the different magical-object types. That is, there is no intermixing of the serial numbers among the MagicWands, the Broomsticks, and the Owls. The serial numbers are incremented sequentially through the instance variable idNum defined here and the static variables defined for each of the concrete magical-object classes presented in the next section.

```
public abstract class Enchanted {

    public int idNum;
    public String schoolID;
    public String itemType;
```

```
    public Enchanted( String forWhichSchool, String itemType ) {
        schoolID = forWhichSchool;
        this.itemType = itemType;
    }

    public int getIdNum() { return idNum; }
    public void print() { System.out.println( idNum + " " + schoolID ); }
    public String toString() {
        return schoolID + "_" + itemType + "_" +  idNum;
    }
}
```

2.10   THE CONCRETE CLASSES FOR MAGICAL OBJECTS

The goal of this section is to present the three concrete extensions of the Enchanted class. We will start with the Broomstick class.

In the definition of the Broomstick class shown below, note the important role played by the static variable nextBroomstickNum that is initialized to 1. This static variable, along with the instance variable idNum inherited from the parent class Enchanted, ensure that each broomstick that is ordered carries a unique id. This id is a concatenation of the school name and the unique serial number that is given to each broomstick. Note how the static variable nextBroomstickNum is incremented by the constructor to store the serial number that will be given to the next broomstick.

```
public class Broomstick extends Enchanted {

    public static int nextBroomstickNum = 1;

    public Broomstick( String forWhichSchool ) {
        super( forWhichSchool, "Broomstick" );
        idNum = nextBroomstickNum++;
    }
}
```

Paralleling the Broomstick class, we next show the definition for the MagicWand class. The role that was played by the nextBroomstickNum variable in the former class is now played by the static variable nextMagicWandNum. As the reader should expect by now, this static variable together with the instance variable idNum inherited from the parent class Enchanted ensure that each magic wand that is ordered will have a unique id associated with it. To remind the reader, this id is a concatenation of the school name and the unique serial number that is given to each magic wand. The static variable nextMagicWandNum is incremented by the constructor to store the serial number that will be given to the next magic wand.

```
public class MagicWand extends Enchanted {

    public static int nextMagicWandNum = 1;

    public MagicWand( String forWhichSchool ) {
        super( forWhichSchool, "MagicWand" );
        idNum = nextMagicWandNum++;
    }
}
```

What follows next is the definition of the Owl class. It works in exactly the same manner as the Broomstick and the MagicWand classes presented above.

```
public class Owl extends Enchanted {

    public static int nextOwlNum = 1;

    public Owl( String forWhichSchool ) {
        super( forWhichSchool, "Owl" );
        idNum = nextOwlNum++;
    }
}
```

2.11   THE CONCRETE Factory CLASSES

This section presents three concrete factory classes derived from the abstract root class Factory of Section 2.7. These concrete factories are BroomstickFactory, MagicWandFactory, and OwlEmporium.

A concrete factory class must implement the deliverItem() method declared in the parent abstract class Factory. As the reader can see in the definition of the BroomstickFactory shown below, the implementation of deliverItem() calls the locally defined private method deliverBroomstick() whose implementation code first checks whether the stock currently held by the factory store is empty. If not empty, it delivers the next available broomstick from that stock. However, if that stock has been used up, it fires up the replenishBroomstickStock() method for producing a fresh batch of the broomsticks for the store.

Note also that of the three methods defined for the BroomstickFactory class shown below, only the deliverItem() method is public, the other two being private. This is in keeping with the interface made public in the root class Factory. *A concrete factory class must not expose any methods by making them public if they are not in the root class* Factory. In other words, the clients of the Factory hierarchy must not be able to access any factory methods that are NOT in the root class Factory.

```
import java.util.*;

public class BroomstickFactory extends Factory {

    public BroomstickFactory( String schoolName ) { super(schoolName); }

    public Broomstick deliverItem() {
        return deliverBroomstick();
    }
    private Broomstick deliverBroomstick() {
        if ( store.checkBroomstickStockIsEmpty() )
            replenishBroomstickStock();
        return store.deliverOneBroomstickToClient();
    }
    private void replenishBroomstickStock() {
        System.out.println( "Replenishing stock with "
                            + store.batchSize() + " broomsticks" );
        ArrayList<Broomstick> freshStock = new ArrayList<Broomstick>();
        for ( int i = 0; i < store.batchSize(); i++ ) {
            freshStock.add(new Broomstick( store.forWhichSchool() ));
        }
        store.acquireMoreBroomsticksFromFactory(freshStock);
        store.initializeBroomstickStock();
    }
}
```

The definition of the MagicWandFactory class shown next parallels that of BroomstickFactory shown above. In keeping with the spirit of the Abstract Factory pattern, we again insist that only the inherited deliverItem() method be public and any other methods be private to the class so that there is no possibility of a client directly accessing any of locally defined functionality for this factory. The key locally defined method that cannot be accessed directly by clients is deliverMagicWand(); any calls to deliverItem() get translated into calls to this local method. As in the BroomstickFactory class, this local method first delivers the items from the factory store, and when the stock maintained by the store is empty, the locally defined replenishMagicWandStock() replenishes the stock.

```
import java.util.*;

public class MagicWandFactory extends Factory {

    public MagicWandFactory( String schoolName ) { super(schoolName); }

    MagicWand deliverItem() {
        return deliverMagicWand();
    }
```

```
    private MagicWand deliverMagicWand() {
        if ( store.checkMagicWandStockIsEmpty() )
            replenishMagicWandStock();
        return store.deliverOneMagicWandToClient();
    }
    private void replenishMagicWandStock() {
        System.out.println( "Replenishing stock with "
                            + store.batchSize() + " magic wands" );
        ArrayList<MagicWand> freshStock = new ArrayList<MagicWand>();
        for ( int i = 0; i < store.batchSize(); i++ ) {
            freshStock.add(new MagicWand( store.forWhichSchool() ));
        }
        store.acquireMoreMagicWandsFromFactory(freshStock);
        store.initializeMagicWandStock();
    }
}
```

Since the definition for the OwlEmporium presented below parallels exactly the definitions shown above for the BroomstickFactory and MagicWandFactory classes, it speaks for itself.

```
import java.util.*;

public class OwlEmporium extends Factory {

    public OwlEmporium( String schoolName ) { super(schoolName); }

    Owl deliverItem() {
        return deliverOwl();
    }
    private Owl deliverOwl() {
        if ( store.checkOwlStockIsEmpty() ) replenishOwlStock();
        return store.deliverOneOwlToClient();
    }
    private void replenishOwlStock() {
        System.out.println( "Replenishing stock with "
                            + store.batchSize() + " owls" );
        ArrayList<Owl> freshStock = new ArrayList<Owl>();
        for ( int i = 0; i < store.batchSize(); i++ ) {
            freshStock.add( new Owl( store.forWhichSchool() ));
        }
        store.acquireMoreOwlsFromEmporium(freshStock);
        store.initializeOwlStock();
    }
}
```

2.12   THE CLIENT CLASS Diagon AlleyRetailer

This section presents the executable class, DiagonAlleyRetailer, in our demonstration. The purpose of this class is to order the magical objects made available by the factories

using the interface declared in the `Factory` abstract class. The class does this by providing to its users a text-based interactive tool that prompts the users for the objects they wish to order. The client class calls on the `deliverItem()` method defined in the `Factory` interface to order the items from the individual product-specific factories. However, before the objects are ordered, we must first instantiate each of the concrete factories needed for the production of the magical objects. As a comment block in the class definition mentions, a reader is likely to find it odd that a Diagon Alley retailer is constructing instances of the concrete factory classes. We do this purely for programming convenience and, as described in Section 2.13, leave it to the reader to create a more elaborate demonstration of the Abstract Factory pattern in which the instantiation of the factories is independent of the retailers.

With regard to ordering specific objects, the user interface in this class prompts the user to enter 1 if he/she wants to order a broomstick, 2 if the order is for a magic wand, and 3 for an owl. The number 4, if entered by a user, is reserved to terminate the ordering interaction. Subsequently, the user is prompted for whether or not he/she wants to see what he/she actually ordered. Note how we use the `isAssignableFrom()` method of `java.lang.Class` to dynamically determine the class types of the items ordered by a customer.

From the call syntax used for instantiating the concrete factory classes in the code shown below, it should be clear that we are expecting a user to order only the Hogwarts-specific objects from the three object families shown in Figure 2.1. However, that can easily be changed by using a different string argument in the call to the factory class constructors. We leave it as an exercise for the reader in Section 2.13 to create an interactive session that would get the factories to send school-specific objects for any of the three schools.

```java
import java.util.*;

public class DiagonAlleyRetailer {

    public static void main( String[] args ) {

        ArrayList<Enchanted> itemsOrdered = new ArrayList<Enchanted>();

        // To keep the demonstration code simple, we construct instances
        // of the concrete factory classes here (despite the fact that
        // it seems odd for the client class to be instantiating factory
        // classes):
        Factory broomfac = new BroomstickFactory( "Hogwarts" );
        Factory wandfac = new MagicWandFactory( "Hogwarts" );
        Factory owlfac = new OwlEmporium( "Hogwarts" );

        while( true ) {
            System.out.println( "\n\nTo order an enchanted broomstick, "
                            + "enter 1"
                            + "\nTo order a magic wand, enter 2"
                            + "\nTo order an owl, enter 3"
                            + "\nTo quit ordering, enter 4\n");
            Scanner sc = new Scanner(System.in);
            int in = sc.nextInt();
            if ( in == 1 ) itemsOrdered.add( broomfac.deliverItem() );
            if ( in == 2 ) itemsOrdered.add( wandfac.deliverItem() );
```

```
            if ( in == 3 ) itemsOrdered.add( owlfac.deliverItem() );
            if ( in == 4 ) break;
        }
        System.out.println( "Number of items ordered: "
                                        + itemsOrdered.size() );
        System.out.println( "\n\nWould you like to see what you "
                        + "ordered? "
                        + "\n Answer \"y\" for yes and \"n\" "
                        + "for no: " );
        Scanner sc = new Scanner(System.in);
        String yORn = sc.next();
        System.out.println();
        if ( yORn.equals( "y" ) ) {
            ListIterator<Enchanted> iter = itemsOrdered.listIterator();
            while ( iter.hasNext() ) {
                Object item = iter.next();
                if (Broomstick.class.isAssignableFrom(item.getClass())) {
                    System.out.println( "Item ordered: "
                                    + "one broomstick " + item  );
                    continue;
                }
                if (MagicWand.class.isAssignableFrom(item.getClass())) {
                    System.out.println( "Item ordered: "
                                    + "one magic wand " + item  );
                    continue;
                }
                if (Owl.class.isAssignableFrom(item.getClass())) {
                    System.out.println( "Item ordered: "
                                    + "one owl " + item  );
                    continue;
                }
            }
        }
        System.out.println( "Goodbye!!" );
    }
}
```

2.13   PLAYING WITH THE CODE

Download the class files for this pattern from the book website into a separate directory. Compile the code with the command

```
    javac *.java
```

and execute the DiagonAlleyRetailer class by

```
    java DiagonAlleyRetailer
```

The code will interact with you by asking you to specify the objects you wish to order. Subsequently, it will print out for you the objects you just ordered. Under the hood, the different Factory classes working together with the FactoryStore will make sure that the store is always replenished with the objects should your order empty out the currently held stock.

To gain deeper insights, you may wish to extend the demonstration code on your own along the following lines:

- An odd thing about the demonstration code presented in this chapter is that a Diagon Alley retailer gets to create instances of the individual factories. As mentioned earlier, this was done for programming convenience in order to keep the overall demonstration small. What is really needed is an executable class at a higher level of functionality that would spawn the factories and allow different retailers to be instantiated at the same time. The retailers instantiated in this manner would engage independently with the factories for the production of the magical objects. If you are up to it, create this more elaborate version of the demonstration. However, do keep in mind the issue raised in the item that follows.

- We implemented FactoryStore as a Singleton class (see Chapter 6 for what that means), but did not do the same for the individual concrete factories. Fortunately, that worked out for us because our demonstration had only a single retailer. However, just imagine the consequences of there being multiple retailers implemented in the same manner as the DiagonAlleyRetailer class! Each retailer would try to create a separate factory for the same magical object family. Using the Singleton pattern, change the implementation of the individual concrete factory classes so that only one factory is allowed to exist for each magical object family.

- In the definition of the FactoryStore class, N is the number of items that a factory builds should the stock for that object run out in the store. The reader may wish to experiment with different values for N, including $N = 1$. Obviously, when $N = 1$, an order for a magical object will always land in the factory itself.

- At this time, we have a single client for the demonstration of the Abstract Factory code — the DiagonAlleyRetailer class — and we make the assumption that this client will always order objects that are customized for Hogwarts. Expand the DiagonAlleyRetailer class so that the customization can be carried out with regard to any of the three schools. Now you may wish to also expand the dialog between the DiagonAlleyRetailer class and the human user of that class so that the choice of customization is part of the dialog.

- The demonstration code is much too simple with regard to school-specific customization of the magical objects. As you saw in the definition of the Enchanted hierarchy, the root interface of that hierarchy includes the instance variable schoolID that is used to associate the name of the school with the objects ordered by the students of that school. For more realistic customizations, you would need to extend the concrete object classes — MagicWand, Broomstick, and Owl — into school-specific versions of the same. If you are up to it, expand the scope of the demonstration code so that it achieves school-specific customizations in this manner.

3

BUILDER

3.1 BUILDING COMPLEX OBJECTS

We consider an object to be complex if it consists of several parts, if building the object involves a long sequence of assembly steps, and if preconditions exist that must be satisfied before each step can be executed. These preconditions will, in general, be of the two types described below.

The first type relates to the state of the partially built object before a new step can be executed. Think about building a house. The foundations must be in place before you can start on the superstructure.[1] In general, when the number of parts and the number of assembly steps are large (as in, say, the construction of an aircraft engine), one may have to resort to an algorithmic search for the best ordering of the steps so that such precondition constraints on the individual steps are not violated.

The second type of preconditions associated with the individual assembly steps may loosely be referred to as logistical. These preconditions relate to fixturing, tooling, and so on. Consider the case of a toy builder whose job it is to assemble different versions of a complex mechanical toy — a plastic version, a wooden version, and a metal version. Even when the sequencing of the assembly steps in all three cases is the same, the three different versions of the toy will entail different types of tooling and fixturing and, if there are nuts and bolts involved, it is also possible that the bolts would need to torqued differently for the different versions.

An interesting difference exists between the two sources of complexity mentioned above. Regarding the first source of complexity, it could happen that a feasible order in which every step will see its preconditions satisfied simply does not exist. When that happens, you cannot proceed with the assembly. And regarding the second source of complexity, the fulfillment of the logistical preconditions will depend on the resources available to the builder. In general, the logistical preconditions will be different for the different

---

[1] Such preconditions on the assembly steps are also referred to as *precedence constraints*.

Designing with Objects: Object-Oriented Design Patterns Explained with Stories from Harry Potter, First Edition. Avinash C. Kak.

variants of the same object — a point made clear by the previously stated example of assembling three different variants of the same mechanical toy.

Given these different aspects of building complex objects, one can argue that, in general, customers who want such objects built ought not to interface directly with the builders. What is needed in such situations is an entity — let's call this entity a *director* — that has a good sense of whether or not the prevailing circumstances would allow for an object to be built. The director may issue a call for building an object in its entirely, or in a piecemeal fashion, depending on what conditions related to object assembly can be fulfilled at the moment.

These are exactly the kinds of problems that are handled by the Builder pattern in the software context. When creating instances from a complex class, we may have to deal with certain constraints on some or all of the steps invoked by the constructor in the class. For example, it could happen that one of the steps requires a piece of information that must be fetched from a database and that different databases need to be used for different variants of the instances. It may also be the case that some of the databases require that the party making a request for information present certain security credentials for authentication. Additionally, we may have to deal with the situation that some of the subsequent steps in instance construction depend on what exactly is made available by the database used. Given this complexity, we should not allow the clients to directly issue calls for instance construction, since they may not be in a position to determine whether or not all of the conditions associated with the different steps can be satisfied. We would therefore need to interpose a director between the clients and the builders. The director would keep tabs on what conditions can be satisfied at any given time and ask the builders to proceed accordingly — in a piecemeal fashion if necessary.

3.2   INTENT AND APPLICABILITY

When object construction involves algorithmic steps, the intent of the Builder pattern is to organize the object construction details in an efficient representational hierarchy and insulate the clients from the complexity of how the objects are put together.

The pattern should be used when

- object construction involves algorithmic detail regarding how its different parts come together and when this detail is independent of the choice of the parts for the different customizations of the objects;
- you must mask the algorithmic construction details of object construction from the clients of a class hierarchy;
- it is possible to think of all of the objects desired from a class hierarchy by the clients as different customizations of a generic form so that you can place the construction steps for the generic form in a base class and the customization steps in the different subclasses.

3.3   INTRODUCTION TO THE BUILDER PATTERN

As the reader must have inferred from the opening section of this chapter, this pattern is about constructing instances and their variants from a class that is complex in the following

ways: (1) Each instance is composed of several parts that are in non-trivial relationships vis-à-vis one another; (2) The clients are interested in a small number of variants of a generic instance; and (3) The complexity of instances is such that a client cannot be expected to know whether or not all the conditions for instance construction can be satisfied at any given time. The last reason requires that we insulate the object builders from the clients by interposing a director in-between. It would be the director's job to know whether or not the prevailing conditions would allow for an instance to be constructed in at least a piecemeal fashion, if not in one fell swoop.

The Builder pattern teaches us that the algorithmic portion of instance construction is best handled by creating a class hierarchy whose root contains the basic construction knowledge common to all the instances and whose subclasses then provide customizations for the different kinds of instances. We can think of the code in the root class — which we will refer to as the base class in the rest of this section — as the generic instance creation code. In Figure 3.1, the base class is shown as the abstract class `Builder`.

For creating different variants of the objects, the Builder pattern takes advantage of polymorphism and method overriding. The generic instance creation code in the base class is likely to call on ancillary methods of the same class for those steps that need to be customized for the different kinds of instances. These ancillary methods in the base class may be overridden in the derived classes for instance customization. For constructing an instance corresponding to one of the derived classes, the base-class slice of the derived-class object would be constructed according to the generic algorithm in the base class definition, with the ancillary methods executed according to their definitions in the derived class.[2]

With regard to the role of the director, it is this entity's job to stay on top of whether or not the conditions exist in order to issue a call for instance construction to a concrete builder. A sophisticated implementation of the director may allow for instance creation to proceed in a piecemeal fashion if so dictated by the prevailing conditions and available resources — assuming the constructor definitions can be decomposed into a sequence of function calls whose output can be stored in persistent memory. Regardless of how the instances are created, the director's main role is to insulate the builders from the clients.

One thing about the Builder pattern that bears emphasis is that the director, although aware of the overall needs of the individual concrete builders, is not privy to the fine details related to instance construction. That knowledge resides only in the concrete subclasses of the base builder class. Nonetheless, the role of the director is critical because only the director knows when a specific builder can be called upon to construct an instance for a client.

The relationship between the root abstract class Builder, the concrete Builder subclasses, the director class, and the client class is shown in Figure 3.1.

---

[2]Consider two classes `Base` and `Derived`, with the latter a subclass of the former. A call to the constructor of `Derived` will, implicitly or explicitly, call on a constructor for `Base` for constructing the base-class slice of the derived-class instance under construction. Now assume that the base-class constructor calls on a method `foo()` that possesses different definitions in the base class and the derived class. The question then becomes which version of `foo()` will be used in constructing the base-class slice of the derived-class instance. In Java, it is the derived-class version of `foo()`. See Section 15.16 of Chapter 15 of [2] for an example that illustrates this point.

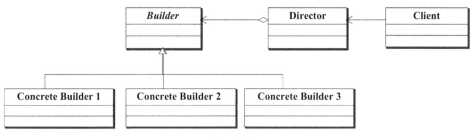

Fig. 3.1

3.4   THE BUILDER PATTERN IN REAL-WORLD APPLICATIONS

Applications involving instantiations of complex objects — their complexity being such that you would not want to expose the clients to it — can benefit from the Builder pattern.

We are talking about objects that require multi-step construction possibly with precedence constraints on the execution of the steps. In such applications, the notion of a director in the Builder pattern can be used to create a much-easier-to-deal-with interface for the clients for instance construction.

We are also talking about complex objects whose instantiation involves a large number of parameters whose values may not become available in one fell swoop. This may call for building an object gradually, in the sense that you start up a process that accumulates information related to the parameters as and when such information becomes available, and then, when all of the needed information is there, it issues a call for instantiating the object. The logic needed for instantiating objects in this manner is facilitated by the interaction that can be set up between the director and the concrete builders in the Builder pattern. What's more, the Builder pattern shows us how variants of the instances can easily be produced with a set of concrete builders that customize the logic placed in the base builder class.

For a more specific example, consider a software tool for online customer profiling. A profiler starts out by collecting information on a customer's surfing habits in order to gauge the individual's lifestyle preferences.[3] The surfing habits are subsequently analyzed by software for constructing a customer profile that expresses his or her preferences for food, clothing, consumer products, and so on. From a software perspective, you can think of a profile as an object whose construction will generally require a large number of parameters — the actual number depending on how many dimensions are used for characterizing a customer. Although it is relatively easy to develop a profile for a customer who has logged in with an account name and a password, such is not the case when a company is trying to create a profile for whomsoever is at the IP address where the hits are coming from. Now the parameters of interest must be gleaned with much greater care. The first order of business would be to determine whether there is any coherence at all to the surfing patterns at a particular IP address. (What if the IP address is used by several people, as would be the case for a public machine in a library?) Subsequently, the profiler would attempt to figure out if the user at the other end is an adult or a child, a male or a female, and so on.

---

[3] Such information may subsequently be used for targeted advertisement aimed at the customers.

The important point here is that, in general, a customer profiler needs to be aware of the precedence constraints on the steps involved in the collection and processing of data for the parameters of interest. The Builder pattern is ideal for this sort of object construction. The Builder pattern would make it easier to place all potential customers in a small number of categories, each corresponding to a subclass of a base profile class.

3.5   HARRY POTTER STORY USED TO ILLUSTRATE THE BUILDER PATTERN

Our demonstration of the Builder pattern is based on using potions as the objects to be concocted by a hierarchy of builder classes. We will specifically be interested in the making of the following three potions: the Draught of Peace Potion, the Wit Sharpening Potion, and the Love Potion. Our root abstract builder class, normally called Builder, will be called `PotionMaker`. As shown in Figure 3.2, this root class will be extended into three concrete potion-making classes, called `DraughtOfPeacePotionMaker`, `WitSharpeningPotionMaker`, and `LovePotionMaker`. Each of these concrete classes knows how to prepare the ingredients needed for its respective potion and, what's even more important, *its knowledge regarding how to make the different potions is limited to using just those ingredients.*

Each concrete potion-making class will inherit from the root interface `PotionMaker` two abstract methods, `makePotion()` and `getResult()`, the former for ensuring that any constraints on the order in which the ingredients are mixed are observed and the latter for making it possible for whomsoever has access to this concrete class to fetch the potion made.

The Draught of Peace potion requires two ingredients: moonstones and hellebore. The difficult thing about this potion is that the ingredients must be processed in just the right way for the potion to do its magic. The potion starts with the moonstone ingredient that must be powdered. The powder must be stirred exactly three times counterclockwise. Subsequently, the potion must be allowed to simmer for exactly seven minutes. It is only then that you add exactly two drops of the syrup of hellebore to the potion.

The Wit Sharpening Potion, on the other hand, requires three ingredients: ginger roots, scarab beetles, and armadillo bile. The ginger roots must be sliced, the scarab beetles

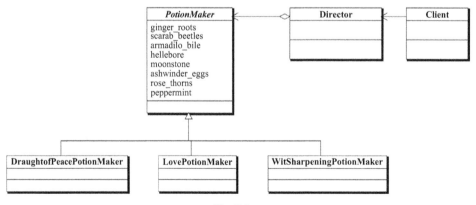

Fig. 3.2

mashed, and the armadillo bile measured out to be exactly one cup, with the ingredients added in the order listed.

And, finally, the Love Potion requires four ingredients: ashwinder eggs, rose thorns, peppermint, and moonstones. The ashwinder eggs must be used frozen and the other three ingredients powdered. The ingredients must be added in the order listed here.

Our demonstration of the Builder pattern will involve an entity that is not in Harry Potter — an entity named `Director` that is also shown in Figure 3.2. When a client needs a potion, it sends its request to the `Director`. It's the `Director`'s job to make sure that all of the ingredients for the potion are on hand before asking a concrete potion maker to supply the potion wanted by the client. After checking on the availability of the ingredients, the `Director` instance invokes the `makePotion()` method on an instance of the appropriate concrete `PotionMaker` class for making the potion and then invokes the `getResult()` method on the same instance for retrieving the potion for the client.

3.6   A TOP-LEVEL VIEW OF THE PATTERN DEMONSTRATION

The class diagram shown in Figure 3.3 is a top-level view of all the classes in our demonstration of the Builder pattern. In addition to the classes shown earlier in Figure 3.2, we now also show three other helper classes: `Ingredient`, `Potion` and `PotionMakingFeasibilityViolation`. Of these, what the classes `Ingredient` and `Potion` stand for is directly implied by their names.

The role of the helper class `PotionMakingFeasibilityViolation` is particularly interesting. We want each concrete potion-making class to only possess knowledge of how to make its own potion. Additionally, we also require each concrete potion-making class to strictly follow the recipe in adding the various ingredients. We will use `PotionMakingFeasibilityViolation` as a class whose instances can be thrown as exceptions when a potion maker is asked to create a potion outside of its competence or when, say through chance, the ingredients for a potion are not combined strictly according to the recipe.

With regard to the overall design shown in Figure 3.3, the base Builder class `PotionMaker` pools together the knowledge that is common to all the concrete extensions of the base class. In our demonstration, we will assume that this common knowledge consists of (a) the names — only the names — of all of the ingredients that go into the different potions; (b) the fact that every concrete potion maker must implement a method called `makePotion()`; and (c) the fact that every concrete potion maker must also provide an implementation for a method called `getResult()` that returns the potion made. *The knowledge regarding how to prepare the ingredients and how to combine them will be considered to be specialized and will only reside in the concrete extension of the base* `PotionMaker` *class.*

This important aspect of the design — that all knowledge regarding how to prepare and combine the ingredients remain confined to the concrete extensions of the base class `PotionMaker` — is taken care of by having all the `prepareAndAdd` methods return `false` in the base class itself. In this manner, by default, a concrete potion maker will only display competence in the processing of those ingredients for which it overrides the `prepareAndAdd` methods of the base class. With regard to the other `prepareAndAdd` methods, the potion maker would be explicit in professing ignorance.

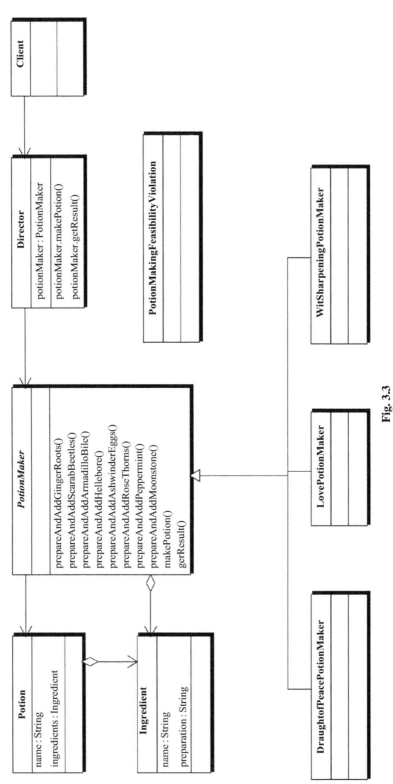

Fig. 3.3

The `Director`, also shown in Figure 3.3, can be expected to be aware of the ingredient needs for each of the concrete `PotionMaker` classes. In keeping with the mandate of the Builder pattern, the `Director`, however, will not know about the fine details of how the concrete classes prepare the ingredients and the sequencing constraints on the mixing of the different ingredients. In order to test the role of the `Director`, we will randomize the available ingredients at any given time and examine the behavior of that class. We would expect that the `Director` would not issue a call for potion making to a concrete `PotionMaker` until all of the ingredients needed by the latter are available.

Considering that the number of classes involved in our demonstration is rather large, the following summary of the roles played by the more prominent classes would perhaps be helpful to the reader:

- The demonstration involves a root builder class, which in our case is `PotionMaker`, that knows about all of the individual parts (in our case, the ingredients) that go into the building of the objects (in our case, making of the potions). We declare the names of all the ingredients in the `PotionMaker` class.

- We provide the root builder class, `PotionMaker`, with default implementations for how to prepare each part (that is, each ingredient). In our case, the default implementations will simply declare its inability to prepare a part (in our case, its inability to prepare an ingredient).

- We provide the abstract root builder class with an instance creation method (in our case, the potion-making method called `makePotion()`) whose implementation in the root class just throws an exception. Therefore, a concrete potion maker obtained by subclassing from the root `PotionMaker` class *must* provide an override for the default implementation inherited from the root class.

- We extend the root builder class into concrete builder classes for the different types of objects needed by the clients. In our case, that boils down to extending the abstract root `PotionMaker` class into concrete potion-making classes.

- In the implementation of each concrete potion-making class, we provide override implementations for those ingredient preparation methods that are needed for the potion. And in the override for the `makePotion()` method, we make sure that all of the constraints, such as those on the order in which the ingredients are combined, are fulfilled.

- We define a `Director` class that completely insulates a client from the internal details of the potion-making hierarchy of classes. The `Director` knows about the overall needs of the concrete potion-making classes. It asks a concrete potion-maker class to make a potion only when all of the ingredients for that potion are on hand.

3.7   THE ABSTRACT CLASS PotionMaker

`PotionMaker` is the base builder class in our demonstration of the Builder pattern.

In the implementation shown below, note that this abstract class knows about all of the ingredients that would go into any of the potions that any concrete potion maker would want to use. Also note that all of the `prepareAndAdd` methods have been given the default behavior of returning `false`. This is to ensure that unless a concrete potion maker overrides a particular `prepareAndAdd` method for a given ingredient, it will be able to honestly declare its lack of knowledge concerning the preparation of that ingredient.

Finally, note the abstract method declarations for `makePotion()` and `getResult()`. The override implementations for the `makePotion()` method, to be shown in the concrete subclasses derived from `PotionMaker`, will make sure that any constraints on the order in which the ingredients are combined and any intermediate processing steps on the individual ingredients are fulfilled. The override implementations for `getResult()` will be expected to return the potion made by a call to the `makePotion()` method.

```java
import java.util.*;

public abstract class PotionMaker {

    protected Ingredient ginger_roots;
    protected Ingredient scarab_beetles;
    protected Ingredient armadillo_bile;
    protected Ingredient hellebore;
    protected Ingredient moonstone;
    protected Ingredient ashwinder_eggs;
    protected Ingredient rose_thorns;
    protected Ingredient peppermint;

    protected Potion potionMade;

    public abstract Set<String> neededIngredients();

    protected boolean prepareAndAddGingerRoots()
            throws PotionMakingFeasibilityViolation { return false; }
    protected boolean prepareAndAddScarabBeetles()
            throws PotionMakingFeasibilityViolation { return false; }
    protected boolean prepareAndAddArmadilloBile()
            throws PotionMakingFeasibilityViolation { return false; }
    protected boolean prepareAndAddHellebore()
            throws PotionMakingFeasibilityViolation { return false; }
    protected boolean prepareAndAddAshwinderEggs()
            throws PotionMakingFeasibilityViolation { return false; }
    protected boolean prepareAndAddRoseThorns()
            throws PotionMakingFeasibilityViolation { return false; }
    protected boolean prepareAndAddPeppermint()
            throws PotionMakingFeasibilityViolation { return false; }
    protected boolean prepareAndAddMoonstone()
            throws PotionMakingFeasibilityViolation { return false; }
    public abstract void makePotion()
            throws PotionMakingFeasibilityViolation;
    public abstract Potion getResult();
}
```

3.8   THE CONCRETE EXTENSIONS OF PotionMaker

As stated earlier, each concrete potion-making class derived from `PotionMaker` provides override methods for only those `prepareAndAdd` methods that are relevant to the potion

that the concrete class is in charge of. In this section, we present three concrete extensions of the base `PotionMaker` class of the previous section.

We start with the concrete class `DraughtOfPeacePotionMaker` for making the Draught of Peace potion. As mentioned in Section 3.5, this potion requires two ingredients, moonstones and hellebore, that must be processed in just the right way (as already described in that section) for the potion to do its magic.

In the class definition that follows, note how the constraint on the order in which the two ingredients are mixed is enforced in the logic of the code for the method `prepareAndAddHellebore()`. Should `prepareAndAddHellebore()` be invoked before `prepareAndAddMoonstone()`, the former will throw an exception. In other words, the hellebore ingredient can be mixed in only after moonstone has been added to the potion. That the ingredients are added in the correct order is ensured by the correct order of invocation of the methods `prepareAndAddMoonstone()` and `prepareAndAddHellebore()` in the override for the `makePotion()` method.

The override for the `getResult()` method first makes sure that all of the ingredients have been added and then returns a `Potion` instance of the desired kind.

```java
import java.util.*;

public class DraughtOfPeacePotionMaker extends PotionMaker {

    public Set<String> neededIngredients() {
        return new HashSet<String>(Arrays.asList("moonstone","hellebore"));
    }

    protected boolean prepareAndAddMoonstone()
                    throws PotionMakingFeasibilityViolation {
        moonstone = new Ingredient( "moonstone", "to be powdered");
        System.out.println( "Moonstone powdered and added to the potion");
        System.out.println( "Stirred potion three times counterclockwise");
        System.out.println( "Allowed the potion to simmer for exactly "
                                                    + "seven minutes");
        return true;
    }
    protected boolean prepareAndAddHellebore()
                throws PotionMakingFeasibilityViolation {
        if ( moonstone == null ) {
            throw new PotionMakingFeasibilityViolation(
                    "\nMoonstone must be powdered and added "
                    + "before hellebore can be added to the potion.\n" );
        }
        hellebore = new Ingredient( "hellebore", "add as a syrup");
        System.out.println(
            "Added two drops of the syrup of hellebore to the potion");
        return true;
    }
    public void makePotion() throws PotionMakingFeasibilityViolation{
        prepareAndAddMoonstone();
        prepareAndAddHellebore();
    }
    public Potion getResult() {
```

```
        if ( moonstone != null  &   hellebore != null ) {
            potionMade = new Potion( "Draught Of Peace",
            new ArrayList<Ingredient>( Arrays.asList( moonstone,
                                                      hellebore )));
            System.out.println(
               "\nDraught of Peace Potion made by "
                            + "DraughtOfPeacePotionMaker.java\n" );
            return potionMade;
        } else {
            System.out.println(
               "DraughtOfPeacePotionMaker unable to make the potion" );
            return null;
        }
    }
}
```

We next show the implementation for the concrete potion-making class that creates the Wit Sharpening potion. As mentioned earlier in Section 3.5, this potion requires three ingredients: ginger roots, scarab beetles, and armadillo bile. These ingredients must be added to the potion in a specific order that was described in that section.

As in the definition of the previous potion-making class, note how the class shown below makes sure that the ingredients are added to the potion in the correct order. That order, as stated in Section 3.5, requires that prepareAndAddGingerRoots() be called first, followed by a call to prepareAndAddScarabBeetles(), followed, finally, by a call to prepareAndAddArmadilloBile(). Any violation of this order causes an exception to be thrown, as the reader can see from the implementation code in the prepareAndAddScarabBeetles() and prepareAndAddArmadilloBile() methods. That the ingredients are added in the correct order is ensured by the implementation code in the override for the makePotion() method.

The override for the getResult() method first makes sure that the three ingredients for the Wit Sharpening potion have been added and then returns a Potion instance of the desired type.

```
import java.util.*;

public class WitSharpeningPotionMaker extends PotionMaker {

    public Set<String> neededIngredients() {
        return new HashSet<String>(Arrays.asList("ginger_roots",
                                   "scarab_beetles","armadillo_bile"));
    }

    protected boolean prepareAndAddGingerRoots()
                throws PotionMakingFeasibilityViolation {
        ginger_roots = new Ingredient( "ginger_roots", "slicing");
        System.out.println(
                    "Ginger roots sliced and added to the potion");
        return true;
```

```
    }
    protected boolean prepareAndAddScarabBeetles()
            throws PotionMakingFeasibilityViolation {
        if ( ginger_roots == null ) {
            throw new PotionMakingFeasibilityViolation(
                    "Ginger roots must be sliced and added before "
                + "scarab beetles can be added to the potion" );
        }
        scarab_beetles = new Ingredient( "scarab_beetles", "mashing");
        System.out.println(
                    "Scarab beetles mashed and added to the potion");
        return true;
    }
    protected boolean prepareAndAddArmadilloBile()
            throws PotionMakingFeasibilityViolation {
        if ( ginger_roots == null | scarab_beetles == null ) {
            throw new PotionMakingFeasibilityViolation(
                "Ginger roots and scarab beetles must be  added "
                + "before armadillo bile can be added to the potion" );
        }
        armadillo_bile = new Ingredient( "armadillo_bile",
                                         "measure out a cup");
        System.out.println(
            "Armadillo bile measured out and added to the potion");
        return true;
    }
    public void makePotion() throws PotionMakingFeasibilityViolation{
        prepareAndAddGingerRoots();
        prepareAndAddScarabBeetles();
        prepareAndAddArmadilloBile();
    }
    public Potion getResult() {
        if ( ginger_roots != null
                &   scarab_beetles != null
                &  armadillo_bile != null ) {
            potionMade = new Potion( "Wit Sharpening Potion",
                new ArrayList<Ingredient>(
                 Arrays.asList( ginger_roots,
                                scarab_beetles,
                                armadillo_bile)));
            System.out.println(
                            "\nWit sharpening potion made by "
                        + "WitSharpeningPotionMaker.java\n" );
            return potionMade;
        } else {
            System.out.println(
                "WitSharpeningPotionMaker unable to make the potion" );
            return null;
        }
    }
}
```

Next we present the implementation of the concrete potion-making class that creates the Love potion. As mentioned earlier in Section 3.5, the Love potion requires four ingredients: ashwinder eggs, rose thorns, peppermint, and moonstones. These ingredients must be added to the potion in a specific order that was described in Section 3.5.

As with the previous two potion-making classes, note how the class shown below enforces the ordering constraint on the addition of the four ingredients. This ordering constraint, as stated in Section 3.5, requires that the following methods be called in the order they are listed here:

```
prepareAndAddAshwinderEggs()
prepareAndAddRoseThorns()
prepareAndAddPeppermint()
prepareAndAddMoonstone()
```

As the reader can see in the implementation code for `prepareAndAddRoseThorns()`, `prepareAndAddPeppermint()`, and `prepareAndAddMoonstone()`, any violation of the order in which these four methods are called would cause an exception of type `PotionMakingFeasibilityViolation` to be thrown. That the ingredients are added in the correct order is ensured by the implementation code in the override for the `makePotion()` method.

As in the other two concrete classes in this section, the override for the `getResult()` method first makes sure that all of the ingredients have been added and then returns a `Potion` instance of the desired kind.

```java
import java.util.*;

public class LovePotionMaker extends PotionMaker {

    public Set<String> neededIngredients() {
        return new HashSet<String>(Arrays.asList("ashwinder_eggs",
            "rose_thorns","peppermint"));
    }

    protected boolean prepareAndAddAshwinderEggs()
            throws PotionMakingFeasibilityViolation {
        ashwinder_eggs = new Ingredient( "ashwinder_eggs", "frozen" );
        System.out.println(
                    "Frozen ashwinder eggs added to the potion" );
        return true;
    }
    protected boolean prepareAndAddRoseThorns()
            throws PotionMakingFeasibilityViolation {
        if ( ashwinder_eggs == null ) {
            throw new PotionMakingFeasibilityViolation(
                "You must first add frozen ashwinder eggs "
            + "to the love potion before you can add rose "
            + "thorns" );
        }
        rose_thorns = new Ingredient( "rose_thorns", "powdered" );
        System.out.println( "Rose thorns added to the potion" );
        return true;
```

```java
    }
    protected boolean prepareAndAddPeppermint()
            throws PotionMakingFeasibilityViolation {
        if ( rose_thorns == null ) {
            throw new PotionMakingFeasibilityViolation(
                    "Before you can add peppermint to the " +
                    "love potion, you must first add rose thorns" );
        }
        peppermint = new Ingredient( "peppermint", "powdered" );
        System.out.println( "Peppermint powder added to the potion" );
        return true;
    }
    protected boolean prepareAndAddMoonstone()
            throws PotionMakingFeasibilityViolation {
        if ( peppermint == null ) {
            throw new PotionMakingFeasibilityViolation(
                    "YBefore you can add moonstone to the " +
                    "love potion, you must first add peppermint" );
        }
        moonstone = new Ingredient( "moonstone", "powdered");
        System.out.println(
                        "Moonstone powdered and added to the potion");
        return true;
    }
    public void makePotion() throws PotionMakingFeasibilityViolation{
        prepareAndAddAshwinderEggs();
        prepareAndAddRoseThorns();
        prepareAndAddPeppermint();
        prepareAndAddMoonstone();
    }
    public Potion getResult() {
        if ( ashwinder_eggs != null &
             rose_thorns != null  &
             peppermint != null &
             moonstone != null ) {
            potionMade = new Potion( "Love potion",
                        new ArrayList<Ingredient>(
                            Arrays.asList( ashwinder_eggs,
                                           rose_thorns,
                                           peppermint,
                                           moonstone)));
            System.out.println(
                    "\nLove potion made by LovePotionMaker.java\n" );
            return potionMade;
        } else {
            System.out.println(
                    "LovePotionMaker unable to make the potion" );
            return null;
        }
    }
}
```

3.9   THE Director CLASS

In keeping with the mandate of the Builder pattern, the `Director` class defined in this section satisfies the following three requirements:

- It isolates a client from the potion makers. By isolation in this context, we mean the following: A client would request a potion merely by naming it. We do not expect the client to know what ingredients go into the potion. It is the job of the `Director` to translate a client's request into a form that would be understood by the potion makers.
- The `Director` asks a concrete `PotionMaker` class to supply a potion *only after all of the ingredients for that potion have become available.*
- Although the `Director` class must be aware of the overall requirements of the individual potion makers, it must *not* be privy to the fine details concerning the making of the potions. As explained in the previous section, this fine detail in our demonstration relates to the order in which the ingredients are mixed for creating a potion.

As the reader will see in Section 3.13 where we define the `Client` class, the first requirement is rather easy to satisfy. It is facilitated by the fact that all potion-making requests from a client are sent to the `Director`, and each request only mentions the name of the potion desired.

In order to satisfy the second requirement, the `Director` class maintains two different containers, `all_ingredients` and `availableIngredients`, the first declared at the beginning of the class definition and the second declared separately in each of the three `if` blocks for deciding when to issue a potion-making call for each of the three different potions. As its name implies, the `all_ingredients` container is a list — actually a set — of all of the ingredients that are used by all the potion-making classes in this demonstration. The second container, `availableIngredients`, chooses the ingredients randomly from the first by calling the method `update_available_ingredients()`. Consider the first container as simply a naming list for all of the ingredients. *An ingredient does not become available for a potion unless it is in the second container, the `availableIngredients` container.*

In each of the potion-making `if` blocks in the class definition, the `Director` patiently waits in a `while` loop until all of the needed ingredients become available in order to fulfill a client request for a potion.

With regard to satisfying the third requirement mentioned above, it is clear that whereas the `Director` is aware of the overall needs of the individual potion makers in terms of the ingredients they require, it has no direct knowledge of the fine details that go into the making of the potions — in keeping with the mandate of the Builder pattern. As the reader already knows, the fine detail in our demonstration refers to the ordering constraints on the mixing of the ingredients.

```
import java.util.*;

public class Director {

  private static Set<String> all_ingredients =
     new HashSet<String>(Arrays.asList("ginger_roots","scarab_beetles",
                                  "armadillo_bile","hellebore",
```

```
                                     "moonstone","ashwinder_eggs",
                                     "rose_thorns","peppermint"));
private static Set<String> update_available_ingredients() {
    Set<String> availables = new HashSet<String>();
    Iterator<String> iter = all_ingredients.iterator();
    while (iter.hasNext()) {
        String ingredient = iter.next();
        if (Math.random() < 0.7) {
            availables.add(ingredient);
        }
    }
    return availables;
}


public static void  makePotion( String clientRequest ) {
    PotionMaker potionMaker = null;
    if ( clientRequest.equalsIgnoreCase("Wit Sharpening Potion")){
        System.out.println("\n\nDIRECTOR will try to get the Wit " +
                            "Sharpening Potion made\n");
        Set<String> availableIngredients = update_available_ingredients();
        potionMaker = new WitSharpeningPotionMaker();
        Set<String> neededIngredients = potionMaker.neededIngredients();
        System.out.println("   NEEDED INGREDIENTS: " + neededIngredients);
        System.out.println("   Available ingredients: "
                                              + availableIngredients);
        while (!availableIngredients.containsAll( neededIngredients ) ) {
            try {
                Thread.sleep(3000);
            } catch(InterruptedException e){}
            availableIngredients = update_available_ingredients();
            System.out.println("   Available ingredients: "
                                              + availableIngredients);
        }
    } else if (clientRequest.equalsIgnoreCase(
                              "Draught of Peace Potion")){
        System.out.println("\n\nDIRECTOR will try to get the Draught "
                            + "of Peace Potion made\n");
        Set<String> availableIngredients = update_available_ingredients();
        potionMaker = new DraughtOfPeacePotionMaker();
        Set<String> neededIngredients = potionMaker.neededIngredients();
        System.out.println("   NEEDED INGREDIENTS: " + neededIngredients);
        System.out.println("   Available ingredients: " +
                                              availableIngredients);
        while (!availableIngredients.containsAll( neededIngredients ) ) {
            try {
                Thread.sleep(3000);
            } catch(InterruptedException e){}
            availableIngredients = update_available_ingredients();
            System.out.println("   Available ingredients: " +
                                              availableIngredients);
        }
    } else if ( clientRequest.equalsIgnoreCase("Love Potion") ) {
```

```
                    System.out.println("\n\nDIRECTOR will try to get the Love Potion "
                                                          + "made\n");
                    Set<String> availableIngredients = update_available_ingredients();
                    potionMaker = new LovePotionMaker();
                    Set<String> neededIngredients = potionMaker.neededIngredients();
                    System.out.println("  NEEDED INGREDIENTS: " + neededIngredients);
                    System.out.println("   Available ingredients: " +
                                                          availableIngredients);
                    while (!availableIngredients.containsAll( neededIngredients ) ) {
                        try {
                            Thread.sleep(3000);
                        } catch(InterruptedException e){}
                        availableIngredients = update_available_ingredients();
                        System.out.println("   Available ingredients: " +
                                                          availableIngredients);
                    }
            } else {
                System.out.println(
                            "Client request not understood. Exiting" );
                System.exit(0);
            }
            System.out.println("  \nDIRECTOR now has all the needed ingredients\n");
            try {
                potionMaker.makePotion();
                potionMaker.getResult();
            } catch( PotionMakingFeasibilityViolation e ) {
                System.out.println( e.getMessage() );
            }
        }
    }
}
```

3.10   THE Potion CLASS

We now present the Potion class. The goal of our demonstration of the Builder pattern is to create instances of this class. A Potion instance is made up of Ingredient instances that, as the reader knows, must be combined in just the right order for a potion to have the desired magical quality.

```
import java.util.*;

public class Potion {
    String name;
    List<Ingredient> ingredients;

    public Potion( String name, List<Ingredient> ingredients ) {
        this.name = name;
        this.ingredients = ingredients;
    }
}
```

3.11   THE Ingredient CLASS

This section presents the Ingredient class. Instances of this class are the ingredients that go into a potion. Since each ingredient must be processed in some fashion before it is added to the potion, the class includes an instance variable called preparation whose value expresses how the ingredient should be prepared.

```
public class Ingredient {
    String name;
    String preparation;
    public Ingredient( String name, String prep ) {
        this.name = name;
        this.preparation = prep;
    }
    public String toString() { return name; }
}
```

3.12   THE PotionMakingFeasibilityViolation CLASS

In order to fulfill the mandate of the Builder pattern, a concrete builder class must enforce various constraints on how the parts are assembled into objects, which in our case translates into the order in which the ingredients are added to a potion. A concrete potion-making class must throw an exception when these constraints are violated. This section defines the exception class for that purpose.

```
public class PotionMakingFeasibilityViolation extends Exception {

    public PotionMakingFeasibilityViolation() {
        super();
    }
    public PotionMakingFeasibilityViolation(String arg0) {
        super(arg0);
    }
}
```

3.13   THE Client CLASS

As mentioned earlier, an important role of the Director class is to serve as a translator of the requests for potions from the clients — the requests merely naming the potions desired — into a form that would be understood by the potion makers. A client is not expected to know what ingredients go into the potions. As mentioned in Section 3.9, this translation is an important aspect of how the Director isolates a client from the builders. As shown in the definition of Client in this section, a client communicates with just the Director and that too by just naming the potion wanted.

```
public class Client {
    public static void main( String[] args ) {

        // Each call shown below succeeds only after the Director has
        // ascertained that all the ingredients needed for the potion
        // in question are available.  Each call prints out how the
        // potion was actually made.
        Director.makePotion( "Wit Sharpening Potion");
        Director.makePotion( "Draught of Peace Potion");
        Director.makePotion( "Love Potion" );
    }
}
```

3.14   PLAYING WITH THE CODE

Download the class files for this pattern from the book website into a separate directory. Compile the code with the command

```
javac *.java
```

and execute the Client class by

```
java Client
```

Given the code in the main() of Client, executing the class Client will yield the following sort of output. Note that the output will vary from one run to another on account of the randomization of the availability of the ingredients that you see in the Director class in Section 3.9.

```
DIRECTOR will try to get the Wit Sharpening Potion made

    NEEDED INGREDIENTS: [ginger_roots, armadillo_bile, scarab_beetles]
    Available ingredients: [ginger_roots, armadillo_bile, ashwinder_eggs,
                                                          rose_thorns]
    Available ingredients: [ginger_roots, armadillo_bile, hellebore,
                               moonstone, scarab_beetles, peppermint]

DIRECTOR now has all the needed ingredients

Ginger roots sliced and added to the potion
Scarab beetles mashed and added to the potion
Armadillo bile measured out and added to the potion

Wit sharpening potion made by WitSharpeningPotionMaker.java
```

```
DIRECTOR will try to get the Draught of Peace Potion made

    NEEDED INGREDIENTS: [hellebore, moonstone]
    Available ingredients: [ginger_roots, armadillo_bile, moonstone,
                                    scarab_beetles, ashwinder_eggs]
    Available ingredients: [ginger_roots, armadillo_bile, moonstone,
                    scarab_beetles, peppermint, ashwinder_eggs, rose_thorns]
    Available ingredients: [ginger_roots, peppermint, ashwinder_eggs,
                                                        rose_thorns]
    Available ingredients: [ginger_roots, armadillo_bile, hellebore,
                            moonstone, scarab_beetles, peppermint]

DIRECTOR now has all the needed ingredients

Moonstone powdered and added to the potion
Stirred potion three times counterclockwise
Allowed the potion to simmer for exactly seven minutes
Added two drops of the syrup of hellebore to the potion

Draught of Peace Potion made by DraughtOfPeacePotionMaker.java



DIRECTOR will try to get the Love Potion made

    NEEDED INGREDIENTS: [peppermint, ashwinder_eggs, rose_thorns]
    Available ingredients: [ginger_roots, peppermint, ashwinder_eggs,
                                                        rose_thorns]

DIRECTOR now has all the needed ingredients

Frozen ashwinder eggs added to the potion
Rose thorns added to the potion
Peppermint powder added to the potion
Moonstone powdered and added to the potion

Love potion made by LovePotionMaker.java
```

The output shown above starts with the Director wanting to get the Wit Sharpening potion made for the client. However, before a call to the WitSharpeningPotionMaker can be issued, the Director must be sure that all of the ingredients for this potion are on hand. The Director compares the list of the ingredients needed for the potion with the list of ingredients actually available at the moment. If you look at the logic in the update_available_ingredients() method of the Director class in Section 3.9, a fresh list of the available ingredients is generated every 3 seconds by randomly selecting from the list of all known ingredients. In the output shown above, it is in the second

round that the `Director` has all of the ingredients needed for the Wit Sharpening potion. The rest of the output is along the same lines.

To gain deeper insights into the Builder pattern, you may wish to extend the demonstration code on your own along the following lines:

- You could expand the `PotionMaker` hierarchy by creating concrete subclasses for some other potions mentioned in Harry Potter. If you don't remember the names of the potions, just try Googling a string like "potions harry potter" to see a large number of potions-related resources on the web. You will find websites that not only name the potions but also list their ingredients and the steps you have to go through to make them.

- Many readers are likely to say that the `Director` class as currently implemented is brain dead. You see, in the current demonstration, the `Director` examines the list of the ingredients currently available and then, should this list not contain all of the ingredients needed for a potion, examines the next list of the available ingredients. Looking at the successively generated lists of the available ingredients continues until the `Director` sees a list with all of the needed ingredients. This way of acquiring the needed ingredients does not represent any reality — even in the world of magic. A more realistic `Director` would grab the ingredients as they become available and, when all the ingredients for a potion are on hand, would issue a call for the potion to be made. One way to implement this more sophisticated logic would be to create a multithreaded implementation of the code in which the `Director` would interact with each potion maker in a separate thread. See if you can do that.

- The access control used in the hierarchy of builder classes — meaning in the `PotionMaker` hierarchy — leaves much to be desired. As programmed, nothing prevents a client from bypassing the `Director` and directly calling the public `makePotion()` method declared in the root interface `PotionMaker`. In a more watertight demonstration, the `PotionMaker` classes would check where the request for making a potion was coming from and make sure that only the `Director` was allowed that privilege. Expand the code in the `PotionMaker` hierarchy of classes to incorporate this safety feature.

4

FACTORY METHOD

4.1 REVISITING THE CONCEPT OF A FACTORY IN SOFTWARE

All of the comments made in Section 2.1 of Chapter 2 apply to this chapter also. As mentioned there, the main purpose of a factory in a software context is to increase the separation between the producers and the consumers of the objects constructed from certain designated classes. The Abstract Factory pattern of Chapter 2 dealt with efficient production of a family of related objects through a family of related factories, with a client having to program to only two interfaces, one at the root of the object hierarchy and the other at the root of the factory hierarchy. The Factory Method pattern we take up in this chapter, on the other hand, is concerned about how to construct instances through method calls — these being known as factory methods — that, in turn, call the constructors, instead of calling the constructors directly, and how the factory method code can be organized efficiently for a hierarchy of classes.

When the main mechanism provided to a client for acquiring an instance of a class is by calling a factory method, you can incorporate in the software the following sorts of features: (1) an ability to control access to the class beyond what is possible by placing its constructor in the private or the protected section of the class; (2) an ability to check on the availability of resources (computational, network related, and other) for the construction of an instance before a call to the constructor is actually issued; (3) an ability to subject instance creation to how many such instances were previously created by the same client or by all the clients together; and so on.

Upon hearing this, a reader might argue: why not place all of this code in the constructor itself? To answer, the reasons for using a factory method may vary from one application of a class to another. If so needed, such application-dependent variability can be taken care of by providing multiple factory methods for the same class.

If instance construction is to be regulated by a factory method, you are then faced with the question of how to best write code for such methods — *especially if you are dealing with not just one class but with a class along with its subclasses.* If at all possible, you would like to create a uniform factory interface whose methods can be used for constructing

Designing with Objects: Object-Oriented Design Patterns Explained with Stories from Harry Potter, First Edition. Avinash C. Kak.

all of the different types of objects, even those that correspond to the subclasses of the main object classes. Ideally, you would like to make it possible for a client to use the same factory method call for constructing objects of all of the different types — obviously with the expectation that the client would invoke the method on the different implementations of the factory interface. It is this issue of how to construct a uniform factory interface for an object class hierarchy that is addressed in this chapter by the Factory Method pattern.

4.2   INTENT AND APPLICABILITY

The intent of the Factory Method pattern is to provide a root interface that defines the factory methods that the clients can call for constructing objects from a class hierarchy, with the different concrete realizations of the root interface providing override implementations for the different object types.

You should consider using this pattern when

- you want the clients of a class hierarchy to call certain designated methods for constructing objects, as opposed to calling the constructors directly;
- the code for the object construction methods can be organized in such a way that all of the objects (corresponding to the different classes in a class hierarchy) can be constructed by override definitions for one or more abstract methods declared in a root interface;
- you need to create a separation between the object class hierarchy and the code that defines the methods for constructing objects from that hierarchy.

4.3   INTRODUCTION TO THE FACTORY METHOD PATTERN

Let us say that the software you make available to your clients includes two classes, A and B, whose instances are the software artifacts of interest to your clients. Let's further say that your code also makes available a separate class — let's call it `ArtifactMaker` — whose factory methods `makeArtifactA()` and `makeArtifactB()` return instances of types A and B, respectively. Obviously, for reasons mentioned in Section 4.1, we are assuming that the clients are not given direct access to the constructors of the classes A and B. It is the factory methods that call the constructors of these classes for actual instance production. If this is how your software is organized, it is likely to work just fine assuming that A and B are unrelated classes.

But now let's consider the case when the two artifact classes A and B are related, in the sense that they are both small variations on a more generic class and could therefore be derived from a root class where you'd place all the code common to both A and B. This is where the Factory Method comes into play. This pattern teaches us a couple of important things about how to best organize the factory-method based object production code in this case. First, as illustrated in Figure 4.1, instead of just one `ArtifactMaker` class that contains the factory methods for both A and B, the pattern says that it is better to have a hierarchy of artifact-maker classes that parallels the hierarchy for the classes whose instances are desired by the clients. Second, as also shown in Figure 4.1, the pattern calls for the roots of both the artifact-maker class hierarchy and the artifact-class hierarchy to be pure interfaces. That allows the clients of the software to acquire the desired instances by programming to just the interface of the artifact-maker class hierarchy. Doing so satisfies a

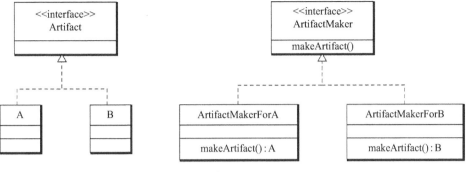

Fig. 4.1

basic tenet of good object-oriented programming, which is to program to just the interfaces. Since the artifact-maker class hierarchy is also likely to be programmed to just the interface of the artifact hierarchy, the developer of the software for the classes A and B would acquire greater freedom with regard to any future alterations to the artifact hierarchy code.

Let's now see how the factory method hierarchy on the right in Figure 4.1 can be used to yield objects while giving the clients a uniform interface for constructing all of the different types of objects. As shown in the figure, in the interface `ArtifactMaker`, we declare a method named `makeArtifact()` with the expectation that there will be a concrete class implementing this interface for each object class in the hierarchy on the left. In the figure, we have denoted these concrete classes as `ArtifactMakerForA` and `ArtifactMakerForB`. We will expect that `ArtifactMakerForA` will send to class A the client's request for an instance of that class after ascertaining that the request can indeed be fulfilled. And the same would go for the role of the class `ArtifactMakerForB` vis-à-vis the class B.

4.4   THE FACTORY METHOD PATTERN IN REAL-WORLD APPLICATIONS

Factory Method is one of the most extensively used patterns in the object-oriented software for modern applications. You'll see this pattern being used wherever there is a need to disallow direct access to a constructor for any of the reasons mentioned previously in Section 4.1. The factory methods typically have names like `makeX()` and they ultimately call the appropriate constructors for the instances needed by the clients.

In addition to the reasons stated in Section 4.1, another important reason for routing constructor calls through factory methods in real-world applications is the resulting convenience in the customization of the behavior of a class vis-á-vis the type of the data elements participating in the class. A classic example of this are the `Iterator` classes in Java and other languages. You need an instance of an `Iterator` class because you want to iterate through a collection of objects. By iterating through a collection, we mean starting at, say, the first element, visiting each element in turn, until reaching the last element. What is important here is that, since the `Iterator` object you need must be specific to both the collection and the element type in the collection, it is not convenient to construct an iterator though the usual mode of a constructor call. At the least, you would need to provide each different combination of the container type and the element type with its own constructor. Java therefore provides a factory method for the purpose of constructing `Iterator` objects.

For example, if you need an `Iterator` instance for an `ArrayList` container, you obtain the former by invoking the factory method `listIterator()` on the latter.

4.5   HARRY POTTER STORY USED TO ILLUSTRATE THE FACTORY METHOD PATTERN

Let's say we have clients who need magic wands and remembralls. Also, let's say that these magical artifacts can be represented by the hierarchy shown in Figure 4.2. A straightforward approach to satisfying this need would be to equip the classes for magic wands and remembralls with appropriate constructors. A client could then call on these constructors directly to construct any number of instances of these enchanted objects.

Although the solution described above would be the one used in many cases, there can be situations where such a solution would create too direct a coupling between the implementation of the class hierarchy in which the `MagicWand` and `Remembrall` classes reside and the client class. What follows is an example of such a situation.

Consider a hypothetical case of the Ministry of Magic wanting to place restrictions on the qualifications of the wizards who wish to acquire magical objects and wanting to keep tabs on the number of such objects in the wizarding community. The Ministry of Magic itself has no interest in supplying such objects directly to the folks at large. However, when an artifact maker receives a client's request (the client could be a Diagon Alley retailer placing an order on behalf of a wizard), the Ministry requires that the request be first checked with regard to the qualifications of the wizard desiring the magical object. The Ministry also wants a unique identification number to be assigned to each artifact that is supplied by the artifact makers to the clients.

The sort of checking mentioned above that must be carried out before the magical objects are actually constructed makes a Factory Method based implementation the ideal choice for the object construction software in this case. The makeArtifact() factory methods in the ArtifactMaker hierarchy in Figure 4.3 can make the checks required by the Ministry before invoking the constructors for the magical objects. Here is an example of a check we will incorporate in our demonstration code: We will ensure that when a magic wand is constructed for a wizard, the material at its core — this material holds the enchantment — matches the experience level of the wizard. The Ministry believes that a novice wizard,

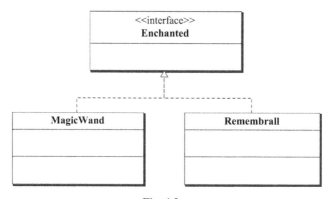

Fig. 4.2

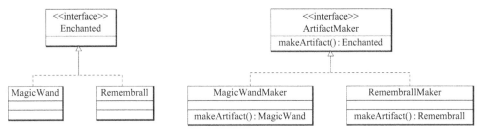

Fig. 4.3

such as a new student at Hogwarts, is generally not able to handle a magic wand that has the dragon's heart strings in its core. A wizard must be able to retain his composure as the wand is used to launch a new spell. If the wizard himself becomes too agitated by the spell he is trying to create, the spell may not last for any duration. For all such reasons, an important responsibility of a magic wand maker is to ensure that any constraints on the wand vis-á-vis its intended user are not violated. With regard to assigning unique identification numbers to the magical objects, we will incorporate that aspect of object construction in the class definitions for the magical objects, although we could just as easily have done that in the factory methods themselves.

4.6   A TOP LEVEL VIEW OF THE PATTERN DEMONSTRATION

Figure 4.4 shows a top-level view of all of the classes in our demonstration of the Factory Method pattern. In addition to the classes in the `Enchanted` and the `ArtifactMaker` hierarchies mentioned in the previous section, we now include the following additional classes: `Client`, `WandCores`, and `ArtifactCannotBeCreated`. Of these, the role of the `Client` class is to exercise the rest of the code. Acting on behalf of a wizard or a witch, a `Client` instance will place a request for one of the `Enchanted` artifacts with the corresponding `ArtifactMaker` class by calling a method declared at the root of the `ArtifactMaker` hierarchy. At the time of placing the order, the client will be expected to also supply the customer's qualifications relevant to the order. For the demonstration, we will limit this interaction between the client and the `ArtifactMaker` hierarchy to the ordering of magic wands only. The magic wand maker would want to know whether the customer who will receive the wand is a novice, an intermediate, or a seasoned wizard or witch.

Note that `Enchanted` in the class diagram is merely a marker interface — that is, an empty interface used to define objects of type `Enchanted`. In the other hierarchy, the artifact-maker hierarchy, the root interface, `ArtifactMaker`, has only one responsibility, which is to declare a `makeArtifact()` method. Since it may not be possible to always construct an object when it is ordered (say, because the smoke needed for a remembrall is not available, or, even if it is available, its enchantment does not succeed for whatever reason), the root class `ArtifactMaker` will declare the `makeArtifact()` method as throwing a special exception called `ArtifactCannotBeCreated`.

The other two classes in Figure 4.4, `WandCores` and `ArtifactCannotBeCreated`, can be thought of as support classes. `WandCores` is an interface class in which we use Java's `enum` to define the following names for wand cores: `phoenixTailFeather`, `unicornTailHair`, `veelaHair`, and `dragonHeartString`. The definition of `WandCores` is

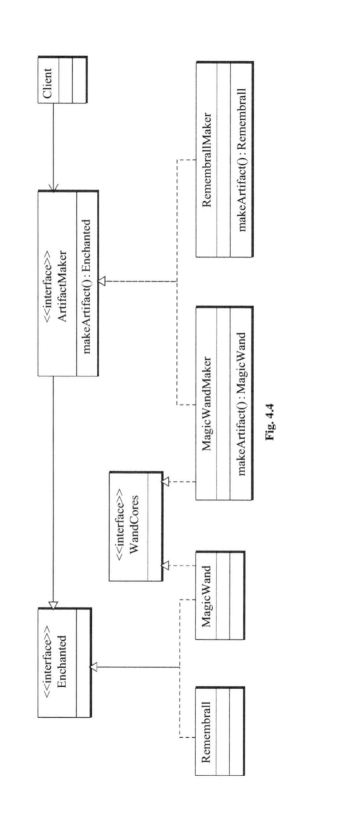

Fig. 4.4

```
public interface WandCores {
    public enum WandCore { phoenixTailFeather,
                           unicornTailHair,
                           veelaHair,
                           dragonHeartString };
}
```

Recall that wands with different cores possess different capabilities. Only the most experienced wizards can be expected to handle a wand whose core consists of a dragon heart string.

The class `ArtifactCannotBeCreated` is used as an exception class in our demonstration. Since an important feature of our demonstration is the enforcement of certain constraints on object construction, we obviously have a need for the code to throw an exception if those constraints cannot be satisfied. The definition of the exception class follows:

```
public class ArtifactCannotBeCreated extends Exception {
    public ArtifactCannotBeCreated( String s ) {super(s);}
}
```

With the definitions of the interface `WandCores` and the class `ArtifactCannotBe-Created` out of the way, the sections that follow present the remaining classes in Figure 4.4.

4.7 THE Enchanted CLASS HIERARCHY

As mentioned in the previous section, `Enchanted` is merely a marker interface whose job is to "pull together" for our demonstration code the magical artifacts that exist in the world of wizards and witches. Our demonstration is based on the assumption that the Ministry of Magic publishes specifications — in the form of class definitions — for all artifacts that are considered to be `Enchanted`. The Ministry also specifies the qualifications a wizard or a witch must possess in order to acquire one of these objects. Being just a marker interface, here is the official definition of `Enchanted`:

```
public interface Enchanted {}
```

We next present the `MagicWand` class from our `Enchanted` hierarchy. Since the most important part of a magic wand is its core — it must be made of material that can hold magic — the class specification places a restriction on the choice of cores. Furthermore, the class makes sure that the core chosen is acceptable with regard to the experience level of the wizard or the witch who will be using the wand. The relationship between the experience level of the user and the core inside the wand is enforced through a `HashMap` container

whose reference is held by the static variable experience_to_wandCore_mapping in the class definition. In the main constructor, we check whether the wand core used in the call to the constructor matches the information stored in the HashMap. If a violation is detected, an exception of type ArtifactCannotBeCreated is thrown.

If a wizard or a witch chooses to order a magic wand without telling the wand maker what his/her experience level is, the Ministry of Magic allows the wand maker to supply a wand whose core is made of veela hairs. Since this is the default construction of a magic wand, we place it in the no-arg constructor of the class.

Also note that the Ministry of Magic requires that each magic wand be stamped with a unique serial number. This requirement is easily taken care of by providing the class with a class variable called nextIdNum and an instance variable idNum. These are used in the no-arg constructor. When a new MagicWand is constructed by the wand maker, the wand maker calls the constructor of the class shown below, which, in turn, calls the no-arg constructor at the outset. And that causes a new serial number to be generated for the new wand.

```java
import java.util.*;

public class MagicWand implements WandCores, Enchanted {

    public int idNum;
    public static int nextIdNum = 1;

    private String owner;
    private String wizardExperienceLevel;
    private WandCore wandCore;

    public static final HashMap<String, WandCore>
            experience_to_wandCore_mapping =
                                    new HashMap<String,WandCore>();

    { experience_to_wandCore_mapping.put( "novice",
                                    WandCore.phoenixTailFeather );
      experience_to_wandCore_mapping.put( "intermediate",
                                    WandCore.unicornTailHair );
      experience_to_wandCore_mapping.put( "advanced",
                                    WandCore.dragonHeartString );
    }

    public MagicWand() {
        idNum = nextIdNum++;
        wandCore= WandCore.veelaHair;
    }
    public MagicWand( String owner, WandCore core,
                        String wizardExperienceLevel)
                            throws ArtifactCannotBeCreated {
        this();
        this.owner = owner;
        this.wandCore = core;
        this.wizardExperienceLevel = wizardExperienceLevel;
```

```
            if ( !experience_to_wandCore_mapping.get(
                        wizardExperienceLevel ).equals( core ) ) {
                throw new ArtifactCannotBeCreated(
                        "wizard's experience not matched to the wand");
            }
        }

    public MagicWand( String owner ) {
        this();
        this.owner = owner;
    }

    public String toString() {
        return "Wand Owner: " + owner + "        Wand Core: "
                        + wandCore + "        Serial Num: " + idNum;
    }

    public int getIdNum() { return idNum; }
    public String getOwner() { return owner; }
    public String getWizardExperienceLevel() {
        return wizardExperienceLevel;
    }
}
```

We next show the Remembrall class whose definition is similar to that of the MagicWand class. What the Ministry of Magic requires in this case is that the ball contain smoke and that the smoke be enchanted. One would expect that both these requirements would be checked by the ArtifactMaker class in charge of supplying remembralls. However, just to be sure, the class checks that the ball is indeed filled with smoke and that the smoke is enchanted. If either of these two conditions is violated, the class throws the ArtifactCannotBeCreated exception.

As with most magical objects in the wizarding kingdom, the Ministry of Magic requires that each Remembrall carry a unique serial number. This is made possible by the static variable nextIdNum that holds the serial number to be used for the next Remembrall instance.

```
public class Remembrall implements Enchanted {
    public int idNum;
    public static int nextIdNum = 1;

    private String owner;

    public Remembrall( String owner, boolean isSmokeAvailable,
                        boolean isSmokeEnchanted )
                                    throws ArtifactCannotBeCreated {
        if (! isSmokeAvailable) {
         throw new ArtifactCannotBeCreated(
                "Smoke not available for making a new remembrall");
```

```
        }
        if (! isSmokeEnchanted) {
            throw new ArtifactCannotBeCreated(
                    "Enchantment not available for the smoke" );
        }
        idNum = nextIdNum++;
        this.owner = owner;
    }

    public String toString() {
        return "Remembrall owner: " + owner + "  Serial Num: " + idNum;
    }

    public int getIdNum() { return idNum; }
    public String getOwner() { return owner; }
}
```

4.8 THE ArtifactFactory CLASS HIERARCHY AND THE FACTORY METHODS CONTAINED THEREIN

Shown below is the root interface of the two concrete artifact-maker classes defined in this section.

This interface says that any concrete class that implements the interface must at least implement the factory method makeArtifact() and that this method must return an Enchanted artifact, unless the artifact ordered by the client cannot be made for some reason, in which case the artifact maker must throw an exception of type ArtifactCannotBeCreated. The reason for an artifact maker's inability to supply a particular Enchanted object may include the nonavailability of the components that go into making the ordered object; not being possible to enchant the object or its critical magic-holding components; etc.

```
public interface ArtifactMaker extends Enchanted {
    public Enchanted makeArtifact( String owner )
                                throws ArtifactCannotBeCreated;
}
```

We next show the MagicWandMaker class. Since this class implements the ArtifactMaker interface, it must provide implementation code for the factory method makeArtifact(String owner) declared in the interface. In our case, this method simply asks the magic wand retailer about the experience level of the wizard for whom the wand is being ordered. Subsequently, it invokes the two-arg version of the factory method for the actual production of the magic wand. As shown, the contract of the two-arg makeArtifact() method is to throw the ArtifactCannotBeCreated exception. This is needed because the MagicWand constructor throws the same exception if it discovers that the wand maker is attempting to supply a non-compliant wand.

Also note the comment lines within each if block. They are meant to serve as place holders for those wand making steps that must be executed by the ArtifactMaker class itself. One of these steps will certainly be making certain that the wand core that is commensurate with the experience level of the wizard is available. Obviously, should any of these steps fail, they would throw the ArtifactCannotBeCreated exception.

Finally note that if the experience level of the wizard ordering a wand is neither novice nor intermediate nor advanced, the wand-maker supplies what could be referred to as a generic magic wand — this is a wand with veela hair core. Such a wand automatically comes into existence by a call to the no-arg constructor of MagicWand.

```java
import java.util.*;

public class MagicWandMaker implements ArtifactMaker, WandCores {

    public Enchanted makeArtifact( String owner )
                                    throws ArtifactCannotBeCreated {
        System.out.println(
        "\n\nEnter the experience level of the wizard as \"novice\","
            + " \"intermediate\", \"advanced\", or \"unknown\" ");
        Scanner sc = new Scanner(System.in);
        String experienceLevel = sc.next();
        return makeArtifact( owner, experienceLevel );
    }


    public Enchanted makeArtifact( String owner,
          String experienceLevel ) throws ArtifactCannotBeCreated {
        if ( experienceLevel.equals( "novice" ) ) {
            // Call procedures for checking on the availability
            //     of phoenix tail feathers.
            // If successful, call the return below, otherwise
            //     throw exception.
            return new MagicWand( owner,
                                WandCore.phoenixTailFeather,
                                experienceLevel );
        } else if ( experienceLevel.equals( "intermediate" ) ) {
            // Call procedures for checking on the availability
            //     of unicorn tail hairs.
            // If successful, call the return below, otherwise
            //     throw exception.
            return new MagicWand(owner,
                                WandCore.unicornTailHair,
                                experienceLevel );
        } else  if ( experienceLevel.equals( "advanced" ) ) {
            // Call procedures for checking on the availability
            //     of dragon heart strings.
            // If successful, call the return below, otherwise
            //     throw exception.
            return new MagicWand( owner,
                                WandCore.dragonHeartString,
                                experienceLevel );
```

```
        } else {
            // Either the user entered an unrecognizable string or
            // nothing at all in response to the prompt for
            // experience level:
            return new MagicWand( owner );
        }
    }
}
```

We next show the `RemembrallMaker` class. As with the previous artifact-maker class, since this class implements the `ArtifactMaker` interface, it must provide implementation code for the factory method `makeArtifact(String owner)` that is declared in the root interface.

The implementation of the factory method `makeArtifact()` in this case calls on a random number generator's boolean output to decide whether or not smoke is available for the remembrall under construction and whether or not the smoke, when available, can be enchanted. Think of both of these calls as stand-ins for there being no ironclad guarantee regarding the availability of smoke or its enchantability. Ordinarily, it would be the remembrall maker's responsibility to verify that both of these conditions are satisfied. However, in this case, the artifact maker ships off a remembrall construction request willy-nilly to the `Remembrall` constructor. As you will recall from the specification of the `Remembrall` class, the `Remembrall` constructor will make sure that both the smoke and its enchantability are in compliance before issuing the unique serial number to the remembrall being constructed.

```java
import java.util.Random;

public class RemembrallMaker implements ArtifactMaker {

    public Enchanted makeArtifact( String owner )
                        throws ArtifactCannotBeCreated {
        Random rand = new Random();
        boolean isSmokeAvailable = rand.nextBoolean();
        boolean isSmokeEnchantmentAvailable= rand.nextBoolean();
        return  new Remembrall( owner, isSmokeAvailable,
                                    isSmokeEnchantmentAvailable );
    }
}
```

4.9   THE Client CLASS

A client in this demonstration is supposed to be a Diagon Alley retailer of magical artifacts. Such clients know that the magical artifacts can only be ordered from certain artifact makers that are tasked with their production. The clients also know that the artifact makers will send the artifacts only if the wizards and the witches are qualified to receive the artifacts they order. They are also aware of the fact that each magical artifact received bears a unique

serial number that is used by the Ministry to keep track of all magical artifacts in the wizarding kingdom.

Shown below is a client that orders a magic wand for Harry and a remembrall for Neville. When the client puts in the order for Harry with the wand maker, the maker will ask the client for Harry's experience level. We are pretending that the client does not know in advance all of the compliance issues related to the ordering of an artifact; the client assumes that that is the responsibility of the wand maker anyway. So the client goes ahead and puts in an order and waits for the wand maker to tell it as to what additional information the wand maker might need so as to be compliant with the latest regulations from the Ministry of Magic.

```java
public class Client {
    public static void main( String[] args ) {
        ArtifactMaker maker1 = new MagicWandMaker();
        try {
            // This is a call to the factory method 'makeArtifact'
            // the MagicWandMaker class:
            MagicWand mw = (MagicWand) maker1.makeArtifact( "Harry" );
            System.out.println( mw );
        } catch( ArtifactCannotBeCreated u ) {}

        ArtifactMaker maker2 = new RemembrallMaker();
        try {
            // This is a call to the factory method 'makeArtifact'
            // of the RemembrallMaker class:
            Remembrall rem =
                    (Remembrall) maker2.makeArtifact( "Neville" );
            System.out.println( rem );
        } catch( ArtifactCannotBeCreated u ) {}
    }
}
```

4.10 PLAYING WITH THE CODE

Download the class files for this pattern from the book website into a separate directory. Compile the code with the command

    javac *.java

and execute the Client class by

    java Client

Given the code in the main() of Client, executing the class Client will cause you to be prompted with the following message:

    Enter the experience level of the wizard as
        "novice", "intermediate", "advanced", or "unknown":

If you enter, say,

    novice

the system will come back with

```
Wand Owner: Harry     Wand Core: phoenixTailFeather     Serial Num: 1

Remembrall Owner: Neville     Serial Num: 1
```

Recall that the code in the `main()` of `Client` orders a magic wand for Harry Potter and a remembrall for Neville Longbottom. That is where the names "Harry" and "Neville" come from in the output shown above. *Whether or not you see the second line shown above depends on the output of the random-number generator in the implementation of the factory method* `makeArtifact()` *in the* `RemembrallMaker` *class.* Recall that we use this random number generator to spit out a random boolean that determines whether or not there is smoke available for the remembrall under construction. If there is no smoke, the `Remembrall` constructor will throw the `ArtifactCannotBeCreated` exception. Since this exception is absorbed by the `Client`, you will not see the second line in such cases.

To gain deeper insights into the Factory Method pattern, you can extend the demonstration code on your own along the following lines:

- Our current demonstration leaves implicit the existence of an entity like the Ministry of Magic that is in charge of maintaining the specifications for the artifacts (by being in charge of the class definitions for the artifacts) and that is also in charge of laying down the conditions under which the artifacts can be supplied to the wizards and the witches. To keep the demonstration code simple, we incorporated these conditions directly in the constructor code in the artifact class definitions. You can make the demonstration more elaborate by actually defining a supervisory class with a name like `MinistryOfMagic` for specifying and storing the artifact construction constraints and also for being the keeper of the unique identification numbers that are assigned to the artifacts.

- In the current demonstration code, the artifact makers merely pass on the customer requests (after ascertaining customer qualifications) to the artifact constructors directly. Our demonstration code could get away with this because we have an artifact maker for each artifact type in the `Enchanted` hierarchy. You can make the demonstration more impressive by creating an object hierarchy of parts that must be assembled by the artifact makers into products for the customers. Now you will need a more distributed implementation of the constraints imposed by the Ministry on the parts, on the assembled objects, and on the qualifications of the wizards and the witches who order the magical objects from the Diagon Alley retailers.

5

PROTOTYPE

5.1 WHY NOT MAKE NEW OBJECTS BY COPYING OLD OBJECTS?

Let's say you are allowed to order chairs directly from a furniture factory that specializes in classic designs named after the French monarchs. And let's say your order is for a Louis XVI chair.

Assuming that the workers at the factory include highly skilled craftsman who can create authentic looking period pieces from scratch with great mastery, and not-so-expensive workers who are good at creating reproductions if given a period piece to copy from, the factory has two choices: It can either ask some of the high-cost workers to create a new chair for you from scratch, or it can ask some of its low-cost workers to make a duplicate from one of the previously made Louis XVI chairs.

Chances are that the factory would choose the latter approach. In order to use this option routinely for all incoming orders, the factory may permanently store away one example of each period piece and refer to it as a *prototype*. Subsequently, fulfilling a customer's order would boil down to asking the low-cost workers to create a reproduction from one of the prototypes.

What is interesting is that creating a new object by copying a prototype has another advantage that is often overlooked. When a worker is asked to create an exact duplicate of another object, it is less likely that the new object thus produced would deviate from what was ordered by the customer — assuming, of course, the customer's order mentioned a specific prototype.

On the other hand, when a new object is created from scratch, there is a greater chance that the final product would not be exactly what the customer had in mind. Assuming that the object is complex, any production-from-scratch will involve giving values to the various attributes of the object. It is not unlikely that when the customer placed his/her order, he/she mentioned only the more prominent of those attributes. However, the attributes specified by the customer may not sufficiently constrain someone who is going to create the object from the ground up. The end result is more likely that when the customer sees the final

Designing with Objects: Object-Oriented Design Patterns Explained with Stories from Harry Potter,
First Edition. Avinash C. Kak.
© 2015 John Wiley & Sons, Inc. Published 2015 by John Wiley & Sons, Inc.

object, he/she will not be fully satisfied, especially if the consequences of the attributes that the customer left unmentioned at the time of placing the order are serious.[1] Other possible errors in the build-from-scratch approach include misunderstanding the customer's specifications, etc.

As will be argued shortly in this chapter, these benefits of object construction by copying, as opposed to object construction from scratch, also apply to the world of software development.

5.2   INTENT AND APPLICABILITY

The intent of the Prototype pattern is to construct new objects by making duplicates from their stored versions.

You should consider using this pattern when

- the cost of constructing an object from scratch significantly exceeds the cost associated with just duplicating a previously stored version of the same;
- the number of different kinds of instances that the clients need to construct from the same class is small so that each kind can be stored away as a prototype;
- the class definitions do not lead to objects that are composed of deeply nested structures (which might create issues in deep copying from the stored prototypes).

5.3   INTRODUCTION TO THE PROTOTYPE PATTERN

As the reader already knows, it is basic to general object-oriented programming that you create a new instance of a class by invoking its constructor. This manner of creating a software object amounts to constructing it from scratch every time. Is that really necessary, one might ask, as we did for the case of physical-world objects in Section 5.1? In the software world, are there any benefits to creating a new object by just cloning a previously constructed object that is still in the memory — assuming, of course, that the state of the object newly requested by a client is the same as the state of an old object that is still in the memory? By state, we mean the values assigned to the instance variables when a new object is constructed from a class.

For small and simple objects — let's say for a class involving instance variables of just the primitive types — constructing an instance from scratch involves no major costs (in terms of, say, the amount of computational effort required) in most cases. Therefore, it makes sense to fulfill a client's request for a new object by creating afresh a new instance by calling the class's constructor — except perhaps for the following caveat: When you give a programmer the freedom to construct an object by a direct invocation of the class's

---

[1] If you have ever hired a contractor to remodel a part of your house, say your kitchen, you have probably already experienced this. If you give your contractor a photograph and a description from an architectural magazine of what exactly you want done in your house, you are less likely to be disappointed than if you only mention to the contractor in general terms how you want the kitchen remodeled. The former is tantamount to duplication and the latter to creating something from scratch.

constructor, you also give the programmer the freedom to make errors in setting the state of the object. When the instance variables are set directly in a constructor call, they are subject to keyboard-entry errors and other errors that may be caused by the programmer making incorrect assumptions about the values to be supplied for the constructor parameters. Researchers who have studied issues related to API complexity[2] have shown that the larger the number of parameters in a function call, and especially if several of the parameters are of the same type, the greater the likelihood of programmer errors in correctly specifying the arguments in calling such functions. So even when the costs associated with actual object construction are minimal, there can be other factors that may speak against constructing an object afresh through constructor calls every time a new instance of a class is needed by a client.

And when the objects are complex, say, because their instance variables are themselves class type objects or because the instance variables require values that must be fetched from resources elsewhere in a network, it may be faster and simpler to supply a new object by simply cloning a previously constructed object.

But, obviously, a clone of a previously constructed instance can be returned as a new instance only if the state of the previously constructed instance is the same as what is required for the new instance.

This implies that only when there exist strong constraints on the states of the instances constructed from a class that it makes sense to use cloning to supply a new instance. For example, if the nature of a class or its application context dictates that all its instances correspond to one of N different states, we could store these N instances in memory as *prototypes* on a permanent basis and then, when a new request for an instance comes in, return a clone of the prototype that best fulfills the client's request.

To show pictorially the distinction between constructing instances directly by invoking constructors and by cloning from one of a small number of prototypes, we depict the former case by Figure 5.1 and the latter by Figure 5.2. When instances are created directly by invoking a class constructor, the state of each instance constructed *can* be unique. So it is possible that each of the N objects shown in Figure 5.1 is unique. On the other hand, the prototype-based instance construction depicted in Figure 5.2 involves creating duplicates from a small number of prototypes. Obviously, the state of every instance created from the same prototype will be identical to that of the prototype. Figure 5.2 shows the case when we have only three prototypes.

It is important to realize that the Prototype pattern does not place a limit on the number of instances that can be constructed from a class. The limit that is placed is on how many *different types of instances*[3] can be created from a class, with each type being represented by one prototype instance. In Figure 5.2 we have grouped together the instances with identical states. When we say that all of the instances correspond to a small number of different

---

[2] See, for example, the article "Some Structural Measures of API Usability" [4]. API (which stands for "Application Programming Interface") of a module is a listing of the functions that can be invoked on the module either by other modules or by a programmer. You can also think of an API as a catalog of the services offered by a module for the benefit of the other modules in a software system and for the benefit of human programmers who wish to use that module.

[3] We are using the word "type" in an informal sense here, as opposed to its more formal meaning when you talk about the type of a variable in a programming language.

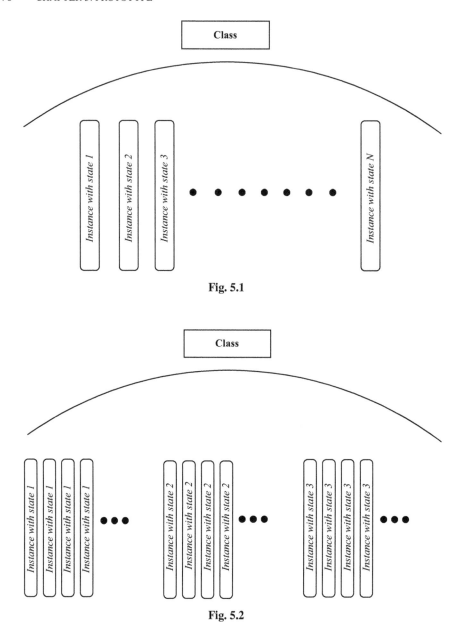

Fig. 5.1

Fig. 5.2

states, what we mean is that the space spanned by all of the values that can be assigned to the instance variables is sparsely populated.

So if the main message of the Prototype pattern is to create new instances by duplicating a prototype instance, how does one actually carry out the duplication needed? Are there any pitfalls in duplicating one instance to create another instance? As it turns out, one must exercise caution when writing code in which the instances are created by duplication as opposed to by invoking a constructor. The reason why that is the case has to do

with how the objects stored in the memory of a computer are accessed. To elaborate, consider the case of two Java classes, *A* and *B*, with the former class possessing an instance variable that holds a reference to an instance of the latter class. Let's say you have constructed an instance of class *A*. We'll call this instance *instanceA*. Obviously, *instanceA* has a variable that points to an instance of type *B*; we will refer to that instance by the name *instanceB*. If you were to duplicate *instanceA* by straightforward byte-by-byte copying, the same variable in the duplicate version of *instanceA* would hold reference to the same *instanceB* object. Depending on your application, this may or may not be what you mean by duplicating an instance in order to create a new instance. In most cases, such a sense of duplication — referred to as *shallow copying* — would result in program misbehavior.

The opposite of *shallow copying* is *deep copying*. When deep copying is employed to create a duplicate instance from, say, *instanceA*, you would need to make sure that any class-type objects pointed to by the instance variables inside *instanceA* undergo their own duplication elsewhere in the memory. *In this manner, you can be assured that a duplicate of an instance is a completely separate object, with no hidden connections with the object from which the duplicate is created.*

Before you can duplicate class-type objects in Java — whether by shallow copying or by deep copying — you have to first make sure that the class from which the original instance was created implements the `Cloneable` interface. Although `Cloneable` is an empty interface, it nevertheless is a signal to the Java compiler that it is permissible to create duplicates of the objects constructed from such a class. Once you declare a class `Cloneable` in this manner, you are then allowed to provide an override implementation for the `clone()` method, which is defined originally for the root class `Object`, that dictates how an instance constructed from the class will be duplicated. In the absence of an override implementation for `clone()`, the system will use the `Object`'s definition of this method — but that definition can only create a byte-by-byte copy of the instance that is being duplicated. In other words, the default instance duplication in Java is byte-by-byte duplication, which amounts to shallow copying of the objects that need to be duplicated. For deep-copying, you have no choice but to provide an override implementation for the `clone()` method inherited from the root class `Object`.

Practically all major object-oriented languages provide facilities for duplicating instances created from class definitions. For example, the role that `clone()` serves in Java is served in C++ by the notion of a copy constructor. The code that is placed in the copy constructor of a class determines the copy semantics for the instances constructed from that class. That is, you may achieve shallow copying or deep copying depending on how you program up the copy constructor of a class in C++.

5.4 THE PROTOTYPE PATTERN IN REAL-WORLD APPLICATIONS

Most major OO languages provide mechanisms for implementing the Prototype pattern. As mentioned previously, Java provides the `Cloneable` interface for this purpose.

Software vendors use this pattern to exercise greater control over the states of the instances created from a class definition if that is important to the proper functioning of an application. Using the Prototype pattern for exercising such control is particularly effective

when only a limited number of the different states is allowed for a class. For such classes, a vendor provides the clients with a Factory Method[4] based front-end for object construction whose job is to first store away the prototype instances for all of the different allowed states for a class and to then supply to the clients duplicates of the prototypes. As to which duplicate a client acquires depends on the object creation request made by the client. The goal would be to provide the client with an instance that comes closest to the needs of the client.

Apart from exercising control over the states of the instances, the Prototype pattern is useful whenever the cost of creating a new instance with a direct constructor call is greater than the cost of cloning off a previously constructed instance. Both ways of object creation require memory allocation — so the cost of memory allocation is not an issue. However, there can be other costs associated with object creation that can be avoided if a client can make do with a clone of an object that was constructed previously. For example, these other costs may relate to an algorithmic estimation of the values for the constructor parameters. In some cases, figuring out these values may involve accessing remote databases, data downloads, data filtering, and so on. So if a client is content with the parameter values used for an instance constructed previously, why not supply the client with a clone of that instance?

5.5   HARRY POTTER STORY USED TO ILLUSTRATE THE PROTOTYPE PATTERN

We will explain the Prototype pattern with the help of dragons from the magical world of Harry Potter. Only a small number of different *types* of dragons exists. They reside in different parts of the world and differ with regard to what they eat, how long they grow, how much they weigh, and so on. Whereas they may be different with regard to a small number of specific traits, what they have in common far exceeds how they are different — they are, after all, all dragons.

For our demonstration of the Prototype pattern, we will define a single `Dragon` class with instance variables for the following three attributes: native range of the dragon, what it likes to eat, and its length in feet. We will create one instance from this class for each of the eight different types of dragons listed below.[5] These eight instances will then serve as the prototypes for the different types of dragons. It will be the job of a manager class to store these prototypes and, subsequently, upon receiving a client request for a dragon, to supply one by making a duplicate from one of the prototypes.

In order to ensure that the clients do not have direct access to the `Dragon` class for creating fresh instances, we will make certain that the class does not have constructors that are public.

Listed below are the eight different kinds of dragons that we will create prototypes for:

---

[4] See Chapter 4 for the Factory Method pattern.

[5] A couple of additional dragon types exists, but the values for the three attributes for those are not fully known. So we will ignore them in our demonstration of the Prototype pattern.

```
Chinese Fireball
        Native range:              China
        Likes to Eat:              Pigs, Humans
        Can grow to length:        25 feet

Hungarian Horntail
        Native range:              Hungary
        Likes to Eat:              Goats, Humans
        Length:                    50 feet

Common Welsh Green
        Native Range:              Wales
        Likes to Eat:              Sheep
        Length:                    18 feet

Norwegian Ridgeback
        Native Range:              Norway
        Likes to Eat:              Large land mammals
        Length:                    35 feet

Hebridean Black
        Native range:              Scotland
        Likes to eat:              Deer, dogs, cattle
        Can grow to length:        30 feet

Peruvian Vipertooth
        Native range:              Peru
        Likes to eat:              Goats, cows, humans
        Can grow to length:        15 feet

Romanian Longhorn
        Native range:              Romania
        Likes to eat:              Unknown
        Can grow to length:        40 feet

Swedish Short-Snout
        Native range:              Sweden
        Likes to eat:              Dogs, humans
        Can grow to length:        22 feet
```

5.6   A TOP LEVEL VIEW OF THE PATTERN DEMONSTRATION

The class diagram in Figure 5.3 presents a top-level view of our demonstration of the Prototype pattern. It is the job of the `PrototypeManagerAndDuplicator` class to first create and store the eight generic instances (the prototypes) of the `Dragon` class, and, to subsequently deliver clones of these prototypes when client requests for dragons are received. As shown in the figure, the `PrototypeManagerAndDuplicator` class is equipped with eight private instance variables for storing references to the eight prototypes. As the reader will see later, these instance variables are initialized automatically when we call `PrototypeManagerAndDuplicator`'s no-arg constructor.

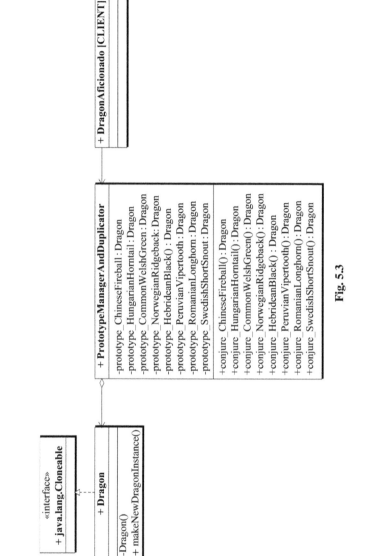

Fig. 5.3

As can be inferred from the visibility marks in the Dragon class in Figure 5.3, the constructor for this class is placed in the private section of the class. This is to forbid any direct construction of the instances of the Dragon class. The only mechanism available for constructing Dragon instances would be through Dragon's makeNewDragonInstance() method that is placed in the public section of the class, as implied by its visibility mark in Figure 5.3.

Figure 5.3 also shows us making the Dragon class cloneable. As shown in the figure, the eight prototype dragons are stored by the class PrototypeManagerAndDuplicator. These prototypes are created and stored before fielding any requests for the supply of dragons. Subsequently, when the PrototypeManagerAndDuplicator class receives a request from a dragon aficionado, the class delivers a clone of the prototype that corresponds to the requested type.

5.7 THE Dragon CLASS

The implementation of the Dragon class is based on the assumption that this class will be called upon to supply an instance for only one of the eight types listed in the set allTypes.

Note the instance variables whatType, nativeRange, likesToEat, and length. The first, whatType, can only be set to one of the eight types in the set allTypes, since otherwise an UnknownDragonException will be thrown. The instance variable nativeRange is set to the default value of Unknown. The three instance variables whatType, nativeRange, and length do not require any special cloning procedures. That is, a byte-by-byte duplication of an instance will exhibit correct behavior with regard to these three instance variables.

However, the instance variable likesToEat holds a reference to a container of type List<String>. It is this instance variable that requires special attention when we clone a Dragon instance in order to create its duplicate. To ensure that the likesToEat instance variable of a cloned Dragon instance does NOT point to the same ArrayList as in the original Dragon instance, notice how in the implementation code for clone(), after calling super.clone(), we call the ArrayList constructor to construct a fresh ArrayList from the contents of the original ArrayList.

Also note that the names of all different Dragon types are stored in a final static set called allTypes. Since we do not want this set to be expanded or altered in any way, we declare it final. Additionally, since this information is common to all Dragon instances, we declare it static.

Additionally, note that the Dragon constructor is declared to be private. At the same time, we equip the class with the public method makeNewDragonInstance() that can return a new Dragon instance by invoking the private constructor. We do not wish for the constructor to be directly accessible outside the class since we want to control how the Dragon instances come into existence. As the reader knows from the top-level view of the demonstration presented in Section 5.6, we use the PrototypeManagerAndDuplicator class to provide new Dragon instances by duplicating them from the prototype instances stored in that class. In the class PrototypeManagerAndDuplicator, we will create the needed prototypes by invoking Dragon's makeNewDragonInstance() method.

Finally, note the "get" and "set" methods, the former to print out the attributes of a specific Dragon instance and the latter to change some of the attributes. *We will use these methods to demonstrate that despite the fact that a Dragon instance requested by a client is created by copying from a prototype, the client can modify the attributes of the acquired instance without affecting either the prototype used or the other instances obtained by duplication from the same prototype.*

```java
import java.util.*;

public class Dragon implements Cloneable {

    private String whatType;
    private String nativeRange = "Unknown";
    private List<String> likesToEat =
                new ArrayList<String>( Arrays.asList( "Unknown" ) );
    private int length;                              // in feet

    private final static Set<String> allTypes =
                                new HashSet<String>(Arrays.asList(
        "Chinese Fireball",
        "Hungarian Horntail",
        "Common Welsh Green",
        "Norwegian Ridgeback",
        "Hebridean Black",
        "Peruvian Vipertooth",
        "Romanian Longhorn",
        "Swedish Short-Snout") );

    private Dragon(String whatType) throws UnknownDragonException {
        try {
            if ( allTypes.contains( (Object) whatType ) ) {
                this.whatType = whatType;
                if ( whatType.equals( "Chinese Fireball" ) ) {
                    nativeRange = "China";
                    likesToEat  =
                        new ArrayList<String>(
                                    Arrays.asList("pigs","humans"));
                    length = 25;
                } else if ( whatType.equals("Hungarian Horntail")) {
                    nativeRange = "Hungary";
                    likesToEat  =
                        new ArrayList<String>(
                                    Arrays.asList("goats","humans"));
                    length = 50;
                } else if ( whatType.equals("Common Welsh Green")) {
                    nativeRange = "Wales";
                    likesToEat  =
                        new ArrayList<String>(Arrays.asList("sheep"));
                    length = 18;
                } else if ( whatType.equals("Norwegian Ridgeback")){
```

```java
            nativeRange = "Norway";
            likesToEat  =
                new ArrayList<String>(
                        Arrays.asList("large land mammals"));
            length = 35;
        } else if ( whatType.equals("Hebridean Black")) {
            nativeRange = "Scotland";
            likesToEat  =
                new ArrayList<String>(
                    Arrays.asList("deer", "dogs", "cattle"));
            length = 30;
        } else if (whatType.equals("Peruvian Vipertooth")) {
            nativeRange = "Peru";
            likesToEat  =
                    new ArrayList<String>(
                      Arrays.asList("goats","cows","humans"));
            length = 15;
        } else if (whatType.equals("Romanian Longhorn")) {
            nativeRange = "Romania";
            length = 40;
        } else if (whatType.equals("Swedish Short-Snout")) {
            nativeRange = "Sweden";
            likesToEat  =
                new ArrayList<String>(
                            Arrays.asList("dogs", "humans"));
            length = 22;
        }
    } else {
        throw new UnknownDragonException(
            "Dragons of type " + whatType + " do not exist");
    }
} catch( ClassCastException e ) {
    e.printStackTrace();
    System.exit(1);
}
}
public static Dragon makeNewDragonInstance( String whatType )
                        throws UnknownDragonException {
    // This is where you can place additional code for
    // authenticating access to the makeNewDragonInstance()
    // method.
    return new Dragon( whatType );
}
public String getAttributes() {
    return whatType + " is native to "
                + nativeRange + ", likes to eat "
                + likesToEat
                + ", and is generally of length "
                + length;
}
public void setHabitat( String range ) {
    nativeRange = range;
```

```
    }
    public void addThingsToEat( String newItem ) {
        likesToEat.add( newItem );
    }
    public Object clone() throws CloneNotSupportedException {
        Dragon d = (Dragon) super.clone();
        d.likesToEat = new ArrayList<String>( likesToEat );
        return d;
    }
    public String toString() {
        return this.getClass().getName() + " of kind " + whatType;
    }
}
```

5.8   THE PrototypeManagerAndDuplicator CLASS

The class we define in this section, `PrototypeManagerAndDuplicator`, is the keeper of the prototypes. This class delivers a clone of one of the prototypes when a dragon of a certain type is requested by a dragon aficionado.

Ideally, the class defined in this section should be based on the Singleton pattern of Chapter 6 since, in general, we would want to enforce the condition that only one instance of this class exists. We will leave that as an exercise for the reader in Section 5.11, "Playing with the Code."

Regarding the class definition shown below, first note that we have declared the class `PrototypeManagerAndDuplicator` to be final because we do not want it to be extended. We want this class to have the final say in the production of `Dragon` instances. As the reader can see, the constructor creates a prototype for each different kind of `Dragon` instance.

For the benefit of the wizards and the witches who wish to conjure up dragons, the class provides the method `conjure()` that takes for its `String` argument the type of `Dragon` desired. If the dragon desired is of the type that exists in the magical world of Harry Potter, a call to `conjure()` is translated into a call to one of the `prototype_xxxx()` methods of this class. As the reader can see, a `prototype_xxxx()` call merely copies the prototype instance and supplies it as a new dragon instance. In the client class `DragonAficionado.java`, shown in the next section, and through the output of the demonstration code shown in Section 5.11, we will demonstrate that a `Dragon` copy created by `prototype_xxxx()` is a deep copy of the original prototype.

```
public final class PrototypeManagerAndDuplicator {
    private Dragon prototype_ChineseFireball;
    private Dragon prototype_HungarianHorntail;
    private Dragon prototype_CommonWelshGreen;
    private Dragon prototype_NorwegianRidgeback;
    private Dragon prototype_HebrideanBlack;
    private Dragon prototype_PeruvianVipertooth;
    private Dragon prototype_RomanianLonghorn;
    private Dragon prototype_SwedishShortSnout;
```

```
public PrototypeManagerAndDuplicator() {
 try {
        prototype_ChineseFireball =
                Dragon.makeNewDragonInstance("Chinese Fireball");
        prototype_HungarianHorntail =
                Dragon.makeNewDragonInstance("Hungarian Horntail");
        prototype_CommonWelshGreen=
                Dragon.makeNewDragonInstance("Common Welsh Green");
        prototype_NorwegianRidgeback =
                Dragon.makeNewDragonInstance("Norwegian Ridgeback");
        prototype_HebrideanBlack =
                Dragon.makeNewDragonInstance("Hebridean Black");
        prototype_PeruvianVipertooth =
                Dragon.makeNewDragonInstance("Peruvian Vipertooth");
        prototype_RomanianLonghorn =
                Dragon.makeNewDragonInstance("Romanian Longhorn");
        prototype_SwedishShortSnout =
                Dragon.makeNewDragonInstance("Swedish Short-Snout");
    } catch( UnknownDragonException e ) {
        e.printStackTrace();
        System.exit(1);
    }
 }
public Dragon conjure_ChineseFireball() {
    Dragon d = null;
    try {
        d = (Dragon) prototype_ChineseFireball.clone();
    } catch( CloneNotSupportedException e) {}
    return d;
}
public Dragon conjure_HungarianHorntail() {
    Dragon d = null;
    try {
        d = (Dragon) prototype_HungarianHorntail.clone();
    } catch( CloneNotSupportedException e) {}
    return d;
}
public Dragon conjure_CommonWelshGreen() {
    Dragon d = null;
    try {
        d = (Dragon) prototype_CommonWelshGreen.clone();
    } catch( CloneNotSupportedException e) {}
    return d;
}
public Dragon conjure_NorwegianRidgeback() {
    Dragon d = null;
    try {
        d = (Dragon) prototype_NorwegianRidgeback.clone();
    } catch( CloneNotSupportedException e) {}
    return d;
}
public Dragon conjure_HebrideanBlack() {
```

```
        Dragon d = null;
        try {
            d = (Dragon) prototype_HebrideanBlack.clone();
        } catch( CloneNotSupportedException e) {}
        return d;
    }
    public Dragon conjure_PeruvianVipertooth() {
        Dragon d = null;
        try {
            d = (Dragon) prototype_PeruvianVipertooth.clone();
        } catch( CloneNotSupportedException e) {}
        return d;
    }
    public Dragon conjure_RomanianLonghorn() {
        Dragon d = null;
        try {
            d = (Dragon) prototype_RomanianLonghorn.clone();
        } catch( CloneNotSupportedException e) {}
        return d;
    }
    public Dragon conjure_SwedishShortSnout() {
        Dragon d = null;
        try {
            d = (Dragon) prototype_SwedishShortSnout.clone();
        } catch( CloneNotSupportedException e) {}
        return d;
    }
    public Dragon conjure( String whatType )
                                throws UnknownDragonException {
     if ( whatType.equals( "Chinese Fireball" ) ) {
       return conjure_ChineseFireball();
     } else if ( whatType.equals( "Hungarian Horntail" ) ) {
         return conjure_HungarianHorntail();
     } else if ( whatType.equals( "Common Welsh Green" ) ) {
         return conjure_CommonWelshGreen();
       } else if ( whatType.equals( "Norwegian Ridgeback" ) ) {
         return conjure_NorwegianRidgeback();
      } else if ( whatType.equals( "Hebridean Black" ) ) {
         return conjure_HebrideanBlack();
      } else if ( whatType.equals( "Peruvian Vipertooth" ) ) {
         return conjure_PeruvianVipertooth();
      } else if ( whatType.equals( "Romanian Longhorn" ) ) {
         return conjure_RomanianLonghorn();
      } else if ( whatType.equals( "Swedish Short-Snout" ) ) {
         return conjure_SwedishShortSnout();
     } else {
         throw new UnknownDragonException(
                                "Unknown dragon type called for" );
     }
    }
}
```

5.9   THE DragonAficionado CLASS

Shown below is the client class for testing the Prototype pattern in our demonstration. Given that instance copying is central to this pattern and given the issues related to shallow versus deep copying, it is important to test through the client class the copy semantics used by the `PrototypeManagerAndDuplicator` class (and, even more to the point, the copy semantics used by the `clone()` function defined for the `Dragon` class since the prototype manager class merely calls on the override definition of `clone()` in the `Dragon` class to do the copying).

The demonstration in this client class consists of acquiring three `Dragon` instances but with the first and the third instances being the same type of `Dragon`. With the help of the first and the third instances, we show that the copy semantics used in our Prototype pattern demonstration corresponds to deep copying. We show this by changing the `ArrayList` container, which stores the items that a dragon likes to eat, for one of the dragons and then examining the same container for the other dragon of the same type. As the output shown in Section 5.11 demonstrates, even though both the Chinese Fireball dragons, d1 and d3, are constructed by copying from the same prototype, when we modify the `likesToEat` list of d3 by adding "monkeys" to it, the `likesToEat` list for d1 remains unchanged. If the cloning in our implementation had been based on shallow copy semantics, any change in the list for d3 would have caused the same list for d1 to also change.

```
public class DragonAficionado {

    public static void main( String[] args ) {

        PrototypeManagerAndDuplicator ptm =
                            new PrototypeManagerAndDuplicator();

        try {
            Dragon d1 = ptm.conjure( "Chinese Fireball" );
            System.out.println("A dragon of type " + d1 + " conjured.");
            System.out.println( d1.getAttributes() + "." );

            Dragon d2 = ptm.conjure( "Hungarian Horntail" );
            System.out.println("A dragon of type " + d2 + " conjured.");
            System.out.println( d2.getAttributes() + "." );

            Dragon d3 = ptm.conjure( "Chinese Fireball" );
            System.out.println( "A new dragon of type "
                                            + d3 + " conjured." );
            d3.addThingsToEat(  "monkeys" );
            System.out.println( d3.getAttributes() + "." );

            System.out.println( "Attributes of the first Chinese "
                                        + "Fireball dragon: " );
            System.out.println( d1.getAttributes() + "." );
        } catch ( UnknownDragonException e ) {
            e.printStackTrace();
        }
```

```
    }
}
```

5.10   THE UnknownDragonException CLASS

Since the Prototype pattern is based on the idea that all of the instances that are allowed to be constructed from a class can be categorized into a small number of distinct types on the basis of the values assigned to the instance variables, we need a mechanism to forbid an attempt at instance creation that tries to give unacceptable values to the instance variables.

In our demonstration, a client can request only one of the eight different kinds of dragons. So we are faced with the question of how the Dragon and the other associated classes should handle a client request for a dragon type that is outside of what is programmed into the Dragon class. In the demonstration here, we want an exception to be thrown in such cases. The exception class defined below is for that purpose.

```
public class UnknownDragonException extends Exception {

    public UnknownDragonException() {
        super();
    }
    public UnknownDragonException(String message) {
        super(message);
    }
}
```

5.11   PLAYING WITH THE CODE

Download the class files for this pattern from the book's website into a separate directory. Compile the code with the command

```
javac *.java
```

and execute the DragonAficionado class by

```
java DragonAficionado
```

In light of the code in the main() of the DragonAficionado class, when you execute this class, you will see the following output:

```
A Chinese Fireball dragon was conjured.  Chinese
Fireball dragon is native to China, likes to eat [pigs, humans],
and is generally of length 25.

A Hungarian Horntail dragon was conjured.  Hungarian
Horntail is native to Hungary, likes to eat [goats,
humans], and is generally of length 50.
```

```
A Chinese Fireball dragon was conjured. Chinese Fireball
is native to China, likes to eat [pigs, humans, monkeys],
and is generally of length 25.

Attributes of the first Chinese Fireball dragon:
Chinese Fireball is native to China, likes to
eat [pigs, humans], and is generally of length 25.
```

For additional insights regarding the Prototype pattern, you may wish to extend the demonstration code for this pattern along the following lines:

- Ideally, only one instance of the class `PrototypeManagerAndDuplicator` should be allowed. However, our demonstration did not do that since, in keeping with the alphabetic ordering of the patterns in each part of this book, we have not yet covered the Singleton pattern. However, after the reader has learned the Singleton pattern, you may wish to implement the `PrototypeManagerAndDuplicator` class as a singleton.

- The current demonstration code does not include a way for the `Dragon` class to authenticate access from `PrototypeManagerAndDuplicator` for the purpose of constructing the eight generic instances of `Dragon`. So, with the current implementation, any outside class would be able to call on the `makeNewDragonInstance()` method of `Dragon` to create additional prototypes for the eight `Dragon` types. What we really need is an authenticated access to the `makeNewDragonInstance()` method of `Dragon`. Toward that end, you would need to insert additional code at the place indicated in the definition of the `makeNewDragonInstance()` method of `Dragon` class. See if you can do that.

6

SINGLETON

6.1 SINGULAR OBJECTS

In most cases the higher the level of abstraction at which you model physical reality, the smaller the number of model instantiations you need. And, if you happen to be a person with a religious bent of mind, you are likely to believe that, at the highest level, there is only one entity – a singular entity – that explains it all. But that's taking us far from the main subject matter of this book — object-oriented design. Considering that this book is neither about metaphysics, nor about religion, let's not dwell any further on modeling the reality at the highest levels.

In general, though, whether or not you have a singular object depends on the scope of what it is you are trying to model. Let's say you are trying to construct a mental model of the administrative people in a university. If the scope of your model is limited strictly to one university, there will exist but a singular object in your mind for the role "University President." However, that would obviously not be the case if your model were to encompasses several universities in a certain geographic region.

6.2 INTENT AND APPLICABILITY

The intent of the Singleton pattern is to ensure that the clients of a class are not able to construct more than a certain designated number of objects — typically only one — from the class definition.

You should consider using this pattern when

- the reality of what a class is supposed to model is such that only one instance of the class can be allowed to exist at any given time and any subsequent attempts at object construction must return the same previously constructed object;
- or, in a variant of the pattern, the physical reality places constraints on the total number of instances that are allowed to exist at any given time;

Designing with Objects: Object-Oriented Design Patterns Explained with Stories from Harry Potter, First Edition. Avinash C. Kak.

- or, in another variant of the pattern, you want a class to honor only a single request for instance construction and throw an exception for all subsequent requests;
- and, in yet another variant of the pattern, you not only want to place constraints on how many instances of a class are allowed to exist at any given time, but also on how many instances are allowed to be constructed from the subclasses of the class.

6.3   INTRODUCTION TO THE SINGLETON PATTERN

When a modeling process requires that there exist only one of an object that is deemed to be singular, how does one prevent inadvertent creation of multiple versions of the same object? Obviously, someone must create the very first instance of such an object and the mechanism that prevents multiple such objects from coming into existence must become effective immediately after the first instance is created. These are the issues that are addressed by the Singleton pattern. The main purpose of this pattern is to ensure that there exists only one instance of a class at any given time. It's straightforward to generalize an implementation of the pattern to the case such that, at any time, there will exist only N instances of a class for a designated value of N.

When a class implements the Singleton pattern, after a client has constructed one instance, any subsequent attempts at instance construction must either return the same instance that was constructed originally or throw an exception that warns the user that the contract of the class is being violated. As already mentioned, such implementations can be extended in a straightforward manner to allow the construction of a maximum of N instances from a class at any given time.

At this point, a reader might ask: Does there not exist some similarity between the overall goal of the Prototype pattern of the previous chapter and the Singleton pattern of the current chapter — assuming you use the Singleton pattern to establish a limit on the maximum number of instances that can be constructed from a class? Not really. Note that the Prototype pattern places no limits at all on the total number of instances you can construct from a class. That pattern says only that the instances you construct correspond to one of a small number of the stored prototypes. As long as you create instances just by copying from the prototypes, you are allowed any number of instances by the Prototype pattern. The Singleton pattern, on the other hand, places a strict limit on the total number of instances of a class that is allowed to exist at any given time. Most commonly, the Singleton pattern insists that there be only one instance made from a class.

6.4   THE SINGLETON PATTERN IN REAL-WORLD APPLICATIONS

A software vendor uses the Singleton pattern when it is necessary to enforce the condition that there exist only one instance of a class. Consider a class meant for representing a connection between an application and a relational database. An instance of such a class can be used to communicate SQL commands to the database. If there are two or more calls for instantiating such a class at different places in a software system and all of these calls refer to the same database, you are likely to want all such calls to return the same connection object. Such an object would be instantiated by the first call for its creation.

For another example, consider an object-oriented approach to the design of systems software that controls the hardware in your computer. This software is likely to place limits on how many serial port[1] instances are allowed to be constructed from a class that represents the serial port abstraction. The number of such instances at any time must not exceed the actual number of serial ports on a machine. If a machine has only one serial port, which is commonly the case, you'd want only one instance to be created from the serial port class. Similar arguments would apply to an object-oriented approach to the creation of multiple threads or multiple processes in a program that requires concurrency.[2] Since each process and each thread consumes system resources, you would not want the software to allow for creating more than a certain number of them in resource constrained environments.

With regard to the role played by a Singleton class vis-à-vis the rest of the software in an application, you can think of an instance constructed from such a class as serving like a global variable *with state*. Obviously, the state would depend on all of the instance variables in the class definition. If you also equip the class with a method for changing the state, then a change made to the Singleton instance at any point would be immediately visible through all of the other variables that hold references to the instance.

6.5   HARRY POTTER STORY USED TO ILLUSTRATE THE SINGLETON PATTERN

We will define a class called `MinisterForMagic` for demonstrating the Singleton pattern. Obviously, only one Minister for Magic can exist at any given time.

As a reader of Harry Potter would recall, the Ministry of Magic is the governing body of the wizarding world in Britain. It carries out law enforcement in the wizarding communities; is in charge of the Hogwarts School of Magic for training new wizards and witches; makes sure that no improper use of magic is carried out (especially by underage wizards and witches and, even more especially, against the muggles); and makes sure that the muggles do not find out about the wizarding world. On occasion, if things get out of hand and muggles get a glimpse of the world of magic (as was the case when the Dursleys witnessed how Harry made his obnoxious Aunt Marge float like a balloon to the ceiling of the living room), the Ministry of Magic immediately rushes in and performs memory charms on the muggles to make them forget what they saw. As the title implies, the Minister of Magic, who is sometimes appointed and at other times elected, supervises the Ministry of Magic.

6.6   A TOP LEVEL VIEW OF THE PATTERN DEMONSTRATION

The class diagram in Figure 6.1 presents a top-level view of our demonstration of the Singleton pattern. As can be inferred from the visibility marks in the `MinisterForMagic` class, we place the constructor for this class in its private section. This is to prevent the clients of this class from directly constructing its instances. For public instance creation, the class provides the `makeInstanceOfMinisterForMagic()` method. As

---

[1] We are talking about the old-style RS-232 compliant serial ports that you still find on many machines for data transfer and diagnostics.

[2] For example, GUI (Graphical User Interface) programs frequently require concurrency in their execution for superior user experience.

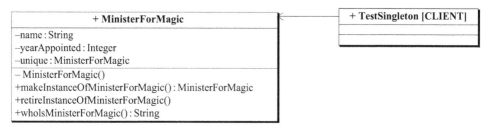

Fig. 6.1

explained later, this method ensures that only a single instance of this class is ever constructed — and that happens at the first request received for such an object. Any subsequent calls to the method will return the same instance. We test the behavior of the `MinisterForMagic` class in the class `TestSingleton`. As to how we do that will be explained in Section 6.8.

6.7   THE MinisterForMagic CLASS

So what attributes should be placed in the class `MinisterForMagic`? If our goal was limited to conveying just the essence of the Singleton pattern, we could do so with an empty class, that is, a class devoid of any instance variables related to the duties and other aspects of the individual holding this high office. However, just for the sake of greater "realism," we will place two instance variables in the class: one for the name of the minister and the other for the year of appointment.

The class definition shown below has the constructor of the class in its private section. This prevents anyone from constructing an instance of the class directly by calling its constructor. The only available means for constructing an instance of the class is through the public method `makeInstanceOfMinisterForMagic()`. This method first checks whether a binding for the static variable `unique` already exists. It's only when there is no previously created instance of the class assigned to `unique` that `makeInstanceOfMinisterForMagic()` goes ahead and makes an instance by calling the private constructor for the class. The role played by the private static variable `unique` is obviously central to the operation of this pattern — this variable holds a reference to the one and only one Minister for Magic that is allowed to exist at any given time.

Also note the public static method `retireInstanceOfMinisterForMagic()` to destroy a previously constructed instance of `MinisterForMagic`. Obviously, after a call to this method, we can once again create the next version of an instance of this class, as we will demonstrate in `TestSingleton.java`.

It's interesting to note that the unique instance of `MinisterForMagic` is not created until it is needed by a client of this class. This is sometimes referred to as *lazy instantiation*.

The class definition shown below makes sense only if you ignore the fact that other countries besides Great Britain may have their own Ministers for Magic. For example, Bulgaria and Norway are definitely known to have their own Ministers for Magic. In fact, the Bulgarian Minister for Magic, Mr. Oblansk, was invited to the World Cup Final for Quidditch in 1994. Therefore, strictly speaking, for the class presented here, its name ought to be `BritishMinisterForMagic` so as not to offend other countries.

```
public class MinisterForMagic {
    private String name;
    private int yearAppointed;
    private static MinisterForMagic unique;

    private MinisterForMagic(String name, int yearAppointed){
        this.name = name;
        this.yearAppointed = yearAppointed;
    }
    public static MinisterForMagic makeInstanceOfMinisterForMagic(
                                        String name, int year) {
        if ( unique == null )
            unique = new MinisterForMagic( name, year );
        return unique;
    }
    public static void retireInstanceOfMinisterForMagic() {
        unique = null;
    }
    public String whoIsMinisterForMagic(){
        return name;
    }
}
```

6.8   THE TestSingleton CLASS

With regard to the class defined in the previous section, we must now demonstrate that it allows only one instance of the class to exist at any time.

In the test code in the main() of the TestSingleton class shown below, we try to construct two supposedly different instances, minster_1 and minster_2, of the MinisterForMagic class by calling makeInstanceOfMinisterForMagic() twice with different arguments. As we show in Section 6.10, the second call returns the same object that the first call created. In other words, the second call is ignored with regard to its wanting to create a new instance of MinisterForMagic.[3] As also presented in Section 6.10, after we call the retireInstanceOfMinisterForMagic() method to destroy the instance created by the first call to makeInstanceOfMinisterForMagic(), we can once again create another instance of the MinisterForMagic class.

```
public class TestSingleton {
    public static void main( String[] args ) {
        MinisterForMagic minister_1 =
            MinisterForMagic.makeInstanceOfMinisterForMagic(
                                        "Cornelius Fudge", 1990);

        MinisterForMagic minister_2 =
            MinisterForMagic.makeInstanceOfMinisterForMagic(
```

[3]Since the second call to makeInstanceOfMinisterForMagic() is with different values for the instance variables, one could argue that this invocation of makeInstanceOfMinisterForMagic() should throw an exception. We revisit this issue in Section 6.10 where we leave its implementation as an exercise for the reader.

```
                                        "Pius Thicknesse", 1996);
        if ( minister_1 == minister_2 )
            System.out.println( "The two ministers are the same" );

        System.out.println("The name of the Minster: "
                            + minister_1.whoIsMinisterForMagic() );
        System.out.println("The name of the Minster: "
                            + minister_2.whoIsMinisterForMagic() );

        MinisterForMagic.retireInstanceOfMinisterForMagic();

        minister_2 = MinisterForMagic.makeInstanceOfMinisterForMagic(
                                "Pius Thicknesse", 1996);
        System.out.println("The name of the Minster: "
                            + minister_2.whoIsMinisterForMagic() );
    }
}
```

6.9   VARIATIONS ON THE SINGLETON PATTERN

This section presents some variations on the Singleton pattern as discussed so far.

The implementation shown below is useful if you want the Singleton class to honor only a single request for an instance and you want all subsequent client requests to cause an exception to be thrown. The exception class needed for such a case is also defined below.

```
class UnauthorizedInstanceException extends Exception {
    public UnauthorizedInstanceException() {
        super();
    }
    public UnauthorizedInstanceException( String message ) {
        super( message );
    }
}

class Singleton {
    static boolean instanceExists = false;

    public Singleton() throws UnauthorizedInstanceException {
        if ( instanceExists ) {
            throw new UnauthorizedInstanceException(
                    "Unique instance constructed previously."
                + " New instance creation request denied." );
        } else {
            instanceExists = true;
            System.out.println("Unique instance of Singleton created");
        }
    }
}
```

```
class TestSingleton {
    public static void main( String[] args )
    {
        // First attempt works fine:
        try {
            Singleton obj_1 = new Singleton();
        } catch( UnauthorizedInstanceException u ) {
            System.out.println( u.getMessage() );
        }

        // Second attempt causes an exception to be thrown:
        try {
            Singleton obj_2 = new Singleton();
        } catch( UnauthorizedInstanceException u ) {
            System.out.println( u.getMessage() );
        }
    }
}
```

You can place this code in any file, compile the file with the `javac` command and execute it by

      `java TestSingleton`

to see what we mean by the `Singleton` class honoring just one client request for an instance.

For another variant of the pattern, what if we want a class extended from a singleton class to also act like a singleton? Shown below is a complete working example that illustrates how a subclass derived from a singleton class can also be made to behave like a singleton. Note how we now place the constructor for the base class `Singleton` not in the private section of the class, but in the protected section so that it is visible to a subclass of `Singleton`.

```
class Singleton {
    protected static Singleton unique;
    protected Singleton(){}
    public static Singleton makeInstanceOfSingleton() {
        if ( unique != null )
            return unique;
        else {
            unique = new Singleton();
            return unique;
        }
    }
}
class SingletonExtended extends Singleton {
```

```
    private static SingletonExtended unique;
    public static SingletonExtended makeInstanceOfSingletonExtended() {
        if ( unique != null )
            return unique;
        else {
            unique = new SingletonExtended();
            return unique;
        }
    }
}

class TestSingletonExtended {
    public static void main( String[] args )
    {
        Singleton obj_1 = Singleton.makeInstanceOfSingleton();
        Singleton obj_2 = Singleton.makeInstanceOfSingleton();
        if ( obj_1 == obj_2 )
            System.out.println(
                    "The two Singleton objects are the same" );
        SingletonExtended obj_3 =
                SingletonExtended.makeInstanceOfSingletonExtended();
        SingletonExtended obj_4 =
                SingletonExtended.makeInstanceOfSingletonExtended();
        if ( obj_3 == obj_4 )
            System.out.println(
                    "The two SingletonExtended objects are the same" );
    }
}
```

You can place this code in any file, compile the file with the `javac` command and execute it by

```
java TestSingletonExtended
```

to verify for yourself that the two ostensibly different instances created first from the parent class and then from the extended class are the same in each case.

6.10   PLAYING WITH THE CODE

We will now show the output for the main presentation of the Singleton pattern in Sections 6.6 through 6.8. Download into a separate directory the class files for the code shown in these sections and compile the code with the command

```
javac *.java
```

and execute the `TestSingleton` class by

```
java TestSingleton
```

Given the code in the `main()` of `TestSingleton` of Section 6.8, executing this class will produce the following output:

```
The two ministers are the same

The name of the Minster: Cornelius Fudge
The name of the Minster: Cornelius Fudge
The name of the Minster: Pius Thicknesse
```

If you look at the definition of `TestSingletonClass` in Section 6.8, there are three attempts at constructing a `MinisterForMagic` instance in the `main` of that class. As you can see in the output shown above, the second attempt, although with a different name and a different year of appointment for the minister, yields the same instance that was created by the first attempt. The first output line "The two ministers are the same" is the result of comparing the instances created in the first two attempts. The "Pius Thicknesse" output line is evidence that after we have "retired" the instance created in the first attempt, we are free again to create a new instance of `MinisterForMagic`.

For gaining additional insights regarding the Singleton pattern, you may wish to extend the code shown along the following lines:

- In Section 6.9 we talked about variations on the Singleton pattern. In accordance with the first example in that section, rewrite the `MinisterForMagic` class of Section 6.7 so that it honors only one request for instantiation. That is, after returning the instance created at the first request received from a client, it should throw an exception.
- Again as explained in Section 6.9, extend the `MinisterForMagic` class so that a subclass derived from it also behaves like a Singleton class.
- You may wish to create an expanded version of the Singleton pattern demonstration here so that it allows a maximum of N number of instances of the class to be made. Any additional requests for instantiation should return one of the previously constructed N instances. If you actually do this, reflect on the differences between your expanded implementation of the Singleton pattern and the Prototype pattern presented in the previous chapter.

7

ADAPTER

7.1 GETTING THINGS TO WORK TOGETHER

When traveling abroad, you need an adapter when you are unable to connect your laptop's power plug with the hotel's wall socket. What you desperately need in that situation is an example of a mechanical adapter for an electrical function. On one side, it has the required number of prongs whose shapes and configuration satisfy the electrical code of the country you find yourself in and, on the other, the socket holes that you use in your home country. Other examples of mechanical adapters include pipe sections with different diameters at the two ends for joining two pipes that are not of the same diameter; camera lens mount adapters that allow third-party lenses that come with their own lens mounts to be mated with cameras; and so on.

You have a more sophisticated adapter when one system wants to use the services offered by another system, but the mode of interaction used by one is not comprehensible to the other. For such systems to work together, you need to interpose an adapter between the two. The adapter's job is to translate the requests from one system into a language that the other can understand. Before Ethernet became the protocol of choice for exchanging digital information in local area networks, these sorts of adapters were commonly employed when, say, a computer whose network interface understood the Ethernet protocol needed to be hooked into a Token Ring network of PCs. In the early years of computer networking, adapters were also needed for higher-level packet forwarding in wide area networks when a computer whose communication interface was based on the TCP/IP protocol wanted to exchange information with another computer in an AppleTalk or IPX based network. But, now, practically all packet forwarding is carried out with the TCP/IP protocol.

In the software context, as you will see in this chapter, an adapter is what you need when you try to use a vendor-supplied class (because it has the desired functionality) whose interface is incompatible with how that functionality is invoked in your own software.

Designing with Objects: Object-Oriented Design Patterns Explained with Stories from Harry Potter,
First Edition. Avinash C. Kak.
© 2015 John Wiley & Sons, Inc. Published 2015 by John Wiley & Sons, Inc.

7.2   INTENT AND APPLICABILITY

The intent of the Adapter pattern is to make it possible for a client to use a new class to augment the services being provided by an existing class (or to even replace an existing class) with the client having to make only minimal changes to its own code.

Referring to the old class as the *adaptee class* and the new class as the *adapter class*, you should consider using this pattern when

- it is possible to make the adapter class a subclass of the adaptee class;
- or, it is possible for the adapter class to implement the interface that the client code is programmed to, and for the adapter class to then call on an instance of the adaptee class, or one of its subclasses, for using the adaptee's services selectively in the new versions of those services;
- or, in a variant of the pattern, it is possible for the adapter to implement the interface the client code is programmed to, and that, subsequently, the adapter can make a run-time selection from multiple possible adaptee classes.

7.3   INTRODUCTION TO THE ADAPTER PATTERN

When talking about the Adapter pattern, it is convenient to use the notion of a "Target interface," this being the interface that your own code is programmed to for using a class supplied by a vendor. Let's now say that you want to switch to a different vendor whose more up-to-date class offers an enhanced version of the same functionality that you are currently using through the Target interface. Unfortunately, the interface of the class from the new vendor is different. So how do we solve this problem? Using the Adapter pattern, the new vendor could create an adapter class that, on the one hand, would implement the Target interface that you are accustomed to and that, on the other, would invoke the code in the new class. Subsequently, you may need to make only a one-line change in your own code in order to use the upgraded functionality offered through the adapter class.

We illustrate this idea with the help of Figures 7.1 and 7.2. The class diagram in Figure 7.1 shows a client needing the functionality defined in the Target interface and,

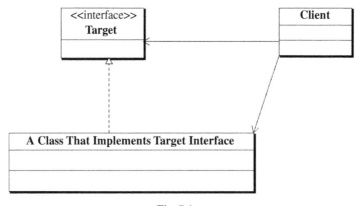

Fig. 7.1

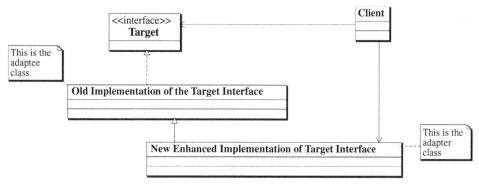

Fig. 7.2

for that purpose, the client uses the class shown at the bottom of the figure. At some point, the client wants to switch to another vendor and finds one that provides a closely related but not identical functionality. This is illustrated with the class diagram in Figure 7.2. The client can use this new class provided the new vendor is willing to modify it so that it can serve as an adapter class that either directly implements the Target interface or that extends the previous class if the previous class is going to remain in the system. (What Figure 7.2 shows is the latter case.) As you'll see through the demonstration code in this chapter, chances are that the modifications needed in the new class are relatively trivial — mostly in the nature of changing the class header and defining simple methods that call on the main body of the code in the new class for doing heavy lifting. In either case, the client would need to make only minimal changes to its own code (as minimal as changing just one statement) when the client switches from the first vendor to the second. As shown in Figure 7.2, we refer to the old class as the adaptee class and the new class as the adapter class.

7.4 THE ADAPTER PATTERN IN REAL-WORLD APPLICATIONS

Let's say your company is involved in writing software for an industrial controller needed for manufacturing certain kinds of products. For example, think about creating a controller software package for the 6-DoF (six degrees of freedom) pick-and-place arm robots that are now widely used in manufacturing. There are a very large number of such robots out there, but they all work on the same principles — the principles of kinematic control. To explain briefly what that means: The main goal of a controller is to send the robot end-effector (think of your hand as your arm's end-effector) to specific 3D coordinates (which accounts for 3 DoF) and with a specific orientation (which accounts for the other 3 DoF). Assuming that we are dealing with what are known as articulated robots, the controller's main job is to figure out the extent of rotation by the motors at the rotary joints between the successive links of the robot for a given position and orientation of the end-effector. The joint rotations estimated by the controller must be fed into the low-level function calls for controlling the joint motors. In other words, the controller software must be written with respect to a specific API that describes the function calls for the motors.

In writing such software, your company will have to choose between the following two options: The company may choose to create a separate software package for each different

robot type out there, *or the company may choose to create a single controller package for a low-level API of its own design and then provide adapters, based on the Adapter pattern, for the different types of robots.* Since the controller software is likely to be complex, just imagine how much easier your company's job would be if there is only one such package to maintain. The adapters are likely to be much simpler compared to the main controller package. By treating them as independent pieces of software, you would be eliminating the individual robot dependencies from your own controller package. So a bug report is likely to be specific to just the adapter designed for a particular robot type. Obviously, if your controller works as advertised for the other customers, it is less likely that you have a bug in the controller software itself.

7.5   HARRY POTTER STORY USED TO ILLUSTRATE THE ADAPTER PATTERN

Our demonstration of the Adapter pattern is based on the DADA (Defense Against Dark Arts) teaching needs of the Hogwarts School of Magic. This teaching position is believed to have been cursed by Voldemort when, in his younger days, his application for the job was rejected. Ever since, there has been a veritable parade of DADA instructors through Hogwarts. For the purpose of our demonstration we will imagine that this high turnover has created a logistical problem for the school. We will further imagine that the school administration requires each new instructor for DADA to conform to the school-specified basic teaching syllabus for this class before injecting any additional topics of his or her own choice.

Now consider the following situation: The school has just lost its DADA teacher. So the school hires a new teacher, who, as it turns out, also wants to educate the students about the moral dimensions of the practice of the dark arts. The school would like to accommodate the new teacher's desire, but, being short on resources, does not wish to make too many changes to its own records and school administration protocols. How can the school bring this about? With the Adapter pattern, as you will see in the rest of this chapter.

More generally, we can certainly expect that each new teacher will teach DADA slightly differently — since each teacher will make his or her own decisions about how much time to devote to important related issues such as the morality of practicing the dark arts and the dangers associated with such practice. We therefore need to let each teacher customize the basic DADA teaching interface to his or her own way of doing the job. An adapter class is ideal for such customization. By deriving from the previous teacher's class (which we may think of as the adaptee class), each new teacher's adapter class would allow us to construct the same type of teacher instances as in the previous years. This would make it possible for Hogwarts to have to make only minimal changes to its code when a new teacher joins the school for teaching DADA.

7.6   A TOP LEVEL VIEW OF THE PATTERN DEMONSTRATION

Figure 7.3 presents the class diagram for our demonstration of the Adapter pattern. (To be more precise, this diagram describes the main demonstration of the pattern. Sections 7.11 and 7.12 present two other ways of implementing the Adapter pattern.) We will use the methods declared in the interface `TeachingDADA` to represent at a high-level what a DADA teacher must teach the students at Hogwarts.

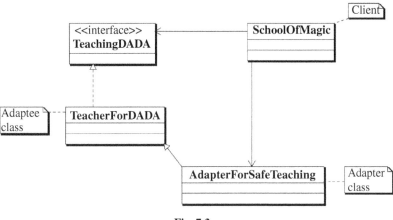

Fig. 7.3

We will assume that the old teacher had implemented the `TeachingDADA` interface in a class called `TeacherForDADA`. As you will see later in that class, the old teacher taught the class in a very generic fashion, or, you might say, in a matter-of-factly fashion. His class did not address the issue of morality at all, did not warn the students that the practice of dark arts could lead to the destruction of their souls, and could result in their disfigurement.

The new teacher who is hired implements his teaching syllabus through an adapter class called `AdapterForSafeTeaching` that extends the old teacher's class `TeacherForDADA`. The new class is the adapter class vis-à-vis the adaptee class `TeacherForDADA` and the Target interface `TeachingDADA`.

For the School of Magic, implemented in a client class called `SchoolOfMagic`, we will use the basic teaching interface `TeachingDADA` to define a teacher instance through the following declaration:

    TeachingDADA teacher;

If the school had renewed the contract of the previous teacher (assuming that the teacher was still available), it would have set the `teacher` instance variable to the object returned by a call to the constructor for `TeacherForDADA`. However, we know that the old teacher is no longer available and the new teacher is going to teach the same course a bit differently. In order to make the switch from the old teacher to the new teacher in our software demonstration, all that the school has to do is to change the binding of the variable `teacher` to an instance of `AdapterForSafeTeaching`. That works because, as shown in Figure 7.3, the adapter class `AdapterForSafeTeaching` is derived from the `TeacherForDADA` (which in turn implements the Target interface `TeachingDADA`). Therefore, an instance of `AdapterForSafeTeaching` is also of type `TeachingDADA`.

While the adapter class `AdapterForSafeTeaching` will provide implementations for all of the methods in the Target interface `TeachingDADA`, the former will also include additional functionality through the following methods:

    doTeachPowerOfLove()
    doTeachHowDarkMagicCanHarmTheCaster()
    doTeachAboutProtectiveDevices()

These methods are needed by the adapter class since they will be called in its override implementations for the methods declared originally in the `TeachingDADA` interface.

To repeat, we use `TeacherForDADA` as the adaptee class and, for the adapter class, we use `AdapterForSafeTeaching`. As you would expect, in addition to providing additional functionality, the adapter class adapts to the adaptee class in such a way that the client, `SchoolOfMagic`, has to change only a single line in its code as it switches from the adaptee class to the adapter class.

7.7   THE TARGET INTERFACE: TeachingDADA

Shown in this section is the `TeachingDADA` interface that is published by the Hogwarts School of Magic. This interface spells out at a high level what the school's expectations are regarding what a DADA teacher should teach. Although there exist many forms of the dark arts, the interface will focus on just the following five:

Cruciatus Curse: This curse causes excruciating pain. It is one of the three Unforgivable Curses, the other two being the Avada Kedavra Curse and the Imperius Curse.

Horcrux: A Horcrux is an inanimate object or a living being in which a dark wizard can deposit a portion of his/her soul for safekeeping with the intention of achieving immortality.

Petrificus Totalus: This curse causes a victim to fall into a state of stone-like unconsciousness.

Sectumsempra: This curse is meant to slash a victim. The slash marks on the victim follow the motion of the attacker's wand. If the wand is held stationary as it points to a specific limb, the curse can cause the limb to separate from the body.

Avada Kedavra: This is one of the three Unforgivable Curses and it causes instant death. As mentioned earlier, the other two Unforgivable Curses are the Cruciatus Curse, already described, and the Imperius Curse, which causes a victim to act like a slave of the individual inflicting the curse.

A wizard can call upon several means to defend himself against the harm that can be caused by the dark arts. For example, the Shield Charm can cause some of the not-so-strong curses to either become weaker or to even rebound on the attacker. Then there is the sneakascope, a small spinning glass top that makes shrill sounds if it detects someone with evil intentions in the vicinity. Curse-specific defenses also exist. For example, one can defend oneself against the Avada Kedavra curse by ducking behind a wall or some other object. The shielding object used in this manner will burst into flames when the Avada Kedavra curse hits it. The school expects a DADA teacher to instruct the students in such defensive techniques.

The teaching interface we show below says simply that a teacher will provide instruction in how to defend oneself if one is confronted with any of the instances of the dark arts that are indicated by the names of the methods.

```
public interface TeachingDADA {
```

```
    void defenseAgainstCruciatusCurse();

    void defenseAgainstPetrification();

    void defenseAgainstSectumsempra();

    void defenseAgainstAvadaKedavra();

    void awarenessOfHorcrux();
}
```

7.8   THE TeacherForDADA CLASS

The previous DADA teacher at Hogwarts is represented by the class shown below. Although it conforms to the TeachingDADA interface specified by the school, this class focuses primarily on the teaching of the dark arts and mentions little of why it is immoral to practice such arts.

In our demonstration, the act of teaching how to defend oneself should one become a victim of a dark curse consists of the class (an instance of this class, to be more precise) printing out relevant educational messages.

```
public class TeacherForDADA implements TeachingDADA {

    public void defenseAgainstCruciatusCurse(){
        System.out.println(
            "This curse inflicts extreme pain. The overall "
          + "effect of the curse depends on the state of the "
          + "mind of the caster and how intent the caster is "
          + "on inflicting torture. "
        );
        System.out.println(
            "No specific counter-curse is known for this curse. "
          + "One could try the shield charm Protego Horribilis. "
          + "An individual expecting to be hit with this curse "
          + "could also carry around a sneakoscope, which is a "
          + "miniature glass spinning top that emits shrill "
          + "sounds when someone with evil intent is in the "
          + "vicinity. "
        );
    }
    public void awarenessOfHorcrux(){
        System.out.println(
            "A horcrux can be a living being or an object. A dark "
          + "wizard wanting immortality stores a portion of "
          + "his/her soul in a horcrux. "
        );
        System.out.println( "Can be destroyed with basilisk's venom. ");
```

```
    }
    public void defenseAgainstPetrification(){
        System.out.println(
            "Petrification turns a living being into a stone-like "
          + "state of unconsciousness. "
        );
        System.out.println(
            "Can be revived with mandrake restorative draught. "
        );
    }
    public void defenseAgainstSectumsempra(){
        System.out.println(
            "Sectumsempra curse causes a victim's skin to be "
          + "slashed according to the motions of the wand held "
          + "by the caster.  However, if the caster does not "
          + "move the wand but only points it at a limb of the "
          + "victim, the victim may lose that limb. "
        );
        System.out.println(
            "There exists a counter curse to Secturmsempra --- "
          + "it is called Vulnera Sanentur.  Snape used the "
          + "counter curse when Harry threw the Sectumsempra"
          + " curse at Draco Molfoy. "
        );
    }
    public void defenseAgainstAvadaKedavra() {
        System.out.println(
            "This darkest of the dark arts is the killing curse. "
        );
        System.out.println(
            "Is blocked by the power of love.  That is, if you are "
          + "'shielded' by the love given to you by people in your "
          + "past or at present, this darkest of the curses will"
          + "be deflected off you. Harry was shielded against this "
          + "curse because his mother made the ultimate sacrifice "
          + "of love for him. The only other being who is known to "
          + "possess a shield against this curse was Voldemort "
          + "because of his Horcruxes. This curse can also"
          + "be blocked if a victim hides behind a solid object. "
          + "The object will burst into flames when hit by the "
          + "curse.  The curse hits a victim in the form of a "
          + "green bolt of lightning. "
        );
    }
}
```

7.9   THE AdapterForSafeTeaching CLASS

The adapter class presented in this section stands for the new DADA teacher who must, obviously, conform to the TeachingDADA interface specified by the school and, to the

extent possible, also utilize the teaching materials declared in the `TeacherForDADA` class, which corresponds to how the previous teacher taught DADA.

Note how the adaptation has been implemented in the class definition that follows. For each of the methods declared in the `TeachingDADA` interface, the adapter class shown below uses a combination of the implementation defined in the adaptee class `TeacherForDADA` and the new functionality defined here. For example, the implementation of the method `defenseAgainstCruciatusCurse()` first calls on two locally defined methods for teaching the morality issues related to the casting of the Cruciatus Curse on someone, and then calls upon the material in the implementation inherited from the parent class `TeacherForDADA` for the rest of the educational material related to the teaching of this curse.

In this manner, the new teacher, as represented by the `AdapterForSafeTeaching` class, manages to inject the moral dimensions of engaging in the dark arts before actually launching into the various acts and artifacts of such arts and how one should defend oneself against them.

```
public class AdapterForSafeTeaching extends TeacherForDADA {

    public void defenseAgainstCruciatusCurse(){
        doTeachHowDarkMagicCanHarmTheCaster();
        doTeachPowerOfLove();
        super.defenseAgainstCruciatusCurse();
    }
    public void awarenessOfHorcrux(){
        doTeachHowDarkMagicCanHarmTheCaster();
        doTeachPowerOfLove();
        super.awarenessOfHorcrux();
    }
    public void defenseAgainstPetrification(){
        doTeachAboutProtectiveDevices();
        super.defenseAgainstPetrification();
    }
    public void defenseAgainstSectumsempra(){
        doTeachHowDarkMagicCanHarmTheCaster();
        super.defenseAgainstSectumsempra();
    }
    public void defenseAgainstAvadaKedavra() {
        doTeachHowDarkMagicCanHarmTheCaster();
        super.defenseAgainstAvadaKedavra();
    }
    void doTeachPowerOfLove() {
        System.out.println(
            "The magic of love can conquer the darkest magic"
        );
    }
    void doTeachHowDarkMagicCanHarmTheCaster() {
        System.out.println(
            "Use of Dark Magic can corrupt the soul and body of "
          + "the caster.  An evil wizard may use such magic  to "
```

```
            + "prolong his own life and to obtain great power. A "
            + "practice of such arts can make a wizard look deformed "
            + "and inhuman. "
        );
    }
    void doTeachAboutProtectiveDevices() {
        System.out.println(
            "Don't forget to take along the Sneakoscope detector "
          + "as a general protection against curses and spells. "
        );
    }
}
```

7.10   THE CLIENT CLASS SchoolOfMagic

We now present the client class SchoolOfMagic. Recall that the Hogwarts School of Magic is the client in our demonstration of the Adapter pattern. Implicit in our demonstration is the fact that this client previously employed a DADA teacher whose teaching of the material was according to the definition of the various methods shown in the class TeacherForDADA of Section 7.8.

When the new teacher was hired to replace the old teacher, the new teacher not only wanted to teach about the dark arts and how to defend oneself against them, but also about the morality of engaging in such arts against others. Toward that end, the class presented in the previous section corresponds to the new teacher. As we showed in that section, the new class is an adaptation of the new teaching of DADA to how it was taught previously.

So, in the definition of the client class below, we set the variable teacher to an instance of the adapter class AdapterForSafeTeaching. It would be correct to assume that previously, while DADA was being taught by the old teacher, the teacher variable was set to an instance of TeacherForDADA.

It is important to realize that when the school hired the new teacher, only one line in the client class shown below needed to be changed — this is the line in which we set the teacher variable. The rest of the code remained exactly as it was for the previous teacher.

```
public class SchoolOfMagic {

    TeachingDADA teacher;

    public SchoolOfMagic() {
        teacher = new AdapterForSafeTeaching();
    }
    public void teachDefenseAgainstDarkArts() {
        teacher.defenseAgainstPetrification();
        System.out.println( "\n\n");
        teacher.defenseAgainstCruciatusCurse();
        System.out.println( "\n\n");
        teacher.awarenessOfHorcrux();
        System.out.println( "\n\n");
        teacher.defenseAgainstPetrification();
```

```
        System.out.println( "\n\n");
        teacher.defenseAgainstSectumsempra();
        System.out.println( "\n\n");
        teacher.defenseAgainstAvadaKedavra();
    }
    public static void main(String[] args) {
        SchoolOfMagic hogwarts = new SchoolOfMagic();
        hogwarts.teachDefenseAgainstDarkArts();
    }
}
```

That completes the demonstration code for the Adapter pattern. To be more precise, that completes the demonstration code for the *Class Adapter* version of the Adapter pattern (as to what that means, see the next section). Normally, at this point in a chapter, the next section would be labeled "Playing with the Code," where the output produced by the executable class of the pattern demonstration would be presented. We depart from that formula in this chapter since we need to make the reader aware of two other ways in which the Adapter pattern can be implemented. The output produced by executing the code you have seen so far will be presented in Section 7.13 of this chapter.

7.11   OBJECT ADAPTER

As the reader will recall, the purpose of the Adapter pattern is to enable a client to use a new class to either replace an existing class, or to augment its functionality, with only minimal changes to the client-side code. So, as stated earlier, we think of the old class as the adaptee class and the new class as the adapter class. The adapter class must adapt to the adaptee while, at the same time, possibly augmenting the functionality provided by the old class.

What we have demonstrated so far in this chapter is referred to as the *Class Adapter* method of implementing the Adapter pattern. Two other ways exist in which to implement this pattern: the *Object Adapter* approach and the *Pluggable Adapter* approach. In this section, we will explain what we mean by an *Object Adapter*. The next section will then go into *Pluggable Adapter*.

In the Class Adapter approach presented in the previous sections of this chapter, the adapter class was subclassed from the adaptee class and overrode its methods. In the Object Adapter approach presented in this section, the adapter will NOT be subclassed from the Adaptee. On the other hand, the adapter will now construct an instance of the adaptee and then call on that instance to gain access to the functionality that the adapter needs from the adaptee as it provides additional functionality to the client (which is the School of Magic in our case).

In our demonstration of the Object Adapter approach, we will use the same TeachingDADA interface as shown previously. Recall that that interface spells out the school's minimal expectations of what it wants a DADA teacher to cover in the classroom. We will also use the same TeacherForDADA class as before for our representation of the old teacher. As for the client, we will again use the same SchoolOfMagic class as was shown previously. So the only new class in our demonstration of the Object Adapter approach is AdapterForSafeTeaching. Recall, this represents the new teacher.

The new version of the adapter class is shown below. In accordance with the above explanation, instead of subclassing from TeacherForDADA, we now use an instance variable of type TeacherForDADA. Subsequently, we invoke the various methods declared in the interface TeachingDADA on that variable to bring in the functionality defined in the adaptee class TeacherForDADA.

```java
public class AdapterForSafeTeaching  implements TeachingDADA {

    TeachingDADA oldTeacher = new TeacherForDADA();

    public void defenseAgainstCruciatusCurse(){
        doTeachHowDarkMagicCanHarmTheCaster();
        doTeachPowerOfLove();
        oldTeacher.defenseAgainstCruciatusCurse();
    }
    public void awarenessOfHorcrux(){
        doTeachHowDarkMagicCanHarmTheCaster();
        doTeachPowerOfLove();
        oldTeacher.awarenessOfHorcrux();
    }
    public void defenseAgainstPetrification(){
        doTeachAboutProtectiveDevices();
        oldTeacher.defenseAgainstPetrification();
    }
    public void defenseAgainstSectumsempra(){
        doTeachHowDarkMagicCanHarmTheCaster();
        oldTeacher.defenseAgainstSectumsempra();
    }
    public void defenseAgainstAvadaKedavra() {
        doTeachHowDarkMagicCanHarmTheCaster();
        oldTeacher.defenseAgainstAvadaKedavra();
    }
    void doTeachPowerOfLove() {
        System.out.println(
                "The magic of love can conquer the darkest magic");
    }
    void doTeachHowDarkMagicCanHarmTheCaster() {
        System.out.println( "Use of Dark Magic can corrupt the soul "
                + "and body of the caster.  An evil wizard "
                + "may use such magic  to prolong his own "
                + "life and to obtain great power. A "
                + "practice of such arts can make a wizard "
                + "look deformed and inhuman.");
    }
    void doTeachAboutProtectiveDevices() {
        System.out.println( "Don't forget to take along the "
                + "Sneakoscope detector as a "
                + "general protection against curses "
                + "and spells. ");
    }
}
```

Regarding the relative merits of Class Adapters and Object Adapters, here are some of the advantages of the former: A Class Adapter makes it easier for the adaptee's functionality to simply flow through. To explain this point further, if in the Class Adapter demonstration the `AdapterForSafeTeaching` class of Section 7.9 did not override all of the methods of the adaptee class `TeacherForDADA`, the non-overridden methods of the latter would still be available to the client class `SchoolOfMagic`. This reduces the workload on the adapter if it wants to affect only minimal changes to the services offered by the adaptee.

As for the advantages of Object Adapters, in object adaptation as shown in the class definition in this section, the adapter constructs an instance of the adaptee and then selectively uses the latter's functionality with or without augmentation. Since an Object Adapter constructs an instance of the adaptee, it can polymorphically access the functionality in any of the subclasses of the adaptee (assuming that we have a hierarchy of adaptee classes). This obviously cannot be done with a Class Adapter. With a Class Adapter, the adapter can only let through the functionality of the chosen adaptee class.

7.12   PLUGGABLE ADAPTER

So far we have presented two different approaches to the implementation of the Adapter pattern: the Class Adapter approach and the Object Adapter approach. The previous section also presented the relative advantages of these two different approaches.

Now we demonstrate a third approach — a *Pluggable Adapter*. This approach allows us to change dynamically (that is, at runtime) the choice of the adaptee class. In the previous two demonstrations, the adaptee class remained fixed.

We will explain the third approach with the help of the following assumption: Let's say there are two different kinds of DADA teachers, *vecchio* and *nuovo*, with the latter more likely to inculcate in the students the immorality of the practice of the dark arts. As to what type of a DADA instructor the school may hire during a given year depends entirely on the whim of the headmaster. A headmaster may feel old-fashioned for some reason and decide that, during the coming year, the dark arts be taught purely as they are, that is, without also going into the moral dimensions related to their practice. On the other hand, the same headmaster may have some sort of an epiphany and decide that DADA teaching during the coming year should also address the moral aspects of the practice of the dark arts.

Therefore, the new teacher to be hired may be called upon to adapt to either the *vecchio* style of teaching DADA or the *nuovo* style. To capture this in a program, we are going to need two different adaptee classes that we will name `TeacherVecchio` and `TeacherNuovo`. Since the decision regarding what style of DADA teaching the incoming teacher would need to conform to depends completely on the headmaster's state of mind on the day the decision is made, it would be safe to say that the choice of the adaptee would only be known at runtime.

The demonstration that follows shows how the client class `SchoolOfMagic` can easily switch between the two choices available as adaptee classes. The new instructor, in the form of an instance of the `PluggableAdapterForDADATeaching` class, will adapt to whatever choice is made at runtime regarding the adaptee class. A top level view of this demonstration is shown in the class diagram of Figure 7.4.

As the reader would imagine, the crux of this demonstration lies in showing how the `PluggableAdapterForDADATeaching` class allows for the choice of the adaptee class to be switched at runtime between `TeacherNuovo` and `TeacherVecchio`. As to how that is accomplished, note the following most interesting feature of the

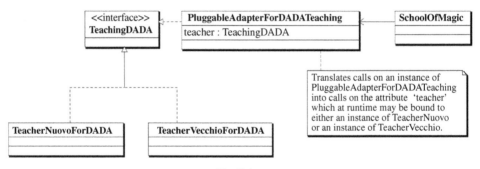

Fig. 7.4

PluggableAdapterForDADATeaching class: the interface TeachingDADA plays two different roles in the class definition simultaneously. On the one hand, the class implements the interface TeachingDADA, and, on the other, it possesses an instance variable of type TeachingDADA. We want the pluggable adapter class to implement the TeachingDADA interface since that is how the client class SchoolOfMagic accepts a DADA instructor through its instance variable teacher. Remember, a new DADA instructor is an instance constructed from the adapter class. But implementing the TeachingDADA interface implies that PluggableAdapterForDADATeaching class is now obligated to provide implementations for all of the methods declared in that interface. This is where the private instance variable teacher of the adapter class comes in handy. In the implementation code for the methods of TeachingDADA in the adapter class shown below, we simply invoke the same method names on the instance variable teacher that is declared in the adapter class. *This is the key to the runtime adaptation property of the Pluggable Adapter. The school headmaster can choose either type of teacher at runtime and the Pluggable Adapter will provide the functionality as defined for that teacher.*

```
public class PluggableAdapterForDADATeaching implements TeachingDADA {

    private TeachingDADA teacher;

    public PluggableAdapterForDADATeaching( TeachingDADA adaptee ) {
        teacher = adaptee;
    }
    public void defenseAgainstCruciatusCurse() {
        teacher.defenseAgainstCruciatusCurse();
    }
    public void defenseAgainstPetrification() {
        teacher.defenseAgainstPetrification();
    }
    public void defenseAgainstHorcrux() {
        teacher.defenseAgainstHorcrux();
    }
    public void defenseAgainstSectumsempra() {
        teacher.defenseAgainstSectumsempra();
    }
```

```
    public void defenseAgainstAvadaKedavra() {
        teacher.defenseAgainstAvadaKedavra();
    }
}
```

Shown below is the code for the first of the two adaptee classes, the TeacherVecchio class:

```
public class TeacherVecchioForDADA implements TeachingDADA {

    public void defenseAgainstCruciatusCurse(){
        System.out.println(
            "This curse inflicts extreme pain. The overall effect "
            + "of the curse depends on the state of the mind of the "
            + "caster and how intent the caster is on inflicting "
            + "torture. "
        );
        System.out.println(
            "No specific counter-curse is known for this curse.  "
            + "One could try the shield charm Protego Horribilis. "
            + "An individual expecting to be hit with this curse "
            + "could also carry around a sneakoscope, which is a "
            + "miniature glass spinning top that emits shrill sounds "
            + "when someone with evil intent is in the vicinity. "
        );
    }
    public void awarenessOfHorcrux(){
        System.out.println(
            "A horcrux can be a living being or an object. A dark "
            + "wizard wanting immortality stores a portion of his/her "
            + "soul in a horcrux. "
        );
        System.out.println( "Can be destroyed with basilisk's venom. ");
    }
    public void defenseAgainstPetrification(){
        System.out.println(
            "Petrification turns a living being into a stone-like state "
            + "of unconsciousness. "
        );
        System.out.println(
            "Can be revived with mandrake restorative draught. "
        );
    }
    public void defenseAgainstSectumsempra(){
        System.out.println(
            "Sectumsempra curse causes a victim's skin to be slashed "
            + "according to the motions of the wand held by the caster.  "
            + "However, if the caster does not move the wand but only "
            + "points it at a limb of the victim, the victim may lose "
            + "that limb. "
        );
```

```
        System.out.println(
            "There exists a counter-curse to Secturmsempra --- it is "
          + "called Vulnera Sanentur.  Snape used the counter curse "
          + "when Harry threw the Sectumsempra curse at Draco Molfoy. "
        );
    }
    public void defenseAgainstAvadaKedavra() {
        System.out.println(
            "This darkest of the dark arts is the killing curse. "
        );
        System.out.println(
            "Is blocked by the power of love.  That is, if you are "
          + "'shielded' by the love given to you by people in your "
          + "past or at present, this darkest of the curses will"
          + "be deflected off you. Harry was shielded against this "
          + "curse because his mother made the ultimate sacrifice of "
          + "love for him. The only other being who is known to "
          + "possess a shield against this curse was Voldemort "
          + "because of his Horcruxes. This curse can also be blocked "
          + "if a victim hides behind a solid object.  The object will "
          + "burst into flames when hit by the curse.  The curse hits "
          + "a victim in the form of a green bolt of lightning. "
        );
    }
}
```

Next we show the second of our two adaptee classes, the TeacherNuovoForDADA class:

```
public class TeacherNuovoForDADA implements TeachingDADA {

    public void defenseAgainstCruciatusCurse(){
        doTeachHowDarkMagicCanHarmTheCaster();
        doTeachPowerOfLove();
        System.out.println(
            "This curse inflicts extreme pain. The overall "
          + "effect of the curse depends on the state of the mind "
          + "of the caster and how intent the caster is on "
          + "inflicting torture. "
        );
        System.out.println(
            "No specific counter-curse is known for this curse. "
          + "One could try the shield charm Protego Horribilis.  An "
          + "individual expecting to be hit with this curse could "
          + "also carry around a sneakoscope, which is a miniature "
          + "glass spinning top that emits shrill sounds if when "
          + "someone with evil intent is in the vicinity. "
        );
    }
    public void awarenessOfHorcrux(){
        doTeachHowDarkMagicCanHarmTheCaster();
        doTeachPowerOfLove();
```

```
        System.out.println(
            "A horcrux can be a living being or an object. A dark "
          + "wizard wanting immortality stores a portion of his/her "
          + "soul in a horcrux. "
        );
        System.out.println( "Can be destroyed with basilisk's venom. " );
}
public void defenseAgainstPetrification(){
    doTeachAboutProtectiveDevices();
    System.out.println(
            "Petrification turns a living being into a stone-like "
          + "state of unconsciousness. "
    );
    System.out.println(
                "Can be revived with mandrake restorative draught. ");
}
public void defenseAgainstSectumsempra() {
    doTeachHowDarkMagicCanHarmTheCaster();
    System.out.println(
            "Sectumsempra curse causes a victim's skin to be slashed "
          + "according to the motions of the wand held by the caster. "
          + "However, if the caster does not move the wand but only "
          + "points it at a limb of the victim, the victim may lose "
          + "that limb. "
    );
    System.out.println(
            "There exists a counter-curse to Secturmsempra --- it is "
          + "called Vulnera Sanentur.  Snape used the counter-curse "
          + "when Harry threw the Sectumsempra curse at Draco Molfoy. "
    );
}
public void defenseAgainstAvadaKedavra() {
    doTeachHowDarkMagicCanHarmTheCaster();
    System.out.println(
            "This darkest of the dark arts is the killing curse."
    );
    System.out.println(
            "Is blocked by the power of love.  That is, if you are "
          + "'shielded' by the love given to you by people in your "
          + "past or at present, this darkest of the curses will"
          + "be deflected off you. Harry was shielded against this "
          + "curse because his mother made the ultimate sacrifice of "
          + "love for him. The only other being who is known to "
          + "possess a shield against this curse was Voldemort "
          + "because of his Horcruxes. This curse can also be blocked "
          + "if a victim hides behind a solid object.  The object will "
          + "burst into flames when hit by the curse.  The curse hits "
          + "a victim in the form of a green bolt of lightning. "
    );
}
void doTeachPowerOfLove() {
    System.out.println(
```

```
                          "The magic of love can conquer the darkest magic. ");
    }
    void doTeachHowDarkMagicCanHarmTheCaster() {
        System.out.println(
            "Use of Dark Magic can corrupt the soul and body of the "
          + "caster. An evil wizard may use such magic to prolong his "
          + "own life and to obtain great power. A practice of such "
          + "arts can make a wizard look deformed and inhuman. "
        );
    }
    void doTeachAboutProtectiveDevices() {
        System.out.println(
            "Don't forget to take along the Sneakoscope detector as a "
          + "general protection against curses and spells. "
        );
    }
}
```

Finally, we show the client class `SchoolOfMagic` needed for demonstrating the Pluggable Adapter. Before going through the definition shown below, the reader may wish to review the comments made earlier regarding the adaptee classes `TeacherNuovo` and `TeacherVecchio` to understand why they both needed to descend from the same root interface `TeachingDADA` and why this interface must declare all of the services expected by the client from its DADA teachers. The reader may also wish to review the earlier discussion related to the `PluggableAdapter` class to understand why it must also implement the root interface of the adaptee classes. As mentioned earlier, this is to enable dynamic binding for the `teacher` instance variable in the client class `SchoolOfMagic` shown below and, thus, for dynamic determination of which adaptee's services will be used by the school. In the code below, note the two possible choices for the `teacher` instance variable. The user is prompted for the choice to be made for the adaptee class at runtime. As you would expect, the teaching services you get in the method `teachDefenseAgainstDarkArts()` depend on which adaptee was selected.

```
import java.util.*;

public class SchoolOfMagic {

    TeachingDADA teacher;

    public SchoolOfMagic() {
        System.out.println(
            "\n Pretend you are the Headmaster of the Hogwarts School"
          + "\n of Magic. You are drawn to both the old-style DADA"
          + "\n teaching, with its focus exclusively on how a wizard"
          + "\n can defend himself or herself against the dark arts,"
          + "\n and the new-style teaching of the same subject that"
          + "\n also addresses the moral dimensions of engaging in"
```

```
                    + "\n the dark arts.  You have a habit of waiting until the"
                    + "\n last minute before deciding whether the new teacher"
                    + "\n you are hiring should conform to the old style or the"
                    + "\n new style.  Well, that moment is here. If you would"
                    + "\n like for the new teacher to conform to the old style,"
                    + "\n enter number 1.  Otherwise enter number 2:" );
                Scanner sc = new Scanner(System.in);
                int in = sc.nextInt();
                if ( in == 1 ) {
                    teacher = new PluggableAdapterForDADATeaching(
                                        new TeacherNuovoForDADA() );
                } else if (in == 2) {
                    teacher = new PluggableAdapterForDADATeaching(
                                        new TeacherVecchioForDADA() );
                } else {
                    System.out.println("Wrong answer. Exiting");
                    System.exit(0);
                }
            }
        public void teachDefenseAgainstDarkArts() {
            teacher.defenseAgainstPetrification();
            System.out.println( "\n\n");
            teacher.defenseAgainstCruciatusCurse();
            System.out.println( "\n\n");
            teacher.awarenessOfHorcrux();
            System.out.println( "\n\n");
            teacher.defenseAgainstPetrification();
            System.out.println( "\n\n");
            teacher.defenseAgainstSectumsempra();
            System.out.println( "\n\n");
            teacher.defenseAgainstAvadaKedavra();
        }
        public static void main(String[] args) {
            SchoolOfMagic hogwarts = new SchoolOfMagic();
            hogwarts.teachDefenseAgainstDarkArts();
        }
    }
}
```

If you execute the version of the SchoolOfMagic class shown above, you will be prompted for your choice of the adaptee class you'd like to make. If you enter number 1, the system will choose an instance of TeacherVecchioForDADA as the adaptee. And if you enter 2, the system will choose an instance of TeacherNuovoForDADA for the same. How the teaching specified by root interface TeachingDADA is carried out by the new teacher will depend on your choice for the adaptee class.

7.13   PLAYING WITH THE CODE

The class files for this pattern have been placed in the following three directories at the course website:

1. ClassAdapterDemonstration
2. ObjectAdapterDemonstration
3. PluggableAdapterDemonstration

Download these files into your own three separate directories. In each directory, you can compile the code with the command

```
javac *.java
```

and run the executable class SchoolOfMagic class by

```
java SchoolOfMagic
```

Assuming that you are running the code in Sections 7.6 through 7.10 for the Class Adapter demonstration, given the code in the main() of the SchoolOfMagic class in Section 7.10, executing this class should produce the following output:

```
Don't forget to take along the Sneakoscope detector as a
general protection against curses and spells.
Petrification turns a living being into a stone-like state
of unconsciousness. Can be revived with mandrake restorative
draught

Use of Dark Magic can corrupt the soul and body of the
caster.  An evil wizard may use such magic to prolong his
own life and to obtain great power.  A practice of such
arts can make a wizard look deformed and inhuman.  The
magic of love can conquer the darkest magic. This curse
inflicts extreme pain. The overall effect of the curse
depends on the state of the mind of the caster and how
intent the caster is on inflicting torture.  No specific
counter-curse is known for this curse.  One could try the
shield charm Protego Horribilis.  An individual expecting
to be hit with this curse could also carry around a
sneakoscope, which is a miniature glass spinning top that
emits shrill sounds when someone with evil intent is in
the vicinity.

....
....
....
```

For additional insights, you could try to extend the code for this pattern along the following lines:

- All of our methods in the three implementations of the Adapter pattern return void. We could get away with it because we used the text that is printed out by the methods as standing for what the teachers would teach. You may wish to create alternative demonstrations in which the methods return values. Placing constraints on the values

acceptable to the client, program your adapter class vis-à-vis the adaptee classes in such a way that any new functionality picked up in the adapter class satisfies the client constraints.

- Our implementations of the Adapter pattern were made simple by the fact that we used the same data types in the adapter and the adaptee classes. What if this pattern is needed in situations where that is not the case? Let's say the client wants to replace an old software package with a new one (because the new package adds to the functionality provided by the old one) but is faced with the problems caused by incompatibilities between the data types used in the two packages. Now you would need a more sophisticated adapter class since it must also translate the data types from the new software package to those used in the adaptee class. See if you can create a demonstration of this idea.

PART II

STRUCTURAL PATTERNS

The Structural Patterns are about creating new objects through a collaboration between multiple classes. The resulting representational structures are more complex than what you saw for the Creational Patterns. Nonetheless, the solutions provided by the Structural Patterns are such that we can write instance creation code that is just as straightforward as it was for the Creational Patterns. As with the Creational Patterns, these solutions continue to obey the tenets of good object-oriented programming described in Chapter 1.

The representational issues that require inter-class collaboration for instance production are unique to each of the seven Structural Patterns. Also unique to each pattern is the extent of collaboration needed. When a pattern allows for an arbitrary number of classes to work together, the representational efficiency of the solution provided by the pattern is not compromised.

For the sort of respresentational issues addressed by the Structural Patterns, let's say your application involves a class that needs to be mixed with a potentially large number of embellishments and assume that the clients of the class want to mix and match the embellishments in arbitrary ways. How should one represent the embellishments vis-à-vis the basic class so that the instances incorporating the embellishments can be produced efficiently? For another representational issue, let's say we have a class that is a composition over several smaller classes, but, as it happens, all of the classes involved are of the same fundamental type. Is there some way to exploit the type similarity of all of the classes so that they (including the large class) can all be manipulated with a common interface? For yet another representational issue that is best addressed by multiple classes collaborating together, is it possible for there to be one organization in charge of specifying the data abstractions required for modeling a domain and another in charge of supplying the implementations for the behaviors associated with those abstractions? What about the representational issues that arise when you want to augment the services provided by an existing class with those from a new class but the two classes are programmed to different interfaces? And so on.

In what follows, we will briefly list the seven Structural Patterns that address these sorts of questions:

Designing with Objects: Object-Oriented Design Patterns Explained with Stories from Harry Potter,
First Edition. Avinash C. Kak.

Adapter: Let us say you want to use a new class for augmenting the services being provided by an existing class or for replacing an existing class. When the interface to which the new class is programmed is not exactly the same as for the existing class, this pattern gives us three different solutions to the problem of how to best incorporate the new class in your software.

Bridge: There can be situations when it is necessary to decouple the implementation of a class from its high-level definition. This could, for example, happen when one organization is in charge of publishing the specifications for a class and another organization is charged with the responsibility of creating an implementation according to those specifications. The Bridge pattern shows how such decoupling can be achieved.

Composite: The Composite pattern shows us not only how a subclass type can be composed of objects of the superclass type (which, in and of itself, is hardly any news to those well versed in object-oriented programming) but also how the objects of the subclass type — including the objects that are composites over the superclass types — can be manipulated through just the interface declared in the superclass.

Decorator: Let's say that the clients of a class would like to see it embellished in different ways. A seemingly simple solution to this problem would be to extend the basic class for each possible embellishment. In some cases that may work fine. However, when the number of embellishments is large and their combinations arbitrary, a representational framework based on pure inheritance can become cumbersome. This is where the Decorator pattern comes to our rescue. This pattern gives you a compact representational structure in which the class that contains the core functionality needed by your clients is allowed to be augmented with a nested layering of embellishments with no constraints on the order or the depth of nesting.

Facade: You will find this pattern useful if you do not want your software to suffer from the following problem that is common to many applications that run on your computer: You must master an application at the expert level even if your needs vis-à-vis that application will never exceed that of a novice. This pattern shows how you can create different usage views of a complex class. So, for a complex application, you could have one usage view for novices and another for experts.

Flyweight: This pattern is useful when, from all the objects that may be needed by your clients, you can tease out a small number of core forms and consider the rest to be embellishments thereof. If that can be done, you can use this pattern to significantly reduce the total number of classes you would need to define in order to span all of the embellishments expected by the clients. The pattern gives you a representational structure that is efficient with regard to the production of the instances and with regard to any future changes to the software.

Proxy: Proxies are everywhere these days. It is rather common for businesses to use what are known as *proxy servers* to channel all outgoing and incoming traffic. As you would expect, a proxy object is a stand-in for the real thing. As stand-ins for real things, proxy objects are also commonly used in remote method invocation protocols. Let's say you want to invoke a method on an object that actually resides on a server at some distant location. How can you do that? This is done by maintaining local proxies for the distant objects.

8

BRIDGE

8.1 CONCEPTS AND THEIR IMPLEMENTATION

It would seem that coming up with a new concept and then implementing it are two sides of the same coin. Thinking of the two as being inseparable applies to much of what we accomplish in our everyday lives. We think of something, in response to a need or otherwise, and then we proceed to act on it. In such situations, we ourselves are the concept creators and the implementers.

However, there are other examples, just as numerous, when those who dream up new concepts and those who implement them are not the same. For example, there are different entities involved in the conceptualization of a house (initially through a set of concept diagrams and then through architectural layouts) and its eventual construction.

What is interesting is that when the conceptualization and the implementation are carried out by two different entities, the entities cannot operate completely independently of each other. Those who create new concepts must possess a good sense of the abilities of the implementers. After all, what's the point of coming up with a plan that is so far out that it cannot be implemented by anyone? This suggests a need for a direct link between those who are involved in creating new concepts and those in charge of implementing them. The link would allow concept creators to convey their ideas to those engaged in the implementation of those ideas and, subsequently, to check that the implementations are carried out according to the specifications laid out by the creators of the concepts.

That brings us to the main focus of the Bridge pattern. The pattern shows us how it is possible to have two different entities in object-oriented software, one in charge of specifying the concepts and the other charged with the task of implementing those concepts, and how the two entities can be linked together in a structure you might refer to as a "bridge."

Designing with Objects: Object-Oriented Design Patterns Explained with Stories from Harry Potter, First Edition. Avinash C. Kak.
© 2015 John Wiley & Sons, Inc. Published 2015 by John Wiley & Sons, Inc.

8.2   INTENT AND APPLICABILITY

If we think of a class along with its attributes as defining a data abstraction, the intent of the Bridge pattern is to decouple an abstraction from the implementation of the behaviors we want to associate with the abstraction.

You should consider using this pattern when

- the entity charged with specifying the abstractions is independent of the entity whose responsibility is to provide the implementation code for the behaviors associated with the abstractions;
- there is a need to allow for independent extensions of the abstractions and their implementations;
- there is a need to "hide" from the clients the details of how the abstractions used in the client code are actually implemented.

8.3   INTRODUCTION TO THE BRIDGE PATTERN

This pattern draws attention to one of the major shortcomings of traditional inheritance-based class hierarchies: They suffer from the fact that the implementation code in the hierarchy is permanently bound to the concept abstraction hierarchy. As the reader knows, in a traditional hierarchy of classes, you have the most general classes at the top and the more specialized classes further down the hierarchy. Usually, all of the code needed to create an instance from a class is a combination of the code inherited by that class from its parents and ancestors and the code defined specifically for that class.

This permanent binding between the implementation code and the concept abstractions makes it more difficult to modify and/or optimize the implementation after you have written the code for a hierarchy of classes. Such permanent bindings may also make it more difficult to extend the concept abstraction hierarchy in some cases.

The Bridge pattern teaches us how it is possible to keep separate a hierarchy of concept abstractions from a hierarchy of implementation classes for the concepts involved. This allows the implementation code for the concept abstractions to be maintained separately from the concept abstractions themselves. This also allows for the possibility of there being two separate organizations, one that is in charge of publishing the concept abstractions at a high level of description, and the other that is in charge of providing the implementation code for the abstractions.

Before explaining how the Bridge pattern allows for the implementation code to be separated from a class hierarchy, let's briefly revisit a conventionally programmed class hierarchy as shown in Figure 8.1. When you create such a hierarchy with the traditional methods, you will place in the root class A the most general of the attributes and the behaviors to be inherited by all other classes in the hierarchy. Subsequently, when you write code for, say, the class B, you'll take advantage of the attributes and the behaviors that this class inherits from its parent class and write any additional code needed to particularize those attributes and behaviors to B; and so on. This creates a permanent binding between the concept abstractions and the code that implements the functionality associated with the abstractions. Ordinarily, this is not a problem, since the software vendor supplying the concept abstractions is likely to be the same as the

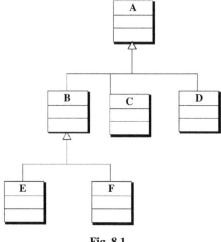

Fig. 8.1

one in charge of providing the implementation code. And, if needed, a client using this software library can always customize the library to his/her particular needs by subclassing from it with additional concept abstractions and the associated implementation code.

However, situations do arise in which you would be better off creating an implementation hierarchy that is independent of the concept hierarchy, yet connected with it. That is, in some situations, we want to just *declare* the functionality we need in one class hierarchy and then place in a different class hierarchy the code for implementing that functionality, with the two hierarchies being independent of each other. To explain what the word *independent* means here, let's consider for a moment the case of there being just one concept class. Let's see with the help of the following example how we may separate the declaration of the class from its implementation.

The class Hello shown below wants to provide to its clients a functionality under the name sayHello(). However, the actual implementation for that functionality is provided by another class named Hello_impl, also shown below. All that the class Hello does is to ask an instance of Hello_impl to do the needful with regard to the behavior associated with sayHello().

```
######################### class Hello #########################
class Hello {
    private Hello_Impl imp = new Hello_Impl();
    public Hello( Hello_Impl impl ) {
        this.imp = imp;
    }
    public void sayHello() {
        imp.sayHello();
    }
}
```

```
##################### class Hello_Impl #####################
class Hello_Impl {
    public void sayHello() {
        System.out.println( "Here is a hello from class Hello " +
                           " -- it was supplied by class Hello_Impl" );
    }
}


##################### class Client #####################
class Client {
    public static void main(String[] args) {
        Hello h = new Hello( new Hello_Impl() );
        h.sayHello();
    }
}
```

Figure 8.2 is a class diagram for the code shown above. If we extend this separation between
a concept (expressed as a class, obviously) and its implementation to the hierarchy of
Figure 8.1, the overall implementation of that hierarchy would look like what is shown
in Figure 8.3, where the names of the implementation classes carry the suffix $\_Impl$. We
would place in the root implementation class A_Impl, which would possibly be abstract,
the declarations of the functionality expected to be provided by all other classes in the
implementation hierarchy. As a trivial example of this, let's say that each concept class
has an instance variable called name and we expect every class to provide a "get" method
that returns the value of name in the instance constructed from that class. With software
design based on the Bridge pattern, it is the implementation hierarchy that must provide
this functionality. So the abstract implementation class at the root, A_Impl in our example
in Figure 8.3, must declare a method with a name like getName().

Of course, there is also the issue of how to link the concept hierarchy with the implementation hierarchy. As the reader will see in this chapter, in the Bridge pattern this link is
established by a direct associational connection between the root of the concept hierarchy
and the root of the implementation hierarchy. Figure 8.3 illustrates this link between the
two root classes. As the reader will see later, a call to the constructor of a concept class,
let's say it is class B, supplies implicitly to the constructor of the concept root an instance
of the corresponding implementation class, B_Impl. The reference to this implementation
object is held by an instance variable that is defined at the root of the concept hierarchy,
the instance variable being of the type that is the root of the implementation hierarchy.
Through polymorphism, any methods invoked on the implementation object thus created
would correspond to the functionality needed in the concept class B. This important detail

Fig. 8.2

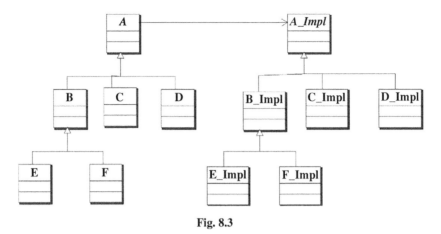

Fig. 8.3

concerning the operation of the Bridge pattern should become clear as we take the reader through the demonstration in this chapter.

8.4   THE BRIDGE PATTERN IN REAL-WORLD APPLICATIONS

To appreciate how this pattern is used in actual applications, it's good to first become familiar with the notion of an E-API, which stands for *Extension API*.[1] The more familiar API is an example of a *Service API* and is denoted S-API when there is a need to distinguish it from E-APIs. An S-API typically consists of a listing of the methods, in the form of method signatures, that are provided by a software module. Those wishing to utilize the functionality offered by a module can call these methods in accordance with the declarations made in the S-API.

An E-API of a module, on the other hand, is a declaration of the methods that the module *expects* will be implemented by other software artifacts that are frequently referred to as *plugins*. The purpose of a plugin is to extend the functionality of a module with additional capabilities. Those who create implementation code for the plugins for a given software module only need to look at the E-APIs of the module. In other words, if you are a plugin developer, you may have no need to look at the source code for the module as long as you have access to its E-APIs.

Obviously, if, as a plugin developer, the E-API that you are interested in involves a hierarchy of classes whose constructors call methods from a parallel hierarchy of implementation classes to be provided by a plugin, the code that you create will have to provide this implementation hierarchy.

Such plugin-based design is now widely used in software engineering. Perhaps the most popular examples of such design are the Eclipse IDE for software development, the EJB container framework for the Java platform, and so on.

It follows from the discussion in Section 8.3 that a plugin along with the concept hierarchy exposed through an E-API constitute an implementation of the Bridge pattern.

---

[1] As previously mentioned in this book, the acronym 'API' stands for "Application Programming Interface." An API is a list of method declarations for utilizing the functionality offered by a software package.

8.5   HARRY POTTER STORY USED TO ILLUSTRATE THE BRIDGE PATTERN

For our demonstration of the Bridge pattern, we will consider a concept hierarchy that involves some of the magical creatures, in particular the humanoids, in Harry Potter. The demonstration will be based on: Dementors, Goblins, and House Elves. We show this hierarchy in Figure 8.4.

The Bridge pattern tells us that there are several advantages to implementing the class hierarchy of Figure 8.4 in the manner shown in Figure 8.5. In the latter diagram, we keep the implementation code in a separate hierarchy by creating for each class in the original hierarchy a corresponding implementation class.

When the implementation code is organized in the manner shown in Figure 8.5, it can become easier to extend a concept hierarchy, *especially when it is possible for a new concept to use an existing implementation*. To explain this point, say that after we have programmed up the implementation of the `Humanoid` hierarchy as shown in Figure 8.5, we want to create a `Human` hierarchy as a subcategory of the `Humanoid` hierarchy. (A human is a humanoid but not vice versa.) Let's also say that the vendor of the concept hierarchy wishes to create sub-categories of this new `Human` category that would correspond to the `Dementor`, `Goblin`, and `HouseElf` subcategories of the humanoids.[2] With the new uncoupled implementation shown in Figure 8.5, the vendor may now proceed as shown in Figure 8.6. Since it is likely that a `Human_Dementor` will share many characteristics with the humanoid `Dementor`, much of the code in `Dementor_Impl` written originally will now be directly usable in the definition of the class `Human_Dementor_Impl`. The same would go for the classes `Human_Goblin_Impl` and `Human_Elf_Impl`. It may even be possible that when we construct an instance of `Human_Dementor`, we are able to use the implementation class `Dementor_Impl` directly for that purpose. That is, we may not even have

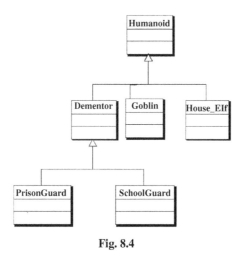

Fig. 8.4

---

[2] Assume that the human version of dementors is less scary and therefore less likely to require that you eat a ton of chocolate should you accidentally encounter one.

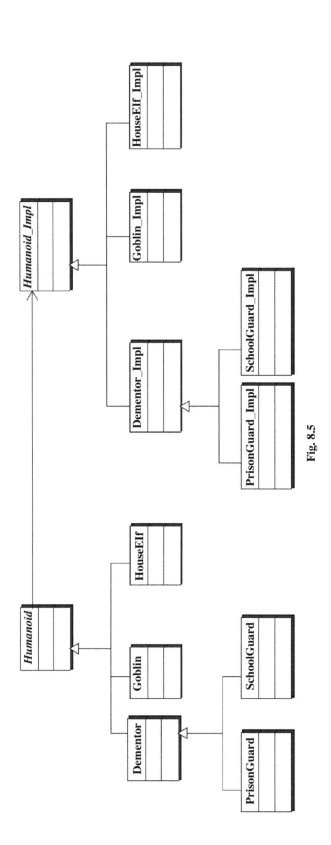

Fig. 8.5

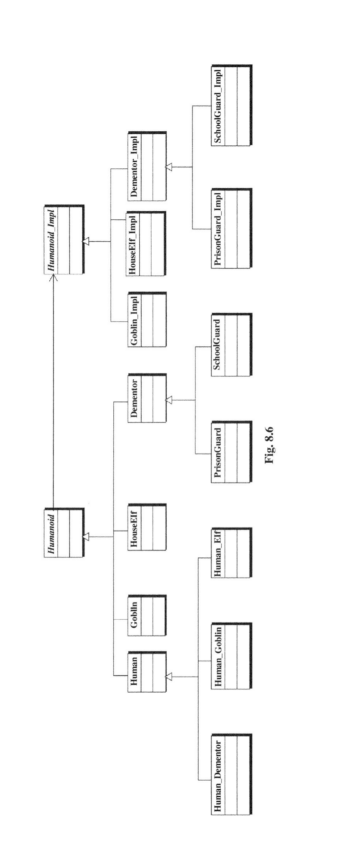

Fig. 8.6

to create a separate implementation class called Human_Dementor_Impl. The same might work for the newly created Human_Goblin and Human_Elf classes. It is to emphasize this point that the class diagram in Figure 8.6 does not show separate implementation classes for Human_Dementor, Human_Goblin, and Human_Elf.

For the client class, our demonstration will use the Ministry of Magic, since it is the job of this ministry to keep track of the humanoids in the world of wizardry. This class will be named MinstryOfMagic and it will create different instances of the Dementors, Goblins, and the House Elves.

8.6   A TOP LEVEL VIEW OF THE PATTERN DEMONSTRATION

Figure 8.7 presents a top-level view of our demonstration of the Bridge pattern. As shown in the figure, in keeping with our earlier discussion, on the one hand, we have the Humanoid hierarchy that consists of the root abstract class of the same name and its subclasses Dementor, HouseElf, and Dementor. And, on the other, we have the implementation hierarchy, consisting of the abstract root class Humanoid_Impl and its concrete subclasses HouseElf_Impl, Goblin_Impl, and Dementor_Impl. The goal of the client class MinistryOfMagic is to construct instances of the magical creatures HouseElf, Goblin, and Dementor *without being aware of how exactly the instances are created.*

This last point is particularly important to the Bridge pattern: a client of the pattern should *not* have to know that the functionality provided by the software is encoded in a separate implementation class hierarchy that is independent of the hierarchy in which the classes are declared. In other words, whether the Humanoid is programmed as a traditional purely inheritance-based class hierarchy or whether it is programmed in the form of a Bridge pattern should be of no consequence to the client.

8.7   THE Humanoid CLASS

This section presents the abstract root of the concept hierarchy — the Humanoid class. We declare this class to be abstract simply because, in general, you would not want to construct instances directly from this class. As a concept, Humanoid is abstract in the same sense that a class like Bird is abstract. With a bird hierarchy of classes, you would want to construct instances of the more concrete subclasses of Bird, such as BlueJay, Finch, etc. The purpose of the abstract root class Bird would be merely to capture the general properties of all birds. The same thing goes here for the abstract root class Humanoid.

Probably the most noteworthy thing about the class definition shown below is that it has an instance variable called imp of type Humanoid_Impl. This is the only direct link between the concept hierarchy rooted at Humanoid and the implementation hierarchy rooted at Humanoid_Impl.

```
import java.util.*;

public abstract class Humanoid {

    private Humanoid_Impl impl;
```

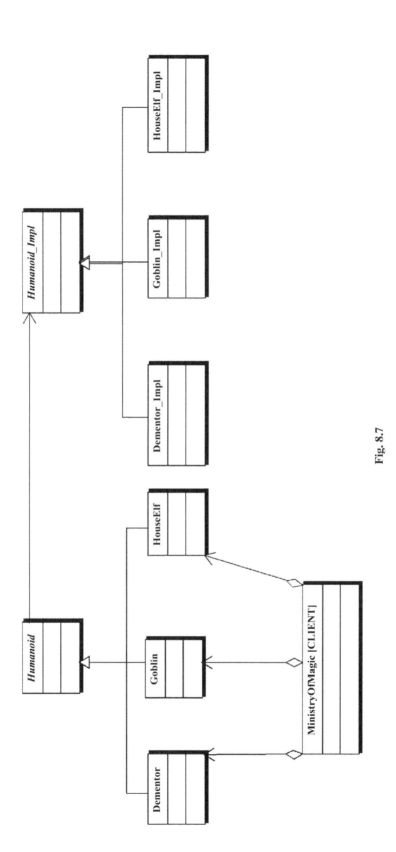

Fig. 8.7

```
    protected Humanoid( Humanoid_Impl impl ) {
        this.impl = impl;
    }
    protected void registerWithMinistryOfMagic( String category ) {
        impl.registerWithMinistryOfMagic( category );
    }
    protected void unRegisterWithMinistryOfMagic( String category ) {
        impl.unRegisterWithMinistryOfMagic( category );
    }
    protected int howManyRegistered() {
      return impl.howManyRegistered();
    }
    protected String getName(){
        return impl.getName();
    }
    protected String getServingAs(){
        return impl.getServingAs();
    }
    public List<String>  getAppearance( String category ) {
        return impl.getAppearance(category);
    }
    public List<String>  getBehavior( String category ) {
        return impl.getBehavior(category);
    }
}
```

8.8   THE Dementor, Goblin, AND HouseElf CLASSES

Since the three concrete classes in the Humanoid hierarchy have very similar definitions, we will present them together in this section.

With regard to the definition of the Dementor class shown below, note how the constructor sends an instance of the implementation class Dementor_Impl to the root class constructor. This is the mechanism used for giving the correct value to the instance variable imp in the root class Humanoid shown in the previous section.

With regard to the method definitions, although most of these methods have the same names as in the parent class Humanoid, they really are not the same methods. (That is, we are *not* providing override definitions for the parent methods here.) When the method names here are the same as in the parent class, the parent methods require a class type argument, but the corresponding methods here are no-arg methods. (In other words, even when the method names are the same between the parent class and the class defined here, their signatures are different.)

```
import java.util.List;

public class Dementor extends Humanoid {

    public Dementor(  String occupation ) {
```

```
            super( new Dementor_Impl( occupation ) );
        }
        public void registerWithMinistryOfMagic() {
            registerWithMinistryOfMagic( "Dementor" );
        }
        public void unRegisterWithMinistryOfMagic() {
            unRegisterWithMinistryOfMagic( "Dementor" );
        }
        public void printName(){
            String name = getName();
            System.out.println( "The name of the dementor is: " + name );
        }
        public void printServingAs(){
            String name = getServingAs();
            System.out.println( "The dementor is serving as: " + name );
        }
        public String  getAppearance() {
            List<String> list = getAppearance( "Dementor" );
            return  list.toString();
        }
        public String  getBehavior() {
            List<String> list = getBehavior( "Dementor" );
            return  list.toString();
        }
    }
```

We next present the Goblin class in our Humanoid concept hierarchy. As with the Dementor class, note how the Goblin constructor sends an instance of the implementation class Goblin_Impl to the root class constructor for Humanoid. This mechanism gives the correct value to the instance variable imp in the root class Humanoid. The comment made earlier regarding the method definitions of the Dementor class apply here also. In particular, we are referring to the fact that although several of the Goblin methods have the same names as in the parent class Humanoid, they really are not the same methods since their signatures are different. So the methods of the same name in the Goblin class are *not* meant to override the corresponding methods in the Humanoid class.

```
import java.util.List;

public class Goblin extends Humanoid {

    public Goblin(  String name, int age ) {
        super( new Goblin_Impl( name, age ) );
    }
    public void registerWithMinistryOfMagic() {
        registerWithMinistryOfMagic( "Goblin" );
    }
    public void unRegisterWithMinistryOfMagic() {
        unRegisterWithMinistryOfMagic( "Goblin" );
    }
```

```java
    public void printName(){
        String name = getName();
        System.out.println( "The name of the Goblin is: " + name );
    }
    public String  getAppearance() {
        List<String> list = getAppearance( "Goblin" );
        return  list.toString();
    }
    public String  getBehavior() {
        List<String> list = getBehavior( "Goblin" );
        return  list.toString();
    }
}
```

Finally, we present the HouseElf class. Except for the name of the class and the changes that result from the different class name, the code shown below is exactly the same as presented for the Dementor and the Goblin classes.

```java
import java.util.*;

public class HouseElf extends Humanoid {

    public HouseElf(  String name, int age ) {
        super( new HouseElf_Impl( name, age ) );
    }
    public void registerWithMinistryOfMagic() {
        registerWithMinistryOfMagic( "House Elf" );
    }
    public void unRegisterWithMinistryOfMagic() {
        unRegisterWithMinistryOfMagic( "House Elf" );
    }
    public void printName(){
        String name = getName();
        System.out.println( "The name of the House Elf is: " + name );
    }
    public String  getAppearance() {
        List<String> list = getAppearance( "House Elf" );
        return  list.toString();
    }
    public String  getBehavior() {
        List<String> list = getBehavior( "House Elf" );
        return  list.toString();
    }
}
```

8.9   THE Humanoid_Imp CLASS

This is the root class of the implementation hierarchy. First of all, note that this class is abstract, in the same manner as the root class of the concept hierarchy, Humanoid, was

abstract. We do not expect to create instances directly from this class. This class defines, from an implementation perspective, what it means for an entity to be a Humanoid in as general a manner as possible. Therefore, there is no Dementor-specific, Goblin-specific, etc., information in the implementation code in this root class.

Note the static variables of this class, these being registeredHumanoids, behavior, and appearance. These variables are used for storing general category-wide information. That is, things that are generally known about all of the concrete concepts in the concepts hierarchy will be stored in these variables. As you will see, two of these static variables, behavior and appearance, will be initialized separately in the individual implementation classes HouseElf_Impl, Goblin_Impl, and Dementor_Impl. Since these static variables store hash tables, the information is stored in the form of <key,value> pairs, where the key is the name of the species and the value a list of attributes for that species.

Also note that this class comes with two different constructors, one that takes two arguments, name and age, and the other that takes only one argument, servingAs. The reason for this is that some types of humanoids in Harry Potter do not have individual names; they are referred to primarily through what it is they do at the moment. This is particularly true of dementors. They are used mostly as guards (in the Azkaban prison, for example), for carrying out search operations, and so on. The one-arg constructor allows us to instantiate a Humanoid_Impl on the basis of just the occupation.

After the two constructors, we have three "get" methods. These are called in the Humanoid hierarchy to retrieve information related to Humanoid instances. These are followed by the two methods named register() and unRegister() for registering and unregistering a humanoid with the Ministry of Magic. Even though both are instance methods, they manipulate the static database bound to the variable registeredHumanoids. Both of these methods take the humanoid category as their sole argument.[3]

Next we have the *abstract* method howManyRegistered() in the class definition. This method is abstract because its definition depends on specific humanoid species on which it is invoked. By placing just the header of the method in the root class defined below, we can invoke it on instances of type Humanoid_Impl. Obviously, the actual implementation code that will be executed will correspond to the definition of the method in the individual implementation classes.

```
import java.util.*;

public abstract class Humanoid_Impl {

    private String name;
    private int age;
    private String servingAs;

    // In the <key,value> pairs shown below,  the key is the name of
    // the humanoid and the value the name of the species.  Of the
    // three static variables defined below, behavior and appearance
    // are initialized in the child classes of the
    // Humanoid_Impl class.
```

---

[3]Note that the species-specific classes like Dementor also define the register() and unRegister() methods that take no arguments. The bodies of those methods call the one-argument register() and unRegister() methods that are defined for the root class Humanoid_Impl shown here.

```java
    protected static Map<String, String> registeredHumanoids
                                = new HashMap<String,String>();
    protected static Map< String, List<String>> behavior
                            = new HashMap<String,List<String>>();
    protected static Map< String, List<String>> appearance
                                = new HashMap<String,List<String>>();

    public Humanoid_Impl( String name, int age ) {
        this.name = name;
        this.age = age;
    }
    public Humanoid_Impl( String occupation ) {
        this.servingAs = occupation;
    }

    public String getName() { return name; }
    public int getAge() { return age; }
    public String getServingAs() { return servingAs; }

    public void registerWithMinistryOfMagic( String category ) {
        registeredHumanoids.put( name,  category  );
    }
    public void unRegisterWithMinistryOfMagic( String category ) {
        if ( registeredHumanoids.containsKey( name ) ) {
            if (registeredHumanoids.get( name ).equals(category)) {
                registeredHumanoids.remove( name );
            }
        }
    }
    public abstract int howManyRegistered();

    // The set methods shown below are used in the individual Impl
    // subclasses for the initialization of the static variables
    // defined earlier in this class definition:
    public static void setAppearance(String category, List<String> list){
        appearance.put( category, list );
    }
    public static void setBehavior(String category, List<String> list) {
        behavior.put( category, list );
    }

    // The get methods defined below are called in the root class
    // Humanoid to retrieve information in the databases stored in
    // the static variables defined earlier for this class:
    public  List<String> getAppearance( String category ) {
        return appearance.get( category );
    }
    public  List<String> getBehavior( String category ) {
        return behavior.get( category );
    }
}
```

8.10   IMPLEMENTATION CLASSES FOR THE Dementor, Goblin, AND HouseElf CLASSES

Shown below is the implementation class `Dementor_Impl`. The constructor for this concrete class calls the one-arg constructor of the parent class `Humanoid_Impl`. Also note the initialization of the static variables `behaviors` and `appearance` in the two-statement segment of the class definition that is within curly brackets.

Since we are defining a concrete class that is subclassed from the abstract class `Humanoid_Impl`, it is incumbent upon us to provide an implementation for the abstract method `howManyRegistered()` declared in the root class `Humanoid_Impl`. The implementation shown here is specific to the `Dementor_Impl` class.

```java
import java.util.*;

public class Dementor_Impl extends Humanoid_Impl {

    public Dementor_Impl( String occupation ) {
        super( occupation );
    }
    {
        setBehavior( "Dementor", new ArrayList<String>(
                                    Arrays.asList( "soulless",
                                                   "prison guard duty",
                                                   "immortal"
                                                 ) ) );
        setAppearance( "Dementor", new ArrayList<String>(
                                    Arrays.asList( "10 feet tall",
                                                   "no eyes",
                                                   "hole for mouth"
                                                 ) ) );
    }

    public int howManyRegistered() {
        int n = 0;
        for (Map.Entry<String, String>
                    entry: registeredHumanoids.entrySet()) {
            if ( "Dementor".equals( entry.getValue() ) ) n++;
        }
        return n;
    }
}
```

We next present the implementation class `Goblin_Impl`. Whereas the constructor for `Dementor_Impl` called its parent class's one-arg constructor for the initialization of the parent-class slice of the subclass instance, the `Goblin_Impl` constructor calls the two-arg constructor of the parent class for doing the same. The reason for this difference is that, as mentioned earlier, whereas the dementors are mostly known through one attribute — their occupation (such as serving as prison guards) — the goblins are more likely to be known through their personal attributes such as name and age.

With regard to the initialization of the static variables behaviors and appearance, the code here is the same as in the Dementor_Impl class, as shown by the two-statement segment of the class definition that is within curly brackets. The implementation of the howManyRegistered() abstract method inherited from the parent class follows the same logic as in the Dementor_Impl class, although its precise details are specific to the Goblin_Impl class.

```java
import java.util.*;

public class Goblin_Impl extends Humanoid_Impl {

    public Goblin_Impl( String name, int age ) {
        super( name, age );
    }
    {
        setBehavior( "Goblin", new ArrayList<String>(
                            Arrays.asList( "no wands",
                                           "goblin magic only",
                                           "banking"
                                         ) ) );
        setAppearance( "Goblin", new ArrayList<String>(
                            Arrays.asList( "long thin fingers",
                                           "large domed heads",
                                           "large black eyes"
                                         ) ) );
    }
    public int howManyRegistered() {
        int n = 0;
        for (Map.Entry<String, String>  entry:
                            registeredHumanoids.entrySet()) {
            if ( "Goblin".equals( entry.getValue() ) ) n++;
        }
        return n;
    }
}
```

Finally, we present the implementation class HouseElf_Impl. Since its definition closely parallels that of the previous class Goblin_Impl, the code shown needs no further explanation.

```java
import java.util.*;

public class HouseElf_Impl extends Humanoid_Impl {

    public HouseElf_Impl( String name, int age) {
        super( name, age);
    }
```

```
    {
        setBehavior( "House Elf", new ArrayList<String>(
                                    Arrays.asList( "obedient",
                                                   "pliant",
                                                   "loyal"
                                                 ) ) );
        setAppearance( "House Elf", new ArrayList<String>(
                                    Arrays.asList( "small",
                                                   "spindly arms",
                                                   "large head"
                                                 ) ) );
    }
    public int howManyRegistered() {
        int n = 0;
        for (Map.Entry<String, String>  entry:
                            registeredHumanoids.entrySet()) {
            if ( "House Elf".equals( entry.getValue() ) ) n++;
        }
        return n;
    }
}
```

8.11   THE CLIENT CLASS MinistryOfMagic

This is the executable class for our demonstration of the Bridge pattern. In the main() of this class, we construct instances of HouseElf, Goblin, and Dementor and we register them with the MinistryOfMagic. We also print out the various characteristics of the different types of humanoids.

What is interesting is that the output produced in the main() of the class shown below is obtained by invoking methods directly on the constructed instances of the different types of Humanoids. However, as the reader should know by now, these calls are in reality processed by the code in the implementation hierarchy headed by the Humanoid_Impl abstract class. For example, when we register a HouseElf, the actual code for that is in the Humanoid_Impl class. Similarly, when we print out the name of a HouseElf, the actual code for that is again in the HouseElf_Impl class.

The fact that all of the calls on the Humanoid instances are translated into invocation of the code in the Humanoid_Impl hierarchy becomes all the more remarkable when you realize that the only direct connection between the abstraction hierarchy under Humanoid and the implementation hierarchy under Humanoid_Impl is the instance variable imp in the abstract Humanoid class.

```
public class MinistryOfMagic {
    public static void main( String[] args ) {

        // House Elves:
        HouseElf elf1 = new HouseElf( "Dobby",  15 );
        elf1.registerWithMinistryOfMagic();
```

```
elf1.printName();
HouseElf elf2 = new HouseElf( "Hokey",  15 );
elf2.registerWithMinistryOfMagic();
elf2.printName();
int n = elf2.howManyRegistered();
System.out.println( "Number of elves registered: " + n );
HouseElf elf3 = new HouseElf( "Kreacher",  8 );
elf3.registerWithMinistryOfMagic();
elf3.printName();
n = elf2.howManyRegistered();
System.out.println( "Number of elves registered: " + n );
elf2.unRegisterWithMinistryOfMagic();
n = elf2.howManyRegistered();
System.out.println( "Number of elves registered: " + n );
System.out.println( "Appearance of a house elf: "
                              + elf2.getAppearance() );
System.out.println( "Behavior of a house elf: "
                              + elf2.getBehavior() );

//Goblins:
Goblin gob1 = new Goblin( "Griphook", 23 );
gob1.registerWithMinistryOfMagic();
gob1.printName();
System.out.println( "Number of goblins registered: "
                          + gob1.howManyRegistered() );

//Dementors:
Dementor dem1 = new Dementor( "Azkaban Guard" );
dem1.registerWithMinistryOfMagic();
dem1.printServingAs();
System.out.println( "Number of dementors registered: "
                          + dem1.howManyRegistered() );
    }
}
```

8.12   PLAYING WITH THE CODE

Download the class files for this pattern from the book website into a separate directory.
Compile the code with the command

```
javac *.java
```

and execute the MinistryOfMagic class by

```
java MinistryOfMagic
```

Given the code in the main() of MinistryOfMagic, executing this class will produce the
following output:

```
The name of the House Elf is: Dobby
The name of the House Elf is: Hokey
Number of elves registered: 2
The name of the House Elf is: Kreacher
Number of elves registered: 3
Number of elves registered: 2
Appearance of a house elf: [small, spindly arms, large head]
Behavior of a house elf: [obedient, pliant, loyal]
The name of the Goblin is: Griphook
Number of goblins registered: 1
The dementor is serving as: Azkaban Guard
Number of dementors registered: 1
```

In order to gain additional insights into the Bridge pattern, you may wish to extend the code for this pattern on your own along the following lines:

- Earlier it was mentioned that the Bridge pattern can make it easier to extend a concept hierarchy. Figure 8.6 shows that one could conceive of a Human subcategory of the Humanoid class and then further extend the Human class to Human_Dementor, Human_Goblin, and Human_Elf classes, these being more human equivalents of the true humanoids Dementor, Goblin, and HouseElf. Modify the code for the demonstration presented in this chapter along these lines and see as to what extent you can re-use the code already presented in the implementation classes Dementor_Impl, Goblin_Impl, and HouseElf_Impl.
- In the client class MinistryOfMagic, the references to all of the Humanoid instances we created were held by variables specific to those instance types. This would ordinarily be considered to be a poor programming practice.[4] For example, here are the statements related to the creation of the first humanoid, a HouseElf, in the main() of MinistryOfMagic:

```
HouseElf elf1 = new HouseElf( "Dobby",  15 );
elf1.registerWithMinistryOfMagic();
elf1.printName();
```

Since a HouseElf is a Humanoid, could we have declared the variable elf1 to be of type Humanoid? If you do not know the answer, see what happens if you change the type of elf1 from HouseElf to Humanoid. Give reasons for what you see.

---

[4]When using the Java Collections Framework, let's say you are using an ArrayList to hold your objects. The recommended programming practice is that a reference to an instance of the ArrayList container be held by a variable of the more general type; that is, a variable of type List in this case. The advantage of this recommendation is that if, at a later time, you want to change your actual container to a LinkedList because of its faster performance for random insert and delete operations, all you'd need to do in your code would be to make a one-line change to switch over to the new container.

9

COMPOSITE

9.1 RELATIONSHIPS THAT LOOP BACK

The relationships between different types of objects that are easiest to grasp are usually strictly hierarchical. Such relationships are also easy to visualize since they can be displayed in the form of trees. Consider the taxonomies that have been created for biological organisms and plants.[1] In such taxonomies, the membership in a category is based on shared evolutionary history and the primary relationship between the categories is one of shared descent from the nearest common ancestor. Such taxonomies are strictly hierarchical and can therefore be displayed as trees.

Let's now talk about relationships between different types of man-made physical objects and between different types of abstract notions. Although we are free to use any criteria we wish for membership in the different categories and for what constitutes a relationship between the categories, we would want the criteria to serve some useful purpose. As to what that purpose would be depends on the application domain for which you are trying to model the physical objects (or the abstract notions).

As it turns out, the modeling required for both the man-made objects and the abstract notions — modeling that serves some useful purpose — is also often strictly hierarchical. As anyone who has done even a bit of object-oriented programming knows, a most commonly used relationship between object categories is that of inheritance in which the descendants of a parent category inherit the attributes of the parent. In spirit at least, a purely inheritance-based relationship between the categories for the case of man-made objects (and abstract notions) is similar to the relationships in the taxonomies based on evolutionary history for the case of natural objects.

Although we have many examples of strictly hierarchical models for man-made objects and abstract notions, there also abound examples when such is *not* the case. That is, when we model man-made objects and abstract notions, some of the relationships may require

---

[1] A taxonomy refers to how we categorize the objects in a domain. It must specify the criteria for membership in the different categories and it must also specify what constitutes a relationship between any two categories.

Designing with Objects: Object-Oriented Design Patterns Explained with Stories from Harry Potter,
First Edition. Avinash C. Kak.
© 2015 John Wiley & Sons, Inc. Published 2015 by John Wiley & Sons, Inc.

looping back from a specialized category to a more general category in a modeling diagram. These loop-back links typically involve *containment* of some sort — a relational concept that is also referred to as *aggregation, composition,* and *has-a*.[2]

Consider the following simple example: Let's say we want to model the relationships between seat-like objects — objects that people sit on when they don't want to stand or lie down. We can think of `seat` as a generic abstract object that we endow with the property *"can be used for sitting on."* Through inheritance, that is, through `is-a` relationships, we can now specify more concrete object categories such as `chair`, `stool`, `sofa`, and so on, as subcategories of the root category `seat`. So far our inter-category relationships are purely hierarchical and can be displayed as a tree, with `seat` at the root and with the concrete categories as the children of the root.

However, given the fact that modular furniture is not that uncommon anymore and that extended sitting areas can be devised by joining together seats in different configurations, we can conceive of another object category that we may refer to as a `combo_seat`.[3] Since a `combo_seat` is, after all, a seat, it is also a subcategory of `seat`. At the same time, though, a `combo_seat` is an aggregation of other `seat` objects. Therefore, in a depiction of the relationships in a domain where `combo_seat` objects are used, we must show a link from the `combo_seat` back to the generic class `seat`. This link would obviously be a containment link — an *associational* link in the jargon of class diagrams. So our overall depiction of the categories would show inheritance links from `seat` to each of `chair`, `stool`, `sofa`, `combo_seat`, and so on, and then a loop-back from `combo_seat` to the generic class `seat`.

As you will see in this chapter, the Composite pattern takes advantage of these loop-backs in a class diagram for a more efficient organization of the instance generation code for the classes.

9.2   INTENT AND APPLICABILITY

The intent of the Composite pattern is to manipulate all objects, even those that are compositions over other smaller objects, in a uniform manner through the code placed in the same interface.

You should use this pattern when

- all classes — even those that involve compositions over other classes — are of the same fundamental type;
- the clients of a class hierarchy want to use the same root interface for manipulating all objects, including the objects that involve compositions over other smaller objects;
- you can place in the root interface the protection needed to deal with situations when the behaviors that are intended specifically for complex classes are invoked on objects constructed from other classes.

---

[2]As mentioned in Chapter 1, the relationships of *composition* and *aggregation* are not synonymous in object-oriented modeling. See Chapter 1 for the difference between the two.

[3]If you have seen a modular unit in a furniture catalog or in someone's living room, its being composed of two or more pieces is not always easy to discern — at least not with the naked eye. If you search Google Images with a string like "modular seat," you'll see several examples of furniture that look like integral pieces but are really composed of smaller units.

9.3 INTRODUCTION TO THE COMPOSITE PATTERN

As you know from Chapter 1 and as also mentioned in Section 9.1, when we think of a large entity as being made up of smaller entities, we may refer to the former as a composition — or, as a composite — of the latter. In general, a composite may involve disparate elements. And, in general again, the large entity itself is likely to be very different from the smaller elements that constitute it. Such a composition is shown in Figure 9.1. This class diagram tells us that we may think of a car as being a composite of four wheels, an engine, a transmission, and a body.

The Composite pattern is *not* meant for what is exemplified by Figure 9.1. To see the sort of a composite that this pattern is meant for, let's consider creating a class diagram for the folks who work in a factory. Some of these employees will be ordinary workers, some shop foremen, some computer operators, some secretaries, and some managers. A manager would be someone who supervises a bunch of workers, foremen, computer operators, a secretary, and so on. So when we define the `Manager` class — we are thinking of the class definitions as standing for the roles played by the individuals, as opposed to just the individuals — it must include references to the individuals supervised by a manager. To construct a class diagram for this case, we first note that all individuals who work in a factory, including the managers, are employees of the organization that owns the factory. Even though a `Manager` is basically an `Employee`, we must nevertheless endow the `Manager` class with instance variables for the other employees who are under the supervision of a manager. Although we would depict `Manager` as a specialization of `Employee` in a class diagram, we would also want to show that the role of a manager involves a composite over other `Employees`. These facts are captured by the class diagram of Figure 9.2.

In the class diagram in Figure 9.2, the arrowed links express our extending the `Employee` class through inheritance. What these links imply is that a `Worker` is an `Employee`, a `Foreman` is an `Employee`, as is a `Secretary`, and as is a `Computer Operator`. And even more to the point, although a `Manager` is also an `Employee`, its definition involves a composite over an arbitrary number of `Worker`, `Foreman`, `Computer Operator`, and `Secretary` instances. This last fact is expressed by the filled-diamond at the `Manager` end of the link that goes from the `Manager` back to the `Employee`. *It is this sort of a composite that is the focus of the Composite pattern.* The multiplicity notation '1..*' at the `Employee` end of the composition link from `Manager` means that a `Manager`

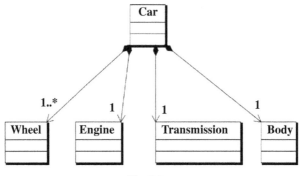

Fig. 9.1

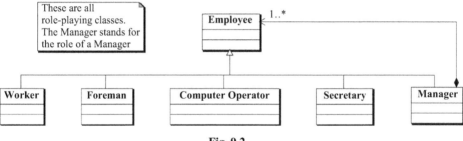

Fig. 9.2

role involves a composite over an arbitrary number of `Employee` roles, as long as the manager is supervising at least one other employee.

Since all classes shown in the modeling diagram of Figure 9.2 are of type `Employee`, we can raise the following question: Is it possible to manipulate all objects that are created from the concrete classes in the class diagram with just the interface defined in the root `Employee` class? *It is this question that is answered by the Composite pattern.*

The Composite pattern tells us that all objects constructed from a class hierarchy of the sort shown in Figure 9.2 can be created, accessed, and manipulated through the interface defined for just the root class `Employee`. What is particularly remarkable here is that that includes the objects constructed from the class `Manager` whose definition incorporates a composite over other `Employee` objects. You might ask that since the `Manager` class can be expected to have many more responsibilities than the non-supervisory `Employees`, how is it possible to manipulate even the `Manager` objects through the `Employee` interface? Therein lies the secret of the Composite pattern.

According to the Composite pattern, you endow the `Employee` class in Figure 9.2 with all of the behaviors that are needed by any of its descendants, including the `Manager` class, but with a default definition that, in general, warns the clients if those behaviors are invoked on objects inappropriately. For illustration, let's say we want to define a method called `hireSecretary()` that enables a `Manager` instance to hire a new secretary. But, since it may make no sense to allow a `Foreman` instance to hire a secretary, we will define this method for the root class `Employee` with a default definition that merely throws an exception and displays a warning message. On the other hand, this method can be overridden in the `Manager` class to present the functionality needed in that class for hiring a secretary.

9.4 THE COMPOSITE PATTERN IN REAL-WORLD APPLICATIONS

This pattern is useful in any application in which you want to treat in a uniform manner the basic classes and any larger classes that involve composites over the basic classes. Most commonly, you would only want to do this with respect to specific computations involving the different classes as explained below.

Let us say you are writing code for a large class C_{large} that, through its instance variables, is associated with a number of more basic classes $C_1, C_2, \cdots$, that were previously defined in a possibly different context. Your application requires for you to traverse all of the objects contained in an instance of C_{large} with respect to some elemental property p_{elem}. But, unfortunately, calculation of this property was not made a part of the implementation of $C_1, C_2, \cdots$ when they were defined. Assuming that the calculation of

p_{elem} requires the same implementation in all of the component classes $C_1, C_2, \cdots$, an easy way to solve this problem (that would entail only minimal changes to the component classes $C_1, C_2, \cdots$) is to first define an abstract root class C_{new_root} with the code that calculates p_{elem} as needed in the component classes incorporated in it.[4] Subsequently, you will make *all* other classes, C_i, $i = 1, 2, \cdots$, and C_{large}, descend from the new root C_{new_root}. In the C_{large} class you are working on, you'd obviously need an override implementation of the root class method that calculates p_{elem} since this method would need to traverse over the component objects. Subsequently, you'll be able to manipulate your C_{large} objects through the interface defined in C_{new_root} and calculate p_{elem} by calling the method you defined in C_{new_root}. This would constitute a Composite-pattern-based solution to the problem.

For a specific example, consider the case of object modeling software used in discrete-parts manufacturing. Let's say you have just created a class for a new shape that is partly an aggregation over simpler shapes represented by more basic classes. Let's further say you would like to measure some property of this new shape — a property whose computation is not currently in the class definitions for the basic shapes. A Composite-pattern-based approach outlined in the previous paragraph is one way to solve this problem.

9.5   HARRY POTTER STORY USED TO ILLUSTRATE THE COMPOSITE PATTERN

The composition that we'll be interested in for our demonstration of the Composite pattern is that of the Ministry of Magic. In particular, we will focus on the role of the Minister for Magic, especially with regard to his or her supervision of the different wizards who work in the Ministry. These include obliviators, aurors, and various department heads. The job of an obliviator is to perform a memory charm on a muggle if he or she has witnessed any magic by a wizard or a witch. The charm makes the muggle forget what he might have seen by way of magic. The job of an auror is to capture Death Eaters, these being wizards who have switched over to the dark side. The Minister also hires and fires the heads of the various departments within the ministry. Some of the more prominent departments in the ministry are the Department of Magical Law Enforcement, the Department of Magical Accidents and Catastrophes, and the Department of Magical Transportation. The departments that are large are further broken down into offices, with each office serving a separate function. For example, the Department of Magical Law Enforcement is composed of the Improper Use of Magic Office, the Auror Office, the Wizengamot (it's more of a high court than an office), and so on.

Figure 9.3 is a straightforward depiction of the fact that the role of the Minister for Magic includes exercising supervisory authority over the other employees of the ministry as mentioned above. This depiction, however, fails to capture the fact that the Minister is himself a wizard and shares many of his traits with all of the other employees in the figure.

Therefore, since all of the entities in the class diagram of Figure 9.3 are merely different types of `Wizard`, a more complete depiction of the relationships in Figure 9.3 is shown in

---

[4]A reader might ask what if the calculation of p_{elem} requires access to the instance variables of the component classes. We assume that the component classes have defined the "`get`" methods for accessing the values of those variables. You could place do-nothing implementations for such methods in the newly created root class and take advantage of method overriding to automatically invoke the correct "`get`" methods on the component classes at runtime.

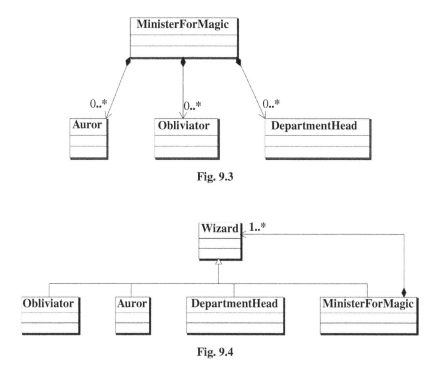

Fig. 9.3

Fig. 9.4

Figure 9.4. Expressing the class relationships as in Figure 9.4 — and especially focusing on the fact that all of the classes in Figure 9.4, even those that are complex, are of the same type as the more elemental class `Wizard` — allows us to benefit from the Composite pattern. With the Composite pattern, our goal would be to define all of the functionality for all of the classes in the hierarchy, including the more complex class `MinisterForMagic`, in the root class `Wizard`. The implementation of the `Wizard` class we show later in this chapter does exactly that.

9.6   A TOP LEVEL VIEW OF THE PATTERN DEMONSTRATION

Figure 9.5 presents a top-level view of our demonstration of the Composite pattern. For the sake of programming convenience, we have defined some key wizard qualifications in the form of enums in a separate interface called `WizardTraits`. We will have more to say about these enums in the next section. Suffice it to say here that these enums give us a vocabulary for the qualifications of the wizards for the different jobs in the Ministry of Magic.

The diagram in Figure 9.5 includes the class `UnauthorizedAccessException` that plays an important role in the working of the Composite pattern. Recall that we wish to place in the root class `Wizard` all of the behaviors that would be needed by any of its descendants, and that includes the rather complex class `MinisterForMagic`. Obviously, several of the behaviors appropriate for the Minister would be inapplicable to the other wizards. To take care of this problem within the framework of the Composite pattern, for the behaviors in the Wizard class that are meant specifically for `MinisterForMagic`, we give them default implementations that merely

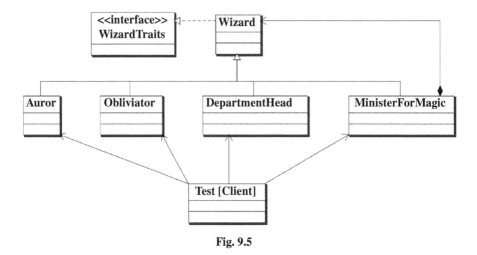

Fig. 9.5

throw the exception `UnauthorizedAccessException`. As you would expect, the `MinisterForMagic` class overrides these default definitions as appropriate. The definition of the `UnauthorizedAccessException` class is straightforward. As shown below, perhaps the only remarkable thing about the exception class is its name. The name would indicate to a client the nature of the violation that caused this exception to be thrown.

```
public class UnauthorizedAccessException extends Exception {
    public UnauthorizedAccessException() { super(); }
    public UnauthorizedAccessException(String arg0) { super(arg0); }
}
```

Finally, note the class `Test` in Figure 9.5. It is in this class that we test the demonstration code for the Composite pattern. You can think of `Test` as the client class for the `Wizard` hierarchy.

9.7   THE WizardTraits INTERFACE

The role of `WizardTraits` is merely to serve as a helper interface for the root class `Wizard` and for some of the other classes in this demonstration. As mentioned earlier, the purpose of this interface is to create a vocabulary for the qualifications of the wizards vis-à-vis the jobs in the Ministry of Magic. We use Java enums to define four different types of wizard qualifications: `WizardryLevel`, `SchoolGraduatedFrom`, `HogwartsHouse`, and `WizardryStrength`. The demonstration assumes that when any of these qualification types is not known for a wizard, it is set to `Unknown`.

```
public interface WizardTraits {
    public static enum WizardryLevel  {
```

```
            Novice, Intermediate, Advanced, Master, Unknown }
    public static enum SchoolGraduatedFrom {
            Hogwarts, Durmstrang, Beauxbatons, HomeSchooled, Unknown }
    public static enum HogwartsHouse {
            Gryffindor, Hufflepuff, Ravenclaw, Slytherin, Unknown }
    public static enum WizardryStrength {
            Transfiguration, DADA, Charms, Spells, Flying, Unknown }
}
```

9.8 THE Wizard CLASS

As should be obvious by now, the Composite pattern can be expected to be useful for efficiently implementing a class hierarchy when, in a whole-parts relationship, the whole as well as the parts are of the same fundamental type. When that condition is met, it is possible to declare all of the functionality — for the parts as well as the whole — in the root class that defines the fundamental type. This functionality can then be selectively overridden in the classes that descend from the fundamental type. The Wizard class serves as the fundamental type in this demonstration.

The Wizard class defined in this section includes all of the functionality needed (at least as far as this demonstration is concerned) for all of the objects that can be constructed from any of its subclasses. But note that the method definitions shown are the default definitions, to be overridden in the subclasses as appropriate. When a method is not overridden in a subclass, its default definition as presented below applies. As the reader can see, the default definitions merely throw an exception, with a message to the effect that the method is being used in a manner for which it was not intended. The exception thrown consists of an instance of the specially defined class UnauthorizedAccessException whose definition was presented in Section 9.6.

As shown below, the definition of the class begins with six instance variables that characterize a Wizard. The first two of these, firstName and lastName, we expect every Wizard instance to possess. These therefore go into the definition of the Wizard constructor that follows the declaration of the six instance variables. The rest of the instance variables — schoolGraduatedFrom, wizardryLevel, strongAt, and houseAssigned — are optional. We initialize them with the default Unknown as shown. What follows the constructor are the "get" and the "set" methods for the four optional instance variables. The rest of the class defines the overall functionality for the class hierarchy.

Since the root classes in typical class hierarchies are abstract (or, for the case of Java, frequently interfaces), an important question that arises is whether we could have made Wizard abstract. The only reason we did not declare Wizard to be abstract is because of the following code fragment that appears in the client class Test that you will see in Section 9.13:

```
    new Wizard( "Peter", "Pettigrew" )
```

In the definition of the class Test where this code fragment appears, we need to supply an Auror with the name of a Death Eater wizard. Since we did not define Death Eater as a separate subclass of Wizard, we had no choice but to use the generic class Wizard for the purpose.

```
import java.util.*;

public class Wizard implements WizardTraits {

    private String firstName;
    private String lastName;
    private SchoolGraduatedFrom schoolGraduatedFrom =
                               SchoolGraduatedFrom.Unknown;
    private WizardryLevel wizardryLevel = WizardryLevel.Unknown;
    private WizardryStrength strongAt = WizardryStrength.Unknown;
    private HogwartsHouse houseAssigned = HogwartsHouse.Unknown;

    public Wizard( String fname, String lname ) {
        firstName = fname; lastName = lname;
    }
    public String toString() { return firstName + " " + lastName; }

    // get and set methods for the optional instance variables:
    public WizardryLevel getWizardryLevel() { return wizardryLevel; }
    public void setWizardryLevel( WizardryLevel wl ) {
        wizardryLevel = wl;
    }
    public SchoolGraduatedFrom getSchoolGraduatedFrom() {
        return schoolGraduatedFrom;
    }
    public void setSchoolGraduatedFrom( SchoolGraduatedFrom sch ) {
        schoolGraduatedFrom = sch;
    }
    public HogwartsHouse getHouseAssigned() { return houseAssigned; }
    public void setHouseAssigned( HogwartsHouse house ) {
        houseAssigned = house;
    }
    public WizardryStrength getWizardryStrength() { return strongAt; }
    public void setWizardryStrength( WizardryStrength strength ) {
        strongAt = strength;
    }


    // Functionality to be overridden in the Obliviator
    public boolean isAllowedToPerformMemoryCharm()
                        throws UnauthorizedAccessException {
        throw new UnauthorizedAccessException(
                "Only obliviators allowed to perform Memory Charm" );
    }
    public void alterMuggleMemory( String muggleName )
                        throws UnauthorizedAccessException {
        throw new UnauthorizedAccessException(
                "Only obliviators allowed to perform Memory Charm" );
    }


    // Functionality to be overriden in the Auror class:
    public boolean isAurorInGoodStanding()
```

```
                       throws UnauthorizedAccessException {
    throw new UnauthorizedAccessException(
                    "This question can only be asked of an auror" );
}
public boolean acceptOrderToCaptureDeathEater( Wizard wiz )
                       throws UnauthorizedAccessException {
    throw new UnauthorizedAccessException(
                       "Only an auror can accept such an order" );
}


// Functionality to be overridden in the DepartmentHead class:
public String getDepartmentInChargeOf()
                       throws UnauthorizedAccessException {
    throw new UnauthorizedAccessException(
                    "Only a dept head can be asked for this info" );
}
public void assignOfficesToDepartmentHead( List<String> offices )
                       throws UnauthorizedAccessException {
    throw new UnauthorizedAccessException(
                       "Only a dept head can be assigned offices" );
}
public void reassignDepartment( String newDept )
                       throws UnauthorizedAccessException {
    throw new UnauthorizedAccessException(
               "Only a dept head can be assigned a new department" );
}
public List<String> listOfficesInChargeOf()
                       throws UnauthorizedAccessException {
    throw new UnauthorizedAccessException(
               "Offices  can only be listed for a department head" );
}


// Functionality to be overridden in the MinisterForMagic class:
public void issueOrderToCaptureDeathEater()
                       throws UnauthorizedAccessException {
    throw new UnauthorizedAccessException(
               "Only the minister for magic can issue such an order" );
}
public void appointWizardAsObliviator(Wizard w)
                       throws UnauthorizedAccessException {
    throw new UnauthorizedAccessException(
          "Only the minister for magic can appoint "
                                     + "a wizard as obliviator" );
}
public void appointWizardAsAuror(Wizard w)
                       throws UnauthorizedAccessException {
    throw new UnauthorizedAccessException(
       "Only the minister for magic can appoint a wizard as auror" );
}
public void appointDepartmentHead(Wizard w)
                       throws UnauthorizedAccessException {
    throw new UnauthorizedAccessException(
```

```
                          "Only the minister for magic can appoint a dept head" );
      }
      public void listEmployeesWorkingAtMinistry()
                            throws UnauthorizedAccessException {
          throw new UnauthorizedAccessException(
             "This method can only be called on a minister for magic" );
      }
  }
```

9.9   THE Auror CLASS

An Auror's job is to apprehend Death Eaters. A Death Eater is a wizard who has switched over to the dark side. Death Eaters fought on behalf of Lord Voldemort during the First and the Second Wizarding Wars. They caused much destruction and killed many innocent wizards, witches, and muggles. For obvious reasons, you have to be an exceptionally capable wizard to become an auror. You must certainly have mastered DADA (Defense Against Dark Arts). After a candidate is accepted for an auror's position, he/she is put through three years of rigorous training in magical combat and forensic investigation.

In the implementation shown below, we state only two requirements for a wizard to qualify as an auror: the wizardry expertise possessed must be at the level of "Master," and DADA must be one of the main strengths of the wizard. The qualifications of a wizard for the Auror's position are checked only the first time he/she is asked to apprehend a Death Eater. The implementation also assumes that an auror is not expected to handle more than five Death Eaters at any one time.

```
import java.util.*;

public class Auror extends Wizard {

    private List<Wizard> deathEatersAssigned = new ArrayList<Wizard>();
    private boolean hasPreviousExperienceInDealingWithDeathEaters
                                                          = false;

    public Auror( String firstname, String lastname ) {
        super( firstname, lastname );
    }

    public boolean isAurorInGoodStanding()
                    throws UnauthorizedAccessException {
        if (!this.getWizardryLevel().equals(
                WizardTraits.WizardryLevel.Master)) {
            System.out.println(
              "This wizard is not qualified to capture a Death Eater");
            return false;
        }
        if (!this.getWizardryStrength().equals(
                WizardTraits.WizardryStrength.DADA ) ) {
            System.out.println(
```

```
                "This wizard is not qualified to capture a Death Eater");
            return false;
        }
        for (SchoolGraduatedFrom school : SchoolGraduatedFrom.values()){
            if ( school.equals( this.getSchoolGraduatedFrom() ) ) {
                return true;
            }
        }
        System.out.println(
                "This wizard is not qualified to capture a Death Eater");
        return false;
    }


    public boolean acceptOrderToCaptureDeathEater(Wizard deathEater)
                                throws UnauthorizedAccessException {
        if ( !hasPreviousExperienceInDealingWithDeathEaters ) {
            if ( isAurorInGoodStanding() ) {
                deathEatersAssigned.add( deathEater );
                hasPreviousExperienceInDealingWithDeathEaters = true;
                System.out.println(
                    "Order to capture " + deathEater + " accepted" );
                return true;
            }
        } else if (deathEatersAssigned.size()  < 5) {
            deathEatersAssigned.add( deathEater );
                System.out.println(
                    "Order to capture " + deathEater + " accepted" );
            return true;
        }
        System.out.println(
            "Order to capture " + deathEater + " was not accepted" );
        return false;
    }
}
```

9.10   THE Obliviator CLASS

An Obliviator is another type of Wizard that is under the supervision of the Minister
for Magic. As you will see later in Section 9.12, the definition of the MinisterForMagic
class includes an instance variable that stores references to the Obliviators working for
the minister.

An Obliviator's job is to perform memory charms on muggles who happened to have
witnessed magic that they were not supposed to see. To be hired as an Obliviator, a
wizard must, at the least, be good at charms and must have gone through formal schooling
in wizardry.

An Obliviator performs the memory charm on a muggle by invoking its
alterMuggleMemory() method shown in the class definition below — the muggle on
whom the memory charm is to be carried out is supplied as an argument to the method.

This method first checks whether the wizard on which the method is invoked is qualified to perform the charm. It does this by invoking the isAllowedToPerformMemoryCharm() method that is a part of the class definition. After this check is conducted, the chosen muggle's memory is altered by the wizard uttering an incantation that consists of the word "*Obliviate*" followed by the name of the muggle. For special effect, the implementation shown below actually sounds out the incantation.[5] It does this with the help of the speech synthesis function espeak(). For platforms that do not support voice synthesis with espeak, the alterMuggleMemory() method just prints out the message that the memory charm was performed on the designated muggle.

```java
import java.io.*;

public class Obliviator extends Wizard {

    public Obliviator( String firstname, String lastname ) {
        super( firstname, lastname );
    }
    public boolean isAllowedToPerformMemoryCharm()
                    throws UnauthorizedAccessException {
        if ( this.getSchoolGraduatedFrom().equals(
                WizardTraits.SchoolGraduatedFrom.HomeSchooled ) )
            return false;
        if (! this.getWizardryStrength().equals(
                WizardTraits.WizardryStrength.Charms ) )
            return false;
        for (SchoolGraduatedFrom school : SchoolGraduatedFrom.values()){
            if ( school.equals( this.getSchoolGraduatedFrom() ) ) {
                return true;
            }
        }
        return false;
    }
    public void alterMuggleMemory( String muggleName )
                    throws UnauthorizedAccessException {
        if ( !isAllowedToPerformMemoryCharm() ) {
            System.out.println(
              "This wizard is not qualified to perform memory charm" );
            System.exit(0);
        }
        try {
            Process p = Runtime.getRuntime().exec( "which espeak" );
            BufferedReader stdInput =
                new BufferedReader(
                        new InputStreamReader( p.getInputStream()));
            BufferedReader stdError =
                new BufferedReader(
```

---

[5]When you run this demonstration on a machine that supports speech synthesis with Jonathan Duddington's espeak library, you will actually hear the incantation "Obliviate Aunt Marge." On Linux machines, you can use your package manager to install this library if it is not already there.

```
                                new InputStreamReader( p.getErrorStream()));
            String reply = stdInput.readLine();
            String error = stdError.readLine();
            if  ( reply.contains("/espeak")  )  {
                String incantation = "Obliviate" + muggleName;
                incantation = incantation.replaceAll(" ", "");
                Runtime.getRuntime().exec(
                    "espeak -s80 -p99 -a200 -k20 " + incantation );
            } else {
                if (error != null) System.out.println( error );
                System.out.println("Memory Charm cast on Aunt Marge");
            }
        } catch ( IOException e ) {
            e.printStackTrace();
            System.exit(-1);
        }
    }
}
```

9.11   THE DepartmentHead CLASS

As previously mentioned, the Ministry of Magic is divided into several departments, with an officially designated Department Head in charge of each department. As you will see in the next section, the definition of the `MinisterForMagic` class includes a variable that points to the Department Heads under the supervision of the minister.

The implementation of the `DepartmentHead` class overrides those methods of the parent `Wizard` class that are especially relevant to a wizard serving the role of a department head. We assume that it is a department head's responsibility to keep track of the offices in his/her department. For that purpose, for the rudimentary demonstration here, we provide the `DepartmentHead` class with a set container called `officesInChargeOf`.

The reader will also notice that we have provided the class with a method named `assignOfficesToDepartmentHead()` for assigning new offices to a department head. Supposedly any client of this class could invoke this method on a `DepartmentHead` instance. In and of itself, that makes no sense. One would think that only a higher official, such as the Minister for Magic himself/herself, would have the authority to assign a new office to a department head. So in a cleaner implementation, this method would be placed in the `MinisterForMagic` class. Another argument that could be made with regard to this method would be that even if one were to place this method where it currently is, its sender should be checked before the method is executed. That is, a department head should first verify that the method was invoked by an appropriate authority before executing the method. Similar arguments could be made for the `reassignDepartment()` method. On the other hand, it makes perfect sense to place the method `listOfficesInChargeOf()` method here.

```
import java.util.*;

public class DepartmentHead extends Wizard {
```

```
    private String nameOfDepartment;
    private Set<String> officesInChargeOf = new HashSet<String>();

    public DepartmentHead(String firstname, String lastname,
                                              String deptName){
        super( firstname, lastname );
        nameOfDepartment = deptName;
    }
    public String getDepartmentInChargeOf()
                    throws UnauthorizedAccessException {
        return nameOfDepartment;
    }
    public void assignOfficesToDepartmentHead( List<String> offices )
                            throws UnauthorizedAccessException {
        officesInChargeOf.addAll( offices );
    }
    public List<String> listOfficesInChargeOf()
                throws UnauthorizedAccessException {
        return new ArrayList<String>( officesInChargeOf );
    }
    public void reassignDepartment( String newDept )
                    throws UnauthorizedAccessException {
        nameOfDepartment = newDept;
    }
}
```

9.12   THE Minister For Magic CLASS

The class defined here is for the role of the Minister for Magic. Presumably, the individual holding this position is elected by the wizards and the witches of the United Kingdom (UK). Presumably also, the Ministry of Magic is funded by the taxes collected from the world of wizardry in the UK. When a new muggle Prime Minister is elected, an important job of the Minister for Magic is to inform the Prime Minister about the existence of the world of wizardry in the UK.

Section 9.5 listed some of the more important departments that are in the Ministry of Magic. That section also mentioned that some of the larger departments are subdivided into offices, with each office serving a separate function. The implementation of the MinisterForMagic shown below is based on the assumption that whereas the department heads keep track of the employees assigned to them, the hiring and firing decisions regarding the more critical employees — such as the aurors, the obliviators, the department heads, etc., — remain vested in the minister.

The implementation code shown below makes sure that there can only be one Minister for Magic. This is accomplished by using the Singleton pattern presented earlier in Chapter 6. The Singleton pattern requires that the constructor for the class be placed in its private section. That way a client of the class will not be able construct an instance at will. The instance construction facility is now provided through a static method named makeInstanceOfMinisterForMagic(). The logic in this method makes certain that

the private constructor of `MinisterForMagic` class is called only once — the first time `makeInstanceOfMinisterForMagic()` is invoked. Subsequently, the method returns the same previously constructed `MinisterForMagic` instance that was constructed in the first call to `makeInstanceOfMinisterForMagic()`.

For our simple demonstration here, we provide the `MinisterForMagic` class with the methods to hire individual wizards for the important positions of obliviators, aurors, and department heads. The class also includes a method to list the names of all such wizards hired by the minister.

```java
import java.util.*;

public class MinisterForMagic extends Wizard {

    private Set<Obliviator> obliviators = new HashSet<Obliviator>();
    private Set<Auror> aurors = new HashSet<Auror>();
    private Set<DepartmentHead> deptHeads =
                                    new HashSet<DepartmentHead>();

    // This will hold the reference to the only one minister that
    // is allowed to be constructed from this class:
    private static MinisterForMagic theMinister;

    //NOTE: This constructor is private because we want to make sure
    //      it is not possible to construct more than one Minister
    //      for magic
    private MinisterForMagic( String firstname, String lastname ) {
        super( firstname, lastname );
    }

    public static MinisterForMagic makeInstanceofMinisterForMagic(
                                    String fname, String lname ) {
        if ( theMinister == null )
            theMinister = new MinisterForMagic( fname, lname );
        return theMinister;
    }

    public void appointWizardAsObliviator(Wizard w)
                        throws UnauthorizedAccessException {
        obliviators.add( (Obliviator) w);
    }
    public void appointWizardAsAuror(Wizard w)
                        throws UnauthorizedAccessException {
        aurors.add( (Auror) w );
    }
    public void appointDepartmentHead(Wizard w)
                        throws UnauthorizedAccessException {
        deptHeads.add( (DepartmentHead) w );
    }
    public void listEmployeesWorkingAtMinistry()
```

```
                        throws UnauthorizedAccessException {
        Iterator<Obliviator> it1 = obliviators.iterator();
        Iterator<Auror> it2 = aurors.iterator();
        Iterator<DepartmentHead> it3 = deptHeads.iterator();
        while (it1.hasNext()) System.out.print( it1.next() + "   ");
        while (it2.hasNext()) System.out.print( it2.next() + "   ");
        while (it3.hasNext()) System.out.print( it3.next() + "   ");
    }
}
```

Since it extends the `Wizard` class, the `MinisterForMagic` class defined above is of
the same fundamental type as `Wizard`. At the same time, the `MinisterForMagic` class
incorporates compositions over other `Wizard` instances. The variables in the class that hold
references to composites are `obliviators`, `aurors`, and `deptHeads`.

9.13   THE CLIENT CLASS Test

This is the client class for the `Wizard` hierarchy. The class first constructs instances of the
different types of wizards that the Minister for Magic would be interesting in hiring and
sets values for their various attributes, such as the school attended, the wizarding strength,
and so on. Subsequently, the client class tests the main ability that is expected of each
of the wizards created. For example, the `Obliviator` instance is tested for its ability to
perform a memory charm on Aunt Marge.[6] Finally, the client class shown below constructs an instance of `MinisterForMagic` and gets the minister to hire the wizard instances
constructed previously.

```
import java.util.*;

public class Test {
    public static void main( String args[] ) throws Exception {

        Obliviator obl = new Obliviator( "Moomy", "Memsucker" );
        obl.setSchoolGraduatedFrom(
                        WizardTraits.SchoolGraduatedFrom.Hogwarts);
        obl.setWizardryStrength(WizardTraits.WizardryStrength.Charms);
        obl.alterMuggleMemory( "Aunt Marge" );                        //(A)

        Auror auror = new Auror( "Bootsie", "Bangerbolt" );
        auror.setSchoolGraduatedFrom(
                        WizardTraits.SchoolGraduatedFrom.Beauxbatons);
        auror.setWizardryLevel( WizardTraits.WizardryLevel.Master );
        auror.setWizardryStrength( WizardTraits.WizardryStrength.DADA );
        auror.acceptOrderToCaptureDeathEater(
```

---

[6]As mentioned in Section 9.10, if your machine is equipped with Jonathan Duddington's speech synthesis library,
you will actually hear the incantation that the obliviator will use to perform the memory charm on Aunt Marge.

```
                    new Wizard( "Peter",  "Pettigrew" ) );          //(B)

        DepartmentHead deptHead =
            new DepartmentHead("Amelia", "Bones",
                                            "MaginalLawEnforcement");
        deptHead.assignOfficesToDepartmentHead(
          new ArrayList<String>(
                        Arrays.asList("Auror Office","Wizengamot")));
        System.out.println( deptHead.listOfficesInChargeOf() );    //(C)
        deptHead.assignOfficesToDepartmentHead( new ArrayList<String>(
            Arrays.asList("Wizengamot","Misuse Of Muggle Artifacts")));
        System.out.println( deptHead.listOfficesInChargeOf() );    //(D)

        MinisterForMagic minister =
            MinisterForMagic.makeInstanceofMinisterForMagic("Cornelius",
                                                        "Fudge");

        minister.appointWizardAsObliviator( obl );
        minister.appointWizardAsAuror( auror );
        minister.appointDepartmentHead( deptHead );
        minister.listEmployeesWorkingAtMinistry();                 //(E)
    }
}
```

9.14   PLAYING WITH THE CODE

Download the class files for this pattern from the book website into a separate directory. Compile the code with the command

```
javac *.java
```

and execute the Test class by

```
java Test
```

Given the code in the `main()` of `Test`, executing that class will first produce the sound for the incantation "Obliviate Aunt Marge" assuming your computer has the previously mentioned speech synthesis library installed, and then print out the following output:

```
Order to capture Peter Pettigrew accepted
[Wizengamot, Auror Office]
[Misuse Of Muggle Artifacts, Wizengamot, Auror Office]
Moomy Memsucker   Bootsie Bangerbolt   Amelia Bones
```

where the four lines of the output correspond to the statements labeled (B), (C), (D), and (E), respectively, in the code shown for `Test`. Line (A) produces the sound of the incantation mentioned above.

For additional insights into the Composite pattern, you can extend the demonstration code in this chapter along the following lines:

- If you are not able to hear any sound effects when you execute the client class `Test`, try to replace the system call to `espeak()` in the `alterMuggleMemory()` method of the `Obliviator` class by the speech synthesizer function in your machine.
- Create another subclass of `Wizard` for the Death Eaters. Obviously, since we would not expect the Minister for Magic to knowingly hire a Death Eater, incorporation of this new class should not alter your code for the `MinisterForMagic` class. However, now you will be able to replace the following statement in the `main()` of the client class `Test`:

```
auror.acceptOrderToCaptureDeathEater(
                       new Wizard("Peter", "Pettigrew"));
```

by something like

```
auror.acceptOrderToCaptureDeathEater(
                       new DeathEater("Peter", "Pettigrew"));
```

This would free you to declare the class `Wizard` abstract, which would conform to the normal practice of keeping the top of the class hierarchies abstract.

10

DECORATOR

10.1 ONION AS A METAPHOR

An onion is often used as a metaphor when layers of seemingly not-too-relevant detail must be peeled away in order to see the ultimate truth. Not surprisingly, the human personality has been described as an onion by several psychologists. Supposedly, the outermost layers of our persona are meant for our everyday interactions with folks with whom we have mostly a work relationship. The layers further down are reserved for people whom we consider to be our friends. And, the innermost layers — these are the layers where our core beliefs and values reside — are meant for only those we are closest to.

The metaphor can also be used to describe physical objects — the Russian nesting doll being a classic example — and software objects, as you will soon see. Among physical objects, we also have the example of the party gifts that are wrapped multiple times for heightening the suspense as each layer is unwrapped to reveal either a tantalizing clue about the gift or to pose a question about it.

As you would guess, the primary reason for using the metaphor in our everyday lives is to draw attention to the existence of the layers that envelope something of interest. It is interesting to note that in its common usage the metaphor is unlikely to also draw our attention to the degree of isolation provided by each enclosing layer for all of the enclosed layers, or the order in which the layers occur, or even the number of layers. Sometimes these additional aspects of the onion metaphor are constrained implicitly by the nature of the domain. For example, for the case of the Russian nesting dolls, while the number of layers varies from one maker of the dolls to another, the order of the layers is fixed by the sizing constraint — the constraint that each doll must fit inside the next larger doll.

It is these additional aspects of the onion metaphor — in particular the extent to which we can control the choice and the order of the layers — that are important when the metaphor is used for the modeling of abstract objects in software development. The purpose of using the metaphor in a software context is for you to first write code for some

Designing with Objects: Object-Oriented Design Patterns Explained with Stories from Harry Potter,
First Edition. Avinash C. Kak.
© 2015 John Wiley & Sons, Inc. Published 2015 by John Wiley & Sons, Inc.

basic functionality and to then provide additional code in the form of embellishments that can be wrapped around the basic functionality. The Decorator pattern teaches us how you can write this sort of code in a way that gives the clients maximum freedom with regard to how they mix and match the embellishments for customizing the behavior of the software to their needs.

10.2   INTENT AND APPLICABILITY

The intent of the Decorator pattern is to give the clients the ability to add multiple embellishments to the core functionality offered by a class without constraining the order in which the embellishments are added.

You should consider using this pattern when

- the core functionality offered by a class can be embellished by calling on other classes;
- the clients want the freedom to mix and match the embellishments for enhancing the core functionality from a class;
- the alternative of creating a subclass for each different combination of the embellishments results in too many subclasses.

10.3   INTRODUCTION TO THE DECORATOR PATTERN

Let's say that the code you have written for some basic functionality needs to be embellished in different ways for different usage scenarios. A straightforward way to solve this problem would be to create a separate variant of your basic functionality for each usage scenario. In Figure 10.1, the class at the root represents the basic functionality and its subclasses the various embellished versions of the basic functionality.

However, this seemingly straightforward approach is likely to run into a roadblock if your customers seek combinations of embellishments. For each combination desired by your customers, you would need to create a new extension in your class hierarchy, as shown in Figure 10.2. Just imagine what a large and complex class hierarchy you would need to create with a purely inheritance-based implementation of Figure 10.2 if you have more than

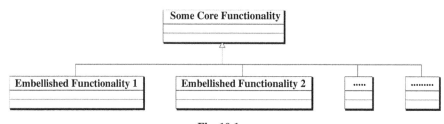

Fig. 10.1

a trivial number of distinct embellishments and your customers expect you to provide for every possible combination of them.

However, as we show in this chapter, with an approach based on the Decorator pattern — feasible when all of the embellishments implement the same interface as the original functionality — you'd only need to create one subclass for each embellishment as shown in Figure 10.3, thus avoiding the potentially exponential growth in the number of subclasses in the class diagram of Figure 10.2. Subsequently, a client of your software would be able to call on the embellishment classes in any arbitrary sequence. *That is because the Decorator pattern allows for a recursive incorporation of the embellishments, while placing no constraints on either the choice of the embellishments or the order in which they are sequenced.*

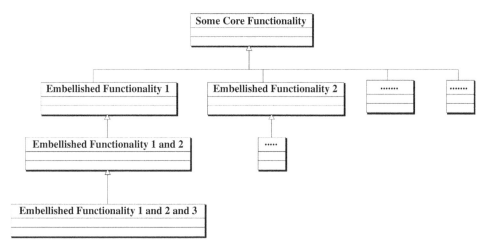

Fig. 10.2

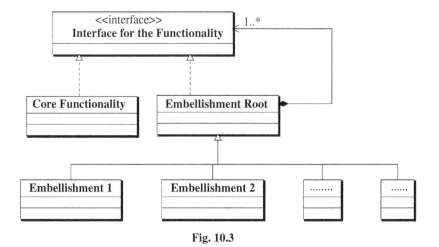

Fig. 10.3

Starting with Section 10.5, the rest of this chapter will explain these ideas with greater clarity using a story from Harry Potter that appears to be ideally suited for illustrating the Decorator pattern.

10.4   THE DECORATOR PATTERN IN REAL-WORLD APPLICATIONS

Java IO (Input/Output) classes constitute perhaps the oldest example of a fairly extensive use of the Decorator pattern in modern OO software. To illustrate this use of the Decorator, and, even more particularly, to illustrate why one would want to use Decorator classes in Java IO, let's consider the act of writing the integer 98 to a disk file.[1] From the standpoint of the programming involved, one is likely to think that there couldn't possibly be much to writing an innocuous integer like 98 to a file. But, as it turns out, there is more to it than meets the eye.

Let's say the integer 98 is the value of a local variable `anInt`. Now the question is whether you want the value of `anInt` to be written as two ASCII characters, 9 and 8, to the file. Or whether you wish for the integer to be written to the file in the form it is stored in the memory of the computer — a 4-byte bit pattern in most systems whose hex representation would be '00000062'. In addition, you would also need to make a decision regarding whether your program should buffer the stream used for writing to the disk file. If you were writing a sequence of integers to a file in a loop construct and the number 98 was one such integer, you would enhance the performance of your program if you choose the buffered option.

Java handles all of these variations on file IO with the help of the Decorator pattern. For example, one of the core functionality classes in Java IO is `FileOutputStream` — this class knows how to write raw bytes to a file. Subsequently, if you want the outgoing bytes to be buffered and for the information to show up in the file in the form of ASCII characters, you would make the following sort of a call in your program:

```
int anInt = 98;
PrintStream pbs = new PrintStream(
                    new BufferedOutputStream(
                        new FileOutputStream("out.dat")));
pbs.print( anInt );
pbs.close();
```

where the calls `BufferedOutputStream()` and `PrintStream()` are the decorator wrappings for the core functionality provided by the stream that is constructed by `FileOutputStream()`.

Another successful application of the Decorator pattern is the Zend_Form in the PHP-based Zend platform for serving out dynamically created web content. Zend_Form is used for dynamically emitting both the HTML markup for displaying a form in a user's browser and the data that goes into the form. Obviously, each client of the Zend platform would want to customize the look of the form and how the data are displayed therein in order to project a brand identity. The developers of the Zend platform chose a Decorator-based

---

[1]This example is taken from Chapter 6 of [2].

design for Zend_Form to give their clients the flexibility they needed with regard to form customization. The reader may wish to visit the "decorators-with-zend-forms" web page at Zend's home page for additional information on their approach to the use of the Decorator pattern. It is especially instructive to see the distinction they make between what they refer to as the content decorators, these being for the information that is displayed in a form, and the decorators for how the form looks to a user.

10.5   HARRY POTTER STORY USED TO ILLUSTRATE THE DECORATOR PATTERN

Consider a class whose primary function is to deliver a letter to Harry Potter while he is living with the Dursleys. Under normal circumstances, the letter would be placed in regular muggle mail with Harry's name on the envelope along with the house address of the Dursley residence. In fact, that is exactly what was first attempted by Hogwarts when the school needed to inform Harry that he had been admitted. A class that would accomplish this could be defined as follows:

```
class DeliverMsgToHarryPotter {
    String message = "Dear Harry, You have been admitted to Hogwarts." +
                    "Contgratulations!";
    public deliverMessage() {
        // Place the message in envelope with Harry's name
        // and Dursleys address on it.
    }
}
```

But, if the above direct method for delivering the message does not work — what if Mr. Dursley is in the habit of intercepting any regular mail that arrives for Harry! — we would need to think of another way of informing Harry that he has been admitted to Hogwarts. Hogwarts could try dropping the envelope through the chimney of the house at a time when the Dursleys, along with Harry, are sure to be eating their breakfast. This could be achieved by extending the class shown above:

```
class DeliverMsgThruChimney extends DeliverMsgToHarryPotter {
    public deliverMessage() {
        super.deliverMessage();
        // The call to parent class's deliverMessage()
        // will get the message and the envelope ready.
        // The new code here will drop the envelope
        // down the chimney.
    }
}
```

Note how the deliverMessage() of the derived class calls the deliverMessage() method of the parent class for doing the core work of placing the message in an envelope and for putting the correct address on the envelope. After that, the deliverMessage() of the derived class drops the envelope down the chimney chute of the Dursley house.

But what if Mr. Dursley intercepted this delivery mode also? Hogwarts could try slipping the envelope through the crack under the front door. This could be done by a class similar to the one shown above that again relies on the `DeliverdMsgToHarryPotter` class for the core work of placing the letter inside an envelope and addressing the envelope correctly:

```
class DeliverMsgThruDoorCrack extends DeliverMsgToHarryPotter {
    public deliverMessage() {
        super.deliverMessage();
        // The call to parent class's deliverMessage()
        // will get the message and the envelope ready.
        // The new code here will slip the envelope
        // under the front door of the Dursley house.
    }
}
```

But, as we know, after intercepting the door-crack-based message delivery, Mr. Dursley will seal the cracks under all the outside doors and windows of the house. To deal with this situation, Hogwarts could invoke yet another method — this one based on concealment. The envelope prepared by the `DeliverMsgToHarryPotter` class could be placed inside another envelope. Although the outside envelope would still bear Harry Potter's name, it could be made to look goofy, as if it came from a local toy store promoting its wares and things meant for kids who are about to go to high school. This could be accomplished with a class like:

```
class DeliverMsgThruConcealment extends DeliverMsgToHarryPotter {
    public deliverMessage() {
        super.deliverMessage();
        // The call to parent class's deliverMessage()
        // will get the message and the envelope ready.
        // The new code here will conceal the envelope
        // inside another envelope and make the
        // outer envelope look like it came from a local
        // toy store.
    }
}
```

In a similar manner, one could think of other delivery modes, each defined by a separate class that extends the basic class `DeliverMsgToHarryPotter`. Each new mode would result in making yet another addition to the class hierarchy shown in Figure 10.4.

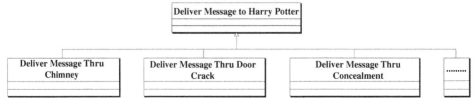

Fig. 10.4

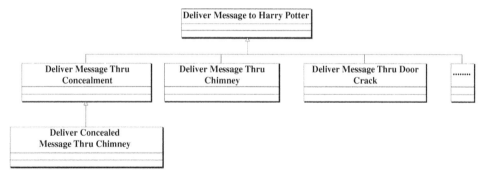

Fig. 10.5

As you dream up new delivery modes in order to deal with Mr. Dursley's intransigence, constructing a new class for each new mode will prove to be inefficient — because it implies an ever-expanding list of classes derived from the parent class `DeliverMsgToHarryPotter`. *This inefficiency becomes even more glaring if you want to combine some of the previously defined delivery modes in order to create new ones.* What if Hogwarts decides to send the message through the chimney but the real message-bearing envelope is placed inside a concealing envelope. With the present scheme of having to create a new class for each new message delivery mode, we would need to extend the hierarchy in the manner shown in Figure 10.5.

As you can see, this approach to combining message delivery modes is unwieldy. Each combination of the message delivery modes requires us to tinker with and expand the original source code. That is not good. Instead, what we would like to do is to think of a way of organizing the software so that we have the freedom to combine the different message delivery modes in arbitrary ways without the need to change the source code in any way.

Programming problems like this that involve arbitrary combinations of different embellishments to some core functionality are best solved with the Decorator pattern. Central to this pattern is the notion of *recursive invocations* of the embellishments that allow for them to be nested arbitrarily. For example, if in order to frustrate Mr. Dursley we wanted to place the concealing envelope inside another concealing envelope, we can do so with the Decorator pattern without having to create a special class that would carry out this double concealment. What's more, a Decorator-based design would allow us to truly imitate a Russian nesting doll by concealing the original envelope to the n-th degree, with one envelope placed inside another, that resides inside yet another, and so on, without having to define any additional classes at all.

As shown in Figure 10.6, the Decorator pattern requires that we first define a root interface that declares the basic functionality that needs to be implemented. In our demonstration, this interface will be called `MessageDelivery`. Subsequently, we define an abstract class called `MessageDeliveryDecorator` that implements the interface `MessageDelivery` and, at the same time, has a constructor that takes an argument of type `MessageDelivery`. This fact will allow the instances created from the concrete subclasses of `MessageDeliveryDecorator` to be nested recursively. As for implementing the core functionality that was declared in `MessageDelivery`, the class `CoreMessageDeliveryClass` takes care of that. This class also implements the root interface `MessageDelivery`. Because the core functionality class and the recursively embellished classes all implement the same interface — which in our case is

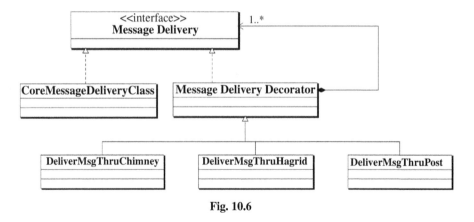

Fig. 10.6

MessageDelivery — it is possible to wrap any arbitrary nesting of the embellishments around the core functionality.

10.6   A TOP LEVEL VIEW OF THE PATTERN DEMONSTRATION

Figure 10.7 presents a top-level view of our demonstration of the Decorator pattern. Ignoring for a moment the client class Test and the links emanating therefrom, the class diagram in Figure 10.7 is just a more detailed version of the diagram presented in Figure 10.6. The class hierarchy descends from the root interface MessageDelivery, which is defined as follows:

```
public interface MessageDelivery {
    public void deliverMessage();
}
```

This interface plays a critical role in the Decorator pattern's ability to allow for arbitrary nesting of the embellishments corresponding to the classes that are derived from the abstract class MessageDeliveryDecorator. A message meant to be delivered to Harry Potter is an instance of the class CoreMessageDeliveryClass. This message is "delivered" using one or more of the subclasses of MessageDeliveryDecorator and the delivery modes can be chained in an arbitrary manner, as we will show in the client class Test in Section 10.9. Here is an example of the chaining of the message delivery modes from the main() of Test:

```
MessageDelivery m3 = new DeliverMsgThruHagrid(
                     new DeliverMsgThruChimney(
                         new CoreMessageDeliveryClass() ) );
m3.deliverMessage();
```

which shows the delivery mode for the message as Hagrid taking the envelope over to the Dursleys and dropping it through their chimney.

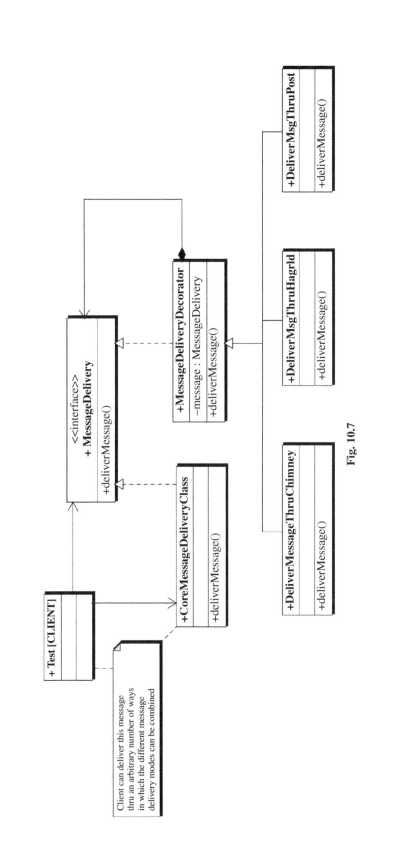

Fig. 10.7

As to how the Decorator pattern allows us to create arbitrary chains of message delivery modes from the descendants of the class `MessageDeliveryDecorator`, note the following in the class diagram of Figure 10.7: The constructor for the abstract class `MessageDeliveryDecorator` takes an argument of type `MessageDelivery`, as do all of the concrete subclasses of this class. Add to this the fact that the core functionality class `CoreMessageDeliveryClass` is also of type `MessageDelivery` and its constructor, as shown in the figure, also takes an argument of type `MessageDelivery`. Therefore all instances constructed from the concrete classes shown in Figure 10.7 (except, of course, for the client class `Test`) are of type `MessageDelivery`. We can therefore construct an instance, of, say, `DeliverThruPost` and supply to its constructor an instance of type `CoreMessageDeliveryClass`. This would automatically embellish the functionality provided by the core delivery class with the additional functionality provided by the `DeliverThruPost` delivery class. Along the same lines, we can wrap an instance of `DeliverMsgThruHagrid` around an instance of `DeliverMsgThruChimney`, which in turn would be a wrapper around an instance of `CoreMessageDeliveryClass`. As the reader can see, this notion of recursive wrappings can be nested to an arbitrary extent.

10.7   THE CoreMessageDeliveryClass CLASS

An instance of this class defines the endpoint of the recursive wrappings (or the nested wrappings or the nested embellishments) created through instances of type `MessageDeliveryDecorator`. These wrappings are all of type `MessageDelivery`, which is also the type of the instances created from the class shown below.

```
public class CoreMessageDeliveryClass implements MessageDelivery {
    public void deliverMessage() {
        System.out.println( "Dear Harry, You have been admitted to "
                        + "Hogwarts. Congratulations!" );
    }
}
```

10.8   THE DECORATOR CLASSES

The concrete Decorator classes are all derived from `MessageDeliveryDecorator`, which as defined below is an abstract class. As mentioned earlier, central to the Decorator pattern is the fact that the class shown below both implements the `MessageDelivery` interface and includes a constructor that takes an argument of the same type. Additionally, an instance of type `MessageDeliveryDecorator` contains an instance variable of the type `MessageDelivery`. These facts make it possible to construct an instance of type `MessageDeliveryDecorator` — this instance will in actuality be constructed from a concrete subclass of `MessageDeliveryDecorator` since the class shown below is abstract — and have this object serve both as an instance of type `MessageDelivery` and contain another object of the same type — a fact central to the Russian nesting dolls effect (or the onion effect) achieved with the Decorator pattern.

```
public abstract class MessageDeliveryDecorator
                          implements MessageDelivery {

    private MessageDelivery message;

    public MessageDeliveryDecorator( MessageDelivery m ) {
        message = m;
    }

    public void deliverMessage() {
        message.deliverMessage();
    }
}
```

We next present the DeliverMsgThruChimney class — a concrete subclass of the abstract parent MessageDeliveryDecorator shown above — that defines one of the specific modes for message delivery. In order to allow for recursive embellishments, note how the constructor takes a single argument of type MessageDelivery that is used to give a value to the instance variable message inherited from the parent class MessageDeliveryDecorator.

Also note how the override implementation for the deliverMessage() method calls on the parent class's method of the same name. That would cause the method deliverMessage() to be invoked on the instance that is wrapped by the current instance. The endpoint of such recursive invocations is defined by an instance of CoreMessageDeliveryClass, as previously mentioned, and this accounts for the onion effect achieved by the Decorator pattern.

```
public class DeliverMsgThruChimney extends MessageDeliveryDecorator {
    public DeliverMsgThruChimney(MessageDelivery m) {
        super(m);
    }
    public void deliverMessage() {
        super.deliverMessage();
        System.out.println( "This message is being sent through the "
                          + "chimney of Harry Potter's home" );
    }
}
```

Shown next is DeliverMsgThruHagrid that is another subclass of the abstract MessageDeliveryDecorator. Since, except for the differences implied by its name, the definition of the class shown below is exactly the same as that of the DeliverMsgThruChimney presented above, the reason for why the constructor is supplied with an argument of type MessageDelivery should be clear to the reader. Also clear to the reader should be the purpose served by the deliverMessage() method calling on the parent class's method of the same name.

```
public class DeliverMsgThruHagrid extends MessageDeliveryDecorator {
    public DeliverMsgThruHagrid(MessageDelivery m) {
        super(m);
    }
    public void deliverMessage() {
        super.deliverMessage();
        System.out.println( "This message was carried by Hagrid" );
    }
}
```

That brings us to the third and final concrete subclass derived from the abstract class
MessageDeliveryDecorator — the DeliverMsgThruPost class for delivering a message to Harry Potter by regular post. Its definition parallels exactly those of the previous
two subclasses that define the two other modes for delivering a message to Harry Potter.

```
public class DeliverMsgThruPost extends MessageDeliveryDecorator {
    public DeliverMsgThruPost(MessageDelivery m) {
        super(m);
    }
    public void deliverMessage() {
        super.deliverMessage();
        System.out.println( "This message is being sent via the Postal "
                            + "Service");
    }
}
```

10.9   THE CLIENT CLASS Test

The Test class shown below illustrates the onion metaphor on which the Decorator pattern
is based. Note especially the third delivery mode for sending the message to Harry Potter.
It calls for Hagrid to take the message over to where the Dursleys live and to drop the
envelope through the chimney.

```
public class Test {
    public static void main(String[] args) {
        MessageDelivery m1 = new DeliverMsgThruPost(
                            new CoreMessageDeliveryClass() );
        m1.deliverMessage();
        System.out.println();

        MessageDelivery m2 = new DeliverMsgThruChimney(
                            new CoreMessageDeliveryClass() );
        m2.deliverMessage();
        System.out.println();
```

```
        MessageDelivery m3 = new DeliverMsgThruHagrid(
                            new DeliverMsgThruChimney(
                            new CoreMessageDeliveryClass() ) );
        m3.deliverMessage();
        System.out.println();
    }
}
```

10.10   PLAYING WITH THE CODE

Download the class files for this pattern from the book website into a separate directory. Compile the code with the command

```
    javac *.java
```

and execute the Test class by

```
    java Test
```

Given the code in the `main()` of `Test`, executing this class should produce the following output (except for the annotations like "*first delivery mode*"):

first delivery mode:

```
    Dear Harry, You have been admitted to Hogwarts. Congratulations!
    This message is being sent via the Postal Service
```

second delivery mode:

```
    Dear Harry, You have been admitted to Hogwarts. Congratulations!
    This message is being sent through the chimney of Harry Potter's home.
```

third delivery mode:

```
    Dear Harry, You have been admitted to Hogwarts. Congratulations!
    This message is being sent through the chimney of Harry Potter's home.
    This message was carried by Hagrid.
```

To gain additional insights, you can extend on your own the code for this pattern and do so along the following lines:

- A straightforward way to extend the demonstration code would be to add additional message delivery modes. As a Harry Potter reader would recall, an attempt was also

made to deliver the admission message to Harry when the Dursley family was staying overnight in a roadside hotel as Mr. Dursley was trying to get away from their house so as to not receive the letters.

- Another way to extend the code would be to disallow certain recursive calls on the delivery modes. For example, if the message is going to be delivered ultimately by dropping the envelope down the chimney at Number 4 Privet Drive, you obviously would not want to send the letter to, say, the hotel mentioned above.

11

FACADE

11.1 HIDING COMPLEXITY

Most people associate facades with buildings and think of a facade as the front of a building. And for many, the word "facade" also has a strong association with the fake fronts of the buildings — typically a saloon, a general store, a jailhouse, and so on — in the old Hollywood movies of the wild west. People watching these old Westerns obviously think of what they see as actual buildings and not just facades constructed on film sets in studio backlots.

When used as a metaphor, we could say that the facade of an object is what its designer has chosen for how the object will be experienced by the humans. In general, this would only make sense when there is much more to an object than just the facade. If an object can easily be experienced in its entirety, it probably does not make sense to associate a facade with it.

When using "facade" as a metaphor for abstract objects in the memory of a computer, it is interesting to reflect on an important difference between its usage for such objects and its normal usage for physical objects such as buildings: Whereas a building will generally possess only a single facade, an abstract object can be endowed with any number of facades. *It is this fact that is taken advantage of when the Facade pattern is used in software development.*

As you will see in this chapter, when software objects are endowed with facades, we can use them in different ways in different applications or for different categories of users.

11.2 INTENT AND APPLICABILITY

The intent of the Facade pattern is to create different usage views for a complex system of classes.

You should use this pattern when

Designing with Objects: Object-Oriented Design Patterns Explained with Stories from Harry Potter, First Edition. Avinash C. Kak.
© 2015 John Wiley & Sons, Inc. Published 2015 by John Wiley & Sons, Inc.

- the expected user community for your software includes people with diverse backgrounds;

- the software you are developing is meant to be used in different ways in different application contexts;

- you are working on a complex application that requires an entry point — a simple interface — to give the users a taste of the capabilities of the software.

11.3 INTRODUCTION TO THE FACADE PATTERN

The Facade pattern is about creating different usage views of a system of classes for different categories of users. With software design based on this pattern, what each user would see would be a front-end designed specifically for the category to which the user belongs. Such facades can be expected to alleviate the frustration that most of us experience when using software applications for even the simplest of reasons. Many of these applications expect you to acquire expert-level familiarity with them before you can put them to any use at all, no matter how trivial.

To elaborate, many of us are drawn to newfangled computer tools for editing photos, videos, documents, and so on, but are discouraged by the steep learning curve associated with developing even a beginner-level familiarity with them. Don't you think these tools would appear less formidable if they had different front ends for different categories of users? Let's consider the case of document processing software. If all you wanted to do was to write simple letters and short reports, with just the most basic formatting and no embedded multimedia objects, wouldn't it be wonderful if the software provided you with a specially designated but highly intuitive user interface that you could use to get simple jobs done quickly — as opposed to you getting lost in layers upon layers of menus and buttons meant for creating all kinds of special effects by a trained user?[1] This is obviously not the case with much of today's software. For most applications today, the full complexity of the entire application is thrown at you willy-nilly. The result often is nothing but frustration for at least the beginner users. The alternative that many users would prefer would require a complex software application to offer multiple usage views — facades — as shown in Figure 11.1. Such compartmentalized

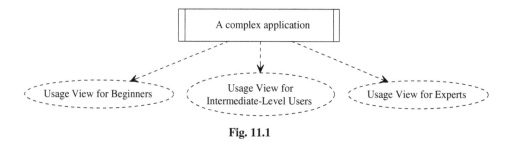

Fig. 11.1

---

[1] You yourself may not have a need for such easy-to-use interfaces to software, but think of your older relatives who may be intimidated by anything on a computer that goes beyond touching an app.

usage views could also make it easier to let the expert users customize the application to their needs with changes of the sort you would not want the beginners to even think about.

11.4   THE FACADE PATTERN IN REAL-WORLD APPLICATIONS

In the open-source community, it is not uncommon for the developers to offer their own versions of the interfaces for complex modules, these interfaces being for specific usages of the modules. For open-source software, these simpler and limited-utility interfaces are examples of the Facade pattern.

The `FileIO` Java class[2] mentioned at the end of Chapter 10 of [2] is meant to be a facade, in the sense that it offers a simple interface for certain specific IO tasks and saves the user the bother of having to wade through all of the classes in the `java.io` package in order to figure out what combination of basic IO and wrapper classes to use. As was mentioned in a different context in the previous chapter, the large number of wrapper classes in the `java.io` package can be combined in different ways for the same end result. As shown in the program `WriteIntToFile.java` in Chapter 6 of [2], if your goal is to write the value of an integer-valued variable to a disk file as a sequence of ASCII digits, there exist at least six different combinations of the wrapper classes that produce the same end result. In the simpler interface provided by the `FileIO` class, there is only one function to call, `writeOneInt()`, for that purpose. Two other examples of the Facade pattern that are also in Chapter 6 of [2] are the `TerminalIO` and the `FileReaderData` classes for the IO operations implied by their names.

11.5   HARRY POTTER STORY USED TO ILLUSTRATE THE FACADE PATTERN

Our demonstration of the Facade pattern is based on the Floo network in Harry Potter. The wizarding community uses this network to travel, almost instantaneously, from one place to another. The network itself is managed by the Floo Network Authority in the Department of Magical Transportation of the Ministry of Magic. It is their job to set up the network, to extend it, and, during times of danger, to monitor it and keep track of who is traveling in the network.

To travel from one location to another in a Floo network, you toss a handful of the enchanted Floo powder into a lit fireplace. As the flames turn emerald green, you step into the fireplace and state clearly your destination. Suddenly you find yourself whizzing past the fireplaces of the wizards that are on the way to your destination. The Floo network also lends itself to a few other modes of magical transportation. For example, you do not have to physically transport your entire body from where you are to the destination. If you only wanted to chat with someone at the other end, all you'd need to do would be to stick just your head into the flames while the rest of the body stayed firmly at the starting point. Just

---

[2]The Solution Manual for [2] presents the implementation code for the FileIO class. The book itself shows only the class API.

your head would then travel to the destination. It would appear in the flame at the other end and engage in a conversation with an individual there.

It would be safe to assume that running and managing the Floo network is a complex job for the wizards of the Floo Network Authority at the Ministry of Magic, not the least because they must also conjure up extensions to the current network as the wizarding community expands. Although much of this complexity would not be visible to an underage wizard who merely wants to travel from one place to another, some complexity is likely to be encountered by an experienced wizard who has many enemies and who wishes to know the precise route he will be traveling in the network. Obviously, a wizard would not want to be routed through an enemy's fireplace. We know from reading Harry Potter that as wizards travel through the network at high speeds, they can see blurry images of the rooms as they pass through the enroute fireplaces. Therefore, it is entirely possible that experienced wizards sitting in those rooms could intercept someone passing through their fireplaces. (There is no mention of such intercepts, or even the possibility of such intercepts, by J.K. Rowling. We will make this assumption, nonetheless, because it *could* be true and because it allows us to add interesting features to our demonstration here.)

In our use of Floo networks here, we will make the following assumptions:

- An underage wizard should not have to deal with any of the complexity of a Floo network. Such a wizard should simply be able to use the network to travel from one place to another.

- A seasoned wizard should be able to query the network for the routing that will be used to get to the destination in order to make sure that the route is clear of the houses that may be occupied by enemies.

- A warlock (we will refer to all the wizards in the Floo Network Authority and all wizards with superior powers, such as Dumbledore, Lord Voldemort, etc., as warlocks) should be be able to create a new Floo network. Obviously, a warlock must also be able to use the network in all of the ways in which a regular wizard can.

What that means is that our Floo network must allow for different types of usages by the three different types of wizards listed above. For obvious reasons, we do not want an underage wizard to access the type of usage that is meant specifically for the grown-up wizards and the warlocks. The same applies to the grown-up wizards vis-á-vis the type of usage meant specifically for the warlocks.

How do we that? As will be shown in this demonstration, we can create three different usage views — or facades — of a Floo network and make sure that each category of users is allowed access to only that usage view which is meant specifically for that category.

These three different facades will be subclassed from a root abstract class called `Facade`, as shown in Figure 11.2.

We will place the basic usage of a Floo network in the abstract root class `Facade`. By basic usage we mean the services that are expected by all, such as the ability to travel from one place to another. By inheritance, this usage will be available in all three usage views of the network. *We will also declare some of the more advanced usage in the root class, but we will make sure that this functionality cannot be utilized in those usage views where it is not allowed.*

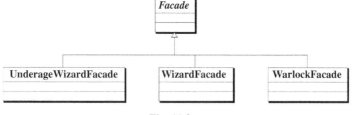

Fig. 11.2

11.6 A TOP LEVEL VIEW OF THE PATTERN DEMONSTRATION

The class diagram in Figure 11.3 is a top-level view of our demonstration of the Facade pattern. Central to the demonstration is the role played by the Network class shown at left. The existing built-in Floo network is modeled by this class, as are any new extensions to the network. Each place (or, more precisely speaking, each fireplace) that is accessible in the network is considered to be an instance of the Node class. And each direct connection between a pair of Node instances is represented by an instance of the Link class.[3] A sequence of nodes and links that constitutes a travel path in the network is represented by an instance of the Path class.

We will make a distinction between the built-in network consisting of all the well known places mentioned in Harry Potter and an ad-hoc network that a warlock working for the Floo Network Authority at the Ministry of Magic might want to create from a set of new locations. The built-in network is based on the following locations in and around London:

- Diagon Alley
- Knockturn Alley
- Gryffindor Commons

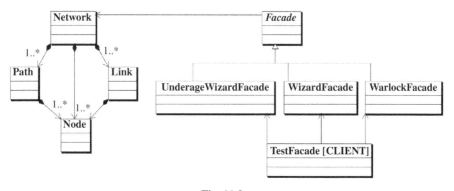

Fig. 11.3

---

[3] In graph theory, direct connections between nodes are also commonly referred to as arcs and edges.

- DADA Professor's Office
- Dolores Umbridge's Office
- The Burrow
- Ministry of Magic Atrium
- 12 Grimmauld Place

So that we can play with different connectivity patterns in the network, we will associate a probability with any two nodes being connected directly. Therefore, when you execute the code for this demonstration, what specific network you end up with would depend on chance in a manner that will be explained later.[4]

Regarding the Facade classes, the basic functionality defined in the abstract root `Facade` will allow everyone in the wizarding world to travel through the built-in network. The additional functionality meant for grown-up wizards, and made available through the `WizardFacade` class, will consist of allowing a wizard to query the network for the route that will be taken by his travel and to also query the network regarding whether a particular place (which may be occupied by an enemy) will be on the route. In addition to these two functionalities, the `WarlockFacade` class will allow a Floo Network Authority wizard to conjure up new Floo networks.

If you wish to view the built-in Floo network, it can be done by calling the method `displayBuiltinFlooNetwork()` of the `Facade` class. It will produce a display like:

```
Total number of nodes in the network: 8

Displaying the network:

Number of direct connections in the network:  15

Direct connection:   Diagon Alley <=> DADA Professor's Office:  18
Direct connection:   Diagon Alley <=> The Burrow:  62
Direct connection:   Knockturn Alley <=> Gryffindor Commons:  36
....
....


Displaying the neighborhoods in the network:

Gryffindor Commons: [Knockturn Alley, DADA Professor's Office,
                Ministry of Magic Atrium, 12 Grimmauld Place]

12 Grimmauld Place: [Knockturn Alley, Gryffindor Commons,
  DADA Professor's Office, Dolores Umbridge's Office, The Burrow]
....
....
```

---

[4]You can suppress this aspect of the demonstration by setting the variable p in the code for the `initializeBuiltInNetwork()` method of the `Network` class to 1. The variable p is the probability that any given pair of nodes in the built-in network is connected directly. See Section 11.8 for further comments regarding this randomness.

The first part of this display shows the individual links in the network, each link being a direct connection between a pair of locations. Each direct connection displayed in this manner also shows the distance between the two endpoints of that connection. The second part of the display shows the neighborhoods around each of the locations. For example, since Gryffindor Commons is directly connected to Knockturn Alley, DADA Professor's Office, Ministry of Magic Atrium, and Number 12 Grimmauld Place, all of these places constitute the neighborhood for Gryffindor Commons. The full output produced by `displayBuiltinFlooNetwork()` of the Facade class for the built-in network is shown in Section 11.12.

11.7   THE ABSTRACT ROOT CLASS Facade

This section presents the root class of the facade hierarchy, the abstract class `Facade`. As stated earlier, the main purpose of this root class is to define the basic usage of the built-in network that was introduced in the previous section.

```
public abstract class Facade {

    private static boolean builtinNetworkInitialized = false;

    public void initializeBuiltinNetwork() {
        if (builtinNetworkInitialized) return;
        builtinNetworkInitialized = true;
        Network.initializeBuiltInNetwork();
    }
    public void displayBuiltinFlooNetwork() {
        initializeBuiltinNetwork();
        Network.displayNetwork();
        System.out.println( "\nDisplaying direct connection "
                        + "neighborhoods in the network:\n");
        Network.displayNeighborhoods();
    }
    public boolean doesDestinationExistInBuiltinNetwork(
                                        String destination) {
        initializeBuiltinNetwork();
        return Network.isLocationInNetwork( new Node(destination) );
    }
    public Path travelByBuiltinFlooNetwork( String startLocation,
                                        String endLocation ) {
        initializeBuiltinNetwork();
        Path bestPath = null;
        try {
            bestPath = Network.findShortestPath( startLocation,
                                        endLocation, false );
        } catch(Exception e) {
            e.printStackTrace();
            System.exit(1);
        }
```

```
        return bestPath;
    }
    public abstract Network constructNewFlooNetwork(
                            String[] placeNames) throws Exception;
    public abstract boolean checkForLocationOnShortestPath(
                String start, String destination, String place )
                                             throws Exception;
    public abstract boolean doesGivenPathPassThroughLocation(
                                    Path path, String location )
                                             throws Exception;
}
```

Regarding the methods in the class definition shown above, note that when the demonstration code in this chapter is first fired up, the built-in network must be initialized. This is accomplished by the method `initializeBuiltinNetwork()`. All other methods defined above first call the `initializeBuiltinNetwork()` method. However, since we do not want to initialize the built-in network more than once, we ensure that that is the case through the static boolean variable `builtinNetworkInitialized` that itself is initialized to false. The very first time `initializeBuiltinNetwork()` is called, this boolean variable will be set to true. Any subsequent calls to `initializeBuiltinNetwork()` will return immediately without doing anything.

Another method, `doesDestinationExistInBuiltinNetwork()`, presented in the class definition is useful to anyone who is planning to travel to a new destination. Such an individual would want to know whether this destination is a stop on the network.

Finally, we have the method `travelByBuiltinFlooNetwork()`, which is probably the most important method provided by the root class. It is this method that you'd need to call in order to transport yourself to the desired destination. This method calculates your path to the destination by searching for the shortest path to take in the network. The shortest path calculation, as presented in Section 11.8, is based on the famous Dijkstra's algorithm.

Notice also that this root class contains just declarations for the three methods — `constructNewFlooNetwork()`, `checkForLocationOnShortestPath()`, and `doesGivenPathPassThroughLocation()` — with the expectation that the derived classes will implement these methods. Regarding the purpose of these three abstract methods, what `constructNewFlooNetwork()` accomplishes should be obvious by its name. Only the warlocks working for the Floo Network Authority are allowed to construct (or conjure up) new networks.

Regarding the other two methods that are only declared in this class, the reader is probably curious about them since their names sound so similar. These two methods accomplish very different things. The `checkForLocationOnShortestPath()` method is supposed to first search for the shortest path to the destination in the network and then determine if a particular location happens to be on the shortest path. The second method, `doesGivenPathPassThroughLocation()`, is supposed to check for whether a certain location exists on the path that is supplied to the method as its first argument. Both of these methods would be important to wizards who are concerned about running into enemies while traveling in the network, especially if they have dangerous enemies and they do not want their travel paths to pass through the fireplaces of the houses where their enemies live.

11.8   THE Network CLASS

This section presents the `Network` class that is used for modeling the Floo network and any new extensions to the network conjured up by the folks who work for the Floo Network Authority.

The class definition starts with the following static variables that are used to store all of the information related to the built-in network:[5]

```
networkAddressesBuiltIn
networkLocationsBuiltIn
neighborhoodBuiltIn
networkArcsBuiltIn
```

We store the addresses for the built-in network in `networkAddressesBuiltIn`. Each built-in address for a stop in the network is converted into an instance of `Node` and stored in the list `networkLocationsBuiltIn`. We also store separately each direct link, meaning each pair of nodes that are directly connected, in the list `networkArcsBuiltIn`. Finally, we store each neighborhood separately in the hash `neighborhoodBuiltIn` of <key,value> pairs in which each key is a node in the network and the corresponding value a list of the nodes that constitute the neighborhood for the key. For any given node, its neighborhood is a list of the other nodes that are directly connected to the given node. For ordinary uses of the built-in network — meaning using the network just for transportation — we expect the users to interact with the information stored in just these static variables.

After the static variables, the `Network` class contains instance variables that store information related to any new networks that the wizards may conjure up at runtime — assuming they are authorized to do so. The instance variables are `networkAddresses`, `networkLocations`, `networkNodesHash`, `neighborhoods`, and `networkLinks`.[6]

After defining the static and the instance variables mentioned above, the definition of the `Network` class includes implementations for the following two methods:

```
initializeBuiltInNetworkNodes()
initializeBuiltInNetwork()
```

A call to the first simply creates an instance of `Node` for each address and a call to the second then proceeds to actually create a network from the `Node` instances that are output by the first call. The `Node` class is presented in Section 11.9. A most important aspect of network creation is the randomness that is used to decide which nodes to connect directly and what distance values to assign to such direct connections. Before explaining how this

---

[5]These static variables were not declared `final` because we want the wizards working for the Floo Network Authority to be able to make changes to the built-in network.

[6]The Network class has been given very similar attributes that operate on a class-wide basis and on a per-instance basis. As mentioned earlier, an intentional aspect of this class design is to provide two different kinds of services: services meant to be called on the built-in network and services meant to be called on new experimental networks that can be conjured up by the folks at the Ministry of Magic. The former types of services are based on the attributes defined as static variables and the latter on the attributes defined as instance variables.

randomness is introduced, note that when a direct connection is made between two Node instances, we say that there is a Link between them. The Link class is also defined in Section 11.9.

Regarding how randomness is introduced in network connections, let's examine the code in the definition of the method initializeBuiltInNetwork(): we visit each Node instance in the for loop and, standing at each node, we examine all other Node instances one at a time in order to decide whether we should construct a direct link to that node from where we are standing. That decision is made by tossing a loaded coin that shows heads with probability p and tails with probability $1 - p$. If we see the head, we connect, otherwise we do not. In computer code, tossing a loaded coin can be simulated by firing up a pseudorandom number generator that spits out real numbers that are uniformly distributed between 0 and 1. If the number produced by the pseudorandom number generator is less than p, we can construe that as a loaded coin showing heads with probability p. The call to initializeBuiltInNetwork() also assigns distances to these links. In the implementation shown below, these distances are random numbers between 0 and 100.[7]

Since a wizard might wish to look at a map of the entire Floo network, the Network class must provide a method for doing so. The built-in network can be viewed through the static methods displayNetwork() and displayNeighborhoods(). These two methods show the network in two different yet complementary ways. The first, displayNetwork(), displays each direct link separately, listing the start Node, the end Node, and the distance inbetween. On the other hand, displayNeighborhoods() displays the network one neighborhood at a time. As stated earlier, a neighborhood consists of a Node along with all the other Node instances that are directly connected to the former. It is easier to get a sense of the local connectivity available at a Node instance when you can directly see its neighborhood, as produced by the second display.

It goes without saying that the most important function of the Network class is to create routes in the network between a given start Node and a given destination Node. Toward that end, the class includes the static method findShortestPath() for finding the shortest path between any two Node instances in the built-in network. The same functionality for newly conjured-up networks is provided by the instance method findShortestPath2(). Both of these methods use basically the same code for implementing the Dijkstra's algorithm for finding the shortest paths in a graph. Nonetheless, *we have chosen to keep them separate to make it easier for a reader to extend the demonstration code along the lines indicated in Section 11.12, "Playing with the Code."*

So far our discussion has been mostly about the static methods that work specifically on the built-in network. The last section of the class contains instance methods meant for working with new networks that can be created by constructing new instances of the Network class. The instance versions of the network initialization routines are different because of the difficulties associated with the entry of all of the information needed for the instantiation of a new network.

---

[7]The readers are likely to say that the built-in network, by its very definition, should have no randomness in it. Built-in, after all, means that you have certain locations that are fixed stops in the network. Note that the randomness we are talking about for the built-in network does NOT alter the network after it is initialized. After a built-in network is brought into existence through calls to the two initialization routines, it operates as a fixed and unchangeable network for the rest of the time the code is running. So the randomness is only from one run of the demonstration to another. We believe such randomness is educational, in the sense that it allows us to investigate how the performance of the different algorithms, such as the shortest path algorithm, depends on the network topology.

```
import java.util.*;

public class Network {

    //Static variables that store information on the built-in network:
    private static List<String> networkAddressesBuiltIn =
            new ArrayList<String>( Arrays.asList(
                                    "Diagon Alley",
                                    "Knockturn Alley",
                                    "Gryffindor Commons",
                                    "DADA Professor's Office",
                                    "Dolores Umbridge's Office",
                                    "The Burrow",
                                    "Ministry of Magic Atrium",
                                    "12 Grimmauld Place"
                                   ) );
    private static List<Node> networkLocationsBuiltIn =
                                            new ArrayList<Node>();
    private static Map<Node, ArrayList<Node>> neighborhoodsBuiltIn =
                            new HashMap<Node, ArrayList<Node>>();
    private static List<Link> networkArcsBuiltIn =
                                            new ArrayList<Link>();


    // Instance variables for extensions to the floo network:
    private List<String> networkAddresses = new ArrayList<String>();
    private List<Node> networkLocations = new ArrayList<Node>();
    private Map<String,Node> networkNodesHash =
                                        new HashMap<String,Node>();
    private Map<Node, ArrayList<Node>> neighborhoods =
                            new HashMap<Node, ArrayList<Node>>();
    private List<Link> networkLinks = new ArrayList<Link>();


    // Static methods for services from the built-in floo network:
    private static void initializeBuiltInNetworkNodes() {
        Iterator<String> lit =
                            networkAddressesBuiltIn.listIterator();
        while (lit.hasNext()) {
            networkLocationsBuiltIn.add( new Node( lit.next()) );
        }
        System.out.println(
                "Total number of nodes in the network: "
                        + networkLocationsBuiltIn.size() + "\n");
    }
    public static void initializeBuiltInNetwork(){
        initializeBuiltInNetworkNodes();
        double p = 0.6;
        Object[]  arr = networkLocationsBuiltIn.toArray();
        for(int i=0; i < arr.length; i++){
            for(int j=i; j < arr.length; j++){
```

```
                if ( (j != i) &&  (Math.random() < p) ) {
                    Node nn1 = (Node) arr[i];
                    Node nn2 = (Node) arr[j];
                    networkArcsBuiltIn.add(
                        new Link(nn1, nn2,  (int)(100*Math.random())));
                    List<Node> neighborhood =
                                    neighborhoodsBuiltIn.get( nn1 );
                    if (neighborhood == null) {
                        neighborhoodsBuiltIn.put(
                          nn1,new ArrayList<Node>(Arrays.asList(nn2)));
                    }else {
                        neighborhood.add( nn2 );
                    }
                    neighborhood = neighborhoodsBuiltIn.get( nn2 );
                    if (neighborhood == null) {
                        neighborhoodsBuiltIn.put(
                          nn2,new ArrayList<Node>(Arrays.asList(nn1)));
                    }else {
                        neighborhood.add( nn1 );
                    }
                }
            }
        }
    }
    public static void displayNetwork() {
        System.out.println( "Displaying the network:\n" );
        int s = networkArcsBuiltIn.size();
        System.out.println(
            "Number of direct connections in the network: " + s + "\n" );
        Iterator<Link> lit = networkArcsBuiltIn.listIterator();
        while (lit.hasNext()) {
            System.out.println( lit.next() );
        }
    }
    public static void displayNeighborhoods() {
        System.out.println("   Displaying neighborhoods constructed:\n");
        for ( Object key: neighborhoodsBuiltIn.keySet() ) {
            System.out.println( "    " + key + ": "
                                    + neighborhoodsBuiltIn.get(key) );
        }
    }
    public static int getDirectConnectionDistanceBetweenTwoNodes(
                                    Node nn1, Node nn2 ) {
        Link dc = null;
        dc = new Link( nn1, nn2 );
        for (Link conn: networkArcsBuiltIn) {
            if (dc.equals(conn)) {
                return conn.getDirectDistance();
            }
        }
        return -1;
    }
```

```
//Shortest path calculation based on Dijkstra's algorithm:
public static Path findShortestPath( String place1,
                String place2, boolean debug )  throws Exception {
    Node start = new Node(place1);
    Node destination = new Node(place2);
    if ( !Network.isLocationInNetwork( start ) ||
                !Network.isLocationInNetwork( destination ) )
        throw new Exception(
            "Either the start or the destination node does not "
          + "exist in the shortest path calculation");
    Set<Node> keyset = neighborhoodsBuiltIn.keySet();
    boolean keymatch = false;
    for (Node key: keyset) {
        if (start.equals(key) ) keymatch = true;
    }
    if (!keymatch) throw new Exception(
                "Start node is disconnected from the network");
    List<Path> pathsToDestExplored = new ArrayList<Path>();
    Collection<Node> visitedNodes = new HashSet<Node>();
    List<Path> listOfPaths = new ArrayList<Path>();
    Path initialPath = new Path( start );
    if (debug) System.out.println( "The initial path is: "
                                            + initialPath );
    listOfPaths.add( initialPath );
    int i = 0;
    boolean somePathExtended = false;
    while (visitedNodes.size() <
                        (networkLocationsBuiltIn.size() -1)) {
        somePathExtended = false;
        if (listOfPaths.size() == 0) break;
        i++;
        Path pathArray[] = new Path[ listOfPaths.size() ];
        listOfPaths.toArray( pathArray );
        Arrays.sort( pathArray );
        listOfPaths.clear();
        for (Path pa: pathArray ) {
            listOfPaths.add(pa);
        }
        List<Path> newListOfPaths = new ArrayList<Path>();
        for (Path pa: listOfPaths ) {
            if (pa.getLastNode().equals(destination)) {
                pathsToDestExplored.add(pa);
            } else {
                newListOfPaths.add(pa);
            }
        }
        listOfPaths = newListOfPaths;
        if (listOfPaths.size() == 0) break;
        Path path = listOfPaths.get(0);
        Node nn = path.getLastNode();
        boolean nodeAlreadyExpanded = false;
```

```java
            for (Node seen: visitedNodes) {
                if (nn.equals(seen)) {
                    nodeAlreadyExpanded = true;
                    break;
                }
            }
            if (nodeAlreadyExpanded) {
                listOfPaths.remove(0);
                if (listOfPaths.size() == 0) break;
                continue;
            }
            visitedNodes.add(nn);
            List<Node> neighbors = null;
            boolean hasNeighbors = false;
            for ( Object key: neighborhoodsBuiltIn.keySet() ) {
                if (nn.equals( (Node) key )) {
                    neighbors = neighborhoodsBuiltIn.get( key );
                    if (neighbors != null) hasNeighbors = true;
                }
            }
            if (!hasNeighbors) continue;
            for (Node nei: neighbors ) {
                Path newpath = new Path( path );
                newpath.extendPath( nei );
                listOfPaths.add( newpath );
                somePathExtended = true;
            }
            listOfPaths.remove(0);
            if (!somePathExtended) break;
        }
        if (pathsToDestExplored.size() == 0)
            throw new Exception( "There exists no path between "
                        + start + " and " + destination );
        Path pathsToDestExploredArray[] =
                            new Path[pathsToDestExplored.size()];
        pathsToDestExplored.toArray( pathsToDestExploredArray );
        Arrays.sort( pathsToDestExploredArray );
        return pathsToDestExploredArray[0];
    }
    public static boolean isLocationInNetwork( Node location ) {
        for ( Node ele: networkLocationsBuiltIn ) {
            if (location.equals( ele )) return true;
        }
        return false;
    }

    // Instance methods for services from extensions to Floo net:
    public void setNetworkAddressesAndLocations( String[] places ) {
        for (String place: places) {
            networkAddresses.add( place );
            Node nn = new Node(place);
            networkLocations.add(nn);
```

```
            networkNodesHash.put(place, nn);
    }
}
public void setNetworkLink( String place1, String place2,
                              int distance ) throws Exception {
    if (!networkAddresses.contains(place1) ||
                  !networkAddresses.contains(place2))
        throw new Exception(
                      "Incorrect name entered for place name");
    Link newlink = new Link(networkNodesHash.get(place1),
                        networkNodesHash.get(place2), distance);
    for (Link ln: networkLinks) {
        if (ln.equals(newlink)) {
            throw new
               Exception("Link created previously --- not allowed");
        }
    }
    networkLinks.add( newlink );
}
public void createNeighborhoods() throws Exception {
    if (networkLocations.size() == 0 || networkLinks.size() == 0)
        throw new Exception( "Either the nodes or the arcs have "
                         + "not yet been initialized in the "
                         + "network");
    for (Node node: networkLocations) {
        for (Link dc: networkLinks) {
            if ( node.equals( dc.getStartNode() ) ) {
                List<Node> neighborhood = neighborhoods.get(node);
                if (neighborhood == null) {
                    neighborhoods.put( node,
                        new ArrayList<Node>(
                          Arrays.asList(dc.getDestinationNode())));
                }else {
                    neighborhood.add( dc.getDestinationNode());
                }
            }
            if ( node.equals( dc.getDestinationNode() ) ) {
                List<Node> neighborhood = neighborhoods.get(node);
                if (neighborhood == null) {
                    neighborhoods.put( node, new ArrayList<Node>(
                              Arrays.asList(dc.getStartNode())));
                }else {
                    neighborhood.add( dc.getStartNode());
                }
            }
        }
    }
}

// When you define a network instance one neighborhood at a time,
// you have got to make sure that the direct distances between the
// nodes are consistent from one neighborhood definition to another.
```

```java
public void defineOneNeighborhood( String place,
        String[] neighbors, int[] distances) throws Exception {
    if (networkLocations.size() == 0)
        throw new Exception("The nodes have not yet been "
                        + "initialized in the network");
    if (neighbors.length != distances.length)
        throw new Exception( "The number of neighbors and "
                        + "the numbers of distances must "
                        + "be the same");
    ArrayList<Node> newneighbors = new ArrayList<Node>();
    Node start = null;
    for (Node nd: networkLocations) {
        if (place == nd.toString()) {
            start = nd;
        }
    }
    if (start == null) {
        start = new Node(place);
    }
    List<Link> newNetworkLinks = new ArrayList<Link>();
    for (int i=0;i<neighbors.length;i++) {
        boolean link_previously_created = false;
        Node destination = new Node(neighbors[i]);
        Link newlink = new Link(start, destination, distances[i]);
        for (Link ln: networkLinks) {
            if ( ln.equals(newlink) ) {
                if (ln.getDirectDistance() != newlink.getDirectDistance
                        ()) {throw new Exception("Link created previously
                        with a " + "different distance--- not allowed in
                        undirected graphs");
                } else {
                    link_previously_created = true;
                    break;
                }
            }
        }
        if (!link_previously_created) {
            newNetworkLinks.add( newlink );
            link_previously_created = false;
        }
        newneighbors.add( destination );
    }
    networkLinks.addAll(newNetworkLinks);
    neighborhoods.put(  start, newneighbors );
}
public void displayNetwork2() {
    System.out.println( "Displaying the network:\n" );
    Iterator<Link> lit = networkLinks.listIterator();
    while (lit.hasNext()) {
        System.out.println( lit.next() );
    }
}
```

```java
public void displayNeighborhoods2() {
    System.out.println("\n    Displaying neighborhoods constructed:\n");
    for ( Object key: neighborhoods.keySet() ) {
      System.out.println( "    " + key + ": " + neighborhoods.get(key) );
    }
}
public  int getDirectConnectionDistanceBetweenTwoNodes2( Node nn1,
                                                         Node nn2 ) {
    Link dc = new Link( nn1, nn2 );
    for (Link conn: networkLinks) {
        if (dc.equals(conn)) {
            return conn.getDirectDistance();
        }
    }
    return -1;
}
// The implementation shown below for the per-instance method for
// shortest path calculation is basically the same as in the static method
// presented earlier. This is for the convenience of a reader who wishes
// to create a best-path calculator as suggested in Section 11.12. Modify
// the code shown below for best-path calculations in newly conjured up
// extensions to the built-in Floo network.
public Path findShortestPath2( String place1, String place2,
                               boolean debug ) throws Exception {
    Node start = new Node(place1);
    Node destination = new Node(place2);
     if ( !isLocationInNetwork2( start ) ||
                 !isLocationInNetwork2( destination ) )
        throw new Exception( "Either the start or the "
                         + "destination node does not exist "
                         + "for shortest path calculation");
    Set<Node> keyset = neighborhoods.keySet();
    boolean keymatch = false;
    for (Node key: keyset) {
        if (start.equals(key) ) keymatch = true;
    }
    if (!keymatch) throw new Exception(
            "Start node is disconnected from the network");
    List<Path> pathsToDestExplored = new ArrayList<Path>();
    Collection<Node> visitedNodes = new HashSet<Node>();
    List<Path> listOfPaths = new ArrayList<Path>();
    Path initialPath = new Path( start, this );
    if (debug) System.out.println( "The initial path is: "
                                          + initialPath );
    listOfPaths.add( initialPath );
    int i = 0;
    boolean somePathExtended = false;
    while (visitedNodes.size() < (networkLocations.size() -1)) {
        somePathExtended = false;
        if (listOfPaths.size() == 0) break;
        i++;
        Path pathArray[] = new Path[ listOfPaths.size() ];
```

```
listOfPaths.toArray( pathArray );
Arrays.sort( pathArray );
listOfPaths.clear();
for (Path pa: pathArray ) {
    listOfPaths.add(pa);
}
List<Path> newListOfPaths = new ArrayList<Path>();
for (Path pa: listOfPaths ) {
    if (pa.getLastNode().equals(destination)) {
        pathsToDestExplored.add(pa);
    } else {
        newListOfPaths.add(pa);
    }
}
listOfPaths = newListOfPaths;
if (listOfPaths.size() == 0) break;
Path path = listOfPaths.get(0);
Node nn = path.getLastNode();
boolean nodeAlreadyExpanded = false;
for (Node seen: visitedNodes) {
    if (nn.equals(seen)) {
        nodeAlreadyExpanded = true;
        break;
    }
}
if (nodeAlreadyExpanded) {
    listOfPaths.remove(0);
    continue;
}
visitedNodes.add(nn);
List<Node> neighbors = null;
boolean hasNeighbors = false;
for ( Object key: neighborhoods.keySet() ) {
    if (nn.equals( (Node) key )) {
        neighbors = neighborhoods.get( key );
        if (neighbors != null) hasNeighbors = true;
    }
}
if (!hasNeighbors) continue;
for (Node nei: neighbors ) {
    Path newpath = new Path( path, this );
    newpath.extendPath2( nei, this );
    listOfPaths.add( newpath );
    somePathExtended = true;
}
listOfPaths.remove(0);
if (!somePathExtended) break;
}
if (pathsToDestExplored.size() == 0)
        throw new Exception("There exists no path between "
                                + place1 + " and " + place2);
Path pathsToDestExploredArray[] =
```

```
                             new Path[ pathsToDestExplored.size() ];
        pathsToDestExplored.toArray( pathsToDestExploredArray );
        Arrays.sort( pathsToDestExploredArray );
        return pathsToDestExploredArray[0];
    }
    public boolean isLocationInNetwork2( Node location ) {
        for ( Node ele: networkLocations ) {
            if (location.equals( ele )) return true;
        }
        return false;
    }
}
```

11.9   THE Node, Link, AND Path CLASSES

Having introduced the Network class in the previous section, our goal here is to present the building blocks of a network — the Node, Link, and the Path classes. We start with the Node class.

As the reader knows, the main purpose of the Node class is to represent a street address as a node in the Floo network. Note the implementations of the equals() and hashCode() methods for this class. The equals() method plays a key role when you store instances of type Node in a container and you are searching for whether one of those nodes is the same as a query node. Calling a predicate such as contains() on a container in the Java Collections Framework with its argument set to a Node will use your definition of equals() to find the truth value for the predicate. The method hashCode() is used to figure out the hash address of an instance of type Node, the hash code being needed for storing instances of type Node in a hash table. The implementation of equals() must be consistent with that of hashCode(). That is, if two instances of type Node are considered to be equal according to the implementation of equals(), their hash codes as spit out by the implementation of hashCode() must be identical.

```
public class Node {
    private String location;
    public Node( String location ) {
     this.location = location;
    }
    public String toString() {
     return location;
    }
    public boolean equals( Node other ) {
     if (location == other.location) {
     return true;
     }
     return false;
    }
    public int hashCode() {
     return  3 ^ 19 + location.hashCode();
    }
}
```

The Link class that follows is for representing the direct links in the Floo network. (We sometimes refer to direct links as *arcs*.) We provide the class with two constructors, one that only needs the two nodes at the two ends of a direct link and the other that requires you to also specify the distance between the nodes. Note also the override definition for the equals() method. As the code shown implies, we consider two Link instances to be the same if the nodes at their two ends are the same, regardless of the order. This amounts to representing a Floo network by an undirected graph. So a link from A to B is the same as a link from B to A.

```java
public class Link {
    private Node start;
    private Node destination;
    private int distance;

    public Link( Node start, Node destination, int distance ) {
        this.start = start;
        this.destination = destination;
        this.distance = distance;
    }
    public Link( Node start, Node destination )  {
        this.start = start;
        this.destination = destination;
    }
    public boolean equals( Link other) {
        if ( ( ( ( start.equals( other.start ) )
            && (destination.equals(other.destination) ) )  ||
                ( ( start.equals( other.destination ) )
            && (destination.equals(other.start) ) ) ) ) {
            return true;
        }
        return false;
    }
    public int getDirectDistance() {
        return distance;
    }
    public Node getStartNode() { return start; }
    public Node getDestinationNode() { return destination; }
    public String toString() {
        return "    Direct connection:    " + start + " <=> "
                            + destination + ": " + distance;
    }
}
```

That takes us to the last of the building-block classes needed for a network — Path. How the Path class is programmed has a great bearing on the code for the implementation of Dijkstra's shortest path algorithm in the Network class.

We must obviously be able to quickly find the shortest path in a list of paths. This task can be easily accomplished if we can sort the list in ascending order of the path lengths and simply return the first path as the one with the shortest length. The easiest way to sort

a collection in Java is to make the class `Comparable`, which is what we have done below. Making a class `Comparable` implies extending the `Comparable` interface and implementing its `compareTo()` method. The implementation code for `compareTo()` tells the system when an instance of `Path` may be considered to be shorter than, equal to, or greater than another instance of `Path`.

Since `Path` is just a sequence of `Node` instances, displaying a path and sequentially searching for a specific node in a path become easy if we also make the class `Iterable`. Toward that end, the `Path` class also implements the `Iterable` interface. This is accomplished by implementing the `iterator()` method of this interface in the definition of the Path class.

As indicated by the instance variables shown in the class definition that follows, a path is stored as a sequence of `Node` instances in the list `nodeSequence` that is initialized to an empty list. For each path, we also maintain its length in the instance variable `pathLength` and the last node that was added to the path as the variable `lastNode`. These three instance variables are all that one needs in order to interact with the built-in Floo network that is brought into existence with the help of the static methods of the `Network` class. When `Path` is used for the new networks created by the instance methods of the `Network` class, we need an additional instance variable in the `Path` class — the instance variable named `network`.

Note the different constructor modes for the `Path` class. Typically, a path comes into existence with a start node. For this we need the first constructor shown. Obviously, the value of `pathLength` for such a path will be the default of 0 since at this point there exists only one `Node` instance on the path. The next constructor, actually more a copy constructor, is useful for constructing a deep copy of a path. The path returned by this constructor is based on fresh memory allocations for the nodes in the argument path. The next three constructors take a `Network` instance as one of the arguments. These do the same thing as the first two constructors but for the special case of newly instantiated networks, as opposed to the built-in network.

Note the implementation for the `compareTo()` method that must be provided since the class implements the `Comparable` interface. It is this implementation that allows us to call `sort()` directly on a list of `Path` instances in the shortest path calculations in the `Network` class.

The method `getLastNode()` retrieves the node that is currently at the head of a path; this is the node that was added most recently to the path. Finally, there is the `iterator()` method from the Iterable interface that is implemented by the `Path` class in order to make this class iterable with respect to the nodes on a path. This method must return an `Iterable` instance that has the methods `hasNext()` and `next()` defined for it. In our case, the object returned by `iterable()` is an instance of the inner class `PathIterathor` whose definition is at the end of the `Path` class.

```
import java.util.*;

public class Path implements Comparable<Path>, Iterable<Node> {
    private List<Node> nodeSequence = new ArrayList<Node>();
    private int pathLength = 0;
    private Node lastNode;
    private Network network;
```

```
public Path( Node nn ) {
    nodeSequence.add(nn);
    lastNode = nn;
}
public Path( Path otherPath ) {
    for (Node nn: otherPath) {
        if (nn == null) continue;
        nodeSequence.add( nn );
        if (nodeSequence.size() == 1) {
            pathLength = 0;
        } else {
            pathLength +=
                Network.getDirectConnectionDistanceBetweenTwoNodes(
                                            lastNode, nn );
        }
        lastNode = nn;
    }
}
public Path( Network network ) {
    this.network = network;
}
public Path( Node nn, Network network ) {
    nodeSequence.add(nn);
    lastNode = nn;
    this.network = network;
}
// The second arg 'network' in the following method is to supply it
// with a reference to the underlying network so that it can
// get access to inter-node distances for calculating path lengths.
public Path( Path otherPath, Network network ) {
    this.network = network;
    for (Node nn: otherPath) {
        if (nn == null) continue;
        nodeSequence.add( nn );
        if (nodeSequence.size() == 1) {
            pathLength = 0;
        } else {
            pathLength +=
                network.getDirectConnectionDistanceBetweenTwoNodes2(
                                            lastNode, nn );
        }
        lastNode = nn;
    }
}
public void extendPath( Node nn ) {
    nodeSequence.add(nn);
    Node oldLastNode = lastNode;
    lastNode = nn;
    // The logic of shortest path calculation ensures
    // that the following statement will only be invoked if
    // there is a direct path between the last node on the path
```

```
        // and the argument node nn:
        pathLength +=
            Network.getDirectConnectionDistanceBetweenTwoNodes(
                                        oldLastNode, lastNode );
    }
    // The following version is for non-static versions of the network.
    // The second arg supplies a reference to the network in which the
    // path is to be extended.
    public void extendPath2( Node nn, Network net ) {
        network = net;
        nodeSequence.add(nn);
        Node oldLastNode = lastNode;
        lastNode = nn;
        pathLength +=
            network.getDirectConnectionDistanceBetweenTwoNodes2(
                                        oldLastNode, lastNode );
    }
    public String toString() {
        String outputString = "";
        for ( Node nn: nodeSequence ) {
            outputString += nn + " : ";
        }
        outputString += " length: " + pathLength;
        return outputString;
    }
    public int getPathLength() {
        return pathLength;
    }
    public int compareTo( Path other ) {
        if ( pathLength < other.pathLength ) {
        return -1;
        } else if ( pathLength > other.pathLength ) {
            return 1;
        }
        return 0;
    }
    public boolean lessThan(Path other ) {
        if ( pathLength < other.pathLength ) return true;
        return false;
    }
    public Node getLastNode() {
        return lastNode;
    }
    public Iterator<Node> iterator() {
        return new PathIterator( nodeSequence.toArray() );
    }


    ////////////////// Inner class: PathIterator //////////////
    class PathIterator implements Iterator<Node> {
        private int index = 0;
        private Object[] pathAsArray = null;
        public PathIterator( Object[] collection ) {
```

```
            pathAsArray = collection;
        }
        public boolean hasNext() {
            return index < pathAsArray.length;
        }
        public Node next() {
            if (hasNext()) {
                return (Node) pathAsArray[index++];
            } else {
                throw new NoSuchElementException();
            }
        }
        public void remove() {
            throw new UnsupportedOperationException();
        }
    }
}
```

11.10   THE THREE CONCRETE Facade CLASSES

As stated earlier, our demonstration of the Facade pattern is based on three usage views of a Floo network for the three different categories of the wizards. These views are the three concrete subclasses of the abstract root Facade: UnderageWizardFacade, WizardFacade, and WarlockFacade.

We now present the first — and the simplest — of these concrete subclasses: the UnderageWizardFacade class. Our definition of this class is simple since the root class Facade, presented earlier in Section 11.7, already defines all of the basic functionality of a Floo network — which is the only functionality that we allow for an underage wizard. The basic functionality refers to using the built-in Floo network for just transportation, which is something you expect every wizard to be able to engage in. Therefore, all that the class definition shown below does is to pass through the functionality already defined in the parent class Facade and to throw exceptions if an underage wizard attempts to call methods that he is not allowed to use.

```
public class UnderageWizardFacade extends Facade {

    public Network constructNewFlooNetwork( String[] placeNames )
                                            throws Exception{
        throw new Exception( "An underage wizard is not allowed to "
                        + "construct a new network");
    }
    public boolean checkForLocationOnShortestPath( String start,
            String destination, String place ) throws Exception {
        throw new Exception( "An underage wizard is not allowed to "
                        + "query the network in this manner");
    }
```

```
    public boolean doesGivenPathPassThroughLocation( Path path,
                           String location ) throws Exception {
        throw new Exception( "An underage wizard is not allowed to "
                           + "query the network in this manner");
    }
}
```

The next class, `WizardFacade`, is meant for grown-up wizards. In addition to making available the basic functionality defined originally in the root class `Facade`, this new class makes it possible for a grown-up wizard to avoid particular addresses in the Floo network that may house enemies. A wizard may invoke this functionality in two different ways:

```
    checkForLocationOnShortestPath()
    doesGivenPathPassThroughLocation()
```

See the end of Section 11.7 for the difference between these two methods and how a grown-up wizard would use them for avoiding enemies in the Floo network.

For obvious reasons, the `WizardFacade` class must not allow a wizard to invoke that functionality of the Network class that is meant specifically for the folks at the Floo Network Authority. We are referring to the ability to instantiate a new network from the Network class. That is, only a warlock should be able to call a method like `constructNewFlooNetwork()` that was originally declared, but not implemented, in the root abstract class `Facade`. As the reader can see from the implementation of the first method shown below, if a regular wizard were to call `constructNewFlooNetwork()`, the method would throw an exception.

```
import java.util.*;

public class WizardFacade extends Facade {
    public Network constructNewFlooNetwork( String[] placeNames )
                                          throws Exception{
        throw new Exception("Only a warlock can construct a new "
                          + "floo network");
    }
    public boolean checkForLocationOnShortestPath( String start,
              String destination, String place ) throws Exception {
        initializeBuiltinNetwork();
        Path path = Network.findShortestPath( start, destination,
                                              false );
        Iterator<Node> it = path.iterator();
        Node node = new Node(place);
        boolean answer = false;
        while (it.hasNext()) {
            if (node.equals( it.next() )) {
                answer = true;
                break;
```

```
            }
        }
        return answer;
    }
    public boolean doesGivenPathPassThroughLocation( Path path,
                                 String place ) throws Exception {
        initializeBuiltinNetwork();
        Iterator<Node> it = path.iterator();
        Node node = new Node(place);
        boolean answer = false;
        while (it.hasNext()) {
            if (node.equals( it.next() )) {
                answer = true;
                break;
            }
        }
        return answer;
    }
}
```

Next we present the last of the three concrete Facade classes. This class, WarlockFacade, is meant to be used by warlocks, these being the wizards with extraordinary powers. We consider all those who work for the Floo Network Authority at the Ministry of Magic to belong to this category. Our focus here is on the ability of the warlocks to conjure up a new Floo network as a possible extension to the existing built-in network.

The two main methods that the class shown below provides for creating a new network are:

```
constructNewFlooNetwork()
constructNewFlooNetworkUsingNeighborhoods()
```

the former for constructing a network, one link at a time, until all of the links have been specified, and the latter for specifying a network one neighborhood at a time, until all of the neighborhoods have been specified. Since the two approaches are different in how a wizard supplies the needed information, the methods that support them are different. The sequence of calls in the two cases are shown in Figure 11.4.

The reader may also wish to note how we use the boolean instance variables in the class to make sure that the network creation methods are not called out of sequence. What we mean by that is that we cannot allow the method setNetworkLink() to be called before constructNewFlooNetwork() is called. That is because the latter must first specify the network addresses so that their corresponding Node instances can be created and put in place before the former can be called for specifying links between the node pairs drawn from the instances created by the first call. By the same token, setNeighborhoodsAndDisplayNetworkCreated() cannot be called before the links are put in place by calls to setNetworkLink() in the sequence of methods on the left in Figure 11.4. Similar reasoning applies to the use of boolean variables to control the order in which the sequence of methods shown on the right is invoked.

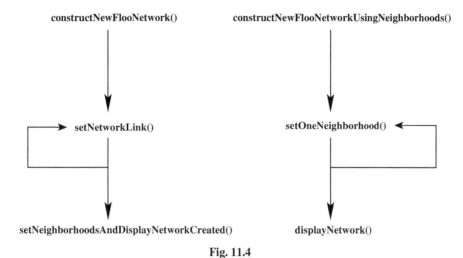

Fig. 11.4

After a warlock has created a new network, he/she would naturally want to analyze the best paths in the network between a given start node and a given destination node. This the warlock can accomplish by calling

```
findShortestPathInNewNetwork()
```

As the implementation code for this method shows, this call is directly translated into the Network class's instance method for finding the shortest paths in a network. Finally, the class includes implementations of the methods

```
checkForLocationOnShortestPath()
doesGivenPathPassThroughLocation()
```

that were declared to be abstract in the root class Facade. The reason for implementing these here is the same as in the WizardFacade class.

```java
import java.util.Iterator;

public class WarlockFacade extends Facade {
    private boolean networkAddressesAndNodesInitialized = false;
    private boolean networkLinksInitialized = false;
    private boolean networkInitialized = false;

    public Network constructNewFlooNetwork(String[] places)
                                                throws Exception{
        Network newnet = new Network();
        newnet.setNetworkAddressesAndLocations( places );
        networkAddressesAndNodesInitialized = true;
        return newnet;
    }
```

```java
public void setNetworkLink( Network net, String place1,
                 String place2, int distance ) throws Exception {
    if (!networkAddressesAndNodesInitialized)
        throw new Exception("Network nodes not yet initialized");
    net.setNetworkLink( place1, place2, distance );
    networkLinksInitialized = true;
}
public Network constructNewFlooNetworkUsingNeighborhoods(
                            String[] places) throws Exception {
    Network newnet = new Network();
    newnet.setNetworkAddressesAndLocations( places );
    networkAddressesAndNodesInitialized = true;
    return newnet;
}
public void setOneNeighborhood( Network newnet, String place,
         String[] neighbors, int[] distances ) throws Exception {
    if (!networkAddressesAndNodesInitialized)
        throw new Exception("Network nodes not yet initialized");
    newnet.defineOneNeighborhood( place, neighbors, distances);
    networkInitialized = true;
}
public void setNeighborhoodsAndDisplayNetworkCreated(
                            Network newnet ) throws Exception {
    if (! networkLinksInitialized )
        throw new Exception( "Network nodes and arcs not "
                        + "initialized");
    newnet.createNeighborhoods();
    networkInitialized = true;
    newnet.displayNetwork2();
    newnet.displayNeighborhoods2();
}
public void displayNetwork( Network newnet ) throws Exception {
    if (!networkInitialized)
        throw new Exception( "Network neighborhoods not yet "
                        + "initialized");
    newnet.displayNetwork2();
    newnet.displayNeighborhoods2();
}
public Path findShortestPathInNewNetwork( Network newnet,
                String place1, String place2 ) throws Exception {
    if (!networkInitialized)
        throw new Exception( "Network has not yet been "
                        + "initialized");
    Path bestPath =
                newnet.findShortestPath2( place1, place2, false );
    return bestPath;
}
public boolean checkForLocationOnShortestPath( String start,
            String destination, String place ) throws Exception {
    initializeBuiltinNetwork();
    Path path = Network.findShortestPath(start,destination,false );
    Iterator<Node> it = path.iterator();
```

```
        Node node = new Node(place);
        boolean answer = false;
        while (it.hasNext()) {
            if (node.equals( it.next() )) {
                answer = true;
                break;
            }
        }
        return answer;
    }
    public boolean doesGivenPathPassThroughLocation( Path path,
                                    String place ) throws Exception {
        initializeBuiltinNetwork();
        Iterator<Node> it = path.iterator();
        Node node = new Node(place);
        boolean answer = false;
        while (it.hasNext()) {
            if (node.equals( it.next() )) {
                answer = true;
                 break;
            }
        }
        return answer;
    }
}
```

11.11   TESTING THE DEMONSTRATION CODE

In the test code shown below, we test the calls for finding the best paths in the built-in Floo network for all three concrete Facade classes. For the WizardFacade class, we also test the calls that a wizard can make to figure out if a certain address happens to be on the route returned by the network as the best route. And, finally, for the WarlockFacade class, we also test the methods that allow a warlock to construct a new network and to determine the shortest paths in the newly conjured up network.

We start with testing the UnderageWizardFacade class. Recall that the usage view represented by this class is meant for interacting with just the built-in class as specified by the static variables of the Network class. The call

```
    facade1.displayBuiltinFlooNetwork()
```

that is invoked on the instance facade1 of the UnderageWizardFacade class is actually handled by the method displayBuiltinFlooNetwork() of the root class Facade. A review of the implementation code for that method in the Facade class in Section 11.7 would reveal that, before the built-in network is actually displayed, it is initialized by calling Network.initializeBuiltInNetwork(). That initialization results in the creation of the Node and Link instances according to the specification of the built-in class. Recall that the links in the built-in network and the lengths of the various links are set randomly.

After the built-in network is initialized and displayed by the call shown above, we ask it to return the best path between "The Burrow" and the "Gryffindor Commons." Finally, as far as this facade is concerned, we do something that is illegal for the underage wizards — we invoke checkForLocationOnShortestPath(). This, as is to be expected, elicits a warning from the system.

For testing WizardFacade, we make the following call

```
facade2.checkForLocationOnShortestPath()
```

on the instance facade2 of the WizardFacade class. The implementation code for the method checkForLocationOnShortestPath() in the WizardFacade class first calls initializeBuiltinNetwork() of the root class Facade to initialize the built-in network.[8] Subsequently, the above call invokes the findShortestPath() method of the Network class to find the route that will be taken to travel from the starting point to the destination. The answer to the question posed by the above call is then answered by scanning through the nodes on this path to see if the node in question happens to be on the path. The second part of the code for testing the WizardFacade class does the same thing as what we have described so far, except that now it computes the best path separately and then asks the method doesGivenPathPassThroughLocation() to find out if a given node is on the path.

Our most extensive testing is for the WarlockFacade class. That is because this facade allows for the most radical things to be done to a network — conjuring up of a new network that could potentially be added to the existing built-in network. We start testing WarlockFacade by invoking the same two methods that we used for testing the WizardFacade class. This we do by calling

```
facade3.checkForLocationOnShortestPath()
facade3.doesGivenPathPassThroughLocation()
```

on the instance facade3 of the WarlockFacade class. As with the WizardFacade test, this produces predictable results. The rest of the testing of the WarlockFacade class consists of creating new networks with this facade. We exercise both ways of specifying a new network: one link at a time and one neighborhood at a time. After a new network is created, we test it by calculating the shortest paths in it.

```
public class TestFacade {
    public static void main( String[] args ) {

        // Test the facade for underage wizards:
        UnderageWizardFacade facade1 = new UnderageWizardFacade();
        System.out.println(
                    "Displaying the Built-In Floo Network:\n\n");
        facade1.displayBuiltinFlooNetwork();
```

---

[8]This call becomes a do-nothing call if the built-in network was initialized by a previous call through any of the other methods in any of the three facades meant for interacting with the built-in network. This is made possible by the role played by the boolean variable builtinNetworkInitialized of the Facade class, as mentioned previously in Section 11.7.

```
System.out.println("\n\nTESTING UnderageWizardFacade:\n");
try {
    Path path = facade1.travelByBuiltinFlooNetwork(
                    "The Burrow", "Gryffindor Commons");
    System.out.println( "    The path found: " + path );
} catch(Exception e)   {
    System.out.println( e.getMessage() );
}


System.out.println( "\n    Make a direct check on whether a "
                + "place will be on the shortest path between "
                + "two specified places in the network:\n");
try {
    boolean answer = facade1.checkForLocationOnShortestPath(
      "The Burrow", "Gryffindor Commons", "Knockturn Alley" );
    System.out.println( "        The answer to whether "
        + "Knockturn Alley is on the best path: " + answer);
} catch(Exception e)    {
    System.out.println( "         " + e.getMessage() );
}


// Test the facade for grownup wizards:
System.out.println("\nTESTING WizardFacade:");
WizardFacade facade2 = new WizardFacade();
System.out.println( "\n    Make a direct check on whether a "
                + "place will be on the shortest path "
                + "between two specified places in the "
                + "network:\n");
try {
    boolean answer = facade2.checkForLocationOnShortestPath(
      "The Burrow", "Gryffindor Commons", "Knockturn Alley" );
    System.out.println( "        The answer to whether  "
        + "Knockturn Alley is on the best path: " + answer);
} catch(Exception e)    {
    System.out.println( "         " + e.getMessage() );
}
System.out.println( "\n    First get the path you will "
                + "travel through the network and then "
                + "and then try to find out if a certain "
                + "location will be on the path");
try {
    Path path = facade2.travelByBuiltinFlooNetwork(
                        "The Burrow", "Gryffindor Commons");
    System.out.println( "        The path found: " + path );
    boolean answer = facade2.doesGivenPathPassThroughLocation(
                            path, "Knockturn Alley" );
    System.out.println( "        The answer to whether "
        + "Knockturn Alley is on the best path: " + answer);
} catch(Exception e)    {
    System.out.println( "         " + e.getMessage() );
}
```

```
// Test the facade for warlocks:
System.out.println("\nTESTING WarlockFacade:");
WarlockFacade facade3 = new WarlockFacade();
System.out.println( "\n    Make a direct check on whether a "
              + "place will be on the shortest path between "
              + "two specified places in the network:\n");
try {
    boolean answer = facade3.checkForLocationOnShortestPath(
                        "The Burrow", "Gryffindor Commons",
                                    "Knockturn Alley" );
    System.out.println( "         The answer to whether "
          + "Knockturn Alley is on the best path: " + answer);
} catch(Exception e)   {
    System.out.println( "          " + e.getMessage() );
}
System.out.println( "\n    First get the path you will "
        + "travel through the network and then "
        + "try to find out if a certain location will be "
        + "on the path");
try {
    Path path = facade3.travelByBuiltinFlooNetwork(
                        "The Burrow", "Gryffindor Commons");
    System.out.println( "         The path found: " + path );
    boolean answer = facade3.doesGivenPathPassThroughLocation(
                                path, "Knockturn Alley" );
    System.out.println( "         The answer to whether  "
          + "Knockturn Alley is on the best path: " + answer);
} catch(Exception e)   {
    System.out.println( "          " + e.getMessage() );
}
System.out.println("\n    Try constructing a new network "
                + "by specifying the arcs individually:");
try {
    Network newnet = facade3.constructNewFlooNetwork(
                new String[]{"nn1", "nn2", "nn3", "nn4"} );
    facade3.setNetworkLink( newnet, "nn1", "nn2", 100 );
    facade3.setNetworkLink( newnet, "nn1", "nn3", 50 );
    facade3.setNetworkLink( newnet, "nn2", "nn4", 80 );
    facade3.setNetworkLink( newnet, "nn3", "nn4", 80 );
    facade3.setNetworkLink( newnet, "nn1", "nn4", 180 );
    facade3.setNeighborhoodsAndDisplayNetworkCreated(newnet);
    Path bestPath = facade3.findShortestPathInNewNetwork(
                                newnet, "nn1", "nn4" );
    System.out.println( "         The solution path: "
                                    + bestPath );
} catch (Exception e) {
    System.out.println( "          " + e.getMessage() );
}
System.out.println("\n    Try constructing a new network by "
                + "specifying the neighborhoods individually:");
WarlockFacade facade3_new = new WarlockFacade();
try {
```

```
        Network newnet =
          facade3_new.constructNewFlooNetworkUsingNeighborhoods(
            new String[]{"nn11", "nn12", "nn13", "nn14", "nn15" } );
        facade3_new.setOneNeighborhood( newnet,
                    "nn11",  new String[]{"nn12", "nn14", "nn15"},
                                    new int[]{100, 50, 180});
        facade3_new.setOneNeighborhood( newnet,
                    "nn12",  new String[]{"nn11","nn13", "nn15"} ,
                                    new int[]{100,75, 50});
        facade3_new.setOneNeighborhood( newnet, "nn13",
 new String[]{"nn12","nn15"} , new int[]{75,80});
        facade3_new.setOneNeighborhood( newnet, "nn14",
      new String[]{"nn11","nn15"} , new int[]{50,80});
        facade3_new.displayNetwork(newnet);
        Path bestPath = facade3_new.findShortestPathInNewNetwork(
                                newnet, "nn11", "nn15" );
        System.out.println( "\n   The solution path: "
                                            + bestPath );
    } catch (Exception e) {
        System.out.println( "          " + e.getMessage() );
    }
   }
}
```

11.12 PLAYING WITH THE CODE

Download the class files for this pattern from the book website into a separate directory. Compile the code with the command

```
javac *.java
```

and execute the TestFacade class by

```
java TestFacade
```

Given the code in the main() of TestFacade, executing this class will produce an output that would look like:[9]

```
Displaying the Built-In Floo Network:

    Total number of nodes in the network: 8

    Displaying the network:

    Number of direct connections in the network: 18
```

[9]Recall, because of the randomization mentioned earlier, no two runs of the output will look exactly the same. As mentioned earlier, the degree of randomization is controlled by the probability variable p in the initializeBuiltInNetwork() method of the Network class. Also note that several of the line breaks shown in the output are a result of the constraints on the width of a printed page.

```
Direct connection:    Diagon Alley <=> Knockturn Alley: 16
Direct connection:    Diagon Alley <=> Gryffindor Commons: 37
Direct connection:    Diagon Alley <=> DADA Professor's Office: 53
Direct connection:    Diagon Alley <=> Dolores Umbridge's Office: 19
Direct connection:    Diagon Alley <=> The Burrow: 94
Direct connection:    Diagon Alley <=> 12 Grimmauld Place: 79
Direct connection:    Knockturn Alley <=> Gryffindor Commons: 78
Direct connection:    Knockturn Alley <=> Dolores Umbridge's Office: 39
Direct connection:    Knockturn Alley <=> The Burrow: 0
Direct connection:    Gryffindor Commons <=> DADA Professor's Office: 95
Direct connection:    Gryffindor Commons <=> Dolores Umbridge's Office: 71
Direct connection:    Gryffindor Commons <=> Ministry of Magic Atrium: 4
Direct connection:    DADA Professor's Office <=> Dolores Umbridge's
                                                          Office: 49
Direct connection:    DADA Professor's Office <=> The Burrow: 44
Direct connection:    DADA Professor's Office <=> Ministry of Magic
                                                           Atrium: 47
Direct connection:    DADA Professor's Office <=> 12 Grimmauld Place: 96
Direct connection:    Dolores Umbridge's Office <=> Ministry of Magic
                                                           Atrium: 59
Direct connection:    Dolores Umbridge's Office <=> 12 Grimmauld Place: 97
```

Displaying direct connection neighborhoods in the network:

Displaying neighborhoods constructed:

```
Gryffindor Commons: [Diagon Alley, Knockturn Alley, DADA Professor's
                            Office, Dolores Umbridge's Office, Ministry
                            of Magic Atrium]
12 Grimmauld Place: [Diagon Alley, DADA Professor's Office,
                                       Dolores Umbridge's Office]
Dolores Umbridge's Office: [Diagon Alley, Knockturn Alley, Gryffindor
            Commons, DADA Professor's Office, Ministry of Magic Atrium,
            12 Grimmauld Place]
Diagon Alley: [Knockturn Alley, Gryffindor Commons, DADA Professor's
                            Office, Dolores Umbridge's Office, The Burrow,
                            12 Grimmauld Place]
DADA Professor's Office: [Diagon Alley, Gryffindor Commons,
                Dolores Umbridge's Office, The Burrow, Ministry of
                Magic Atrium, 12 Grimmauld Place]
Ministry of Magic Atrium: [Gryffindor Commons, DADA Professor's Office,
                                       Dolores Umbridge's Office]
The Burrow: [Diagon Alley, Knockturn Alley, DADA Professor's Office]
Knockturn Alley: [Diagon Alley, Gryffindor Commons, Dolores Umbridge's
                                                   Office, The Burrow]
```

TESTING UnderageWizardFacade:

```
The path found: The Burrow : Knockturn Alley : Diagon Alley :
                                   Gryffindor Commons :  length: 53
```

Make a direct check on whether a place will be on the shortest path
                                    between two specified places in the network:

    An underage wizard is not allowed to query the network in this manner

TESTING WizardFacade:

    Make a direct check on whether a place will be on the shortest path
                                    between two specified places in the network:

        The answer to whether Knockturn Alley is on the best path: true

    First get the path you will travel through the network and then try to
                        find out if a certain location will be on the path
        The path found: The Burrow : Knockturn Alley : Diagon Alley :
                                    Gryffindor Commons : length: 53
        The answer to whether Knockturn Alley is on the best path: true

TESTING WarlockFacade:

    Make a direct check on whether a place will be on the shortest path
                                    between two specified places in the network:

        The answer to whether Knockturn Alley is on the best path: true

    First get the path you will travel through the network and then try to
                        find out if a certain location will be on the path
        The path found: The Burrow : Knockturn Alley : Diagon Alley :
                                    Gryffindor Commons : length: 53
        The answer to whether Knockturn Alley is on the best path: true

    Try constructing a new network by specifying the arcs individually:

    Displaying the network:

    Direct connection: nn1 <=> nn2: 100
    Direct connection: nn1 <=> nn3: 50
    Direct connection: nn2 <=> nn4: 80
    Direct connection: nn3 <=> nn4: 80
    Direct connection: nn1 <=> nn4: 180

    Displaying neighborhoods constructed:

    nn2: [nn1, nn4]
    nn1: [nn2, nn3, nn4]
    nn4: [nn2, nn3, nn1]
    nn3: [nn1, nn4]

    The solution path: nn1 : nn3 : nn4 : length: 130

```
Try constructing a new network by specifying the neighborhoods
                                              individually:


Displaying the network:

Direct connection:    nn11 <=> nn12: 100
Direct connection:    nn11 <=> nn14: 50
Direct connection:    nn11 <=> nn15: 180
Direct connection:    nn12 <=> nn13: 75
Direct connection:    nn12 <=> nn15: 50
Direct connection:    nn13 <=> nn15: 80
Direct connection:    nn14 <=> nn15: 80


Displaying neighborhoods constructed:

nn14: [nn11, nn15]
nn13: [nn12, nn15]
nn12: [nn11, nn13, nn15]
nn11: [nn12, nn14, nn15]


The solution path: nn11 : nn14 : nn15 :  length: 130
```

For additional insights, you can extend the code for this pattern on your own along the following lines:

- You can reduce the size of the Network class significantly by eliminating the distinction between the static built-in network meant for ordinary wizards and the network instances that can be created at runtime by the folks in the Ministry of Magic. Although this distinction makes for an interesting narrative — since you can talk about the main network that must remain fixed for ordinary wizards as they cannot be expected to have the ability to change it — you could try creating your own version of the Facade demonstration without this distinction. If you eliminate this distinction, you will have to figure out other ways to keep network instances from being created by wizards who are not allowed to do so.

- It would be nice to expand the scope of the Node class by including in it an attribute that indicates the degree of desirability of including a node in a path. (The desirability of a node could depend on the perceived safety of the node with regard to the dangers posed by the wizards who live at that address.) The point here is that the shortest path with an undesirable node may be less preferable than a longer path that does not include any undesirable nodes. If you take on this project, you would need to implement a best-path calculator that modifies the logic of the shortest path calculation algorithm in order to take into account the desirability weights associated with the nodes. You'd find it easiest to make these changes to the per-instance version of the shortest path calculator in the Network class. In fact, that per-instance method was placed there specifically for this purpose.

- A demonstration such as the one in this chapter cries out for a GUI-based tool through which a user can interact with the software. The GUI should have buttons that when clicked should display the Floo network. A user should be able to use button clicks to

designate both his/her current address and the desired destination address and have the GUI display the route chosen. An advanced version of such a GUI could also include convenient data-entry mechanisms if a user wanted to create new extensions to the built-in Floo network. If you are up to it, see if you provide a GUI-based tool for interacting with the software shown here.

12

FLYWEIGHT

12.1 THE IDEA OF CUSTOMIZED DUPLICATIONS

Let's say you are in possession of a special object that is known for its unique qualities. Assume that there exists only one such object. If there is a need for additional such objects, why not construct them by copying the object in your possession? The alternative would be to start from scratch for each new copy of the object by specifying values for all its properties, and then actually building it.

Constructing a new copy of an object by duplicating the version in your possession saves you from the possibility of making errors in specifying the properties you would need for building the object from scratch. The chance of making such errors increases with the complexity of the object. When an object possesses either a large number of properties or when the values of some of the properties must be guessed, you may set a value to something that you believe is correct when in fact it is not.

The comments made above are essentially the same as in Section 5.1 of Chapter 5 on the Prototype pattern.

To go beyond the "construction by duplication" idea of the Prototype pattern, let's now consider a situation in which you have customers who want copies of the object in your possession but with variations on that object. Let's say that the singular object in your possession can be thought of as consisting of a core part and some embellishments to the core. And let's further assume that the variants of the object that are desired by your customers require changes only to the embellishments. Now the question is how to best organize the production of new versions of the object so that while the core part is directly duplicated, the embellishments are set according to the preferences expressed by your customers. It is this problem that is addressed by the Flyweight pattern.

Generalizing to the case of multiple objects in your possession, the main idea of the Flyweight pattern can be explained thus: Let's say that all the objects produced by your software consist of a small number of core forms and a large number of ways in which the core forms can be embellished. The Flyweight pattern says that it is best to store in memory all the core forms — these are likely to be instances constructed from one or a small

Designing with Objects: Object-Oriented Design Patterns Explained with Stories from Harry Potter,
First Edition. Avinash C. Kak.
© 2015 John Wiley & Sons, Inc. Published 2015 by John Wiley & Sons, Inc.

number of classes. In order to construct an object for a client, you would quickly duplicate one of the stored core forms and subsequently customize it with the client-specified
embellishment.

12.2   INTENT AND APPLICABILITY

The intent of the Flyweight pattern is to lend efficiency to the production of objects that can
be characterized by relatively invariant *intrinsic state* and a more variable *extrinsic state*.
   You should consider using the pattern when

- the objects constructed from a system of classes can be considered to be embellishments over a small number of core forms, with the core forms determining the intrinsic
state of the objects, and with the embellishments determining the extrinsic state;
- it is cheaper to produce new versions of the core forms by duplication, as opposed to
producing from scratch through constructor calls;
- object customization desired by the clients consists primarily of changing the embellishments;
- it is cheaper to optimize the production of the embellishments than the production of
the core forms.

12.3   INTRODUCTION TO THE FLYWEIGHT PATTERN

Let's consider pizza making as a metaphor for constructing software objects. Assume that
you want to deliver to your customers four very different styles of pizzas: (1) thin crust; (2)
Chicago-style deep-dish; (3) pan-style in which the bottom of the crust is made crisp by
cooking it slightly in oil in a pan; and (4) take-n-bake. As you would expect, the toppings
for each pizza would vary from order to order. If you use the Flyweight pattern, you would
not need to create a separate class for each style and each combination of toppings. *Neither*
would you need to create a single class to represent all the pizzas and have the style of
each pizza and its toppings be taken care of by the instance variables of the class. With
the Flyweight pattern, instead, you would have four classes for the four basic core styles
of pizzas. For each pizza that rolls out of your operation, you would make an instance
from one of these core classes (or, as is more likely, use a copy of an instance created
previously) and then embellish the instance with the toppings as will be explained in this
chapter. The core forms shown in Figure 12.1 correspond to the four basic pizza styles and
the embellishments to the toppings.
   The state information that would be needed for each core form in Figure 12.1 could be
referred to as constituting the *intrinsic parameters* of the objects desired by your customers.
And the additional state information you need in order to customize a core form may be
referred to as constituting the *extrinsic parameters* of the objects. Isolating the intrinsic and
the extrinsic parameters of a pizza-making process allows you to control separately the construction of the core forms of the pizzas and their embellishments, which, one could argue,
could lead to greater efficiencies overall in your pizza delivery business. For example, any
optimization applied to the intrinsic parameters of a core form would require a much more
thorough analysis and understanding (since all of the pizza instances customized from that

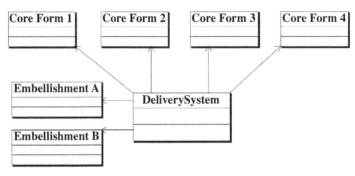

Fig. 12.1

form would be affected). Such is not likely to be the case with any optimizations applied to just the extrinsic parameters since, relatively speaking, only a small number of the final pizza instances may be affected.

12.4 THE FLYWEIGHT PATTERN IN REAL-WORLD APPLICATIONS

A real-world application of these ideas would be a purely object-oriented approach to the representation of text documents and their contents. Each character may appear an arbitrary number of times in a document. For each appearance of a given character, what would vary would be its position in the document and the font style and size used at that position. Each such appearance of a character could be an instance of a core form of that character that is embellished with the extrinsic parameters related to the position of the character and its font style and size. Such a representation of a document would give us independent control over the core forms, on the one hand, and their embellishments — especially those related to font size and style.

12.5 HARRY POTTER STORY USED TO ILLUSTRATE THE FLYWEIGHT PATTERN

Several former heads of Hogwarts are renowned for all the good things they accomplished during their tenure at the school. On account of their fame, people and organizations like to hang their portraits on their walls. These portraits are magical in the sense that the image of the same individual can travel from one portrait to another even when the two portraits are separated by a great distance. For example, in the "Order of the Phoenix" book, Dumbledore talked to the portrait of the former headmaster Professor Everard and asked the professor to go to his portrait in the Ministry of Magic to raise an alarm in order to draw attention to Arthur Weasley who lay injured at the Ministry. At the same time, Dumbledore dispatched the former headmistress Dilys Derwent to her portrait in St. Mungo's hospital to find out if Arthur had been taken to the hospital. In the same story, Dumbledore talked to the portrait of the former headmaster Phineas Nigellus Black and asked him to travel to his portrait at 12 Grimmauld Place to inform his great-great-grandson Sirius Black that Arthur

Weasley had been injured and that Arthur's wife and children, along with Harry Potter, would soon be arriving at the house.

Our demonstration of the Flyweight pattern is based on making portraits of the former heads of Hogwarts. We will assume that making such a portrait involves (1) procuring an image of the headmaster (or headmistress) from an official image archive; (2) imprinting the image on a suitable medium like paper or canvas; and, finally, (3) placing a border around the medium, *the border being the customization of the portrait for a customer*. Therefore, to draw an analogy with our earlier example, we can think of the image in a portrait as the core form and the border as the embellishment. The Flyweight pattern says that, if at all possible, when the image of a former head is procured, it should be stored away so that the same image can be used again for a future portrait request for the same headmaster or headmistress.

If we assume that the wizarding community is rather large and the number of portrait makers rather small, it is possible that a portrait maker would receive a large number of requests for the portraits of the former Hogwarts heads — especially so for those who were popular during their time at the school. So, instead of repeatedly buying the image of the same head from the image archive, it would make more sense for the portrait maker to acquire the image the first time a request is received, store that image in his/her own device of some sort, and then use it to create duplicates with customer-specific borders for subsequent orders involving the same former head. *This is exactly what the Flyweight pattern is supposed to do.*

12.6 A TOP LEVEL VIEW OF THE PATTERN DEMONSTRATION

We will imagine the following scenario through which folks in the wizarding community acquire portraits of the former headmasters and headmistresses of Hogwarts:

1. Various kinds of images, including images of the former heads of Hogwarts, are available from an official image archive — a role that will be played by the `ImageManager` class in our case. The archive sells the images to licensed portrait makers on a buy-once-use-indefinitely basis.

2. Since an image procured by a portrait maker can be used any number of times in the future, he/she must store each acquired image in his/her own database.

3. When a customer requests a portrait, the customer will also, in general, request a border of his/her own choosing for the portrait. Ordinarily, the choice of the border will be based on the colors and other symbols (such as a coat of arms) that are appropriate to the house in which the portrait is to be hung. However, for the sake of simplicity, we will assume that this customization consists merely of placing a wide color border around the image.

Our demonstration of Flyweight is based on the following "actors":

ImageManager: The primary contract of this class is to serve as the official image archive for the wizarding world. This class is supposed to make available to a client

of the class a set of images from which the client can pick and choose. (A client of this class would be a portrait maker.) `ImageManager` makes its images available through a static method called `loadImages()`. When a portrait maker calls

```
ImageManager.loadImages();
```

the portrait maker can acquire — but for inspection only — all of the images available from the archive. Subsequently the portrait maker must choose the image for the portrait order he/she has received and store it in his/her own local database. The portrait maker is only charged for the selected image. As mentioned earlier, the portrait maker need pay only once for an image.[1] After acquiring an image, he/she is free to create as many portraits as he/she wishes from that image.

HeadMasterPortrait: An instance of this class is the portrait that is made from the image that is either ordered from the `ImageManager` class or retrieved from the local storage maintained by the portrait maker. Therefore, an instance of this class is what is delivered by the portrait maker to a customer. Using an image, bought or retrieved, the job of actually creating a new portrait goes to the class `PortraitMakerAssignment`. Each portrait created by `PortraitMakerAssignment` is a combination of the image of a former head of Hogwarts and a border as selected by the customer for whom the portrait is made.

FlyweightImageStore: Recall that at the heart of the Flyweight pattern is the storage of the core parts of the portrait instances created previously, the core parts being the images of the Hogwarts heads, so that the images can be used again in future portraits of the same heads. (To remind the reader again, a portrait is a combination of an image and its border.) `FlyweightImageStore` is the portrait maker's local storage. It is a smart storage system in the sense that it acquires a new image from the `ImageManager` class only if that image was not used previously.

PortraitBorderChoices: Each order for a portrait includes a customization request, the customization consisting of a border of a particular color for the portrait. The class `PortraitBorderChoices` gives us a predefined list of colored borders for that purpose. This class is actually a Java interface. So any constants defined in the class can be accessed by any subclass directly.

PortraitMakerAssignment: A portrait maker uses this class to create a new portrait by constructing an instance of `HeadMasterPortrait`. The `HeadMasterPortrait` constructor must be supplied with the image of the headmaster (or headmistress, as the case may be) and the border to be used with the image. The image of the head is procured from the `FlyweightImageStore` class. As mentioned previously, that class will decide on its own whether it can supply the requested image from its own local store or whether it should purchase it from the official archive. On the other hand, the border is as specified by the customer.

Figure 12.2 shows a top-level view of the code for this demonstration. As mentioned, an order for a new portrait is processed by the class `PortraitMakerAssignment`.

---

[1] Actually paying for the portraits selected will not be a part of the demonstration code.

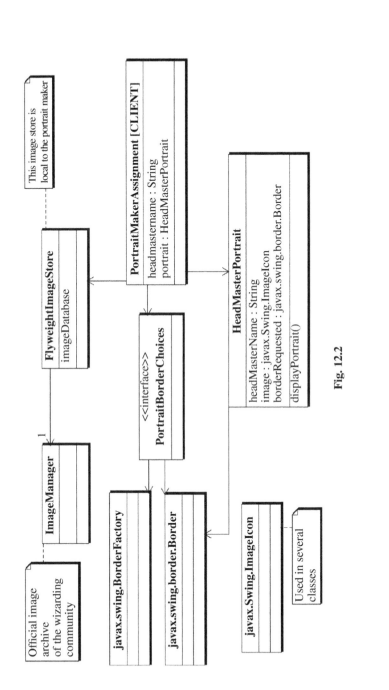

Fig. 12.2

12.7 THE HeadMasterPortrait CLASS

When a portrait maker makes a portrait from an image and the border desired by a customer, the portrait is an instance of the class shown here. When the constructor of this class is called (as it is by the PortraitMakerAssignment class in our demonstration), it must be supplied with both the image of the Hogwarts head and the image border desired by the customer.

```
import javax.swing.*;
import javax.swing.border.*;

public class HeadMasterPortrait  {

    private String headMasterName;
    private ImageIcon image;
    private Border borderRequested;

    public HeadMasterPortrait( String name, ImageIcon picture,
                                            Border border ) {
        headMasterName =name;
        image = picture;
        borderRequested = border;
    }

    public void displayPortrait() throws Exception {
        ImageManager.displaySingleImage( headMasterName,
                                    image, borderRequested );
    }
}
```

12.8 THE FlyweightImageStore CLASS

The purpose of the class defined in this section is to provide storage (used locally by the portrait maker) for the images to be used in the portraits. The images are procured from the image archive whose role is played by the ImageManager class presented in the next section. When an image is procured for the first time, it is stored away in a collection whose reference is held by the variable portraitImages in the implementation shown below.

The two static members of this class, imageDatabase and portraitImages, are both hash tables for storing images. But note that their usage semantics are very different. The imageDatabase store is made available by the image archive as represented by the ImageManager class. On the other hand, portraitImages is the local store maintained by the portrait maker for the images previously acquired from the archive.

With regard to the implementation of the getImage() method, it first checks whether an image is already in the local store portraitImages maintained by the portrait maker. If the requested image is not found there, it is fetched (or, for the sake of the storyline in this demonstration, should we say purchased) from the ImageManager vendor by retrieving the image from its imageDatabase. Any such image is then stored away in the local store portraitImages for future portraits of the same head.

The static method getPortraitImageStoreSize() can tell us how many images have so far been acquired from the ImageManager vendor and stored locally by the portrait maker. The static method howManyImagesOrderedFromImageArchive() can be used to determine how many images were ordered from the archive. Later, in Section 12.13, we will compare the integer values returned by these two methods to establish that our demonstration of the Flyweight pattern works correctly — in the sense that an image that was used previously is not ordered again from the ImageManager class for a new portrait order. Each time an image is ordered from the archive, the value of the integer static variable numberImagesOrderedFromArchive is incremented.

```java
import java.util.*;
import javax.swing.ImageIcon;

public class FlyweightImageStore {

    private static Hashtable<String,ImageIcon> imageDatabase =
                                    ImageManager.loadImages();
    private static Hashtable<String,ImageIcon> portraitImages =
                                    new Hashtable<String,ImageIcon>();
    private static int numberImagesOrderedFromArchive = 0;

    public static ImageIcon getImage( String name )
                                throws ImageNotAvailableException {
        if (portraitImages.containsKey( name ) ) {
           return portraitImages.get( name );
        }
        if ( !imageDatabase.containsKey(name) ) {
         throw new ImageNotAvailableException();
        }
        ImageIcon newImage = imageDatabase.get( name );
        numberImagesOrderedFromArchive++;
        portraitImages.put(name, newImage);
        return newImage;
    }

    public static int getPortraitImageStoreSize() {
        return portraitImages.size();
    }

    public static int howManyImagesOrderedFromImageArchive() {
        return numberImagesOrderedFromArchive;
    }
}
```

12.9   THE ImageManager CLASS

The class ImageManager presented in this section plays the role of the image vendor in our demonstration. Its static method loadImages() makes available the jpeg images in the current directory to others in the form of a hash table in which the names of the former

Hogwarts heads serve as the keys and the `ImageIcon` objects created from the jpeg images as the corresponding values.

By way of service to the wizarding world, the `ImageManager` class also provides a method for displaying the portraits put together by the portrait makers. The class also contains a slide-show method for quickly perusing all of the images in the database — just to see what images are currently in the database. This method, called `slideshow()`, is not used in the Flyweight demonstration presented here, but is available through the `ImageManager` class if the reader is interested in experimenting with it.

Going through the code in the definition of the `ImageManager` class, the reader probably wants to know why we need the static variable `nextPhotoDisplayIndex`. This variable makes it easier to see multiple images together in a terminal window. To elaborate, as you will see in Section 12.12, the `main` of the class `PortraitMakerAssignment` constructs and displays a number of portraits simultaneously in the terminal window of your computer. Ordinarily, all of these portraits would be displayed one on top of the other. However, with the help of the static variable `nextPhotoDisplayIndex`, we associate an integer index with each portrait and subsequently use this index to translate each displayed portrait vis-à-vis the portrait that was displayed previously. This creates a staggered display for the portraits, making it easier to see them all at the same time. Even though the portraits are shown overlapping, the user can click on the portraits that are obscured to bring them to the foreground.

The first method shown in the class definition is `loadImages()`. It is this method that allows the `ImageManager` class to serve as an archive that makes its images available to portrait makers (for a fee, we pretend). This method simply scans the current directory for any jpeg images and presents them to the portrait makers in the form of a hash table whose keys are derived from the names of the jpeg files. It is assumed that the name of each image file is of the form "firstName_lastName.jpg" or of the form "name.jpg". The name of the individual in an image is constructed from the relevant substrings extracted from the name of the image file. In the hash table, each image is then keyed to the name of the individual.

The next method in the class definition has the signature

```
void displaySingleImage( Hashtable<String,ImageIcon> hash, String name)
```

This method displays on your computer screen a single image whose name is specified in the second argument. This name would presumably be that of a previous headmaster or headmistress of Hogwarts. The first argument is the hash table that is constructed by a call to the `loadImages()` method of the class.

The next method has the signature

```
void displaySingleImage( String name, ImageIcon image, Border border)
```

This method is used by a client of the `ImageMaker` class for displaying a "portrait." Recall that a portrait is what a portrait maker creates by imprinting an image on some medium and then placing a border around it.

The next static method is `slideshow()` that is not currently used in the Flyweight demonstration, but has been included in case the user wants to quickly see all of the images that are made available by the `ImageManager` class. This method is essentially a wrapper around a call to a method of the same name in the inner class `SlideShowDisplay`. Our

wrapper method first constructs an instance of the inner class and invokes the inner class's `slideshow()` method on the instance. The inner class uses a timer to display each image for a fixed interval of time; the length of this interval can be changed by changing the value of the variable pause in the inner class.

Note that all of the image display methods use the `javax.swing.Label` class for actually displaying an image. What is nice about this class is that it accepts a text label that can be shown along with the image. The class provides various methods for controlling the placement of the text label in relation to the placement of the images.

```java
import java.util.Hashtable;
import java.util.StringTokenizer;
import javax.swing.*;
import javax.swing.border.*;
import java.awt.*;              //for Graphics, Color, Dimension, etc.
import java.awt.event.*;
import java.io.*;              // for File

public class ImageManager {

    public static int nextPhotoDisplayIndex = 0;

    public static Hashtable<String,ImageIcon> loadImages() {
        File fileobj = new File( "." );
        FilenameFilter jpegOnly = new FilenameFilter() {
            public boolean accept( File dir, String name ) {
                return name.endsWith( ".jpg" );
            }
        };
        String[] allImageFiles = fileobj.list( jpegOnly );
        int numImages = allImageFiles.length;
        Hashtable<String,ImageIcon> hash =
                            new Hashtable<String,ImageIcon>();
        String name = "";
        for (int i=0; i < numImages; i++) {
            int index = allImageFiles[i].lastIndexOf(".");
            String restOfFileName =
                            allImageFiles[i].substring(0,index);
            StringTokenizer st =
                    new StringTokenizer( restOfFileName, "_" );
            while (st.hasMoreTokens() ) {
                name += " " + st.nextToken();
            }
            // Get rid of extra space at the beginning:
            name = name.substring(1);
            hash.put( name, new ImageIcon( allImageFiles[i] ) );
            name = "";
        }
        return hash;
    }
```

```java
public static void displaySingleImage( Hashtable<String,
                ImageIcon> hash, String name) throws Exception {
    if ( ! hash.containsKey( name ) ) {
        throw new Exception("Database does not contain the image "
                        + "named");
    }
    nextPhotoDisplayIndex++;
    JFrame f = new JFrame( "Single Image Display" );
    f.addWindowListener(new WindowAdapter() {
        public void windowClosing(WindowEvent e) {
            System.exit(0);
        }
    });
    Container cPane = f.getContentPane();
    int width = 600;
    int height = 500;
    int displayWidth =
        width - cPane.getInsets().left - cPane.getInsets().right;
    int displayHeight =
        height - cPane.getInsets().top - cPane.getInsets().bottom;
    JLabel label =
    new JLabel( name, (ImageIcon) hash.get(name), JLabel.CENTER );
    label.setVerticalTextPosition(JLabel.BOTTOM);
    label.setHorizontalTextPosition(JLabel.CENTER);
    Border border =
      BorderFactory.createMatteBorder(20, 20, 20, 20, Color.red );
    label.setBorder( border );
    JScrollPane scrollableImage = new JScrollPane( label );
    scrollableImage.setPreferredSize( new Dimension( displayWidth,
                                        displayHeight-8));
    if ( scrollableImage != null ) {
        cPane.add( scrollableImage );
    }
    f.pack();
    f.setSize( 600, 600 );
    f.setLocation( 100*nextPhotoDisplayIndex,
                                100*nextPhotoDisplayIndex);
    f.setVisible( true );
}

public static void displaySingleImage( String name,
                ImageIcon image, Border border) throws Exception {
    nextPhotoDisplayIndex++;
    JFrame f = new JFrame( "Single Image Display" );
    f.addWindowListener(new WindowAdapter() {
        public void windowClosing(WindowEvent e) {
            System.exit(0);
        }
    });
    Container cPane = f.getContentPane();
    int width = 600;
    int height = 500;
```

```java
        int displayWidth =
            width - cPane.getInsets().left - cPane.getInsets().right;
        int displayHeight =
            height - cPane.getInsets().top - cPane.getInsets().bottom;
        JLabel label = new JLabel( name,  image, JLabel.CENTER );
        label.setVerticalTextPosition(JLabel.BOTTOM);
        label.setHorizontalTextPosition(JLabel.CENTER);
        label.setBorder( border );
        JScrollPane scrollableImage = new JScrollPane( label );
        scrollableImage.setPreferredSize(new Dimension( displayWidth,
                                            displayHeight-8));
        if ( scrollableImage != null ) {
            cPane.add( scrollableImage );
        }
        f.pack();
        f.setSize( 600, 600 );
        f.setLocation( 100*nextPhotoDisplayIndex,
                                    100*nextPhotoDisplayIndex);
        f.setVisible( true );
    }

    public static void slideshow() {
        ImageManager.SlideShowDisplay slideshow =
                            new ImageManager.SlideShowDisplay();
        slideshow.slideshow();
    }

    private static class SlideShowDisplay extends JRootPane {
        Timer timer;
        int frameIndex = -1;       //the current frame number
        int numImages;             //number of images to display
        int width;                 //width of the frame's content pane
        int height;                //height of the frame's content pane
        int displayWidth;
        int displayHeight;
        JComponent contentPane;    //the content pane
        ImageIcon images[];        //the images
        String imageNames[];
        boolean finishedLoading = false;
        JScrollPane scrollableImage;
        boolean newFrameAvailable = false;

        private SlideShowDisplay() {
            int pause = 1000;
            numImages = 3;
            width = 600;
            height = 500;

            displayWidth = width - getInsets().left -
                                            getInsets().right;
            displayHeight = height - getInsets().top -
                                            getInsets().bottom;
```

```java
        contentPane = new JPanel() {
            public void paintComponent( Graphics g ) {
                super.paintComponent( g );
                if ( finishedLoading && newFrameAvailable ) {
                    JLabel label = new JLabel(
                                        imageNames[frameIndex],
                                        images[ frameIndex ],
                                        JLabel.CENTER );
                    label.setVerticalTextPosition(JLabel.BOTTOM);
                    label.setHorizontalTextPosition(JLabel.CENTER);
                    Border border =
                        BorderFactory.createMatteBorder(20,20,20,20,
                                                Color.red );
                    label.setBorder( border );
                    scrollableImage = new JScrollPane( label );
                    scrollableImage.setPreferredSize(
                        new Dimension( displayWidth,
                                            displayHeight - 8 ) );
                }
                if ( scrollableImage != null ) {
                    this.removeAll();
                    this.add( scrollableImage, BorderLayout.NORTH );
                }
                this.revalidate();
                //                      this.setVisible( true );
                newFrameAvailable = false;
            }
        };
        contentPane.setBackground(Color.white);
        setContentPane(contentPane);

        timer = new Timer( pause, new ActionListener() {
                public void actionPerformed( ActionEvent evt ) {
                    frameIndex++;
                    if ( frameIndex == numImages )
                        frameIndex = 0;
                    newFrameAvailable = true;
                    contentPane.repaint();
                }
        });
        timer.setInitialDelay( 0 );
        timer.setCoalesce(false);

        new Thread() {
                public void run() {
                    loadImages();
                }
        }.start();
    }
    private void loadImages() {
        File fileobj = new File( "." );
```

```
            FilenameFilter jpegOnly = new FilenameFilter() {
                    public boolean accept( File dir, String name ) {
                        return name.endsWith( ".jpg" );
                    }
            };
            String[] allImageFiles = fileobj.list( jpegOnly );
            numImages = allImageFiles.length;
            System.out.println( "Number of images found "+numImages );
            imageNames = new String[numImages];
            for (int i=0; i < numImages; i++) {
                imageNames[i] = allImageFiles[i];
                System.out.println( allImageFiles[i] );
            }
            images = new ImageIcon[numImages];
            for ( int i = 0; i < numImages; i++ ) {
                images[i] = new ImageIcon( allImageFiles[i] );
            }
            finishedLoading = true;
            timer.start();
        }
    private void slideshow() {
        JFrame f = new JFrame( "slide show" );
        f.addWindowListener(new WindowAdapter() {
            public void windowClosing(WindowEvent e) {
                System.exit(0);
            }
        });
        Container cPane = f.getContentPane();
        cPane.add( this, BorderLayout.CENTER );
        f.pack();
        f.setSize( 600, 550 );
        f.setVisible( true );
    }
  }
}
```

12.10   THE PortraitBorderChoices CLASS

As mentioned earlier, a portrait maker makes a portrait by imprinting an image (acquired originally from the official image archive of the wizarding world, meaning the ImageManager class) on some medium, such as paper, fabric, canvas, etc., and then placing a customer-chosen border around the image. So, basically, a portrait is a combination of an image and a border. This class, which is actually an interface, makes available a collection of predefined borders for our convenience. The borders are 20 pixels wide and matte in appearance.

```
import java.awt.*;
import javax.swing.*;
import javax.swing.border.*;
```

```
public interface PortraitBorderChoices {
    public static final Border redborder =
            BorderFactory.createMatteBorder(20,20,20,20, Color.red);
    public static final Border blueborder =
            BorderFactory.createMatteBorder(20,20,20,20, Color.blue);
    public static final Border magentaborder  =
            BorderFactory.createMatteBorder(20,20,20,20, Color.magenta);
    public static final Border greenborder  =
            BorderFactory.createMatteBorder(20,20,20,20, Color.green);
}
```

12.11   THE ImageNotAvailableException CLASS

Since it is possible that the ImageManager class may not have in its stock the image that is requested by a portrait maker, we need an exception class whose instances can be used as throw objects when requests for such images are received. The exception class shown below serves that purpose.

```
public class ImageNotAvailableException extends Exception {
    public ImageNotAvailableException() {
        super();
    }
    public ImageNotAvailableException(String message) {
        super(message);
    }
}
```

12.12   THE PortraitMakerAssignment CLASS

A PortraitMakerAssignment will serve as our client, in the sense that it will exercise the rest of the code in this demonstration of the Flyweight pattern.

The code below shows a portrait maker receiving four requests for portraits. There are two requests for the same former head — Ambrose Swott — presumably from two different customers. These two portraits have been requested with two different borders. If our Flyweight pattern is working as it is supposed to, the first request for Ambrose Swott's portrait should cause FlyweightImageStore to order his image from ImageManager. However, the second request for the same portrait should only entail fetching the same image from the local store maintained in the FlyweightImageStore class. Since each image ordered from ImageManager is stored away by the FlyweightImageStore class, the check on the number of images in this store and also a check on the number of images actually ordered from the image archive — the ImageManager class — tells us whether or not our implementation of the Flyweight pattern is working correctly. It is important to note that just checking on the number of images stored in the local store maintained by the portrait maker would not suffice. Being a hash table, a repeat insertion of a <key,value> pair — the key being the name of the individual and the value the image object — would

simply replace the old value. Hence we must also check the number of images actually ordered from the `ImageManager` class. Both of these checks are carried out by the last two statements of the implementation shown below. In our case, both of these numbers should be 3 for the four orders that were received by the portrait maker.

```java
import javax.swing.*;
import javax.swing.border.*;

public class PortraitMakerAssignment implements PortraitBorderChoices {

    String headmastername;
    HeadMasterPortrait portrait;

    public PortraitMakerAssignment( String name, Border border ) {
        headmastername = name;
        ImageIcon imageRequested = null;
        try {
            imageRequested =
                        FlyweightImageStore.getImage( headmastername );
        } catch (ImageNotAvailableException e) {
            System.out.println( "This portrait cannot be made since "
                                + headmastername + "'s image is not "
                                + "available from the image archive.");
        }
        if (imageRequested != null)
            portrait =
                new HeadMasterPortrait(name, imageRequested, border);
    }

    public static void main( String[] args ) throws Exception {
        PortraitMakerAssignment job1 =
            new PortraitMakerAssignment("Ambrose Swott", greenborder );
        job1.portrait.displayPortrait();

        PortraitMakerAssignment job2 =
            new PortraitMakerAssignment("Basil Fronsac", redborder );
        job2.portrait.displayPortrait();

        PortraitMakerAssignment job3 =
            new PortraitMakerAssignment("Ambrose Swott", redborder );
        job3.portrait.displayPortrait();

        PortraitMakerAssignment job4 =
            new PortraitMakerAssignment("Phineas Nigellus Black",
                                                    blueborder );
        job4.portrait.displayPortrait();

        System.out.println( "Number of images in the portrait "
                + "maker's image store: "
                + FlyweightImageStore.getPortraitImageStoreSize() );
```

```
        System.out.println( "Number of images ordered from the image "
                          + "archive: "
  + FlyweightImageStore.howManyImagesOrderedFromImageArchive());
    }
}
```

12.13 PLAYING WITH THE CODE

Download the class files for this pattern from the book website into a separate directory. Compile the code with the command

```
javac *.java
```

and execute the PortraitMakerAssignment class by

```
java PortraitMakerAssignment
```

Given the code in the main() of PortraitMakerAssignment, executing this class will produce the following output:

```
Number of images in the portrait maker's image store: 3
Number of images ordered from the image archive: 3

   (Also displayed on your screen will be four
   photos --- the portraits ordered  from the archive --- of the three
   different former heads of Hogwarts.)
```

For additional insights, you may wish to extend the code for this pattern along the following lines:

- As the reader has surely noticed, the slideshow() method in the implementation of the ImageManager was not actually used in the demonstration of the Flyweight pattern. However, it is a useful method that a client of the ImageManager class can use to quickly look through the entire image collection held by the ImageManager class. Modify the demonstration code in order to give the PortraitMakerAssignment class the option to bring up the slide show. To make this extension of the demonstration really useful, it will be best to create a GUI-based interface for the PortraitMakerAssignment class that not only gives the user the option to see the slideshow but to also select the images with mouse clicks.
- In the current demonstration, the client PortraitMakerAssignment "downloads" the entire image collection held by the ImageManager class before choosing the image needed for a portrait. That's unlikely to work well for large collections. It's more likely that the image archive — the ImageManager class — will make available to the portrait makers just the thumbnails of the images in its collection. The portrait makers would be expected to choose the images they want on the basis of what they see in the thumbnails. If you are up to it, modify the demonstration code so that the actual images are held in the private section of the ImageManager class and only the

thumbnails are made available through its public section. Of course, after a portrait maker has chosen an image, the `ImageManager` class would want to supply the image from its privately held collection.

- The borders in the `PortraitBorderChoices` interface are all of uniform color and they are all 20 pixels wide. For a more elaborate demonstration, one could create fancier borders using pixel patterns based on icons and such. If the reader chooses to extend the demonstration in that direction, he/she would find it educational to first go through the Swing "How to Use Borders" tutorial at the official Java site.

12.14   ACKNOWLEDGMENT

The Hogwarts headmaster and headmistress images that are made available by the `ImageManager` class were downloaded from [5].

13

PROXY

13.1 IS IT ALWAYS NECESSARY TO HAVE THE REAL THING?

For the most part, humans want to interact with only real things. When we discover that the object of our attention is fake, we feel duped.

Despite the pejorative sense we associate with "fakes," there do exist real-life situations when what you need are not the real objects themselves, but objects that can serve as stand-ins for the real objects. Speaking loosely, a stand-in is fake for the simple reason that it is not exactly the same as the real thing. Nonetheless, a stand-in can be important when the real thing is unavailable and when it is believed that a stand-in would do just as well. In many situations, such stand-ins are referred to as *proxies*.

Practical considerations that dictate the need for a proxy vary from situation to situation. For example, corporate organizations generally allow for proxy voting by the shareholders when they are unable or unwilling to attend a stakeholders meeting. In proxy voting, you can designate someone else to vote on your behalf. For another example, again in the context of human organizations, the head of an organization may vest his or her authority in a designated *surrogate* — a proxy, really — to perform certain duties at a function.

Although the words "surrogate" and "proxy" carry the same meaning in many contexts, the former generally stands for you designating someone to act on your behalf and the latter for a higher-up designating someone else to act on your behalf.

The notion of a proxy has become hugely important in modern computer networks where, in addition to serving essentially the same purpose as in human organizations, it is also used for controlling access to resources and for allowing users to anonymize themselves in the internet.

13.2 INTENT AND APPLICABILITY

The intent of the Proxy pattern is to provide an object that can serve as a stand-in for the real object.

Designing with Objects: Object-Oriented Design Patterns Explained with Stories from Harry Potter, First Edition. Avinash C. Kak.
© 2015 John Wiley & Sons, Inc. Published 2015 by John Wiley & Sons, Inc.

You should consider using the pattern when

- you need a stand-in object (a proxy) for regulating access to the real object for reasons of security;
- you need a proxy for web caching;
- your clients need a proxy for anonymizing their access to the internet;
- your clients need proxies for the objects that reside in remote hosts in a network so that they can access the services offered by those remote objects through method invocations on their local proxies.

13.3   INTRODUCTION TO THE PROXY PATTERN

The Proxy pattern is about designing interfaces through which clients may access resources that cannot be (or are not allowed to be) reached directly. Probably the most common examples of such interfaces are the proxy servers used by some internet service providers to channel all accesses to the web from their customers. At the least, proxy servers provide caching of the information accessed by the customers. As a result, if one customer downloaded, say, *The New York Times* web page and, within a few seconds, another customer tried to do the same, the second customer will see a cached copy of what was downloaded by the first customer. Such proxy interfaces can also act as security gateways. When used for security, a proxy can authenticate the customers and/or their requests before forwarding the connections to the real server. Implementation of the proxy pattern in such cases boils down to writing a client-server program[1] that acts like a server vis-à-vis the customers whose access to the resources elsewhere in a network needs to be regulated and like a client vis-à-vis the real servers that the customers want to reach.

The notion of a proxy is also foundational to distributed computing in which one machine in a network provides a service that the other machines want to utilize. In what is known as the Service Oriented Architecture (SOA) for distributed computing, as depicted in Figure 13.1, a client wants to invoke a function on an object that resides in the memory of some other machine in a network. However, the client has to first surmount the problem caused by the fact that objects are represented by their memory addresses and the memory addresses do not cross machine boundaries. To get around this difficulty, with an SOA implementation, when first establishing a connection with the server, which is the machine that has the object, the client downloads the proxies (more commonly referred to as the *stubs* in this context) for the remote objects. These proxies on the client side then serve as stand-ins for the server-based remote objects. When a client's machine invokes a method on a remote object (which, more correctly speaking, is a method invocation on the local proxy of the remote object), it is the proxy's job to package the method call (and that may involve packaging, or what is more commonly referred to as *serializing*, the parameters involved in the method call) and ship it off to the remote server. The server must unpack the parameters (or, *deserialize* them), execute the method, compute the result, serialize the result if necessary, and ship the packaged result obtained in this

---

[1] If you are not familiar with client-server programs, you will find examples of different kinds of such programs in Chapter 19 of [2] and Chapter 15 of [6].

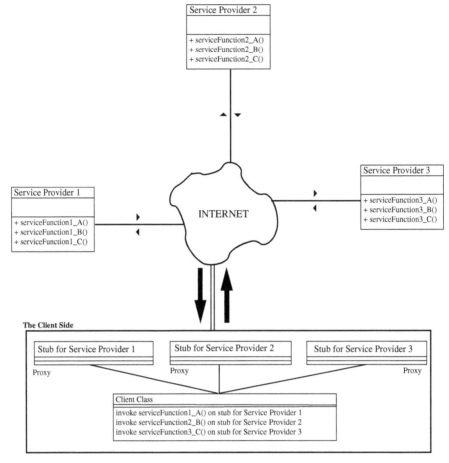

Fig. 13.1

manner back to the client. Obviously, this would only work if the client's machine also has proxies for the objects in the result obtained from the computation on the remote server.

13.4   THE PROXY PATTERN IN REAL-WORLD APPLICATIONS

Squid [7] is probably the world's most popular proxy server for web services. A Squid proxy can be used either for anonymizing oneself or for caching. For anonymizing, you would obviously use such a proxy hosted at a remote location that routes your calls out without revealing your identify. And, when used for caching, an ISP (Internet Service Provider) can improve the quality of its service by temporarily storing in its local memory the web resources requested by the clients so that repeat requests for the same web object can be served out without having to fetch them over and over from their original

sources.[2] Some people also claim that you can improve your personal web surfing experience if you install such a proxy server on your own machine and ask your web browser to route all outgoing requests through the proxy. A proxy server like Squid can also be used by an organization to control what outside resources in the internet can be accessed by the folks on the inside.

With regard to the use of proxies for invoking methods on objects that reside in remote machines in a network, an important example of that is RMI (Remote Method Invocation) in Java. When a proxy is used in this manner, it is sometimes referred to as a *remote proxy*.

13.5   HARRY POTTER STORY USED TO ILLUSTRATE THE PROXY PATTERN

In our demonstration of the Proxy pattern, the Dark Lord Voldemort is the real thing. As the reader will recall, in the first four Harry Potter books, Voldemort lived only in spirit, that is, without a human body. In particular, in the first book, Voldemort lived in spirit through Quirinus Quirrell who taught DADA (Defense Against Dark Arts) at Hogwarts. In the language of the Proxy pattern, Quirrell served as a proxy for Lord Voldemort during Harry Potter's first year at Hogwarts.

As a background for the demonstration code in this chapter, let's briefly review the role Quirrell played vis-à-vis his master Lord Voldemort. Voldemort's desire was for Quirrell to steal the Philosopher's Stone that was owned by the noted alchemist Nicolas Flamel and stored at the Gringotts Wizarding Bank. Voldemort wanted the stone because it could be used to brew an elixir that bestowed immortality on the drinker. (Voldemort obviously believed that gaining immortality would return him to a full life form.) Unfortunately for Voldemort, this plan failed as Dumbledore dispatched Hagrid to remove the stone from Gringotts just before Quirrell was able to break into the vault where the stone was stored.

After retrieving the stone from Gringotts, Dumbledore stored the stone in a secret chamber at Hogwarts, the access to which was guarded by multiple enchantments, each created by a different teacher at Hogwarts. To get to the secret chamber where the stone was hidden, you had to first make your way past a vicious three-headed dog (this was Hagrid's contribution to the stone's protection) and enter a chute through a trap-door guarded by the dog. You dropped down the chute into a room full of Devil's Snare that, as the name implies, tried to wrap itself tightly around you and choke you to death. This enchantment was created by Professor Pomona Sprout, the herbology teacher at Hogwarts. If you survived the Devil's Snare, you found yourself in a room that was full of winged keys in constant flight. The keys darted from wall to wall and bounced off the walls. Only one of these keys opened the door to the next chamber on the way to where the stone was hidden. The keys were charmed to fly by Professor Filius Flitwick who was in charge of teaching the Charms class during Harry Potter's first year at Hogwarts.

Given Harry Potter's well demonstrated mastery as a catcher of the golden snitch in Quidditch games, it was relatively easy for him to spot and grab the correct key by chasing

---

[2]For a large web object, the ISP can also send an HTTP HEAD request to the original source of that object in order to ascertain whether the state of the object has changed. The ISP can continue to serve out its locally stored copy of the object as long as its state (in terms of its size, last-modified date, etc.) remains unchanged.

it on a broomstick that was also in the room. The next challenge on the way to the stone was a chamber that contained Professor Minerva McGonagall's Wizard Chess Board with its towering and enchanted chess pieces. Harry, Ron, and Hermione had no choice but to play their way to get across the chess board to its other side since it was at that end where there was a door that presumably led to the next chamber. The chess board was enchanted to allow Harry, Ron, and Hermione to replace three of the black pieces of their choice. As to how the black side played was up to the trio since the black pieces obeyed their commands, but the white pieces were enchanted to play on their own in opposition to the black pieces. When the white captured a black piece, they showed no mercy — they would haul the captured piece off the board and smash it on the floor. So when Ron decided that the only way to win the game was to let the white queen capture him, he had to let himself be taken down by the queen — much to the consternation of Harry and Hermione.

That left Harry and Hermione to tackle the next protection — a giant mountain troll. But, as it later became known, the troll had been knocked out by Quirrell who was just ahead of them in reaching the stone. So Harry and Hermione were able to simply walk past the troll. That brought Harry and Hermione to the next enchantment protecting the stone — a room with a table that had on it seven bottles of different shapes containing different kinds of potions. (This enchantment was created by Professor Severus Snape who taught Potions at Hogwarts during Harry Potter's first year there.) Regarding the purpose of the seven bottles of potions, what happened was that as soon as Harry and Hermione stepped into the room, purple flames shot up at the door through which they had just entered the room and at the door that led to the next chamber. Of the seven potions, one would let the drinker pass through the flame at the door to the next chamber, one would allow the drinker to pass through the flame at the door through which they had just entered the potions room, two contained harmless wines, but three contained poisons that would kill them. To figure out which bottle contained what sort of a potion, they had to solve a riddle that is known as the Riddle of the Potions. Hermione, with her keen sense of logic, solved the riddle and that allowed Harry to get into the final chamber that contained the stone. Hermione went back to where Ron lay unconscious so that she could revive him and at the same time try to get help from Dumbledore.

The reason for this rather longish review of how the Philosopher's Stone was protected is to impress upon the reader as to why Voldemort's proxy needed to be a capable dark wizard who could be expected to surmount the enchantments used for protecting the Philosopher's Stone.

The goal of our demonstration is not to reenact in full how Quirrell tried to do Voldemort's bidding. On the other hand, our demonstration will focus on the following tiny part of the scene toward the end of Quirrell's attempt to acquire the stone: *Harry has entered the chamber where the stone is actually hidden. At the moment he enters, Harry is shocked to see Quirrell because he had believed all along that it was Professor Snape who was after the stone. Harry expresses his utter amazement to Quirrell,* **only to find out that Quirrell is serving as a proxy for Voldemort.** *From that point on, we witness a struggle between Quirrell who is trying the extract the stone from the Mirror of the Erised (since that is where Dumbledore has hidden the stone) and Harry who is trying his best to keep Quirrell from giving all his attention to the mirror.*

More specifically, our demonstration code tries to capture the moment when Quirrell, acting as Voldemort's proxy, becomes frustrated as he is unable to see the stone in the

Mirror of the Erised, let alone get to the stone. He appeals to his master for help with understanding how the mirror works. Voldemort responds back by saying that Quirrell needs to use Harry for locating the stone. It is this exchange between the proxy Quirrell and the master Voldemort that we capture in the demonstration shown here.

13.6   A TOP LEVEL VIEW OF THE PATTERN DEMONSTRATION

Our demonstration consists of the interaction between a `DarkWizard` and the `DarkLord`, with the former serving as a proxy for the latter as described in the previous section. The `DarkLord` wants his proxy Quirrell to steal the Philosopher's Stone so that he (the Dark Lord) can achieve immortality.

The class diagram in Figure 13.2 provides a top-level view of the demonstration in which an instance of the class `DarkWizard` acts as a proxy for the sole instance of the class `DarkLord` that we are allowed to construct (through the Singleton pattern of Chapter 6). Since the `DarkLord` would want to control his proxy `DarkWizard` in real time, four of the other classes that you see — `TalkToDarkWizard`, `LinkFromDarkWizard`, `TalkToDarkLord`, and `LinkFromDarkLord` — are for establishing a real-time two-way communication link between the two.

We place the attributes that are expected to be possessed by a regular wizard in the abstract class `Wizard`, and, in order to distinguish the dark wizards (and to highlight their unique ability to harm others) from the regular wizards, we define an interface class `DarkWizardTraits`. So a class derived from `Wizard` that also implements the `DarkWizardTraits` interface can be expected to become a `DarkWizard` class, as is the case in the class diagram of Figure 13.2.

When we say that a `DarkWizard` wants to serve as a proxy for the `DarkLord`, we mean that the `DarkWizard` instance wants to do `DarkLord`'s bidding. In our demonstration, Quirrell will serve is an instance of `DarkWizard`.[3] As mentioned earlier, our demonstration will focus on the scene at the end of the first Harry Potter book where Voldemort wanted his proxy Quirrell to steal the Philosopher's Stone from the chamber where Dumbledore had hidden it under multiple enchantments.

13.7   THE ABSTRACT CLASS Wizard

The abstract class `Wizard` presented in this section is at the root of the hierarchy used for demonstrating the Proxy pattern. If the reader is puzzled by the attributes we have mentioned in the definition of the class shown below — you might say that those attributes characterize just the dark wizards — note that we have set them to false by default. In other words, a wizard who is not a dark wizard should *not* be able to cast unforgivable

---

[3]J. K. Rowling does not explicitly label Quirrell as one of the dark wizards. That is probably because dark wizards were first mentioned in the second book of the series, whereas Quirrell lives and dies in the first book. But if we go by the official definition of a dark wizard, Quirrell would certainly be labeled as such. We say so because he tried to kill Harry Potter during a Quidditch match between the Gryffindors and the Slytherins, and killing is one of the three unforgivable curses the practice of which characterizes the dark wizards. The three unforgivable curses were previously mentioned in Chapter 7. A footnote in the next section reviews them again briefly.

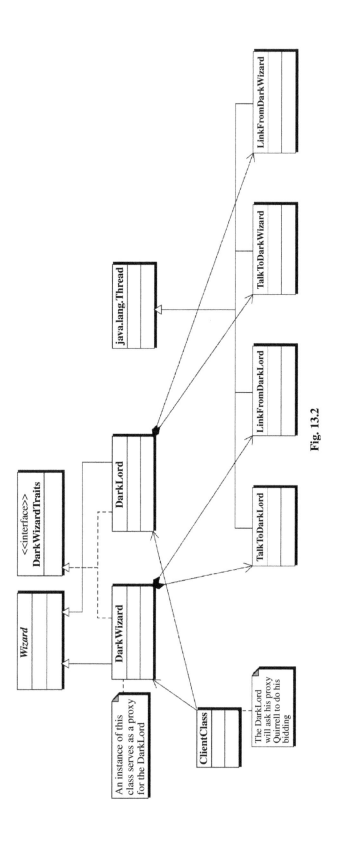

Fig. 13.2

curses; should *not* be able to brew dark potions; and should *not* be able to animate inferi.[4]
The main reason for defining the class through the absence of the negatives (as opposed
to the presence of the positives) is that, in terms of the object instances that are created,
this demonstration involves only the wizards who have gone over to the other side and the
Dark Lord himself. We can capture the notion of a wizard switching over to the dark side
by setting to true the attributes in the class definition shown below.

```
abstract class Wizard {
    protected String name;
    protected boolean canCastUnforgivableCurses = false;
    protected boolean canBrewDarkPotions = false;
    protected boolean canAnimateInferi = false;

    protected Wizard(String name){
        this.name = name;
    }
    public String getName() { return name; }
}
```

13.8   THE DarkWizardTraits INTERFACE

Recall that what sets dark wizards apart from the regular wizards is that the former engage
in one or more of the dark arts the practice of which is normally punishable by banish-
ment to Azkaban, the Wizard prison. At the least, the dark arts include casting the three
unforgivable curses, brewing the dark potions, and animating the inferi, as described in the
previous section.

In our demonstration, a dark wizard must implement the interface shown below. And
that includes the Dark Lord himself. The methods declared in the interface can be used to
selectively endow a dark wizard with the abilities in one or more of the three dark arts that
we described in the previous section. For example, Quirrell has admitted that he was trying
to kill Harry Potter (on behalf of Voldemort), and that, as stated in the previous section,
makes him a dark wizard. We will use the setCanCastUnforgivableCurses() method
shown below to set Quirrell's instance variable canCastUnforgivableCurse to true.

```
public interface DarkWizardTraits {
    void setCanCastUnforgivableCurses(boolean yesOrNo);
    void setCanBrewDarkPotions(boolean yesOrNo);
    void setCanAnimateInferi(boolean yesOrNo);
}
```

---

[4]As mentioned previously in Chapter 7, the three unforgivable curses are the Avada Kedavra Curse (Killing
Curse), the Cruciatus Curse (for inflicting excruciating pain), and the Imperius Curse (for getting a victim to do
the wizard's bidding without questioning). The dark potions include the Drink of Despair that causes a drinker
to see "terrible things" and experience excruciating pain, and the Rudimentary Body Potion that can be used
by a dark wizard to create a rudimentary body that can subsequently be inhabited by a non-corporeal wizard.
Animating the inferi involves creating animated zombies out of dead bodies; the zombies, which have no free
will, can subsequently be used by a dark wizard as soldiers in warfare.

13.9   THE DarkWizard CLASS

As the reader will recall, our demonstration of the Proxy pattern is based on Quirrell, an instance of the DarkWizard class, acting as a proxy for Voldemort as represented by the singular instance of DarkLord. In order for Quirrell to act as a proxy for Voldemort, Quirrell must first establish a communication link with Voldemort. A large portion of the DarkWizard class shown below relates to the facilities for establishing this communication link.

The communication link between an instance of DarkWizard and the singular DarkLord instance consists of four simplex channels, two initiated by a DarkWizard instance and two by the DarkLord.[5] The two simplex channels created by the DarkWizard are through its two inner classes:

```
TalkToDarkLord
LinkFromDarkLord
```

The first inner class, TalkToDarkLord, is for establishing a separate thread for maintaining continuous contact with the DarkLord for the outgoing messages. And the second inner class, LinkFromDarkLord, is for creating a separate thread, which runs concurrently with all other executing threads, for maintaining continuous contact with the DarkLord for his responses to the questions sent to him through the first channel. Each of these channels has a counterpart in the DarkLord's implementation code; we will talk about those when we present the DarkLord class.

Note the role played by the establishCommunicationLinkWithDarkLord() method. It is this method that knows about the fact that the inter-thread communication in Java takes place through piped streams. These streams, called the PipedOutputStream and the PipedInputStream, define the two end-points of a one-way communication link between two threads in Java. Let's say you want thread *A* of a DarkWizard to send data to thread *B* of the DarkLord on an ongoing basis. You must first create a linked pair of input-output piped streams by supplying an instance of the local output stream to the constructor of an input piped stream. You then supply the local end of this pair to the local thread *A* and the remote end of the pair to thread *B* of the DarkLord. Obviously, if you want the DarkWizard to receive answers from the DarkLord on an ongoing basis, a similar pair of piped streams must be created for the down link also.

Let's now focus on the implementation of the TalkToDarkLord inner class. Any message that needs to be sent to the DarkLord is supplied to an instance of this class through its instance method sendMessageToDarkLord(String msg). Note how this method appends the newline character "\n" to the message. There is an important reason for that: The stream that actually writes data into an outgoing piped stream is a DataOutputStream object. For sending a message to the DarkLord, the TalkToDarkLord instance invokes the writeChars() method on the DataOutputStream object. At the other end of this inter-thread communication link, as you will see in the next section, the DarkLord instance will use the readLine() method of a BufferedReader object to read the incoming data. But this method blocks until it sees a newline character at the end of a string. That is, as the readLine() method fetches data from the BufferedReader instance, if it does not see a newline character, it will simply continue to wait for the next appearance of the newline character. So we must make sure that any outgoing message has a newline

---

[5]A simplex channel can send data in only one direction. An ordinary telephone connection between two parties is a duplex connection in which the information can flow *simultaneously* in both directions.

character appended to it, since otherwise the receiving party will not be able to retrieve the message from the communication pipe.[6]

In the class definition shown below, note the invocation of `Thread.sleep()` at various points in the code that is supposed to run in separate threads. Putting the threads to sleep is one of the most effective ways to promote thread cooperation and to prevent thread deadlock. When a thread is put to sleep, however briefly, that gives a chance to another thread waiting for its share of time on the CPU. We have made the sleep times random, as random additions to fixed values. This is to break up any possible deadlocks that might be caused by the timing issues between the threads. In the implementation shown, a certain amount of thread synchronization takes place anyway through how we use the `download.answerReceived` variable in the `assignedTask()` method. However, thread synchronization through variables has the potential of causing a thread deadlock unless one uses a `wait-notify` mechanism. Since we have chosen to not use the `wait-notify` mechanism for synchronization, we resort to manual control by checking the boolean value of the `downlink.answerReceived` variable and by randomizing the sleep times.

An additional item to note in the code that follows is the construction of the unique `DarkLord` instance at the beginning of the class definition. The idea here is that we want all `DarkWizard` instances to be aware of who the `DarkLord` is — as would probably be the case for all of the dark wizards during the period of the Harry Potter series. The reader may wonder about the relationship of this construction to the construction of the `DarkLord` in the client class `ClientClass` in Section 13.11. What is interesting is that because, as the reader will see in the next section, the `DarkLord` class is implemented using the Singleton pattern, there will always be a single `DarkLord` instance regardless of who constructs an instance from the `DarkLord` class. The call `DarkLord.makeInstanceOfDarkLord()` in the code shown below simply returns the `DarkLord` instance constructed in the `main()` of `ClientClass` to be presented in Section 13.11.

Note also how the `answerReceived` instance variable of the `LinkFromDarkLord` class helps us with the serialization of the communication between a `DarkWizard` and the `DarkLord`. The importance of this variable should be evident from how it is used in the method `assignedTask()` of the `DarkWizard`. The `DarkWizard` sets this variable (this is the variable that is referred to as `downlink.answerReceived`) to false before transmitting a new query to the `DarkLord`. Subsequently, when a response is received from the `DarkLord` in the `run()` method of the `LinkFromDarkLord` class, this variable is set to true.

```
import java.io.*;

public class DarkWizard extends Wizard implements DarkWizardTraits {

    private TalkToDarkLord uplink;
    private LinkFromDarkLord downlink;

    private static DarkLord youKnowWho =
                    DarkLord.makeInstanceOfDarkLord( "Voldemort" );
```

---

[6]Given this important role served by the newline character appended to an outgoing message, we must make sure that the string constituting an outgoing message does not contain any newline characters to begin with. In a more foolproof implementation, before appending the newline character at the end of an outgoing message, the message would first be sanitized to ensure that it does not contain any such characters to begin with.

```
public DarkWizard(String name){
    super(name);
}


/////////////////    Inner class TalkToDarkLord   ///////////////
public class TalkToDarkLord extends Thread {
    private DataOutputStream out;
    private String nameOfSender;
    private String outgoingMessage = null;
    public TalkToDarkLord(OutputStream outsm, String nameOfSender){
        this.nameOfSender = nameOfSender;
        out = new DataOutputStream( outsm );
    }
    public void sendMessageToDarkLord(String msg) {
        outgoingMessage = msg + "\n";
    }
    public void run() {
        for (;;) {
            try {
                while (outgoingMessage == null) {
                    sleep(100 + 100 * (long) Math.random() );
                }
                System.out.println( nameOfSender + ":  "
                                            + outgoingMessage );
                out.writeChars( outgoingMessage );
                out.flush();
                outgoingMessage = null;
                sleep( 500 +  1000 * (long) Math.random() );
            } catch( Exception e ) {
                System.out.println( "Error: " + e );
            }
        }
    }
}


///////////////   Inner class LinkFromDarkLord   ///////////////
public class LinkFromDarkLord extends Thread {
    private BufferedReader in;
    public boolean answerReceived = false;
    public LinkFromDarkLord( InputStream istr ) {
        try {
            in = new  BufferedReader(
                        new InputStreamReader(istr, "UTF-16" ));
        } catch(Exception e){ System.out.println( "Error: " + e);}
    }
    public void run() {
        for (;;) {
            try {
                String answer = in.readLine();
                System.out.println( youKnowWho.getName() + ": "
                                            + answer + "\n\n");
```

```
                     answerReceived = true;
                     sleep( 100 + 100 * (long) Math.random() );
                 } catch(InterruptedException e){
                     System.out.println( "InterruptedException: " + e );
                 } catch( IOException e ) {
                     System.out.println( "Error: " + e );
                 }
             }
         }
     }


     ///////////////////   The rest of the DarkWizard code   ////////////
     public void establishCommunicationLinkWithDarkLord() {
         try {
             // for incoming messages:
             PipedOutputStream pout2 = new PipedOutputStream();
             PipedInputStream pin2 = new PipedInputStream( pout2 );
             DarkLord.TalkToDarkWizard  downlink_origin =
                             youKnowWho.new TalkToDarkWizard( pout2 );
             downlink = new LinkFromDarkLord( pin2 );
             // for outgoing messages:
             PipedOutputStream pout = new PipedOutputStream();
             PipedInputStream pin = new PipedInputStream( pout );
             uplink = new TalkToDarkLord( pout, name );
             DarkLord.LinkFromDarkWizard uplink_endpoint =
                 youKnowWho.new LinkFromDarkWizard(pin,downlink_origin);
             uplink.start();
             uplink_endpoint.start();
             downlink_origin.start();
             downlink.start();
         } catch( IOException e ){
             System.out.println(
                 "ERROR in establishing communication link up: " + e);
         }
     }


     public void assignedTask( String goal ){
         establishCommunicationLinkWithDarkLord();
         try {
             uplink.sendMessageToDarkLord( "My Master, Is this your "
                                 + "command that I " + goal + "?");
             while (!downlink.answerReceived) {
                 Thread.sleep(100 + 100 * (long) Math.random() );
             }
         downlink.answerReceived = false;
             uplink.sendMessageToDarkLord( "What does this mirror do? "
                         + "How does it work? Help me, Master!");
             while (!downlink.answerReceived) {
                 Thread.sleep(100 + 100 * (long) Math.random() );
             }
             downlink.answerReceived = false;
             uplink.sendMessageToDarkLord( "Master, the boy is not "
```

```
                                                     + "cooperating!");
        while (!downlink.answerReceived) {
            Thread.sleep(100 + 100 * (long) Math.random() );
        }
        downlink.answerReceived = false;
        uplink.sendMessageToDarkLord( "Master, I can't. "
                            + "My hands!!  My hands!!!");
        while (!downlink.answerReceived) {
            Thread.sleep(100 + 100 * (long) Math.random() );
        }
        downlink.answerReceived = false;
    } catch(InterruptedException e){}
    }


    public void setCanCastUnforgivableCurses(boolean yesOrNo) {
        canCastUnforgivableCurses = yesOrNo;
    }
    public void setCanBrewDarkPotions(boolean yesOrNo){
        canBrewDarkPotions = yesOrNo;
    }
    public void  setCanAnimateInferi(boolean yesOrNo){
        canAnimateInferi = yesOrNo;
    }
}
```

13.10   THE DarkLord CLASS

We now present the implementation of the DarkLord class. As should be clear from the previous section, for Quirrell to act as a proxy for Voldemort, the DarkWizard instance that represents Quirrell must first establish a communication link with the Dark Lord. The DarkLord class must therefore provide enablers for that purpose. As mentioned in our explanation of the DarkWizard class, the communication link between a DarkWizard and the DarkLord consists of four simplex channels, two initiated by an instance of DarkWizard and two by the DarkLord himself. The two simplex channels created by the DarkLord are through the inner classes TalkToDarkWizard and LinkFromDarkWizard.

In the class definition that follows, the first inner class, TalkToDarkWizard, is for establishing a separate thread for maintaining continuous contact with a DarkWizard for the outgoing responses to the queries received from the DarkWizard. And the second, LinkFromDarkWizard, is for creating a separate thread, which runs concurrently with all other executing threads, for maintaining continuous contact with the DarkWizard for his queries. Each of these inner classes has a counterpart in the DarkWizard class, as the reader has seen already.

It is important to note that a communication link between a DarkWizard and the DarkLord is initiated by the DarkWizard. In other words, the DarkLord instance does not initiate contact with a DarkWizard in this demonstration.[7] The DarkWizard does so by

---

[7]Obviously, it would be easy to expand the code so that a communication link can be established by either of the two parties.

calling its method establishCommunicationLinkWithDarkLord(). This method calls
on the appropriate methods from the DarkWizard and the DarkLord classes to set up the
four simplex links that go into a two-way communication link. The DarkWizard class's
establishCommunicationLinkWithDarkLord() method knows about the inner classes
of the DarkLord class through the static variable youKnowWho whose value is the same for
every instance of the DarkWizard class.

The explanation presented in the previous section regarding how each simplex communication link is implemented in a separate thread applies here also. Also applicable here are all of the comments made in that section regarding why the method
setOutgoingMessage(String msg) needs to append the newline character "\n" to each
message from the DarkLord to a DarkWizard instance. And the reasons for why we must
invoke Thread.sleep() at various points in the code that runs in separate threads remain
the same as explained earlier.

An additional item of note is the use of the Singleton pattern for the DarkLord class.
That pattern was presented previously in Chapter 6.

```java
import java.io.*;

public class DarkLord extends Wizard implements DarkWizardTraits {

    private static DarkLord unique = null;

    private DarkLord(String name){
        super(name);
        setCanCastUnforgivableCurses(true);
        setCanBrewDarkPotions(true);
        setCanAnimateInferi(true);
    }
    public static DarkLord makeInstanceOfDarkLord(String darkLordName){
        if (unique == null) unique = new DarkLord(darkLordName);
        return unique;
    }
    public void goal(String g, DarkWizard proxy ) {
        proxy.assignedTask( g );
    }

    ///////////////////   Inner class TalkToDarkWizard   //////////////////
    public class TalkToDarkWizard extends Thread {
        private DataOutputStream out;
        private String outgoingMessage = null;
        public TalkToDarkWizard( OutputStream outsm ) {
            out = new DataOutputStream( outsm );
        }
        public void setOutgoingMessage(String msg) {
            outgoingMessage = msg + "\n";
        }
        public void run() {
            for (;;) {
                try {
                    while (outgoingMessage  == null) {
```

```
                        sleep(100 * (long) Math.random() );
                    }
                    out.writeChars( outgoingMessage );
                    out.flush();
                    outgoingMessage = null;
                    sleep( 100 * (long) Math.random() );
                } catch( Exception e ) {
                    System.out.println( "Error: " + e );
                }
            }
        }
    }


    ////////////////    Inner class LinkFromDarkWizard    //////////////
    public class LinkFromDarkWizard extends Thread {
        private BufferedReader in;
        private TalkToDarkWizard talkdownlink;
        public LinkFromDarkWizard( InputStream istr,
                              TalkToDarkWizard talkdownlink ) {
            this.talkdownlink = talkdownlink;
            try {
                in = new  BufferedReader(
                            new InputStreamReader(istr, "UTF-16" ));
            } catch(Exception e){}
        }
        public void run() {
            for (;;) {
                try {
                    // readLine() blocks until it sees a sequence
                    // of chars that end a newline character
                    String msgReceived = in.readLine();
                    if (msgReceived.contains( "I can't")) {
                        talkdownlink.setOutgoingMessage("KILL HIM!");
                    } else if (msgReceived.contains(
                                    "What does this mirror do")) {
                        talkdownlink.setOutgoingMessage(
                                "Use the boy.....Use the boy...");
                    } else if (msgReceived.contains(
                                    "the boy is not cooperating")) {
                        talkdownlink.setOutgoingMessage(
                                                "SIEZE HIM!!!");
                    } else if (msgReceived.contains(
                                    "Is this your command")) {
                        talkdownlink.setOutgoingMessage(
                                    "Yes, that is correct!");
                    }
                    sleep( 100 );
                } catch(InterruptedException e){
                    System.out.println( "InterruptedException: " + e );
                } catch( IOException e ) {
                    System.out.println( "Error: " + e );
                }
```

```
            }
        }
    }

    /////////////////    The rest of the DarkLord code    /////////////////
    public void setCanCastUnforgivableCurses(boolean yesOrNo) {
        canCastUnforgivableCurses = yesOrNo;
    }
    public void setCanBrewDarkPotions(boolean yesOrNo){
        canBrewDarkPotions = yesOrNo;
    }
    public void  setCanAnimateInferi(boolean yesOrNo){
        canAnimateInferi = yesOrNo;
    }
}
```

13.11   THE ClientClass CLASS

This is the class that tests the code for the Proxy pattern. Recall that our demonstration is based on the DarkLord wanting his proxy Quirrell to steal the Philosopher's Stone from the chamber where Dumbledore has hidden it in the Mirror of Erised. In our demonstration, Quirrell is an instance of the DarkWizard class and Voldemort a one and only one possible instance of the DarkLord class. The demonstration is a snippet of what happens toward the end of the first Harry Potter book when Harry Potter enters the chamber where Dumbledore has hidden the Philosopher's Stone, only to discover that Quirrell has beaten him to that chamber and is trying to figure out how to get the stone out of the mirror.

More specifically, our demonstration is about the proxy Quirrell making an appeal to the DarkLord for help with finding the stone in the mirror. The DarkLord responds that Quirrell needs to use the boy, meaning Harry Potter. It is this conversation between the proxy Quirrell and the master, the DarkLord, that is the focus of our demonstration.

In the implementation shown below, we first construct an instance of the master server class, the DarkLord class. As indicated earlier, there exists one and only one DarkLord. We then construct an instance of the proxy object, which for our demonstration is a DarkWizard instance for the wizard Quirrell and, in the next statement, set its canCastUnforgivableCurses property to true. The final statement in the code shown below amounts to setting Voldemort's goal to the stealing of the Philosopher's Stone through the proxy Quirrell.

When you execute this class, you will see a dialog taking place between the proxy and the master in the terminal window of your computer in which you run this demonstration. We will show this dialog in the next section.

```
public class ClientClass {
    public static void main( String[] args ) {
        DarkLord youKnowWho =
                        DarkLord.makeInstanceOfDarkLord("Voldemort");
        DarkWizard proxy = new DarkWizard("Quirrell");
        proxy.setCanCastUnforgivableCurses(true);
        youKnowWho.goal("steal the Philosopher's Stone",  proxy );
```

```
    }
}
```

13.12   PLAYING WITH THE CODE

Download the class files for this pattern from the book website into a separate directory. Compile the code with the command

```
javac *.java
```

and execute the `ClientClass` class by

```
java ClientClass
```

Given the code in the `main()` of `ClientClass`, executing this class will produce the following output:

```
Quirrell:  My Master, Is this your command that I steal
           the Philosopher's Stone?

Voldemort: Yes, that is correct!


Quirrell:  What does this mirror do? How does it work?
           Help me, Master!

Voldemort: Use the boy.....Use the boy...


Quirrell:  Master, the boy is not cooperating!

Voldemort: SIEZE HIM!!!


Quirrell:  Master, I can't.  My hands!!  My hands!!!

Voldemort: KILL HIM!
```

For additional insights, you can extend the code for this pattern on your own along the following lines:

• In the code as shown, all communications between the Dark Lord and his proxy Quirrell are initiated by the proxy. That is, when the proxy needs to consult the Dark Lord, it invokes the `establishCommunicationLinkWithDarkLord()` method defined for the `DarkWizard` class that brings into existence a two-way communication link with the Dark Lord. You may want to extend the code so that a two-way communication link between the proxy and the master can be established by either party.

- In Section 13.3, we talked about different kinds of proxies. The type actually demonstrated in this chapter is useful when there is a need to create a front-end to a master server, with the front-end handling most of the routine incoming queries (or, at least, the queries for which it has cached the server responses), and with the back-end server focusing on just the exceptional cases. We can also think of another type of a proxy that serves merely as a conduit between the clients on one side and the rest of the internet on the other. This type of a proxy can be used as an anonymizing device for the folks on the client side. Such a proxy can also be used for placing security restrictions on who is allowed to communicate with the outside and what sort of traffic is allowed to pass through. Pretending that the Ministry of Magic has figured out a way to monitor all communications between the Dark Lord and the rest of the wizarding world, modify the inter-thread communication code in this chapter so that you have what would amount to a monitored pipe between a wizard such as Quirrell, on the one hand, and the Dark Lord on the other.

14

CHAIN OF RESPONSIBILITY

14.1 PASSING THE BUCK

In all likelihood you have heard of "query escalation" or "complaint escalation" that some businesses use to handle complaints from irate customers. Folks whose job it is to provide help to the customers are typically arranged in a hierarchy, with people at the bottom qualified to handle the most routine of the problems that are likely to be encountered by customers who cannot or will not read the instructions that come with the products. People at the higher levels of such hierarchical arrangements are asked to step in when those at the lower levels find themselves befuddled by the issues raised by the customers. In business-to-business interactions, especially when important customers are involved, it is not unlikely that the top individual in this hierarchy is the CEO of the organization. The important point to note here is that, generally speaking, a query/complaint escalates to the next higher level at the discretion of the individual handling it at the lower level because, say, he/she is unable to resolve it.

An alternative to a hierarchical organization of people for handling queries and complaints is a hierarchical organization of the topics and a matrix organization of the people. The topic hierarchy is arranged in such a manner that a leaf node at the bottom represents a narrowly defined specific issue and a higher-level node an "integration" of the issues as represented by the descendants of that node. In this approach, before a customer uploads a query, he/she is asked to click on all of the topic categories that best describe the problem faced by the customer. If the category information checked by the customer implies a narrowly defined problem, it may be sent to all the individuals assigned to the relevant leaf nodes of the topic hierarchy with the expectation that one of them will take on the job of handling the query. On the other hand, if the category information checked by the customer implies a more systemic problem that is manifesting itself in multiple ways, the query would be sent to the folks assigned to a level in the topic hierarchy that best corresponds to the information uploaded by the customer. Additionally, when the folks handling a query at a lower level discover that the issue at hand could result in other problems (that the customer may not have yet reported), the query would be escalated to a

Designing with Objects: Object-Oriented Design Patterns Explained with Stories from Harry Potter,
First Edition. Avinash C. Kak.
© 2015 John Wiley & Sons, Inc. Published 2015 by John Wiley & Sons, Inc.

higher level depending on how systemic these other problems are likely to be. We again have query escalation, but now the query can escalate not just one level at a time, but can jump up to any level depending on the extent to which the query is already known to (or is likely to) result in systemic problems.

The second alternative presented above is more complex and is likely to be used only in business-to-business query processing systems. Note, though, that in both approaches, the nodes on a path from any of the leaf nodes of the hierarchies to the root node constitute a *chain of responsibility*. Such chains tend to be static in the sense that any two similar queries propagate up the hierarchy of problem solvers in more or less the same manner. Ideally, one would want chains of responsibility that are *dynamic*, meaning that the chain would vary from query to query, even when two queries are similar, depending on the problem solvers actually available at the moment a query is received and who amongst them would be the best for resolving the issues that need to be addressed; the priority level associated with the query; penalties associated with any delays in query resolution; importance of the customer; and so on. In general, these aspects of a query will not be known in advance and may vary from query to query even from the same customer. The Chain of Responsibility pattern shows us how we can create dynamic chains in software systems that are based on the query escalation metaphor.

14.2   INTENT AND APPLICABILITY

The intent of the Chain of Responsibility pattern is to specify dynamically a chain of objects that should receive a query for its resolution. A query is passed from object to object in the chain until its eventual resolution.

You should use this pattern when

- it is not known at compile time which objects should resolve a query;
- when an object needs to pass a query to the next "higher level" object in a chain, the identity of the best qualified receiving object can only be determined at runtime;
- there exist multiple objects qualified to handle a query, but the object that will accept the query for its resolution is only known at runtime.

14.3   INTRODUCTION TO THE CHAIN OF RESPONSIBILITY PATTERN

As mentioned previously, query escalation systems as generally implemented result in static chains of responsibility. With static chains, all similar queries are pre-programmed to be handled in roughly the same manner by the query escalation system in place. However, ideally, you would want to employ a dynamic approach to resolving the issues with a hierarchy of problem solvers. In a dynamic approach, you would associate with each new query a chain of responsibility that is meant specifically for that query. For constructing such chains, you'd look for the problem solvers who are actually available at the moment the query is received and who best match the issues raised by the query. The chain assigned to a query could also take into account factors such as its technical complexity, the urgency

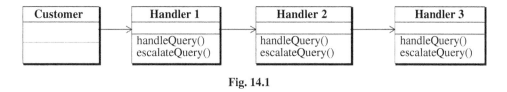

Fig. 14.1

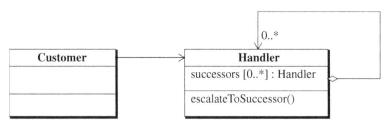

Fig. 14.2

with which the problem must be resolved, the costs associated with the non-resolution of the problem in a timely manner, and so on.

Figure 14.1 shows a customer query being handled by a static chain of responsibility in a software system. Each query handler — an instance of a `Handler` class — can either process the query itself, or, if unable to resolve the issue, can escalate it to the next supposedly more qualified handler in the chain. Such a chain of responsibility would normally be hard-coded at compile time. A static chain of responsibility has the advantage — if it has any advantages at all — that its flow of control is easy to understand. Referring to Figure 14.1, the applicable query-handler method of the `Handler1` would simply invoke the appropriate query-handler method of `Handler2`, and so on. Obviously, once you create such hard-coded links in a chain of potential query responders, you lose flexibility in the processing of the queries.

Figure 14.2, on the other hand, illustrates how one might use a dynamic approach to the creation of a chain of responsibility. Each query handler now maintains a list of other query handlers, bound to the variable named `successors`, who are more qualified to handle the query if it is not resolved locally. The important thing to note in Figure 14.2 is that, for a given query, the variable `successors` is assigned a list of certain designated more qualified query handlers only at runtime. Additionally, it is only at runtime that the next handler for a given query is chosen from this list. As to which specific handler is chosen from any of these lists would depend on the various parameters that are assigned to the query when it is first logged by the query processing system.

14.4   THE CHAIN OF RESPONSIBILITY PATTERN IN REAL-WORLD APPLICATIONS

A typical application of this pattern is in GUI (Graphical User Interface) software. After a GUI — consisting normally of a main window incorporating widgets like buttons, check boxes, text windows, scroll bars, and so on — is instantiated, it is placed in what is

known as the event-processing loop in which it waits for the user's interaction. Subsequently, in response to the user's actions, the GUI invokes what are usually known as *callback functions* or just *callbacks*. A GUI software system typically defines callbacks at different levels of specificity and, usually, only the most specific callback is invoked for a given action by the user. For example, a GUI system may define a general callback for a "Keypress" event that is associated with the pressing of *any* key on the keyboard and a more specific callback for the "Return" event that is associated with the pressing of just the Return key (the same as the Enter key) on the keyboard. If the user actually pressed the Return key, only the callback associated with the "Return" event would be invoked.

In general, the callbacks that are relevant to a widget in a GUI constitute a tree that corresponds to the *containment hierarchy* of the GUI. As the name implies, a widget containing other widgets in a GUI gives rise to a containment hierarchy. With regard to the structure of containment, whereas a widget is allowed to contain multiple widgets, it can only possess a single parent. Obviously, such a hierarchy would be rooted at the main window of the GUI. When a user interacts with a widget, if the widget has no callbacks registered with it, the event goes up the containment hierarchy to the parent of that widget, and so on. *This represents a real-world implementation of the Chain of Responsibility pattern especially when it is only at runtime that the containment hierarchy comes into existence (as would be the case for dynamically generated web pages that are rich in user interaction).* Looking up from the leaf nodes of the containment hierarchy toward the root, we would see chains of event processing agents. What facilitates the passing of an event up these chains is the fact that all potential event handlers are objects of the same basic type — the type from which all of the GUI classes descend.

14.5 HARRY POTTER STORY USED TO ILLUSTRATE THE CHAIN OF RESPONSIBILITY PATTERN

Our demonstration of the Chain of Responsibility pattern is in the context of resolving the violations in the game of Quidditch, a major organized sport of the wizarding world. Given a team of Quidditch players, the school teachers, the referees, the headmaster, and so on, we want to create at runtime a chain of responsibility for the resolution of violations in a Quidditch game. That is, at runtime, we wish to decide whether a given violation by some player should be resolved locally by the referee, or, when the violation is serious, if it should be forwarded by the referee to the teacher supervising the game. Extending the scenario further, we may also think of violations that are so offensive and contentious that they would need to be forwarded by the supervising teacher to the Deputy Headmaster, or, for that matter, to the Headmaster himself.

The critical thing to note is that we want to be able to specify the chain of the officials used for violation reporting and resolution for each game separately and do so at runtime. *So the reporting links cannot be hard coded into the class definitions.* This run-time ability in constructing a chain of responsibility will be achieved in our demonstration by having all potential participants in the chain descend from a root class that we will name Adjudicator. In principle at least, anyone who is an Adjudicator will have the authority to resolve one or more violations.

Here is a list of the Quidditch violations we will include in our demonstration:

1. Seizing an opponent's broom (Blagging)
2. Flying with the intent to collide (Blatching)
3. Locking broom handles to steer opponent off course (Blurting)
4. Hitting a bludger toward the keepers or spectators — however, the former is allowed if the quaffle is within the scoring area (Bumphing)
5. Elbowing the opponents excessively (Cobbing)
6. When a keeper defends a hoop from behind (Flacking)
7. A chaser still in contact with the quaffle as it passes through a hoop (Haversacking)
8. When a chaser tampers with the quaffle (QuafflePocking)
9. When more than one chaser is in the scoring area at the same time (Stooging)
10. Player leaves boundary
11. Push player off the broom
12. Piss off the referee
13. Hit player with club
14. Beater hitting quaffle
15. Throw quaffle out of bounds
16. Non-seeker contacting golden snitch
17. Failure to return after timeout
18. Using wand to enchant during play
19. Team foul
20. Broom tampering
21. Tampering with referee broom

In our demonstration, when a player commits a violation, the need to resolve the violation will be expressed as follows:

```
Player p =  .....
p.resolveViolation( PissOffTheReferee );
```

where we first construct an instance of a `Player` and then call the `resolveViolation()` method on the player while supplying the violation to the method as its argument. The violation `PissOffTheReferee` is the code representation of the 12th violation listed above. As to the chain of responsibility for the resolution of this violation, we will set that up dynamically at the time the `Player` instance is created. Here is an example of how a `Player` instance will be created:

```
Player p = new Player( "Fred Weasley",
                       "Blind Side Beater",
                       new ArrayList<Adjudicator>(
                           Arrays.asList( referee, teacher, deputyHead )));
```

where the first argument to the `Player` constructor is the name of the player, the second argument the position played, and the third argument the chain of responsibility for

the violation supplied as the argument to `resolveViolation()`. In the code fragment shown above, the objects bound to the variables `referee`, `teacher`, and `deputyHead` would be set at runtime and, in general, would vary from player to player. Additionally, these variables would be assigned their own chains of responsibility that would also be set dynamically. Note that you'd create a `Player` instance only when a player has committed a violation that needs to be resolved. So the values chosen for the third argument would implicitly take into account the availability of those who are qualified to resolve the violation committed by the player.

14.6 A TOP LEVEL VIEW OF THE PATTERN DEMONSTRATION

Figure 14.3 presents a top-level view of the code for this demonstration. As should be obvious from the diagram, the class `Adjudicator` plays a most important role in how the code implements the Chain of Responsibility pattern and how it allows us to create chains dynamically. As the reader will see in the next section, dynamic creation of chains of responsibility is made possible by the fact that the `Adjudicator` class possesses an instance variable `successors` that stores a list of other `Adjudicator` instances who are qualified to receive a violation for its resolution. This instance variable is bound at runtime to a list of other `Adjudicator` instances. Since all of the other "actors" in the demonstration — teachers, referees, and so on — are also of type `Adjudicator`, they are allowed to become members of the list that is bound to the instance variable `successors` of any given `Adjudicator`. The `successors` instance variable, defined in the root abstract class `Adjudicator`, is inherited by the five derived classes shown in Figure 14.3. The fact that what is bound to `successors` is an aggregation of the instances of type `Adjudicator` is made evident by the loopback link from the `Adjudicator` class to itself.

For the sake of convenience, we place all Quidditch violations in the interface `Violations` that is presented in the next section. By having the abstract class `Adjudicator` implement this interface and by virtue of the fact that all of the "actors" in our demonstration are subclassed from `Adjudicator` makes all of the violations declared in the interface `Violations` available to all other classes.

The reader is probably puzzled by the fact that the class `Player` is also subclassed from the `Adjudicator`. If our implementation were to reflect a complaint handling system of the sort we talked about in the introduction to this chapter (also see Figure 14.2), you would not expect a customer to be of the same type as a query handler in a business establishment.[1] Subclassing a `Player` from the abstract root `Adjudicator` was done purely for convenience in this demonstration (and to keep the code base from becoming too large). With `Player` as a subclass of `Adjudicator`, we can use the framework established in the latter for escalating the violation to the next available authority. Additionally, this also makes available to the `Player` class all of the violations declared in the interface `Violations`.

The reader might ask: if the `Player` class is also subclassed from `Adjudicator`, how do we keep the players from resolving their own violations? We make sure that a player

---

[1] This analogy between a customer in Figure 14.2 and a player in Figure 14.3 is a stretch because the latter does not submit a violation for its redress by the authorities. A referee in a game of Quidditch would be more akin to a customer in Figure 14.2. Nonetheless, for the sake of keeping the code base for this demonstration from becoming too large, we have chosen to implement it in the fashion shown.

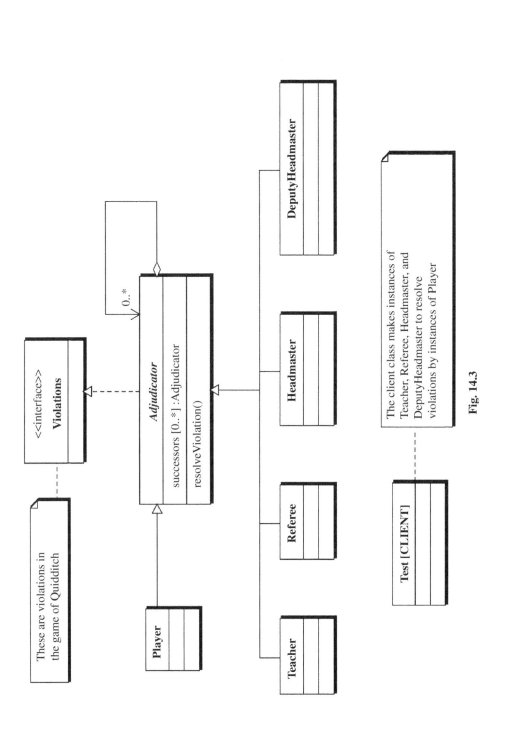

Fig. 14.3

does not resolve his or her own violations by the expedient of not providing the Player class with the `violationsResolved` variable — a fact that will become clear in Section 14.9. As the reader will see after being introduced to the `Adjudicator` class, the value of this variable in the `Player` class will be as it is defined in the root class `Adjudicator` — an empty list.

The executable class for this demonstration is `Test`. This class, presented in Section 14.11, shows us creating chains of responsibility dynamically and binding them to the instance variable `successors` in the objects of type `Adjudicator`.

14.7   THE INTERFACE CLASS Violations

Shown below is a helper interface that stores the mappings between the symbolic names of the violations and the integer values assigned to them. Although it is more convenient to refer to the violations symbolically, the associated integer values make it easier to write the violation handling code.

```
public interface Violations {
    public final int CannotResolveViolations = -1;

    public final int Blagging = 0;        // Seizing an opponent's broom.
    public final int Blatching = 1;       // Flying with the intent to
                                          //    collide.
    public final int Blurting = 2;        // Locking broom handles to
                                          //    steer opponent off course.
    public final int Bumphing = 3;        // Hitting a bludger towards
                                          //    the keepers or spectators.
                                          //    However, the former is
                                          //    allowed if the quaffle is
                                          //    within the scoring area.
    public final int Cobbing = 4;         // Elbowing the opponents
                                          //    excessively.
    public final int Flacking = 5;        // When a keeper defends a
                                          //    hoop from behind.
    public final int Haversacking = 6;    // A chaser still in contact
                                          //    with the quaffle as it
                                          //    passes through a hoop.
    public final int QuafflePocking = 7;// When a chaser tampers with
                                          //    the quaffle.
    public final int Stooging = 8;        // When more than one chaser
                                          //    is in the scoring area
                                          //    at the same time.
    public final int PlayerLeavesBoundary = 9;
    public final int PushPlayerOffTheBroom = 10;
    public final int PissOffTheReferee = 11;
    public final int HitPlayerWithClub = 12;
    public final int BeaterHittingQuaffle = 13;
    public final int ThrowQuaffleOutOfBounds = 14;
    public final int NonSeekerContactingGoldenSnitch = 15;
    public final int FailureToReturnAfterTimeout = 16;
```

```
public final int UsingWandToEnchantDuringPlay = 17;
public final int TeamFoul = 18;
public final int BroomTampering = 19;
public final int TamperingWithRefereeBroom = 20;

public final String[] printViolation = new String[]{"Blagging",
                "Blatching", "Blurting", "Bumphing",
                "Cobbing", "Flacking", "Haversacking",
                "QuafflePocking", "Stooging",
                "PlayerLeavesBoundary",
                "PushPlayerOffTheBroom", "PissOffTheReferee",
                "HitPlayerWithClub", "BeaterHittingQuaffle",
                "ThrowQuaffleOutOfBounds",
                "NonSeekerContactingGoldenSnitch",
                "FailureToReturnAfterTimeout",
                "UsingWandToEnchantDuringPlay", "TeamFoul",
                "BroomTampering", "TamperingWithRefereeBroom"};
}
```

14.8   THE ABSTRACT CLASS Adjudicator

Being abstract, an object of this class would never be constructed. However, anyone who is authorized to resolve game violations is expected to be of type that is derived from this class.

As mentioned previously, what gives an Adjudicator the ability to forward an incoming request for violation adjudication to another Adjudicator are the following two facts:

- The Adjudicator class is equipped with a instance variable called successors through the following declaration:

```
protected List<Adjudicator> successors =
                        new ArrayList<Adjudicator>();
```

Obviously, successors is simply a list of instances of type Adjudicator. This is where we store the receivers of a violation if the current adjudicator in the chain of responsibility must forward it to the next level. For example, if a Referee sees a violation but considers it beyond his/her authority to adjudicate, the Referee instance will forward it to the authorities listed in the successors list. As to who these authorities are would depend on how the Referee instance is created at runtime. When a Referee instance is created, it is supplied with values for its successors instance variable that it inherits from the Adjudicator parent class.

- The constructors for all classes that participate in a Quidditch game take a second argument where we supply one or more values for the successors instance variable.

As you will see in Section 14.10, each different type of an adjudicator will be given a fixed set of violations that it is authorized to resolve. This will be accomplished by assigning a list of values to the variable violationsResolved in the concrete subclasses of

Adjudicator in Section 14.10. So whereas the power of each type of adjudicator is defined at compile time, the chain of adjudicators assigned to resolve a particular violation by a particular player is set at runtime, as will be clear from the discussion in the next section when we introduce the Player class.

As the reader can see, this abstract class has been provided with three different constructors. This is just for convenience. The first constructor is for those Adjudicators who have no successors. That is, the buck will stop with the instances of such adjudicators — but only for those violations that they are knowledgeable about. So if a violation is received by such an Adjudicator but he/she is not competent to handle the violation, the violation will be deemed to be irresolvable. The second constructor is for the case when a single successor is named for an Adjudicator, and the third for the case when a list of successors is named.

Note the predicate canResolveViolations(). If the list of violations stored in the variable violationsResolved is empty and also if the list of successors stored in the variable successors is empty, we say that this Adjudicator will not be able to resolve any violations. Also note the implementation of the method resolveViolation(). If an Adjudicator himself or herself cannot resolve a violation, the violation in question is sent in succession to each of the successors for the Adjudicator. It is deemed resolved by the first successor who can handle it.

```java
import java.util.*;

public abstract class Adjudicator implements Violations {

    protected String name;
    protected List<Adjudicator> successors =
                                    new ArrayList<Adjudicator> ();
    protected List<Integer>  violationsResolved =
                                    new ArrayList<Integer>();
    public Adjudicator( String name ) { this.name = name; }
    public Adjudicator( String name, Adjudicator successor ) {
        this.name = name;
        if (successor != null)
            successors.add( successor );
    }
    public Adjudicator( String name, List<Adjudicator> successors ) {
        this.name = name;
        this.successors = successors;
    }
    public void addAdjudicator( Adjudicator adjudicator ) {
        this.getSuccessors().add( adjudicator );
    }
    public boolean canResolveViolations() {
        if ( violationsResolved.isEmpty()
                & getSuccessors().isEmpty() ) return false;
        return true;
    }
    public boolean resolveViolation( int vio ) {
        boolean vioResolved = false;
        if ( getSuccessors().isEmpty() ) {
            return false;
```

```
        } else {
            ListIterator<Adjudicator> iter =successors.listIterator();
            while ( iter.hasNext() ) {
                vioResolved = false;
                if( iter.next().resolveViolation( vio ) ) {
                    vioResolved = true;
                    break;
                }
            }
        }
        return vioResolved;
    }
    public List<Integer> getViolationsResolved() {
        return violationsResolved;
    }
    public void setSuccessors( List<Adjudicator> successors ) {
        this.successors = successors;
    }
    public List<Adjudicator> getSuccessors() {
        return successors;
    }
    public String toString() {
        if ( this instanceof Player) return "Player";
        if ( this instanceof Referee) return "Referee";
        if ( this instanceof Teacher) return "Teacher";
        if ( this instanceof  DeputyHeadmaster )
            return "Deputy Headmaster";
        if ( this instanceof Headmaster) return "Headmaster";
        return "";
    }
}
```

14.9   THE Player CLASS

This section presents the Player class — important because it represents the folks who commit violations whose resolution by dynamically created chains of responsibility is the focus of our demonstration.

Note how the constructors supply a value for the successor instance variable that is inherited by every Player from the superclass Adjudicator.

Probably the most important part of the definition of the Player class is the method resolveViolation(). In the implementation of this method, we first invoke the predicate canResolveViolations() that is defined for the parent class Adjudicator. This inherited predicate returns false if it finds that the successors list is empty and, at the same time, if the list of violations in the inherited instance variable violationsResolved is empty. Subsequently, it checks if the violation in question is included in the list stored in the inherited instance variable violationsResolved. In contrast with the definition of the other concrete subclasses of Adjudicator, which we present in the next section, the Player class is *not* provided with a static variable named violationsResolved. So it inherits the default value of empty-list for this important variable. What that means is that

a Player instance — even when he/she is, say, a team captain — is not allowed to resolve any violations, even when they are intra-team violations.

By virtue of the above fact, when `resolveViolation()` is invoked on a Player instance, the control will shift to line (A) in the implementation shown below. This might lead a reader to wonder why we did not provide a shorter definition for the method, that is, a definition without the code up to line (A). The reason is to allow an enterprising reader to extend the demonstration code in a way that allows some players to resolve some of the intra-team violations (see Section 14.12).

With regard to the if-else clause at line (A), a call to `resolveViolation()` starts by calling on the implementation of this method as defined for the parent class Adjudicator to process the violation. If the code in the parent class cannot resolve the violation in question, you declare that the violation cannot be resolved by all of those who were inducted at runtime into the chain of responsibility for a given game of Quidditch.

```
import java.util.*;

public class Player extends Adjudicator {

    private String role;    // must be one of Chaser,
                            // Beater, Seeker, and Keeper
    public Player( String name, String role, Adjudicator successor ) {
        super(name, successor);
        this.role = role;
    }
    public Player( String name, String role,
                                    List<Adjudicator> successors ) {
        super(name, successors);
        this.role = role;
    }
    public boolean resolveViolation( int vio ) {
        if ( !canResolveViolations() ) {
            System.out.println( "  It is not possible to resolve "
                            + "this violation" );
            return false;
        } else if ( violationsResolved != null &&
                    violationsResolved.contains( new Integer(vio) ) ) {
            System.out.println( "   Violation " + printViolation[vio]
                        + " resolved by the " + this + " " + name );
            return true;
        } else {
            if ( super.resolveViolation(vio) )                    // (A)
                return true;
            else {
                System.out.println( "   The violation "
                        + printViolation[vio] + " cannot be resolved" );
                return false;
            }
        }
    }
}
```

14.10   THE CLASSES WITH THE AUTHORITY TO RESOLVE VIOLATIONS

We start with the `Referee` class. Note how in contrast with the `Player` class, the `Referee` class is provided with its own static variable `violationsResolved` that stores a list of the violations that a `Referee` is allowed to resolve on his/her own. As mentioned previously in Section 14.8, this amounts to a compile-time declaration of the scope of violation resolution authority for each different type of an Adjudicator. So, whereas the power of each adjudicator type is declared at compile-time, the list of adjudicators pressed into service for resolving a particular violation by a particular player is created at runtime.

Also note how the implementation of the method `resolveViolation()` for `Referee` is much simpler than it was for the `Player` class[2] or for the parent class `Adjudicator`. The implementation in this class first looks for the violation in question in the static variable `violationsResolved`. If the violation is found in that list, then we are done and we can say that `Referee` was able to resolve the violation on his/her own. Otherwise, we forward the violation to the parent class's implementation of `resolveViolation()`, where we simply go through each of the successors stored in the list pointed to by the instance variable `successors` and check if the violation can be handled by any of them. We stop at the first successful resolution of the violation.

```java
import java.util.*;

public class Referee extends Adjudicator {

    private final static List<Integer> violationsResolved =
        new ArrayList<Integer>( Arrays.asList( Blatching, Cobbing,
                QuafflePocking, Haversacking, Flacking, Stooging,
                                        Blurting, Bumphing ) );
    public Referee( String name, Adjudicator successor ) {
        super( name, successor );
    }
    public Referee( String name, List<Adjudicator> successors ) {
        super( name, successors);
    }
    public boolean resolveViolation( int vio ) {
        System.out.println( "    Violation handed over to " + this );
        if ( violationsResolved.contains( new Integer(vio) ) ) {
            System.out.println( "   Violation " + printViolation[vio]
                        + " resolved by the " + this + " " + name );
            return true;
        } else {
            return super.resolveViolation(vio);
        }
    }
}
```

---

[2]As mentioned in the previous section, one reason for why the `resolveViolation()` method in the `Player` class was implemented as shown is to help the reader extend the demonstration along the lines suggested in Section 14.12 so that some players, such as the team captain, can resolve some of the violations by themselves.

Next we present the `Teacher` class. Except for its name and the consequences thereof, the definition of this class is exactly the same as for the `Referee` class. So all the comments made for the `Referee` class apply to this class also.

```java
import java.util.*;

public class Teacher extends Adjudicator  {

    private final static List<Integer> violationsResolved =
        new ArrayList<Integer>( Arrays.asList(
                                  FailureToReturnAfterTimeout ));

    public Teacher( String name, Adjudicator successor ) {
        super( name, successor );
    }
    public Teacher( String name, List<Adjudicator> successors ) {
        super( name, successors );
    }
    public boolean resolveViolation( int vio ) {
        System.out.println( "    Violation handed over to " + this );
        if ( violationsResolved.contains( new Integer(vio) ) ) {
            System.out.println( "    Violation "
                         + printViolation[vio] + " resolved by the "
                               + this + " " + "Professor " + name );
            return true;
        } else {
            return super.resolveViolation(vio);
        }
    }
}
```

Next we present the `DeputyHeadmaster` class. With regard to the code for violation resolution, this class is no different from the `Referee` and the `Teacher` classes. However, there is a significant difference between this class and the other two with regard to how the instances are produced from the class definitions, as we explain next.

The class shown below is based on the Singleton pattern because there can only be one Deputy Headmaster. In line with the explanation provided in Chapter 6, this is ensured by placing the constructor of the class in its private section and by making available a public method called `makeInstanceOfDeputyHeadmaster()` for instance production. If an instance of `DeputyHeadmaster` was previously produced, a call to `makeInstanceOfDeputyHeadmaster()` returns that same instance over and over. However, if an instance of `DeputyHeadmaster` had not been created previously when `makeInstanceOfDeputyHeadmaster()` is called, it creates an instance, stores it away by binding it to the variable `unique` in the definition shown below, and supplies the instance in response to the call.

```java
import java.util.*;

public class DeputyHeadmaster extends Adjudicator {

    private static DeputyHeadmaster  unique;

    private final static List<Integer> violationsResolved =
            new ArrayList<Integer>( Arrays.asList( BroomTampering ) );

    private DeputyHeadmaster( String name, Adjudicator successor ) {
        super( name, successor );
    }
    // Enforce the condition that there can only
    // be one Assistant Headmaster:
    public static DeputyHeadmaster makeInstanceOfDeputyHeadmaster(
                                String name, Adjudicator successor){
        if ( unique == null )
            unique = new DeputyHeadmaster( name, successor );
        return unique;
    }
    public DeputyHeadmaster(String name,List<Adjudicator> successors){
        super(name, successors);
    }
    public boolean resolveViolation( int vio ) {
        System.out.println( "    Violation handed over to " + this );
        if ( violationsResolved.contains( new Integer(vio) ) ) {
            System.out.println( "    Violation "
                + printViolation[vio] + " resolved by the " + this
                                    + " " + "Professor " + name );
            return true;
        } else {
            return super.resolveViolation(vio);
        }
    }
}
```

That brings us to the last of the classes in this section, the Headmaster class. This class is similar to the DeputyHeadmaster class we just presented, in the sense that its implementation is also based on the Singleton pattern — for the same reasons as for the DeputyHeadmaster class. However, there is an important difference between the two classes: Whereas the constructor for the Headmaster class takes only one argument, which is for the name of the headmaster, the DeputyHeadmaster constructor takes two arguments, one for the name and the other for the successor. Our demonstration of the pattern is based on the assumption that the ultimate end point of every chain of responsibility for resolving a Quidditch violation is the Headmaster'. That means that there can be no successors for the wizard occupying this post.

```java
import java.util.*;

public class Headmaster extends Adjudicator {

    private static Headmaster unique;
    private final static List<Integer> violationsResolved =
        new ArrayList<Integer>(
                    Arrays.asList( UsingWandToEnchantDuringPlay ));
    private Headmaster( String name ) {
        super( name );
    }
    // Enforce the condition that there can only be one Headmaster:
    public static Headmaster makeInstanceOfHeadmaster( String name ) {
        if ( unique == null ) unique = new Headmaster( name );
        return unique;
    }
    public boolean resolveViolation( int vio ) {
        System.out.println( "    Violation handed over to " + this );
        if ( violationsResolved.contains( new Integer(vio) ) ) {
            System.out.println( "    Violation "
                + printViolation[vio] + " resolved by the "
                      + this + " " + "Professor " + name );
            return true;
        }
        return false;
    }
}
```

14.11 TESTING THE CODE

The client class shown below demonstrates how you can create chains of responsibility at runtime. Notice the second argument provided to the constructors for Referee, Teacher, and DeputyHeadmaster, and the third argument provided to the constructor for Player. These arguments provide each constructed instance with a successor, meaning the individual(s) who will receive a violation that cannot be resolved by the constructed instance. For the Player instances, the second argument denotes the position played by the player. The rest of the code shows us constructing different Player instances who are accused of having committed different violations. As we invoke the resolveViolation() method on these Player instances, we see the Chain of Responsibility pattern in action.

```java
import java.util.*;

public class Test implements Violations{

    public static void main(String[] args) {
```

```
Headmaster headmaster =
            Headmaster.makeInstanceOfHeadmaster("Dumbledore");
DeputyHeadmaster  deputyHead =
 DeputyHeadmaster.makeInstanceOfDeputyHeadmaster("McGonagall",
                                              headmaster);
Teacher teacher = new Teacher( "Rolanda Hooch", deputyHead );
Referee referee = new Referee( "Severus Snape", teacher );

System.out.println(
          "For player Harry Potter (Violation: Blatching): ");
Player p1 = new Player( "Harry Potter", "seeker", referee );
p1.resolveViolation( Blatching );

System.out.println("\n\nFor player Angelina Johnson " +
                            "(Violation: Haversacking): ");
Player p2 = new Player("Angelina Johnson", "chaser", referee);
p2.resolveViolation( Haversacking );

System.out.println("\n\nFor player Dracy Molfoy "
                    + "(Violation: Using Wand During Play): ");
Player p3 = new Player( "Draco Malfoy", "seeker",
              new ArrayList<Adjudicator>(
                Arrays.asList( referee, teacher, deputyHead )));
p3.resolveViolation(UsingWandToEnchantDuringPlay);

System.out.println("\n\nFor player Viktor Krum "
                        + "(Violation: Broom Tampering): ");
Player p4 = new Player("Viktor Krum","seeker",
              new ArrayList<Adjudicator>(
                Arrays.asList( referee, teacher, deputyHead )));
p4.resolveViolation(BroomTampering);

System.out.println("\n\nFor player Fred Weasley "
                        + "(Violation: Piss off the referee): ");
Player p5 = new Player( "Fred Weasley", "Blind Side Beater",
              new ArrayList<Adjudicator>(
                Arrays.asList( referee, teacher, deputyHead )));
p5.resolveViolation(PissOffTheReferee);
  }
}
```

14.12 PLAYING WITH THE CODE

Download the class files for this pattern from the book website into a separate directory.
Compile the code with the command

```
javac *.java
```

and execute the Test class by

```
java Test
```

Given the code in the `main()` of `Test`, executing this class will produce the following output:

```
For player Harry Potter (Violation: Blatching):
    Violation handed over to Referee
    Violation Blatching resolved by the Referee Severus Snape


For player Angelina Johnson (Violation: Haversacking):
    Violation handed over to Referee
    Violation Haversacking resolved by the Referee Severus Snape


For player Dracy Molfoy (Violation: Using Wand During Play):
    Violation handed over to Referee
    Violation handed over to Teacher
    Violation handed over to Deputy Headmaster
    Violation handed over to Headmaster
    Violation UsingWandToEnchantDuringPlay resolved by the Headmaster
                                            Professor Dumbledore


For player Viktor Krum (Violation: Broom Tampering):
    Violation handed over to Referee
    Violation handed over to Teacher
    Violation handed over to Deputy Headmaster
    Violation BroomTampering resolved by the Deputy Headmaster
                                            Professor McGonagall


For player Fred Weasley (Violation: Piss off the referee):
    Violation handed over to Referee
    Violation handed over to Teacher
    Violation handed over to Deputy Headmaster
    Violation handed over to Headmaster
    Violation handed over to Teacher
    Violation handed over to Deputy Headmaster
    Violation handed over to Headmaster
    Violation handed over to Deputy Headmaster
    Violation handed over to Headmaster
    The violation PissOffTheReferee cannot be resolved
```

For additional insights, you can extend the code for this pattern on your own along the following lines:

- As shown in Figure 14.3, for the sake of programming convenience, we made the Player class a subclass of the Adjudicator class. The convenience was that this made the language of violations directly available in the Player class. Another convenience was that it gave us a uniform mechanism for escalating the violations, starting right from the Players themselves. But, as pointed out in Figure 14.2, you would not

ordinarily expect the objects that generate the queries (or complaints or violations, or however else you wish to refer to the issues that need to be resolved) to be of the same type as the classes that handle the queries. Modify the demonstration code so that there is complete type separation between the players, on the one hand, and the school officials, on the other.

- In the current demonstration code, the players are not allowed to resolve the violations. This is despite the fact that the `Player` class is endowed with the `resolveViolation()` method. The reason a player cannot resolve violations has to do with the fact that the `Player` class does not possess a static variable named `violationsResolved`.[3] However, we can easily think of situations where you would want a player to be able to resolve some of the more minor violations. For example, a team captain might be given the authority to resolve a violation with the proviso that the resolution would stand unless challenged by the opposite-side team captain. Modify the code so that it is possible for a player to engage in violation resolution.

---

[3] In the absence of such a static variable, the `Player` class inherits the variable and its empty-list value from the parent class `Adjudicator`.

PART III

BEHAVIORAL PATTERNS

As the name implies, Behavioral Patterns are about designing classes that work together to provide specific run-time services. Contrast this with what we accomplish with Creational and Structural Patterns. As the reader will recall, Creational Patterns deal with the design of classes and the methods for constructing their instances, while addressing issues related to the need for the following: programming to interfaces, indirection in the production of instances, exercising control over the instances produced, and so on. Structural Patterns are also concerned about designing classes and writing instance production code, but now the representational issues are more complex because of the needed interactions between the classes for the production of the desired instances.

Behavioral Patterns are the most complex of the three. A significant reason for the complexity is the difficulty of tracing the run-time interactions between the classes. When software design is based on the Behavioral patterns, how a class responds to a condition created by user input or by a change in the state of some object depends, in general, on the temporal context of the condition as implied by the states of all other objects relevant to the condition. The run-time flow of execution becomes even less predictable when a pattern allows for a new object to be injected into the system at runtime. While the type of such an object would be known at compile time, how it might influence the flow of execution would not. As the reader would expect, how the resulting dynamic effects manifest themselves varies from pattern to pattern.

What follows is a synopsis of each of the eleven patterns in this part:

Chain of Responsibility: This pattern is about creating dynamically a chain of problem solvers for resolving issues in some domain. Perhaps the closest real-life analogy to what is accomplished by this pattern would be a dynamic version of the query escalation process that some organizations use in their customer help departments. Folks who respond to customer queries are arranged hierarchically. Routine queries are handled by folks at the bottom of the hierarchy, with more complex queries escalating, one step at a time, toward the top of the help department. A dynamic version of such a system would allow for the chain of query-resolution folks to be selected in

Designing with Objects: Object-Oriented Design Patterns Explained with Stories from Harry Potter, First Edition. Avinash C. Kak.
© 2015 John Wiley & Sons, Inc. Published 2015 by John Wiley & Sons, Inc.

real time on a case-by-case basis, depending on the priority to be accorded to a query and the abilities of the folks available.

Command: The communication interactions that are the focus of the Command pattern deal with objects that represent *actions* as opposed to *actors*. Typically, when you write an object-oriented program, you focus on actor objects that are endowed with behaviors as incorporated in the methods defined for the objects. The Command pattern shifts that focus to action objects. The pattern teaches us how you can synthesize large run-time behaviors by synthesizing more elementary behaviors provided by a set of action classes.

Interpreter: The Interpreter pattern shows us how we can use a collection of classes to interpret a language. In most cases, before you can interpret a language, you must parse its sentences in order to identify the subjects, the objects, and the actions involved. Parsing is necessary because it disambiguates the different possible roles that a given word may be able to play in a sentence — the roles corresponding to the usage of the word as a noun, as a verb, as an adjective, etc. With parsing, you can narrow down the range of meanings you may need to associate with a word in a sentence. To zero in on the actual meaning used for a word, you must also understand the context that applies to the usage of that word. While parsing is difficult for free-flowing languages, extracting the context is even more difficult. Both these challenges can only be addressed by placing constraints on the language. Our Harry Potter based demonstration of this pattern involves translating magic-speak into muggle-speak.

Iterator: There are many different ways to store a collection of objects in the memory of a computer. The approaches differ with regard to how computationally efficient they are with respect to the different operations one can carry out on a collection. We are referring to operations such as retrieving objects by address and by value, inserting and deleting objects, and so on. It makes for great programming convenience if a standard idiom is used for iterating through a collection regardless of how it is actually stored in the memory. The Iterator pattern is about creating such standard idioms with the help of an `Iterator` interface. All collections implementing the same `Iterator` interface, regardless of the actual storage mechanism used, will lend themselves to the same programming syntax for iterating through the collections.

Mediator: The Mediator pattern helps us design classes that have the responsibility to coordinate run-time interactions between other classes. In many applications, unfettered direct interactions between a large number of classes can negate any advantages you get by using object-oriented programming for modularizing your code. Too many direct interactions between the classes can imply a large number of inter-class dependencies that may make it more difficult to maintain each class independently of the other classes. The solution in such cases is to use a `Mediator` class and route all object-to-object run-time calls through the `Mediator`. It becomes the job of the `Mediator` to keep track of the state of all other objects and to decide when to allow a certain interaction between the other classes in the system.

Memento: This pattern shows us how the state of an object can be rolled back at run-time to a previous state while respecting the encapsulation properties of the state variables. The cool thing about this pattern is that all of the previous state information can be stored by the client but without the client being able to directly access the state variables and their values. With this pattern, the state is saved in instances of a class whose name is commonly `Memento`. Although a client cannot look inside the

`Memento` instances, the instances are nonetheless available to the class whose states are being saved and possibly rolled back by the client.

Observer: The Observer pattern shows how to orchestrate collaborative run-time interaction among a set of classes in which a distinguished object serves as the keeper of some data that changes with time, with the other objects staying up-to-date with the distinguished object with regard to this data. The distinguished object must allow for the other objects to register themselves with it if they want access to its data. Subscription-based broadcasting is what comes to mind when you think about the Observer pattern. Those who want access to the information being made available must first sign up with the information provider.

State: The State pattern is useful when the run-time behavior of a system as a whole lends itself to discrete characterizations, which we may refer to as its states. As you would expect, such a system would be in only one of those states at any given time and its run-time behavior would only make certain specific state transitions. Consider the scenario of a user interacting with such a system. Assuming that the questions posed by the user correspond to a small number of different contexts, we could have each context correspond to one run-time state of the system and any change in the context of the questions could automatically trigger a state transition. This pattern shows how you should design your software if you want to facilitate a state-based run-time interaction with it (by the clients of your software).

Strategy: Pursuing a goal often involves solving multiple problems along the way. How you choose to solve the problems encountered would, in general, depend on your abilities and resources. We can think of all of the solutions taken together for achieving a goal as constituting a strategy. Focusing on software development, let's say we have a set of classes that work together to achieve a certain end condition. If the functionality provided by each class is rich enough so that it gives us a choice of which specific method to invoke given the available resources, you may be able to string together all of the choices into a collection of strategies. You can then use the strategy pattern for regulating the run-time interactions between the classes in order to achieve the desired goals.

Template Method: This pattern shows how you can program an algorithm as a generic sequence of steps in an abstract base class. The class may provide implementation code for some of the steps, leaving others either merely in the form of declarations or with do-nothing implementations. Those steps that are not fully implemented in the base class would be expected to be implemented in the concrete subclasses of the base class. Subsequently, at runtime, you would be able to achieve a dynamic customization of the algorithm through polymorphic invocation of the methods for which the implementation code is provided by the subclasses.

Visitor: The purpose of the Visitor pattern is to elicit a new (previously unanticipated) run-time behavior from a class hierarchy without having to modify the classes in the hierarchy in any significant way. This is made possible by having the classes in the hierarchy incorporate a Visitor hook. The same hook can be used to elicit different new behaviors by using different Visitor objects.

15

COMMAND

15.1 ACTIONS VERSUS THE ACTORS

Practically every narrative involves actors and their actions. As a writer you have the option of placing your primary focus on either the actors, which is what you'd do if you were writing about heroic figures and their deeds, or their actions. When the latter is the case, the specific actors mentioned become secondary and could be replaced by other comparable actors in your narrative.

It is interesting to see this actions-versus-actors dichotomy in the evolution of programming styles and languages over the years. Programming started out as being primarily procedural — the focus was mainly on actions as specified by functions. However, with the advent of object-oriented programming, the programming focus has shifted to objects — the actors. With the OO style of programming, the first things you think of when you are asked to develop software for a new application are the main classes you are going to need. The instances constructed from these classes serve as the actors at runtime. You endow the classes with methods — the actions — that are needed for the application. The important thing to note here is that the locus of conceptual emphasis in writing code in this manner is on the actors themselves. On the other hand, the actions, in the form of methods, play a subservient role to the actors — subservient in the sense that you first think of the actors and then think of what actions they should be able to carry out.

Despite this actor-centric focus of the object-oriented style of programming, we still need to be able to create software designs where the actions are primary and the actors secondary. That is, while still operating within the object-oriented paradigm, we need to be able to reverse the order of the conceptual focus described above. As you will see in this chapter, we can do that with the Command pattern. This pattern helps us write a class that can synthesize a complex action by pulling together more elementary actions provided by other classes. With the Command pattern, your thinking starts with the actions and how to

Designing with Objects: Object-Oriented Design Patterns Explained with Stories from Harry Potter,
First Edition. Avinash C. Kak.
© 2015 John Wiley & Sons, Inc. Published 2015 by John Wiley & Sons, Inc.

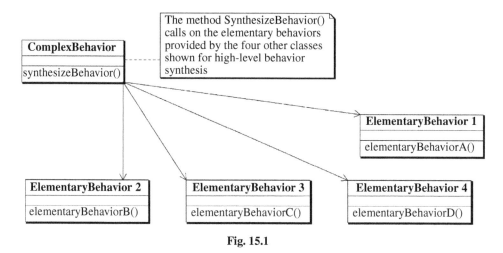

Fig. 15.1

synthesize them, rather than with stateful objects and what actions to assign to them. We illustrate placing the focus on action synthesis in Figure 15.1.

In the rest of this chapter, we will use the term *behaviors* to mean the same thing as *actions* since the former is the standard OO jargon for the latter.

15.2   INTENT AND APPLICABILITY

The intent of the Command pattern is to represent actions as objects and to then synthesize larger actions through compositions over objects that stand for smaller actions. Endowing such objects with properties facilitates operations such as undo, tracking, sorting, logging, etc.

You should use this pattern when

- the problem you are trying to solve requires that, instead of using objects as "nouns" with behaviors, you use objects as "verbs" with properties;
- you need to associate properties with actions — properties related to, say, the context in which an action request is made, the time of the request, the object issuing the request, the priority of the request, and so on;
- your application requires you to synthesize larger actions through compositions over smaller actions while taking into account the properties associated with the smaller actions;
- your application requires you to queue up the action requests and, at any given time, sort the currently pending requests on the basis of, say, their priority levels;
- your application involves a GUI framework and requires an object-oriented approach to the handling of callbacks.

15.3   INTRODUCTION TO THE COMMAND PATTERN

First a bit of vocabulary related to the Command pattern: It uses the word *receiver* to refer to the objects whose more elementary behaviors are pulled together to create a desired larger behavior. The pattern also includes the notion of an *invoker* object for orchestrating the invocation of the synthesized large behaviors.

Keeping in mind the *receiver-invoker* vocabulary, let's now use house construction as a metaphor for creating software in order to illustrate what specifically is achieved by the Command pattern. Obviously, constructing a house requires laying the foundation, putting up the superstructure walls, putting a roof over the structure, and so on. With the traditional approach to object-oriented programming, we would create a class with a name like HouseBuilder, endow it with instance variables in order to give state to the instances constructed from the class, and then equip it with methods that correspond to what goes into building a house. This approach would amount to writing a large monolithic class for constructing a house.

Now consider an approach based on the Command pattern. With the pattern in mind, we realize that each part of the house is likely to be built by one or more tradesmen who specialize in that particular line of work. So, we would designate a FoundationLayer receiver whose job is just to lay the foundation, a Carpenter receiver whose job is to build the floors and the walls, a Roofer receiver to install the roof, and so on. We would pull together all of these jobs in a class with a name like HouseConstruction as shown in Figure 15.2. If real-estate development in your area required that the houses be built in a specific order, or that house building be interleaved with another macro-level activity, such as the installation of fences around the properties on which the houses sit, as depicted in Figure 15.2, we could use an Invoker class to enforce sequencing constraints on the invocations of the different synthesized behaviors (which in this example would be building a house and installing a fence).

The Command pattern asks that all of the major behavior classes — those that represent the behaviors that need to be synthesized by calling on the more elementary behaviors and those that provide the elementary behaviors — descend from a root interface called Command. This is mostly for the convenience of the Invoker class. When all of the invoked commands are of type Command, the Invoker class can deal with them all in a uniform manner. As depicted in Figure 15.2, the Command interface typically declares a method called execute(). So any concrete class that implements the Command interface must provide implementation code for execute(). Going back to our house-building example, the FoundationLayer class would provide an implementation for execute() that would consist of executing the different steps that go into laying the foundation of a new house. By the same token, the execute() of Carpenter would engage in the carpentry needed to build the floors and the walls.

15.4   THE COMMAND PATTERN IN REAL-WORLD APPLICATIONS

What's perhaps the best known real-world application of the Command pattern has much in common with the real-world application of the Chain of Responsibility pattern that we described in Section 14.4 of the previous chapter. We are referring to the processing of the

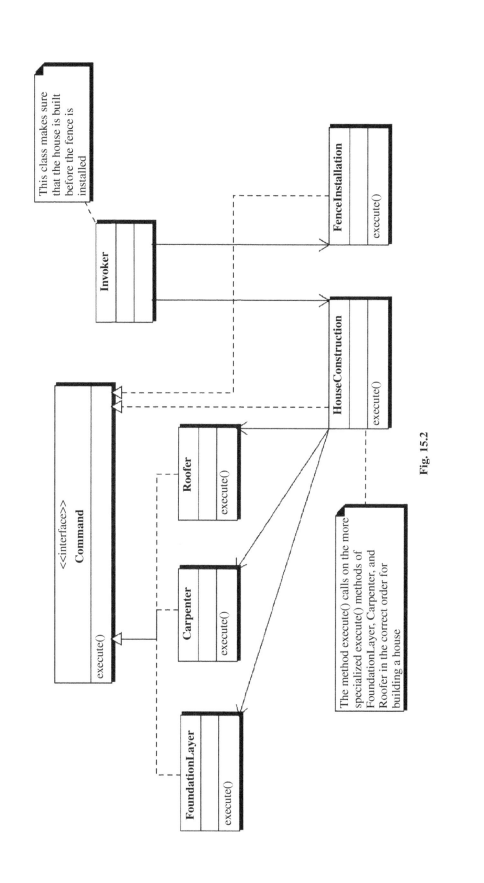

Fig. 15.2

events generating by a user interacting with a GUI. At runtime, as the callbacks associated with the events — the callbacks would be Listener objects in Java — are placed in an event dispatch queue, an event processing loop (generally operating in a separate thread called the Event Dispatch Thread) executes each callback from this queue on a first come first serve basis. The Command pattern can be used with good effect to orchestrate the invocation of these callbacks — especially if one wants to incorporate "undo" and "redo" capabilities in the processing of the events.

When the callback classes implement the Command interface, instead of processing the callbacks in the event dispatch queue in the order in which they were placed there, the Invoker can, at any given time, use the *priority queue* access discipline to select for execution the callback that has the highest priority at that time. The `execute()` method of the Invoker may also call on an ancillary method like `peek()` to first examine the currently available highest-priority callback to make certain that its execution would be appropriate considering the sequence of callbacks already executed. This can be useful for visual programming systems that allow a user to create a new program by manipulating graphical icons.[1] In visual programming, the program fragment associated with a new icon must "harmonize" with the icons already in place. Referring back to the house construction example presented earlier, there exists a strong analogy between constructing a program with a visual programming language and building a house.

15.5   HARRY POTTER STORY USED TO ILLUSTRATE THE COMMAND PATTERN

Our demonstration of the Command pattern is based on the task of protecting Harry Potter. You see, based on the prophecy that Lord Voldemort had heard only partially, he is convinced he can vanquish his nemesis Harry Potter. So Dumbledore makes sure that Harry is protected at all times when away from Hogwarts. Harry needs such protection particularly during the summer months that he must spend with the Dursleys. When Harry is physically inside the house of his aunt and uncle, he cannot be touched by the dark forces because of the natural protection provided to him by living with a close blood relative of his dead mother — in this case his mother's sister. But outside the house, he is vulnerable. To protect him when he is outside the house, Dumbledore asked the duo of Arabella Figg and Mundungus Fletcher to keep an eye on Harry, with the former in charge (since the latter is somewhat unpredictable — being a petty thief and such).

All through the years as Harry was growing up with the Dursleys at Number 4 Privet Drive, Arabella Figg generally did a good job of keeping an eye on Harry, either directly or through her magical cat Mr. Tibbles. However, an extraordinary event took place in the summer of 1995 that called for enhancing the vigil in protecting Harry Potter. Two dementors attacked Harry and his cousin Dudley as they were returning home late in the evening from a neighborhood park. The fact that dementors showed up in Little Whinging to attack Harry caused, as one would expect, much alarm among those who cared for Harry.

---

[1] We are talking about *visual programming languages* as opposed to the *visual programming environments* made available by various IDEs for software development. In the former, you create a functioning program by connecting together program fragments represented by graphical icons. And, in the latter, you yourself create a program but with the help of the IDE that makes sure your programming constructs are legal and that also gives you instant access to the documentation related to the programming language you are using.

So it was decided that Harry was no longer safe with his muggle aunt and uncle for the remainder of the summer. Subsequently, some members of the Order of Phoenix escorted Harry to Number 12 Grimmauld Place, the headquarters of the Order, to keep him out of harm's way the rest of that summer.

Harry's transfer to Number 12 Grimmauld Place raised important issues concerning his security during the transit. First a decision had to be made as to what mode of transportation to use from amongst those available in the wizarding world. There was the Floo network, but that had to be ruled out since it could easily be monitored by the enemy. There was also the option of using a Portkey. But, apparently, setting up a Portkey required prior authorization from the Ministry of Magic. The remaining two choices were apparating to the destination and flying there on their brooms. Since Harry was not old enough to apparate, the choice automatically boiled down to using brooms. But flying on the brooms through wide open spaces was obviously going to expose Harry to potential harm. So the team of wizards and witches that showed up to move Harry to Number 12 Grimmauld Place needed to cover him physically from all sides during the flight to keep him safe from possible threats in midair.

Our demonstration of the Command pattern will consist of writing a class with the name `ProtectHarryPotter` whose main job is to do whatever it takes to protect Harry during the attack by dementors in Little Whinging and during his subsequent journey from the Dursley house to Number 12 Grimmauld Place. The `ProtectHarryPotter` class will define two different types of protections for Harry Potter, one in which the main protection duty is assigned to a single individual who may be a wizard or a witch or even a squib,[2] and, two, in which the protection is provided by a team of wizards and witches working together.

15.6   A TOP LEVEL VIEW OF THE PATTERN DEMONSTRATION

Figure 15.3 shows the class diagram for our demonstration of the Command pattern. The class named `ProtectHarryPotter` is equipped with the functionality that can be used to protect Harry Potter during both situations described in the previous section. Since ultimately Harry can only be protected by the individual actions of the wizards and the witches (and, sometimes, the squibs) who are pressed into service for the job, the `execute()` function of `ProtectHarryPotter` must synthesize the needed protection for Harry by calling on the individual wizards/witches/squibs to do the needful. *This is the essence of the Command pattern*.

The interface `MyPlaces` shown in Figure 15.3 is purely for programming convenience. It allows us to define an enum for the addresses of interest to us in our demonstration. It also allows us to make comparisons of where a wizard, witch, or squib is physically present at any given moment in relation to where he/she needs to be in order to protect Harry Potter. The classes `Wizard` and `Squib` are meant for creating the "actors" for the protection behavior defined in the `ProtectHarryPotter` class. We use the former for modeling the wizards and the witches, and the latter for modeling squibs.

---

[2]In case the reader has forgotten, a squib is someone who is born of wizarding parents but has no magical abilities of his or her own. The fact that squibs understand the wizarding world and that they look like ordinary non-magical people to muggles makes them especially invaluable for the sort of tasks described in this chapter.

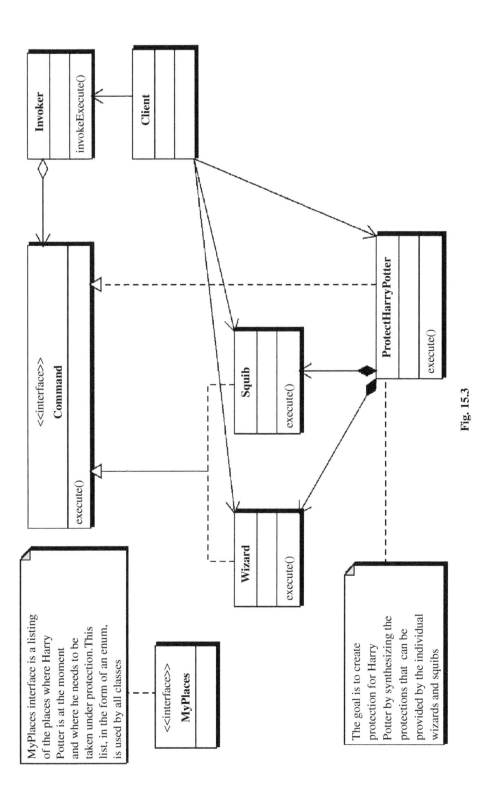

MyPlaces interface is a listing of the places where Harry Potter is at the moment and where he needs to be taken under protection. This list, in the form of an enum, is used by all classes

<<interface>>
MyPlaces

<<interface>>
Command

execute()

Invoker

invokeExecute()

Client

Squib

execute()

Wizard

execute()

ProtectHarryPotter

execute()

The goal is to create protection for Harry Potter by synthesizing the protections that can be provided by the individual wizards and squibs

Fig. 15.3

Since certain conditions must hold before a `Wizard` or a `Squib` can help out with protecting Harry Potter, we need a mechanism for designating the situation when those conditions are not met. The class `UnableToProtectHarryPotterException` serves that purpose. The role of the `Invoker` class is merely to provide storage for objects of type `Command`. In a more elaborate demonstration, the `Invoker` class could be used to make sure that the different commands obey certain prespecified scheduling constraints. Finally, it is the `Client` class in which we test the code for this demonstration.

15.7   THE Command INTERFACE

Shown below is the `Command` interface for this demonstration. As stated previously, the main reason for defining this interface is so that a client (or the `Invoker` class) can manipulate all of the behaviors, synthesized or elementary, in a uniform manner.

As we will mention in Section 15.9, the exception class used in the definition of the interface shown below is meant to signal those situations when it is not possible to protect Harry Potter. For example, if the goal is to keep an eye on Harry in Little Whinging but he has gone away to spend the rest of the summer with the Weasleys at The Burrow, we would need to throw the exception `UnableToProtectHarryPotterException` since the place where Harry is at the moment and the place where protection for Harry is requested are not the same.

```
public interface Command {
    public void execute() throws UnableToProtectHarryPotterException;
}
```

15.8   THE MyPlaces INTERFACE

The goal of the interface defined below, meant more for programming convenience than anything else, is to declare `Place` as an enum with five possible values. This allows us to declare a variable of type `Place`, to give it a value like `Place.Privet_Drive` and to check whether the variable's current value corresponds to one of those declared below.

```
public interface MyPlaces {
    public enum Place { Privet_Drive,
                        The_Burrow,
                        Number_12_Grimmauld_Place,
                        Hogwarts,
                        Hogsmeade
    }
}
```

15.9   THE ProtectHarryPotter CLASS

We now present the `ProtectHarryPotter` class. As its name implies, the main purpose of this class is to provide Harry Potter with the protection he needs when he is not at Hogwarts.

When the danger is such that several wizards and witches (and sometimes squibs) must work together to keep Harry safe, a class such as ProtectHarryPotter *must synthesize the needed protection by calling on the various capabilities of the participating individuals.* As mentioned previously, creating large behaviors from a set of elementary behaviors provided by certain actors is the essence of the Command pattern.

Again as the reader already knows, in the context of the Command pattern, the actors are referred to as the *receivers* since they are the receivers of the commands that must be executed so that a Command object can fulfill its contract to supply the behavior requested. For the ProtectHarryPotter class, the receivers are instances of the Wizard and Squib classes.

The ProtectHarryPotter class contains logic for the following two different situations for protecting Harry: when protection is provided by an individual wizard or squib, and when protection is the result of joint action by a team of wizards and witches. These are the two situations we talked about in Section 15.5.

The class directly calls the execute() of the wizard or the squib for the protection needed in the first of the two situations described above. For the second, the needed protection is synthesized by pooling together the individual capabilities of the participating wizards and the witches. As you see in the class definition shown below, the behavior synthesis needed for the second case is rather straightforward when the elementary behaviors can be executed independently. However, when coordination is required between the elementary behaviors, the implementation of the Command pattern becomes more complex. The extension of our demonstration code to the case when coordination is needed between the more elementary behaviors for synthesizing larger behaviors is left as an exercise for the reader in Section 15.15.

Notice the three constructors in the class definition shown below. The first constructor initializes a ProtectHarryPotter instance with the Wizard instance whose job it is to protect Harry. The second constructor does the same, but now the protection is provided by a Squib. The third constructor is for those situations when a team of wizards and witches is needed for protecting Harry, such as when Harry is being moved to Number 12 Grimmauld Place from Number 4 Privet Drive.

Regarding the code in the execute() method, you can easily identify its parts when the protection is provided by a single wizard, by a single squib, and by a team of wizards and witches. In all of these cases, we check that certain minimal conditions are satisfied so that the task can be accomplished by the receivers. For example, if a wizard is to protect Harry during his stay at Privet Drive, we require that the wizard possess an invisibility cloak (since otherwise the wizard would not be able to do his job). By the same token, when a team of wizards and witches is asked to guard Harry during his transit to Number 12 Grimmauld Place, we require that all of them belong to the Order of the Phoenix.

```java
import java.util.*;

public class ProtectHarryPotter implements MyPlaces, Command {

    private Wizard wizardGuard = null;
    private Squib squibGuard = null;
    private List<Wizard> guards = new ArrayList<Wizard>();
    private String whenProtectionNeeded = null;
```

```
private static Wizard harry = new Wizard( "Harry Potter" );

{
    harry.setCurrentlyLocatedAt( Place.Privet_Drive );
}


public ProtectHarryPotter( Wizard guard ) {
    wizardGuard = guard;
}
public ProtectHarryPotter( Squib guard ) {
    squibGuard = guard;
}
public ProtectHarryPotter( List<Wizard>  guards,
                                String whenProtectoinNeeded ) {
    this.guards = guards;
    this.whenProtectionNeeded = whenProtectoinNeeded;
}
public void execute() throws UnableToProtectHarryPotterException {
    if ( (squibGuard != null)  || (wizardGuard != null) ){
        if (squibGuard != null) {
            squibGuard.setWhomToProtect( harry );
            squibGuard.execute();
        }
        if (wizardGuard != null) {
            wizardGuard.setWhomToProtect( harry );
            wizardGuard.execute();
        }
    }
    if ( (guards.size() != 0) & (whenProtectionNeeded != null) ) {
        if (whenProtectionNeeded !=
                    "take Harry Potter to 12 Grimmauld Place") {
            throw new UnableToProtectHarryPotterException(
                    "The activity during which Harry is to be "
                    + "protected not recognized");
        }
        ListIterator<Wizard> it = guards.listIterator();
        while (it.hasNext()) {
            Wizard wiz = it.next();
            if( wiz.getCanCastDisillusionmentCharm() ) {
                wiz.castDisillusionmentCharm();
                break;
            }
        }
        it = guards.listIterator();
        while (it.hasNext()) {
            Wizard wiz = it.next();
            if( !wiz.getMembershipInOrderOfPhoenix() ) {
                throw new UnableToProtectHarryPotterException(
                        "At least one member of the guards is "
                        + "a traitor to the cause!");
            }
            System.out.println( wiz
```

```
                        + " will fly in formation and deliver Harry Potter"
                        + " to Number 12, Grimmauld Place");
                }
            }
        }
}
```

15.10 THE Wizard CLASS

As mentioned previously, the Command pattern entails the notion of a receiver, which is an object whose elementary behavior is a part of the desired larger behavior. In other words, when we witness the larger behavior, what we are actually seeing is an aggregation of the more elementary behaviors provided by the participating receiver objects. The receivers in our demonstration consist of wizards and witches (both types of instances made from the Wizard class that we present here) and squibs.

The descriptions of the scenarios for protecting Harry Potter, as presented in Section 15.5, should indicate what sort of attributes we need for the Wizard receiver objects. The protection scenario that calls upon a wizard to follow Harry in Little Whinging while staying invisible to the muggles requires that the wizard possess an invisibility cloak. By the same token, the wizards and witches who have volunteered to guard Harry while he is in transit between Number 4 Privet Drive and Number 12 Grimmauld Place must belong to the Order of Phoenix since otherwise they may not be able to see the house at the destination let alone be allowed inside. These requirements on the wizards and witches should explain the elementary behaviors we have defined for the Wizard class below.

```
import java.util.*;

public class Wizard implements MyPlaces, Command {
    private String wizardName;
    private Place currentlyLocatedAt;
    private boolean hasInvisibilityCloak = false;
    private boolean canApparate = false;
    private boolean canCastDisillusionmentCharm = false;
    private boolean hasMembershipInOrderOfPhoenix = false;
    private Wizard whomToProtect;

    public Wizard( String wizardName ) {
        this.wizardName = wizardName;
    }
    public String toString() { return wizardName; }

    public void setCurrentlyLocatedAt( Place place ) {
        currentlyLocatedAt = place;
    }
    public Place getCurrentlyLocatedAt() {
        return currentlyLocatedAt;
    }
```

```java
public void setMembershipInOrderOfPhoenix( boolean truOrFalse ) {
    hasMembershipInOrderOfPhoenix =  truOrFalse;
}
public boolean getMembershipInOrderOfPhoenix() {
    return hasMembershipInOrderOfPhoenix;
}
public void setCanApparate( boolean yesOrNo ) {
    canApparate = yesOrNo;
}
public boolean getCanApparate( ) {
    return canApparate;
}
public void aparateTo( Place destination ) {
    System.out.println( "Apparating to "  + destination );
}
public void aparateFrom( Place destination ) {
    System.out.println( "Apparating from "  + destination );
}
public void setHasInvisibityCloak( boolean yesOrNo ) {
    hasInvisibilityCloak = yesOrNo;
}
public boolean getHasInvisibilityCloak( ) {
    return hasInvisibilityCloak;
}
public void followHarryPotter()
                throws UnableToProtectHarryPotterException {
    if (!hasInvisibilityCloak) {
        throw new UnableToProtectHarryPotterException();
    } else {
        System.out.println( "Following Harry Potter while staying "
                        + "under an invisibility cloak" );
    }
}
public void setCanCastDisillusionmentCharm( boolean yesOrNo ) {
    canCastDisillusionmentCharm = true;
}
public boolean getCanCastDisillusionmentCharm() {
    return canCastDisillusionmentCharm;
}
public void castDisillusionmentCharm() {
    if (canCastDisillusionmentCharm) {
        System.out.println( wizardName
                + " casting Disillusionment Charm on Harry Potter"
                + " to make him difficult to see" );
    }
}
public void setWhomToProtect(Wizard ward) {
    whomToProtect = ward;
}
public void execute() throws UnableToProtectHarryPotterException {
    if ( getCurrentlyLocatedAt()  !=
                        whomToProtect.getCurrentlyLocatedAt() ) {
```

```
            throw new UnableToProtectHarryPotterException( this
                    + " unable to protect Harry Potter! "
                        + " Harry is at a different location.I");
        }
        if ( getHasInvisibilityCloak() ) {
            followHarryPotter();
        }
    }
}
```

15.11   THE Squib CLASS

We now present the second of the receiver classes, Squib, needed for demonstrating the Command pattern. A squib obviously makes for a perfect lookout for protecting Harry in muggle surroundings — squibs look like ordinary non-magical people to the muggles.

As to why this class possesses cat-related methods and attribute, recall from Section 15.5 that when two dementors attacked Harry (and his cousin Dudley) in a dark alley on that summer night, it was Mrs. Figg's cat, Mr. Tibble, who witnessed the attack. The cat rushed home and informed Mrs. Figg. In light of the important role played by the cat in protecting Harry, it seems reasonable that we should endow the Squib class with the cat-related methods and attribute you see in the class definition below. Recall, Mrs. Figg is a squib.

```
public class Squib implements MyPlaces, Command {
    private String squibName;
    private Place currentlyLocatedAt;
    private boolean ownsCat = false;
    private Wizard whomToProtect;

    public Squib( String squibName ) {
        this.squibName = squibName;
    }
    public String toString() { return squibName; }

    public void setCurrentlyLocatedAt( Place place ) {
        currentlyLocatedAt = place;
    }
    public Place getCurrentlyLocatedAt() {
        return currentlyLocatedAt;
    }
    public void setOwnsCat( boolean yesOrNo ) {
        ownsCat = yesOrNo;
    }
    public boolean getOwnsCat( ) {
        return ownsCat;
    }
    public void useCatAsLookout( Wizard target ) {
        System.out.println( "Cat owned by " + squibName
```

```
                            + " keeping an eye on " + (Wizard) target );
    }
    public void setWhomToProtect(Wizard ward) {
        whomToProtect = ward;
    }
    public void execute() throws UnableToProtectHarryPotterException {
        if ( getCurrentlyLocatedAt()   !=
                            whomToProtect.getCurrentlyLocatedAt() ) {
            throw new UnableToProtectHarryPotterException( this
                        + " unable to protect Harry Potter! "
                        + " Harry is at a different location.I");
        }
        if ( getOwnsCat() ) {
            useCatAsLookout( whomToProtect );
        }
    }
}
```

15.12   THE Invoker CLASS

The Invoker class serves as the clearinghouse for all Command objects. So if we wanted to create a sequence of Command instances and execute them serially in one go, we could store them in the class Invoker defined here. The execution of the stored Command instances is triggered by calling the static method invokeExecute() of the class. Although our demonstration does not do so, this class can also be used to enforce any sequencing and precedence constraints that may apply to the stored Command instances.

The implementation of the class shown below is straightforward. If there's anything at all noteworthy about it, it's the last statement of invokeExecute() ending in the initialization of a new empty version of the container that stores the Command instances. As to why, after we are done executing all of the Command instances stored in invokerCommandList, it is time to reinitialize that container so that new Command instances can be stored in it.

```
import java.util.*;

public class Invoker {
    static private List<Command> invokerCommandList =
                                    new ArrayList<Command>();
    static public void addToCommandList( Command command ) {
        invokerCommandList.add( command );
    }

    static public void invokeExecute(){
        ListIterator<Command> iter = invokerCommandList.listIterator();
        while ( iter.hasNext() ) {
            System.out.println();
            try {
                iter.next().execute();
```

```
        } catch(UnableToProtectHarryPotterException e) {
            e.printStackTrace();
        }
    }
    invokerCommandList = new ArrayList<Command>();
}
}
```

15.13   THE UnableToProtectHarryPotterException CLASS

As previously mentioned, certain conditions must be satisfied by an individual whose job it is to protect Harry Potter. For example, for a wizard to keep an eye on Harry during his summers with the Dursleys at Number 4 Privet Drive, the wizard must be physically present at about the same location. So a class like ProtectingHarryPotter must check whether or not such conditions are satisfied by the individuals who are given the task of protecting Harry. Implementing this condition checking logic requires that we be able to deal with the cases when the conditions are violated. This is where an exception class like UnableToProtectHarryPotterException proves useful. When a condition that must be satisfied for protecting Harry is violated, we throw an exception of type UnableToProtectHarryPotterException. The implementation shown below asks its superclass Exception to do all the work related to the notification of the exception.

```
public class UnableToProtectHarryPotterException extends Exception {
    public UnableToProtectHarryPotterException() {
        super();
    }
    public UnableToProtectHarryPotterException(String arg0) {
        super(arg0);
    }
}
```

15.14   THE Client CLASS

A Client of the Command pattern must first create one or more receiver instances and supply them as arguments to the constructor of a behavior-synthesizing Command class like the ProtectingHarryPotter class in our demonstration. The client must also deposit the behavior-synthesizing Command object thus created in an instance of the Invoker class. Subsequently, the client can ask the Invoker class to execute the Command instances stored there.

The client implementation shown below is for the two Harry Potter protection scenarios described earlier in Section 15.5: protecting Harry during his stay with the Dursleys during the summer of 1995, and guarding Harry when he is in transit between Number 4 Privet

Drive and Number 12 Grimmauld Place. The receivers are Arabella Figg and Mundungus Fletcher for the first case, and Mad-Eye Moody, Nymphadora Tonks, and Remus Lupin for the second.[3]

The attributes we have set for the receivers (wizards, witches, and the lone squib) in the class definition shown below are dictated by what is needed for the two different types of protection for Harry Potter (see the logic in the ProtectHarryPotter class). For example, Mundungus Fletcher's role in this demonstration is to follow Harry secretly (by hiding under an invisibility cloak) when Harry is out and about in Little Whinging. So we need to make sure that the Mundungus Fletcher instance of the Wizard class has its hasInvisibilityCloak property set to true. Additionally, a squib or a wizard will not be able to protect Harry in Little Whinging unless the individual is physically present in the same general area. Regarding the protection scenario that requires a team of wizards and witches to guard Harry while he is in transit to Number 12 Grimmauld Place, all of those wizards and witches must belong to the Order of Phoenix since that is a requirement for being able to see the house at the destination and for being allowed inside it.

```
import java.util.*;

public class Client implements MyPlaces {
    public static void main(String[] args) {
        Squib battyOldNeighbor = new Squib( "Arabella Figg" );
        battyOldNeighbor.setCurrentlyLocatedAt(Place.Privet_Drive );
        battyOldNeighbor.setOwnsCat( true );
        Command c1 = new ProtectHarryPotter( battyOldNeighbor );
        Invoker.addToCommandList( c1 );
        Invoker.invokeExecute();

        Wizard sneakThief = new Wizard( "Mundungus Fletcher");
        sneakThief.setHasInvisibityCloak( true );
        sneakThief.setCanApparate( true );
        sneakThief.setCurrentlyLocatedAt(Place.Privet_Drive );
        Command c2 = new ProtectHarryPotter( sneakThief );
        Invoker.addToCommandList( c2 );
        Invoker.invokeExecute();

        Wizard guard1 = new Wizard("Mad-Eye Moody");
        Wizard guard2 = new Wizard("Nymphadora Tonks");
        Wizard guard3 = new Wizard("Remus Lupin");
        guard1.setMembershipInOrderOfPhoenix( true );
        guard1.setCanCastDisillusionmentCharm(true);
        guard2.setMembershipInOrderOfPhoenix( true );
        guard3.setMembershipInOrderOfPhoenix( true );
        List<Wizard> guards = new ArrayList<Wizard>(
                        Arrays.asList(guard1, guard2,guard3));
```

[3]The reader should note that the second case actually involves a dozen or so wizards and witches. But adding code for creating all of those wizards and witches would only clutter up the demonstration, without supplying any additional insights into the Command pattern.

```
        Command c3 = new ProtectHarryPotter( guards,
                        "take Harry Potter to 12 Grimmauld Place" );
        Invoker.addToCommandList( c3 );
        Invoker.invokeExecute();
    }
}
```

15.15   PLAYING WITH THE CODE

Download the class files for this pattern from the book website into a separate directory. Compile the code with the command

```
javac *.java
```

and execute the Client class by

```
java Client
```

Given the code in the main() of Client, executing this class will produce the following output:

```
Cat owned by Arabella Figg keeping an eye on Harry Potter

Following Harry Potter while staying under an invisibility cloak

Mad-Eye Moody casting Disillusionment Charm on Harry Potter to
make him difficult to see

Mad-Eye Moody will fly in formation and deliver Harry Potter to
Number 12, Grimmauld Place

Nymphadora Tonks will fly in formation and deliver Harry Potter
to Number 12, Grimmauld Place

Remus Lupin will fly in formation and deliver Harry Potter to
Number 12, Grimmauld Place
....
....
```

For additional insights, you may consider extending the code for this pattern along the following lines:

- Our implementation of the second security scenario for Harry Potter as described in Section 15.5 is only partially complete. Instead of a dozen wizards and witches who accompany Harry to Number 12 Grimmauld Place, we have only the following three: Mad-Eye Moody, Nymphadora Tonks, and Remus Lupin. Extend the code to create a full security escort for Harry's journey to Number 12 Grimmauld Place.

- The `Wizard` class included some behaviors that are currently not invoked anywhere in the demonstration code in this chapter. For example, the behavior related to a wizard apparating from one place to another is not being used anywhere. However, we know that Mundungus Fletcher usually apparates to Little Whinging when he is asked to report there for guarding Harry Potter. Extend the demonstration to include these additional behaviors in the synthesis of Harry Potter's protection.

- As described in Section 15.9, the `ProtectHarryPotter` class contains logic for the following two different situations regarding protecting Harry Potter: when protection is provided by an individual wizard or squib, and when protection is the result of joint action by a team of wizards and witches. Whereas we invoked the `Command` interface's `execute()` on the individual wizards and the squibs for supplying the protection needed in the first situation, for the second we directly invoked the different protection-enabling behaviors of the participating wizards and witches. In that sense, for the second situation, we violated the spirit of the Command pattern. Extend the demonstration code so that the coordinated action of the different wizards, as required by the second situation, can also be carried out by calling the `Command` interface's `execute()`.

- Our use of the `Invoker` class leaves much to be desired, in the sense that the demonstration of the pattern as presented would work the same even without the `Invoker` class. Extend the demonstration so that it has multiple large-scale behaviors synthesized from the elementary behaviors provided by the receiver classes. For the new behaviors you define, make sure that you would need to enforce sequencing constraints on the order in which the behaviors are called. Put the `Invoker` class to use for enforcing these sequencing constraints.

- If you want to put even more smarts in your `Invoker` class, you could try to give your commands the "undo" feature. Before executing a command, the `Invoker` would store the state of all of the objects participating in the execution of the command. Subsequently, should "undo" be invoked on the just executed command, the objects would all be restored to their original states. You may want to utilize elements of the Memento pattern of Chapter 19 for designing the Invoker class in this case.

16

INTERPRETER

16.1 PARSING VERSUS INTERPRETATION

Understanding a language — any language — is a two-step process. First, you must parse the syntactical units of the language, which in most cases would be the sentences, for the different grammatical components they contain. And then you must comprehend the declarations made or the actions suggested by the grammatical components. The first step, analyzing a sentence for its grammatical components, is called *parsing*. And the second step, inferring from the grammatical components the purpose of a sentence, is called *interpretation*. The Interpreter pattern is about the second step. But, obviously, the second step cannot be carried out without the first step.

The extent of parsing that must be carried out before interpretation can be attempted depends on the application domain. Thinking of just user-interactive applications, at one end of the spectrum you have "personal assistants" like Siri for Apple mobile devices that come fairly close to providing natural language like interfaces (at least with respect to a chosen set of actions) and, at the other, you have command-line interfaces that give the user a specific set of options (which must be expressed in a prescribed manner in the command line) for launching applications. In general, the closer a user interface is to what appears to be a free-flowing natural language, the more complex the parser must be for the interpreter to work well.

A parser typically outputs what is formally referred to as the Abstract Syntax Tree (AST) for the text it is asked to parse and the interpreter then works off the information in the syntax tree. The interior nodes of the tree correspond to the different grammatical components of a sentence. For example, consider the case when the grammar rules (also called *productions*) given to a parser are:[1]

---

[1] We have displayed the grammar rules using an extension of the BNF (Backus Naur Form) notation. In this notation, the symbol '::=' stands for "is defined as"; the symbol '|' for "or"; the symbol '?' for optional; the symbol '*' for arbitrary number of repetitions, including zero; and the pair of matched parentheses '()' for grouping. Note also the implicit role played by concatenation — an expression like 'A B' on the right of '::=' means that the grammatical constituent B must come after the grammatical constituent A. So, you could say, that concatenation plays the role of 'and' along with imposing an order on the two operands. Therefore, the role

Designing with Objects: Object-Oriented Design Patterns Explained with Stories from Harry Potter, First Edition. Avinash C. Kak.

```
Statement              ::=    NounPhrase  VerbPhrase?
NounPhrase             ::=    ( Pronoun | ( Determiner? Adjective*
                                  CompoundNoun ) ) PrepPhrase?
CompoundNoun           ::=    Noun Noun?
PrepPhrase             ::=    Preposition Adjective NounPhrase
VerbPhrase             ::=    Verb (NounPhrase | PrepPhrase)

Noun                   ::=    "charm" | "help" | "wizard" | magic ...
Verb                   ::=    "is" | "cast" | "are" | ...
Adjective              ::=    "good" | "fast" | ...
Preposition            ::=    "of" | "on" | "for" | ...
Determiner             ::=    "the" | "every" | "this" | "a" | "an" | ...
```

When a parser with these rules is asked to parse a sentence like

```
the magic of your charm is of no help.
```

it will produce a syntax tree that can be displayed in the following form:

```
Statement
   NounPhrase
      Determiner : the
      CompoundNoun
         Noun : magic
      PrepPhrase
         Preposition : of
         Adjective : your
         NounPhrase
            CompoundNoun
               Noun : charm
   VerbPhrase
      Verb : is
      PrepPhrase
         Preposition : of
         Adjective : no
         NounPhrase
            CompoundNoun
               Noun : help
```

It is this syntax tree that the interpreter must work with in order to carry out an interpretation of the sentence. In its common usage, the interpretation would tell us what is being conveyed by the sentence, what specific action is mentioned, who the main actor is, what the object of the action is, and so on.

---

played by concatenation is opposite to the role played by the symbol '|', which, taking into account the specific order of the operands, is that of 'or'. A grammar such as the one shown here, in which only a single grammatical entity is on the left of the definition operator '::=' is called a *Context Free grammar*. It is context-free because each rule — which we may think of as a string replacement rule — applies regardless of the context surrounding the left-hand side symbol.

16.2   INTENT AND APPLICABILITY

As implied straightforwardly by its name, the intent of the Interpreter pattern is to generate an interpretation for a given input by examining its different grammatical constituents while taking into account the context.

You should consider using this pattern when

- the grammar is simple — certainly no more complex than a context-free grammar;
- the parse of the input can be represented as a syntax tree;
- the context for the interpretation of each grammatical component can be ascertained relatively easily by examining the surrounding words, phrases, etc.;
- the interpretation can be carried out through simple dictionary lookup for the information at the nodes of the syntax tree.

16.3   INTRODUCTION TO THE INTERPRETER PATTERN

As the opening section of this chapter says, parsing is an essential first step before interpretation can be carried out. What that section neglected to mention was that there is one more issue that must be resolved before one can do a proper job of interpretation: *establishing the context*. You see, even after you have correctly identified the grammatical categories for all of the words, the precise meaning of a sentence like "John went to the bank"[2] can only be determined from the context surrounding the sentence. The word "bank" in this sentence could mean either a financial institution or the edge of a river.

Incorporating context in language interpretation is no easy task and, for the case of natural languages, is still largely an unsolved problem. What compounds the difficulty is that the context is sometimes implied by factors that are not always tangible. In a direct communication between two individuals, it could be implied by difficult-to-describe factors such as the body language, the shared societal and cultural mores, and so on.

The Interpreter pattern as presented by GoF, although mentioning context as something that must be addressed in interpretation, is largely silent about how one should go about representing and utilizing the context. That is because GoF considers the Interpreter pattern to be a poor man's substitute for more "complex" parsers, say of the sort created by automatic parser generators. The pattern, as presented by GoF, seeks to represent a grammar by a set of classes, with each class in charge of a grammatical category. Interpretation consists of assigning the different portions of an input sentence to the different classes and deducing an interpretation on the basis of such assignments.

We take a slightly larger view of the process of interpretation. Considering that parser generators have become so easy to use over the years,[3] we believe that the bar set for the Interpreter pattern can be raised by using the grammatical category classes created by an automatic parser generator. As for the context, we can use the occurrence of certain

---

[2]The reader will find a good collection of such sentences at [8].

[3]The GoF book predates some of the more commonly used parser/lexer generators used today. For example, what eventually became JavaCC was first released in 1996, whereas the GoF book came out in 1994.

words — let's call them trigger words — at the sentence level or the phrasal level to define a context for the interpretation of the individual words. Therefore, as you descend down the syntax tree, you can examine at each node its string value — this is the portion of the input sentence assigned to that node — for the presence of certain trigger words. When such words are detected at a node, you consider that to define a context for all the lower-level nodes. As a result, how a word at a leaf node of the tree is interpreted would depend on the overall string value of some higher level node in the tree. Obviously, this gives us only local control over the context. However, the approach could be generalized to higher levels in the interpretation of multiple sentences simultaneously.

Our explanation of the Interpreter pattern is based on showing how we can automatically convert magic-speak into muggle-speak. We want to translate each sentence of the former into a sentence of the latter. As readers of Harry Potter know, wizards use a language that can be frightening to muggles. Muggles are not supposed to know anything about wizards, witches, dementors, spells, charms, hexes, curses, and so on. Muggles are not even supposed to know that there exist things like magic wands that the wizards use to point at things that they want to cast spells on.

Our Interpreter pattern must therefore first analyze the syntax of a magic-speak sentence and then, taking the context of each word into account, translate each word/phrase into something that would sound harmless to a muggle. Note that we do not have the option of translating magic-speak into gibberish — a random collection of harmless words — because that would arouse suspicion among muggles.

In order to produce translated syntax that makes sense, we must obviously first parse the magic-speak sentences. The demonstration code presented in this chapter includes a parser created by the JavaCC parser/lexer generator. JavaCC makes it possible to directly convert a set of rules in the BNF form into parser code. JavaCC is an abbreviation of "Java Compiler Compiler."

An important aspect of the Interpreter pattern is that it calls for the clients of an interpreter to be able to access all of the interpretation functionality through a common interface even when it is necessary that the input be broken into chunks and each chunk interpreted separately. As to how that can be done, we will illustrate with the help of the demonstration code presented in the rest of this chapter.

Overall, our magic-speak to muggle-speak translator demonstration will require that we first identify the different grammatical portions of magic-speak, recognize the context for each portion, and then make decisions regarding the interpretation and subsequent translation into muggle-speak.

16.4   THE INTERPRETER PATTERN IN REAL-WORLD APPLICATIONS

In practical software development, the Interpreter pattern is meant for applications that are not as complex as those needing full-blown natural-language like interfaces.[4] The likely applications for this pattern are those in which the choices for the verbs, the nouns, the adjectives, etc., and the permissible syntactical relationships among these are fairly limited.

---

[4]Parser generators such as JavaCC can only handle what are known as context-free grammars. Such grammars are inadequate for describing unconstrained natural languages.

The pattern is widely used in compilers that by design must translate a program, written obviously with a set of constraints on the syntax, into a structure suitable for conversion into executable machine code.

As an example of even simpler applications of this pattern, imagine a multi-column display of information that gives a user considerable latitude with regard to how the information is displayed in each column, with regard to which column is the primary controller of the sort order in the display, and even with regard to which specific columns are displayed (assuming that the display comes with a large number of columns, but any user is likely to be interested in only a small subset of them). It may be possible to express all permissible permutations of the choices for the user in the form of a mini-language. Such languages can often be modeled by finite state automata, which implies that they can be parsed with fast algorithms. The output of such parsing can then be submitted to an interpreter based on the pattern described in this chapter.

16.5   HARRY POTTER STORY USED TO ILLUSTRATE THE INTERPRETER PATTERN

As mentioned, our demonstration of the Interpreter pattern consists of translating magic-speak into muggle-speak. When wizards and witches talk to one another in public places that are also frequented by muggles, they have to be extra careful since some of the utterances in the wizarding world can sound frightening (if not nonsensical) to muggles.

Interpreting and translating magic-speak requires that we must first parse the magic-speak sentences to identify their grammatical parts. This is particularly important because, in general, a word can play one of several different grammatical roles in a sentence and how you translate it into a word in another language depends on the role it was playing in the original sentence. As mentioned in Section 16.1, the identification of the grammatical roles played by the words in a sentence can be carried out by examining the syntax tree of the sentence that is generated by a parser. Using the syntax tree, the interpretation/translation of a word from one language into a word in another can at least use the phrase and the sentence level contexts for the word.

For our demonstration, consider the case of two wizards, an older wizard and an underage wizard, in a public place (that is open to muggles also) trying to have a conversation over lunch. The wizards, being wizards after all, obviously want to talk about matters that are important to the wizarding world. However, if muggles overheard snippets of this conversation, they could get scared and may report the wizards to the authorities — especially if there are other ominous and possibly inexplicable things happening in the world at the same time, such as too many owls flying, too many outbursts of shooting stars, and so on.

To guard against such possibilities, the older wizard could put a charm on the space around them so that they are surrounded by an imaginary bubble and any voices passing though the bubble boundaries would be translated into phrases that muggles would consider harmless.[5] With such a charm in place, if the elder wizard, while explaining to the underage wizard how to use the magic wand, said something like:

```
you point with your magic wand when you want to cast a spell
```

---

[5]This would be similar to the Bubble Head charm that was used by Cedric Diggory and Fleur Delacour during the second task of the Triwizard Tournament to form a bubble around their heads so that they could breathe underwater.

this sentence would be heard by the nearby muggles as

```
you point with your little finger when you want to show a picture.
```

The magical bubble surrounding the two wizards would obviously need to parse the original sentence and decide how to make substitutions for the different words and phrases in order to construct a sentence suitable for muggle ears. A parse of the sentence as spoken by the senior wizard may look like:

```
Statement
    NounPhrase
        Pronoun : you
    VerbPhrase
        Verb : point
        PrepPhrase
            Preposition : with
            NounPhrase
                Adjective : your
                CompoundNoun
                    Noun : magic
                    Noun : wand
                PrepPhrase
                    Preposition : when
                    NounPhrase
                        Pronoun : you
                    VerbPhrase
                        Verb : want
                        PrepPhrase
                            Preposition : to
                            VerbPhrase
                                Verb : cast
                                NounPhrase
                                    Determiner : a
                                    CompoundNoun
                                        Noun : spell
```

The charmed bubble surrounding the two wizards would need to examine the syntax tree shown above and decide which words would need to be replaced by other words in order to construct a harmless sentence that would be heard outside the bubble. The reader should see the need for constructing the syntax tree before deciding on the word substitutions. A word such as "spell" has multiple meanings. It could be a verb, standing for spelling a word, or it could be a noun that stands for a magical spell. It is the job of the parser to tell us whether "spell" is being used as a verb or as a noun. Obviously, if "spell" is being used as a noun — as in "a magic spell" — we do not want a muggle to hear the word as such. We could make similar statements about the other more significant words in the magic-speak sentence shown above.

In addition to the grammatical role played by a word, another factor that goes into deciding how to make word substitutions would be the local (or even the sentence or larger level) context for the words. To illustrate this issue, the word "magic" when it is used as a qualifier

for what is obviously a wizarding-world word "wand" may need to be replaced by some non-wizarding-world word, but when the same word appears in a sentence like "the magic of your charm is of no help," that ought to need no replacement.

What this points to is the fact that, in addition to extracting the grammatical role of a word through the syntax tree of the sentence, the interpreter must also examine at least the phrasal context of the word for proper interpretation.

Based on the above explanation, we can say that an interpreter must possess the following two capabilities: (1) It must know how to descend down a syntax tree until it reaches the leaf nodes where the individual words of a sentence reside. (2) When it tries to figure out what rules to use for interpretation, it must take into account the context for the phrase or the word that is currently the focus of interpretation. The interpreter presented in the rest of this chapter possesses both of these capabilities.

16.6   A PARSER FRONT-END FOR THE INTERPRETER PATTERN

Any attempt at direct interpretation, that is, interpretation without any sort of parsing, is bound to be of very limited utility. Without parsing, all you can do is to carry out a keyword-based (or key-phrase-based) interpretation. As you can imagine, that is likely to suffice for only the simplest of applications. In any case, since parser-generators have now become so easy to use, why not take advantage of them for demonstrating the Interpreter pattern? With parsing out of the way with the help of a parser-generator like JavaCC, we can place greater focus on the other challenge in the use of the Interpreter pattern — the context.

Our demonstration of the Interpreter pattern will use JavaCC for generating a parser and a lexer to serve as the front-end to the Interpreter pattern.[6] JavaCC is the world's most popular parser/lexer generator for Java applications. A parser generator is a tool that can convert a set of grammar rules, specified typically using the BNF notation we described earlier in Section 16.1, or some variant thereof, into a parsing program. And a lexer generator is a tool that translates the rules for what combination of the characters constitute the words in the different grammatical categories.[7]

Since parsing is carried out on the output of the lexer, a few words about the lexical analysis of text are in order. A lexer typically scans a sequence of characters left to right, while it groups the characters into *tokens* that, for the case of ordinary text processing, would be the words and the punctuation marks. The tokens that would be produced for a sentence like:

    The magic of your charm is of no help.

---

[6]You need a *lexer* (also called a *lexical analyzer* or a *scanner*) for a parser to do its work. It is a lexer's job to extract the character sequences and punctuation marks from an input text file. Yes, for the simple examples we show here, we could have done away with a lexer since we could have extracted the sentences from a text file with the help of, say, regular expressions. But since the tools that generate parsers come coupled with the tools that generate lexers, we will assume that we are faced with both the lexical analysis of a magic-speak text file and its parsing in order to construct its syntax tree.

[7]For more information on JavaCC, see [9].

would be

```
"The" SPACE "magic" SPACE "of" SPACE "your" SPACE "charm" SPACE
            "is" SPACE "of" SPACE "no" SPACE "help" PERIOD
```

where SPACE is the identifier that the lexer may use for the space character between the words and PERIOD the identifier for the period at the end of the sentence. In addition to supplying the tokens, the lexer also supplies to the parser the grammatical types for the tokens. For the example shown above, the lexer would know that the word "magic" is of grammatical type NOUN; the parser would be sent that information along with the token. As the parser receives the tokens and their grammatical types, it attempts to fit the rules of the grammar to the tokens for the purpose of constructing a syntax tree for the sentence.[8]

When tokens belong to multiple grammatical types, one of the main challenges faced by a parser is how to handle the available type choices. To explain, consider the following sentence:

    Harry and Ron play quidditch.

and this sentence:

    That was a great play by Harry.

In the first case, "play" is a VERB and in the second it is a NOUN. So, let's say, that the parser first considers "play" as a token of type NOUN as the first of the two sentences shown above is being processed. With "play" being processed as a NOUN token, the parser will not be able to parse the entire sentence. That is, as the parser processes the last token in the sentence, it would not be able to find a grammar rule that would accommodate the last word of the sentence. To get around such difficulties, ideally speaking, you would need a parser that is allowed to backtrack and undo its decisions until it reaches a choice point where the parser can use one of the other grammar rules and move forward again. For the first sentence shown above, if backtracking is allowed, the parser would now consider "play" as a VERB token. With this choice, the parser will be able to parse the whole sentence.[9]

---

[8] As the tokens are generated in a left-to-right scan of the input, the lexer typically passes them on to the parser. From the grammar rules it knows, the parser tries to find the rule that best describes the tokens received so far. At the end of processing each token, the parser may behave in one of the following ways: (1) It may either accept or reject the input on the basis of its being legal (or not) using the tokens received so far; (2) It may translate the token directly into an action on the token or on previously received tokens, in the sense that a number token would be converted into its actual numeric value and a token such as PLUS used to invoke the operation of addition on the numeric values supplied by the previous two number tokens; or (3) The parser may construct a portion of the syntax tree for the input received so far. When a parser does not generate a syntax tree, it is said to operate in the "direct interpretation" mode. Direct interpretation parsers are all you need for simple applications such as the calculators that process one line of input at a time, for the interpretation of command lines in programming, and so on. For more complex interpretations, such as required by a looping statement in a programming language, a parser must output a syntax tree that is then converted into machine code.

[9] Since, as mentioned, words can belong simultaneously to multiple grammatical categories, a parser should be allowed to backtrack. But, as experience has shown, when no particular constraints are placed on a sentence to be

The parsers generated by JavaCC come under the category of LL parsers. These parsers process the tokens produced in a left-to-right scan of a sentence and they carry out what is known as a *top-down leftmost derivation* of the parse of the sentence. Since these parsers can also allow for lookahead in the sense explained in the previous footnote, these parsers are more generally categorized as $LL(k)$ parsers where k stands for the number of lookahead tokens. Obviously, the larger the k, the slower the performance of the parser.[10]

JavaCC gives us a couple of different ways of specifying all the information needed for the generation of the lexer and the parser. If all we want from the parser is to find out whether a sentence is legal according to the rules of some grammar, we can place all of the information in a ".jj" file. The same is the case if we want the parser to execute a piece of code as it discovers certain grammatical constituents in the input. However, if we want the parser to return the syntax trees for the input sentences, we are supposed to place all of the information in a ".jjt" file. Here we will only be interested in the latter case. To give the reader a sense of what is placed in a ".jjt" file, we will show in this section such a file for the following grammar:

```
MagicalSpeech   ::=  ( Statement <PERIOD> )+
Statement       ::=  NP VP?
NP              ::=  ( Pronoun | ( ( Determiner )?
                        ( Adjective )* CN ) ) ( PP )?
CN              ::=    Noun ( Noun )?
PP              ::=    Preposition NP
VP              ::=    Verb (NP | PP)
```

where the rules are presented in the BNF form whose basic notation was explained earlier in a footnote in Section 16.1. (To add to the BNF notation shown earlier, the operator '+' means "at least one.") In the rules shown above, NP stands for noun phrase, VP for verb phrase, CN for compound noun, and PP for prepositional phrase. These rules are placed in a ".jjt" file named `magic_speak_parser_specs.jjt` in the manner shown below. As you

---

parsed (that is, when a sentence is allowed to have an arbitrary number of relative clauses, prepositional phrases, and such), arbitrary backtracking can slow down a parser to such an extent as to render it practically useless. *Therefore, the parsers that are used in actual practice either forbid backtracking completely or permit it only to a limited extent.* As you would expect, the greater the restrictions on backtracking, the smaller the set of languages that would be acceptable to the parser. When parsers do allow for limited backtracking, they do so through the mechanism of *lookahead*. For example, if a parser allows a lookahead of N, that means that before committing to a grammatical type at a token for which a choice is available, the parser will also look at all available grammatical types for N tokens up ahead to the right. However, after the parser has made a decision about what grammatical type to associate with a token (or, with a group of consecutive tokens) for which alternative grammatical types are available in this manner, the parser does *not* change that decision. These are the types of parsers generated by JavaCC. You can control the extent of lookahead through the LOOKAHEAD option.

[10] Some very famous programming languages, such as ALGOL and Pascal, are based on $LL(1)$ grammars, meaning they can be parsed by $LL(1)$ parsers. In contrast to LL parsers, you can also have LR parsers. These parsers also require a left-to-right scan of the input character sequences, but they carry out a *top-down rightmost derivation* of the parse. $LR(k)$ parsers, where k again stands for the number of lookahead tokens to the right, are popular for programming languages because they can be implemented very efficiently — more efficiently than LL parsers for several context-free languages. The implementations for both LL and LR parsing are based on pushdown automata, a computational device that is a combination of a finite automaton and a pushdown stack.

see, the file consists of the following four parts: first there is an options part,[11] which is followed by a part where you specify the lexical analyzer rules. The third part of the file is where you specify the grammar rules. And the last part of the file is used for specifying the rules that generate the leaf nodes of the syntax tree.

```
//
// filename:  magic_speak_parser_specs.jjt
//

///////////////////////// Part 1:  Options  /////////////////////////

options {
  JAVA_UNICODE_ESCAPE = true;
  NODE_PREFIX = "AST";
  MULTI = true;
  STATIC = false;
  NODE_DEFAULT_VOID = true;
}

PARSER_BEGIN(Parser)             //The parser class name is "Parser"
import java.io.*;
public class Parser {}
PARSER_END(Parser)

//////////////// Part 2:  Lexical Analyzer Rules  //////////////////

SKIP : {
  " "
| "\t"
```

---

[11] Regarding the options declarations at the beginning of the ".jjt" file shown, setting the NODE_PREFIX to "AST" means that the names of the class files that are generated automatically by the javacc tool will be prefixed by the substring "AST" (without the quotes). This also implies that when you look at all the Java files in your directory for this demonstration of the Interpreter pattern, you can be certain that all files whose names begin with "AST" were auto generated from the contents of this ".jjt" file. However, beware that, while most of the auto-generated files carry the "AST" prefix, there are a few more auto-generated files whose names are, as we will mention later, without this prefix. Getting back to the declarations of options in the ".jjt" file, note in particular the option of setting NODE_DEFAULT_VOID to true. This option controls the conditions under which a class file for a node on the syntax tree would be generated. Setting this option to true implies that a class file would not be generated for a node unless the header of the declaration of the grammatical entity corresponding to the left-hand side of a rule includes a '#' clause. The STATIC option, if set to true, causes the parser class that is generated to be a static class. Setting to true the MULTI option causes the syntax tree nodes to be given the same names as the names that are on the left-hand sides of the productions. If you do not set MULTI to true, all of the nodes will carry the name SimpleNode, the differentiation between the nodes in that case will be based on the 'id' field of the node classes. The JAVA_UNICODE_ESCAPE option, when set to true, results in the auto creation of a class named JavaCharStream for reading the characters in your input. When the same option is set to false, which is the default, a class named SimpleCharStream is produced instead. There are several other options that can be specified at the beginning of the ".jjt" file that we do not need for our demonstration here. These carry names such as BUILD_NODE_FILES, NODE_FACTORY, NODE_SCOPE_HOOK, and so on. See the documentation on JJTree for what the other options do. That brings us to the PARSER_BEGIN -- PARSER_END directive. With this directive, you specify the name to be used for the main parser class that will be generated by JavaCC. What you see between PARSER_BEGIN and PARSER_END is a *stub class* for the parser class that will be generated by the javacc tool.

```
| "\n"
| "\r"
| "\f"
}
TOKEN_MGR_DECLS: {
    public static int commentNestingCounter = 0;
}
SKIP: {
    <"//" (~["\n","\r"])* ("\r\n"|"\r"|"\n") >
}
SKIP: {
    <"/*"> {commentNestingCounter=1;}: INSIDE_COMMENT
}
<INSIDE_COMMENT> SKIP: {
    <"/*"> {commentNestingCounter++;}
}
<INSIDE_COMMENT> SKIP: {
    <"*/"> {commentNestingCounter--;
        if (commentNestingCounter==0) SwitchTo(DEFAULT);}
|
    <~[]>
}
TOKEN :
{
  < NUMBER: (<DIGIT>)+ ( "." (<DIGIT>)+ )? >
|
  < #DIGIT: [ "0"-"9" ] >
}
TOKEN : { < DETERMINER: "the" | "every" | "this" | "a" | "an" > }
TOKEN: { < NOUN: "wand" | "chess" | "spell" | "business" | "beings"
                | "help"  | "mousetraps" | "dementors"
                | "world" | "wizards" | "charm" | "polyjuice"
                | "potion" | "else" | "magic"
                | "pieces" | "problems" > }
TOKEN: { < PRONOUN: "i" | "we" | "this" | "you" | "us" > }
TOKEN: { < ADJ: "magic" | "wizard" | "polyjuice" | "your" | "dark"
                | "fast" | "large" | "dangerous" | "wizarding"
                | "no" | "high" | "animated" | "else"
                | "difficult"> }
TOKEN: { < VERB: "is" | "are" | "have" | "has" | "make"
                | "want" | "cast" | "look" | "play" | "can"
                | "makes" | "point" | "allows"
                | "construct" | "build" | "builds"
                | "stores" | "conquer" >}
TOKEN: { < PREPOSITION: "with" | "when" | "without" | "for"
                        | "about" | "at" | "after" | "to"
                        | "of" | "between" | "but" | "below"
                        | "in" | "into" | "like" | "except"
                        | "following" | "on" | "than" | "over"
                        | "near" | "of" | "like" | "near"
                        | "since" | "up" | "upon" | "within"
                        | "by" > }
```

```
TOKEN : /* words */
{
  < WORD: (<LETTER>)+ >
|
  < #LETTER: ["a"-"z", "A"-"Z"] >
}
/* SEPARATORS */
TOKEN :
{
     < PERIOD: "." >
}

//////////////////////// Part 3:  Grammar Rules  ////////////////////////

ASTMagicalSpeech MagicalSpeech() #MagicalSpeech :
{}
{
    ( Statement() <PERIOD> )+
    { return jjtThis; }
}
void Statement() #Statement :
{ }
{
    NP() ( VP() )?
}
void NP() #NounPhrase :
{}
{
    ( Pronoun() | ( ( Determiner() )? ( Adjective() )* CN() ) ) (PP())?
}
void CN() #CompoundNoun:
{}
{
    Noun() ( Noun() )?
}
void PP() #PrepPhrase :
{}
{
    Preposition() ( (NP() (VP())?) | VP() )
}
void VP() #VerbPhrase :
{}
{
    Verb() (NP() | PP())
}

////////////////// Part 4:  Grammar Leaf Nodes  ///////////////////////

void Noun() #Noun :
{Token t;}
{
    t=<NOUN> {jjtThis.setLexem(t.image);}
```

```
}
void Pronoun() #Pronoun :
{Token t;}
{
    t=<PRONOUN> {jjtThis.setLexem(t.image);}
}
void Determiner() #Determiner :
{Token t;}
{
    t=<DETERMINER> {jjtThis.setLexem(t.image);}
}
void Adjective() #Adjective :
{Token t;}
{
    t=<ADJ> {jjtThis.setLexem(t.image);}
}
void Preposition() #Preposition :
{Token t;}
{
    t=<PREPOSITION> {jjtThis.setLexem(t.image);}
}
void Verb() #Verb :
{Token t;}
{
    t=<VERB> {jjtThis.setLexem(t.image);}
}
```

The rest of this section explains the syntax used in the file shown above for the lexer and the parser rules. This is for the convenience of the reader who wishes to extend the demonstration code in this chapter according to the suggestions made in Section 16.12.

Part 2 of the ".jjt" file shown above, the part labeled "Lexical Analyzer Rules," declares the different token types for the benefit of the lexer. More precisely speaking, the identifiers SKIP, INSIDE COMMENT, TOKEN, etc., define *lexical states*. The lexical analyzer is allowed to be in only one of these states at any given time as the input is scanned from left to right. As to what the lexical analyzer does to the part of the input that is matched with the regular expression that is associated with a lexical state depends on the state itself. For example, any portion of the input that matches the regular expression for the identifier SKIP is simply discarded. And any portion of the input that matches the regular expression for TOKEN is sent as a token to the parser. While certain lexical states — SKIP and TOKEN in the ".jjt" file shown — are provided by JavaCC, you can also define your own lexical states and have the lexical analyzer enter those states when appropriately defined regular expressions match certain designated sequences of characters in the input. The lexical state INSIDE COMMENT is an example of such a user-defined state. Note how the states SKIP and INSIDE COMMENT work together to discard all comment blocks, even nested comment blocks, in the input.

Focusing now on the tokens that are supplied by the lexer to the parser, the definition of such a token must begin with the lexer state identifier 'TOKEN:', which is then followed by the token type name and its specification inside curly braces. Each token type is placed within the '<>' delimiters. Looking at what is perhaps the simplest such token declaration

in the file, we declare PERIOD to be a token and its specification is the punctuation mark '.' that is used to denote the end of a sentence. What is interesting is that the same character is also a part of the NUMBER token that is defined much earlier in the file. So what does that imply with regard to how the character '.' will be recognized lexically? It all depends on the order in which the tokens are specified in the ".jjt" file. If the character '.' shows up surrounded by numeric digit characters, it will be be recognized as a NUMBER token and those characters — meaning the digits along with the period — in the text file will not be available for any further lexical analysis.

The reader may wish to pay particular attention to the NUMBER token.[12] The specification for this token indicates what groupings of characters constitutes a number. To make this definition convenient to write, we use the prefix '#' to designate a local token — in this case the name of the local token is DIGIT. (This token is completely local to the lexer. That is, on account of the prefix '#', the token DIGIT will not be passed on to the parser. Its role is confined to the lexical analysis of the input.) The specification of the DIGIT token uses what is known as a *character-class* in regular expressions.[13] It says that each input character in the range from '0' to '9', both ends inclusive, is to be accepted as a DIGIT token. This definition of the DIGIT token is then used in the main specification of a NUMBER token: a NUMBER is any repetitions of a DIGIT, as long as there is at least one such character, possibly followed by the decimal character '.', that if present, must be followed by at least one additional DIGIT character.

Part 3 of the ".jjt" file, the part labeled "Grammar Rules," is for specifying the grammar rules we showed earlier in this section. Note how exactly the rules of the grammar are laid out in the ".jjt" file. Let's focus on the first rule shown in that part of the file:

```
ASTMagicalSpeech MagicalSpeech() #MagicalSpeech :
{}
{
    ( Statement() <PERIOD> )+
    { return jjtThis; }
}
```

This is the JavaCC way of expressing the following rule in the BNF notation:

```
MagicalSpeech    ::=    ( Statement <PERIOD> )+
```

Note the header of the JavaCC representation of the same rule:

```
ASTMagicalSpeech MagicalSpeech() #MagicalSpeech :
```

This header does multiple things, all at the same time. On the one hand, it purports to be the declaration of a method named MagicalSpeech() that should return an object

---

[12] The token specification syntax uses the operators '+', '*', '|', '?', and '()' in the same manner as in the grammar rules shown earlier.

[13] See the first few sections of Chapter 4 of [6] for a reader-friendly introduction to regular expressions.

of type ASTMagicalSpeech and, on the other, the notation #MagicalSpeech means that we want the parser to output a node for the syntax tree and that this node, to be named MagicalSpeech, will be created by the Java class ASTMagicalSpeech. Without the additional syntactic sugar in the form of #MagicalSpeech, the parser will work just the same, but you will not see a node in the syntax tree with the label MagicalSpeech.

The header is followed by two pairs of curly braces. The first pair holds any local variables that may be used inside the declarations and the executable code within the second pair of curly braces. Any statements inside the second pair of curly braces — such as the statement 'return jjtThis;' — represent the *user action* that needs to be carried out as the parse is taking place. The statement 'return jjtThis;' inside the second pair of curly braces simply says to return the current node of the parse tree. The variable 'jjtThis' always stands for the current node, meaning the node corresponding to the rule that contains the statement with 'jjtThis'.

That brings us to Part 4 of the ".jjt" file. This section, labeled "Grammar Leaf Nodes" in the file shown in this section, contains rules for the leaf nodes of the parse tree. As with the expression of the rules in the "Grammar Rules" section, note how the header of each rule both declares a method, as with the part 'Noun()' in the header for the Noun leaf node, and the fact that we want the parse tree to contain the corresponding node, the latter being done through declarations like '#Noun' in the header. Again as with the rules in the "Grammar Rules" part, each rule involves two pairs of curly braces, the first for declaring any local variables needed inside the second pair of curly braces, and the second for the actual placement of the code that creates a value for the grammatical category. Being leaf nodes, the code inside the second pair of curly braces gets the corresponding token that is shown with the '<>' delimiters and sets the value of the corresponding node in the parse tree by invoking the "image" of the token, the image being merely the character string that corresponds to the token.

As will be mentioned in Section 16.12, the magic_speak_parser_specs.jjt file shown in this section is processed by the jjtree preprocessor that is a part of the JavaCC library.

16.7   A TOP LEVEL VIEW OF THE PATTERN DEMONSTRATION

Figure 16.1 shows the class hierarchy for our demonstration of the Interpreter pattern. The overall orchestration of the interpretation is carried out by the Driver class with the help of the classes that descend from the root interpretation class Interpreter_Sentence. The actual interpretation of the individual nouns, verbs, and adjectives of magic-speak is carried out by the classes Interpreter_Noun, Interpreter_Verb, and Interpreter_Adjective, respectively. *However, the Driver class can access these more focused* Interpreter *classes only through the interface provided by the* Interpreter_Sentence *class.*

As you will see through the explanations in the rest of this chapter, the role played by the Driver class is critical, in the sense that, on the one hand, it knows how to invoke the functionality of the parser generated from the grammar specifications presented in the previous section, and, on the other, it knows how to use the interface provided by the

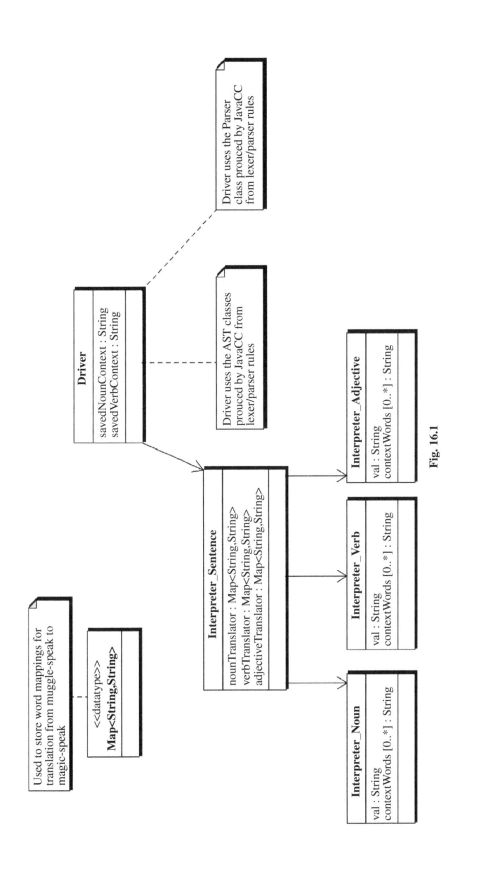

Used to store word mappings for translation from muggle-speak to magic-speak

<<datatype>>
Map<String,String>

Driver uses the Parser class prouced by JavaCC from lexer/parser rules

Driver

savedNounContext : String
savedVerbContext : String

Driver uses the AST classes prouced by JavaCC from lexer/parser rules

Interpreter_Sentence

nounTranslator : Map<String,String>
verbTranslator : Map<String,String>
adjectiveTranslator : Map<String,String>

Interpreter_Adjective

val : String
contextWords [0..*] : String

Interpreter_Verb

val : String
contextWords [0..*] : String

Interpreter_Noun

val : String
contextWords [0..*] : String

Fig. 16.1

Interpreter_Sentence class and trigger the interpretation of the individual words and the phrases in magic-speak sentences.

About the first capability of the Driver class, that is, its knowing how to invoke the parser generated from the ".jjt" file of the previous section, here are the core invocations from the code for Driver that we will show more fully in the next section:

```
Parser parser =  new Parser(inputStream);
ASTMagicalSpeech root = parser.MagicalSpeech();
```

where Parser is the auto-generated class from the grammar specifications in the ".jjt" file and where the second invocation calls the method MagicalSpeech() on the parser to start the process of lexical analysis and parsing. Note how the Parser instance is tied to an InputStream object. As you will see later, this input stream is attached to the file containing the magic-speak sentences.

The second capability of the Driver class is its ability to initiate automatic interpretation, which in our case results in automatic translation of magic-speak into muggle-speak. The Driver does this by making the following invocation on the root node returned by the above call to MagicalSpeech():

```
processForInterpretation(root);
```

It is this call that descends down the syntax tree hanging from the root node and makes appropriate calls to the Interpreter_Sentence *interface while at the same time supplying the context needed for the interpretation.*

The demonstration code for this pattern starts with the following three human-supplied files:

```
magic_speak_parser_specs.jjt
Driver.java
ShowSyntaxTree.java
```

where magic_speak_parser_specs.jjt, as described in detail in the previous section, contains the specifications for the lexer and the parser; where Driver.java contains the code for orchestrating the lexer/parser, on the one hand, and the code for the Interpreter pattern, on the other; and, finally, where ShowSyntaxTree.java contains the code for pretty-printing the abstract syntax tree.

In addition to the three files listed above, there is another bit of human intervention that is needed before you can actually call on the Driver class to process magic-speak: You must "manually" enter some extra code in the automatically produced classes for the leaf nodes of the syntax tree. This additional code is needed to further annotate the syntax tree and to help out with the display of the information when ShowSyntaxTree.java is asked to pretty-print the syntax tree in a window of the terminal screen. This additional code, shown below, goes right before the ending brace of the class definitions for the affected classes.

```
String lexem = "";
public void setLexem( String lex ) { lexem = lex; }
public String getLexem() { return lexem; }
// Override superclass handling:
public String toString() { return super.toString()+ " : " + lexem; }
```

This code fragment must be entered in the following leaf node classes of the syntax tree that are automatically generated by JavaCC:[14]

```
ASTNoun.java
ASTVerb.java
ASTAdjective.java
ASTPronoun.java
ASTPreposition.java
```

16.8 THE Driver CLASS

As mentioned earlier, the `Driver` class has two important roles that it must fulfill simultaneously: (1) It must first construct an instance of the parser, which is represented by the class `Parser` in this demonstration, and then invoke the parser on the file containing magic-speak. In this role, we will also expect the `Driver` to pretty-print the syntax tree for each of the sentences in the magic-speak file. (2) It must invoke a designated method for the interpretation of magic-speak into muggle-speak. The name of this method for our demonstration is `processForInterpretation()` in the definition of the `Driver` class.

To explain the class definition that follows, let's start with its four static variables. The variable `interpretedSentence` is meant to store the interpreted version of a magic-speak sentence. So when a file contains multiple magic-speak sentences, the string value of this variable will change as the sentences in the file are being translated into muggle-speak. The static variable `offset` is used in the pretty-printing of the interpreted sentences. The static variables `savedNounContext` and `savedVerbContext` hold the contextual information for the interpretation of the individual words. As stated earlier, words cannot be interpreted in isolation from other words.[15] As the interpreter descends down the syntax tree, the variables `savedNounContext` and `savedVerbContext` hold the larger phrase level information that is applicable to each word in the phrase. *Word translation then takes place keeping in mind the contextual phrases for each word.* Using the context in this manner is an important aspect of the Interpreter pattern.[16]

---

[14]The interested reader will find at the book website a Perl script named `annotateAST.pl` whose execution will automatically insert the extra code in the leaf node classes.

[15]As mentioned in Section 16.5, when translating magic-speak into muggle-speak, words that are evocative of the wizarding world must be translated into other non-wizarding words but without turning the sentences into gibberish. Therefore, the word "magic" in the phrase "a magic wand" needs to be translated into something more suitable for muggles. However, the same word in a phrase like "the magic of your charm" probably needs no translation/interpretation.

[16]In case the reader is wondering why all of these variables are static, as opposed to being instance variables, it is because we have chosen to do all of the interpretation work inside the static method `main()` of the `Driver` class. It would obviously be trivial to create a different class for the purpose of interpretation and to use the instance variables of that class for storing the sort of information that is in `interpretedSentence`, `offset`, `savedNounContext`, etc., in the discussion here.

With regard to the local variables inside `main()`, the variable `inputStream` is bound to the file containing magic-speak. The name of this file is supplied as a command-line argument to the `Driver` class. The variable `parser` holds a reference to an instance of the `Parser` class. To construct an instance of the `Parser`, we supply to the `Parser` constructor the `inputStream` reference attached to the magic-speak file. By invoking the top-level parser method `MagicalSpeech()` on the parser instance, we parse all of the sentences in the magic-speak file. Subsequently, we display the syntax trees of the sentences by supplying the root of the composite tree for all of the sentences to an instance of `ShowSyntaxTree`.

That brings us to the interpretation of the syntax tree that was constructed by the parser — the raison d'etre of this demonstration. As mentioned earlier, it is the call to the `Driver`'s method `processForInterpretation()`, with the root of the syntax tree supplied as the argument, that causes the translation of magic-speak sentences into muggle-speak sentences.

If you look at the code for the method `processForInterpretation()`, you will see that this method recursively descends down the syntax tree. You originally call this method on the root of the tree; it then calls itself recursively on the children of the root, and so on. Note how, at the direct children of the root, `processForInterpretation()` constructs a new instance of `Interpreter_Sentence`. Since our parser can handle multiple period-delimited sentences in a file, towards that end it creates a new `Statement` node in the parse tree for each new sentence. In the syntax tree, the children of a `Statement` node correspond to the noun-phrase–verb-phrase decomposition of a sentence. So the subsequent 'if' conditionals look for `NounPhrase` and `VerbPhrase` nodes, and, as these nodes are found, `processForInterpretation()` sets the `saveNounContext` and the `saveVerbContext` to the total string value of these non-terminal nodes in the syntax tree. By the string value, we mean the actual terminal strings hanging from the subtrees that correspond to the non-terminal nodes. These string values are fetched by calling the `getStringValue()` method.

As `processForInterpretation()` continues descending down the syntax tree, it will eventually run into the terminal nodes of the tree — these would correspond to the nouns, the verbs, the adjectives, etc., in a sentence. When such nodes are encountered, `processForInterpretation()` asks the instance of `Interpreter_Sentence` constructed at the root node of the sentence to also construct an instance of the actual interpretation classes such as `Interpreter_Noun`, `Interpreter_Verb`, and `Interpreter_Adjective`. These requests include the applicable context as the argument to the `constructXXXNode()` methods.

```java
import java.io.*;

public class Driver {

    static String interpretedSentence = "";
    static String offset = "";
    static String savedNounContext = "";
    static String savedVerbContext = "";

    public static void main(String args[]) {
        InputStreamReader inputStream = null;
```

```java
    try {
        if (args.length == 1) {
            System.out.println("\nReading from file " + args[0]);
            inputStream =  new FileReader(args[0]);
        } else {
            System.out.println(
                          "Usage: java Driver magic_phrases.txt");
            System.exit(-1);
        }

        // Construct parser instance for parsing the file with
        // magic-speak:
        Parser parser =  new Parser(inputStream);
        ASTMagicalSpeech root = parser.MagicalSpeech();
        System.out.println(
                  "\nMagical speech file parsed successfully.\n");

        // Print an indented list of the AST nodes:
        ShowSyntaxTree printer = new ShowSyntaxTree();
        printer.print(root);

        // Now process the AST for the interpretation of
        // magic-speak:
        processForInterpretation(root);
        System.out.println( "\n\nInterpreted sentence(s):\n "
                                  +  interpretedSentence );
    } catch (ParseException pe) {
        System.out.println("Main : " + pe.getMessage());
    }catch (java.io.FileNotFoundException fnfe) {
        System.out.println("Main : " + fnfe.getMessage());
        System.exit(0);
    }
}

private static void processForInterpretation(Node node) {
 Interpreter_Sentence st = new Interpreter_Sentence();
  if (node instanceof ASTStatement ) {
        st = new Interpreter_Sentence();
        interpretedSentence += "\n\n";
    } else if (node instanceof ASTNounPhrase ) {
        String nounContext = getStringValue( node );
        savedNounContext = nounContext;
    } else if (node instanceof ASTVerbPhrase ) {
        String val = getStringValue( node );
        savedVerbContext = val;
    } else if (node instanceof ASTNoun ) {
        st.constructNounNode( node.toString(), savedNounContext );
        interpretedSentence += offset + st.interpretNoun() + "\n";
    } else if (node instanceof ASTVerb ) {
        st.constructVerbNode( node.toString(), savedVerbContext );
        interpretedSentence += offset + st.interpretVerb() + "\n";
    } else if (node instanceof ASTAdjective ) {
```

```
            st.constructAdjectiveNode( node.toString(),
                                           savedNounContext );
            interpretedSentence += offset
                              + st.interpretAdjective() + "\n";
    } else {
        if ( node.toString().contains( ":")) {
            interpretedSentence += offset + node + "\n";
        }
    }
    int count = node.jjtGetNumChildren();
    offset += offset;
    for (int i=0;i<count;i++) {
        Node child = node.jjtGetChild(i);
        processForInterpretation(child);
    }
}

private static String getStringValue( Node node ) {
    String val = "";
    int nn = node.jjtGetNumChildren();
    if (nn == 0) {
        String str = node.toString();
        val += str.substring( 1+ str.indexOf( ':' ) );
    }
    for (int i=0;i<nn;i++) {
        Node child = node.jjtGetChild(i);
        val += getStringValue( child );
    }
    return val;
}
}
```

16.9 THE Interpreter_Sentence CLASS

The root interpretation class Interpreter_Sentence has two primary roles: On the one hand it must store the dictionaries needed for the translation of magic words into muggle words, and, on the other, it must serve as the interface that the Driver class can call on for the interpretation of magic-speak sentences. The implementation of the Interpreter_Sentence class shown below contains logic for both of these roles.

With regard to the second role of the Interpreter_Sentence class, note that the actual interpretation of the individual nouns, the verbs, and the adjectives of magic-speak is carried out by the classes Interpreter_Noun, Interpreter_Verb, and Interpreter_Adjective, respectively, that are subclasses of the root class Interpreter_Sentence. *But the* Driver *class can access these more focused interpreter classes only through the interface provided by the* Interpreter_Sentence *class.*

As the reader will recall from our description of the Driver class, it serves its interpretation role by descending down the syntax tree constructed by the parser. When it encounters

higher level nodes, such as the nodes corresponding to the noun-phrase and the verb-phrase portions of a sentence, it saves away their string values as context that would be helpful for the translation of the actual words hanging from the leaf nodes. And when the `Driver` encounters the leaf nodes of the syntax tree, it uses the applicable context to translate the magic-speak nouns, verbs, and adjectives into magic-speak versions of the same.

Since the interpretation of magic-speak takes place dynamically as the `Driver` visits each node of the syntax tree, the values for the instance variables `mn`, `mv`, and `ma` in the class definition shown below would change depending on which leaf node the `Driver` is visiting. The roles played by these instance variables will become clear when we discuss the methods defined for this class.

In the code shown below, after the declaration of the instance variables and before the method definitions, we create a set called `trigger_words`, and the three dictionaries: `nounTranslator`, `verbTranslator`, and `adjectiveTranslator`. The idea here is that a context for the interpretation of a noun, a verb, or an adjective must contain at least one of the words in the set `trigger_words`. In other words, we do not alter a sentence of magic-speak if the sentence in question is harmless from the standpoint of how it will be received by the muggles.

Although the trigger set and the three dictionaries are very small, they nonetheless suffice for conveying the main points of this demonstration. Obviously, if such a pattern were to be implemented for a real-life application, you would need much larger versions of the trigger set and the three dictionaries.

That brings us to the method definitions in the class. Recall from the description of the `Driver` class that the `Driver` invokes the methods `constructNounNode()`, `constructVerbNode()`, and `constructVerbNode()` of the class presented here when it encounters the leaf nodes of the syntax tree for a magic-speak sentence. As shown below, these methods in turn construct instances of the respective interpretation classes for the nouns, the verbs, and the adjectives, *while supplying the constructors with the applicable context collected from the higher-level nodes in the syntax tree.* The instance of the actual `Interpreter` class returned by each such method is stored in one of the instance variables of the class shown here. Subsequently, when `Driver` needs the results of an interpretation, it calls on one of the last three methods in the class definition, those calls being translated into the calls on the instance variables of the class.

Our implementation of `Interpreter_Sentence` completely isolates the `Driver` class from the actual classes engaged in the task of interpretation. So the `Driver` class only needs to know about the methods defined for the class shown below. *This is an important feature of the Interpreter pattern.*

```java
import java.util.*;

public class Interpreter_Sentence {

    private Interpreter_Noun mn;
    private Interpreter_Verb mv;
    private Interpreter_Adjective ma;

    static protected Set<String> trigger_words = new HashSet<String>();
    static protected Map<String,String> nounTranslator =
```

```
                                   new HashMap<String,String>();
    static protected Map<String,String> verbTranslator =
                                   new HashMap<String,String>();
    static protected Map<String,String> adjectiveTranslator =
                                   new HashMap<String,String>();
    {
        nounTranslator.put("wand", "finger");
        nounTranslator.put("wizards", "people");
        nounTranslator.put("dementors", "greedy businessmen");
        nounTranslator.put("spell", "picture");

        verbTranslator.put("cast", "show");

        adjectiveTranslator.put("magic", "little");
        adjectiveTranslator.put("dark", "ambitious");
        adjectiveTranslator.put("wizarding", "trading");

        trigger_words.addAll( Arrays.asList("wizards", "wand",
                              "spell", "dementors", "wizarding"));
    }

    void constructNounNode( String str, String context ) {
        mn = new Interpreter_Noun( str, context );
    }
    void constructVerbNode( String str, String context ) {
        mv = new Interpreter_Verb( str, context );
    }
    void constructAdjectiveNode( String str, String context ) {
        ma = new Interpreter_Adjective( str, context );
    }
    String interpretNoun() {
        return mn.interpret();
    }
    String interpretVerb() {
        return mv.interpret();
    }
    String interpretAdjective() {
        return ma.interpret();
    }
}
```

16.10   THE WORKER CLASSES FOR INTERPRETATION

As mentioned earlier, although the root interpreter class Interpreter_ Sentence serves as the main interpretation interface for the Driver class, the actual word-level translation from magic-speak to muggle-speak is carried out by the three subclasses of Interpreter_Sentence. Before we go further into the first of these three classes, note again that they are completely isolated from the Driver. That is, these three subclasses are only accessible through the interface provided by the root class Interpreter_ Sentence.

Each class derived from the root interpreter class `Interpreter_Sentence` inherits the `trigger_words` set and the three dictionaries we mentioned in the previous section. So the implementation code in each of these three subclasses consists primarily of comparing the context with what is in the set `trigger_words` and then either actually translating a magic-speak word, if the context calls for a need for translation, or leaving the word alone.

The code shown below for the `Interpreter_Noun` class consists mostly of the constructor and the implementation of the `interpreter()` method. The constructor first extracts the actual noun word that needs to be interpreted from the first argument string by calling

```
val = str.substring( 2 + str.indexOf( ':' ) );
```

As to the structure of the argument in this call, note that the leaf-node values that are supplied by the `Driver` class are in the form

```
Noun :  actual_noun_word
```

for the Noun leaf nodes of the syntax tree. Therefore, in order to retrieve the actual noun word, we must first locate the separator ':' and then start extracting the word starting at two character positions past the location where ':' was found. Subsequently, the constructor splits the context string into an array of strings and tries to see if any of the context words appears in the set `trigger_words` that is inherited from the parent class `Interpreter_Sentence`. If the answer is yes, we set the interpretation flag `muggleAlert` to true.

The implementation of the `interpret()` method first checks that the context-driven interpretation flag `muggleAlert` is on and that the `nounTranslator` actually contains the magic noun that requires translation.

```
public class Interpreter_Noun extends Interpreter_Sentence {

    private String val;
    private String[] contextWords;
    private boolean muggleAlert = false;

    public Interpreter_Noun( String str, String context ) {
        val = str.substring( 2+ str.indexOf( ':' ) );
        contextWords = context.trim().split( "\\s+" );
        for ( String word : contextWords ) {
            if (trigger_words.contains(word)) {
                muggleAlert = true;
                break;
            }
        }
    }
    String interpret() {
        if ( (muggleAlert == true) &&
```

```
                                (nounTranslator.containsKey(val)) ) {
        return "noun interpreted as:  " + nounTranslator.get(val);
    }
    return "noun not interpreted:  " + val;
  }
}
```

Next we show the implementation of the Interpreter_Verb worker class. As was the case with its sibling class Interpreter_Noun, this class also inherits from its parent the trigger_words set and the three dictionaries we listed in our presentation of Interpreter_Sentence. As for Interpreter_Noun, the implementation code in Interpreter_Verb consists primarily of comparing the context with what is in the set trigger_words and then either actually translating a magic-speak word, if the context triggers a need for translation, or leaving the input word alone.

```
public class Interpreter_Verb extends Interpreter_Sentence {

    private String val;
    private String[] contextWords;
    private boolean muggleAlert = false;

    public Interpreter_Verb( String str, String context ) {
        val = str.substring( 2+ str.indexOf( ':' ) );
        contextWords = context.trim().split( "\\s+" );
        for ( String word : contextWords ) {
            if (trigger_words.contains(word)) {
                muggleAlert = true;
                break;
            }
        }
    }
    String interpret() {
        if (  (muggleAlert == true) &&
                            (verbTranslator.containsKey(val)) ){
            return "Verb interpreted as:  " + verbTranslator.get(val);
        }
        return "verb not interpreted:  " + val;
    }
}
```

The code shown below for the Interpreter_Adjective parallels the code shown earlier for Interpreter_Noun and Interpreter_Verb. Therefore, we will not go any further into its explanation.

```java
public class Interpreter_Adjective extends Interpreter_Sentence  {

    private String val;
    private String[] contextWords;
    private boolean muggleAlert = false;

    public Interpreter_Adjective( String str, String context) {
        val = str.substring( 2+ str.indexOf( ':' ) );
        contextWords = context.trim().split( "\\s+" );
        for ( String word : contextWords ) {
            if (trigger_words.contains(word)) {
                muggleAlert = true;
                break;
            }
        }
    }
    String interpret() {
        if ((muggleAlert == true) &&
                            (adjectiveTranslator.containsKey(val))) {
            return "adjective interpreted as:  "
                                    + adjectiveTranslator.get(val);
        }
        return "adjective not interpreted:  " + val;
    }
}
```

16.11   THE UTILITY CLASS ShowSyntaxTree

The utility class ShowSyntaxTree is used for pretty-printing the syntax trees produced by the parser. What you see is a standard implementation for such code. The method getIndentation() returns increasingly larger amounts of white space as the visit() method recursively descends down the tree.

```java
public class ShowSyntaxTree {
    private int indentationIndex = 1;

    private String getIndentation() {
        String indentation = "     ";
        for (int i=0;  i< indentationIndex; i++ ) {
            indentation += "     ";
        }
        return indentation;
    }
    public void print(Node node) {
        System.out.println("\nPrinting the tree ...");
        visit(node);
    }
    private void visit(Node node) {
```

```
        System.out.println( getIndentation() + node.toString() );
        ++indentationIndex;
        int count = node.jjtGetNumChildren();
        for (int i=0;i<count;i++) {
            Node child = node.jjtGetChild(i);
            visit(child);
        }
        --indentationIndex;
    }
}
```

16.12 PLAYING WITH THE CODE

Download the class files for this pattern from the book website into a separate directory. Next, go through the following sequence of steps:

1. You will find in the downloaded code a file named `cleanit_jjt`. This executable file is for deleting from the directory in which your downloaded code resides all those classes that are automatically generated by JavaCC. As you are playing with the code, you will find yourself wanting to revert the directory to its original state every once in a while — especially when you make changes to the lexer or parser specifications in the ".jjt" file. Although not needed for the very first run of the downloaded code, your first step in creating your own demonstrations is likely to be a call to

    ```
    cleanit_jjt
    ```

2. Next, you compile the lexer and the parser specifications in the ".jjt" file by

    ```
    jjtree magic_speak_parser_specs.jjt
    ```

    This call will deposit in your directory several files that we will comment on after we describe the next step.

3. Among the files auto generated by the previous call, you will find one that is named `magic_speak_parser_specs.jj`. You now compile this file with the `javacc` tool by invoking

    ```
    javacc magic_speak_parser_specs.jj
    ```

    The two previous steps will generate and deposit in your directory the following 23 Java files, with each file containing a class whose name is the root name of the file:

    ```
    Parser.java                    // The main parser class
    ParserConstants.java
    ParserTreeConstants.java
    ParseException.java
    JJTParserState.java
    ```

```
ParserTokenManager.java          // The main lexer class
Token.java
TokenMgrError.java
Node.java                         // The interface class
                                  //    for AST nodes
SimpleNode.java                   // Implements Node
JavaCharStream.java               // An adapter class that
                                  //    delivers characters
                                  //    to the lexical
                                  //    analyzer

ASTAdjective.java
ASTCompoundNoun.java
ASTDeterminer.java
ASTMagicalSpeech.java
ASTNoun.java
ASTNounPhrase.java
ASTPreposition.java
ASTPrepPhrase.java
ASTPronoun.java
ASTStatement.java
ASTVerb.java
ASTVerbPhrase.java
```

Of these automatically generated classes, the number of the classes whose names carry the "AST" prefix depends entirely on the complexity of the grammar rules in the ".jjt" file. In general, you will have one AST class for each grammatical symbol that is on the left-hand side of the grammar rules in the ".jjt" file. Of the other auto generated classes listed above, the Node class is a pure interface for the classes that represent the nodes of the syntax tree. The Node interface is implemented by the SimpleNode class to create the basic functionality that must be possessed by all of the nodes of the syntax tree. Subsequently, each of the AST classes extends the SimpleNode class.

The automatically generated Parser class is the main class for parsing a text file containing the magic-speak input and ParserTokenManager is the main class that knows how to carry out the lexical analysis of the input file. As the reader will recall from one of the footnotes in Section 16.6, the name given to the parser class is determined by one of the options declared in the ".jjt" file. As we mentioned there, what you see between the directives PARSER_BEGIN and PARSER_END is a stub class for the parser that is eventually filled out by the javacc tool.

The TokenMgrError class is an exception class; an instance of this class is thrown as the exception if an error is detected by the lexer. Another exception class is ParseException; an exception of this type is thrown when a problem is encountered during parsing. Token is a class defining the tokens to be extracted by the lexer. The following two auto generated classes define the various "constants" used by the lexer and the parser: ParserConstants and ParserTreeConstants. The ParserConstants class associates different integers with the different token types specified in the ".jjt" file; these constants are used in the Token class for the code that is needed for extracting the different tokens from an input file. What ParserContants class does for the terminals of the grammar, the

ParserTreeConstants class does for the nonterminals. The reason for the prefix "Parser" in the names these two classes, is the same as in the names of the classes Parser and ParserTokenManager.

4. You execute the Perl script annotateAST.pl to inject into each leaf-node class the extra code we mentioned earlier in Section 16.7.

5. Now you must compile the Driver class by

```
javac  Driver.java
```

Because of the dependency between the different Java files in your directory, this will cause compilation of all of your Java code in the directory.

6. Finally, you are ready to do an automatic interpretation of magic-speak into muggle-speak by

```
java Driver magic_phrases.txt
```

assuming that the sentences, as can be expected to be spoken by the folks of the wizarding world, are in a file named magic_phrases.txt.

7. If you want to see the grammar you placed in the ".jjt" file in the more readable BNF form, you can invoke

```
jjdoc magic_speak_parser_specs.jj
```

The above command will generate an HTML file that you can view in a browser.

To show the output of the interpretation/translation demonstration for an actual magic-speak sentence, let's say your magic_phrases.txt file contains the following sentence:

```
you point with your magic wand when you want to cast a spell.
```

For the above input, you will see the following output:

```
Reading from file magic_phrases.txt

Magical speech file parsed successfully.

Printing the tree ...
    MagicalSpeech
        Statement
            NounPhrase
                Pronoun : you
            VerbPhrase
                Verb : point
                PrepPhrase
```

```
Preposition : with
NounPhrase
        Adjective : your
        Adjective : magic
        CompoundNoun
            Noun : wand
        PrepPhrase
            Preposition : when
            NounPhrase
                Pronoun : you
            VerbPhrase
                Verb : want
                PrepPhrase
                    Preposition : to
                    VerbPhrase
                        Verb : cast
                        NounPhrase
                            Determiner : a
                            CompoundNoun
                                Noun : spell
```

```
Interpreted sentence(s):

Pronoun :                    you
verb not interpreted:        point
Preposition :                with
adjective not interpreted:   your
adjective interpreted as:    little
noun interpreted as:         finger
Preposition :                when
Pronoun :                    you
verb not interpreted:        want
Preposition :                to
Verb interpreted as:         show
Determiner :                 a
noun interpreted as:         picture
```

As you can see, the magic-speak sentence "*You point with your magic wand when you want to cast a spell.*" was translated successfully into "*You point with your little finger when you want to show a picture.*"

For additional insights, you may consider extending the code for this pattern along the following lines:

- A straightforward exercise in extending this demonstration is to use a larger set of grammatical and lexical analysis rules in the ".jjt" file. This would allow you to do an interpretation of a larger variety of magic-speak sentences into muggle-speak sentences.

- Before a word is translated from magic-speak to muggle-speak, our demonstration considers the context of the word, but only at the level of the local phrase of which

the word is a part. However, in practice, the context must be examined simultaneously at multiple levels, ranging from the phrase in which the word occurs, to the sentence of which the phrase is a part, and to the paragraph and higher-level components of a discourse. As a step in that direction, you could try to expand the scope of the demonstration by analyzing the sentence-level context for the words before making the interpretation/translation decisions.

17

ITERATOR

17.1 STORING OBJECT COLLECTIONS AND INTERACTING WITH THEM

Let's say your application requires you to scan a collection of objects in the memory of your computer, and, every once in a while, to query one of those objects. But, as you must already know, how you interact with a collection depends much on how you store the objects in the memory. If each object could be allocated the same amount of space, you could store the objects in contiguous segments of memory, one after another. A great advantage of doing this is that the time it would take to access any object would become independent of the size of the entire collection. To access the Nth object in the collection, all you would need to do would be to multiply the space occupied by each object by $N - 1$ and you would know which memory location to query for the desired object. This, as the reader surely knows, is how an `array` is stored by a computer program. The store-in-contiguous-segments-of-memory approach works wonderfully well when a collection once created does not need to be modified subsequently.

Let's now consider a situation in which there is something about a collection that places a constraint on the order in which the objects are stored in the memory. For example, let's say you have stored the names of all the employees in your organization in increasing order of their annual remuneration. When you wrote the code originally, you made sure that you had allocated sufficient memory for an array to account for all the individuals in your organization. But, unfortunately for your code, after the code was up and running, your organization hired a few more individuals. Now you are faced with a conundrum. You not only have to add additional members to your collection, you must also insert their names at certain specific places in the collection depending on their annual incomes. Assuming that you want to stick with the array approach to storage, what that means is that you would need to create another version of the source code whose compilation would lead to the object code that would correspond to the current state of the organization. If your code was meant to be used by others, they are not likely to be thrilled by the prospect of having to recompile the sources every time the organization in question hires or fires people.

Designing with Objects: Object-Oriented Design Patterns Explained with Stories from Harry Potter, First Edition. Avinash C. Kak.
© 2015 John Wiley & Sons, Inc. Published 2015 by John Wiley & Sons, Inc.

Obviously, a smart programmer would anticipate such issues and, for the scenario painted above, would use other more flexible forms of storage that would allow for a collection to be modified even as a program is up and running. The flexible forms of storage are all based on linked structures that permit objects to reside in noncontiguous blocks of memory. In the simplest of such structures, called linked lists, you associate a memory address with each object that points to where the next object is located. Given these linking memory addresses, a program can hop from one object to another until reaching the last object, which would be an object that is not linked with anything further downstream. A flexible structure such as this would allow a new object to be inserted anywhere in the collection. All you'd need to do would be to change the previous object's linking memory address — it would now need to point to the newly inserted object — and the newly inserted object's linking memory address would point to the next object. Similar logic would make it trivial to remove any object from the collection.

However, there is a price to pay for the flexibility made possible by linked structures: now it is not possible to access the individual objects in a time that is independent of the size of the collection. When linked structures are used in their full generality, the only way to access any object in a collection is to start at the beginning of the collection, hop from object to object, until you reach the object you are looking for.

It is possible to create storage structures for collections that retain the efficiency of arrays and the flexibility of linked structures, but only up to a point. For example, when allocating memory for an array, you could ask for more memory than you really need at the moment in order to allow for additional items to be placed in the array without having to recompile the source code. For obvious reasons, the success of this approach would depend on your ability to predict the future — a hazardous undertaking even under the best of circumstances.

So far we have only talked about the efficiency and flexibility of storage structures with regard to the simplest of the object access questions: accessing the individual objects in a collection under the implied assumption that the objects are stored in some order in the collection. One can also raise object access and retrieval questions that address the following:

- access the object of a specified value;[1]
- retrieve all objects within a specified range of values;
- access the object that is closest in value to another object in the collection;
- retrieve k objects closest in value to a given object in the collection;
- etc.

The simplest cases of these questions occur when the object values are one dimensional. The storage structures that are the most efficient for the one-dimensional case are typically variants of the binary search tree in which each node stores one of the objects (or, a pointer to one of the objects) and two memory addresses, one for the left child node and the other for the right child node. All of the objects whose values are less than that of the object at the node are in the node's left branch. And all of the objects whose values are greater

---

[1]The value of a scalar object, such as a number or a string, is obvious. The value of a more complex object, such as an instance created from a class, is user defined. In general, for the sort of reasoning that is the focus of this chapter, the value of an instance would depend on one or more of its instance variables.

than that of the object at the node are in the node's right branch. In a common variant of such binary trees, the objects are stored in just the leaf nodes of a binary tree where each node stores just the decision value that separates the objects in the leaf nodes hanging from the left branch from the objects in the leaf nodes hanging from the right branch. When objects are characterized by multidimensional values, the simple binary search tree for the one-dimensional case generalizes to what is known as the *k-d tree* where 'k-d' stands for "k-dimensional."

The important point being made here is that there does not exist a single best way to store a collection in the memory of a computer. If you are creating a software library that involves collections of objects, what storage mechanisms you provide for the collections would depend on what sort of operations your clients want to carry out over the collections and what computational efficiencies the clients expect when they seek answers from the collections.

The Iterator pattern is about designing an interface for accessing the objects in a collection in a manner that insulates the clients from the precise details of how the objects are stored.

17.2 INTENT AND APPLICABILITY

The intent of the Iterator pattern is to provide the clients of your software a way to access the individual objects in a collection in a manner that is independent of how exactly the objects in the collection are stored.

You should use this pattern when

- the interface you provide for iterating through a collection needs to be uniform for different types of collections regardless of how the objects are stored;
- the interface you provide includes run-time support for inserting new objects and deleting existing objects (and your clients expect your interface to make explicit the consequences of dynamic inserts and deletes);
- the iteration functionality you provide needs to allow for traversals to occur in both forward and reverse directions with equal facility;
- the mechanism for iterating through a collection needs to allow for multiple traversals to occur simultaneously.

17.3 INTRODUCTION TO THE ITERATOR PATTERN

As should be clear from Section 17.1, the precise details of how a collection of objects is iterated through depend on the storage structure used for the collection, and, in general, the choice of the storage structure depends on what sorts of operations your clients want to carry out on the collection and what types of questions the collection should provide answers to in a computationally efficient answer.

As one would expect, exposing these collection-specific details to a programmer can only result in programming inefficiency in addition to making the code more unreadable. This is where the Iterator pattern comes to our rescue. The pattern teaches us about the merits of a uniform interface for iterating through different kinds of collections. With an

interface based on the Iterator pattern, the client would not need to know the precise details of how the objects are stored. The client would use exactly the same programming idiom for all the collections that are programmed to a given Iterator based interface.

17.4 THE ITERATOR PATTERN IN REAL-WORLD APPLICATIONS

Iterators are common to all modern object-oriented platforms. Java, for example, comes with the interface class `java.util.Iterator` whose API consists of the following method declarations:

```
boolean hasNext()
T next()
void remove()
```

where T is the type of the object stored in the collection that implements the interface. The method `hasNext()` returns true if the collection has another object ahead; this next object can subsequently be fetched by calling `next()`.[2] The method `remove()` deletes the last object that was returned by calling `next()`.

The Java platform also includes another interface class called `ListIterator` that is derived from `Iterator` and that is intended specifically for iterating through storage structures that are based on linked lists. (Java's `java.util.ArrayList` is an example of such a storage structure.) Including the method declarations inherited from the parent interface `Iterator`, the API of `ListIterator` consists of the following declarations:

```
void add( T  object)
boolean hasNext()
boolean hasPrevious()
T next()
int nextIndex()
T previous()
int previousIndex()
void remove()
void set(T object)
```

Of the method declarations shown above that are besides those inherited from the parent interface `Iterator`, `hasPrevious()` and `previous()` allow a container to be traversed in the reverse direction, in the same manner as `hasNext()` and `next()` allow us to traverse a container in the forward direction. The method `add()` inserts a new object immediately before the object that would be returned by the call to `next()`. The method `set()` replaces the last object returned by `next()` with a new object. Of the other method declarations above, `nextIndex()` and `previousIndex()` return an array-like integer index that

---

[2]The best way to look at the behavior of `hasNext()` and `next()` is to think of the iterator, as it is iterating though the objects in the container, as pointing to the "space" between the consecutive objects. This is purely for convenience in imagining the functioning of the iterator since there is no such thing as "space" between the items stored in the memory of a computer. Situated putatively between two consecutive objects, `hasNext()` returns true if there is indeed another object ahead and `next()` then actually fetches this object.

one may associate with the objects when they are conceptualized as constituting a linear sequential structure (an imaginary array, if you will).

An important consideration that goes into a real-world implementation of the Iterator pattern relates to the consequences of any changes made to a collection as it is being iterated through. Let's say that as a user is iterating through a collection, he/she decides to delete an object. The question then becomes whether the object in question should be deleted immediately or at the end of the iteration loop. Deleting existing objects (or inserting new objects) dynamically, meaning during the course of an iteration, entails a programming overhead that may extract a performance penalty at runtime. On the other hand, doing the same after the iteration loop has completed may create errors of logic at runtime if an object that was previously marked for deletion is accessed as the iteration is progressing.

17.5 HARRY POTTER STORY USED TO ILLUSTRATE THE ITERATOR PATTERN

Iterators are best demonstrated by programs that are rich in the use of collections that require iterating through. We have chosen the story of the Sorting Hat in the first volume of Harry Potter for this purpose. This story requires a number of lists for its telling (through a computer program).

Here is a brief description of what the Sorting Hat is all about and why it serves us well for illustrating the Iterator pattern: When a fresh batch of admittees — referred to as "freshers" in this chapter — first arrives at Hogwarts, one of the first rituals they go through is their placement in one of the four houses at the school. The freshers are always 40 in number and each must be placed in one of the following four houses: Gryffindor, Hufflepuff, Ravenclaw, and Slytherin. Each house has something special about it. As the freshers are informed by the Sorting Hat, Gryffindor is known for the wizards who are brave of heart; Hufflepuff for those who believe in being just and loyal; Ravenclaw for the wizards who are passionate about wit and learning; and, finally, Slytherin for the wizards who would do anything to achieve their goals. In the house placement ritual, each fresher is asked to wear the Hat, which, being bewitched, is able to read the fresher's mind and figure out the best house for the new student. For this, the Hat takes into account a student's preference if he or she has any. You see, some freshers come to Hogwarts with strong opinions about the different houses. This is particularly the case for the freshers who come from wizarding families that are well acquainted with the four houses and their traditions. Another reason for why a new student may have a house preference is that he/she may have formed friendships even before arriving at the sorting ceremony and would like to be in the same house as his/her friends.

Capturing the Sorting Hat ceremony in a computer program involves several collections and a need to iterate through them. We would need to start with a list of the names of the freshers. We would want to sort this list using a criterion that would be useful for naming the best house for each fresher. We would need to maintain a list of the freshers already placed in each house so that the total number of freshers placed in a house does not exceed the number of open spaces available there. And, finally, we would also need a list of the four houses so that our program can iterate through the houses as it tries to emulate the Sorting Hat in order to find the best house for each fresher. How all these lists are accessed and processed would be subject to constraints on the number of spaces available in each house (10 each) and the division of the spaces between the boys and the

girls (each gender gets 5 spaces in each house). The demonstration of the Iterator pattern in this chapter ignores the constraint related to the division of the available spaces between the boys and the girls.

From a programming standpoint, we must make decisions as to what sort of storage structures we should use for the different lists in a computer-program-based re-telling of the Sorting Hat story. We need a storage structure for the freshers when they first arrive at Hogwarts. We also need storage structures for the names already placed in each house since we need to keep track of how many open slots are still available in each house. The house-based student lists had better be implemented as linked lists on account of the fact that these lists come into existence dynamically at runtime as the students are placed in each of the houses. Finally, placing the freshers in the four houses must honor the same constraints as done by the "real" Sorting Hat: it must take into account (1) the student's aptitudes and preferences; (2) what each house is known for; and (3) the slots still available in a house.

17.6 A TOP LEVEL VIEW OF THE PATTERN DEMONSTRATION

Figure 17.1 is a top-level view of the pattern demonstration in this chapter. Focusing first on the Fresher class, since each Hogwarts house is known for a special quality of the wizards who lived there, we must take into account the aptitudes of the incoming students vis-á-vis those qualities at the time of their placement in the houses. Toward that end, we will evaluate the students with respect to the following aptitude-related attributes:

```
aptitudeForBravery
aptitudeForWitAndKnowledge
howFairnessMinded
howGoalOriented
```

We will assume that each of these four attributes is measured on a 100-point scale and that the Sorting Hat can figure out this value when a student is asked to put on the Hat during the sorting ceremony. The values for these attributes will be stored in the instance variables named above for the Fresher class. As the figure shows, the other instance variables of that class are:

```
name
preferredHouse
howStronglyPreferenceWanted
```

where the variable `name` is obviously the name of the fresher. We store the preference of the fresher regarding the house in which he/she would like to be placed in the variable `preferredHouse`. And, we use the variable `howStronglyPreferenceWanted` to store the strength of conviction with which the student wants his/her preference.

We will make reasonable assumptions about how the Sorting Hat places a fresher in a house. To appreciate the assumptions listed below, note that the greater the range of the values taken by an aptitude-related attribute that characterizes the students, the more useful the attribute in the sorting process. Consider, for example, what would happen if all freshers scored equally high on, say, `aptitudeForBravery`. If everyone were to be equally strong

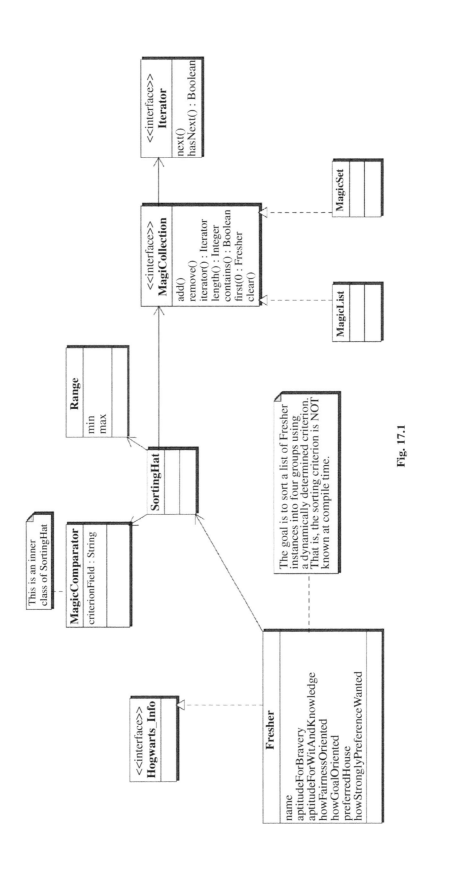

Fig. 17.1

on aptitudeForBravery, then the aptitude for bravery would cease to be a discriminating quality for deciding who should be sent to which house. Keeping this observation in mind, our demonstration is based on the following logic (which we pretend is the logic used by the Sorting Hat) for placing the freshers in the houses:

1. We sort the freshers on the basis of the most discriminating of the four attributes, aptitudeForBravery, aptitudeForWitAndKnowledge, howFairness Minded, and howGoalOriented. This will be the attribute with the largest range of values for the freshers.

2. Subsequently, taking up the students one at a time from the sorted list produced by the previous step, a student is placed in a house through a two-step process, which consists of an initial placement that is followed by a final placement. Regarding these two steps:

    (a) The initial placement consists of placing a student in the house of his/her preference.

    (b) The final placement may alter the initial house placement by taking into account both the rank of the student in the sorted list and the strength of his/her preference. So a student with a low rank on the most discriminating of the aptitude-related attributes and with a low strength-of-preference for the house desired would be highly likely to get moved out of his/her initially assigned house if such a move to another house is needed to balance out the number of students placed in each house.

That brings us to a description of how we use the Iterator pattern in our demonstration. As shown in Figure 17.1, we define a container interface MagicCollection and implement this interface in two containers MagicList and MagicSet. Both of these containers store their objects in the form of linked lists, the only difference between the two being that the latter container will not allow you to store a duplicate of an object that is already in the container since that would be a violation of the set access discipline. With regard to the demonstration of the Iterator pattern, the most important thing about both of these containers is that they implement a method called iterator() that returns an object of type Iterator. Any time we need to iterate through either a MagicList instance or a MagicSet instance, we do so with the help of the hasNext() and next() methods declared in the Iterator interface. These invocations of the Iterator interface through its hasNext() and next() methods constitute our demonstration of the Iterator pattern.

17.7   A UTILITY INTERFACE FOR DEMONSTRATING THE ITERATOR PATTERN

To make it easier for a reader to understand the demonstration code in the rest of this chapter, this section describes how the different Hogwarts houses and the names of the freshers are represented in the code.[3] We represent both of these as Java enum structures in an interface as shown in this section.

---

[3]Remember, we refer to the fresh batch of students admitted to Hogwarts as freshers.

The first enum shown in the interface definition that follows is for the names of the Hogwarts houses. This enum is simple and requires no further explanation. However, the second enum shown, used for the names of the freshers, is more complex. Its complexity arises from the fact that, after declaring the names for the freshers,[4] this enum provides a constructor whose job it is to return an instance of type FresherName. So when the enum returns the instance AbbotHannah, it actually calls on the constructor for doing so, supplying to the constructor the parenthesized arguments that follow each enum value. So for the AbbotHannah instance, the two arguments would be "Hannah" and "Abbot", the first becoming the value for the firstName parameter and the second the value for the lastName parameter in the call to the constructor. The FresherName enum also comes with a toString() method that tells the system how to create a print representation for each instance of the enum. The toString() method creates the print representation from the instance variables firstName and lastName associated with each enum instance. As you would expect, the instance variables acquire their values through the constructor. So if your code has a statement like

```
FresherName name = AbbotHannah;
```

the variable name will be set to the object returned by the constructor for the FresherName enum. This constructor will be called implicitly with the two arguments "Hannah" and "Abbot".

```
public interface Hogwarts_Info {

    public static enum HogwartsHouse { Gryffindor, Hufflepuff,
                                       Ravenclaw, Slytherin}

    public static enum FresherName {
                AbbotHannah            ("Hannah", "Abbot"),
                BonesSusan             ("Susan", "Bones"),
                BootTerry              ("Terry", "Boot"),
                BrocklehurstMandy      ("Mandy", "Brocklehurst"),
                BrownLavender          ("Lavender", "Brown"),
                BulstrodeMillicent     ("Millicent", "Bulstrode"),
                ChangCho               ("Cho", "Chang"),
                CrabbeVincent          ("Vincent", "Crabbe"),
                CreevyColin            ("Colin", "Creevy"),
                FinniganSeamus         ("Seamus", "Finnigan"),
                GoyleGregory           ("Gregory", "Goyle"),
                GrangerHermione        ("Hermione", "Granger"),
                LongbottomNeville      ("Neville", "Longbottom"),
                MacDougalMorag         ("Morag", "MacDougal"),
```

---

[4]These names are mentioned in Chapter 7 of "Harry Potter and the Philosopher's Stone." There should be 40 such names, since that is how many students are admitted to the freshman class at Hogwarts each year. However, JKR has mentioned only 25 names explicitly in that book. Of those, we have included 24 in the definition of the FresherName enum. This was done so that we could invoke the constraint that an equal number of students be placed in each of the four houses.

```
                    MalfoyDraco          ("Draco", "Malfoy"),
                    PatilParvati         ("Parvati", "Patil"),
                    PatilPadma           ("Padma", "Patil"),
                    PerksSallyAnne       ("Sally-Anne", "Perks"),
                    PotterHarry          ("Harry", "Potter"),
                    ThomasDean           ("Dean", "Thomas"),
                    TurpinLisa           ("Lisa", "Turpin"),
                    WeasleyGinny         ("Ginny", "Weasley"),
                    WeasleyRon           ("Ron", "Weasley"),
                    ZabiniBlaise         ("Blaise", "Zabini");
        private final String firstName;
        private final String lastName;
        FresherName( String first_name, String last_name) {
            this.firstName = first_name;
            this.lastName = last_name;
        }
        public String firstName() {return firstName;}
        public String lastName() {return lastName;}
        public String toString() {return firstName + " " + lastName; }
    }
}
```

17.8   THE Iterator INTERFACE

Shown below is the Iterator interface with its two methods: hasNext() and next(). As
we mentioned earlier, it is best to think of an Iterator instance as pointing to the spaces
between the objects that are imagined to be stored along a line. With this mental imagery,
we can think of hasNext() as returning true if there is an object up ahead along the line
and then a call to next() returning that object.

```
public interface Iterator<ItemType> {
    public ItemType next();
    public boolean hasNext();
}
```

17.9   THE Fresher CLASS

As mentioned previously, we refer to the fresh batch of students admitted to Hogwarts as
freshers. Each fresher will be an instance of the Java class Fresher that is defined in this
section. Recall that the core of our demonstration consists of creating a collection of the
freshers and iterating through the collection for the purpose of placing them in the four
houses at Hogwarts.

In order to achieve the objectives stated in Section 17.6, we need to associate with
each fresher a set of attributes that measure in some way the student's bravery, the
sense of justice, the sense of fairness, and the ability to be singleminded in the pursuit of goals. This, as was mentioned earlier in Section 17.6, is accomplished with the

help of the instance variables `aptitudeForBravery`, `aptitudeForWitAndKnowledge`, `howFairnessMinded`, and `howGoalOriented` that you see in the class definition. Obviously, when we instantiate a fresher from the class defined in this section, we need to give values to these attributes. Without taking anything away from our illustration of the Iterator pattern, we will fire up a random number generator for spitting out these values for each new student.

Assigning random values to the aptitude-related attributes of the freshers does create an interesting programming challenge — *the criterion for sorting the students cannot be set in advance.* That is because the effectiveness of these values from the standpoint of sorting the students depends directly on the range spanned by the values. To repeat what was mentioned earlier in Section 17.6, suppose all freshers have very nearly the same score for, say, the aptitude for bravery, then the aptitude for bravery ceases to be effective for deciding who should go where. Therefore, from a programming standpoint, we must first determine which of the four aptitude-related attributes carries the most information with regard to placing the students in the houses. *This can only be done at runtime.*

To explain the programming difficulty created by not knowing at compile time how to sort the students, let's say that we want to sort the students by calling Java's `Arrays.sort()` function. This function requires that we supply it with a `java.util.Comparator` object that knows how to compare any two students.[5] However, in our case, we do not have the luxury of supplying such a comparator object at compile time since the comparison criterion would depend on which of the four aptitude-related attributes shows the largest variation among the freshers that need to be sorted. That information is only known at runtime after we have randomly assigned values to the different aptitude-related attributes of the students.

What we need is an ability to create a dynamic implementation of the interface `java.util.Comparator` that would depend on which of the four aptitude-related attributes of the freshers is most effective for sorting the new students in a given year. As we show in the `SortingHat` class in Section 17.10, this dynamic implementation of the `java.util.Comparator` interface can be carried out with what is known as *Java reflection.* Reflection allows a new Java class to be created or an existing Java class to be modified at runtime.

In the class definition shown below, following the four instance variables that measure a fresher's aptitudes vis-á-vis the houses, we have the following two instance variables that indicate a student's personal house preference and the degree of conviction for that preference: `preferredHouse` and `howStronglyPreferenceWanted`. The next instance variable, `preferredHouseIndex`, is a convenience variable that stores basically the same information as what is stored in `preferredHouse`. Whereas `preferredHouseIndex` stores an integer value, these being integers between 0 through 3, with each integer representing a house, `preferredHouse` stores the actual symbolic name of the house as made available by the `HogwartsHouse` enum defined in the `Hogwarts_Info` interface. The mapping between the integers stored in `preferredHouseIndex` and the house names is:

---

[5]For example, if you wanted to call `Arrays.sort()` to sort a list of strings on the basis of their lengths, you would supply to `Arrays.sort()` as its second argument a `java.util.Comparator` object whose `compare()` method would be programmed to return one of -1, 0, and 1 if the first string is shorter than the second, equal in length to the second, and greater in length to the second, respectively. An alternative strategy would consist of the class that represents the objects to be sorted implementing the `Comparable` interface by providing code for its `compareTo()` method.

```
Griffyndor    =>        0
Hufflepuff    =>        1
Ravenclaw     =>        2
Slytherin     =>        3
```

The integers associated with the house names make it more convenient to generate randomly the initial house preferences of the freshers.

The reader has probably already noticed that the four instance variables that measure a fresher's aptitudes for the four Hogwarts houses are public, whereas the rest of the instance variables are private. The reason for keeping the aptitude-related variables public is to make them directly available (without the intermediary of four additional "get" methods) to the Java reflection based logic in the SortingHat class in Section 17.10.

That brings us to the constructor in the class definition. In keeping with our earlier explanation, the constructor uses a random number generator to assign a value between 50 and 100 to each aptitude-related instance variable of a new student.[6] The constructor then sets the house preference of a fresher by randomly choosing an integer between 0 and 3 and then mapping the integer selected to the actual name of the house. A random number between 0 and 9, both ends inclusive, is used to set the strength of conviction in the house preference chosen.

Next we have three "get" methods and the toString() method for creating a print representation of a fresher. What these methods do should be immediately obvious from their implementations.

That brings us to the code in the main() part of the class. The code there consists of the following sequence of steps that uses the functionality of the SortingHat class of Section 17.7 to sort a MagicCollection of the freshers:

1. We first create an instance called sorter of the SortingHat class.
2. We then create a MagicList, called all_freshers, of all of the freshers whose names are declared in the Hogwarts_Info interface.
3. Next, we call:

```
sorter.makeInitialHousePlacements( all_freshers,
                                   "getPreferredHouseIndex");
```

This call is merely to get an idea of how many students have expressed preferences for each of the four houses. The argument getPreferredHouseIndex causes the preferred house request of a fresher to be returned in the form of an integer index between 0 and 3, with 0 representing Gryffindor, 1 Hufflepuff, 2 Ravenclaw, and 3 Slytherin. The preference counts calculated by the above call are displayed on your terminal screen by calling

```
System.out.println( "Initial house counts: "
                          + sorter.getHouseCounts() );
```

---

[6]This is done with the belief that Hogwarts, being highly conscious of its reputation, is unlikely to admit anyone who scores below 50 on any of the four important aptitude metrics.

4. We now ask `SortingHat` to sort the freshers on the basis of their most discriminating aptitude with regard to what is important to the Hogwarts houses:

```
MagicCollection<Fresher> sortedFreshers = sorter.sortAndRank(
                        all_freshers,
                        "getHowStronglyPreferenceWanted",
                        "setRankWeightedStrengthOfPreference" );
```

5. Now the `SortingHat` class is ready to place the students in the houses. This is done by calling

```
sorter.makeHousePlacements( sortedFreshers,
                        "getPreferredHouseIndex",
                        "rankWeightedStrengthOfPreference");
```

In the description of the `SortingHat` class in the next section, we will describe how the method call shown above works and why it needs the two arguments in addition to the sorted list of the freshers.

The definition of the `Fresher` class follows:

```java
public class Fresher implements Hogwarts_Info {

    public FresherName name;
    public double aptitudeForBravery;
    public double aptitudeForWitAndKnowledge;
    public double howFairnessMinded;
    public double howGoalOriented;
    private int preferredHouseIndex;
    private HogwartsHouse preferredHouse;
    private int howStronglyPreferenceWanted;
    public double rankWeightedStrengthOfPreference;

    public Fresher( FresherName name ) {
        this.name = name;
        this.aptitudeForBravery = 50 + (int) (50 * Math.random());
        this.aptitudeForWitAndKnowledge =
                            50 + (int) (50 * Math.random());
        this.howFairnessMinded = 50 + (int) (50 * Math.random());
        this.howGoalOriented = 50 + (int) (50 * Math.random());
        this.preferredHouseIndex = (int) ( 4 * Math.random() );
        this.preferredHouse =
                    HogwartsHouse.values()[ preferredHouseIndex ];
        this.howStronglyPreferenceWanted =
                            (int) (10 * Math.random() + 1);
    }
```

```
public int getPreferredHouseIndex() {return preferredHouseIndex;}
public int getHowStronglyPreferenceWanted() {
    return howStronglyPreferenceWanted;
}
public double getRankWeightedStrengthOfPreference() {
    return rankWeightedStrengthOfPreference;
}
public void setRankWeightedStrengthOfPreference(double val) {
    this.rankWeightedStrengthOfPreference = val;
}
public String toString() {
    String s = String.format( "%.2f",
                               rankWeightedStrengthOfPreference);
    return name + ":  Preferred House is " + preferredHouse
            + " with preference " +howStronglyPreferenceWanted
            + " and with rank-weighted preference " +  s;
}

public static void main( String[] args ) throws Exception {
    SortingHat<Fresher> sorter = new SortingHat<Fresher>();
    MagicCollection<Fresher> all_freshers =
                                    new MagicList<Fresher>();
    for(int i=0; i < FresherName.values().length; i++) {
        all_freshers.add(
                new Fresher( FresherName.values()[i] ) );
    }
    sorter.makeInitialHousePlacements(all_freshers,
                            "getPreferredHouseIndex");
    System.out.println( "Initial house counts: "
                            + sorter.getHouseCounts() );
    MagicCollection<Fresher> sortedFreshers =
            sorter.sortAndRank( all_freshers,
                    "getHowStronglyPreferenceWanted",
                    "setRankWeightedStrengthOfPreference" );
    sorter.makeHousePlacements(sortedFreshers,
                        "getPreferredHouseIndex",
                        "rankWeightedStrengthOfPreference");
    System.out.println( "Final house counts: "
                            + sorter.getHouseCounts() );
    sorter.displayHousePlacements();
}
}
```

17.10   THE SortingHat CLASS

We now present the SortingHat class in this section. This class is "magical", but only in the sense that it knows how to dynamically determine the best sorting criterion to use

for the new students admitted to Hogwarts.[7] This Java class is smart enough to *not* use the same sorting criterion for every batch of freshers. The class can figure out at runtime the most effective criterion to use for placing a new batch of freshers in the four Hogwarts houses.

Scanning through the code in the class definition presented in this section, the definition begins with the creation of four lists for holding the names of the freshers placed in each of the four houses. For obvious reasons, these lists are named gryffindor, hufflepuff, ravenclaw, and slytherin. We next define a list of these four lists, all_houses, that will later help us iterate through the four house lists. This is followed by an anonymous block of code for the initialization of the lists of house lists.

That brings us to the methods section of the class. The first of these is what gives our class SortingHat its "magical" ability:

```
findMostDiscriminatingField()
```

This method analyzes the numerical scores for the four aptitudes for all of the freshers and finds one that holds the maximal discriminatory power with regard to placing the freshers in the four houses. Recall, as mentioned earlier, if all of the freshers scored more or less equally strongly on, say, the bravery aptitude (as measured by the instance variable aptitudeForBravery), then bravery would cease to be an attribute that could be used for the house placement exercise — despite the fact that the Gryffindor house values bravery the most. So the purpose of the aforementioned method is to determine which of the four aptitudes is maximally discriminating for our purpose. The method depends on the following two methods for its functioning:

```
listAllNumericFields()
getRangeOfAttributeValues()
```

The first of these, listAllNumericFields(), simply returns an array of all of the public numerical instance variables of the class whose instances are stored in the container that is supplied as the argument to findMostDiscriminatingField(). In our case, that would be the Fresher class. For our demonstration code, a call to listAllNumericFields() returns the following list of the instance variables of the Fresher class:

```
aptitudeForBravery
aptitudeForWitAndKnowledge
howFairnessMinded
howGoalOriented
rankWeightedStrengthOfPreference
```

---

[7] In a vast majority of programming scenarios where sorting is needed, the sorting criterion is known at compile time and, therefore, remains fixed from one run of the program to another. What we are trying to do here is uncommon — establishing the sorting criterion at runtime. So it is entirely possible that whereas the aptitude for bravery plays a dominant role in house placement for the students in one run of the demonstration code, it is one of their other aptitudes, say the ability to be singleminded, that becomes the deciding factor in the next.

where the first four are the aptitudes that determine the match between a student and each of the four houses. The last one, `rankWeightedStrengthOfPreference`, is simply there for programming convenience. It shows up at the output of the method `listAllNumericFields()` because it is, as you'd expect, numerical (and also because it is public). We declared `rankWeightedStrengthOfPreference` to be public in the `Fresher` class so that the class `MagicComparator`, which is an inner class to the `SortingHat` class, would be able to access it easily.[8],[9]

That brings us to the second method, `getRangeOfAttributeValues()`, that `findMostDiscriminatingField()` depends on. The job assigned to `getRangeOf AttributeValues()` is to examine each of the instance variables returned by `listAllNumericFields()` and calculate the range of the values taken for that instance variable by all of the freshers. Subsequently, these ranges are used by `findMostDiscriminatingField()` to determine the most discriminating instance variable, meaning the most discriminating aptitude, for the freshers.

Next we consider the implementation of the method `sortAndRank()`. As you would expect, `sortAndRank()` first calls up `findMostDiscriminatingField()` to find the most discriminating of the four aptitudes and then presses into service `java.util.Arrays.sort()` for the actual sorting of the freshers. To make sure that the sorting routine uses the most discriminating of the four aptitudes for sorting, we supply to `sort()` for its second argument an instance of the inner `MagicComparator` comparator class whose constructor is provided with the sorting criterion to use. The sorting is accomplished with the call:

```
java.util.Arrays.sort( (T[]) objArray,
                       this.new MagicComparator<T>(field) );
```

where `objArray` is the array version of the list of freshers and where we need the syntax `this.new` to create an instance of the inner non-static `MagicComparator` class. We defined `MagicComparator` to be an inner call on a per-instance basis for the enclosing class (because the inner class is *not* static). So, in order to create an instance of this inner class, we must create it vis-á-vis the instance of the enclosing class. Note also the argument `field` supplied to the constructor of `MagicComparator`; the value of `field` is set to the name of the most discriminating of the aptitudes for the `Fresher` class. *This is the key to how* `SortingHat` *can alter at runtime the sorting criterion for the students.*

The call to `sortAndRank()` returns a list of the students that is sorted according to their scores on the most discriminating of the four house-admission aptitudes. What is even more important for us here, `sortAndRank()` also deposits in

---

[8]With some additional code, we could keep `rankWeightedStrengthOfPreference` private to `Fresher` and introduce a public 'get' method in the `Fresher` class for its retrieval. If we were to go that route, we would need additional code in `MagicComparator` that would retrieve values by invoking the relevant 'get' methods of the `Fresher` class.

[9]Note that the appearance of `rankWeightedStrengthOfPreference` in the list produced by `listAllNumericFields()` is a non-issue for us since, when `listAllNumericFields()` is called, the values for the instance variable `rankWeightedStrengthOfPreference` are pegged at zero for all of the freshers. In other words, this instance variable will not have a non-zero range to interfere with the selection of the most discriminating aptitude.

each instance object that represents a student a value for a special instance variable rankWeightedStrengthOfPreference.[10] The value of this variable, which plays an important role in the final placement of the freshers in the houses, is a product of the student-expressed strength of preference for the house of his/her choice and the rank calculated on the basis of the most discriminating aptitude. *The point here is that a student's strength of preference is to be given importance only to the extent the student ranks high when all students are sorted according to the most discriminating aptitude.* Let's say we have a fresher who has expressed a desired to be placed in Hufflepuff with a strength of 9 (out of 10). If this fresher scores a high rank — say 2 out of 24 — when he/she is sorted by the most discriminating aptitude, then the preference strength of 9 should carry high weight. But if it turns out that this fresher is close to the bottom of the ranking, say the student is 23 out of 24, then his/her strength of preference should carry less weight. In the first case, we place a value of $9(24 - 2)/24$ in the variable rankWeightedStrengthOfPreference, and in the second case we place the value $9(24 - 23)/24$ in the same variable.

After sortAndRank() has finished, the Sorting Hat is ready to place the freshers in the houses. This is done by making a call to makeHousePlacements(). What this method does is to re-sort the freshers on the basis of the values stored in rankWeightedStrengthOfPreference in order to take into account both the preferences expressed by the freshers and their scores on the most discriminating of the aptitudes. Subsequently, makeHousePlacements() places the freshers in the houses on a "first come, first served" basis as long as there is space in the preferred houses. The phrase "first come" is an informal reference to the freshers who rank high on the final sorted list. A fresher high on the final sorted list is likely to get his/her choice of the house. On the other hand, a fresher low on the final sorted list is likely to not get his/her choice. Recall, each house has only a fixed number of spaces available for the fresh batch of incoming students.

```
import java.util.Comparator;
import java.lang.reflect.*;

public class SortingHat<T> implements Hogwarts_Info {

    // These lists hold the names of the freshers
    // placed in each of the four houses:

    private MagicCollection<T> gryffindor = new MagicList<T>();
    private MagicCollection<T> hufflepuff = new MagicList<T>();
    private MagicCollection<T> ravenclaw = new MagicList<T>();
    private MagicCollection<T> slytherin = new MagicList<T>();

    private MagicCollection<T>[] all_houses = new MagicList[4];
    {
        all_houses[0] = gryffindor;
        all_houses[1] = hufflepuff;
        all_houses[2] = ravenclaw;
        all_houses[3] = slytherin;
```

---

[10]For a tutorial introduction to Java Reflection, see [10].

```
}

////////////////         Methods         ////////////////////
/**
 * This method tells us which of the four public
 * instance variables (that describe the aptitudes of an
 * incoming student) defined for the Fresher class shows
 * the largest range over all the 24 freshers.  The
 * larger the range of values for such an instance
 * variable, the greater its usefulness for
 * discriminating between the freshers with regard to
 * their placement in the four houses.
 */
public String findMostDiscriminatingField(MagicCollection<T> coll)
                                                  throws Exception {
    String mostDiscriminatingField = null;
    Class<?> cl = coll.first().getClass();
    MagicCollection<String> atts = listAllNumericFields( cl );
    if (atts.length() == 0) {
        throw new NumericalAttributesNotFoundException();
    }
    Iterator<String> itatt = atts.iterator();
    while (itatt.hasNext()) {
        System.out.print( itatt.next() + "  ");
    }
    System.out.println();
    Range[] ranges = new Range[ atts.length() ];
    double rangeSpan = 0;
    Iterator<String> itatt2 = atts.iterator();
    int i = 0;
    while (itatt2.hasNext()) {
        String attsitem = itatt2.next();
        ranges[i] = getRangeOfAttributeValues(attsitem, coll);
        if (i == 0) {
            rangeSpan = ranges[0].max - ranges[0].min;
            mostDiscriminatingField = attsitem;
        } else {
            double rangeForThisAttribute =
                               ranges[i].max - ranges[i].min;
            if (rangeForThisAttribute > rangeSpan) {
                rangeSpan = rangeForThisAttribute;
                mostDiscriminatingField = attsitem;
            }
        }
        i++;
    }
    if (mostDiscriminatingField == null) {
        throw new MostDiscriminatingFieldNotFoundException();
    }
    //comparisonFieldName = mostDiscriminatingField;
    return mostDiscriminatingField;
}
```

```
/**
 *   This method returns those fields of the argument class that
 *   are numerical in nature.  Finding such fields is important
 *   because it is one of the numerical fields that is used for
 *   establishing the sorting criterion.
 */
public MagicCollection<String> listAllNumericFields(Class<?> cl) {
    Field[] flds = cl.getFields();
    MagicCollection<String> fieldNames = new MagicList<String>();
    for (int i=0; i < flds.length; i++) {
        int mod = flds[i].getModifiers();
        if (!Modifier.isStatic(mod)){
            Type type = flds[i].getGenericType();
            if (   "int".equals(type.toString())
                 | "float".equals(type.toString())
                 | "double".equals(type.toString())) {
                fieldNames.add(flds[i].getName());
            }
        }
    }
    return fieldNames;
}


/**
 * Returns as a Range instance the range of values that correspond
 * to the designated attribute.
 */
public Range getRangeOfAttributeValues( String attribute,
                                 MagicCollection<T> coll) {
    Range range = new Range();
    Iterator<T> it = coll.iterator();
    int i=0;
    while (it.hasNext()) {
        T candidatei = it.next();
        Class<?> cl = candidatei.getClass();
        Field fd = null;
        try {
            fd = cl.getField( attribute );
        } catch (SecurityException e) {
            e.printStackTrace();
        } catch (NoSuchFieldException e) {
            e.printStackTrace();
        }
        double val = 0.0;
        Object objVal = null;
        try {
            Type type = fd.getGenericType();
            objVal = fd.get( candidatei );
            if ( "int".equals(type.toString()) ) {
                val = ( (Integer) objVal ).intValue();
                if (i == 0) {
```

```
                      range.min = range.max = val;
                  } else {
                      if (val < range.min) {
                          range.min = val;
                      }
                      if (val > range.max) {
                          range.max = val;
                      }
                  }
              } else if ("float".equals(type.toString())) {
                  val = ( (Float) objVal).floatValue();
                  if (i == 0) {
                      range.min = range.max = val;
                  } else {
                      if (val < range.min) {
                          range.min = val;
                      }
                      if (val > range.max) {
                          range.max = val;
                      }
                  }
              } else if ("double".equals(type.toString())) {
                  val = ( (Double) objVal).doubleValue();
                      if (i == 0) {
                          range.min = range.max = val;
                      } else {
                          if (val < range.min) {
                              range.min = val;
                          }
                          if (val > range.max) {
                              range.max = val;
                          }
                      }
              } else if ( "string".equals( type.toString() ) ) {
                  range.symbolicVals.add( objVal.toString());
              }
          } catch (IllegalArgumentException e) {
          e.printStackTrace();
          } catch (IllegalAccessException e) {
              e.printStackTrace();
          }
          i++;
      }
      return range;
}

public void makeInitialHousePlacements(MagicCollection<T> arr,
                            String criterion ) throws Exception{
    Class<?> clarr = arr.first().getClass();
    Method m = clarr.getMethod( criterion );
    Iterator<T> it = arr.iterator();
    while( it.hasNext() ) {
```

```
            T f = it.next();
            switch ( ((Integer) m.invoke(f,
                                    (Object[]) null)).intValue() ) {
                case 0: gryffindor.add(f); break;
                case 1: hufflepuff.add(f); break;
                case 2: ravenclaw.add(f); break;
                case 3: slytherin.add(f); break;
            }
        }
    }

    public MagicCollection<T> sortAndRank(MagicCollection<T> coll,
            String wherePreferences, String whereToSetRankedPrefs)
                                                throws Exception {
        Class<?> clarr = coll.first().getClass();
        Method m1 = clarr.getMethod( wherePreferences );
        Method m2 = clarr.getMethod( whereToSetRankedPrefs,
                                                double.class );
        String field = findMostDiscriminatingField(coll);
        System.out.println( "Most discriminating field is: " + field);
        Object[] objArray = new Object[ coll.length() ];
        Iterator<T> it_for_coll = coll.iterator();
        int i = 0;
        while (it_for_coll.hasNext()) {
            objArray[i] = (T) it_for_coll.next();
            i++;
        }
        java.util.Arrays.sort( (T[]) objArray,
                            this.new MagicComparator<T>(field) );
        MagicCollection<T> sortedFreshers = new MagicList<T>();
        for (int j=0; j<objArray.length; j++) {
            double weightedpref =
                ( (objArray.length - j) / (1.0 * objArray.length))
                *
                (((Integer) m1.invoke((T)objArray[j])).intValue());
            m2.invoke( (T) objArray[j], weightedpref );
            sortedFreshers.add((T) objArray[j]);
        }
        return sortedFreshers;
    }

    public void makeHousePlacements(MagicCollection<T> coll,
                    String getPreferredHouseIndex,
                    String rankWeightedPriority) throws Exception {
        gryffindor.clear();
        hufflepuff.clear();
        ravenclaw.clear();
        slytherin.clear();
        Class<?> elementClass = coll.first().getClass();
        Object[] objArray = new Object[ coll.length() ];
        Iterator<T> it_for_coll = coll.iterator();
        int i = 0;
```

```java
        while (it_for_coll.hasNext()) {
            objArray[i] = (T)  it_for_coll.next();
            i++;
        }
        java.util.Arrays.sort( (T[]) objArray,
                this.new MagicComparator<T>( rankWeightedPriority ) );
        MagicCollection<T> furtherSortedObjArr = new MagicList<T>();
        for (int j=0; j<objArray.length; j++) {
            furtherSortedObjArr.add((T) objArray[j]);
        }
        double average = coll.length() / all_houses.length;
        Method m = elementClass.getMethod( getPreferredHouseIndex );
        Iterator<T> it = furtherSortedObjArr.iterator();
        while (it.hasNext()) {
            T item = it.next();
            int wantedHouse =
                ((Integer) m.invoke(item, (Object[]) null)).intValue();
            if (all_houses[wantedHouse].length() < average ) {
                all_houses[wantedHouse].add( item );
            } else {
                for(int j=0; j<all_houses.length;j++) {
                    if (j == wantedHouse) continue;
                    if (all_houses[j].length() >= average ) {
                        continue;
                    } else {
                        all_houses[j].add(item);
                        break;
                    }
                }
            }
        }
    }


public String getHouseCounts() {
 return "House counts:  Gryffindor=" + gryffindor.length()
                    + " Hufflepuff=" + hufflepuff.length()
                    + " Ravenclaw=" + ravenclaw.length()
                    + " Slytherin="  + slytherin.length() ;
}

public void displayHousePlacements() {
    for(int i=0; i<all_houses.length;i++) {
        switch(i) {
            case 0: System.out.println("Gryffindor:"); break;
            case 1: System.out.println("Hufflepuff:"); break;
            case 2: System.out.println("Ravenclaw:"); break;
            case 3: System.out.println("Slytherin:"); break;
        }
        Iterator<T> it = all_houses[i].iterator();
        while (it.hasNext()) {
            T f = it.next();
            System.out.println("        " + f + "  placed in: "
```

```
                                        + HogwartsHouse.values()[i] );
            }
        }
    }


    /**
     * This enclosed class serves as a comparator object for the
     * sorting algorithm. This class assumes that you have already
     * called an appropriate method to discover the field that must
     * be used as the sorting criterion for the instances.  The name of
     * that field is supplied as an argument to the constructor of
     * MagicComparator.  When Array.sort is called on an array of
     * instances, the second argument to that method is an instance
     * of the comparator class shown below:
     */
    public class MagicComparator<T1> implements Comparator<T1> {
        private String criterionField;
        public MagicComparator(String criterionField ) {
            this.criterionField = criterionField;
        }
        public int compare( T1 f1, T1 f2) {
         Class<?> cl = f1.getClass();
            Field fd = null;
            try {
                fd = cl.getField(criterionField);
            } catch(NoSuchFieldException e) {
                e.printStackTrace();
            } catch(SecurityException e){
                e.printStackTrace();
            }
            double yy = 0.0;
            double zz = 0.0;
            try {
                yy = fd.getDouble(f1);
                zz = fd.getDouble(f2);
            } catch(IllegalArgumentException e){
                e.printStackTrace();
            } catch(IllegalAccessException e){
                e.printStackTrace();
            }
            // The -1, 0, 1 values returned below produce sorting
            // in a value decreasing order:
            if (yy == zz) { return 0;}
            if(yy < zz) {return 1;}
            return -1;
        }
    }
}
class MostDiscriminatingFieldNotFoundException extends Exception {}
class NumericalAttributesNotFoundException extends Exception {}
```

17.11   THE MagicCollection INTERFACE

This section presents the root interface for the collection classes in our demonstration. At the least, any such interface must provide a method for inserting a new object in a collection, a method for removing an existing object, and a method that makes it possible to iterate over the collection. These methods are typically named add(), remove(), and iterator(). Whereas the first two method do directly what their names imply, the last generally returns an object — typically referred to as the Iterator — whose methods allow you to conveniently iterate over a collection.

Shown below is the interface for the collection classes used in this chapter. In addition to the methods named above, the interface shown below also includes the following convenience methods: length(), contains(), first(), and clear(). The method length() reports back to the number of objects in a collection; the method contains() tests whether or not a particular object is already in a collection; the method first() returns a reference to the first object in the collection; and the method clear() empties out a collection. Note that what first() returns would also be returned by the first call to the next() method of the iterator object returned by iterator().

```
public interface MagicCollection<T> {
    public void add( T x );
    public void remove(T x);
    public Iterator<T> iterator();
    public int length();
    public boolean contains( T item );
    public T first();
    public void clear();
}
```

17.12   THE MagicList AND MagicSet CLASSES

This section first presents the MagicList implementation of the MagicCollection interface. Most of the iterator examples we use in the Sorting Hat demonstration are based on iterating through MagicList based collections. Another implementation of the MagicCollection interface that is presented next is the MagicSet class.

The storage mechanism used in MagicList is that of a linked list. We imagine the objects stored in a MagicList collection as "hanging" from a sequence of interlinked nodes, with each node being an instance of the Node class that is defined as a nested class of MagicList. The nodes are linked through the next instance variable of the Node class. The item instance variable of the Node class holds a reference to the object that is "hanging" from that node.

The MagicList class is provided with two instance variables, head and tail, of type Node, that help us reach any desired element of the list. The instance variable head holds a reference to the Node instance at the head of the linked list and the instance variable tail holds a reference to the Node instance at the tail end of the same. At the outset, both of these instance variables are initialized to null. This initialization represents an empty MagicList. We can visualize the linked list as growing from left to right, with head always

pointing to the Node instance at the left end of the linked list and the tail always pointing to the last Node instance at the right end of the linked list. Since the code shown for add(), remove(), and contains() uses the standard idioms for such functions in linked-list type of data structures, it requires no further elaboration.

Regarding the implementation of iterator(), recall that this method must return an object of type Iterator. This is done by calling the constructor of an anonymous class of type Iterator. The anonymous class has an instance variable named ptr of type Node that initially holds a reference to the same object as the instance variable head of the enclosing class. Looking at the implementation of hasNext() and next(), initially hasNext() returns true if ptr is non-null. A subsequent call to next() returns the object held by the Node instance at the beginning of the linked list. Thereafter, each invocation of next() retrieves the object in the Node instance to which ptr points and, at the same time, changes the value of the reference held by ptr to ptr.next.

The other features of the MagicList class include the fact that it keeps a count of the objects stored in the list. This count is automatically incremented and decremented when you call add() and remove() on an instance of the MagicList, respectively. The MagicList class also includes implementation for the toString() method that is convenient during code debugging as it prints out the entire list. The implementation of toString() for MagicList depends, in turn, on the toString() implementation for the inner Node class, and that, in turn, depends on there being a toString() implementation for the object type that is stored in a MagicList.

```
public class MagicList<T> implements MagicCollection<T>{

    protected class Node {
        T item;
        Node next = null;
        Node( T item ) { this.item = item; }
        public String toString() { return (String) item; }
    }
    protected Node head = null;
    protected Node tail = null;
    private int length = 0;
    public  MagicList() {}
    public T first() { return head.item; }
    public void add( T item ) {
        if ( head == null ) {
            head = new Node( item );
            length++;
            tail = head;
        } else {
            tail.next = new Node( item );
            length++;
            tail = tail.next;
        }
    }
    public void remove( T item ) {
        Node ptr = head;
```

```java
        Node ptr_prev = ptr;
        while (ptr != null) {
            if ((ptr == head) && (ptr.item == item)) {
                head = ptr.next;
                length--;
                return;
            } else if (ptr.item == item) {
                ptr_prev.next = ptr.next;
                length--;
                return;
            } else {
                ptr_prev = ptr;
                ptr = ptr.next;
            }
        }
    }
    public boolean contains( T item ) {
        Node ptr = head;
        while (ptr != null) {
            if (ptr.item == item) return true;
            ptr = ptr.next;
        }
        return false;
    }
    public void clear() {
        head = null;
        tail = null;
        length = 0;
    }
    public Iterator<T> iterator() {
        return new Iterator<T>() {
            protected Node ptr = head;
            public boolean hasNext() { return ptr != null; }
            public T next() {
                if (ptr != null) {
                    T item = ptr.item;
                    ptr = ptr.next;
                    return item;
                } else {
                    throw new RuntimeException();
                }
            }
        };
    }
    public int length() {
        return length;
    }
    public String toString() {
        String result = "";
        Iterator<T> it = iterator();
        while ( it.hasNext() ) {
            T node = it.next();
```

```
            result += node + "\n";
        }
        return result;
    }
}
```

This brings us to the second implementation of the `MagicCollection` interface in our demonstration — the `MagicSet` class. As the reader knows, a set is simply a list that does not allow duplicates to be stored. If a method like `add()` is called to store the same item again in a set, it should simply return without modifying what is currently stored. We use `MagicSet` in only the utility class `Range` that is presented in the next section.

As shown in the class definition that follows, a `MagicSet` is again a sequence of `Node` instances, where `Node` is a nested class of `MagicSet`. Each `Node` instance holds a reference to the object stored at that `Node` instance and points to the next `Node` instance. The only difference between the implementations of `MagicList` and `MagicSet` is in how `add()` is implemented. The `add()` method of `MagicSet` first checks whether the new object to be inserted is already in the set. If it is, the call to `add()` just returns without doing anything.

```
public class MagicSet<T> implements MagicCollection<T>{
    protected class Node {
        T item;
        Node next = null;
        Node( T item ) { this.item = item; }
        public String toString() { return (String) item; }
    }
    protected Node head = null;
    protected Node tail = null;
    private int length = 0;
    public MagicSet() {}
    public T first() { return head.item; }
    public void add( T item ) {
        if ( contains( item ) ) {
            return;
        }
        if ( head == null ) {
            head = new Node( item );
            length++;
            tail = head;
        } else {
            tail.next = new Node( item );
            length++;
            tail = tail.next;
        }
    }
    public void remove( T item ) {
        Node ptr = head;
        Node ptr_prev = ptr;
```

```
        while (ptr != null) {
            if ((ptr == head) && (ptr.item == item)) {
                head = ptr.next;
                length--;
                return;
            } else if (ptr.item == item) {
                ptr_prev.next = ptr.next;
                length--;
                return;
            } else {
                ptr_prev = ptr;
                ptr = ptr.next;
            }
        }
    }
    public boolean contains( T item ) {
        Node ptr = head;
        while (ptr != null) {
            if (ptr.item == item) return true;
            ptr = ptr.next;
        }
        return false;
    }
    public void clear() {
        head = null;
        tail = null;
        length = 0;
    }
    public Iterator<T> iterator() {
        return new Iterator<T>() {
            protected Node ptr = head;
            public boolean hasNext() { return ptr != null; }
            public T next() {
                if (ptr != null) {
                    T item = ptr.item;
                    ptr = ptr.next;
                    return item;
                } else {
                    throw new RuntimeException();
                }
            }
        };
    }
    public int length() {
        return length;
    }
    public String toString() {
        String result = "";
        Iterator<T> it = iterator();
        while ( it.hasNext() ) {
            T node = it.next();
            result += node + "\n";
```

```
        }
        return result;
    }
}
```

17.13   THE CLASS Range

The Range class shown below is a utility class used for returning the result produced by the method getRangeOfAttributeValues() in the class SortingHat. A range is defined as the (min, max) interval for a numerical attribute. The range for a symbolic attribute is defined as the set of all possible symbolic labels taken on by the attribute.

```
public class Range {
    public double min = 0;
    public double max = 0;
    public MagicSet<String> symbolicVals = null;
}
```

17.14   PLAYING WITH THE CODE

Download the class files for this pattern from the book website into a separate directory. Compile the code with the command

```
    javac *.java
```

and execute the Fresher class by

```
    java Fresher
```

Given the code in the main() of Fresher, executing this class will produce the following output:

```
Initial house counts: House counts:  Gryffindor=4 Hufflepuff=6 Ravenclaw=6
                                                                Slytherin=8

Most discriminating field is: howFairnessMinded

Final house counts: House counts:  Gryffindor=6 Hufflepuff=6 Ravenclaw=6
                                                                Slytherin=6


Gryffindor:

        Colin Creevy:  Preferred House is Gryffindor with preference 10 and
```

with rank-weighted preference 7.50 placed in: Gryffindor

Vincent Crabbe: Preferred House is Gryffindor with preference 1 and
with rank-weighted preference 0.88 placed in: Gryffindor

Draco Malfoy: Preferred House is Gryffindor with preference 1 and
with rank-weighted preference 0.83 placed in: Gryffindor

Ginny Weasley: Preferred House is Gryffindor with preference 8 and
with rank-weighted preference 0.67 placed in: Gryffindor

Sally-Anne Perks: Preferred House is Slytherin with preference 2 and
with rank-weighted preference 0.25 placed in: Gryffindor

Seamus Finnigan: Preferred House is Slytherin with preference 5 and
with rank-weighted preference 0.21 placed in: Gryffindor

Hufflepuff:

Mandy Brocklehurst: Preferred House is Hufflepuff with preference 9
and with rank-weighted preference 4.88 placed in: Hufflepuff

Cho Chang: Preferred House is Hufflepuff with preference 6 and with
rank-weighted preference 4.75 placed in: Hufflepuff

Padma Patil: Preferred House is Hufflepuff with preference 10 and
with rank-weighted preference 4.17 placed in: Hufflepuff

Lisa Turpin: Preferred House is Hufflepuff with preference 6 and
with rank-weighted preference 3.75 placed in: Hufflepuff

Millicent Bulstrode: Preferred House is Hufflepuff with preference 3
and with rank-weighted preference 2.75 placed in: Hufflepuff

Lavender Brown: Preferred House is Hufflepuff with preference 9
and with rank-weighted preference 2.63 placed in: Hufflepuff

Ravenclaw:

Dean Thomas: Preferred House is Ravenclaw with preference 6 and
with rank-weighted preference 6.00 placed in: Ravenclaw

Ron Weasley: Preferred House is Ravenclaw with preference 6 and
with rank-weighted preference 3.00 placed in: Ravenclaw

Morag MacDougal: Preferred House is Ravenclaw with preference 2 and
with rank-weighted preference 1.33 placed in: Ravenclaw

Hermione Granger: Preferred House is Ravenclaw with preference 4 and
with rank-weighted preference 1.33 placed in: Ravenclaw

```
Susan Bones:  Preferred House is Hufflepuff with preference 3 and with
        rank-weighted preference 0.28  placed in: Ravenclaw

Hannah Abbot:  Preferred House is Slytherin with preference 2 and
        with rank-weighted preference 0.19  placed in: Ravenclaw


Slytherin:

    Terry Boot:  Preferred House is Slytherin with preference 10 and
            with rank-weighted preference 9.58  placed in: Slytherin

    Parvati Patil:  Preferred House is Slytherin with preference 9 and
            with rank-weighted preference 5.25  placed in: Slytherin

    Gregory Goyle:  Preferred House is Slytherin with preference 6 and
            with rank-weighted preference 2.75  placed in: Slytherin

    Harry Potter:  Preferred House is Slytherin with preference 3 and
            with rank-weighted preference 2.13  placed in: Slytherin

    Blaise Zabini:  Preferred House is Slytherin with preference 4 and
            with rank-weighted preference 1.00  placed in: Slytherin

    Neville Longbottom:  Preferred House is Slytherin with preference 3
            and with rank-weighted preference 0.50  placed in: Slytherin
```

For additional insights, you may consider extending the code for this pattern along the following lines:

- As mentioned in our discussion of the makeHousePlacements() method of the SortingHat class, that method first re-sorts the students on the basis of the values of rankWeightedStrengthOfPreference. Subsequently, the method scans through this re-sorted list of the freshers and first tries to place a fresher in his/her preferred house choice assuming the house still has a vacancy. If the house is full, the method then looks at the other three houses and places the fresher in the first house found with a vacancy. With this logic, a fresher who scores higher on the most discriminating of the aptitude traits has a greater likelihood of being placed in the house of his/her choice. If you think about it, in real life this would be much too lame a way to place a student in a house if he/she cannot get the house of his/her choice. More sophisticated placement logic would examine all of the aptitude scores of the students and find the best matching house that still has a vacancy. Modify the code in makeHousePlacements() of SortingHat so that the final house placement is based all of the aptitude scores for a student.
- This chapter's demonstration of the Iterator pattern uses MagicSet only in the utility class Range. A MagicSet is used there to store all possible values for those instance variables that take symbolic values (as opposed to numerical values). The current demonstration code, however, does not use these symbolic values in any decision

making regarding what house should be assigned to a new student. If you decide to extend the demonstration code in such a way that the instance variables with symbolic values have a say in the house placement decisions, you will find yourself using the `MagicSet` storage more extensively.

- To create a more robust version of the code shown in this chapter, you can try replacing the following declarations in the `SortingHat` class

```
private MagicCollection<T> gryffindor = new MagicList<T>();
private MagicCollection<T> hufflepuff = new MagicList<T>();
private MagicCollection<T> ravenclaw = new MagicList<T>();
private MagicCollection<T> slytherin = new MagicList<T>();
```

by

```
private MagicCollection<T> gryffindor = new MagicSet<T>();
private MagicCollection<T> hufflepuff = new MagicSet<T>();
private MagicCollection<T> ravenclaw = new MagicSet<T>();
private MagicCollection<T> slytherin = new MagicSet<T>();
```

By using sets instead of lists, your code will be better protected against the possibility that you might inadvertently place the same student twice in the same house.

- An important issue not addressed by this demonstration is that of *robust iterators*. An iterator is robust if it does the right thing even when a collection changes (by the addition of a new object or deletion of an existing object) as it is being iterated through. *The iterator use in our demonstration is based on the assumption that a collection being iterated through does not change during the course of iterations.* A simple way to make an iterator robust is to have it track the state of the collection during the iterations. One could, for example, define a collection-modified flag that would be set to true if either the `add()` or the `remove()` functions (for either the collection itself or for the iterator if the `Iterator` class provides for such functions) are called during the iterations. A change in the state of a collection as detected by a change in the boolean value of the flag could either cause the iterator to adapt itself to the new state or, if that is not feasible, to throw an exception. Creating robust iterators that are thread-safe for multi-threaded operations poses its own challenges. At the least, you may have to synchronize the calls to `next()` and `hasNext()`. If you are up to it, you may wish to create robust iterators for this demonstration.

17.15   CREDITS

The code shown for the various methods in both `MagicList` and `MagicSet` classes is based on the implementations of similar classes in the Java Collections Framework. In particular, the author has used code fragments of the programs published by Gilad Bracha, Martin Odersky, David Stoutamire, and Philip Wadler when they first came up with their Generic Java extension to the Java platform.

18

MEDIATOR

18.1 THE ROLE OF MEDIATION IN COLLABORATIVE PROBLEM SOLVING

As an example of collaborative problem solving, let's consider a court trial in which the guilt or the innocence of an accused is decided by a committee of wise men and women sitting around a large table. To complete the imagery, we assume that the accused is sitting at one end of the table and the witnesses at the other. The wise men and women ask questions of the witnesses and the accused and do so in no particular order. The wise folks are also allowed to talk to one another if such conversations are germane to establishing the guilt or the innocence of the accused.

This problem-solving effort involves several individuals interacting simultaneously with the accused and the witnesses. That is, the interaction between the committee and those sitting at the two ends of the table has no particular order to it. This interaction is likely to involve communications at the whim of those charged with judging the accused.

While a court trial operating in the manner described above may solve the problem, it is not as efficient as what you see in a modern court in which the court protocol serves as a *mediator* for regulating the interaction between the individuals participating in a trial. It would be realistic to say that all communication in a modern trial is directed through the court itself. Every exchange of information during a trial must be in accord with the rules of the court, since otherwise the judge would disallow it.

People generally associate mediators with dispute resolution. We will not be interested in those kinds of mediators in this chapter. Our interest here is in mediators that bring order to the interaction between the agents participating in collaborative problem solving.

Designing with Objects: Object-Oriented Design Patterns Explained with Stories from Harry Potter,
First Edition. Avinash C. Kak.
© 2015 John Wiley & Sons, Inc. Published 2015 by John Wiley & Sons, Inc.

18.2   INTENT AND APPLICABILITY

The intent of the Mediator pattern is to define an object that can bring order to the interactions between the other objects in a software system.

You should consider using this pattern when

- there is a need to structure the interactions between the objects in a software system;
- the complexity of the inter-object interactions is such that the consequences of allowing objects to directly invoke methods on other objects may implicitly create dependencies between the classes that make it more difficult to modify the classes individually;
- it is possible to articulate precisely the conditions that must hold for each interaction between the objects and it is feasible to encapsulate these conditions in a mediator object;
- it is feasible to have all objects route their interactions with other objects through a designated mediator object.

18.3   INTRODUCTION TO THE MEDIATOR PATTERN

The main purpose of the Mediator pattern is to regulate the interactions between various objects in a system. These objects *could* invoke methods on one another directly, but, as with the modern court trial mentioned in Section 18.1, it is likely to be more efficient if such method invocations are directed through a mediator. The pattern designates a mediator class whose role is to keep track of the overall state of a system that involves several objects. Depending on the state, the mediator class may allow certain interactions between the objects while disallowing others. As the reader would expect, a mediator class acting in this manner brings order to the interconnections between the objects in a complex system. We can also expect that the efficiencies brought about through such mediation become more important the greater the frequency with which the objects need to call on one another.

When the objects in a system interact, it is likely to be the case that certain preconditions would need to hold before one object can invoke a method of another object. And, when one object executes a method of another object, that could establish the enabling preconditions for additional object interactions subsequently. Instead of each object having to check for itself whether or not the right conditions exist for it to call a method of another object, we can let a mediator keep track of the overall state of the system with regard to all of the participating objects. The various objects can then check with the mediator before invoking any methods and also inform the mediator about the consequences of the methods invoked by them.

It is reasonable to assume that forcing all inter-object interactions to go through a mediator in this manner would make a system consisting of a large number of interacting classes more scalable. It would also make such a system more reusable, in the sense that if a particular implementation for the mediator class is found to be unsuitable for whatever reason, one could extend the class and use the derived class to control the interaction between the other classes.

The Mediator pattern involves a generic `Mediator` interface that declares the various methods and the constraints that must be observed by any interaction between the classes that are subject to mediation. As to the specifics of how the interactions are regulated, that depends on how a concrete realization of the `Mediator` interface is implemented. To explain this point further, let's say we want to define a `Mediator` interface that would specify through its method declarations and constraints how the various entities engaged in a court trial should interact. This `Mediator` interface may be implemented in different ways by the different courts in a country. Considering the courts in the United States, different courts use different procedures and standards for admitting evidence and proving a defendant's guilt. As a case in point, the burden of proving the defendant's guilt is on the prosecution in criminal cases, whereas it is on the plaintiff in civil cases. Additionally, when the prosecution seeks to establish a fact, it must do so "beyond a reasonable doubt." On the other hand, in a civil case, when the plaintiff seeks to establish a fact, it must do so with a "preponderance of evidence." Therefore, while the different courts may use the same `Mediator` interface, they must use different implementations for the methods declared in the interface. The conceptual class diagram of Figure 18.1 should make this point clear — that `Mediator` is merely an interface and that one would realize it according to what is needed for orchestrating the interactions between the relevant objects.

18.4 THE MEDIATOR PATTERN IN REAL-WORLD APPLICATIONS

The Mediator pattern plays an important role in keeping organized the flow of control in software intended for complex graphical user interfaces that are now commonplace.

In GUI programming, in general, each graphical object you see on a screen is an instance constructed from a class. When a user selects an object by, say, clicking on it, that is likely to enable one or more of the other objects for further interaction by the user. If a user clicks on, say, a "Weather Reports" button in a newspaper GUI, that may show the current weather in a panel and enable several other buttons for conveying to the user other aspects of a weather report, such as forecasts spanning different time durations, weather maps of different kinds, and so on. The click on the "Weather Reports" button may also cause advertisements to be displayed in different panels and popups. Subsequently, when the user clicks on, or otherwise selects, one of the newly enabled graphical objects for a second interaction with the GUI, that could result in its own set of enabled and disabled objects (in addition to its own set of popups and adverts); and so on.

If each graphical object that was subject to direct input by the user had to keep track of all of the other objects that would need to be informed so that they could either enable or disable themselves, or all the other popups and panels that would need to be told what it is they should display, just imagine the tangle of linkages you would create in the GUI software. Just think of how difficult it would be to alter the behavior of such a GUI for adding some new functionality. The Mediator pattern can take much of this complexity out of the software. With the Mediator pattern, each object would communicate to the designated mediator object the information regarding its changed state. It would be the mediator's job to determine as to what other objects should become aware of that information and how they should change their states.

In this manner, the mediator would become a centralized repository of all information regarding how the different objects in the GUI should interact with one another. Such a

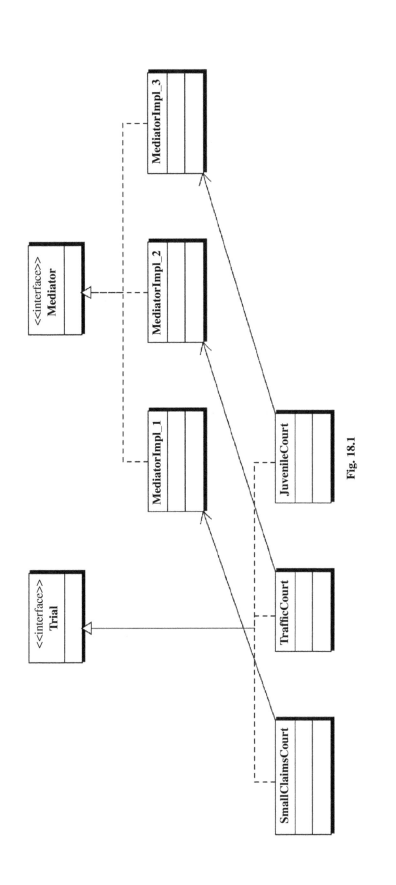

Fig. 18.1

centralized approach would lend itself to representation by a set of easy-to-follow UML diagrams. A developer wishing to alter the behavior of the GUI would only need to consult those diagrams in order to decide what aspects of the mediator to change for adding any new functionality — all other object classes would remain untouched.

18.5   HARRY POTTER STORY USED TO ILLUSTRATE THE MEDIATOR PATTERN

Our demonstration of the Mediator pattern is based on Harry Potter's trial at the Wizengamot, the high court of the wizarding law. This court is housed in the Ministry of Magic. This particular trial was charged with deciding whether Harry Potter was guilty of having performed underage magic in the presence of muggles when he conjured up a Patronus to ward off the dementors who were attacking him and his cousin Dudley. The chief prosecutor at this trial was the Minister for Magic, Cornelius Fudge. The defense was led by Dumbledore who also served as the principal defense witness. There was one additional defense witness, Mrs. Arabella Figg, who lives in the town of Little Whinging in the vicinity of Dursleys where Harry Potter spent his summers. The attack on Harry and Dudley took place not far from the Dursleys' when the boys were on their way back home one summer night.

18.6   A TOP LEVEL VIEW OF THE PATTERN DEMONSTRATION

The class diagram in Figure 18.2 is a top-level view of our demonstration of the Mediator pattern.

The goal in our demonstration here is certainly not to capture every aspect of Harry Potter's court trial. Instead, our goal is only to show how a mediator class can orchestrate the interaction between the court and the witnesses. In the simplified model of the court proceedings for our demonstration, the mediator's job will be to ensure that the trial proceeds sequentially through the following steps:

1. Statement of the charge against Harry Potter
2. Presentation of the evidence that supports the charge
3. Interrogation of the witnesses
4. Interrogation of the defense witnesses by the prosecution
5. Interrogation of the prosecution witnesses by the defense
6. Rendering of the judgment on the basis of those witness reports that were found to be credible

The mediator will bring order to the interaction between the classes by keeping track of the state of the court trial and by placing constraints on state transitions. The trial itself will be represented by the interface `Trial`. We will use the interface `TrialElements` to store some of the basic vocabulary of a court trial (but only at the level of simplicity required by our demonstration). It is in `TrialElements` we will define the `TrialState` data type,

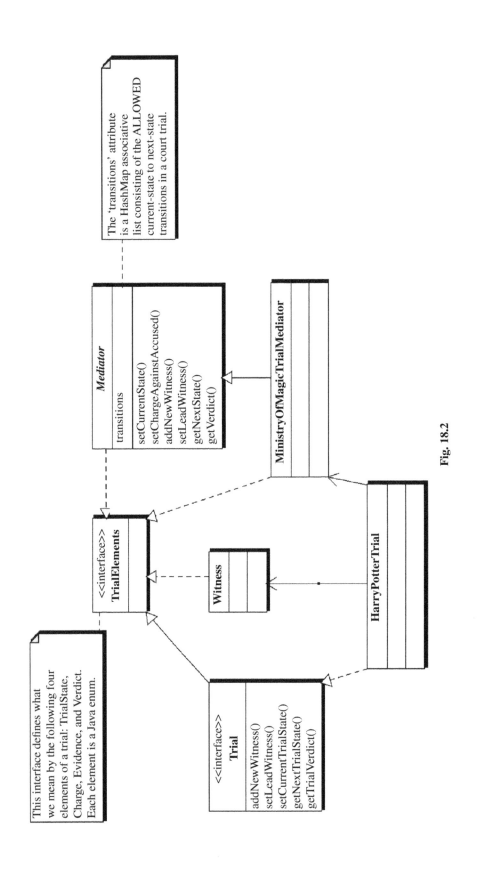

The 'transitions' attribute is a HashMap associative list consisting of the ALLOWED current-state to next-state transitions in a court trial.

Mediator

transitions

setCurrentState()
setChargeAgainstAccused()
addNewWitness()
setLeadWitness()
getNextState()
getVerdict()

MinistryOfMagicTrialMediator

<<interface>>
TrialElements

Witness

HarryPotterTrial

This interface defines what we mean by the following four elements of a trial: TrialState, Charge, Evidence, and Verdict. Each element is a Java enum.

<<interface>>
Trial

addNewWitness()
setLeadWitness()
setCurrentTrialState()
getNextTrialState()
getTrialVerdict()

Fig. 18.2

in the form of an enum, and its various permissible values, those being the different states of a trial.

Our demonstration is based on the following states of a court trial:

```
ChargeBeingFiled
EvidenceBeingPresented
WitnessesBeingQuestioned
WitnessBeingQuestionedByProsecution
WitnessBeingQuestionedByDefense
WitnessTestimoniesCompleted
JudgmentsBeingRendered
TrialCompleted
```

The constraints on state transitions will be expressed by storing the permissible transitions as an associative list in a `Map` structure whose elements are `<key,value>` pairs, in the form of `<TrialState, TrialState>`, with the first element of the pair denoting the current state of the court trial and the second element the next permissible state. This `Map` structure will be stored as the value of the static variable `transitions` you see in the `Mediator` interface (actually an abstract class) in the diagram.

In addition to storing the `transitions Map`, `Mediator` will declare a number of methods that can be used by an instance of `Trial`. Perhaps the most important of these is the `getNextState()` method that is called at the completion of the current state in order to determine what the next state of the trial should be. This function should evidently honor the next-state transitions stored in the `transitions` Map. Initiating a state transition requires that the end of the current state be recognized. As to how one does that and, for the states involving the witness testimony, how the credibility, or lack thereof, of a witness's testimony is established, is left to the concrete realizations of the abstract `Mediator` class. In our simple demonstration here, since our focus is just on how a mediator can be programmed, we will not worry too much about the fine details related to establishing the credibility of the testimonies offered by the witnesses.

Our demonstration's goal is to show how the `MinistryOfMagicTrialMediator` implements the methods in the `Mediator` abstract class and to then show how these methods are used in the `HarryPotterTrial` class to carry out a well orchestrated interrogation of the witnesses. Comparing the class diagram of Figure 18.2 with the more general such diagram of Figure 18.1, our demonstration here includes only one concrete realization of the `Mediator` abstract class and only one concrete realization of the `Trial` interface.

18.7   THE ABSTRACT CLASS Mediator

The definition of the `Mediator` interface, which is actually an abstract class, starts with the declaration of the `transitions` as an associative list of `<TrialState, TrialState>` pairs in which the first element is the current state of a trial and the second element the state that comes next. Next, the interface declares a number of convenience methods that can be used in a `Trial` instance to set and retrieve the values of the more important variables involved. Finally, the `Mediator` interface declares the most important method, `getNextState()`, that would presumably be implemented differently by the different concrete realizations of this abstract class for the different court systems.

```
public abstract class Mediator implements TrialElements {

    public static java.util.Map<TrialState, TrialState> transitions =
                    new java.util.HashMap<TrialState,TrialState>();

    {
        transitions.put( TrialState.ChargeBeingFiled,
                    TrialState.WitnessesBeingQuestioned );
        transitions.put( TrialState.WitnessesBeingQuestioned,
                TrialState.WitnessBeingQuestionedByProsecution );
        transitions.put( TrialState.WitnessesBeingQuestioned,
                    TrialState.WitnessBeingQuestionedByDefense );
        transitions.put(
                    TrialState.WitnessBeingQuestionedByProsecution,
                    TrialState.WitnessBeingQuestionedByDefense );
        transitions.put( TrialState.WitnessBeingQuestionedByDefense,
                TrialState.WitnessBeingQuestionedByProsecution );
        transitions.put(
                    TrialState.WitnessBeingQuestionedByProsecution,
                    TrialState.WitnessTestimoniesCompleted );
        transitions.put( TrialState.WitnessBeingQuestionedByDefense,
                    TrialState.WitnessTestimoniesCompleted );
        transitions.put( TrialState.WitnessTestimoniesCompleted,
                    TrialState.JudgmentBeingRendered );
        transitions.put( TrialState.JudgmentBeingRendered,
                    TrialState.TrialCompleted );
    };

    public abstract void setCurrentState( TrialState state );
    public abstract void setChargeAgainstAccused( Charge ch );
    public abstract void addNewWitness( Witness w );
    public abstract void setLeadWitness( Witness lw );
    public abstract void setAvailabilityOfDefenseWitnesses(boolean b);
    public abstract void setAvailabilityOfProsecutionWitnesses(
                                                boolean b);
    public abstract Verdict getVerdict();
    public abstract TrialState getNextState( TrialState
                                currentState ) throws Exception;
}
```

18.8   THE INTERFACE TrialElements

The purpose of the TrialElements interface is to provide a central repository of the "jargon" of a court trial — in the extremely simplified sense that our demonstration uses the notion of a court trial. This we do with the help of Java enums.

Our first enum, TrialState, defines the different phases that a court trial must go through. We insist that a court trial must at any time be in one of the eight states whose names are the permissible values for a variable of type TrialState. As the reader saw in

the previous section, our `Mediator` abstract class recognizes these eight states The other declarations shown below define what it means to be a `Charge` against an accused, what it means for something to constitute `Evidence`, and what it means for something to be a `Verdict`.

```
public interface TrialElements  {

    public static enum TrialState {
                         ChargeBeingFiled,
                         EvidenceBeingPresented,
                         WitnessesBeingQuestioned,
                         WitnessBeingQuestionedByProsecution,
                         WitnessBeingQuestionedByDefense,
                         WitnessTestimoniesCompleted,
                         JudgementBeingRendered,
                         TrialCompleted
    }

    public static enum Charge { ConjuredPetronusInMugglePresence,
                         UsedHoverCharmOnMuggle,
                         OtherUnderageUsesOfMagic
    }

    public static enum Evidence { AccusedNotAtPlaceOfCrime,
                            LifeOfAccusedInDanger;
    }

    public static enum Verdict { Guilty,
                         NotGuilty,
                         UnableToReachVerdict
    }
}
```

18.9   THE MinistryOfMagicTrialMediator CLASS

You have already seen the `Mediator` interface in the form of an abstract class. An important component of that interface is the specification of what transitions are allowed when a trial progresses through its different phases. In that interface, we refer to each phase of a trial as a state of the trial. Another very important part of the `Mediator` interface was the declaration of the `getNextState()` method. This is a key method that any concrete subclass of `Mediator` must implement. Obviously, how this method is implemented will be different for different kinds of trials and different types of courts. At the least, one can expect the different courts to use different procedures and standards for establishing the proof of a fact presented in the court by either the prosecution or the defense.

We now present a concrete realization of the `Mediator` interface. This realization, `MinistryOfMagicTrialMediator`, is meant specifically for Harry Potter's trial at the

Ministry of Justice. The most important part of this concrete realization of `Mediator` is the implementation of the

```
TrialState getNextState( TrialSttate current_state )
```

method. In addition to returning the next state in accordance with the `transitions` specification in the root `Mediator` interface, `MinistryOfMagicTrialMediator` also provides the following place-holder for implementing the evidentiary logic needed for establishing the veracity of the testimony provided by a witness in accordance with the court procedures:

```
boolean corroborateWitnessTestimony( Evidence testimony )
```

Our implementation of this method is merely a place-holder since all it does is return true for the evidence presented. A full-blown implementation of such a method would take us far from the main goal of this demonstration, which is to focus on the Mediator pattern from the standpoint of how a `Mediator` object regulates the interaction between the other classes.

The implementation code shown in the class definition below starts with defining a set of instance variables; their names make them self-explanatory. The mediator keeps track of the witnesses already heard by the court and the list of all the witnesses available through the two instance variables `setOfWitnesses` and `witnessesHeardByTheCourt`. Also note the role played by the two instance variables `defenseWitnessesAvailable` and `prosecutionWitnessesAvailable`. As the reader will see later when we present the `Witness` class, each witness is either a prosecution witness or a defense witness. A prosecution witness is interrogated by the defense and a defense witness interrogated by the prosecution.[1]

The instance variables are followed by the implementation of the methods declared in the `Mediator` interface. It is through these methods that a `Trial` instance interacts with the mediator. The different "set" methods are for initializing the `MinistryOfMagicTrialMediator` instance used in a particular trial. The `getVerdict()` method is for retrieving the verdict reached by the logic in the `getNextState()` that is described next.

Most of the logic in the `getNextState(currentState)` method is simple: it looks at what is allowed by the `transitions` associative list in the root interface `Mediator` and returns the next `TrialState` that is dictated by that associative list. If there is any complexity at all to this method, it is with regard to how the witnesses are "processed." We first make a determination of whether a witness is a prosecution witness or a defense witness. In either case, we check the value of the instance variable `testimonyCorroboratedUponExamination` for the witness in question to determine the veracity of the testimony. The value of this variable is set by calling the method `corroborateWitnessTestimony()` of the class presented below. As mentioned earlier,

---

[1] As described by J. K. Rowling, the Wizengamot, the high court of the wizarding world, does not directly support the notions of prosecution and defense. But one can safely infer from the description of the trial that the Minister for Magic is the chief prosecutor and Dumbledore the chief defense "attorney" while also, at the same time, serving as the lead defense witness.

our implementation of this method is trivial since it always returns true. To that extent, it is just a place-holder that a reader could use for implementing more elaborate logic that may either return true or false depending on the testimony.

The reader should also note the logic in `getNextState()` for deciding what verdict to issue on the basis of the testimonies supplied by the witnesses. The logic is simple: a single negated testimony from the defense witnesses negates the defense of the accused. By the same token, a single negated testimony from the prosecution witnesses negates all of the prosecution case. If the case presented by the defense fails, the accused is considered guilty as charged. If the case presented by the prosecution fails, the accused is considered to be not guilty as charged. If both the defense and the prosecution cases turn out to be valid or if they both fail, the accused is let go with the verdict `UnableToReachVerdict`.

```java
import java.util.*;

public  class MinistryOfMagicTrialMediator extends Mediator
                                    implements TrialElements {
    private TrialState currentState;
    private Charge charge;
    private Set<Witness>  setOfWitnesses = new HashSet<Witness>();
    private Set<Witness>  witnessesHeardByTheCourt =
                                        new HashSet<Witness>();
    private boolean defenseWitnessesAvailable;
    private boolean prosecutionWitnessesAvailable;
    private Witness leadWitness;
    private Witness currentWitness;
    private Verdict verdict;

    public void setCurrentState( TrialState state ) {
        currentState = state;
    }
    public void setChargeAgainstAccused( Charge ch ) { charge = ch; }
    public void setAvailabilityOfDefenseWitnesses(boolean b) {
        defenseWitnessesAvailable = b;
    }
    public void setAvailabilityOfProsecutionWitnesses(boolean b) {
        prosecutionWitnessesAvailable = b;
    }
    public void setLeadWitness( Witness lw ) { leadWitness = lw; }
    public Verdict getVerdict() { return verdict; }
    public void addNewWitness( Witness wt ) {
        setOfWitnesses.add( wt );
    }

    public TrialState getNextState( TrialState currentState )
                                            throws Exception {
        if ( currentState == TrialState.ChargeBeingFiled ) {
            List<Charge> listOfCharges =
                                Arrays.asList( Charge.values() );
            Set<Charge> setOfCharges =
```

```
                            new HashSet<Charge>( listOfCharges );
    if (! setOfCharges.contains( charge ) ) {
        throw new Exception(
                "Charge against the accused not recognized" );
    }
} else if ( currentState ==
                    TrialState.WitnessesBeingQuestioned ) {
    System.out.println("List of all witnesses: "
                                        + setOfWitnesses );
    System.out.println("The remaining witnesses available: "
                    + remainingWitnesses() );
    if (remainingWitnesses().size() > 0) {
        if (leadWitness != null) {
            currentWitness = leadWitness;
            leadWitness = null;
        } else {
            currentWitness =
                (Witness) remainingWitnesses().toArray()[0];
        }
        witnessesHeardByTheCourt.add(currentWitness);
        System.out.println("Next witness to be questioned: "
                            + currentWitness);
    } else {
        return TrialState.WitnessTestimoniesCompleted;
    }
    if (currentWitness.getWhoseWitness() == "prosecution") {
        System.out.println(
                    "    This is a prosecution witness --- "
                    + "will be questioned by defense");
        return TrialState.WitnessBeingQuestionedByDefense;
    } else {
        System.out.println("   This is a defense witness --- "
                    + "will be questioned by prosecution");
        return TrialState.WitnessBeingQuestionedByProsecution;
    }
} else if ( currentState ==
        TrialState.WitnessBeingQuestionedByProsecution ) {
    System.out.println("   DEFENSE WITNESS: Witness being "
                    + "questioned by prosecution: "
                    + currentWitness);
    if ( !currentWitness.initialTestimonyPresented )  {
        currentWitness.initialTestimonyPresented = true;
        currentWitness.testimonyCorroboratedUponExamination =
            corroborateWitnessTestimony(
                            currentWitness.getTestimony() );
    } else {
        throw new Exception( "Something has gone wrong with "
                    + "the sequencing of court procedures");
    }
    return TrialState.WitnessesBeingQuestioned;
} else if ( currentState ==
                TrialState.WitnessBeingQuestionedByDefense ) {
```

```
    System.out.println("PROSECUTION WITNESS: Witness being "
                    + "questioned by defense: "
                    + currentWitness);
    if ( !currentWitness.initialTestimonyPresented )  {
        currentWitness.initialTestimonyPresented = true;
        currentWitness.testimonyCorroboratedUponExamination =
            corroborateWitnessTestimony(
                            currentWitness.getTestimony() );
    } else {
        throw new Exception( "Something has gone wrong with "
                    + "the sequencing of court procedures");
    }
    return TrialState.WitnessesBeingQuestioned;
 } else if ( currentState ==
                    TrialState.WitnessTestimoniesCompleted ) {
return TrialState.JudgementBeingRendered;
} else if  ( currentState ==
                        TrialState.JudgementBeingRendered ) {
    boolean prosecutionWitnesses = true;
    boolean defenseWitnesses = true;
    for (Witness wit : setOfWitnesses ) {
        if ( wit.getWhoseWitness() == "prosecution" )  {
            if (wit.testimonyCorroboratedUponExamination) {
                continue;
            } else {
                prosecutionWitnesses = false;
            }
        } else if ( wit.getWhoseWitness() == "defense" )  {
            if (wit.testimonyCorroboratedUponExamination) {
                continue;
            } else {
                defenseWitnesses = false;
            }
        }
    }
    if ( (!prosecutionWitnessesAvailable )
                        & (defenseWitnesses == true) ) {
        verdict = Verdict.NotGuilty;
    } else if ( (!prosecutionWitnessesAvailable )
                        & (defenseWitnesses == false) ) {
        verdict = Verdict.Guilty;
    } else if ( (!defenseWitnessesAvailable )
                    & (prosecutionWitnesses == true) ) {
        verdict = Verdict.Guilty;
    } else if ( (!defenseWitnessesAvailable )
                    & (prosecutionWitnesses == false) ) {
        verdict = Verdict.NotGuilty;
    } else if ( (prosecutionWitnesses == true)
                        & (defenseWitnesses == false) ) {
        verdict = Verdict.Guilty;
    } else if ( (prosecutionWitnesses == false)
                        & (defenseWitnesses == true) ) {
```

```
                verdict = Verdict.NotGuilty;
            } else {
                verdict = Verdict.UnableToReachVerdict;
            }
        }
        return transitions.get( currentState );
    }

    public boolean corroborateWitnessTestimony( Evidence testimony ) {
        // This is just a place-holder at the moment since the logic
        // encoded here would not be important to demonstrating the
        // main ideas of the Mediator pattern.
      return true;
    }

    public Set<Witness>  remainingWitnesses() {
        Set<Witness> remaining = new HashSet<Witness>();
        for ( Witness w : setOfWitnesses ) {
            if ( ! witnessesHeardByTheCourt.contains(w) ) {
                remaining.add(w);
            }
        }
        return remaining;
    }
}
```

18.10   THE Witness CLASS

Central to what is accomplished by MinistryOfMagicTrial is the examination of the testimonies provided by the witnesses. As the reader would recall from our presentation of the Mediator interface and the MinstryOfMagicTrialMediator class, we must know beforehand whether a witness is a defense witness or a prosecution witness, a fact indicated by the instance variable whoseWitness of the Witness class shown below. The instance variable initialTestimonyPresented is used in the mediator logic in the MinistryOfMagicTrialMediator class to mark the completion of a witness's testimony so that the same witness is not called again.

The boolean instance variable testimonyCorroboratedUponExamination is set to true if the testimony presented by a Witness is considered to be true by the court, otherwise it is set to false. Remember, the minimum condition for a NotGuilty verdict is that all defense witnesses have provided true testimony and at least one prosecution witness has provided false testimony. By the same token, the minimum condition for a Guilty verdict is that all prosecution witnesses have provided true testimony and at least one defense witnesses has provided false testimony.

The "get" method getTestimony() is called by the getNextState() method in MinistryOfMagicTrialMediator when supplying the argument needed in the call to corroborateWitnessTestimony().

```
public class Witness implements TrialElements {
    private String name;
    private Evidence testimony;
    private String whoseWitness;
    public boolean initialTestimonyPresented = false;
    public boolean testimonyCorroboratedUponExamination;
    public Witness(String name, Evidence testimony, String whoseSide) {
        this.name = name;
        this.testimony = testimony;
        this.whoseWitness = whoseSide;
    }
    public String getWhoseWitness() {
        return whoseWitness;
    }
    public Evidence getTestimony() { return testimony; }
    public String toString() { return name; }
}
```

18.11 THE Trial INTERFACE

The goal here is to define a minimal interface for a `Trial` class. The interface is based on the assumption that a trial can be divided into distinct phases and each phase represented as one of the eight states declared in the super-interface `TrialElements`. The method declarations in this interface speak for themselves.

```
public interface Trial extends TrialElements {
    public void addNewWitness(Witness w);
    public void setLeadWitness(Witness lw);
    public TrialState getNextTrialState( TrialState currentState )
                            throws Exception;
    public void setCurrentTrialState( TrialState state );
    public Verdict getTrialVerdict();
}
```

18.12 THE HarryPotterTrial CLASS

The class shown in this section, `HarryPotterTrial`, is meant to demonstrate the working of the concrete mediator class `MinistryOfMagicTrialMediator`.

The implementation shown below declares three instance variables that are critical to the execution of the Harry Potter trial — any trial for that matter. We have an instance variable `mediator` whose value is set by the constructor to an instance of `MinistryOfMagicTrialMediator`. The other two instance variables store the current

state of the trial and what the next state will be upon completion of the current state. In main(), we start with the currentState, which is set to ChargeBeingFiled just before the while loop, and then, by setting nextState to currentState, we cycle through all the states of the trial until the state TrialCompleted is reached. As the reader has already seen from our presentation of the MinistryOfMagicTrialMediator, when the trial is in the states that call for interrogating the witnesses, we accumulate the evidence needed to reach one of the three final verdicts: Guilty, NotGuilty, and VerdictCannotBeReached.

With regard to the rest of the code presented below, note how we set the predicate setAvailabilityOfDefenseWitnees to true and the predicate setAvailability ofProsecutionWitnesses to false. This mirrors the description of the trial by J. K. Rowling. Basically, the trial consists of the Minister of Magic Cornelius Fudge leveling the charge at Harry Potter, presenting the evidence for the charge, and Dumbledore and Mrs. Figg serving as defense witnesses, with the former as the lead witness. There are no prosecution witnesses.

The two witnesses needed for the trial, Dumbledore and Mrs. Figg, are constructed in the body of main(), where the former is also set as the lead witness. (In our simple demonstration, lead witness means merely that he/she will be the first witness to be interrogated.)

```
public class HarryPotterTrial implements Trial {
    private Mediator mediator;
    private TrialState currentState;
    private  TrialState nextState;
    public HarryPotterTrial() {
        mediator = new MinistryOfMagicTrialMediator();
        mediator.setChargeAgainstAccused(
                            Charge.ConjuredPetronusInMugglePresence);
        mediator.setAvailabilityOfDefenseWitnesses(true);
        mediator.setAvailabilityOfProsecutionWitnesses(false);
    }
    public void addNewWitness(Witness w) {
        mediator.addNewWitness(w);
    }
    public void setLeadWitness(Witness lw) {
        mediator.setLeadWitness( lw );
    }
    public TrialState getNextTrialState( TrialState currentState )
                                                throws Exception {
        return mediator.getNextState( currentState );
    }
    public void setCurrentTrialState( TrialState state ) {
        currentState = state;
        mediator.setCurrentState( state );
    }
    public Verdict getTrialVerdict() {
        return mediator.getVerdict();
    }
```

```
public static void main(String[] args) {
      try {
            HarryPotterTrial trial = new HarryPotterTrial();
            Witness dumbledore = new Witness( "Dumbledore",
                        Evidence.LifeOfAccusedInDanger, "defense");
            Witness figg = new Witness( "Figg",
                        Evidence.LifeOfAccusedInDanger, "defense");
            trial.addNewWitness( dumbledore );
            trial.addNewWitness( figg );
            trial.setLeadWitness(dumbledore);
            trial.setCurrentTrialState(TrialState.ChargeBeingFiled);
            while (trial.currentState != TrialState.TrialCompleted) {
                trial.nextState =
                        trial.getNextTrialState(trial.currentState);
                trial.setCurrentTrialState( trial.nextState );
            }
            System.out.println( "The final trial state is: "
                                          + trial.nextState );
            System.out.println( "The verdict is: "
                                          + trial.getTrialVerdict() );
      } catch(Exception e) {
            e.printStackTrace();
      }
   }
}
```

18.13 PLAYING WITH THE CODE

Download the class files for this pattern from the book website into a separate directory. Compile the code with the command

```
javac *.java
```

and execute the HarryPotterTrial class by

```
java HarryPotterTrial
```

Given the code in the main() of HarryPotterTrial, executing this class will produce the following output:

```
List of all witnesses: [Dumbledore, Figg]
The remaining witnesses available: [Dumbledore, Figg]
Next witness to be questioned: Dumbledore

    This is a defense witness --- will be questioned by prosecution
    DEFENSE WITNESS: Witness being questioned by prosecution:
                                        Dumbledore
```

```
List of all witnesses: [Dumbledore, Figg]
The remaining witnesses available: [Figg]
Next witness to be questioned: Figg

   This is a defense witness --- will be questioned by prosecution
   DEFENSE WITNESS: Witness being questioned by prosecution: Figg

List of all witnesses: [Dumbledore, Figg]
The remaining witnesses available: []
The final trial state is: TrialCompleted

The verdict is: NotGuilty
```

For additional insights, you may consider extending the code for this pattern along the following lines:

- Our implementation of the method `corroborateWitnessTestimony()` used to corroborate the testimony of a witness in `MinistryOfMagicTrialMediator` was trivial for reasons explained in our presentation of that class. However, as you are playing with the code, you might find it interesting to experiment with more elaborate logic for corroborating a witness's testimony.

- The reader may ask what the class `MinistryOfMagicTrialMediator` is mediating between. The mediation is between the `HarryPotterTrial` class and the `Witness` class from the standpoint of how these two classes interact. In general, we could have an arbitrary number of witnesses and the trial process would need to interact with all of them. The mediator class helps give organization to that interaction. If you are up to it, you can introduce a larger set of classes to demonstrate the usefulness of the mediator class. For example, you could have a separate `Verdict` class and a separate framework consisting of several classes for the corroboration of witness testimonies. If you do that, you will obviously have a much more impressive demonstration of the power of the Mediator pattern.

19

MEMENTO

19.1 RECALLING THE PAST

You have surely experienced recalling a moment from the past — especially if the moment was special in some way — upon seeing an object like the stub of a concert ticket, a shell collected from a beach, a photo, etc. All such objects when they bring back old memories serve as mementos of the times gone by. You may think of them as keepers of special memories.

Recalling what was true at a previous time is also important in the software that goes into computer applications for creative work such as writing, drawing, animation, and so on. The simplest form of such recall occurs in "undo" operations that make it possible for a user to restore an object to its previous state. At its simplest, an "undo" must restore the work to what it looked like prior to the latest change. More sophisticated versions of this operation take the work back to any of its previous states by a recursive invocation of "undo".

One might think that restoring software objects to their previous states would be simple since one could use time-stamped tokens for recording the object states as they change and then, with the help of the tokens, recall the old states later. Unfortunately, the problem of restoring an object to one of its previous states does not always lend itself to such an easy solution. As to why, *the state may involve parameters that are not directly accessible to the user for a simple rollback.*

To elaborate, as the reader knows, in object-oriented software, it is common for the state of an object — or some part of it — to reside in the object's private section. If you want your software to permit the old states of an object to be saved for future "undo" operations by a user, you are faced with the conundrum of how to save those portions of the state that are not meant to be directly accessible by the user. If you insist that the information held in the private portion of the state remain inaccessible to the user, a simple-minded approach to user-initiated rollback is not going to work. Additionally, consider the case when a document processing tool used by a company involves security parameters that control who has what access rights to the different portions of a document. After these parameters are set as a document is being created, unsetting of those parameters through

Designing with Objects: Object-Oriented Design Patterns Explained with Stories from Harry Potter,
First Edition. Avinash C. Kak.
© 2015 John Wiley & Sons, Inc. Published 2015 by John Wiley & Sons, Inc.

an ordinary implementation of "undo" may not work if the user creating the document does not possess appropriate security credentials. For another example, let's say a large multi-media document being created involves importing objects from other locations in a network. If the rules concerning object imports and source attribution are not accessible to the user creating the document, an ordinary implementation of the "undo" logic might get confused by the fact that not all of the document state is directly available to the user for restoring the document to its previous state.

Therefore, it is clear that, in general, not everything about the changing state of an object can be assumed to be directly accessible to the user of a software system. That makes it challenging for the state of the object to be rolled back to an earlier state at the user's end. How does one get around this difficulty? How does one store away all of the information related to the previous states of an object without making that information accessible to a user, yet making it available for rolling back the state of the object?

It is this challenge that is answered by the Memento pattern. The pattern shows us how we can set up a recall mechanism for software objects in which the changes and their associated parameters are stored as "mementos" *in such a way that, while a user cannot peer inside them directly, the "mementos" are nevertheless available for restoring the objects to their previous states.*

19.2   INTENT AND APPLICABILITY

The intent of the Memento pattern is to enable the client of a class to save the previous states of its instances but without violating the encapsulation constraints dictated by the access control modifiers private/protected/package in the definition of the class.

You should consider using this pattern if

- you want to give the clients of your software the ability to roll back the state of the objects (assuming that your software creates objects whose states change with time);

19.3   INTRODUCTION TO THE MEMENTO PATTERN

As the opening section of this chapter makes clear, we want a client to be able to roll back the current state of an object to one of the previous states. What's important here is that we want the client to possess this facility without having direct access to the changes themselves. As you will see, the Memento pattern accomplishes this by storing all previous states of the object as instances of a class that is commonly named Memento. The client software is not able to directly peer inside any instances of Memento. Nonetheless, the client software can use those Memento instances to roll back the state of the object to what it was at a previous time.

In the vocabulary that is usually associated with this pattern, the class whose instances need to be rolled back to their previous states is referred to as the Originator class. It is the changing states of an instance of the Originator class that are stored as instances of a Memento class. In general, a client of Originator will not be able to look inside, let alone alter in any way, the Memento instances even when these instances are stored at the client's site. Another way of saying the same thing is that the Memento pattern does not violate any

encapsulation constraints related to the Originator objects even as it gives the clients the freedom to roll back the state of such objects. The relationship between the Originator, the Memento, and the Client classes is as displayed in Figure 19.1.

The rest of this section illustrates the difficulty of rolling back the state of an Originator object with the help of a made-up code example. The Originator class shown below has three instance variables, all in its private section. Focusing on just the x and the y variables, let us say that only x can be set by the public constructor, the other instance variable, y, being set by the private function f():

```
Class Originator {
    private int clockTick;
    private int x;
    private int y;
    public X( int time, int xx) {
        clockTick = time;
        x = xx;
        y = f(x);
    }
    private int f(int xx) {
        //  some code for processing xx
        //  returns an int
    }
}
```

This class allows a client to construct a new instance at each clock tick. (In the rest of the explanation of the Memento pattern, we will refer to clock ticks by the made-up word clockTick.) The state of each instance constructed from this class is obviously characterized by the clockTick that corresponds to the time when the instance was created and the values of the instance variables x and y at that moment.

Let's say that at some point in time the client wants to restore the instance constructed at that moment to its state at a previous clockTick. If the fact that the instance variables

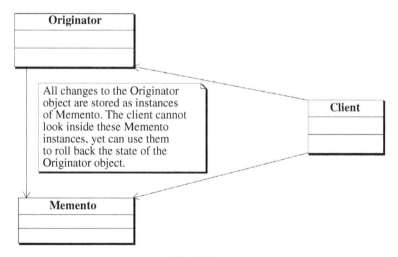

Fig. 19.1

(and also the function $f()$ that is used in setting the value of y) are in the private section of the class was not an issue, the client could simply store the values of the state variables and directly restore the desired previous state. However, that will not be possible in this case because of the visibility constraints on the instance variables. A reader might argue that if all state changes are brought about by constructor calls, why not just store the constructor arguments and then restore the object to its state at a previous time by issuing a constructor call with its arguments set to the values used at that time? That this approach to rolling back the state of an object may not work should be clear from the case when, in the above example, we set the instance variable y by y=rand(x). We can expect that every call to rand() even with the same x will return a different value for y. Think of y=rand(x) as a metaphor for any of a large number of things that may occur when setting the state of an object — things that may not always be visible to the client of a class.

19.4 THE MEMENTO PATTERN IN REAL-WORLD APPLICATIONS

Probably the most common usage scenarios for the Memento pattern are in applications dealing with document processing, computer art, and other similar creative pursuits. In document processing, the state information related to an evolving document must include both the keystroke content of the document, any formatting information related to the layout of the content, and any additional information, such as that related to security and accessibility. While much of this state would be directly visible to a user, there will be several aspects of the state — likely to be held in the private sections of the objects involved — that would not. The user-inaccessible portion of the state may refer to the parameters used in operations that control how the font sizes and the document layout change automatically as the window size is changed under user control, how the menu options shown to the user change with changes made to the document, the display of the annotation tools made available to the user, and so on. With regard to "undo" in this context, the simplest case of rollback occurs when the user makes an error in the document — this could be a keystroke error or a formatting error — and you want the computer to change the document back to what it was before the error occurred. As previously mentioned, a more sophisticated version of such "undo" includes recursive rollback that allows a user to go backward in time, one step at a time, and restore the document to how it was at each of these earlier moments. The same considerations apply to software meant for creating computer art.

19.5 HARRY POTTER STORY USED TO ILLUSTRATE THE MEMENTO PATTERN

Our demonstration of the Memento pattern is based on certain happenings at Hogwarts that take place near the end of the third book in the Harry Potter series when Hermione Granger uses her Time-Turner to go backward in time by three hours in order to save the lives of Sirius Black and the hippogriff Buckbeak. If you have read Prisoner of Azkaban, you will recall that, near the end of the story, Lucious Malfoy (who has no affection for Hagrid, the keeper of the magical creatures at Hogwarts) is injured by Buckbeak while approaching the hippogriff with disrespect. Subsequently, Malfoy lodges a complaint with the Ministry of Magic about how unsafe it is for the students to be in the vicinity of Buckbeak during their

classes with Hagrid. Under the influence of Lucius's father, the Ministry makes a decision to put Buckbeak to death, despite Hagrid's pleas as to the unfairness of this verdict.

That brings us to the moment when the execution party, made up of the Minister for Magic, Cornelius Fudge, the Executioner Walden Macnair, and the Headmaster Dumbledore, shows up at Hagrid's cabin to behead the hippogriff.

But Buckbeak is saved by Hermione Granger and Harry Potter through the magic of Hermione's Time-Turner. It is not only Buckbeak who is saved, also saved is Sirius Black, who has been hounded by dementors ever since his escape from Azkaban. Harry and Hermione get the freed Buckbeak to fly Sirius out of Hogwarts.

Central to the rescue of both Buckbeak and Sirius Black is Hermione using her Time-Turner to go backward in time by three hours. *Going backward in time to an earlier reality is the same thing as restoring the state of an object to what it was at an earlier time.* Using this going-backward-in-time story for explaining the Memento pattern does create an interesting side issue: When Hermione gives three turns to her Time-Turner and travels backward in time by three hours, from that moment on you have to allow for two *parallel* time flows to take place, until they meet again in exactly three hours.[1]

In order to keep track of the events in the two time flows separately, our demonstration of the Memento pattern will use a class named `HogwartsHappening` to store narratives of the significant happenings at Hogwarts. For example, when the execution party shows up at Hagrid's cabin for Buckbeak's execution, a narrative of that happening will be stored away in an instance of `HogwartsHappening`. When an instance of this class is created for a given happening, in addition to the narrative, we will also store in the instance the time associated with that happening. The time will be recorded through the instance variable `clockTick` of the class. Using `clockTicks` would allow us to sequence the instances of `HogwartsHappening` on a time line. That would then permit us to go forward and backward in time.

In keeping with how the two time flows unfold in Prisoner of Azkaban, a client of the `HogwartsHappening` class will construct a sequence of the instances of this class, one for each `clockTick` in each time flow separately. As the instances are constructed in the first time flow (we may think of that as the main time flow), the changing states of these instances will be automatically stored away at the client site in the form of the instances of a class named `Memento` that will be defined as an *inner class* of `HogwartsHappening`. By being put away as the inner-class `Memento` instances, we ensure that the client would have no direct access to the stored states of the `HogwartsHappening` instances. Eventually, at some point, in order to follow the script laid out in Prisoner of Azkaban, the client would want to reset the state of the latest `HogwartsHappening` object to what it was at `clockTick` 0, which is exactly three hours earlier. Any `HogwartsHappening` instances constructed subsequently would correspond to the parallel time flow that leads to Buckbeak and Sirius Black making their escape.

Our demonstration will consist of creating a small sequence of happenings starting at roughly three hours before the moment Hermione gives three turns to her Time Turner:

ClockTick 1: We will start the happenings clock when Harry, Ron, and Hermione set out under Harry's invisibility cloak to visit Hagrid to express their sympathy and

---

[1] A dreamer of time travel would want to allow for "parallel universes" to exist if it is possible to go forward and backward in time. One could say that the two time flows created by Hermione's action with the Time-Turner exist in two parallel universes that merge again three hours later.

solidarity in his moment of grief; Hagrid has just been informed by the Ministry of Magic that his favorite creature, the hippogriff Buckbeak, will be executed later that evening.

ClockTick 2: The next happening we record is when the execution party knocks at the door to Hagrid's cabin and Hagrid asks Harry, Ron, and Hermione to quickly leave his cabin through the back door.

ClockTick 3: As Harry, Ron, and Hermione are making their way back to the castle, Ron's rat Scabbers starts to act up, ostensibly because Hermione's magical cat Crookshanks is nearby. (As we later find out, Crookshanks knows Scabbers's true identity: the rat is actually Peter Pettigrew, who was an Animagus, meaning who could turn himself into an animal at will. Again as we later find out, it was Peter Pettigrew who had betrayed Harry's parents to Lord Voldemort.) Scabbers makes his way to a large hole in the roots of the Whomping Willow tree, followed by a very large dog (actually Sirius Black, also an Animagus) along with Ron who is dragging, followed by Crookshanks the cat, followed by Harry, and, finally, followed by Hermione. This hole in the roots of the Whomping Willow tree leads to an underground tunnel that is a secret passage to Shrieking Shack just outside the Hogsmeade village.

ClockTick 4: The whole party — Harry, Ron, Hermione, Sirius, Crookshanks, and Scabbers — find themselves in an upstairs room in the Shrieking Shack in Hogsmeade.

ClockTick 5: ....

ClockTick 6: ....

And here is the re-traced sequence of events after Hermione goes back in time by giving three turns to her Time-Turner machine:

ClockTick 1: Hermione and Harry are in a broom closet. They can hear footsteps outside that sound like three people going down the steps to Hagrid's cabin. As it turns out, these are the footsteps of Harry, Ron, and Hermione walking under the invisibility cloak in the original sequence of events.

ClockTick 2: While still inside the broom closet, Hermione and Harry puzzle over Dumbledore's rather cryptic mention that they could save two lives, not just Buckbeak's, by the time-travel adventure they were on. They put two and two together and come to the conclusion that, if successful, they could save both Buckbeak and Sirius Black.

ClockTick 3: Hermione and Harry set off for Hagrid's cabin, doing their best to not be discovered crossing the lawn behind the castle by keeping in the shadows of the trees. They arrive at a point where they can see the front door to the cabin. Hiding behind a tree, they can see themselves from the original time flow, along with Ron, knocking at the door.

ClockTick 4: Later they see themselves leaving the cabin through the back door as the execution committee enters the cabin. Harry and Hermione catch sight of McNair looking at Buckbeak through a window. Since the back door to the cabin is open, they can also hear the conversation taking place inside. They decide that the time has come to mount a rescue for Buckbeak. So Harry darts to where Buckbeak is tethered

to the fence, untethers the rope, and pulls Buckbeak into the trees at the edge of the forest where he would not be visible from Hagrid's cabin. The execution committee steps out of the cabin with the idea of carrying out Buckbeak's execution, but is surprised to not see the hippogriff anywhere.

ClockTick 5: ....

ClockTick 6: ....

19.6   A TOP LEVEL VIEW OF THE PATTERN DEMONSTRATION

As explained in the previous section, our demonstration of the Memento pattern is based on using the HogwartsHappening class as the Originator class. (Section 19.3 stated what we mean by the Originator class.) Figure 19.2 presents the class diagram for our demonstration. As the note attached to the Memento class says, it is an inner class of HogwartsHappening, which gives HogwartsHappening free access to the private members of Memento. *This ploy also prevents any outside class directly accessing the state information stored in an instance of* Memento.

Note the public methods listed for the HogwartsHappening class, in particular the methods saveStateToMemento() and restoreStateFromMemento(), the former for saving the current state of an instance of HogwartsHappening and the latter for restoring the current instance to an earlier state.

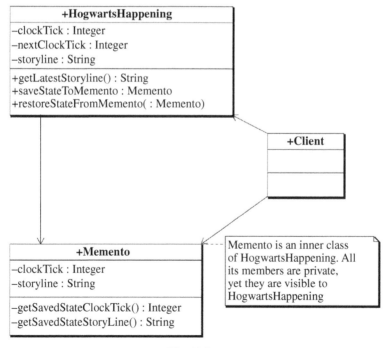

Fig. 19.2

In the `Client` class, we create instances of `HogwartsHappening` for each significant event as the story unfolds starting at the moment three hours prior to Hermione giving three turns to her Time-Turner machine. We associate an integer index, as the value of the instance variable `clockTick`, with each instance of `HogwartsHappening`. As these instances are created, they are stored locally by a client as `HogwartsHappening.Memento` objects. However, being objects of type `HogwartsHappening.Memento`, the client would not be able to peer inside the stored instances. Nonetheless, by calling an appropriate method of `HogwartsHappening`, the client would be able to restore the current instance of this class to the state stored at an earlier time.

In this manner, at the instant Hermione gives three turns to her Time-Turner machine, we can go back in time to that earlier moment that was three hours back. Subsequently, the new instances of `HogwartsHappening` would correspond to the other time flow in which both Buckbeak and Sirius Black make a getaway.

19.7   THE HogwartsHappening CLASS AND THE INNER Memento CLASS

We now present the two conjoined classes `HogwartsHappening` and `Memento`. With the latter class being inner to the former and, at the same time, with the latter class containing no public instance variables, it becomes easy to fulfill one of the main requirements of the Memento pattern: A client of `HogwartsHappening` should be able to save and restore the states of the instances of `HogwartsHappening` *without having direct access to the state information*.

Focusing first on just the `HogwartsHappening` class in the implementation code shown in this section, in addition to equipping the class with the two instance variables, `clockTick` and `storyline`, we also provide it with a class variable named `nextClockTick`. This allows us to sequentially create `HogwartsHappening` instances with just the `storyline` arguments and to let the class figure out on its own what value to use for `clockTick` for the next instance of `HogwartsHappening`. You may think of the class variable `nextClockTick` as the keeper of how many `clockTicks` we have already used; it can therefore tell us which `clockTick` would apply to the next `storyline`. Note how the no-arg constructor is used to increment the static variable `nextClockTick`. As the reader surely knows already, the no-arg constructor is automatically called as the first thing when any of the other two constructors is called by a client of this class. So no matter how we create an instance of `HogwartsHappening`, the static variable `nextClockTick` will be incremented.

Next, note the implementation of the two public methods

```
saveStateToMemento()
restoreStateFromMemento(Memento memento)
```

When a client of the `HogwartsHappening` class invokes `saveStateToMemento()` on an instance of the class, an instance of the inner class `Memento` is created and the state of the `HogwartsHappening` instance saved in the `Memento` instance created. However, since the `Memento` class has no public methods at all, the contents of the `Memento` instances are not visible to the client. Even though the client cannot peer inside the `Memento` instances to examine the saved states of the `HogwartsHappening` objects, the client can call the

public method `restoreStateFromMemento()` of the `HogwartsHappening` class to roll back the state of the latest `HogwartsHappening` instance to what it was at some previous value of `clockTick`.

With regard to the implementation of the inner class `Memento`, the most noteworthy thing here is that all of its members are private. Therefore, anything at all stored away in `Memento` instances is only accessible to the methods of the enclosing `HogwartsHappening` class. So while a client may store locally the instances of the `Memento` class, the client would be unable to alter in any way these objects.

```
public class HogwartsHappening {
    private int clockTick;
    private static int nextClockTick = 1;
    private String storyline;

    public HogwartsHappening() {
        clockTick = nextClockTick++;
    }
    public HogwartsHappening( int clockTick, String story ) {
        this.clockTick = clockTick;
        nextClockTick = clockTick + 1;
        this.storyline = story;
    }
    public HogwartsHappening( String story ) {
        this();
        this.storyline = story;
    }
    public String getLatestStoryline() {
        String answer = "Storyline at time " + clockTick
                            + ":  " + storyline;
        return answer;
    }
    public Memento saveStateToMemento() {
        return new Memento( clockTick, storyline );
    }
    public void restoreStateFromMemento(Memento memento) {
        nextClockTick = memento.getSavedStateClockTick() + 1;
        clockTick = memento.getSavedStateClockTick();
        storyline = memento.getSavedStateStoryLine();
    }

    public static class Memento {
        private final int clockTick;
        private final String storyline;

        private Memento( int clockTick, String story ) {
            this.clockTick = clockTick;
            this.storyline = story;
        }
```

```
        private int getSavedStateClockTick() {
            return clockTick;
        }
        private String getSavedStateStoryLine() {
            return storyline;
        }
    }
}
```

19.8   THE Client CLASS

The Client class is where we want to create stateful HogwartsHappening instances —
instances that change with the passage of time. We encode time by giving successively
larger integer values to the instance variable clockTick of the HogwartsHappening class.
Given such a time-progressive sequence of HogwartsHappening instances, at some point
in time, the client may decide to rollback the instance state to what it was at some earlier
time. For convenience, the client would want to store locally the instance states at all times,
yet — if the intent of the Memento pattern is to be followed — we don't want the client to
have direct access to those states.

In the Client class shown below, the Memento instances returned by the calls to
the saveStateToMemento() method of the HogwartsHappening class are saved as
<key,value> pairs in a hash called savedStates. The keys are the clockTick integers
for the different storyline narratives and the values the corresponding Memento instances
as returned by saveStateToMemento(). Subsequently, when the client wants to restore
the state of the latest HogswartHappening instance to an earlier state, all that the client
has to do is to call restoreStateFromMemento() with its argument set to the Memento
object that corresponds to the desired clockTick.[2] The Client class also provides a convenience variable called latestStoryline where you can store the latest plot line before
creating a HogwartsHappening instance for it.

The rest of the code in main() is for first creating in the main time flow a sequence
of HogwartsHappening objects, each corresponding to a particular clockTick and
each with its own story narrative. At the end of this sequence, which corresponds
to Hermione giving three turns to her Time-Turner machine, we restore the state of
the latest HogwartsHappening instance to what it was three hours back, meaning at
clockTick 0. This is accomplished through the restoreStateFromMemento() command that is invoked on the latest incarnation of the HogwartsHappening instance.
After issuing this command, on account of the argument supplied to the command, the
clockTick is reset to 0 and any subsequent calls to the HogwartsHappening constructor
create a new sequence of instances of that class with the new narrative that corresponds to
Buckbeak and Sirius Black making a clean escape to freedom.

---

[2]Each storyline, along with the associated clockTick, defines the state of a HogswartsHappening instance.
You may also refer to it as the instantaneous state of a HogwartsHappening object that is constantly evolving
with each clockTick.

```
import java.util.*;

public class Client {

    public static void main(String[] args) {
        String latestStoryline;
        Map<Integer, HogwartsHappening.Memento> savedStates =
                    new HashMap<Integer, HogwartsHappening.Memento>();

        // At clockTick 0:
        latestStoryline = "This is the beginning of the story of "
                    + "Buckbeak coming close to being put\n"
                    + "to death and his eventual escape "
                    + "with help from Harry and\n"
                    + "Hermione";
        HogwartsHappening hh =
                    new HogwartsHappening( 0, latestStoryline );
        savedStates.put( 0, hh.saveStateToMemento() );

        //THE ORIGINAL SEQUENCE OF EVENTS:

        // At clockTick 1:
        latestStoryline = "Harry, Ron, and Hermione set out under "
                    + "Harry's invisibility cloak to\n"
                    + "visit Hagrid to express their sympathy "
                    + "and solidarity in his moment\n"
                    + "of grief; he has just been informed by "
                    + "the Ministry of Magic that his\n"
                    + "favorite creature, the hippogriff "
                    + "Buckbeak, will be executed later that\n"
                    + "evening.\n";
        hh = new HogwartsHappening(latestStoryline );
        savedStates.put( 1, hh.saveStateToMemento() );

        // At clockTick 2:
        latestStoryline = "The execution party knocks at the door to "
                    + "Hagrid's cabin and Hagrid asks\n"
                    + "Harry, Ron, and Hermione to quickly leave "
                    + "his cabin through the back door.\n";
        hh = new HogwartsHappening(latestStoryline );
        savedStates.put( 2, hh.saveStateToMemento() );

        // At clockTick 3:
        latestStoryline = "As Harry, Ron, and Hermione are making "
                    + "their way back to the castle,\n"
                    + "Ron's rat Scabbers starts to act up, "
                    + "ostensibly because Hermione's magical\n"
                    + "cat Crookshanks is nearby. "
                    + "(As we later find out, Crookshanks\n"
                    + "knows Scabber's true identity: the rat is "
                    + "actually Peter Pettigrew, who was\n"
```

```
                        + "an Animagus, meaning one who could turn "
                        + "himself into an animal at will.\n"
                        + "Again as we later find out, it was Peter "
                        + "Pettigrew who had betrayed\n"
                        + "Harry's parents to Lord Voldemort.) "
                        + "Scabbers makes his way to a large\n"
                        + "hole in the roots of the Whomping Willow "
                        + "tree, followed by a very large dog\n"
                        + "(actually Sirius Black, also an Animagus) "
                        + "along with Ron who is dragging,\n"
                        + "followed by Crookshanks the cat, followed "
                        + "by Harry, and, finally, followed by\n"
                        + "Hermione.  This hole in the roots of the "
                        + "Whomping Willow tree leads to an\n"
                        + "underground tunnel that is a secret passage "
                        + "to Shrieking Shack just outside the Hogsmeade "
                        + "village.\n";
hh = new HogwartsHappening(latestStoryline);
savedStates.put( 3, hh.saveStateToMemento() );


// At clockTick 4:
latestStoryline = "The whole party --- Harry, Ron, Hermione, "
                + "Sirius, Crookshanks, and\n"
                + "Scabbers --- find themselves in an "
                + "upstairs room in the Shrieking Shack\n"
                + "in Hogsmeade.\n";
hh = new HogwartsHappening(latestStoryline);
savedStates.put( 4, hh.saveStateToMemento() );


//...
//...


//THE RE-TRACED SEQUENCE OF EVENTS AFTER HERMIONE
//GOES BACK IN TIME BY GIVING THREE TURNS TO HER
//TIME-TURNER MACHINE:

hh.restoreStateFromMemento( savedStates.get(0) );


// At clockTick 1:
latestStoryline = "Hermione and Harry are in a broom closet. "
                + "They can hear footsteps\n"
                + "outside that sound like three people "
                + "going down the steps to Hagrid's\n"
                + "cabin. As it turns out, these are the "
                + "footsteps of Harry, Ron, and Hermione\n"
                + "walking under the Invisibility Cloak "
                + "in the original time flow.\n";
hh = new HogwartsHappening(latestStoryline);
savedStates.put( 1, hh.saveStateToMemento() );


System.out.println( hh.getLatestStoryline() );
```

```
// At clockTick 2:
latestStoryline = "While still inside the broom closet, "
                + "Hermione and Harry puzzle over\n"
                + "Dumbledore's rather cryptic mention that "
                + "they could save two lives, not\n"
                + "just Buckbeak's, by the time travel "
                + "adventure they were on.  They put\n"
                + "two and two together and realize that "
                + "what Dumbledore meant: If they\n"
                + "are successful, they could save both "
                + "Buckbeak and Sirius Black, with\n"
                + "the former helping the latter escape.\n";
hh = new HogwartsHappening(latestStoryline);
savedStates.put( 2, hh.saveStateToMemento() );


// At clockTick 3:
latestStoryline = "Hermione and Harry set off for Hagrid's "
                + "cabin, doing their best not to be\n"
                + "discovered crossing the lawn behind the "
                + "castle by keeping in the shadows\n"
                + "of the trees.  They arrive at a "
                + "point where they can see the front door\n"
                + "to the cabin.  Hiding behind a tree, "
                + "they can see themselves from the\n"
                + "original\n time flow, along with Ron, "
                + "knocking at the door.\n";
hh = new HogwartsHappening(latestStoryline);
savedStates.put( 3, hh.saveStateToMemento() );


// At clockTick 4:
latestStoryline = "Later they see themselves leaving the "
                + "cabin through the back door as the\n"
                + "execution committee enters the cabin.  "
                + "Harry and Hermione catch sight of\n"
                + "Mcnair looking at Buckbeak through a "
                + "window.  Since the back door to the\n"
                + "cabin is open, they can also hear the "
                + "conversation taking place inside.  They\n"
                + "decide that the time has come to mount "
                + "a rescue for Buckbeak.  So Harry\n"
                + "darts to where Buckbeak is tethered to "
                + "the fence, untethers the rope, and\n"
                + "pulls Buckbeak into the trees at the edge "
                + "of the forest where he would not\n"
                + "be visible from Hagrid's cabin.  The "
                + "execution committee steps out of the\n"
                + "cabin with the idea of carrying out "
                + "Buckbeak's execution, but is surprised\n"
                + "to not see the hippogriff anywhere.\n";
hh = new HogwartsHappening(latestStoryline);
savedStates.put( 4, hh.saveStateToMemento() );
```

```
        // ...
        // ...

        System.out.println( hh.getLatestStoryline() );
    }
}
```

19.9   PLAYING WITH THE CODE

Download the class files for this pattern from the book website into a separate directory. Compile the code with the command

```
    javac *.java
```

and execute the Client class by

```
    java Client
```

Given the code in the main() of Client, executing this class will produce the following output:

```
Storyline at time 1: Hermione and Harry are in a broom
    closet.  They can hear footsteps outside that sound like
    three people going down the steps to Hagrid's cabin.  As it
    turns out, these are the footsteps of Harry, Ron, and
    Hermione walking under the Invisibility Cloak in the
    original sequence of events.

...
...


Storyline at time 4: Later they see themselves leaving
    the cabin through the back door as the execution committee
    enters the cabin.  Harry and Hermione catch sight of Mcnair
    looking at Buckbeak through a window.  Since the back door
    to the cabin is open, they can also hear the conversation
    taking place inside.  They decide that the time has come to
    mount a rescue for Buckbeak.  So Harry darts to where
    Buckbeak is tethered to the fence, untethers the rope, and
    pulls Buckbeak into the trees at the edge of the forest
    where he would not be visible from Hagrid's cabin.  The
    execution committee steps out of the cabin with the idea of
    carrying out Buckbeak's execution, but is surprised to not
    see the hippogriff anywhere.

...
...
```

For additional insights, you may consider extending the code for this pattern along the following lines:

- The current implementation of the Memento pattern has the "annoying" behavior that after a user has rolled back the state of the latest instance of HogwartsHappening, the savedStates hash maintained by the Client class does NOT wipe out all the stored states subsequent to the rollback point. The saved states corresponding to the different values of clockTick are simply overwritten as they become available. Since this creates a mixture of the expired and the new states in the savedStates store, it would be unacceptable in a production version of the Memento pattern. The fix for this problem is, however, trivial. Try fixing the problem.

- A user rolls back the state of the current instance of HogwartsHappening by invoking

```
restoreStateFromMemento( savedStates.get(0) );
```

What that implies is that, for any given rollback of the state, the user must be able to recall the time index associated with the previous state to which a rollback is desired. But, obviously, given a very long sequence of states, most users would have trouble remembering the clockTick values associated with the different instances of the HogwartsHappening class. If you are up to it, you could make a user's life easier by creating an inverted index of the keywords associated with the storylines in the different states and the corresponding values of clockTick. A user could then look up this index and decide which previous clockTick to use for the rollback. If a user has multiple keywords for the storyline of interest, by taking a set intersection of the ClockTick entries returned by the inverted index for the different keywords, the user is highly likely to zero in on the relevant clockTick value.

20

OBSERVER

20.1 SUBSCRIPTION-BASED BROADCASTING

The flow of information in a network can take various forms, the most common being *point-to-point* and *broadcast*.[1] With the former, the sender of information designates a specific receiver. And, with the latter, the information made available by the sender can be received simultaneously by all those who can access the sender in the network — unless we are talking about *subscription-based broadcasting*. In subscription-based broadcasting, each party wishing to receive the information being made available by a sending party must register itself with the latter. An example of general broadcasting would be a radio station in your area, and an example of subscription-based broadcasting would be a cable television network.

Several of the run-time behaviors between the objects created by a software system can be understood in terms of how information flows between the objects. Consider, for example, the case in which a certain object — to be referred to as the "Observable" — makes available some time-varying information that is desired by other objects. Each object that seeks this information and its updates from the Observable could certainly send a request to the Observable on a one-on-one basis and do so periodically in order to stay current with the latest updates at the Observable. This approach may work perfectly well if the number of the receiving objects is small and known at compile time.

However, from the standpoint of the computational overhead involved, the Observable is likely to find it more efficient if it can provide its information to the other objects in a subscription-based broadcast mode — especially if the receiving objects are not known at compile time. In this mode, the objects that wish to receive information from the

---

[1] How information actually flows in networks such as the internet is more complex than what is described here. At the least, it involves one more mode known as *multicasting*. A more complete description of how information flows in computer networks can be found in Chapter 15 of [6].

Designing with Objects: Object-Oriented Design Patterns Explained with Stories from Harry Potter, First Edition. Avinash C. Kak.

Observable would register themselves with it. The Observable's contract would be to broadcast any updates to the information it holds to all of the objects that have subscribed to its service. The Observer pattern teaches us how to best implement this logic.

20.2   INTENT AND APPLICABILITY

The intent of the Observer pattern is to enable dissemination of information from a designated object to all other objects that register with the provider of the information.

You should consider using this pattern when

- your application needs an object — call it the Observable — that can serve as a central repository of time varying information important to several other objects;
- the objects in your application need a mechanism to disseminate the information that they possess to other objects — possibly by posting it at the Observable;
- the objects that wish to stay synchronized with the Observable come into existence only at runtime;
- for the sake of computational efficiency, the Observable would like to update the information at only those objects that register with it.

20.3   INTRODUCTION TO THE OBSERVER PATTERN

As mentioned in the opening section of this chapter, certain inter-object behaviors at runtime are best understood in terms of how information flows between the objects. When an `Observable` object serves as a repository of some special information (which may be time-varying) that is desired by other objects, we would want the `Observable` to operate in a broadcast mode in which all of the other objects that want to stay up-to-date with the `Observable`'s information are required to register with it. These other objects that want to receive information from the `Observable` are referred to as the `Observer` objects. And the `Observers` keeping up-to-date with the `Observable` is referred to as *synchronization*.

As to what may cause the information made available by the `Observable` to change with time, that could be something resulting from a change in the state of the application itself (that is usually the case in GUI frameworks where this pattern finds extensive use) or it could be because one of the `Observers` has posted new information at the `Observable` for the purpose of its dissemination to all other `Observers`.

According to the pattern, the `Observable` class should provide registration facilities for an object to sign up as an `Observer` and, when so needed, to 'un-sign' subsequently if the `Observer` no longer wishes to receive the information provided by the `Observable`. The `Observable`'s main job, however, is to broadcast the latest changes to the information it keeps to those who have registered to receive such information. It is up to the `Observers` to, first, subscribe to the synchronization services provided by the `Observable`, and to then receive the latest state of the data store maintained by the `Observable`. Figure 20.1 depicts the relationship between the `Observable` and the `Observers`.

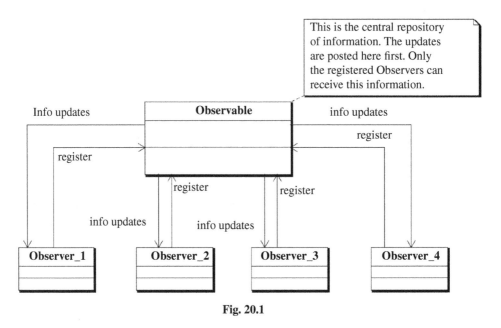

This is the central repository of information. The updates are posted here first. Only the registered Observers can receive this information.

Fig. 20.1

20.4   THE OBSERVER PATTERN IN REAL-WORLD APPLICATIONS

In one form or another, the Observer pattern plays an important role in how event processing is carried out in practically all modern GUI frameworks. In Java, for example, an interaction by a user with a GUI component "generates" an event that can only be trapped by objects that have implemented a designated Listener interface. For example, when a user clicks the mouse on a GUI button, the resulting event produced by the button can be trapped by any object whose class has implemented the ActionListener interface. If we were to draw a parallel with the Observer pattern, the Listener objects would be the Observers, and the event-generating object whose events are being trapped by the Listeners would correspond to the Observable object.

Java also comes with a class Observable and an interface Observer, both in the java.util package, that are directly based on the Observer pattern. To take a quick look at the methods for the Observable class:

```
void addObserver(Observer o)
protected void clearChanged()
int countObservers()
void deleteObserver(Observer o)
void deleteObservers()
boolean hasChanged()
void notifyObservers()
void notifyObservers(Object arg)
protected void setChanged()
```

where the first method, addObserver(), as its signature implies, adds a new Observer that will be notified of any changes to the Observable object. For an object to become

an `Observer` vis-á-vis an `Observable` object, the former must implement the `Observer` interface that contains just the following method declaration:

```
void update(Observable o, Object arg)
```

So any Java class can serve as an `Observer` if it provides implementation code for the `update()` method as declared above. As for the role played by the argument `arg`, it is supplied to the single object notification method of the `Observable`, as will be explained shortly.

The second method in the `Observable` class, `clearChanged()`, is invoked after all of the observers have been notified about the latest change to the `Observable` object. This method is called automatically by the `notifyObservers()` method. Subsequently, any invocations of the `hasChanged()` method on the `Observable` object will return false. The method `setChanged()` when invoked on an `Observable` object marks it as having changed. After `setChanged()` is invoked, the predicate `hasChanged()` will again return true. Note the signatures of the two methods named `notifyObservers()`:

```
void notifyObservers()
void notifyObservers(Object arg)
```

These are the methods that notify the observers about any changes to the `Observable` object. Regarding the difference between these two, recall that each `Observer` implements the `update(Observable o, Object arg)` method. Invocation of this method on an `Observer` instance is how the instance receives the latest update from the `Observable` object. When `notifyObservers(Object arg)` is invoked on the `Observable`, that automatically causes the invocation of `update(Observable o, Object arg)` on the `Observer` instances that have registered with the `Observable`. On the other hand, if the notification of the observers is carried out by an application invoking `notifyObservers()` on the `Observable` object, that is tantamount to calling `update(Observable o, null)` on the `Observer` instances. The behavior of the other methods listed above for the `Observable` class should be evident from their names.

Large websites that are accompanied by mirrored websites serve as another good example of what could be implemented with the Observer pattern. In such linked websites, you have a master website serving as the `Observable` where the information is posted originally. All that the mirrored sites do is to stay in sync with the master site.

20.5 HARRY POTTER STORY USED TO ILLUSTRATE THE OBSERVER PATTERN

Our demonstration of the Observer pattern is based on how the Death Eaters communicated with the Dark Lord and how he summoned them to his side. As the reader perhaps knows, the Dark Lord had imprinted a Dark Mark on the left forearm of his most trustworthy followers. When the Dark Lord wanted his followers to apparate to his side, he would touch the mark with his magic wand either on his own forearm or on that of any of his followers in his vicinity. The Death Eaters could also signal Voldemort by pressing on their own Dark Mark. From a programming standpoint, the mark served as a communication

channel and the Dark Lord touching the mark amounted to his sending a message to the Death Eaters.

To remind the reader about the Dark Mark, the mark, which looked like a a skull with a snake protruding from its mouth, was burned by Voldemort into the inside left forearm of his most loyal followers. When the Dark Lord had lost his powers, the mark faded into a dull gray. But then when he started to regain his powers, the mark began to acquire an increasingly clearer and darker color. The mark gave its wearers a burning sensation when Voldemort wanted the followers to apparate to his side.

To base a demonstration of the Observer pattern on the above narrative, we must make the Dark Lord the `Observable` and the Death Eaters the `Observers` since it is the Dark Lord's wish that the Death Eaters stay "synchronized" with him — assuming that they are loyal to the Dark Lord. Since an expression of loyalty may be construed as registering with the `Observable`, the `Observable` class must make it possible for an `Observer` instance to register with it since only the registered `Observers` receive messages from the `Observable`. We will therefore endow the `Observable` class with two methods with names like `registerWithObservable()` and `unRegisterWithObservable()`.

We must also deal with the issue of establishing a communication link between the `Observable` and an `Observer`. Whereas, in the world of magic, the Dark Lord would just know how to send a message to a loyal Death Eater regardless of the latter's location, that is not such an easy thing to bring about in the world or programming. In our demonstration, a newly registered `Observer` would need to let the `Observable` know how to communicate with it. So, when we construct an instance of an `Observer`, we provide it with the two endpoints of a communication pipe, with one endpoint intended for the Dark Lord to put his message in and with the other endpoint to be kept by the `Observer` for retrieving those messages from.

That still leaves open the question of who is going to instantiate the `Observable` and the `Observers`. There are several scenarios we can conjure up for the purpose. The scenario that would be closest to the world of magic would require the `Observable` to be instantiated at the system initialization time in the form of a `DarkLord` instance and have it running continuously as a background server process. An `Observer` (which in our case would be an instance of a `DeathEater`) wanting to register with the `DarkLord` would send an appropriate message to the server process to that effect. The server process would fork off a child client process for each such `DeathEater`. In the main server process, there would exist a continuously running loop for broadcasting the `DarkLord`'s messages to the `DeathEater` instances through the client sockets in all of the currently running child processes. This approach would create separate programs for the Dark Lord and for the Death Eaters. The main advantage of such an implementation would be that we do not have to worry about who will instantiate the `DarkLord` and who will instantiate the `DeathEater` instances, in the sense that `DarkLord` would become a continuously running server process on a machine and the `DeathEaters` would be — you could say — self-instantiating (a `DeathEater` instance would be instantiated by whosoever is executing the `DeathEater` class).

However, in order to keep the code base and its explanation compact, object instantiations in the demonstration presented in the rest of this chapter will not be based on the approach described above (despite the fact that it has a lot going for it). We will leave that type of an implementation to an exercise for the reader in Section 20.12, "Playing with the Code." Object instantiations in our demonstration will be based on defining a separate class for that purpose, as mentioned in the next section.

20.6 A TOP LEVEL VIEW OF THE PATTERN DEMONSTRATION

As mentioned in the previous section, our demonstration of the Observer pattern is based on how the Dark Lord stays in touch with his followers — the Death Eaters. As mentioned there, the Dark Lord used the Dark Mark as a signaling mechanism to indicate to his followers that they were needed by his side. We can obviously think of the Dark Mark as a sort of communication pipe between the Dark Lord and the Death Eaters. To draw a parallel between how the Dark Lord signaled the Death Eaters and our demonstration here, we can say that the burning sensation at the site of the mark on the forearm was a *message* a Death Eater would *receive* from the Dark Lord when the latter wanted to summon the former.

Thinking of the Dark Lord as the `Observable`, the Death Eaters as the `Observers`, our demonstration shows how we can use the inter-thread communication pipes in a multithreaded implementation of the `Observable` and the `Observer` classes to enable the `Observable` to immediately transmit its wishes to the `Observers`. With multithreading, the Dark Lord will scan through all of the Death Eaters who have registered with him and use the piped streams associated with the Death Eaters to immediately send them his summons. Figure 20.2 presents the class diagram for the code for this demonstration.

We will assign one thread to a singular instance of a class called `DarkLord` — the `Observable` in our demonstration. We will assign a separate thread to each instance of a class called `DeathEater`; this is the class for the `Observer` objects in our demonstration. By having these threads running concurrently, we will create an ongoing real-time interaction between the `DarkLord` and the various instances of the `DeathEater` class. The interaction will consist of the `DarkLord` "expressing" his wishes that would then be communicated in real-time to every `DeathEater` instance who has registered with the `DarkLord` instance.

As to the issue of who will instantiate the `DarkLord` and the `DeathEater` instances, it would be reasonable to assume that forces even larger than the Dark Lord decide who will or will not be a Death Eater. It is for that reason that our demonstration entails a class called `GodProcess`. The `GodProcess` class instantiates `DarkLord` as an instance of type `Observable` and has it running continuously in one thread. The `GodProcess` class also instantiates `Observer` objects in the form of `DeathEater` instances. Each `DeathEater` instance is also run continuously in a separate thread. When a `DeathEater` instance is launched, it is provided with the two endpoints of a piped stream that is used for inter-thread communication in Java. The `DarkLord` acquires one endpoint of the piped stream when the `DeathEater` instance registers with the `DarkLord`, with the other endpoint held by the `DeathEater` instance.

20.7 THE Observer INTERFACE

Shown below is the `Observer` interface. Since the Death Eaters are the observers in our demonstration, this interface is implemented by the `DeathEater` class that we present in Section 20.10.

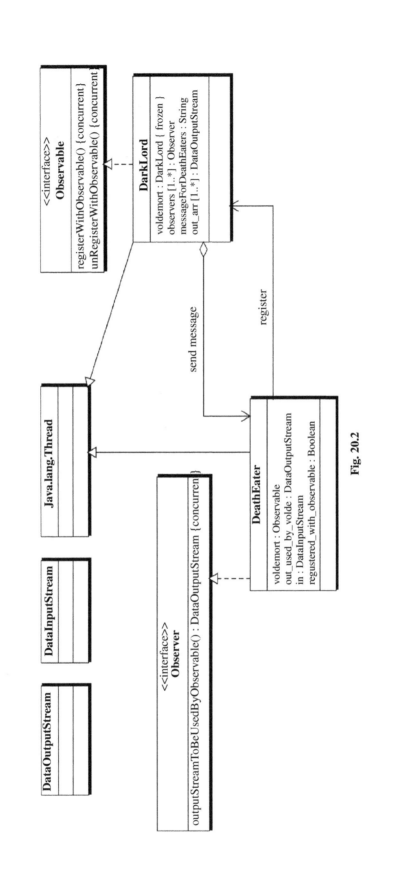

Fig. 20.2

The purpose of this interface is to just declare the `outputStreamToBeUsedBy` `Observable()` method. As its name implies, when the `Observable`, in the form of a singular instance of type `DarkLord` in our case, wants an `Observer` to receive its messages, the `Observable` will invoke this method on the corresponding `Observer` instance. The `DataOutputStream` object delivered by this method is meant to be a wrapper around a `PipedOutputStream` object whose job is to place a message meant for an `Observer` in an inter-thread communication pipe. The corresponding `DeathEater` will then receive the message from the other end of the same pipe.

```java
import java.io.*;

public interface Observer extends Runnable {
    DataOutputStream outputStreamToBeUsedByObservable();
}
```

20.8   THE Observable INTERFACE

The `Observable` interface must obviously declare the functionality that can be used by an `Observer` to register and unregister with an `Observable` object. Presumably, with our Harry Potter-based demonstration of the pattern, when an `Observer` object believes that it is loyal to the `Observable`, it will register with the `Observable`. Subsequently, it will receive messages from the `Observable`. On the other hand, when an `Observer` object no longer believes that it can remain loyal to the `Observable`, it will call on the latter's unregister method. Subsequently, no further messages from the `Observable` will be sent to that `Observer`. Shown below is the `Observable` interface for this demonstration. It declares two methods, `registerWithObservable()` and `unRegisterWithObservable()`, that can be called by an `Observer` object to to express its loyalty, or lack thereof, to the Dark Lord.

```java
public interface Observable  {
    abstract void registerWithObservable( Observer observer );
    abstract void unRegisterWithObservable( Observer observer );
}
```

20.9   THE DarkLord CLASS

We now present the `DarkLord` class. In addition to being an implementation of the `Observable` interface, this class extends the `Thread` class. A class that extends the `Thread` class (or a class that implements the `Runnable` interface) can be used as a multithreadable class. The code that is placed in the `run()` method of such a class is executed in a new thread. This works for us since we want the `DarkLord` to run continuously in a separate thread while the `DeathEater` instances are executing in their own threads. To make

certain that no single thread dominates the CPU, not even the DarkLord thread, we put this thread to sleep for a few seconds in each cycle of the code in the run() method. The main work that is carried out in each traversal through the while loop in run() is the invocation of the notifyObservers() method to notify the registered Observer instances, which are running in their own threads, that the DarkLord has a new message for them.

The design of the DarkLord class shown below is based on the Singleton pattern of Chapter 6. That is because we want to enforce the constraint that there can only be one instance of the Dark Lord. That should explain why the constructor is in the private section of the class. So the only way to create an instance of the DarkLord class is by calling the makeInstanceOfDarkLord() method.

The instance construction method is followed by the implementations for the registerWithObservable() and unRegisterWithObservable() methods. Since this class implements the Observable interface, it is required to provide implementations for these two methods. The first of these inserts an Observer instance in the list observers maintained by the DarkLord, and the second removes the argument Observer from the same list when that observer no longer wishes to receive information updates from the DarkLord.

The current DeathEater members in the list observers are sent messages through the notifyObservers() method. Note the following statement in the implementation of this method

```
DataOutputStream out = observer.outputStreamToBeUsedByObservable();
```

As mentioned earlier, when an Observer is first created, it is provided with two endpoints of an inter-thread communication pipe. One of these is meant to be used by others for sending information to the thread in which the Observer code is running and the other is for use by the same thread to receive the information sent to it. The statement shown above allows the unique DarkLord instance to get hold of the communication endpoint through which the messages can be sent to the observer.

Finally, the reader will notice that we have declared several of the methods as synchronized. A thread executing a synchronized method cannot be taken off the CPU by the thread-scheduling algorithm. It is well known that when different threads share a data object, the threads stepping on one another as they interact with the common object can corrupt the data object. In our case, the threads share the observers list.

```
import java.util.*;
import java.io.*;

public class DarkLord  extends Thread implements Observable  {

    private static ArrayList<Observer> observers =
                                        new ArrayList<Observer>();
    private static DarkLord voldemort;
    private DataOutputStream out;
    private ArrayList<DataOutputStream> out_arr;
    private String messageForDeathEaters =
```

```
                    "Bring me Harry Potter --- dead or alive";
private static int messageID = 0;

private DarkLord(){
    super();
}
public static synchronized DarkLord makeInstanceOfDarkLord() {
    if (voldemort == null) {
        voldemort = new DarkLord();
    }
    return voldemort;
}
public synchronized void registerWithObservable( Observer observer ) {
    observers.add( observer );
    System.out.println( "        The loyal " + observer
                    + " has registered with the Observable");
    int howMany = observers.size();
    System.out.println( "        Now the Dark Lord has  "
                            + howMany + " followers\n");
}
public synchronized void unRegisterWithObservable(Observer observer) {
    observers.remove( observer );
    System.out.println( "        The disloyal " + observer
                    + " has unregistered with the Observable");
    int howMany = observers.size();
    System.out.println( "        Now dark lord has  " + howMany
                    + " followers\n");
}
private synchronized void notifyObservers() {
    int this_mesg_id = messageID++;
    Iterator<Observer> it = observers.iterator();
    while (it.hasNext()) {
        Observer observer = it.next();
        try {
            DataOutputStream out =
                    observer.outputStreamToBeUsedByObservable();
            System.out.println("        Dark Lord sending message "
                + this_mesg_id + " to Death Eater " + observer);
            out.writeUTF( messageForDeathEaters + " <mesg_id: "
                            + this_mesg_id + ">");
            out.flush();
        } catch( IOException e ) {
            System.out.println(
                    "Error at sending end of pipe: " + e );
        }
    }
}
public void run() {
    int i = 0;
    while (true) {
        int howMany = observers.size();
        System.out.println( "\n\nRun " + i++ + " of the Observable "
```

```
                                        + "with " + howMany + " observers");
            notifyObservers();
            try {
                Thread.sleep(3000);
            } catch(InterruptedException e) {}
        }
    }
}
```

20.10   THE DeathEater CLASS

We now present the DeathEater class. Instances of this class are the followers of the Dark Lord. They want to hear from the DarkLord as soon as his messages become available, which happens when the Dark Lord touches with his magic wand the Dark Mark on his left forearm or on the left forearm of one of his followers. As stated earlier, the Dark Mark serves as a communication channel, and the act of touching the mark amounts to the Dark Lord sending a message to the Death Eaters.

Like the DarkLord class, the DeathEater class is also multithreadable since it extends Thread. Recall that our goal is to have the unique DarkLord instance as well as each of the DeathEater instances running in separate threads.

Regarding the code in the run() method of this class (it is this code that is executed in a separate thread for each DeathEater instance), note the variables startTime and currentTime. The former is set to the time at the moment a DeathEater instance is created and the latter to the time when the statement

```
long currentTime = System.currentTimeMillis();
```

in run() is executed. Since the code in run() is basically a while loop, the value acquired by currentTime will be what it is in a given iteration of the loop. Let's now consider the instance variable loyaltyDurationTimePeriod. In order to demonstrate that an Observer (in actuality a DeathEater instance) will receive messages from the Dark Lord *only when* the former is loyal to the latter, the DeathEater's loyalty to the DarkLord is turned off periodically. As to how long a DeathEater instance stays loyal, it is the length of the time that it takes to execute the code in run() plus the time for which the getMessageFromObservable() function is invoked at the end of each run in the loop. As the reader can see, the getMessageFromObservable() function is invoked for a time interval equal to the value of loyaltyDurationTimePeriod.

With regard to the values taken by loyaltyDurationTimePeriod, we set it to a random number between 800 milliseconds and 1300 milliseconds at the very outset. Being a random number, each DeathEater instance will have a different value for loyaltyDurationTimePeriod. This is for the sole purpose of ensuring that not all of the DeathEater instances act in lockstep with regard to their declaration of loyalty (or lack thereof) to the Dark Lord. Obviously, the demonstration would work even if we did allow for this lockstep scenario to develop, but it certainly would not be realistic from the standpoint of how we may expect the world of magic to function.

Regarding the code in the `getMessageFromObservable()` method, we divide the `loyaltyDurationTimePeriod` time interval into four quarters and put a `DeathEater` instance thread to sleep in every alternating quarter. This ensures that the other threads in our demonstration will get a fair chance at the CPU. When the `DeathEater` instance is awake, its main job is to check for any messages from the Dark Lord. Obviously, should there be a message, the `DeathEater` instance retrieves it and displays it on the console. The reader will notice that `getMessageFromObservable()` is NOT a synchronized method. Therefore, the thread in which this method is being executed cannot place a lock on it to prevent the other threads from cutting in. We do not care if another thread cuts in while a given thread is retrieving a message from the Dark Lord since we can be sure that the message would ultimately be retrieved after the given thread is back at the CPU.

Let us now focus on the following code segment in `getMessageFromObservable()`:

```
BufferedInputStream buffin = new BufferedInputStream(in);
if (buffin.available() > 0) {
    String messageReceived = in.readUTF();
    System.out.println( "         " + this
        + " received message from Dark Lord: " + messageReceived );
}
```

where the object `in` is a `DataInputStream` object that is supplied as the argument to the `BufferedInputStream` constructor and on which we invoke the method `readUTF()`. The reason we need to create a `BufferedInputStream` instance from the `DataInput Stream` object is to get around the difficulty caused by the fact that the IO provided by the latter is of the blocking variety. That is, a call such as `readUTF()` on a `DataInputStream` object will block until some data becomes available in the stream. Consequently, should it happen that there is no message to be read from the `DarkLord`, ordinarily a call to `readUTF()` will simply hang until such a message becomes available. By constructing an instance of a `BufferedInputStream` as a wrapper for the `DataInputStream` object, you can invoke the `available()` method on the `BufferedInputStream` instance to find out if the `DataInputStream` object contains bytes ready to be read.[2]

```
import java.io.*;

public class DeathEater extends Thread implements Observer {

    private DataInputStream in;
    private DataOutputStream out_used_by_volde;
    private Observable voldemort;
    private boolean loyalty_to_dark_lord;
    private boolean registered_with_observable;
    private long startTime = System.currentTimeMillis();
```

---

[2]What we achieve with the `BufferedInputStream` here is the same thing that we achieve with the `peek()` methods in C and C++ I/O. A `peek()` method, always nonblocking, allows you to find out if an input stream has any bytes available to be read.

```java
private int loyaltyDurationTimePeriod =
                            2000 + (int) (Math.random()*500);
private String name;

public DeathEater( String name, Observable observable, OutputStream ostr,
                                            InputStream istr ) {
    this.name = name;
    voldemort = observable;
    out_used_by_volde = new DataOutputStream( ostr );
    in = new DataInputStream( istr );
}
public DataOutputStream outputStreamToBeUsedByObservable() {
    return out_used_by_volde;
}
public String toString() {
    return name;
}
public void run() {
    int j = 0;
    while (true) {
        System.out.println( "\n           " + this
                                    + " starting run " + j++);
        long currentTime = System.currentTimeMillis();
        long diffTime = currentTime - startTime;
        int which_interval =
                    (int) diffTime / loyaltyDurationTimePeriod;
        if( which_interval % 2 == 1) {
            loyalty_to_dark_lord = false;
            System.out.println( "         " + this
                                    + " is no longer loyal to Dark Lord");
        } else {
            loyalty_to_dark_lord = true;
            System.out.println( "         " + this
                                    + " declares loyalty to Dark Lord");
        }
        if (loyalty_to_dark_lord) {
            if (!registered_with_observable) {
                registered_with_observable = true;
                voldemort.registerWithObservable( this );
            }
        } else {
          if (registered_with_observable) {
                registered_with_observable = false;
                voldemort.unRegisterWithObservable( this );
            }
        }
        getMessageFromObservable(loyaltyDurationTimePeriod);
    }
}
public void getMessageFromObservable( int howLong ) {
    int quarter = howLong / 4;
    for (int i=0;i<4;i++){
```

```
         if (i%2 == 0) {
            if (registered_with_observable) {
                long curr = System.currentTimeMillis();
                while (System.currentTimeMillis() <
                                        curr + quarter) {
                    try {
                        BufferedInputStream buffin =
                                    new BufferedInputStream(in);
                        if (buffin.available() > 0) {
                            String messageReceived = in.readUTF();
                            System.out.println( "        " + this
                                + " received message from "
                                + "Dark Lord: "
                                + messageReceived );
                        }
                    } catch( IOException e ) {
                        System.out.println(
                          "Error at receiving end of pipe: " + e);
                    }
                }
            } else {
                long timeAtTheMoment = System.currentTimeMillis();
                while ( (System.currentTimeMillis()
                                - timeAtTheMoment) < quarter  )
                    ;
            }
        } else {
            try {
                sleep(quarter);
            } catch( InterruptedException e ){}
        }
    }
}
}
```

20.11   THE GodProcess CLASS

Earlier, in Section 20.5, we talked about the issue of who was going to instantiate the DarkLord and DeathEater classes in our demonstration of the Observer pattern. Object instantiations would not have merited any special discussion if we had opted for a more network-centric implementation of the pattern in which the unique DarkLord instance would act as a server and the DeathEater instances as the clients vis-á-vis the server. In that kind of an implementation, the DarkLord and the DeathEater classes would have become separate programs that could work in separate processes on the same machine or in separate computers in a network.

Our demonstration, on the other hand, uses a more compact program that is based on multithreading to achieve the desired collaboration between the different classes. This requires a somewhat different approach to the construction of the instances of the classes

involved. With our multithreaded design, note that we could have placed all of the object instantiation code in the main() of, say, the DarkLord class. But since that would have created the sense of the DarkLord having complete control over when a DeathEater would be loyal to him, we decided against that approach to object instantiation. Instead, our demonstration uses a separate class, called GodProcess, that is charged with the responsibility of object instantiation. We present this class now.

In the implementation of GodProcess shown below, note that this class only has static variables and methods. The first such variable is voldemort that is set to the unique instance of the DarkLord class that we are allowed to make.

This class also maintains a list called observers whose role is *different* from a list of the same name maintained by the voldemort instance. The observers list that is maintained by voldemort, as defined in the class DarkLord, is for Voldemort to know who his loyal followers are. When a DeathEater stops being loyal to the DarkLord instance, his/her name is automatically taken off the observers list maintained by voldemort. On the other hand, the observers listed created below is the list of all of the DeathEater instances created so far by GodProcess.

The static method addNewObserver() is used by GodProcess to create a new DeathEater instance. Note how this method creates the two endpoints of an inter-thread communication pipe and gives them both for safekeeping to the DeathEater instance.

Since all of the instances created by this class are multithreadable objects, all that the main() of this class has to do is to launch the threads by invoking start() on the constructed instances. Calling start() changes the state of each thread from 'born' to 'runnable'. Subsequently, the thread scheduler program of the system can schedule the threads for time on the processor(s) available to the system.

```java
import java.io.*;
import java.util.*;

public class GodProcess extends Thread {
    static Observable voldemort = DarkLord.makeInstanceOfDarkLord();
    static ArrayList<Observer> observers = new ArrayList<Observer>();

    static void addNewObserver( String name, Observable observable ) {
        try {
            PipedOutputStream pout = new PipedOutputStream();
            PipedInputStream pin      = new PipedInputStream(pout);
            observers.add( new DeathEater( name, observable, pout, pin ));
        } catch(IOException e){
            System.out.println( "Error in creating a pipe: " + e);
        }
    }

    public static void main( String[] args ) {
        addNewObserver( "Malfoy", voldemort );
        addNewObserver( "Wormtail", voldemort );

        ((Thread) voldemort).start();

        Iterator<Observer> it = observers.iterator();
```

```
      while (it.hasNext()){
          ((Thread) it.next()).start();
      }
   }
}
```

20.12 PLAYING WITH THE CODE

Download the class files for this pattern from the book website into a separate directory. Compile the code with the command

```
javac *.java
```

and execute the GodProcess class by

```
java GodProcess
```

We will present the sort of output you will see when you execute the GodProcess class. This output that is presented below was obtained with each iteration of the while loop in the run() method of the DarkLord class being put to sleep for 3000 milliseconds and with each loop in the run() of the DeathEater class lasting roughly 2200 milliseconds.

To understand the output shown below, note that the DarkLord puts out a message for the followers only when at least one of the followers has declared his/her loyalty to the master. Since the DeathEater instances switch their loyalties approximately every 2200 milliseconds, it turns out that in the first iteration of the DarkLord loop, there are no loyal followers. Yes, we do start that loop with two loyal DeathEater instances, but the DarkLord thread does not see that because, presumably, when it gets its turn on the CPU to check on the status of the followers, they have already switched their loyalties. It is for this reason that there is no DarkLord message with ID 1 in the output shown below.

In the next iteration of the DarkLord loop, the one labeled 'Run 1', the Worm Tail DeathEater has expressed his loyalty to the Dark Lord, but the latter does not notice it since the loops in the DarkLord instance and the DeathEater instances run with different periods and since the Dark Lord checked on the loyalties of the followers before Worm Tail declared his loyalty to the Dark Lord. It is in 'Run 2' of the DarkLord loop, that the Dark Lord notices that Worm Tail is loyal to him. This message is received by Worm Tail after going through one cycle of loyalty change.

```
Run 0 of the Observable with 0 observers:

      Malfoy starting run 0
      Malfoy declares loyalty to Dark Lord
      The loyal Malfoy has registered with the Observable
      Now the Dark Lord has  1 followers

      Wormtail starting run 0
```

```
Wormtail declares loyalty to Dark Lord
The loyal Wormtail has registered with the Observable
Now the Dark Lord has  2 followers

Wormtail starting run 1
Wormtail is no longer loyal to Dark Lord
The disloyal Wormtail has unregistered with the Observable
Now the Dark Lord has  1 followers

Malfoy starting run 1
Malfoy is no longer loyal to Dark Lord
The disloyal Malfoy has unregistered with the Observable
Now the Dark Lord has  0 followers
```

Run 1 of the Observable with 0 observers:

```
Wormtail starting run 2
Wormtail declares loyalty to Dark Lord
The loyal Wormtail has registered with the Observable
Now the Dark Lord has  1 followers

Malfoy starting run 2
Malfoy is no longer loyal to Dark Lord
```

Run 2 of the Observable with 1 observers:

```
Dark Lord sending message 2 to Death Eater Wormtail

Wormtail starting run 3
Wormtail is no longer loyal to Dark Lord
The disloyal Wormtail has unregistered with the Observable
Now the Dark Lord has  0 followers

Malfoy starting run 3
Malfoy declares loyalty to Dark Lord
The loyal Malfoy has registered with the Observable
Now the Dark Lord has  1 followers

Wormtail starting run 4
Wormtail declares loyalty to Dark Lord
The loyal Wormtail has registered with the Observable
Now the Dark Lord has  2 followers

Wormtail received message from Dark Lord: Bring me
                    Harry Potter --- dead or alive <mesg_id: 2>
```

Run 3 of the Observable with 2 observers:

```
Dark Lord sending message 3 to Death Eater Malfoy
Dark Lord sending message 3 to Death Eater Wormtail
Malfoy received message from Dark Lord: Bring me
                    Harry Potter --- dead or alive <mesg_id: 3>
```

```
Wormtail received message from Dark Lord: Bring me
                       Harry Potter --- dead or alive <mesg_id: 3>

Malfoy starting run 4
Malfoy is no longer loyal to Dark Lord
The disloyal Malfoy has unregistered with the Observable
Now the Dark Lord has  1 followers

Wormtail starting run 5
Wormtail is no longer loyal to Dark Lord
The disloyal Wormtail has unregistered with the Observable
Now the Dark Lord has  0 followers
```

Run 4 of the Observable with 0 observers:

```
Malfoy starting run 5
Malfoy declares loyalty to Dark Lord
The loyal Malfoy has registered with the Observable
Now the Dark Lord has  1 followers

Wormtail starting run 6
Wormtail declares loyalty to Dark Lord
The loyal Wormtail has registered with the Observable
Now the Dark Lord has  2 followers

Malfoy starting run 6
Malfoy is no longer loyal to Dark Lord
The disloyal Malfoy has unregistered with the Observable
Now the Dark Lord has  1 followers

. . . . .
. . . . . .
```

For additional insights, you may consider extending the code for this pattern along the following lines:

- There is an asymmetry to the communications between the Dark Lord and the Death Eaters in the current demonstration — it is one-sided, from the Dark Lord to the Death Eaters. The DeathEater class creates the two endpoints of an inter-thread communication pipe, with one endpoint used by the DarkLord class to send a message to a DeathEater instance and other used by the DeathEater to receive that message. But what if a Death Eater needed to initiate communications with the Dark Lord? One way to do that would be to establish another inter-thread communication pipe with its own two endpoints. This could be done by endowing the DarkLord class with a four-argument constructor similar to what we have for the DeathEater class. If you are up to it, expand the DarkLord class in this manner and provide the rest of the code that would enable a Death Eater to send messages to the Dark Lord.
- In the current demonstration, the communication link between the Dark Lord and a Death Eater is based on an inter-thread pipe. Earlier in Section 20.5, we talked about another approach to implementing such communications — inter-process

communications. This would require that you implement this demonstration as two separate programs that could then be executed in two or more separate processes. On the one hand, you would have a server process in which you would execute the `DarkLord` class and, on the other, any number of `DeathEater` processes. As for the inter-process communications, you can use a variety of approaches. The interested reader is referred to Chapter 19 of [2] to see the different possibilities for inter-process communications in C++ and Java. If an intrepid reader decides to implement the code in a scripting language like Perl or Python, the reader might want to look up Chapter 15 of [6] to see how inter-process communications can be set up with those scripting languages.

21

STATE

21.1 CONTEXTUAL DEPENDENCE OF BEHAVIORS

Many of our personal behaviors depend on the context. Think of how you greet your family members at different times of a day. When you see them in the morning, you are likely to be short in your greetings as you will probably be in a *state* marked by an urgent need for a cup of tea or coffee. On the other hand, when you come home from work, and especially if your day did not go well, you could be in an agitated *state* of mind and how you greet others may sound even less friendly. The point here is that your behavior regarding how you greet others will depend on the context in which you engage in that behavior.

The same thing happens at a societal level. A community of people collectively is more likely to be responsive to the needs of the less fortunate during the holiday season than at other times.

The idea of the State pattern is to efficiently represent context-based dependencies of behaviors in object-oriented software. We want to refer to a given context through its *state* at any given time and then talk about how a class (or classes) behaves with respect to that state.

In general, in object-oriented programming, it is not uncommon to talk about the instances constructed from a class as being in a particular state, the state being defined by the values assigned to the instance variables. But that's *not* what we mean by *state* in this chapter. The notion of *state* used in this chapter resides at a higher level — a more global level — of conceptualization. If we had to draw an analogy with a comparable concept in purely procedural programming, what we mean by state in this chapter would be akin to using a global variable whose conditional evaluation in a control structure like `if-then` or `switch` would result in the execution of different segments of the code. Unfortunately, if these mechanisms of procedural programming are used directly in object-oriented code for injecting a global context, you are likely to end up with software that is difficult to debug and maintain. Hence the need for the State pattern.

The State pattern shows us how to program classes whose behavior depends strongly on the context chosen from a small set of high-level contexts. As you will see, with the State

Designing with Objects: Object-Oriented Design Patterns Explained with Stories from Harry Potter, First Edition. Avinash C. Kak.

pattern, each state becomes a separate class unto itself. All the classes that represent the different states present themselves to the rest of the software through a common interface. Subsequently, any state-specific functionality can be invoked through the interface.

21.2   INTENT AND APPLICABILITY

The intent of the State pattern is to enable the state of the global context to alter the behavior of a software system.

You should consider using this pattern when

- the global context for the operation of a system of classes possesses a small number of discrete characterizations that may be referred to as states;
- the global context can change at runtime and, when it does change, the run-time behavior exhibited by the software should change accordingly;
- the part of the behavior that is independent of the global context can be placed in the root class of a state-based abstraction hierarchy and the rest of the behavior in the subclasses, with each subclass specific to one state.

21.3   INTRODUCTION TO THE STATE PATTERN

The State pattern teaches us that all context-independent behaviors in an object-oriented system be abstracted out into a root class and that subsequently we create different concrete realizations of the root class, one for each context.

The alternative — having a monolithic class whose methods provide context-dependent behavior through a set of `if-then` blocks or `switch` statements — is likely to result in software that is difficult to maintain and upgrade because much of the control code for regulating the behavior is likely to be the same in the different methods. Any time you have code duplication that can be avoided — shall we refer to it as *gratuitous duplication*? — it can become a source of bugs in software. Let's say you have a large number of methods in a given class, each method with a large number of `switch` statements for dealing with the context. Now assume that at some later point in time you want to make your software responsive to a new context. You must now edit each of the methods and make nearly the same change in all of them for creating code that addresses the new context. Forgetting to do so in any of the methods would be a serious error.

With the State pattern, on the other hand, you will simply create a new concrete realization of the abstract class with context-dependent behaviors for the new context. Since all code related to the new context will be in the new subclass, you are less likely to commit an error caused by having to do the same thing over and over and forgetting to do it once.

21.4   THE STATE PATTERN IN REAL-WORLD APPLICATIONS

The software used by e-commerce websites for multi-step business transactions lends itself to modeling with the State pattern. The different states of a transaction may consist of the following: (1) choosing the items that need to be ordered; (2) placing an order; (3) making a payment; (4) arranging for shipping; and so on. Although each state of a transaction will

have elements that are unique, all of the states will share certain common behaviors, such as the behavior that allows a customer to bail out without completing a transaction, the behavior to save a transaction midstream (in a way that would allow for its continuation in a future session), and so on.

These common behaviors would obviously possess different implementations in the different states of a transaction. The logic required for saving an ongoing transaction just after an item has been selected is different from what it takes to save a transaction after, say, the credit card information has been processed. When transaction processing software is based on the State pattern, the common behaviors are all declared as abstract methods in the root transaction class. Its concrete subclasses, each corresponding to a different state, then provide state-specific implementations for these common behaviors — in addition to incorporating whatever additional functionality outside of the common behaviors is needed in each state.

Another application of the State pattern is in graphics software meant for drawing visual patterns on a virtual canvas and for editing images. Drawing typically requires a user to select a pen or a brush as a tool, to choose one of the permissible states for the tool, and to execute the strokes with the tool for the desired visual effects. The different states may correspond to the different colors and textures in a palette. Such software can be designed with a main draw class that would declare the basic stroke production methods, leaving the details of how the various visual effects are created by the strokes to the subclasses of the draw class, each subclass corresponding to a different state. Yet another application along the same lines is the image editing software. One can again conceive of the main editor class whose behavior would be regulated by the state selected for its operation. A user would again select a tool, such as a brush, whose actions with regard to, say, pixel smoothing and re-coloration would depend on which palette is chosen for the brush. Different choices from a palette would correspond to the different states of the tool.

21.5 HARRY POTTER STORY USED TO ILLUSTRATE THE STATE PATTERN

Our demonstration of the State pattern is based on writing a set of classes that can be used by a client to elicit information regarding DADA (Defense Against Dark Arts) teaching at Hogwarts. Since how DADA was taught varied considerably from year to year, we will use the year of instruction for setting the state of the context. A client interested in using our classes to get information related to DADA teaching in a particular year would need to place the system in the state corresponding to that year.

As you perhaps know, DADA teaching at Hogwarts was jinxed by Lord Voldemort when he was not selected for the job. As a result, no DADA instructor has ever lasted for more than a year. What's worse, at the end of each year, the DADA instructor invariably met some tragic end. Another important fact related to DADA teaching at Hogwarts is that, without fail, the DADA teachers made Harry Potter's life difficult inside the classroom and outside.

The goal of our demonstration is to write a program that can answer questions about the teaching of DADA at Hogwarts. These questions can be about who the teacher was in a particular year, personality quirks of the teacher, how the year ended for the teacher, and so on. Since the answers to these questions vary from year to year, we can refer to each year as a state. So we will define the following seven states: `Year1`, `Year2`, ..., `Year7`.

TABLE 21.1

State (Year)	Teacher	Termination Circumstance
Year 1	Quirinus Quirrell	Possessed by Voldemort ... died.
Year 2	Gilderoy Lockhart	Exposed for taking credit for acts of wizardry carried out by others. Ended up without memory in St. Mungo's Hospital for Magical Maladies.
Year 3	Remus Lupin	Forced to step down after Snape revealed Lupin was a werewolf.
Year 4	Alastor Moody (impersonated by Barty Crouch Jr.)	Barty Crouch Jr. was administered a Dementor's kiss and hauled off to Azkaban. Alastor Moody went back to retirement.
Year 5	Dolores Umbridge	Retrieved in an injured state from the Forbidden Forest and returned to the Ministry of Magic.
Year 6	Severus Snape	Put to death by Voldemort in his quest to gain possession of EldeWand.
Year 7	Amycus Carrow	Sent to Azkaban after the fall of Voldemort.

As a reader familiar with Harry Potter would recall, the teachers who taught DADA and how the year ended for each of them were as shown in Table 21.1.

21.6   A TOP LEVEL VIEW OF THE PATTERN DEMONSTRATION

Our goal in this demonstration is to ensure that when a question related to DADA teaching is posed to the software, its answer is supplied by a class that represents the state of the context as determined by the year to which the question applies. Toward that end, we will define seven state-specific classes with names like DADA_Year1, DADA_Year2, and so on. Each such class will contain all of the information (as far as this demonstration is concerned) for the year to which the class corresponds. All these classes will implement the root state interface defined in DADA_State. The demonstration itself would consist of DADA-teaching related questions being raised in the executable class of the code, named Hogwarts. These questions will be in the form of method invocations on an instance of a class called TeachingDADA. Before the questions are raised, the TeachingDADA instance would be supplied with the year to which the questions apply. We expect the TeachingDADA instance to use the context class appropriate to the year, but through just the interface DADA_State defined for all the context state classes.

You can think of the TeachingDADA class as serving as a font-end to the hierarchy of the state classes rooted at DADA_State. A client can only interact with TeachingDADA. The client is not expected to know how the DADA-related information is organized in the software, let alone know about state based organization of the software.

The pattern demonstration is illustrated by the class diagram shown in Figure 21.1. The important thing to note in this diagram is that the methods that define the functionality of TeachingDADA are the same as those for the interface DADA_State. Therefore, the methods that will be implemented in the concrete realizations of the state DADA_State will also be the same. So how do these methods in TeachingDADA relate to the same methods in

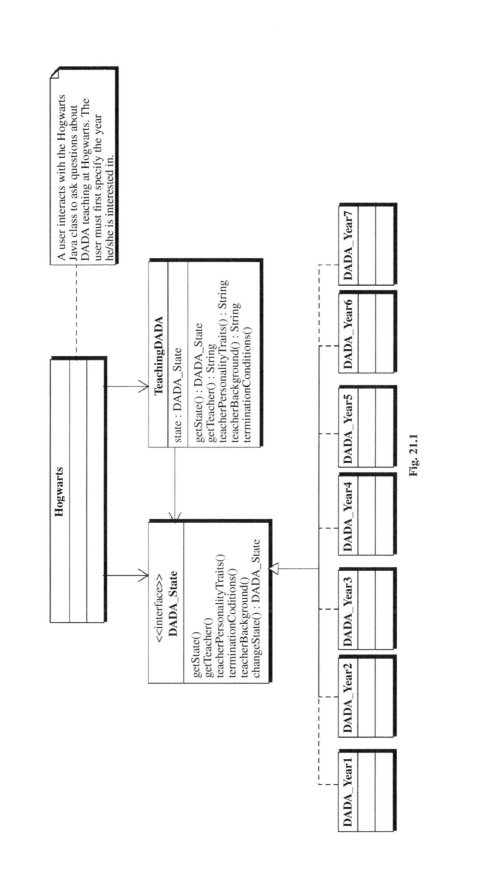

A user interacts with the Hogwarts Java class to ask questions about DADA teaching at Hogwarts. The user must first specify the year he/she is interested in.

Hogwarts

TeachingDADA

state : DADA_State

getState() : DADA_State
getTeacher() : String
teacherPersonalityTraits() : String
teacherBackground() : String
terminationConditions()

<<interface>>
DADA_State

getState()
getTeacher()
teacherPersonalityTraits()
terminationConditions()
teacherBackground()
changeState() : DADA_State

DADA_Year1

DADA_Year2

DADA_Year3

DADA_Year4

DADA_Year5

DADA_Year6

DADA_Year7

Fig. 21.1

DADA_State (and to the implementation of the latter set of methods in the concrete state classes)? The relationship is through the private variable state in the class TeachingDADA. So when a method listed under TeachingDADA is invoked (of course, on an instance of TeachingDADA), we transfer the execution to an invocation of the same method on the variable state that is instantiated to one of the states. *It is in this manner, the functionality of* TeachingDADA *becomes predicated on which state the system is in, or, to say it more precisely, on which of the concrete states the* TeachingDADA *variable* state *is bound to.*

Notice the method changeState() in the DADA_State interface. In many practical applications characterized by the notion of a state, only certain state transitions are allowed. The method changeState() is supposed to capture the state transitions that are allowed in our demonstration. By placing this method declaration in the DADA_State interface, we force each of the concrete state classes to declare what the next allowed state would be should there be a need to exit the state they represent. An alternative approach would be to declare the root DADA_State as an abstract class and to declare all the state transitions there as a data structure. We will mention this alternative approach to changing the state in Section 21.11, "Playing with the Code."

21.7   THE DADA_State INTERFACE

To revisit our main goal in this demonstration, we want to create a computer program that provides information to a user about the teaching of DADA during the seven years of the Harry Potter series of books. By information we mean the name of the teacher, any well-known quirks about the teacher, the circumstances in which the year ended for the teacher, and so on. We want to base the demonstration code on the notion of a state — the state of the context in which the DADA-related questions are posed.

Shown below is the root interface for the state classes. So any concrete state class must implement these methods. As you will see later in Section 21.9, the methods that are included here are the same for which we need functionality in the main utility class TeachingDADA that the clients interact with. The interplay between the methods of that class and any concrete state classes implementing the interface shown below was explained previously in Section 21.6.

The interface also includes a method named changeState(). Whereas the most direct method for the demonstration code to set the state of the context is through the year supplied by the client, we also want to make it possible for the state of the context to switch to the next state should the client make a request to that effect. This point will become clearer after the reader sees changeState() being called in the client code in the definition of the class Hogwarts in Section 21.10.

```
import java.util.List;

public interface DADA_State {
    public String getState();
    public String getTeacher();
    public String teacherPersonalityTraits();
    public List<String> terminationConditions();
    public String teacherBackground();
    public DADA_State changeState();
}
```

21.8   THE YEAR-BY-YEAR IMPLEMENTATION CLASSES FOR THE STATE

Since the state in our demonstration is determined by the year for which a client requires information regarding DADA teaching, we have a total of seven states for the seven years spanned by the seven books of the Harry Potter series. The previous section presented the DADA_State interface that declares the basic functionality that a user expects when he/she seeks DADA-related information for any of the seven years. This section presents the seven concrete state classes that implement the DADA_State interface for each of the seven years.

Shown below is the first of these concrete state classes. As shown, this class is based on Quirinus Quirrell being the first DADA teacher.

```java
import java.util.*;

public class DADA_Year1 implements DADA_State {

    private String teacher = "Quirinus Quirrell";

    public String getState() {
        return "Year1";
    }
    public String getTeacher() {
        return teacher;
    }
    public String teacherPersonalityTraits(){
        return "jittery and nervous; wore a turban to hide "
            + "Voldemort's visage at the back of his head";
    }
    public List<String> terminationConditions() {
        List<String> list =
            new ArrayList<String>(Arrays.asList(
                    "Possessed by Voldemort",
                    "Fought Harry Potter in the dungeons",
                    "Died as Voldemort flees his body at the end"));
        return list;
    }
    public String teacherBackground() {
        return "Was previously a muggles studies instructor";
    }
    public DADA_State changeState() {
        return new DADA_Year2();
    }
}
```

Shown below is the second state class that implements the DADA_State interface. This implementation, for Harry's second year at the school of magic, is based on Gilderoy Lockhart being the instructor that year.

```java
import java.util.*;

public class DADA_Year2 implements DADA_State {

    private String teacher = "Gilderoy Lockhart";

    public String getState() {
        return "Year2";
    }
    public String getTeacher() {
        return teacher;
    }
    public String teacherPersonalityTraits(){
        return "Boastful, narcisstic, superficial ";
    }
    public List<String> terminationConditions() {
        List<String> list =
                new ArrayList<String>(Arrays.asList(
                    "Accidently put a charm on himself",
                    "Lost his memory at the end",
                    "Ended up in St. Mungo's Hospital " +
                        "for Magical Maladies"));
        return list;
    }
    public String teacherBackground() {
        return "Authored several books on magic";
    }
    public DADA_State changeState() {
        return new DADA_Year3();
    }
}
```

Shown below is the third state class that implements the DADA_State interface. This implementation, for Harry's third year at the school of magic, is based on Remus Lupin being the instructor that year.

```java
import java.util.*;

public class DADA_Year3 implements DADA_State {

    private String teacher = "Remus Lupin";

    public String getState() {
        return "Year3";
    }
    public String teacherPersonalityTraits(){
```

```
            return "was revealed to be a werewolf by Snape; "
                + "an excellent teacher; taught Harry the "
                + "Petronous charm; recommended eating chocolate "
                + "to relieve the effects of dementors if "
                + "present nearby ";
    }
    public String getTeacher() {
        return teacher;
    }
    public List<String> terminationConditions() {
        List<String> list =  new ArrayList<String>(Arrays.asList(
                "Forced to step down after Snape reveals " +
                                        "Lupin as a werewolf"));
        return list;
    }
    public String teacherBackground() {
        return null;
    }
    public DADA_State changeState() {
        return new DADA_Year4();
    }
}
}
```

The implementation shown below, for Harry's fourth year at Hogwarts, parallels those of the three previous classes in this section. Central to the definition is the fact that while Alastor Moody was the officially designated DADA instructor for that year, the class was actually taught by his impersonator Barty Crouch Jr.

```
import java.util.*;

public class DADA_Year4 implements DADA_State {

    private String teacher =
                "Alastor Moody -- impersonated by Barty Crouch Jr.";

    public String getState() {
        return "Year4";
    }
    public String teacherPersonalityTraits(){
        return "Bartemius Crouch Jr. used the polyjuice potion to "
            + "impersonate Alastor Moody so effectively that no one "
            + "could tell the difference until the very end of the "
            + "year when other circumstances gave the former away; "
            + "Moody was a retired gruff wizard who had a wooden "
            + "leg, had an erie looking magical eye that could see "
            + "in all directions, and who in his younger days was "
            + "known to have been a ferocious pursuer of the "
```

```
                + "wizards who had gone over to the dark side. "
                + "Crouch Jr.'s impersonation did not belie any of "
                + "these personality traits of Moody";
    }
    public String getTeacher() {
        return teacher;
    }
    public List<String> terminationConditions() {
        List<String> list =  new ArrayList<String>(Arrays.asList(
                    "At the end of the year, Barty Crouch, Jr. was "
                + "administered the truth serum since his "
                + "behavior was inconsistent with what was "
                + "expected of Moody",
                    "His true identity revealed, he was administered "
                + "the Dementor's kiss and hauled away to Azkabahn",
                    "Moody was freed; he went back to retirement" ));
        return list;
    }
    public String teacherBackground() {
        return null;
    }
    public DADA_State changeState() {
        return new DADA_Year5();
    }
}
```

We now present the next concrete implementation of the DADA_State interface — this one is for Harry's fifth year at Hogwarts. Dolores Umbridge was the instructor during that year.

```
import java.util.*;

public class DADA_Year5 implements DADA_State {

    private String teacher = "Dolores Umbridge";

    public String getState() {
        return "Year5";
    }
    public String teacherPersonalityTraits(){
        return "Not conversant with the practical side of DADA;  "
                + "made students learn by just reading the book; "
                + "an agent of the Ministry of Magic, sent to Hogwarts "
                + "by the ministry to deal with Harry Potter's "
                + "assertion (which was supported by Dumbledore) that "
                + "Voldemort had returned to power; imposed harsh "
                + "punishment on Harry Potter to get him to disavow "
                + "his belief in Voldemort's return ; hated by most "
```

```
              + "students and staff" ;
    }
    public String getTeacher() {
        return teacher;
    }
    public List<String> terminationConditions() {
        List<String> list =  new ArrayList<String>(Arrays.asList(
            "Removed from Hogwarts after the Ministry of Magic "
          + "admitted to the fact that Voldemort had returned to "
          + "power",
            "Was hauled away to the forbidden forest in an "
          + "injured state",
            "Eventually returned to the Minstry of Magic"));
        return list;
    }
    public String teacherBackground() {
        return null;
    }
    public DADA_State changeState() {
        return new DADA_Year6();
    }
}
}
```

What follows is the implementation of the DADA_State interface for the sixth year of Harry's stay at Hogwarts that saw Severus Snape teaching DADA.

```
import java.util.*;

public class DADA_Year6 implements DADA_State {

    private String teacher = "Severus Snape";

    public String getState() {
        return "Year6";
    }
    public String teacherPersonalityTraits(){
        return "Wanted to be a DADA teacher, but mostly taught "
              + "potions, until the sixth year when he got his wish; "
              + "An expert potions maker; An oppressive teacher;  "
              + "Was always rough on Harry Potter";
    }
    public String getTeacher() {
        return teacher;
    }
    public List<String> terminationConditions() {
        List<String> list =  new ArrayList<String>(Arrays.asList(
            "Used his magical powers to make Voldemort believe in "
          + "his loyalty to the Dark Lord",
            "At the end, Voldemort puts him to death believing that "
```

```
                    + "by doing so he would gain possession of the ElderWand",
                      "Passes on his memories to Harry Potter as he is dying",
                      "His loyalty to the good side, often in doubt, "
                    + "is finally restored by Harry Potter"));
            return list;
        }
        public String teacherBackground() {
            return "His being in love with Lily Potter and his hating "
                + "James Potter had much to do with his emotions "
                + "vis-à-vis Harry";
        }
        public DADA_State changeState() {
            return new DADA_Year7();
        }
    }
```

Finally, here is the implementation of the DADA_State interface for the seventh year of the Harry Potter story when Harry did not actually attend Hogwarts:

```
import java.util.*;

public class DADA_Year7 implements DADA_State {

    private String teacher = "Amycus Carrow";

    public String getState() {
        return "Year7";
    }
    public String teacherPersonalityTraits(){
        return "A Death Eater; Fought on the side of Voldemort; "
            + "Tortured students for punishment; ";
    }
    public String getTeacher() {
        return teacher;
    }
    public List<String> terminationConditions() {
        List<String> list =  new ArrayList<String>(Arrays.asList(
                            "Arrested after Voldemort's fall",
                            "Presumably sent to Azkaban" ));
        return list;
    }
    public String teacherBackground() {
        return null;
    }
    public DADA_State changeState() {
        return null;
    }
}
```

21.9   THE TeachingDADA CLASS

As the reader will recall, our demonstration of the State pattern is based on constructing a mini "educational tool" that can respond to a user's questions about DADA teaching at Hogwarts. The sort of questions that can be posed are defined in the interface DADA_State, and the concrete classes that implement this interface are named DADA_YearX for X from 1 through 7. The interface for the state classes and its seven concrete implementations were presented in the previous two sections.

In addition to those state classes, we also need a class that can serve as a "front end" for user interaction. That role is served by the TeachingDADA class shown below. It is in an instance of this class that you specify the context of a user's queries through one of the seven state classes. After the state of the context is fixed, the TeachingDADA object automatically directs the DADA-related user queries to the applicable concrete state class.

You can think of TeachingDADA as defining the context generally and of the seven state classes of the previous section as the means to making the context specific. The precise mechanism for making the context specific consists of first instantiating one of the seven state classes and then supplying that as an argument to the constructor of the TeachingDADA class. Note how the TeachingDADA class *isolates the state classes from a client of the software.*

The TeachingDADA class has an instance variable state of type DADA_State. Any questions posed to an instance of TeachingDADA (that is, any methods invoked on an instance of this class) are translated into method invocations on the state chosen through the instance variable state.

```java
import java.util.List;

public class TeachingDADA {

    private static DADA_State state;

    public TeachingDADA( DADA_State state ) {
        this.state = state;
    }
    public String getState() {
        return state.getState();
    }
    public String getTeacher(){
        return state.getTeacher();
    }
    public String teacherPersonalityTraits() {
        return state.teacherPersonalityTraits();
    }
    public List<String>  terminationConditions() {
        return state.terminationConditions();
    }
    public String teacherBackground() {
        return state.teacherBackground();
    }
}
```

21.10   THE Hogwarts CLASS

So far we have defined a set of state classes and the class TeachingDADA in which one of those state classes is used to make the context specific. As mentioned in the previous section, TeachingDADA defines the context generally. The specificity that the context must acquire before a user's questions about DADA teaching can be answered is through one of the concrete state classes. The TeachingDADA class translates the method invocations on itself into the corresponding method invocations on the chosen state class.

We now define a client class that poses DADA-related queries to the TeachingDADA class. We call this class Hogwarts because, conceivably, what we show here could be a small part of a much larger class, named after the school itself, that is meant for supplying all kinds of information about Hogwarts.

In the class definition that follows, we construct an instance of a concrete state class and feed it as the argument to the constructor of TeachingDADA. Subsequently, we "simulate" the process of a user asking questions by invoking methods on the constructed instance of TeachingDADA. It goes without saying that a more realistic scenario for the use of this pattern would entail a GUI-based interaction with a human user. Depending on the information supplied by the user, an expanded version of the class shown here would automatically construct an instance of the applicable state class and use that to construct an instance of TeachingDADA. After that, the user could be presented with a menu of items on which the system has information related to DADA teaching for the year selected by the user. The user clicking on any of those items would cause the invocation of a method specific to that item on the instance of TeachingDADA.

```
public class Hogwarts {

    public static void main(String[] args) {
        // If the human is interested in finding about DADA during
        // the first year of Harry Potter's stay at
        // Hogwarts, instantiate the concrete state DADA_Year1
        // and supply it as an argument to the context
        // class TeachingDADA() as shown below:
        DADA_State year1 = new DADA_Year1();
        TeachingDADA  dada_class = new TeachingDADA( year1 );
        System.out.println( dada_class.getTeacher() );
        System.out.println( dada_class.teacherPersonalityTraits() );
        System.out.println( dada_class.terminationConditions() );

        // If the human is interested in finding about DADA during
        // the second year of Harry Potter's stay at
        // Hogwarts, instantiate the concrete state DADA_Year2 and
        // supply it as an argument to the context
        // class TeachingDADA() as shown below:
        DADA_State year2 = new DADA_Year2( );
        dada_class = new TeachingDADA( year2 );
        System.out.println( dada_class.getTeacher() );
        System.out.println( dada_class.teacherBackground() );
        // and so on ...

        // Experiment with state switching:
```

```
            DADA_State  new_state = year2.changeState();
            dada_class = new TeachingDADA( new_state );
            System.out.println( dada_class.getTeacher() );
            System.out.println( dada_class.teacherBackground() );
            // and so on ...
    }
}
```

21.11   PLAYING WITH THE CODE

Download the class files for this pattern from the book website into a separate directory. Compile the code with the command

```
    javac *.java
```

and execute the Hogwarts class by

```
    java Hogwarts
```

Given the code in the main() of Hogwarts, executing this class will produce the following output:

```
    Quirinus Quirrell

    jittery and nervous; wore a turban to hide Voldemort's
    visage at the back of his head

    [Possessed by Voldemort, Fought Harry Potter in the dungeons,
                Died as Voldemort flees his body at the end]

    Gilderoy Lockhart

    Authored several books on magic

    Remus Lupin

    null
```

For additional insights, you may consider extending the code for this pattern along the following lines:

- Recall that the method changeState(), declared first in the root interface DADA_State in Section 21.7 and then implemented in each of the seven concrete state classes in Section 21.8, captures the state transitions that are allowed. This way, each concrete state class knows the next state when there needs to be an exit from the state the class represents. An alternative approach to the representation of state transitions

in our code would be to declare the root DADA_State as an abstract class and to have it contain all of the state transitions in one place in some convenient data structure, as was, for example, done in our demonstration of the Mediator pattern code. See if you can create an implementation that is based on this other approach to the representation of state transitions.

- The list of questions defined in the root interface DADA_State in Section 21.7 is pretty minimal for the question answering educational tool that is supposedly the goal of our demonstration. How about expanding this list to give more power to the demonstration of the pattern?

- As mentioned in our description of the Hogwarts class, in order to be more convincing, what our demonstration needs is a GUI-based interaction between the human user, the TeachingDADA class, and the seven state classes. If you are up to it, create this GUI front-end to the demonstration code along the lines described in Section 21.10. If you are not familiar with how to write GUI code in Java, you might wish to look up Chapter 17 of [2].

22

STRATEGY

22.1 STRATEGIES IN THE PURSUIT OF GOALS

It goes without saying that if you pursue a difficult goal, you will encounter challenges along the way.

As a case in point, consider a young woman who has just been admitted to a university and whose goal is to earn a bachelor's degree. She must obviously surmount a large number of problems in order to meet the goal, not the least of which are the need to do well in her classes and to make certain that she has the financial means to cover the tuition and her room and board. If she is expected to work part time to defray a portion of the cost of her education, she would need to balance the number of hours worked each week against the course load. She would obviously need to formulate a *strategy* for how to best achieve the end goal given the competing demands on her time.

What's interesting is that, in most cases, the number of solutions available to such a student for each problem expected to be encountered would be rather small. For example, with respect to the time spent working, the available solutions are likely to lend themselves to characterizations such as "a quarter-time job," "a half-time job," etc. Along the same lines, the solutions to the problem of how large an academic load to carry in a semester would be in terms of the number of credit hours she should sign up for. When she chooses a solution for each of these problems, all the solutions taken together would constitute her *strategy* for the semester. Since the total number of available strategies is likely to be small (and that fact plays an important role in the Strategy pattern, as you will soon see), before starting each semester the student should be in a position to easily analyze (consciously or subconsciously) the strategies available for the semester and choose the one that would work the best for that semester.

In general, a *strategy* is the combination of your solution choices for each of the problems you will face in your pursuit of a goal. That is, if you expect to encounter N problems on your way to the goal and you make a choice for how to solve each of those problems, the N solutions taken together would constitute your *strategy* for reaching the goal. In general,

Designing with Objects: Object-Oriented Design Patterns Explained with Stories from Harry Potter, First Edition. Avinash C. Kak.

there will exist multiple strategies for reaching the goal and you will choose one based on your abilities and resources.

22.2   INTENT AND APPLICABILITY

For problems that involve multiple steps whose solutions are subject to choice, the intent of the Strategy pattern is to first define an abstract root class that contains a generic strategy. Subsequently, the subclasses derived from the root provide strategy-specific overrides for the various steps listed in the generic strategy.

You should consider using this pattern when

- the overall problem that your code solves is complex — in the sense that it consists of multiple steps and there exists choice for tackling the steps;
- stringing together specific solution choices for the different steps of the overall problem can be characterized as a strategy;
- you can conceive of a generic overall strategy that may be nothing more than a declaration of the sequence in which the various steps must be tackled.
- you can place a generic overall strategy in an abstract root class and then have its strategy-specific subclasses provide overrides for the various steps of the problem.

22.3   INTRODUCTION TO THE STRATEGY PATTERN

The Strategy pattern addresses the issue of how to best organize the code when the problem it needs to solve is complex and requires a multi-step solution — *especially when choices exist for tackling the individual steps.* Lumping all of the code together in such situations can make for a body of software that requires frequent conditional evaluations in order to figure out the best choice to make for each of the steps that goes into the overall solution. Such code is likely to be difficult to comprehend, debug, and maintain.

Now consider the case when the different alternatives for tackling each of the steps can be organized into a small number of categories. To the extent that these categories represent alternative approaches for getting the job done, we can refer to them as strategies in the sense defined in the opening section of this chapter. If each of the strategies could be separated out into a class by itself, and if each such class was an implementation of an interface whose method declarations represented the different steps of the overall solution, we are likely to end up with code that is much easier to comprehend, debug, and maintain. This approach would amount to an implementation of the Strategy pattern.

As illustrated by Figure 22.1, the Strategy pattern shows us how one can implement a run-time selection of strategy for achieving a goal. You first formulate a generic strategy in terms of the abstract method calls that address the various problems expected to be encountered in reaching the goal. When this strategy is executed at runtime through an instance of a specific concrete strategy class, the method calls in the generic strategy would be executed according to the implementation code in the concrete strategy class chosen.

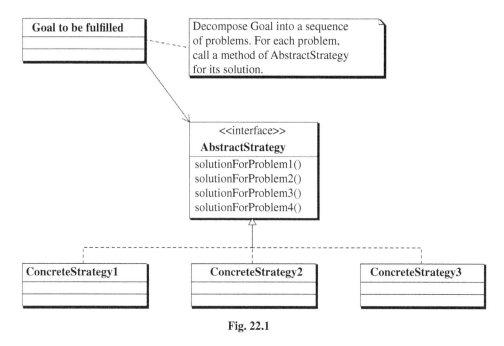

Fig. 22.1

In this manner, you customize a generic strategy to one that is concrete on the basis of certain run-time parameters that indicate what "abilities" and "resources" are available for reaching the goal.

22.4   THE STRATEGY PATTERN IN REAL-WORLD APPLICATIONS

In terms of the code organization achieved, what is accomplished by the Strategy pattern is very much the same as what is achieved by the State pattern presented in the previous chapter. If you stretch your imagination and think of each state as standing for a strategy, you can see the conceptual similarity between the two patterns. Therefore, it is possible for all of the real-world applications we described for the State pattern as also being implementable with the Strategy pattern.

Despite this similarity between the State and the Strategy patterns, there exists an important difference between the two — that of the notion of state transitions for the case of the State pattern. In general, any time one talks about a system being in a state, one is also likely to talk about the system transitioning from one state to another. As a case in point, recall from Section 21.4 of the previous chapter how a business transaction server can be modeled with the State pattern. As mentioned there, a business transaction goes from one state to another state in a specific order — all the way from the first state, in which the customer selects the items to order, to the last state in which the he/she supplies the shipping information. A software implementation based on the State pattern is likely to automatically detect the end of each state and to then place the system in the next state as dictated by the permissible state transitions for the system. *The notion of state transitions is not relevant to the Strategy pattern.* The purpose of the Strategy pattern is simply to take you

from a set of input conditions to the output as dictated by the strategy you chose. The circumstances that prevail when the output is reached would usually not lend themselves to further processing by one of the other strategies.

You might say that the Strategy pattern is more goal focused and the State more process focused. For the State pattern, the process can — at least in principle — continue to cycle through a set of states forever. On the other hand, the Strategy pattern will first help you choose a particular strategy given your resources and abilities, and then take you from your starting condition to the end goal.

Consider a software system in which a set of classes must work together to achieve a certain end goal. However, the functionality that is invoked from the classes may depend on what hardware and software resources are available for achieving the goal. If the classes are sufficiently rich — in the sense that they can provide for different ways of getting to the same endpoint, with the choices depending on the available resources — you should be able to use the Strategy pattern to orchestrate the run-time interactions between the classes.

22.5   HARRY POTTER STORY USED TO ILLUSTRATE THE STRATEGY PATTERN

Our demonstration of the Strategy pattern is based on the second task of the Triwizard Tournament for choosing the best young wizard or witch among the competing schools. Ordinarily, each of the three schools of magic is represented by a champion in the tournament. All of the students who wish to compete are allowed to put their names in the Goblet of Fire, and on a designated day the Goblet picks out for each school the student who would be its champion in the tournament. The champions compete at three tasks chosen by a committee that includes the headmasters of the competing schools.

The normal rules under which the tournament is conducted were violated in 1994 when the Goblet of Fire was made to believe (as a result of the Confundus Charm placed on the Goblet by Barty Crouch Jr., who was impersonating Alastar Moody as the DADA teacher) that there would be four schools participating in the tournament that year. Since Barty Crouch Jr. had also placed Harry Potter's name in the Goblet and since Harry was the only one associated with the fourth fictitious school, the Goblet spat out his name as the fourth champion — much to everyone's consternation. Since the Goblet spitting out a name constituted a magical contract that bound the student to compete, Harry Potter had no choice but to participate in the Tournament. As a consequence, there were four champions competing in the Tournament: Fleur Delacour for the Beauxbatons Academy of Magic, Viktor Krum for the Durmstrang Institute, and Cedric Diggory and Harry Potter for Hogwarts.

For the second task — the demonstration code in this chapter is based on this task — the champions were told that the golden egg they had retrieved in the first task would give them a clue to what they were required to do for the task. While that sounded simple, the problem was that when the champions opened the egg, it just wailed and shrieked and made on sense at all. So the first challenge for the champions was to figure out how to get the egg to reveal the clue it contained. As it turned out, at least for Harry Potter, this puzzle was solved by Cedric Diggory telling him how to get the egg to cooperate — by opening it under water. Cedric, who was supplied this information by the DADA teacher Alastor Moody (in reality by Barty Crouch Jr. who was pretending to be Alastor Moody), was an honorable individual. He felt he had to share this crucial piece of information with Harry in order to reciprocate Harry's help in the first task. Although Cedric shared the information

with the best of intentions, the irony is that that's exactly what Barty Crouch Jr. wanted him to do so that Harry would not drop out of the Tournament.

As to the clue revealed by the egg, it said that the champions had to swim underwater to merpeople's village under the large lake at Hogwarts (known as Black Lake), retrieve from that location someone who was close to them, and do so within one hour. So the next major challenge for the champions was to figure out how to swim under water for such a long time. It is this specific part of the Tournament — solving the problem of swimming under water for a long time — that we use to name the different strategies in our demonstration of the Strategy pattern.

The champions chose different solutions for swimming under water. Both Cedric Diggory and Fleur Delacour decided to use the Bubble Head Charm, which meant surrounding your head under water with a bubble of air. On the other hand, Viktor Krum chose Transfiguration, which meant transforming yourself into a creature of the sea for the duration of the competition — Viktor chose to turn himself into a shark. (Unfortunately for Viktor, his transfiguration was only partially successful; only his head became that of a shark, with the rest of him remaining unchanged.) And, finally, Harry Potter decided to chew gillyweed, which caused him to grow gills for breathing under water and fins for swimming faster. How Harry came upon this idea is a story unto itself that we will not go into here.

With regard to the demonstration presented in this chapter, what is important is that each solution to the problem of underwater breathing had a bearing on the other problems involved in solving the second task. These other problems included fending off grindylows (these are small magical creatures with long fingers that they use to snare their prey), locating the merpeople village and the hostages in the village, freeing the hostages who had been tied to the tail of a stone merperson (this meant cutting the ropes used to tie the hostages), and so on. For example, with his transfiguration into a shark, it was not possible for Viktor Krum to use his shark teeth to cut the ropes that bound Hermione Granger, the "object" that he was supposed to retrieve from under the lake. Harry had to draw his attention to a nearby rock with sharp edges that had done the job for Harry and could now be used by Viktor.

In our demonstration code, we will name the strategies after the method used for breathing underwater, since that is basic to success in the second task of the tournament. The strategies, however, will include solutions for all of the problems encountered in the completion of the second task of the tournament. Whether or not a champion is able to execute the solutions in a strategy would depend on his/her abilities and the resources at his/her disposal.

22.6   A TOP LEVEL VIEW OF THE PATTERN DEMONSTRATION

The Strategy pattern teaches us how to formulate a "plug and play" approach to the run-time selection of a concrete strategy for achieving a goal. With this pattern, we first construct a generic abstract strategy for achieving the goal using general method declarations in a root abstract strategy class. Subsequently, through a concrete strategy class chosen at runtime, we obtain a working solution that is best with regard to the abilities and the resources available for achieving the goal.

Figure 22.2 presents the class diagram for our demonstration of the Strategy pattern. Note in particular the role played by the abstract class `StrategyAbstractRoot` that is the parent of three concrete strategy classes. The parent class declares and, for programming convenience, also provides default definitions for the functionality that all concrete strategy

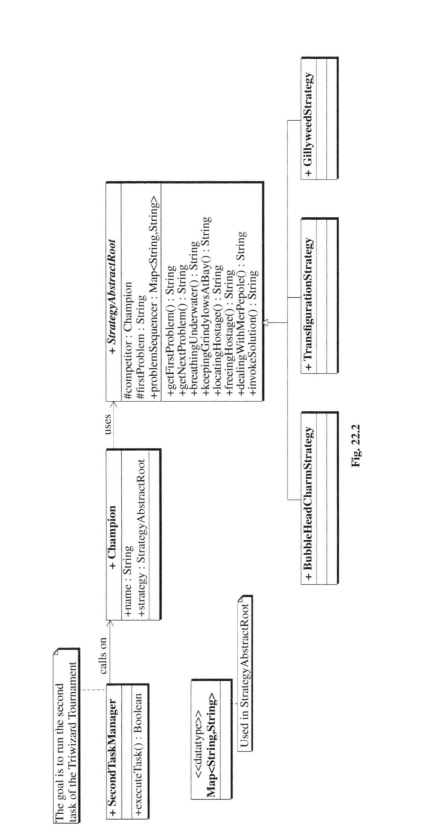

Fig. 22.2

classes must possess. In all concrete strategy classes, choosing a strategy would imply choosing a method for breathing under water, finding a way to keep the grindylows at bay, locating the merpeople village and the hostages in the village, finding a way to cut the ropes that bind the hostages to the stone merperson, and, finally, finding a way to deal with the merpeople if they try to obstruct safe retrieval of the hostages. The concrete strategy classes must, first and foremost, prescribe a way to swim under water, and, secondarily, also provide solutions for dealing with the other problems encountered during the second task.

The specific strategy a champion selects depends, obviously, on the abilities of the champion. For example, if a champion did not know how to carry out transfiguration, the champion would not be able to use the Transfiguration strategy. Along the same lines, if a champion was not aware of the fact that ingesting gillyweed gives you gills for breathing underwater, the champion would not even think of using the Gillyweed strategy.

Therefore, for this demonstration, it is important that we be able to specify whether or not a champion has what it takes to solve each of the problems in the task. This is where the class `Champion` comes in. This class is equipped with a set of boolean attributes whose truth values indicate whether a champion would be able to solve the problems that will be encountered. Although, for the sake of keeping the demonstration simple, we default-set all of these attributes to true in the `Champion` class, when constructing specific champion instances, we can customize these attributes for each champion depending on his/her individual abilities and solution choices. The class `Champion` comes with 'set' methods that can change the default values for these boolean instance variables.

In order to understand the overall organization of the code and how the different classes in Figure 22.2 collaborate, the reader would need to appreciate the relationship between the following three entities: (1) the *problems*; (2) the *methods* as declared in the root strategy class `StrategyAbstractRoot`; and (3) the *strategies*. The *problems* are what the champions encounter as they execute the second task of the Tournament, the first of these being the problem of breathing under water. The *methods* declared in the `StrategyAbstractRoot` class are for providing solutions to the problems. The methods return strings that state how a problem would be solved under a given strategy. Finally, a *strategy* is composed of the solutions, these being the descriptions provided for the methods declared in the root strategy class.

In case the reader is curious as to where the problems that the champions will face in the second task of the Tournament are cataloged in our demonstration code, it is in the `StrategyAbstractRoot` class. The `HashMap` container `problemSequencer` of this class that you will see in the next section defines all of the problems of the second task.

The overall execution of the second task of the Tournament is orchestrated by the client class `SecondTaskManager`. As the reader will see later in Section 22.10, this orchestration is an interplay between the following two methods: `executeTask(champion)` of the class `SecondTaskManager` and `invokeSolution(problem, champion)` of the class `StrategyAbstractRoot` (which is inherited by all concrete strategy classes). The `executeTask()` method takes up each of the problems, in the sequence dictated by the method `getNextProblem()` of the `StrategyAbstractRoot` class, and seeks its solution by calling `invokeSolution()`, also of the same class.

Hopefully the reader is able to see from this top-level description of the demonstration that the Strategy pattern is useful when you have a number of different strategies for reaching a goal and when all of the strategies can be described in terms of the same set of methods that would, in general, possess different implementations in the different strategies. When such is the case, we can define an abstract root strategy class and equip it with

the declarations of the aforementioned methods. The concrete strategy classes containing implementation code for the methods may then be derived from the abstract root strategy class. This allows a solution for reaching the goal to be described in a generic fashion in terms of the method declarations in the abstract root strategy class. Dynamic bindings created at runtime to an instance of a concrete strategy class can then customize the generic solution to that particular strategy.

Regarding the *generic solutions* that can be created out of just the problem-solving method declarations in the root class StrategyAbstractRoot, in the material that follows, the reader should pay close attention to how the invokeSolution() method of the root strategy class and the executeTask() method of the SecondTaskManager class work in tandem to give us a *generic solution to reaching the goal* — which in our case is for a champion to retrieve a hostage from the merpeople village under the Black Lake at Hogwarts.

22.7   THE ABSTRACT ROOT CLASS FOR STRATEGIES: StrategyAbstractRoot

Much of what was said in the previous section dealt with the design of the class we present in this section. That was because this class plays a central role in our demonstration.

Regarding the implementation code shown below, recall from the previous section that the main purpose of the root strategy class StrategyAbstractRoot is to declare the methods that when taken together define a generic strategy. These methods are declared in the last five statements of this class. Purely for the sake of programming convenience, we also provide default implementations for these methods — they all return null. That is, by default, a concrete strategy will not provide a non-null solution for a method unless it provides an override implementation for the method.

Task execution for fulfilling the goal of the tournament requires that we take up the problems in the sequence in which they will be encountered by the champions, with the first problem obviously being that of breathing under water. This sequencing of the problems is regulated by the HashMap problemSequencer and the method getNextProblem() shown in the class definition.

The invokeSolution(problem, champion) method tells us how a champion may solve the problem that is supplied to it as its first argument. This method returns non-null — actually a string that indicates the solution to the problem under the strategy on which the method is invoked — only when a champion has the ability to solve the problem in question. So you could say that the method invokeSolution() is the link between the Champion class and the Strategy classes.

```
import java.util.*;

public abstract class StrategyAbstractRoot {

    protected Champion competitor;
    protected String firstProblem = "breathingUnderwater";

    protected static Map<String,String> problemSequencer =
                            new HashMap<String,String>();
```

```
{
    problemSequencer.put("breathingUnderwater",
                                    "keepingGrindylowsAtBay");
    problemSequencer.put("keepingGrindylowsAtBay",
                                        "locatingHostage");
    problemSequencer.put("locatingHostage", "freeingHostage");
    problemSequencer.put("freeingHostate",
                                        "dealingWithMerpeople");
}


public static String getNextProblem( String problem ){
    return problemSequencer.get(problem);
}
public String invokeSolution(String problem, Champion champ) {
    if (problem == "breathingUnderwater"
            && champ.getHasSolutionForBreathingUnderwater()  ) {
        return this.breathingUnderwater();
    } else if (problem == "keepingGrindylowsAtBay"
            && champ.getHasSolutionForKeepingGrindylowsAtBay()  ) {
        return this.keepingGrindylowsAtBay();
    } else if (problem == "locatingHostage"
            && champ.getcanLocateHostage() ) {
        return this.locatingHostage();
    } else if (problem == "freeingHostage"
            &&  champ.getCanFreeHostage() ) {
        return this.freeingHostage();
    } else if (problem == "dealingWithMerpeople"
            &&   champ.getCanDealWithMerpeople()  ) {
        return this.dealingWithMerpeople();
    } else {
        return null;
    }
}
public String getFirstProblem() { return firstProblem; }
public String breathingUnderwater(){ return null; }
public String keepingGrindylowsAtBay() { return null; }
public String locatingHostage() { return null; }
public String freeingHostage() { return null; }
public String dealingWithMerpeople() { return null; }
}
```

22.8   THE CONCRETE STRATEGY CLASSES

This section presents the three concrete strategy classes derived from the abstract root class presented in the previous section.

We start with the BubbleHeadCharmStrategy as a concrete extension of the root StrategyAbstractRoot. This concrete class represents the strategy that was used by Cedric Diggory and Fleur Delacour for breathing under water and for solving the other problems associated with the retrieval of the hostages from the underwater merpeople village.

As for the override implementations for the problem-solving methods in the root class StrategyAbstractRoot, what we show are simple string declarations of what is involved in each solution. Obviously, these override definitions could be made more elaborate — at the risk of distracting us from the main point of this demonstration, which is to show how the various classes interact in order to achieve the behavior called for by the Strategy pattern.

Recall that a concrete strategy class inherits the instance variables competitor, of type Champion, and firstProblem, of type String, from the root strategy class. Also inherited from the root class is the HashMap container problemSequencer and the method getNextProblem(). These inherited instance variables and methods allow the SecondTaskManager class to put to work a concrete strategy class, such as the one shown below, for orchestrating the behavior of a champion executing the second task of the tournament. An important role played in this orchestration is by the method invokeSolution() that is also inherited by the class shown below from StrategyAbstractRoot. As was mentioned in Section 22.6, the overall orchestration of the execution of the second task of the tournament is achieved by an interplay of the executeTask() of the SecondTaskManager class and the method invokeSolution() that the class shown below inherits from its root class. This interplay will become clear after you have seen the implementation of the SecondTaskManager class in Section 22.10. Shown below is the definition of the BubbleHeadCharmStrategy class with its override implementations for the problem solving methods of the root abstract strategy class.

```
public class BubbleHeadCharmStrategy extends StrategyAbstractRoot {

    public String breathingUnderwater() {
        return "Create a magical bubble of air around your head "
            + "for breathing underwater";
    }
    public String keepingGrindylowsAtBay() {
        return "Stay clear of grindylows";
    }
    public String locatingHostage(){
        return "Ask underwater magical creatures for help with the "
            + "directions";
    }
    public String freeingHostage() {
        return "The rope used to tie the hostage may not be that "
            + "easy to untie. Cut it with a sharp rock.";
    }
    public String dealingWithMerPeople() {
        return "Threaten merpeople by pointing the wand at them if "
            + "necessary";
    }
}
```

Next we define the concrete strategy class GillyweedStrategy that again extends the root class StrategyAbstractRoot. It is this strategy that was used by Harry Potter for

breathing under water and for dealing with the other problems that he encountered in rescuing his friend Ron Weasley and Fleur Delacour's younger sister Gabrielle from the bottom of Black Lake. Since the code in the class shown below is similar to what was shown above, we will not comment on it further, except to again mention the interplay between the `invokeSolution()` method, which the class shown below inherits from the root strategy class, and the `executeTask()` method that we will define in the `SecondTaskManager` class for, first, the specification of a generic goal-achieving solution in terms of the methods in the root strategy class and, subsequently, the run-time customization of this solution through the concrete strategy presented below. As stated earlier, Section 22.10 will make this interplay clearer.

```java
public class GillyweedStrategy extends StrategyAbstractRoot {

    public String breathingUnderwater() {
        return "Eat gillyweed just prior to entering water";
    }
    public String keepingGrindylowsAtBay() {
        return "Cast the Relashio spell on grindylows; Ordinarily "
            + "this spell releases a shower of fiery sparks from "
            + "the tip of the wand and attack the enemy; "
            + "Underwater, the wand releases jets of boiling "
            + "water. ";
    }
    public String locatingHostage(){
        return "Ask magical creatures underwater for directions "
            + "--- especially Moaning Myrtle";
    }
    public String freeingHostage() {
        return "Use a sharp rock to the cut the ropes used to tie "
            + "the hostage";
    }
    public String dealingWithMerPeople() {
        return "Threaten merpeople by pointing your wand at them";
    }
}
```

Presented next is the last of the three strategies used by the champions for breathing under water and for dealing with the other problems that arose in attempting to retrieve the hostages from the bottom of the lake at Hogwarts. This strategy, based on transfiguration, was used by Viktor Krum to turn himself into a shark. As with the other two concrete strategy classes, the class shown below also provides override implementations for the problem solving methods of the abstract root strategy.

```java
public class TransfigurationStrategy extends StrategyAbstractRoot {

    public String breathingUnderwater() {
```

```
        return "If transfigured into a shark, breathe like a shark";
    }
    public String keepingGrindylowsAtBay() {
        return "Scare the grindylows by baring your shark fangs at "
            + "them";
    }
    public String locatingHostage(){
        return "Scare the underwater magical creatures into giving "
            + "your directions";
    }
    public String freeingHostage() {
        return "Do not use your shark teeth to free the hostage; "
            + "your shark head will prevent you from doing that. "
            + "Instead listen to Harry's suggestion and use the "
            + "sharp-edged rock lying on the lake bed";
    }
    public String dealingWithMerPeople() {
        return "Since you look so scary, order the merpeople to "
            + "stay away from you";
    }
}
```

22.9   THE Champion CLASS

The three concrete strategy classes defined in the previous section should make it clear as to what one gains by programming up a goal-achieving solution in terms of the problem-solving functionality expressed in a root abstract strategy class and how such a goal-achieving solution can be then be customized to different specific strategies at runtime.

Obviously, strategies are meant to be used by agents. These in our case are the champions participating in the Triwizard Tournament. Equally obviously, a strategy can only be used if a champion has the ability and the resources needed for that strategy. So we need a representation that would allow us to express whether or not a champion has what it takes to execute a particular strategy. That should explain the definition of the Champion class presented in this section.

Earlier in Section 22.6, we also mentioned how our demonstration used the interplay between the invokeSolution() method of the root strategy class and the executeTask() method of the SecondTaskManager class to be presented in the next section to show, first, the creation of a goal-achieving solution in terms of the problem-solution methods in the root strategy class and, then, the run-time customization of this solution to any concrete strategy that is derived from the root strategy class. Both the invokeSolution() method of the root strategy class and the executeTask() method of the SecondTaskManager class take a Champion instance as an argument. When we invoke invokeSolution() on a strategy object, it has to be on behalf of a champion and it must take into account whether or not the champion can solve the problem that is supplied as the first argument to invokeSolution(). Similarly, when we invoke executeTask() in the main() of SecondTaskManager class, we are referring to the execution of a task by a champion.

The class definition shown below starts with instance variables to be used for naming a champion and for naming the strategy used by the champion for the second task of the Triwizard Tournament. The next five instance variables are meant to be used for declaring whether or not a champion can solve the problems that will be encountered during the execution of the second task. Merely for programming convenience, we default initialize them to true. That is, unless set otherwise by one of the set methods of the Champion class, we assume that a champion has the abilities to solve all of the problems that will be encountered during the second task.

```
public class Champion {
    private String name;
    private StrategyAbstractRoot strategy;

    // The following 'ability' instance variables are default-
    // initialized to true for programming convenience.  They
    // can, however, be set to 'false' by one of the 'set'
    // methods of this class.
    private boolean hasSolutionForBreathingUnderwater = true;
    private boolean hasSolutionForKeepingGrindylowsAtBay = true;
    private boolean canLocateHostage = true;
    private boolean canFreeHostage = true;
    private boolean canDealWithMerpeople = true;

    public Champion( String name, StrategyAbstractRoot strategy ) {
        this.name = name;
        this.strategy = strategy;
    }
    public String getName() {
        return name;
    }
    public StrategyAbstractRoot getStrategy() {
        return strategy;
    }
    public void setHasSolutionForBreathingUnderwater( boolean b ) {
        hasSolutionForBreathingUnderwater = b;
    }
    public boolean getHasSolutionForBreathingUnderwater( ) {
        return hasSolutionForBreathingUnderwater;
    }
    public void setHasSolutionForKeepingGrindylowsAtBay( boolean b ) {
        hasSolutionForKeepingGrindylowsAtBay = b;
    }
    public boolean getHasSolutionForKeepingGrindylowsAtBay( ) {
        return hasSolutionForKeepingGrindylowsAtBay;
    }
    public void setcanLocateHostage( boolean b ) {
        canLocateHostage = b;
    }
    public boolean getcanLocateHostage() {
```

```
        return canLocateHostage;
    }
    public void canFreeHostage(boolean b) {
        canFreeHostage = b;
    }
    public boolean getCanFreeHostage() {
        return canFreeHostage;
    }
    public void canDealWithMerpeople(boolean b) {
        canDealWithMerpeople = b;
    }
    public boolean getCanDealWithMerpeople() {
        return canDealWithMerpeople;
    }
}
```

22.10   THE SecondTaskManager CLASS

We now present the SecondTaskManager class whose job is to provide us with the executeTask() method mentioned previously. We want this method to return true only if all of the problems that are encountered during the execution of the second task are solved successfully.

Being a client class, this class also includes main() in which we construct Champion instances and have them use the different concrete strategies for solving the second task of the tournament.

In the code shown below, we first define the static method executeTask() with the Champion instance supplied to it as its only argument. Note that the very first thing the implementation does is determine the strategy selected by the champion. Next, we determine the first problem that must be solved under this strategy. Recall, a strategy is composed of solutions to the sequence of problems that are encountered during the execution of a task. Each problem has a specific solution under a given strategy, but that solution can be employed only if the champion has the abilities and the resources needed for the solution. So in the while loop we call invokeSolution() to find out if the champion can solve each of the problems that will be encountered. If in any of the iterations of the while loop, it turns out that a solution does not exist for a problem, we exit the loop and report failure.

That takes us to the code in main(). As the reader can see, we construct instances for each of the four champions who participated in the second task of the tournament. Note how for the "Fleur Delacour" instance we set its HasSolutionForKeepingGrindylowsAtBay ability to false through the invocation of the corresponding set method. As the reader would expect, this causes the "Fleur Delacour" instance to fail at finishing the second task.

```
public class SecondTaskManager {

    public static boolean executeTask( Champion champ ) {
        StrategyAbstractRoot strategy = champ.getStrategy();
        String firstProblem = strategy.getFirstProblem();
        boolean solution = true;
        String problem = firstProblem;
```

```
    while(solution) {
        String solution_description =
                        strategy.invokeSolution(problem, champ);
        if (solution_description == null) {
            solution = false;
            break;
        }
        problem =StrategyAbstractRoot.getNextProblem( problem );
        if (problem == null) break;
    }
    return solution;
}

public static void main( String[] args ) {

    Champion champ = new Champion( "Cedric Diggory",
                            new BubbleHeadCharmStrategy() );
    boolean succeeded = executeTask(champ);
    if (succeeded) {
        System.out.println(champ.getName() +
                            " succeeded at the second task");
    } else {
        System.out.println(champ.getName()
                            + " failed at the second task");
    }
    champ = new Champion( "Fleur Delacour",
                            new BubbleHeadCharmStrategy() );
    champ.setHasSolutionForKeepingGrindylowsAtBay(false);
    succeeded = executeTask(champ);
    if (succeeded) {
        System.out.println( champ.getName() +
                            " succeeded at the second task");
    } else {
        System.out.println( champ.getName()
                            + " failed at the second task");
    }
    champ = new Champion( "Victor Krum",
                            new TransfigurationStrategy() );
    succeeded = executeTask(champ);
    if (succeeded) {
        System.out.println( champ.getName() +
                            " succeeded at the second task");
    } else {
        System.out.println( champ.getName() +
                                " failed at the second task");
    }
    champ = new Champion("Harry Potter", new GillyweedStrategy());
    succeeded = executeTask(champ);
    if (succeeded) {
        System.out.println( champ.getName() +
                            " succeeded at the second task");
    } else {
```

```
        System.out.println( champ.getName() +
                              " failed at the second task");
        }
    }
}
```

22.11   PLAYING WITH THE CODE

Download the class files for this pattern from the book website into a separate directory. Compile the code with the command

```
javac *.java
```

and execute the SecondTaskManager class by

```
java SecondTaskManager
```

Given the code in the main() of SecondTaskManager, executing this class will produce the following output:

```
Cedric Diggory succeeded at the second task

Fleur Delacour failed at the second task

Victor Krum succeeded at the second task

Harry Potter succeeded at the second task
```

For additional insights, you may consider extending the code for this pattern along the following lines:

- Our override implementations for the problem-solving methods of the root class StrategyAbstractRoot are triggered by the abilities possessed by the champions. The Champion class has been equipped with "set" methods for setting these abilities for the individual champions and "get" methods for retrieving the same. But notice that, for programming convenience, the Champion class also sets all of the abilities to true by default, the idea being that the client class would explicitly set those abilities to false that are not true for a champion. Create another version of this demonstration by giving default values of false to all of the attributes of a champion in the definition of the class Champion. Now you will have to explicitly set the attributes that are true for each champion.

- In the current demonstration, the output of invoking a strategy by a champion produces a very terse report that merely states whether or not a champion succeeded at the task assigned to him or her. An example of this output was presented in this section when we showed the result of executing the class SecondTaskManager. If you are up to it, modify and extend the demonstration code so that it produces longer narratives that state how exactly a champion succeeded (or failed) at the task.

23

TEMPLATE METHOD

23.1 CUSTOMIZABLE RECIPES

If you are a world traveler, you might have noticed that when you walk into an ethnic-food restaurant, the food that you get does not taste exactly the same as it does in the country of origin of that ethnicity. As you might guess, the main reason for that is the need to customize the original recipes to local taste preferences since otherwise the food would not sell. If the original recipes make the food too spicy for the local palate, their customization must go easy on the spices.

Thinking of recipes in general, let's talk about algorithms since you can think of them as recipes. It is commonly the case that in your attempt to solve a new problem you come to the realization that the problem could be solved by a well-known algorithm if some of its steps could be customized to deal with the peculiarities of your data. What is interesting is that many standard algorithms that lend themselves to any customization at all will usually also make clear which of the steps are open to change so that the overall solution can still be considered to be according to the algorithm.

Consider, for example, the commonly used sorting algorithms such as `quicksort`, `mergesort`, `heapsort`, etc. These algorithms, characterized by different worst-case space-time tradeoffs, differ with regard to how they process the data for sorting. However, all such algorithms have one thing in common: they all need a comparator function that tells the algorithms how to order any two elements of the data. Comparator functions must be specified with care for sorting class type objects, since how to compare two different instances constructed from a class is for the programmer to decide. Plugging a comparator function into a sorting algorithm is an example of its customization to the data at hand.

In the context of customization of algorithms, the purpose of the Template Method pattern is to customize the behavior of a method by defining its invariant part in a base class and its variable parts in the subclasses derived from the base class. That's a top-down look

Designing with Objects: Object-Oriented Design Patterns Explained with Stories from Harry Potter,
First Edition. Avinash C. Kak.
© 2015 John Wiley & Sons, Inc. Published 2015 by John Wiley & Sons, Inc.

at what the Template Method pattern is about. For a bottom-up look, let's say that you have an algorithm whose several steps depend on either the context in which the algorithm is invoked, or on the types of objects that the algorithm is asked to work on, or any number of other things. Considering the algorithm to be a sequence of steps, we place in an abstract base class those steps that are always the same regardless of the context or the object type or any other factor that may affect the operation of the algorithm. With regard to the other steps, we only declare them in the base class, while providing their implementation in the different subclasses of the base class, with each subclass corresponding to a different context, a different object type, and so on. Subsequently, when we instantiate the algorithm by constructing an instance of one of its concrete subclasses, we can be certain that the algorithm will use the base-class code for the invariant steps and the subclass code for the remaining steps.

23.2   INTENT AND APPLICABILITY

The intent of the Template Method pattern is to place the invariant steps of an algorithmic solution to a problem — these would presumably be all of the essential steps that are fundamental to the definition of the algorithm — in a base class and then have the subclasses provide overrides for the different possible customizations of the base class code.

You should consider using this pattern when

- the algorithmic solution you want to use needs to be customized for dealing with the different data types, operational contexts, computational resources, etc.;
- the customizations you need do not alter the fundamental character of the algorithm itself, but may alter some of the low-level details related to operations on the data elements involved, how the computational resources are used, the mode of interaction with the environment, and so on.

23.3   INTRODUCTION TO THE TEMPLATE METHOD PATTERN

Basic to the Template Method pattern is our ability to express an algorithmic solution to a problem as a sequence of more elementary method calls declared in a root class. In general, some of these more elementary methods may be given do-nothing implementations in the root class. However, when at runtime the same algorithm is invoked through an instance of a subclass derived from the root class, the root-class method calls — including those that had do-nothing implementations in the root class — would be translated into calls on their override definitions in the subclass. This allows us to define algorithms in a generic fashion in a root class. Subsequently, at runtime, such algorithms are capable of exhibiting customized behavior according to the subclass-based override definitions of the generic method calls in the root class.

More specifically, let's say that an algorithmic solution requires steps A, B, and C. We may visualize the algorithmic solution as follows:

```
Algorithm:
            Step A
            Step B
            Step C
```

For a solution based on the Template Method pattern, we define a root class, which we may name something like `GenericSteps`, and equip the class with methods named, let's say, `method_for_A()`, `method_for_B()`, and `method_for_C()`. In the class `GenericSteps` itself, we define these methods as possessing do-nothing implementations:

```
class GenericSteps:
    protected void method_for_A() { return null;)
    protected void method_for_B() { return null;)
    protected void method_for_C() { return null;)
```

Subsequently, we specify multiple subclasses of `GenericSteps`, with the subclasses differing with respect to the implementations for some or all of the three steps. So we could have the following:

```
class Approach_1                    | class Approach_2
        extends GenericSteps:       |         extends GenericSteps:
  void method_for_A() {             |     void method_for_A() {
    //  procedure for A             |       // different procedure for A
  }                                 |     }
  void method_for_B() {             |     void method_for_B() {
    // procedure for B              |       // different procedure for B
  }                                 |     }
  void method_for_C() {             |     void method_for_C() {
    // procedure for C              |       // different procedure for C
  }                                 |     }
```

An algorithmic solution to some problem may now be specified at compile time in terms of the method calls in the root class `GenericSteps`. Subsequently, at runtime, the same algorithm may be invoked through either of the subclasses shown above, the choice depending on the context related to the use of the algorithm. We refer to this approach to the declaration of the algorithmic steps in a root class and to placing multiple alternative implementations of the steps in the different subclasses of the root as the *templatization* of an algorithm.

At a high enough level of description, there are many conceptual similarities between the Strategy pattern of the previous chapter and the Template Method pattern of this chapter. Fundamental to both is the delineation of a multi-step solution to a problem in a base class, with its concrete subclasses providing override implementations for those steps that are relevant to different specific customizations of the base class code. In that case, what's the difference between Strategy and Template Method, a reader might ask?

There are two differences between the two patterns: (1) One difference relates to how each is likely to be implemented in practice. For the Strategy pattern, one is likely to invoke the solution steps in the concrete strategy subclasses through the intermediary of the chosen

strategy. On the other hand, when using the Template Method pattern, one is more likely to depend directly on the polymorphic invocations of the concrete subclass methods as we explain in this chapter. (2) The second difference relates to how much of the base class code is meant to be overridden in the subclasses. In Strategy, a subclass is likely to provide override implementations for *all* of the algorithmic steps in the base class (*since the solutions to all of the steps taken together constitutes a strategy*). In Template Method, on the other hand, much of the algorithm would be implemented in the base class and each subclass would then provide overrides for just those steps that define a particular customization of the algorithm. Therefore, you could say, the metaphor of "recipe customization" in Section 23.1 is a good way to talk about the Template Method. *The essential parts of a recipe defined in a base class must remain invariant even as the subclasses change some of the details of the recipe for its different customizations.*

23.4 THE TEMPLATE METHOD PATTERN IN REAL-WORLD APPLICATIONS

Note that the basic concept that the Template Method pattern is based on goes to the heart of object-oriented programming — the concept being that of *polymorphism*. Being one of the cornerstones of object-oriented programming, you are likely to see this concept being used virtually everywhere in object-oriented software. Polymorphism allows us to manipulate the objects instantiated from the different subclasses in a class hierarchy through the methods declared in the root class. So when the same method is invoked on a collection of objects constructed from different subclasses, through polymorphism we are ensured that the method definition used for each object corresponds to the implementation of the method in the subclass from which the object was constructed.

Here are a couple of well-known examples of software systems in which high-level tasks defined in the root interfaces are executed through polymorphic invocation of methods in the manner described above: processing of low-level events in Qt and the processing of all events in the wxWindows. Qt and wxWindows are both C++-based platforms for GUI (Graphical User Interface) programming.

The Template Method pattern goes beyond the basic notion of polymorphism only in the sense that it focuses on the root class defining an algorithm as a sequence of more elementary method calls, with some of these more elementary methods being defined in the root class itself, while others are expressed merely as abstract declarations with the expectation that the subclasses would provide their concrete implementations.

Probably the most famous example of the polymorphic invocation of methods in the algorithmic sense is the support for the sorting utilities in object-oriented languages. For example, the Java Collections Framework provides sorting algorithms that by default use what is known as the *natural order* for the elements to be sorted.[1] If you are not satisfied with the sorting results produced by natural ordering, you can call the sort methods with an additional `Comparator` argument for how the elements should be compared pairwise for sorting. So if your code invokes `Collections.sort()`, with the collection to be sorted supplied as the first argument to the method and with a `Comparator` object as its second argument, the execution of the sorting routine at runtime would follow the logic defined

---

[1] A class possesses a natural order if you have defined the `compareTo()` method for the class.

in the `Collections` class. However, for any element to element comparisons, Java would use the criterion you supplied through the `Comparator` object.

23.5   HARRY POTTER STORY USED TO ILLUSTRATE THE TEMPLATE METHOD PATTERN

Our demonstration of the Template Method pattern consists of writing a computer program that generates stories about Harry Potter going back to school at the end of each summer. These stories are about the events that take place during Harry's last few days with the Dursleys, his journey to Hogwarts, and the term initiation ceremonies at the school. In Harry Potter books, these stories, different for each year, serve as lead-ins for what happens during the rest of that year.

More specifically, our goal is to write a program with an "algorithmic" flavor — even though the "algorithm" itself will be a trivial sequence of only three steps — in such a way that its generic steps stay the same from year to year, while the details of how those steps are implemented vary. The steps that stay the same form an ordered sequence and correspond to the generation of narratives for the following stories:

1. the end of the summer holidays,
2. the travel to Hogwarts, and
3. the welcome ceremonies at Hogwarts.

The narrative generators for these three stories will consist of a sequence of storyline generators. Although the names of the storyline generators would also remain constant from year to year, the storylines they produce will be specific to each year. For example, consider the storyline generator for getting to Platform Nine and Three-Fourth at the King's Cross Station. Getting to that platform is a part of the travel to Hogwarts at the beginning of each school year (the second story listed above). So, whereas you need getting-to-the-platform storyline generator for each year, the storyline produced is different from year to year. For example, for the first year, the storyline must account for the fact that Harry is completely clueless about how to get to the platform and how Mrs. Weasley, who per chance notices Harry looking bewildered, tells him how he must deliberately "crash" into the barrier between the platforms 9 and 10. And, in year 2, the storyline related to getting to the magical platform is made complicated by the fact that the house-elf Dobby has put an enchantment on the barrier to keep it from opening when Harry follows the same procedure that he had used in his first year.

For an example of how the narrative generators for the three stories listed above are decomposed into more elementary storyline generators, consider the first of the three items listed above. This is for the end of summer holidays when Harry Potter is still with the Dursleys. Denoting this story generator by `endOfSummerHolidays`, it will consist of the following two storyline generators: `endOfSummerWithDursleys` and `acquiringSchoolSupplies`. To synthesize the narrative for `endOfSummerHolidays`, we must first fetch the storyline for `endOfSummerWithDursleys` and then do the same for `acquiringSchoolSupplies`. Joining the two storylines would constitute the story for `endOfSummerHolidays`. We will use the Template Method pattern to deal with the fact that the two storylines vary from year to year. We will first create a root class — `EndOfSummerStories` — that will returns null for the storylines for both of

these steps. We will then extend the root class into concrete subclasses for the different years Harry spent at Hogwarts. We will do the same for generating the other two stories. The story generators for those will be denoted `travelToHogwarts` and `welcomeCeremoniesAtHogwarts`.

We may refer to the above as the templatization of the generation of the narratives for the end-of-summer and beginning-of-school-year stories in Harry Potter.

23.6   A TOP LEVEL VIEW OF THE PATTERN DEMONSTRATION

In the class diagram shown in Figure 23.1, the root of the story-generating classes is the abstract class `EndOfSummerStories` in which we define the three methods listed below that form the basic steps of our rudimentary "algorithm" for creating the narratives related to Harry Potter going back to school at the end of summer holidays. We also place in the abstract class other methods that play supporting roles vis-á-vis the three main story-generating methods. To highlight this distinction, which is important to seeing how the code shown demonstrates the Template Method pattern, we have redrawn just the abstract root `EndOfSummerStories` in Figure 23.2, where the storyline generation methods that support the main story generators are displayed with an offset. As displayed in Figure 23.2, the three main methods that form our story generator algorithm are:

    endOfSummerHolidays()

    travelToHogwarts()

    welcomeCeremonyAtHogwarts()

Each of these main story-generating methods relies on storyline generators that, as the reader will see in the next section, only have null implementations in the abstract root class itself. That is because the behavior of the storyline generators changes from year to year; so, they must be overridden for each year Harry Potter went to Hogwarts. For example, the storyline methods for the story generator `endOfSummerHolidays()` are:

    endOfSummerWithDursleys()

    acquiringSchoolSupplies()

So whereas the main story generator `endOfSummerHolidays()` must be called for each year's end of summer story, it is the override definitions for the two storyline methods shown above that will make the story specific to that year. Our demonstration code includes these override definitions for just the first two years of Harry Potter's stay at Hogwarts. These two years are represented by the two classes `EndOfSummerYear1` and `EndOfSummerYear2` shown in Figure 23.1. (We could obviously have defined the rest of the concrete classes needed in the same manner for each of the remaining years Harry Potter went to Hogwarts.)

The executable class for this demonstration is `TestStoryGenerator`, also shown in Figure 23.1. Its role is to create instances of `EndOfSummerStories` that can then be queried for the stories for the year corresponding to the concrete subclass chosen for creating an instance of type `EndOfSummerStories`, as you will see in Section 23.10.

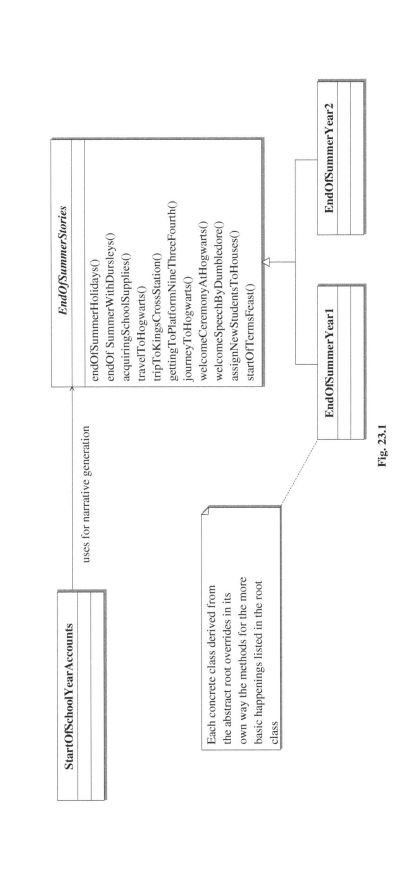

Fig. 23.1

StartOfSchoolYearAccounts

uses for narrative generation

EndOfSummerStories

endOfSummerHolidays()
endOf SummerWithDursleys()
acquiringSchoolSupplies()
travelToHogwarts()
tripToKingsCrossStation()
gettingToPlatformNineThreeFourth()
journeyToHogwarts()
welcomeCeremonyAtHogwarts()
welcomeSpeechByDumbledore()
assignNewStudentsToHouses()
startOfTermsFeast()

EndOfSummerYear1

EndOfSummerYear2

Each concrete class derived from
the abstract root overrides in its
own way the methods for the more
basic happenings listed in the root
class

Fig. 23.2

23.7   THE ABSTRACT ROOT OF NARRATIVE GENERATION CLASSES

Shown below is EndOfSummerStories, the abstract root of the story generation classes for the different years of Harry Potter's stay at Hogwarts. Shown for each of the three basic steps that stay invariant from year to year — endOfSummerHolidays(), travelToHogwarts(), and welcomeCeremonyAtHogwarts() — are the more detailed storyline generation steps defined through method calls.[2] For example, the more detailed storyline generation steps that go into the narrative generator travelToHogwarts() consist of calls to the following three methods: tripToKingsCrossStation(), gettingToPlatformNineThreeFourth(), and journeyToHogwarts(). Earlier, in the previous section, we indicated the storyline generation steps by their offset depiction in Figure 23.2. As the reader can see, each of the storyline generators has a null implementation in the code shown below. We obviously want that to be the case since the storyline generators are year specific. So they would need to be overridden by year-specific extensions of the class shown below.

```
public abstract class EndOfSummerStories {

    public String endOfSummerHolidays() {
        String howDidSummerEnd    =   endOfSummerWithDursleys();
        String acquiringSchoolSupplies = acquiringSchoolSupplies();
```

[2]In addition to referring to the entire demonstration as a Template Method based 3-step algorithm for generating stories, we can also refer to the three methods, endOfSummerHolidays(), travelToHogwarts(), and welcomeCeremonyAtHogwarts(), as "template methods" or as "templatized methods". Each method has its implementation defined in the base class, but some of the steps in the implementation for each must be provided by the customization code in the concrete subclasses. The base class implementations of the template methods shown here are admittedly trivial — an issue we have commented on in the first of the bulleted points in Section 23.10.

```
            return "\nLeaving Dursleys at the end of summer: "
                + howDidSummerEnd + "\n"  + acquiringSchoolSupplies;
    }
    protected String endOfSummerWithDursleys() { return null; }
    protected String acquiringSchoolSupplies() { return null; }

    public String travelToHogwarts() {
        String goToStationScript  =  tripToKingsCrossStation();
        String platformScript    =
                                gettingToPlatformNineThreeFourth();
        String boardTrainScript   =  journeyToHogwarts();
        return "\nTravel to Hogwarts: " + goToStationScript
            + "\n" + platformScript + "\n" + boardTrainScript;
    }
    protected String tripToKingsCrossStation(){ return null; }
    protected String gettingToPlatformNineThreeFourth() {return null;}
    protected String journeyToHogwarts() { return null; }

    public String welcomeCeremonyAtHogwarts() {
        String speech = welcomeSpeechByDumbledore();
        String sortingHatNarrative =  assignNewStudentsToHouses();
        String feastScript  =  startOfTermFeast();
        return "\nWelcome ceremony at Hogwarts: "
            +  speech + "\n" + sortingHatNarrative + "\n" + feastScript;
    }
    protected String welcomeSpeechByDumbledore() { return null; }
    protected String assignNewStudentsToHouses() { return null; }
    protected String startOfTermFeast() { return null; }
}
```

23.8   CONCRETE CLASSES FOR NARRATIVE GENERATION

The abstract root class EndOfSummerStories presented in the previous section showed how the overall story generator is expressed as a sequence of three narrative generation steps and then how each such step is further broken into a sequence of more detailed storyline generation steps, with each of those implemented as a null-returning method. Now, for each year Harry spent at Hogwarts, we must derive concrete subclasses from the root class with override implementations for the null-returning methods in the root class. The code shown below is the concrete subclass for the first year of Harry's time at Hogwarts.

```
public class EndOfSummerYear1 extends EndOfSummerStories {
    public String endOfSummerWithDursleys() {
        return  "\n\tAt the beginning of summer, Harry's living space"
            + "\n\tin the Dursley house is a small dark cupboard"
            + "\n\tunder the stairs. But that changed when letters"
            + "\n\taddressed specifically for Harry started arriving."
            + "\n\tThe address that each letter bore on the front was"
```

```
        + "\n\tHarry's exact location in the house.  The letters"
        + "\n\twere magical, in the sense that they kept on"
        + "\n\tcoming into the house despite Mr. Dursley's every"
        + "\n\tattempt to block them out. The letters --- they"
        + "\n\tall had the same message --- announced Harry's"
        + "\n\tadmission to Hogwarts. Eventually, the message"
        + "\n\twas personally delivered to Harry by Hagrid, the"
        + "\n\tgroundskeeper at Hogwarts.";
}
public String acquiringSchoolSupplies() {
    return  "\n\tFor getting the school supplies, Hagrid takes"
        + "\n\tHarry Potter to Diagon Alley for the school"
        + "\n\tsupplies.  First they visit Gringots, the bank for"
        + "\n\twizards and witches, where they withdraw the money"
        + "\n\tneeded and then the other shops for the actual"
        + "\n\tsupplies such as black robes, a wand, books, etc.";

}
public String tripToKingsCrossStation(){
    return  "\n\tMr. Dursley has to go to London anyway to take"
        + "\n\tDudley to the hospital to have his tail removed"
        + "\n\tsurgically; so he agrees to take Harry Potter"
        + "\n\t along to the train station";
}
public String gettingToPlatformNineThreeFourth(){
    return  "\n\tMolly Weasley shows Harry how to get to Platform"
        + "\n\tNine Three-Fourth by deliberately 'crashing' into"
        + "\n\ta magical barrier between the platforms 9 and 10";
}
public String journeyToHogwarts() {
    return  "\n\tHarry, finding an empty compartment at the end of"
        + "\n\tthe train, has trouble hoisting his large heavy"
        + "\n\ttrunk on to the train. He accomplishes the task"
        + "\n\twith help from the Weasley brothers Fred and"
        + "\n\tGeorge. He finds himself in the compartment with"
        + "\n\tthe youngest of the Weasley brothers, Ron, who"
        + "\n\tlater becomes one his two best friends at"
        + "\n\tHogwarts";
}
public String assignNewStudentsToHouses() {
    return  "\n\tThe first years put on the magical Sorting Hat,"
        + "\n\twhich reads their minds and figures out as to"
        + "\n\twhich house each student belongs to. Harry Potter"
        + "\n\tand his soon-to-be best friends Ron Weasley and"
        + "\n\tHermione Granger are all sorted into the"
        + "\n\tGryffindor House.";
}
public String welcomeSpeechByDumbledore() {
    return  "\n\tDumbledore's speech: '.........Nitwit! Blubber!"
        + "\n\tOddment! Tweak!' Thank you!";
}
public String startOfTermFeast() {
```

```
        return  "\n\tIn the Great Hall, the four long tables, one for"
              + "\n\teach house, are laid with golden plates and"
              + "\n\tgoblets for the students and a large variety of"
              + "\n\tdelicious dishes.";
    }
}
```

What the class `EndOfSummerYear1` does for year 1 is done for year 2 by the concrete class `EndOfSummerYear2` that is shown below. The class `EndOfSummerYear2` provides overrides for the null-returning methods of the abstract root class EndOfSummerStories for Year 2 of Harry Potter's stay at Hogwarts.

```
public class EndOfSummerYear2 extends EndOfSummerStories {

    public String endOfSummerWithDursleys() {
        return  "\n\tFor his first summer back from Hogwarts, Harry"
              + "\n\tmissed his school very much. Back in the clutches"
              + "\n\tof his uncle, aunt, and their enoromously fat"
              + "\n\tson, Harry was not even allowed access to any of"
              + "\n\tthe possessions he had brought back with him from"
              + "\n\tschool.  Even his own Hedwig was kept caged all"
              + "\n\tthe time --- so that Harry would not use her to"
              + "\n\tcarry messages to any of his school friends. It"
              + "\n\twas so bad that even his birthday was completely"
              + "\n\tignored by the Dursleys. To cap it all, near the"
              + "\n\tend of summer, Harry had to put up with a joke"
              + "\n\tplayed on him by his arch enemy Dacro Malfoy who"
              + "\n\tsent his house elf Dobby over to 4 Privet Drive"
              + "\n\tto persuade Harry to not go back to Hogwarts. As"
              + "\n\tHarry discovered, Dobby had been intercepting all"
              + "\n\tof Harry's mail, which made his summer even more"
              + "\n\tmiserable than it would have been normally.";
    }
    public String acquiringSchoolSupplies() {
        return  "\n\tHarry lived with the Weasleys at the Burrow"
              + "\n\tduring the last month of the summer.  On a chosen"
              + "\n\tday, the Weasley family along with Harry, headed"
              + "\n\tby Floo Powder to Diagon Alley for buying school"
              + "\n\tsupplies for the coming year. This happened to be"
              + "\n\tHarry's  first (and not the most pleasant)"
              + "\n\tintroduction to travel by Floo Powder. Harry"
              + "\n\tlanded in the Borgin and Burges shop (devoted to"
              + "\n\tmerchandising in the Dark Arts artifacts) in"
              + "\n\tKnockturn Alley, from where he eventually found"
              + "\n\this way (with help from Hagrid who happened to be"
              + "\n\tin the same alley) back to Diagon Alley.  There"
              + "\n\tthey met up with the Weasleys and Hermione Granger"
              + "\n\tand they all headed to Flourish and Blotts, the"
              + "\n\tbookshop for the school books. The school books"
```

```
            + "\n\tfor the second years were mostly by the same"
            + "\n\tauthor --- Gilderoy Lockhart --- a supposedly"
            + "\n\tcelebrity wizard who was going to be the next"
            + "\n\tprofessor of DADA (Defense Against Dark Arts) at"
            + "\n\tHogwarts. Unfortunately for this professor, he"
            + "\n\twas later found to be more hubris than substance."
            + "\n\tMuch of what he had claimed for himself in his"
            + "\n\tbooks turned out to not be true.";
    }
    public String tripToKingsCrossStation(){
        return  "\n\tThe Weasleys, along with Harry, get a late start for"
            + "\n\tthe trip to the station --- mostly due to dawdling by"
            + "\n\tthe kids. Arthur had just gotten the car going when it"
            + "\n\tsuddenly occurred to George that he had forgotten to"
            + "\n\ttake along his box of fireworks. They were barely on"
            + "\n\tthe road again when Fred realized that he had not packed"
            + "\n\this broomstick. And, then, when it seemed like they were"
            + "\n\tfinally on the road, the car had to be turned around"
            + "\n\tagain because Ginny had forgotten her diary in the"
            + "\n\thouse.  As a result of all these delays, the party"
            + "\n\tarrived at the station with barely any time left to get"
            + "\n\tto the platform.";
    }
    public String gettingToPlatformNineThreeFourth(){
        return  "\n\tThe party had only fifteen minutes left to get to the"
            + "\n\tplatform. You couldn't just race to the platform since"
            + "\n\tpassing through the magical barrier required that you"
            + "\n\tnot be noticed by the muggles.  The end result was that"
            + "\n\tHarry and Ron, the last to attempt charging through the"
            + "\n\tbarrier could not make it. The barrier did not open to"
            + "\n\tlet them through.";
    }
    public String journeyToHogwarts() {
        return  "\n\tSince Harry and Ron missed the train, Ron decided that"
            + "\n\tthey could fly to Hogwarts in his father's enchanted"
            + "\n\tcar. The car did get them to Hogwarts but, as their luck"
            + "\n\twould have it, it crashed into the Whomping Willow tree"
            + "\n\tin the Hogwarts grounds.  As was to be expected, the"
            + "\n\ttree attacked the car by hitting it with its branches."
            + "\n\tFortunately, Ron was able to reverse the car from under"
            + "\n\tthe tree.  When the car stopped again, it ejected them"
            + "\n\tand tossed their luggage out on the grounds and flew"
            + "\n\toff into darkness.  Harry and Ron made their way into"
            + "\n\tthe castle, only to discover that their flying car had"
            + "\n\tbeen noticed by a few muggles --- something considered "
            + "\n\tto be a very serious infraction by the Ministry of"
            + "\n\tMagic. The result was that they received a warning from"
            + "\n\tProfessor Dumbledore to never let anything like that"
            + "\n\thappen again.";
    }
    public String assignNewStudentsToHouses() {
        return  "\n\tBecause Harry and Ron missed the train to Hogwarts (and"
```

```
                + "\n\tbecause they had to take Ron's father's magical car to"
                + "\n\tfly to Hogwarts), they both missed the term initiation"
                + "\n\tceremony in the Great Hall and that included the sorting"
                + "\n\tceremony.";
    }
    public String welcomeSpeechByDumbledore() {
        return  "\n\tFor the same reasons that Harry and Ron missed the"
                + "\n\tsorting ceremony, they also missed the opening speech"
                + "\n\tby  Dumbledore.";
    }
    public String startOfTermFeast() {
        return  "\n\tAs was the case with the sorting ceremony, Harry and"
                + "\n\tRon also missed out on the start of term feast in the"
                + "\n\tGreat Hall.  After they were apprehended by Professor"
                + "\n\tSnape at the entrance steps to the school while the"
                + "\n\tsorting ceremony was taking place inside the Great"
                + "\n\tHall, Harry and Ron were led to Snape's office in the"
                + "\n\tdungeons where they were to detained to face their house"
                + "\n\tteacher Professor McGonagall and, later, the principal"
                + "\n\tProfessor Dumbledore.";
    }
}
```

23.9   THE EXECUTABLE CLASS

As should be clear by this time, the Template Method pattern is for creating algorithmic implementations in which there exist choices regarding how exactly the various steps of the algorithm are executed at runtime. In our demonstration of algorithmic generation of narratives for Harry Potter's end-of-summer stories, the choices depend on the run-time selection of the year Harry attended Hogwarts. The class EndOfSummerYear1, meant for Harry Potter's first year at Hogwarts, provided the implementations of those algorithmic steps that had null-returning definitions in the root class EndOfSummerStories. The class EndOfSummerYear2 did the same for the second year. We now present a class, TestStoryGenerator, for exercising the templatized implementation of the story-generation algorithm in the root class EndOfSummerStories.

The first section of the code shown below is for generating the stories for Harry Potter's first year at Hogwarts and the second section for the second year. In the first section, we construct an EndOfSummerStories instance by calling on the constructor of the subclass EndOfSummerYear1. In the rest of the section, we invoke the three generic narrative generators on it — endOfSummerHolidays(), travelToHogwarts(), and welcomeCeremonyAtHogwarts(). In the second section, we use the constructor for EndOfSummerYear2() for year 2 and invoke the same three narrative generators on the instance thus created. As the reader would expect, the two sections generate two different narratives, one for each of the two years.

Note that, ideally, we should have supplied the root class EndOfSummerStories with a top-level method whose job would be to call each of the three main story generators for a demonstration of the algorithmic production of the overall story for each year. Instead,

for simplicity's sake, we show the invocation of the three story generators separately in the implementation presented below.

```java
public class TestStoryGenerator {

    public static void main(String[] args) {

        EndOfSummerStories forYear1 = new EndOfSummerYear1();
        String story = forYear1.endOfSummerHolidays();
        System.out.println( story );
        story = forYear1.travelToHogwarts();
        System.out.println( story );
        story = forYear1.welcomeCeremonyAtHogwarts();
        System.out.println( story );

        EndOfSummerStories   forYear2 = new EndOfSummerYear2();
        story = forYear2.endOfSummerHolidays();
        System.out.println( story );
        story = forYear2.travelToHogwarts();
        System.out.println( story );
        story = forYear2.welcomeCeremonyAtHogwarts();
        System.out.println( story );
    }
}
```

23.10   PLAYING WITH THE CODE

Download the class files for this pattern from the book website into a separate directory. Compile the code with the command

```
javac *.java
```

and execute the TestStoryGenerator class by

```
java TestStoryGenerator
```

Given the code in the main() of TestStoryGenerator, executing this class will produce the following output:

```
                        YEAR 1

Leaving Dursleys at the end of summer:

At the beginning of summer, Harry's living space in the
Dursley house is a small dark cupboard under the stairs.
```

```
But that changed when letters addressed specifically
for Harry started arriving.   The address that each
letter bore on the front was Harry's exact location
in the house.  The letters were magical, in the sense
        ....
        ....
        ....


Travel to Hogwarts:

Mr. Dursley has to go to London anyway to take Dudley to
the hospital to have his tail removed surgically; so he
agrees to take Harry Potter along to the train station.
Molly Weasley shows Harry how to get to Platform Nine
        ....
        ....
        ....


Welcome ceremony at Hogwarts:

Dumbledore's speech: '.........Nitwit! Blubber! Oddment!
Tweak!' Thank you!

The first years put on the magical Sorting Hat, which
        ....
        ....

                        YEAR 2

Leaving Dursleys at the end of summer:

For his first summer back from Hogwarts, Harry missed
his school very much. Back in the clutches of his uncle,
aunt, and their enoromously fat son, Harry was not even
allowed access to any of the possessoins he had
brought back with him from school.  Even his own Hedwig
        ....
        ....
        ....


Travel to Hogwarts:

The Weasleys, along with Harry, get a late start for
the trip to the station --- mostly due to dawdling by
the kids. Arthur had just gotten the car going when it
suddenly occurred to George that he had forgotten to
        ....
        ....
        ....


Welcome ceremony at Hogwarts:
```

```
For the same reasons that Harry and Ron missed the
sorting ceremony, they also missed the opening speech
by  Dumbledore.
        ....
        ....
        ....
```

For additional insights, you may consider extending the code for this pattern along the following lines:

- The demonstration code in this chapter does not do full justice to the idea of "recipe customization" described in Section 23.1 since the base-class implementation code for the three generic steps of the overall story production algorithm — `endOfSummerHolidays()`, `travelToHogwarts()`, and `welcomeCeremonyAtHogwarts()` — is rather lame. In order to make this sort of a demonstration more respectable, you might think of a finer grained decomposition of the stories and their generation by a hierarchy of steps, with the steps at the root staying invariant for all the stories. With a finer decomposition of the stories, you'll be able to provide a user with a richer experience with your story generator through the sort of features mentioned in the last bullet in this section.
- The two concrete extensions of the abstract root narrative-generating class `EndOfSummerStories` that are in the current demonstration code take care of just the first two years of Harry Potter's stay at Hogwarts. For a complete demonstration of this sort, it would be nice if extensions similar to `EndOfSummerYear1` and `EndOfSummerYear2` could be written up for the other years also.
- You may want to create a more complex version of this demonstration in which the algorithmic steps would depend on some parameter related to how a user wants to interact with the code. For example, if all a user wanted was a summary storyline for each happening, the steps invoked for the story-generating methods would be different from those invoked for the more complete stories. Another extension of the current demonstration along the same lines would be to create stories that only mention certain characters of interest to the user interacting with the code. For example, what if a user wanted to see only the storylines that mention Hermione Granger and Harry Potter together?

24

VISITOR

24.1 HOOKS, GOOD AND EVIL

In the world of software, there are good hooks and then there are evil hooks. In general, a hook is a piece of code that alters the "standard" behavior of a software library. An event-based hook may, for example, intercept your mouse clicks, keystrokes, packets coming in through a network interface, etc., before passing them on to their actual destinations.

With good hooks, such interceptions can be used for a variety of purposes ranging from debugging to packet filtering. Examples of good hooks include the mechanism used by the `iptables` tool in Linux platforms for real-time packet filtering needed for firewalls; the Microsoft Windows library that allows for an application to install its own functions to monitor designated events; the `add-hook` function made available by the Gnu Emacs editor software for its customization; and so on.

However, with evil hooks, the same interceptions can be used for surreptitiously capturing your personal information as you interact with your computer. Examples of evil hooks include those used by the trojans that seek to obtain elevated privileges in your computer via a rootkit. People inadvertently install such trojans in their computers by clicking on spam-borne attachments.

There are various ways to devise hooks that modify the run-time behavior of a software system. Consider, for example, the hooks that alter how the software responds to events — we are talking about GUI events, network interface events, and so on — by redirecting the flow of execution to a function other than where it was meant to go originally. Such redirection can be carried out with a wrapper library whose API is indistinguishable from that of the original library. The method definitions in the wrapper library would evidently go beyond the functionality incorporated in the original library. Hooks may also be created by first locating function entry points in the object code (with, say, a debugger or a disassembler) and then redirecting those pointers to other functions — the hook functions. When one has access to the source code, it becomes a simple matter to install hooks in the software by including in the sources new conditional statements that can alter the originally envisioned flow of execution by the software. Such hooks are frequently used

Designing with Objects: Object-Oriented Design Patterns Explained with Stories from Harry Potter,
First Edition. Avinash C. Kak.
© 2015 John Wiley & Sons, Inc. Published 2015 by John Wiley & Sons, Inc.

for analyzing the data conditions that prevail locally in the software for debugging and analysis.

The Visitor pattern shows how it is possible to give a class hierarchy new behaviors — behaviors unanticipated at the time the classes were originally created — *provided the classes in the hierarchy incorporate a Visitor hook.* For simple classes, the hook itself is likely to possess a trivial implementation. However, the hooks become more elaborate for complex classes that involve composites over other classes.

24.2   INTENT AND APPLICABILITY

The intent of the Visitor pattern is to provide a mechanism that allows additional functionality to be associated with a class hierarchy without actually modifying the hierarchy in any significant way.

You should consider using this pattern when

- your clients, who use your software in different applications, would like to see additional application-specific functionality from your classes;
- your code would become unmanageable if you added to your source code all of the different types of application-specific functionality needed by your clients;
- you or your clients are willing to encode the additional functionality in appropriate Visitor classes (using Visitor classes would make the added functionality external to the original code);
- you are willing to write the source code with "accept" hooks incorporated in it.

24.3   INTRODUCTION TO THE VISITOR PATTERN

Let's say that you have created a class hierarchy and made it available to your clients. Subsequently, you receive a client request for some additional functionality from the hierarchy. In general, enhancing the functionality of the software would require endowing the classes with new methods. Obviously, a direct solution to the problem would entail modifying the original source code.

With the Visitor pattern, however, you have an alternative. If you wrote the original hierarchy with `accept()` "hooks" incorporated in it, you may be able to use the Visitor pattern to incorporate in your classes additional functionality *from the outside*, so to speak, without altering the original source code in any significant way. Of course, a discerning reader would ask: What if you did not write your original classes with the `accept()` hooks? Depending on your application, that may not be a problem because you can always subclass from the original classes and include the `accept()` hooks in the subclasses.[1] Such subclass

---

[1] At this point, the reader might ask that if we are going to be subclassing from the original classes anyway, why not incorporate the new functionality desired by the clients in those subclasses? Also, extending the original classes either amounts to changing the original sources or to creating a new library. Those are indeed good points.

definitions would be rather trivial since they would only need to define the `accept()` method calls.

The `accept()` hook that must be placed in the original class hierarchy (or in the subclasses derived from the original classes) takes for its argument an instance of a class commonly called `Visitor`. The newly desired behavior is then provided through a combination of the code in the `accept()` hooks and the code in the implementation of the `Visitor` classes, as you will see in this chapter's demonstration. The classes that are thus given new behaviors without significant modifications to their implementations are usually referred to as `Element` classes in a presentation of the Visitor pattern.

To further clarify, let's say that we want a tool that would print out the value of a certain private attribute of the instances constructed from a given class in a hierarchy of `Element` classes. We will assume that this attribute is in the private section of the classes and cannot be displayed directly, although the classes in the hierarchy do provide "get" methods to access such attributes — a "get" method is only required to fetch a piece of information and not also print it. Assuming you wrote the original `Element` classes to include methods such as

```
public void accept(Visitor visitor) {
    visitor.visit(this);
}
```

you would be able to provide the needed print functionality in the `Visitor` class without having to alter the original classes. For situations where the new behavior you desire is for a complex class that is a composite over other classes, the `accept()` hook you would need to place in your original source code may be as elaborate as:

```
public void accept(Visitor visitor) {
    Iterator<Obliviator> it1 = some_collection.iterator();
    while (it1.hasNext()) {
        visitor.visit( it1.next() );
    }
    // more code
}
```

Obviously, the code fragment shown above would produce the desired result only if all of the classes involved in the collection lend themselves to Visitor-based elicitation of new behaviors.

As you may be able to infer from the code fragments shown above, the `accept(Visitor)` hook allows a `Visitor` instance to be 'injected' into an `Element` instance at runtime. What this 'injection' returns depends on how the `visitor.visit(arg)` method is implemented. If the new behavior you wish to create for a class through the Visitor pattern involves the instance variables of the class (as it most likely will), the `Visitor` instance would need to access those variables from the outside. If those instance variables happen to be in the private section of the class and you

---

So if the original sources did not include a `Visitor` hook, one would need to carry out a cost-benefit analysis of the alternative approaches available for augmenting the functionality of a class hierarchy.

have not equipped the class with "get" methods to retrieve their values, incorporating the accept(Visitor) hook in the class may not be a useful thing to do.

As for the Visitor instance used in the accept(Visitor) hook, in general one constructs a Visitor hierarchy whose root is likely to be an abstract class like

```
public interface Visitor {
    void visit(....);
    void visit(....);
    ....
    void visit( ....);
}
```

where the different declarations of the visit() method are for the different classes in the Element class hierarchy. This interface is then implemented by the different Visitor classes for the different types of interactions between a Visitor instance and the classes in the Element hierarchy. In other words, we are likely to see a Visitor hierarchy like the one shown in Figure 24.1 where each concrete class, such as Visitor1, Visitor2, and so on, would specialize in its role vis-á-vis the Element hierarchy. For example, we could use Visitor1 to print out the values of one or more of the attributes in the Element classes. By the same token, we could use Visitor2 to provide us with a memory footprint of the instances, and so on.

As the reader can see, what the Visitor pattern accomplishes is through an interaction between the hook accept(Visitor) placed in the classes of the Element hierarchy and how the various visit() methods in the Visitor class hierarchy are implemented.

In summary, then, the purpose of the Visitor pattern is to elicit new behaviors from a collection of classes — we refer to them as Element classes for explanatory convenience — without having to significantly modify the classes themselves. This however requires that we place in the classes of the Element hierarchy a hook, a method really, whose header will generally look like accept(Visitor visitor). The desired new behavior can be

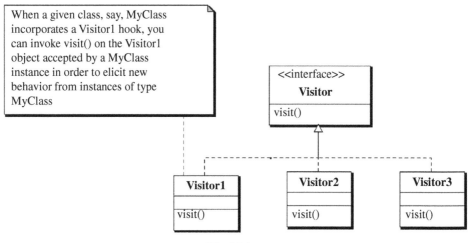

Fig. 24.1

witnessed by first constructing a `Visitor` instance — this instance would presumably have the competence to supply the new behavior — and to then invoke `accept()` on an instance of the `Element` class from which the new behavior is sought.

24.4 THE VISITOR PATTERN IN REAL-WORLD APPLICATIONS

The Visitor pattern has emerged as one way to embed "external functionality" in the system of classes produced by the object-oriented lexer/parser generators in modern compilers. Two well known examples of such generators are JavaCC (Java Compiler Compiler) and ANTLR (Another Tool for Language Recognition). As previously mentioned in Chapter 16, the goal of a lexer generator is to create an executable program, called a *lexer*, that is based on your high-level description of the rules for grouping the individual characters in an input file into tokens. When you apply a lexer thus constructed to an input file, it will output a stream of tokens extracted from that file. Along the same lines, and again as mentioned previously in Chapter 16, the goal of a parser generator is to create another piece of executable code, called a *parser*, that can apply the rules of a user-specified grammar to the tokens output by the lexer. In all modern compilers, the lexers generally use regular expressions for a lexical analysis of the input and the parsers are generally based on context-free grammars.

As stated in Chapter 16, the end-result of parsing an input is a syntax tree whose non-leaf nodes correspond to the various grammatical categories and whose leaf nodes correspond to the different tokens extracted from the input by the lexer. If your goal is limited to figuring out whether or not a given input is a legal construct according to the rules of the grammar, a successful parse of the input suffices to establish that. However, frequently, we need to go beyond just establishing the grammatical correctness of the input. We may also need to scan the syntax tree and take some action at each node depending on what portion of the input is represented by that node.

That's where the Visitor pattern comes in. If the parser generator can spit out the parser classes in such a way that they all have the `accept(Visitor visitor)` *hooks incorporated in them, one can subsequently subject the syntax tree to different kinds of analysis without having to modify the parser classes.* This is exactly what is accomplished by the open-source tool JTB (Java Tree Builder). The Visitor classes that JTB spits out are generic in the sense that they let you visit each node of the syntax tree but without doing anything at the nodes. By overriding the automatically generated Visitor classes, you can manipulate the syntax tree in several useful ways that may range from just pretty-printing the tree to searching for grammatical category-specific information at the nodes.

24.5 HARRY POTTER STORY USED TO ILLUSTRATE THE VISITOR PATTERN

As the reader will recall from our presentation of the Composite pattern in Chapter 9, the Ministry for Magic is divided into several departments, with an officially designated Department Head in charge of each department. The departments include the Department

of Magical Law Enforcement, the Department of Magical Accidents and Catastrophes, the Department of Magical Transportation, and so on. Several of the departments are further divided into offices. For example, the Department of Magical Law Enforcement contains the Auror Office, the Improper Use of Magic Office, besides others.

Our demonstration of the Visitor pattern will use a modified (and, also, simplified) version of the class hierarchy we created for demonstrating the Composite pattern in Chapter 9. That hierarchy is interesting because of the complexity of the `MinisterForMagic` class in relation to that of the other classes in the hierarchy. Since the Minister for Magic, while being a `Wizard` himself, supervises different kinds of `Wizards` who work in the ministry, we expressed the `MinisterForMagic` class as a composite over the other wizards who work in the ministry. The class hierarchy in Chapter 9, shown again in Figure 24.2 for the reader's convenience, involved the following `Wizard` classes: `Obliviator`, `DepartmentHead`, and `Auror`.

An important feature of the Composite pattern demonstration in Chapter 9 was that we defined all of the functionality for *all* of the classes in the hierarchy, including the more complex class `MinisterForMagic`, in the root class `Wizard` itself. That `Wizard` class was given the behaviors we needed for demonstrating the Composite pattern. However, from the standpoint of our needs in this chapter, the two behaviors that the `Wizard` class of Chapter 9 did *not* possess were:

1. A method to print out the names of the wizards who work in the Ministry of Magic. For an individual wizard, it would be the name of the wizard himself. However, for a more complex object, like the one constructed from the class `MinisterForMagic`, we may want such a method to *also* print out the names of all of the wizards who report to the Minister. That we would want a print utility, when invoked on an instance of `MinisterForMagic`, to print out the names of all the wizards who report to the minister seems like a reasonable thing to do considering that — as the reader would recall from Chapter 9 — the `Wizard` classes are all meant to model the roles played by the individuals rather than the individuals themselves. In any case, the code for such a utility would show how to fetch information from the members of a composite when it happens to be a part of the class definition.

2. A method to print out the name of the house that was assigned to a wizard when he attended Hogwarts.

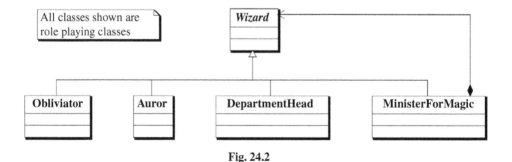

Fig. 24.2

The goal of our demonstration in this chapter is to give the `Wizard` hierarchy these two additional behaviors through the use of the Visitor pattern.

24.6   A TOP LEVEL VIEW OF THE PATTERN DEMONSTRATION

The Visitor pattern requires that we place `accept(Visitor)` hooks in all of our classes shown in Figure 24.2 and then define a set of concrete `Visitor` classes that would examine the instances of the classes in Figure 24.2 through the hooks. In keeping with how the Visitor pattern is generally implemented, we endow the hierarchy of Figure 24.2 with the hook by first defining an `Element` interface with just the following statement in it:

```
public interface Element {
    void accept(Visitor visitor);
}
```

and then 'hanging' the entire hierarchy from this interface, as shown in Figure 24.3. This forces every concrete class hanging from the `Element` root to implement the hook `accept(Visitor)`. For simple classes this implementation may look as simple as

```
public void accept(Visitor visitor) {
    visitor.visit(this);
}
```

The implementation would obviously be more elaborate for more complex classes, such as the `MinisterForMagic` class in our case.

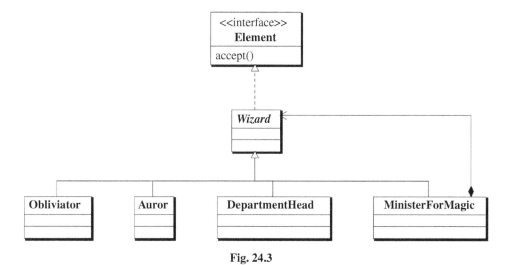

Fig. 24.3

With the `Visitor` classes included, the overall class diagram for our demonstration of the pattern is as shown in Figure 24.4. As shown in the diagram, we use two different concrete extensions of the `Visitor` interface. *This we do in order to demonstrate that the* `accept(Visitor)` *hooks incorporated in the* `Wizard` *class hierarchy are so generic that they can be used with arbitrary* `Visitor` *instances, as long as they are constructed from a class that implements the* `Visitor` *interface and as long as the implementation code in the concrete* `Visitor` *classes accesses information that the* `Element` *class hierarchy makes available on a public basis through its "get" and other such methods.* The two concrete Visitor classes that we use are named:

```
VisitorForPrintingWizardNames

VisitorForPrintingHouseNames
```

The first of these, `VisitorForPrintingWizardNames`, seeks to print out the names of the wizards and the second, `VisitorForPrintingHouseNames`, is for printing out the names of the houses at Hogwarts that the wizards belonged to when they went to school there.

The important thing to understand here is how the `accept(Visitor visitor)` hook in each `Element` class works in concert with the functionality in a concrete `Visitor` class, the end result being that the `Visitor` instance supplied to the `accept()` method elicits from the `Element` instance the desired new functionality.

24.7 THE Visitor INTERFACE

The `Visitor` interface declares a set of methods to be implemented by the concrete Visitor classes that implement this interface. Ordinarily, this set includes a `visit()` method for each class in the `Element` hierarchy. This allows every concrete `Element` class to allow a `Visitor` instance access to its public innards through `accept(Visitor)` hooks that, in the simplest of cases, are implemented as

```
public void accept(Visitor visitor) {
    visitor.visit(this);
}
```

At runtime, the statement `visitor.visit(this)` invokes the applicable version of `visit()` on the instance of the Element class.

```
public interface Visitor {
    void visit(Auror element);
    void visit(DepartmentHead element);
    void visit(Obliviator element);
    void visit(MinisterForMagic element);
}
```

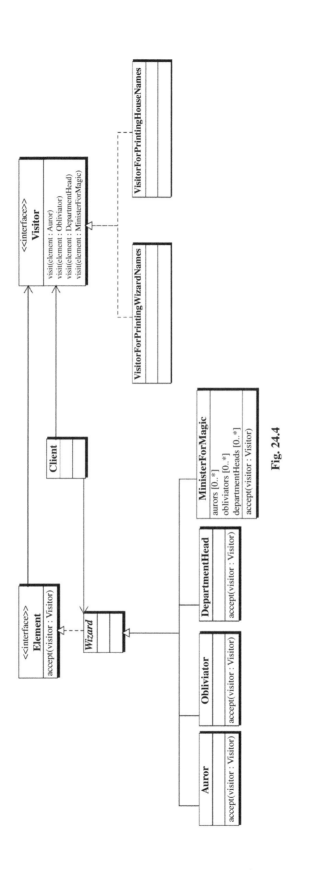

Fig. 24.4

24.8   TWO CONCRETE IMPLEMENTATIONS OF THE Visitor INTERFACE

The Visitor interface requires that its implementation by a class provide code for a visit() method for each of the classes in the Element hierarchy. That way when we inject a Visitor instance into an instance of an Element class at runtime through the accept(Visitor) hook, we can make a call such as visit(this) on the injected Visitor instance in order to elicit the behavior we want from the Element instance in question.

Shown below are the visit() methods that fetch the actual names of the wizards. With regard to the use of the argument element as a string to be printed out directly — or after it is joined with other strings — by System.out.println(), there is an implicit assumption here that the Wizard classes have all implemented the toString() method that returns the name of the Wizard in question when the context requires a string value for a Wizard instance.

```
public class VisitorForPrintingWizardNames implements Visitor {

    public void visit(Auror element) {
        System.out.println(element);
    }
    public void visit(Obliviator element) {
        System.out.println(element);
    }
    public void visit(DepartmentHead element) {
        System.out.println(element);
    }
    public void visit(MinisterForMagic element) {
        System.out.println("     Minister for Magic: " + element);
    }
}
```

As mentioned earlier, the demonstration code in this chapter is meant to highlight the point that after a class hierarchy has incorporated the accept(Visitor) generic hook, subsequently any new behavior can be elicited from the classes by creating an appropriate Visitor class. Toward that end, what we showed above was one concrete Visitor class that seeks to print out the names of the wizards. We next present another concrete Visitor class, this one for printing out the names of the houses assigned to the wizards when they attended Hogwarts.

```
public class VisitorForPrintingHouseNames implements Visitor {
    public void visit(Auror element) {
        System.out.println( "     House assigned to " + element
                            + " : " + element.getHouseAssigned() );
    }
    public void visit(Obliviator element) {
        System.out.println( "     House assigned to " + element
                            + " : " + element.getHouseAssigned() );
    }
```

```
    public void visit(DepartmentHead element) {
        System.out.println( "      House assigned to " + element
                                 + " : " + element.getHouseAssigned() );
    }
    public void visit(MinisterForMagic element) {
        System.out.println( "      House assigned to " + element
                                 + " : " + element.getHouseAssigned() );
    }
}
```

24.9   A RE-IMPLEMENTATION OF THE Wizard HIERARCHY OF THE COMPOSITE PATTERN

As mentioned previously, our demonstration of the Visitor pattern is based on the class hierarchy we developed for the Composite pattern in Chapter 9. As the reader will recall, the Composite pattern shows us that, as long as all of the objects are of the same fundamental type, we can declare all of the functionality for all of the classes — including the classes that involve composites over smaller classes — in the root interface of the hierarchy. That root interface in our demonstration of the Composite pattern was Wizard.

What we need for demonstrating the Visitor pattern in this chapter is a simpler version of the Wizard class hierarchy of Chapter 9 so that we can focus on the issues relevant to the Visitor pattern and not be distracted by the bells and whistles that were relevant to Chapter 9 but are not needed here.

This section therefore presents a simpler version of the earlier Wizard hierarchy, while at the same time incorporating in the classes of the hierarchy the accept(Visitor visitor) hook. Subsequently, this hook can be used for eliciting new behaviors from the hierarchy, subject, of course, to any visibility constraints on the attributes of the classes involved.

In addition to simplifying the earlier Wizard hierarchy, we also "hang" the hierarchy from a new interface called Element as defined below. The main purpose served by this retrofitting of the Element interface to the Wizard hierarchy is that it ensures that the implementation of the interface becomes a part of the contract of the hierarchy. That would make it mandatory for all concrete classes in the hierarchy to provide an implementation for the accept() method of the interface either directly or through inheritance.[2]

```
public interface Element {
    void accept(Visitor visitor);
}
```

Implementation of this interface opens up the hierarchy to access by Visitor objects.

---

[2]We could certainly have combined the Element interface here with the Wizard abstract class we will present next in a single abstract root interface for the rest of the Wizard hierarchy.

In the new definition of the Wizard class shown below, the reader will notice that, despite its implementing the Element interface, the class does not provide an implementation for the accept(Visitor) hook. That is because the Wizard class is abstract. Since our demonstration only requires more specialized wizards — aurors, obliviators, the minister for magic, and so on — we have no particular need to make Wizard a concrete class.

In keeping with the "rules" of the Composite pattern, the Wizard class shown below provides all of the functionality that is expected for any of the Wizard instances, be it an Auror, a DepartmentHead, or a MinisterForMagic. At the same time, in accordance with the Composite pattern, for the functionality that makes sense only for the composite class MinisterForMagic, it provides implementations whose default behavior is to throw the UnauthorizedAccessException exception. The implementation of the class begins with three instance variables. The first two of these, firstName and lastName, we expect every Wizard instance to possess. These therefore go into the definition of the Wizard constructor that follows the definition of the instance variables. The third instance variable, houseAssigned, is optional for each wizard. We initialize it with the default Unknown as shown. What follows the constructor is the toString() method that allows us to conveniently print out the name of a wizard, and the 'get' and 'set' methods for the optional instance variable houseAssigned. Note how the methods that only make sense for the MinisterForMagic subclass throw the UnauthorizedAccessException exception.

```
public abstract class Wizard implements Element {

    private String firstName;
    private String lastName;
    private String houseAssigned = "Unknown";

    public Wizard( String fname, String lname ) {
        firstName = fname; lastName = lname;
    }

    public String toString() { return firstName + " " + lastName; }

    public String getHouseAssigned() { return houseAssigned; }
    public void setHouseAssigned( String house ) {
        houseAssigned = house;
    }

    public void appointWizardAsObliviator(Wizard w)
                        throws UnauthorizedAccessException {
        throw new UnauthorizedAccessException( "Only the minister "
                + "for magic can appoint a wizard as obliviator" );
    }
    public void appointWizardAsAuror(Wizard w)
                        throws UnauthorizedAccessException {
        throw new UnauthorizedAccessException( "Only the minister "
                    + "for magic can appoint a wizard as auror" );
    }
```

```
    public void appointDepartmentHead(Wizard w)
                        throws UnauthorizedAccessException {
        throw new UnauthorizedAccessException( "Only the minister "
                                + "for magic can appoint a dept head" );
    }
    public void listEmployeesWorkingAtMinistry()
                        throws UnauthorizedAccessException {
        throw new UnauthorizedAccessException( "This method can only "
                                + "be called on an instance of MinsterForMagic" );
    }
}
```

That takes us to the first of the four extensions of the abstract class Wizard — the Auror class. As was the case with the version of the Wizard class shown above vis-á-vis the same class in the Composite pattern, the Auror class presented below is a much simpler version of the same that was presented in Chapter 9. The simplicity of Auror here is, obviously, a direct consequence of the simplicity of the Wizard abstract class used in our demonstration. Since our focus here is primarily on how the hook accept(Visitor) would be implemented in each of the concrete classes of the Element hierarchy, the Auror class shown below is a trivial extension of the Wizard class presented above. Apart from the constructor, all that we place in this class is the mandatory implementation of the accept(Visitor) hook that is inherited from the Element interface by way of the Wizard class. Note that the implementation of the hook merely invokes the method visit() of the Visitor object, supplying to the method for its only argument the instance of the Auror class on which accept() is invoked. This obviously assumes that the Visitor object supplies code for a method called visit() whose argument is of type Auror.

```
public class Auror extends Wizard {
    public Auror( String firstname, String lastname ) {
        super( firstname, lastname );
    }
    public void accept(Visitor visitor) {
        visitor.visit(this);
    }
}
```

Next we present the second of the four extensions of the abstract class Wizard — the DepartmentHead class. As was the case with the Auror class, the DepartmentHead class presented below is a much simpler version of the same class that was presented in Chapter 9. Paralleling Auror, our implementation of DepartmentHead is the minimum it can be for the demonstration of the Visitor pattern. As with Auror, the only notable thing here is that the class provides an implementation for the hook method accept(Visitor) that it inherits from the Element interface via the Wizard class.

```
public class DepartmentHead extends Wizard {

    private String nameOfDepartment;

    public DepartmentHead( String firstname, String lastname,
                                                String deptName   ) {
        super( firstname, lastname );
        nameOfDepartment = deptName;
    }
    public String getDepartment() { return nameOfDepartment; }
    public void accept(Visitor visitor) {
        visitor.visit(this);
    }
}
```

That brings us to the third of the four extensions of Wizard — the Obliviator class. As was the case with Auror and DepartmentHead all that we place in this class, apart from the constructor, is the required implementation of the accept(Visitor) hook that is inherited from the Element interface by way of Wizard.

```
public class Obliviator extends Wizard {

    public Obliviator( String firstname, String lastname ) {
        super( firstname, lastname );
    }
    public void accept(Visitor visitor) {
        visitor.visit(this);
    }
}
```

We are now ready to present the most complex of the classes in the Wizard hierarchy — the MinisterForMagic class. As the reader knows, in the Wizard hierarchy, the MinisterForMagic class is special because, while it is also a Wizard class, it is nonetheless a composite of the other three concrete Wizard classes: Auror, DepartmentHead, and Obliviator. The implementation we present here for the MinisterForMagic class is a much simpler version of the same class presented earlier in Chapter 9 since our goal here is only to focus on the workings of the Visitor pattern.

The fact that MinisterForMagic is a composite over other simpler classes makes the implementation of the accept(Visitor) hook a bit more elaborate. Now the accept(Visitor) must be propagated to the elements of the composite that an instance of MinisterForMagic is. Consider, for example, the purpose of the VisitorForPrintingWizardNames class. This Visitor class seeks to print out the names of all the wizards on which it is asked to act upon through the hook accept(Visitor visitor). When we invoke such a method on a MinisterForMagic instance, we want it to print out the name of the minister *and* the names of

all of the wizards who report to the minister.[3] So when we ask an instance of VisitorForPrintingWizardNames to do its job on an instance of MinisterForMagic, we need to pass this Visitor instance to the Wizard instances that are associated with the MinisterForMagic instance. That is what the reader will see in the implementation shown below.

Apart from the Visitor-related aspects, the implementation shown below for MinisterForMagic enforces the fact that there can only be one Minister for Magic. As was explained in the Composite pattern, this is accomplished by using the Singleton pattern of Chapter 6. The Singleton pattern requires that the constructor for the class be placed in the private section of the class and the instance construction facility be provided through a static method with a name like makeInstanceOfMinisterForMagic(). The logic in this method makes certain that the private constructor is called only once — the first time we call the method makeInstanceOfMinisterForMagic(). Subsequently, the previously constructed copy of the MinisterForMagic is supplied.

Also note that, for our simple demonstration, we provide the MinisterForMagic class with just the methods to appoint individual wizards for the important positions of obliviators, aurors, and department heads. For testing the working of the Visitor pattern logic, the class also includes a method to list the names of all wizards hired by the minister.

```java
import java.util.*;

public class MinisterForMagic extends Wizard {

    private Set<Obliviator> obliviators = new HashSet<Obliviator>();
    private Set<Auror> aurors = new HashSet<Auror>();
    private Set<DepartmentHead> deptHeads =
                                    new HashSet<DepartmentHead>();

    // This will hold the reference to the one and only one minister
    // that is allowed to be constructed from this class:
    private static MinisterForMagic theMinister;

    //NOTE: This constructor is private because we want to make sure
    //       it is not possible to construct more than one Minister
    //       for Magic
    private MinisterForMagic( String firstname, String lastname ) {
        super( firstname, lastname );
    }

    public static MinisterForMagic makeInstanceofMinisterForMagic(
                                    String fname, String lname ) {
        if ( theMinister == null )
            theMinister = new MinisterForMagic( fname, lname );
        return theMinister;
```

---

[3] As was mentioned previously, we think of MinisterForMagic as representing a role rather than an individual. So one could argue that when VisitorForPrintingWizardNames works on an instance of that role, it should print out the names of all of the wizards under the Minister in addition to printing out the name of just the Minister.

```
    }

    public void appointWizardAsObliviator(Wizard w)  {
        obliviators.add( (Obliviator) w);
    }
    public void appointWizardAsAuror(Wizard w) {
        aurors.add( (Auror) w );
    }
    public void appointDepartmentHead(Wizard w) {
        deptHeads.add( (DepartmentHead) w );
    }
    public void listEmployeesWorkingAtMinistry()  {
        Iterator<Obliviator> it1 = obliviators.iterator();
        Iterator<Auror> it2 = aurors.iterator();
        Iterator<DepartmentHead> it3 = deptHeads.iterator();
        while (it1.hasNext()) System.out.print( it1.next() + "    " );
        while (it2.hasNext()) System.out.print( it2.next() + "    ");
        while (it3.hasNext()) System.out.print( it3.next() + "    ");
    }
    public void accept(Visitor visitor) {
        visitor.visit(theMinister);
        Iterator<Obliviator> it1 = obliviators.iterator();
        Iterator<Auror> it2 = aurors.iterator();
        Iterator<DepartmentHead> it3 = deptHeads.iterator();
        System.out.print("\n      The obliviators in the Ministry: ");
        while (it1.hasNext()) {
            visitor.visit( it1.next() );
        }
        System.out.print("\n      The aurors in the Ministry: ");
        while (it2.hasNext()) {
            visitor.visit( it2.next() );
        }
        System.out.print(
                  "\n      The department heads in the Ministry: ");
        while (it3.hasNext()) {
            visitor.visit( it3.next() );
        }
    }
}
}
```

We now present UnauthorizedAccessException, the last class of the Wizard hierarchy. Regarding the importance of this class, recall that our demonstration of the Visitor pattern is based on a simplified version of the Wizard hierarchy of the Composite pattern of Chapter 9. The Composite pattern requires that all of the behaviors for all of the specialized Wizard classes be declared in the root class Wizard itself. This obviously would include the behaviors for a more complex class like the MinisterForMagic. But, obviously, there will exist behaviors meant only for an instance of MinisterForMagic — these behaviors would simply make no sense for the other classes derived from the root Wizard. This is where the exception class defined below comes in. If a method defined in the root Wizard

is called on an instance of a subclass for which the method makes no sense, we want an exception to be thrown. This exception will be of the type shown below.

```
public class UnauthorizedAccessException extends Exception {
    public UnauthorizedAccessException() {
        super();
    }
    public UnauthorizedAccessException(String arg0) {
        super(arg0);
    }
}
```

24.10   THE EXECUTABLE CLASS Client

The role of the `Client` class is to exercise the Visitor pattern. It must construct instances of different types of wizards, especially a wizard that is an instance of `MinisterForMagic` (since that is the most complex class in our `Wizard` hierarchy) and then it must invoke `accept(Visitor visitor)` on these instances to demonstrate the workings of the `Visitor` objects supplied.

As mentioned earlier, what makes the Visitor pattern particularly interesting is that all you need to incorporate in a class hierarchy whose behavior you wish to augment with the help of Visitor objects is to have the classes implement a generic hook that is commonly named `accept(Visitor visitor)`. Subsequently, this hook can be used by first constructing an appropriate `Visitor` object and then 'injecting' it through the hook into a class whose behavior needs to be augmented.

To illustrate that, our demonstration in this chapter includes two `Visitor` classes that were presented in Section 24.8. One of these was for printing out the names of the wizards at the Ministry of Magic and the other for printing out the names of the houses that the wizards had been assigned during their time at Hogwarts. In the code we show below, you will see the `Client` constructing these two different types of visitors and then 'injecting' them into the `Wizard` instances through their `accept(Visitor visitor)` hooks.

The class definition shown below starts by constructing instances of an `Obliviator`, an `Auror`, a `DepartmentHead`, and, finally, a `MinisterForMagic`. Since the first three wizards are part of the composition that the role `MinisterForMagic` is made of for this demonstration, we get them appointed at the ministry by invoking the appropriate 'appoint' methods on the `MinisterForMagic` instance. We then invoke the `listEmployeesWorking AtMinistry()` method on the `MinisterForMagic` instance to see all the employees currently at the ministry.

Next, we call on the `accept(Visitor visitor)` hook of the `MinisterForMagic` instance, with visitor set to an instance of `VisitorForPrintingWizardNames` class, in order to print out the names of all the wizards who work in the ministry. As you'll recall from the implementation of the hook in `MinisterForMagic`, this invocation of `accept(Visitor visitor)` is propagated to all of the wizards working in the ministry. We then repeat the above experiment with the `VisitorForPrintingHouseNames` visitor vis-á-vis the `MinisterForMagic` instance.

Finally, we inject the VisitorForPrintingWizardNames visitor into just the Obliviator instance to illustrate that the visitor prints out the name of the obliviator wizard, just as we would expect.

```java
public class Client  {
    public static void main(String[] args) throws Exception {

        Obliviator obl = new Obliviator( "Blasted", "Brainsucker" );
        obl.setHouseAssigned( "Gryffindor" );

        Auror auror = new Auror( "Bootsie", "Slickbottom" );
        auror.setHouseAssigned( "Slytherin" );

        DepartmentHead deptHead = new DepartmentHead( "Amelia",
                                "Bones", "MargicalLawEnforcement");

        MinisterForMagic minister =
            MinisterForMagic.makeInstanceofMinisterForMagic("Cornelius",
                                                "Fudge");
        minister.appointWizardAsObliviator( obl );
        minister.appointWizardAsAuror( auror );
        minister.appointDepartmentHead( deptHead );

        System.out.print("\nListing employees at the ministry:   ");
        minister.listEmployeesWorkingAtMinistry();

        System.out.println("\n\nOutput from 'Print Wizard Names' "
                    + "Visitor from the MinisterForMagic instance:");
        minister.accept( new VisitorForPrintingWizardNames() );

        System.out.println("\n\nOutput from 'Print House Names' "
                    + "Visitor from the MinisterForMagic instance:");
        minister.accept( new VisitorForPrintingHouseNames());

        System.out.print("\n\nOutput from 'Print Wizard Names' "
                    + "Visitor from the Obliviator instance:   ");
        obl.accept( new VisitorForPrintingWizardNames() );
    }
}
```

24.11   PLAYING WITH THE CODE

Download the class files for this pattern from the book website into a separate directory. Compile the code with the command

```
javac *.java
```

and execute the Client class by

```
java Client
```

Given the code in the main() of Client, executing this class will produce the following output:

```
Listing employees at the ministry:

    Blasted Brainsucker    Bootsie Slickbottom    Amelia Bones

Output from 'Print Wizard Names' Visitor from the MinisterForMagic
instance:

    Minister for Magic: Cornelius Fudge

    The obliviators in the Ministry: Blasted Brainsucker

    The aurors in the Ministry: Bootsie Slickbottom

    The department heads in the Ministry: Amelia Bones


Output from 'Print House Names' Visitor from the MinisterForMagic
instance:

    House assigned to Cornelius Fudge : Unknown

    The obliviators in the Ministry:
                House assigned to Blasted Brainsucker : Gryffindor

    The aurors in the Ministry:
                House assigned to Bootsie Slickbottom : Slytherin

    The department heads in the Ministry:
                House assigned to Amelia Bones : Unknown


Output from 'Print Wizard Names' Visitor from the Obliviator
instance:
    Blasted Brainsucker
```

For additional insights, you may consider extending the code for this pattern along the following lines:

- Our demonstration used two different concrete extensions of the Visitor interface to demonstrate the very important point that the accept(Visitor) hooks incorporated in the Wizard class hierarchy are so generic that they can be used with arbitrary Visitor instances. See if you can create additional classes that also implement the Visitor interface with the intention of eliciting additional behaviors from the Wizard hierarchy.
- Since we retrofitted the Visitor pattern to a simplified version of the code that was originally written for the Composite pattern in Chapter 9, we created a separate root

class `Element` from which we "suspended" the `Wizard` hierarchy. Since the only reason for the `Element` root is to enforce the requirement that all classes that want to permit inspection by a `Visitor` object implement the hook `accept(Visitor visitor)`, we could certainly have incorporated the implementation of `Element` in the `Wizard` class itself. If you are up to it, modify `Wizard` so that it serves the roles of both the current `Element` and the `Wizard`.

REFERENCES

1. Erich Gamma, Richard Helm, Ralph Johnson, and John Vlissides, *Design Patterns: Elements of Reusable Object-Oriented Software*. Addison Wesley, 1994.

2. Avinash C. Kak, *Programming with Objects: A Comparative Presentation of Object-Oriented Programming with C++ and Java*. John-Wiley, 2003.

3. Unified Modeling Language (UML), http://www.omg.org/spec/UML/Accessed on September 22, 2014.

4. Girish M. Rama and Avinash C. Kak, Some Structural Measures of API Usability, *Software – Practice and Experience*, 2013.

5. Harry Potter Headmaster Portraits, http://harrypotter.wikia.com/wiki/Headmaster_portraits/ Accessed on November 6, 2014.

6. Avinash C. Kak, *Scripting with Objects: A Comparative Presentation of Object-Oriented Scripting with Perl and Python*. John-Wiley, 2008.

7. Squid - Optimising Web Delivery, http://www.squid-cache.org Accessed on September 22, 2014.

8. The Wordplay Web Site, http://www.fun-with-words.com Accessed on November 6, 2014.

9. Java Compiler Compiler (JavaCC) – Java Parser Generator, https://javacc.java.net/ Accessed on November 6, 2014.

10. The Reflection API, http://docs.oracle.com/javase/tutorial/reflect/ Accessed on September 22, 2014.

11. Gilad Bracha, Martin Odersky, David Stoutamire, and Philip Wadler, Making the future safe for the past: Adding genericity to the Java Programming Language. October. OOPSLA 98.

INDEX

\# for protected visibility, UML, 17
.jj file, 298
.jjt file, 298
* for representing multiplicity, UML, 15
\+ for public visibility, UML, 17
− for private visibility, UML, 17
1..* UML, 15
12 Grimmauld Place, 180, 215
2..* UML, 17

Abstract
  Factory, 19
  Factory vs. Factory Method, 22, 59
abstract
  class, 7
  method, 8
Abstract Syntax Tree, 290, 297, 457
abstract syntax tree, 293
accept(), 454
access control modifiers, 8
achieving immortality, 106
actions vs. actors, 272
Adaptee, 103
adaptee, 104, 105
Adapter, 103
adapter, 104, 105

  mechanical, 101
AdapterForSafeTeaching, 111
add(), 344, 345
add-hook, 453
addNewObserver(), 400
Adjudicator, 256, 258, 261
advertisement, targeted, 42
aggregation, 143
  UML, 13, 16
Alastor Moody, 408, 413, 424
ALGOL, 298
algorithm, shortest path, 182
alterMuggleMemory(), 153
Amycus Carrow, 408, 416
Animagus, 376
animating inferi, 237
annotateAST.pl Perl script, 318
anonymizing proxy, 233
ANTLR, 457
API, 126, 324
apparate, 277, 289, 389
AppleTalk, 101
Application Programming Interface, 126
Arabella Figg, 276, 287
arc, 179, 194
armadillo bile, 43, 48

array, 321
ArrayList, 62
Arrays.sort(), 331
Arthur Weasley, 215
ArtifactCannotBeCreated, 63, 65
ArtifactMaker, 63
ASCII, 164
ashwinder eggs, 43, 50
assignedTask(), 239
assignOfficesToDepartmentHead(), 155
  bidirectional, 15
  binary, 15
  multiplicity, 14
association, UML
  reflexive, 15
  rolename, 14
associative list, 359
AST, 290, 317
attribute, 8, 10
  representation, UML, 16
  UML, 12
  visibility, UML, 17
Aunt Marge, 92
Auror, 146, 152, 458, 465
  Office, 146, 458
Avada Kedavra Curse, 106, 237
Azkaban, 237, 408

Backus Naur Form, 290
Barty Crouch Jr., 408, 413, 424
base class, 8, 9
Beauxbatons Academy of Magic, 424
behavior, 273
Behavioral Patterns, 3, 249
binary
  association, UML, 15
  tree, 323
binding, dynamic, 118
Black Lake, 425, 431
Blagging, 257
Blatching, 257
BNF, 290, 293, 298
Bridge, 123
broadcasting, 386
Broomstick, 23, 31
BroomstickFactory, 24, 32
Bubble Head charm, 294, 425
BubbleHeadCharmStrategy, 429, 430
Buckbeak, 374
buffered output, 164
BufferedInputStream, 397
BufferedOutputStream, 164

Builder, 19
Bulgarian Minister for Magic, 93
Bumphing, 257

callback, 256
canResolveViolations(), 262, 263
Cedric Diggory, 294, 424, 429
chain
  dynamic, 254
  static, 254
Chain of Responsibility, 249
Champion, 433
changeState(), 410
Charge, 361
charm
  Bubble-Head, 294
  memory, 146, 153
  Shield, 106
checkForLocationOnShortestPath(), 182,
    201, 204
Chicago-style pizza, 213
child class, 8
class, 8
  enclosing, 379
  hierarchy, 8, 9
  inner, 379
  method, 8, 11
  relationship
    HasA, 14
    IsA, 14
  responsibility, UML, 14
  variable, 8
Class Adapter Pattern, 111
Class Adapter vs. Object Adapter, 113
clear(), 344
clearChanged(), 389
Client, 63, 71, 279, 380, 470
client-server programs, 231
clock tick, 373
clockTick, 373
clone(), 77, 81
Cloneable, 77
cloning, 75
Cobbing, 257
Collections.sort(), 440
Command, 250, 274, 279
Comparable, 195, 331
Comparator, 440
compareTo(), 195, 331, 440
complaint escalation, 253
composite, 144

composition, 143, 144
    UML, 13, 15
conceptual perspective, UML, 13
concrete class, 9
Confundus Charm, 424
const, C++, 17
constructNewFlooNetwork(), 182, 200
constructNewFlooNetworkUsing
    Neighborhoods(), 200
constructor, 9
    private, 81, 93
containment hierarchy, 256
contains(), 344
context, 292, 296
    dependent behavior, 406
    free grammar, 291, 293, 457
control, kinematic, 103
controller for robot, 103
copy constructor, C++, 77
core form, 215
CoreMessageDeliveryClass, 167, 168, 170
Cornelius Fudge, 357, 368, 375
corroborateWitnessTestimony(), 362, 366,
    370
Creational Patterns, 3, 249
Crookshanks, 376
Cruciatus Curse, 106, 109, 237
curse
    Avada Kedavra, 106, 237
    Cruciatus, 106, 109, 237
    Imperius, 106, 237
    Killing, 237
    Petrificus Totalus, 106
    Sectumsempra, 106
    unforgivable, 106
customer profiling, 42

DADA, 104, 152, 233, 407
DADA
    Professor's Office, 180
DADA_State, 408
DADA_Year1, 408, 411
DADA_Year2, 408, 411
DADA_Year3, 412
DADA_Year4, 413
DADA_Year5, 414
DADA_Year6, 415
DADA_Year7, 416
dark
    arts, 106
    potions, 237
    side, 146

Dark
    Lord, 233, 389
    Mark, 390
DarkLord, 235, 394
DarkWizard, 235, 239
DarkWizardTraits, 235
data member, 10
DataInputStream, 397
DataOutputStream, 239, 393
Death Eater, 146, 149, 152, 389
DeathEater, 390
deep copy, 77, 84
Defense Against Dark Arts, 104, 152, 233,
    407
defenseAgainstCruciatusCurse(), 109
Degrees of Freedom, 103
deliverBroomstick(), 32
deliverItem(), 27, 32
deliverMessage(), 165
DeliverMsgThruChimney, 165, 170, 171
DeliverMsgThruHagrid, 170, 171
DeliverMsgThruPost, 172
DeliverMsgToHarryPotter, 165
DeliverThruPost, 170
Dementor, 130, 132, 139
dementor, 127, 375
Dementor_Impl, 130, 132, 137
Department of Magical Accidents, 458
Department of Magical Accidents and
    Catastrophes, 146
Department of Magical Law Enforcement,
    458
Department of Magical Transportation, 146,
    177, 458
DepartmentHead, 146, 155, 458, 465
DeputyHeadmaster, 266
derived class, 9
deserialization, 232
Devil's Snare, 233
Diagon Alley, 25, 179
DiagonAlleyRetailer, 25, 35
Dijkstra's algorithm, 182
Dilys Derwent, 215
Director, 45, 52
disassembler, 453
displayBuiltinFlooNetwork(), 180, 204
displayNeighborhoods(), 184
displayNetwork(), 184
displaySingleImage(), 220
Dobby, 441
doesDestinationExistInBuiltinNetwork(),
    182

doesGivenPathPassThroughLocation(), 182, 201, 204
DoF, 103
dog, three-headed, 233
Dolores Umbridge, 408, 414
    Office, 180
doTeachAboutProtectiveDevices(), 105
doTeachHowDarkMagicCanHarmTheCaster(), 105
doTeachPowerOfLove(), 105
Dragon, 78, 81
dragon, native range, 78
DragonAficionado, 87
dragonHeartString, 63
Draught of Peace Potion, 42
DraughtOfPeacePotionMaker, 42, 47
Drink of Despair, 237
Driver, 304, 307, 308
Dudley, 276, 357
Dumbledore, 178, 215, 233, 234, 357, 362, 368
Durmstrang Institute, 424
Dursleys, 92, 165, 276, 357
dynamic
    binding, 11, 118
    chain, 254

E-API, 126
Eclipse IDE, 126
EJB container framework, 126
EldeWand, 408
Element, 455
elixir, 233
embellishment, 215
Employee, 144
Enchanted, 30, 63, 65
enclosing class, 379
end-effector, 103
endOfSummerHolidays(), 442, 444
EndOfSummerStories, 442, 444
EndOfSummerYear1, 445
EndOfSummerYear2, 447
enum, 147, 277, 279, 328, 359, 360
equals(), 193
espeak(), 154
establishCommunicationLinkWithDark
    Lord(), 238
Ethernet, 101
ethnic food, 437
event dispatch queue, 276
Evidence, 361
evil hook, 453

evolutionary history, 142
exception
    ArtifactCannotBeCreated, 63, 65
    ImageNotAvailableException, 226
    ParseException, 317
    PotionMakingFeasibilityViolation, 55
    TokenMgrError, 317
    UnableToProtectHarryPotterException, 279, 286
    UnauthorizedAccessException, 147–149, 464, 469
    UnknownDragonException, 88
execute(), 274
executeTask(), 427, 431
execution committee, 376
executioner, 375
extended class, 9
Extension API, 126
extrinsic parameters, 214

Facade, 181
facade, 175
Factory, 24, 27
    hierarchy, 24
factory
    abstract, 19, 22
    concept in software, 21
    method, 19, 22, 60
FactoryStore, 27
FileOutputStream, 164
Filius Flitwick, 233
final, 10, 11
    a declaration, 81, 84
    Java, 17
findMostDiscriminatingField(), 335
findShortestPath(), 204
finite
    automaton, 298
    state automata, 294
fireplace, 177
firewall, 453
First Wizarding War, 152
first(), 344
Flacking, 257
Fleur Delacour, 294, 424, 429, 431, 434
Floo
    network, 177, 277
    Network Authority, 177
    powder, 177
Forbidden Forest, 408
forensic investigation, 152
Fresher, 330, 333

fresher, 330
frozen, UML, 17
fully qualified name, 11
function entry points, 453

Gamma, 2
generalization, UML, 13
getHouseCounts(), 333
getImage(), 218
getIndentation(), 315
getLastNode(), 195
getMessageFromObservable(), 396, 397
getNextProblem(), 427, 428
getNextState(), 359, 362
getPortraitImageStore(), 219
getRangeOfAttributeValues(), 336
getResult(), 42, 45, 46
getStringValue(), 308
getter method, 18
gettingToPlatformNineThreeFourth(), 444
getVerdict(), 362
Gilderoy Lockhart, 408, 411
gillyweed, 425
GillyweedStrategy, 431
ginger roots, 43, 48
Goblet of Fire, 424
Goblin, 133, 139
goblin, 127
Goblin_Impl, 130, 133, 138
GodProcess, 400
GoF, 2
golden
    egg, 424
    snitch, 234
good hook, 453
graphical user interface, 255
Grimmauld Place, 280
grindylow, 425
Gringotts Wizarding Bank, 233
Gryffindor, 235, 325
Gryffindor
    Commons, 179, 204
GUI, 255, 440

Hagrid, 233, 374
Hagrid's
    cabin, 375
Harry Potter, 4
HarryPotterTrial, 368
has-a, 143
HasA relationship, 14
hasChanged(), 389

hashCode(), 193
hasNext(), 195, 324, 328, 330, 345
hasPrevious(), 324
Haversacking, 257
HEAD, HTTP, 233
header, 10
Headmaster, 256, 267
HeadMasterPortrait, 216
heapsort, 437
hellebore, 42, 47
Hello, 124
Hello_impl, 124
Hermione Granger, 235
Hermione Granger, 374, 425
hippogriff, 374, 377
history, evolutionary, 142
Hogsmeade village, 376
Hogwarts, 6, 104, 165, 215, 233, 374, 418,
    424
Hogwarts
    School of Magic, 92, 106
HogwartsHappening, 375
hook, Visitor, 454
Horcrux, 106
Hospital for Magical Maladies, 408
house elf, 127
HouseElf, 130, 134, 139
HouseElf_Impl, 130, 138, 139
howManyImagesOrderedFromImageClearing
    House(), 219
howManyRegistered(), 135, 138
HTML markup, 164
Hufflepuff, 325
Humanoid, 130
Humanoid_Impl, 130, 135, 137, 139

IDE, 126, 276
ImageIcon, 220
ImageManager, 215, 216, 220
ImageNotAvailableException, 226
immortality, 106
Imperius Curse, 106, 237
impersonator, 413
implementation perspective, UML, 13
implements, 9
Improper Use of Magic Office, 146, 458
in.readUTF(), 397
indefinite number, UML, 15
inferi, 237
Ingredient, 43, 55
inheritance, 9
initializeBuiltInNetwork(), 180, 182

inner class, 379
instance, 10, 11
    method, 10, 11
    variable, 10
instantiation, 10
interface, 10
    Cloneable, 77
    Command, 274, 279
    Comparable, 195, 331
    DADA, _State, 408
    Iterable, 195
    Iterator, 328, 330
    java.util.Comparator, 331
    java.util.Iterator, 324
    ListIterator, 324
    MagicCollection, 328
    marker, 63, 65
    MessageDelivery, 167, 170
    MyPlaces, 277, 279
    Observable, 393
    Observer, 389, 391
    Runnable, 393
    TeachingDADA, 104
    Trial, 357, 367
    TrialElements, 357, 360
    Violations, 258, 260
    Visitor, 456, 460
interpretation, 290
Interpreter, 250
interpreter(), 313
Interpreter_Adjective, 304, 310, 314
Interpreter_Noun, 304, 310, 313
Interpreter_Sentence, 304, 310, 311
Interpreter_Verb, 304, 310, 314
intrinsic parameters, 214
invisibility cloak, 282, 287, 376
invokeExecute(), 285
Invoker, 274, 276, 279, 289
invoker, 274
invokeSolution(), 427, 428, 431
iptables, 453
IPX, 101
IsA relationship, 14
isAllowedToPerformMemoryCharm(), 154
ISP, 233
Iterable interface, 195
Iterator, 62, 324, 328, 330
iterator(), 195, 328, 344, 345
iterator, robust, 352

J. K. Rowling, 4, 6, 235
Java Collections Framework, 141

Java Compiler Compiler, 457
Java IO classes, 164
Java Tree Builder, 457
java.io package, 177
java.util.Arrays.sort(), 336
java.util.Comparator, 331
java.util.Iterator, 324
JAVA_UNICODE_ESCAPE option, 299
JavaCC, 292, 293, 457
javacc tool, 299
JavaCharStream class, 299
javax.swing.Label, 221
jjtree preprocessor, 304
Johnson, 2
journeyToHogwarts(), 444
JTB, 457

k-d tree, 323
Katharine McBride, 4
Killing curse, 237
kind, UML
    in, 18
    inout, 18
    out, 18
kinematic control, 103
King's Cross Station, 441
Kneazle cat, 276
Knockturn Alley, 179

lazy instantiation, 93
length(), 344
lexer, 296, 457
lexical
    analyzer, 296
    state, 302
Link, 179, 194
linked list, 322
LinkFromDarkLord, 235, 238
LinkFromDarkWizard, 235, 242
List<String>, 81
listAllNumericFields(), 335
ListIterator, 324
listiterator(), 62
listOfficesInChargeOf(), 155
Little Whinging, 276, 289, 357
LL parser, 298
LL(1) parser, 298
LL(k) parser, 298
loadImages(), 216, 220
look and feel
    customizable, 23
    GUI, 22

lookahead, parsing, 298
loop-back in a relationship, 143
Lord Voldemort, 233
Lord Voldemort, 152, 178, 276, 407
Louis the 16th, 73
Love Potion, 42, 50
LovePotionMaker, 42
LR parser, 298
LR(k) parser, 298
Lucious Malfoy, 374

Mad-Eye Moody, 287
magic
  speak, 293
  wand, 62
magic_speak_parser_specs.jjt file, 299
magical
  combat, 152
  creatures, 374
  maladies, 408
MagicalSpeech(), 306, 308
MagicCollection, 328
MagicComparator, 336
MagicList, 328, 344
MagicSet, 328, 347
MagicWand, 23, 31, 66
MagicWandFactory, 24, 33
MagicWandMaker, 68
make(), 61
makeArtifact(), 63, 68, 70
makeHouseAssignments(), 337
makeInitialHouseAssignments(), 333
makeInstanceOfDarkLord(), 239, 394
makeInstanceOfDeputyHeadmaster(), 266
makeInstanceOfMinisterForMagic(), 93,
  156, 467
makeNewDragonInstance(), 81
makePotion(), 42, 45, 46, 52, 55
making pizzas, 213
Map, 359
marker interface, 63, 65
mechanical adapter, 101
Mediator, 250, 355, 359
Memento, 250
memory charm, 146, 153
mergesort, 437
merpeople, 425
MessageDelivery, 167, 170
MessageDeliveryDecorator, 167, 168, 170
method, 11
  class, 11
  factory, 19, 59

instance, 11
  overriding, 40
  static, 11
Minerva McGonagall, 234
Minister for Magic, 92, 146, 362, 375
MinisterForMagic, 92, 93, 146, 147, 157,
  458, 467
Ministry of Magic, 92, 146, 177, 215, 357,
  408, 458
  Atrium, 180
MinistryOfMagic, 130, 139
MinistryOfMagicTrialMediator,
  363, 370
Mirror of the Erised, 234
moonstone, 42, 47
mountain troll, 234
Mr. Dursley, 6, 174
Mr. Oblansk, 93
Mr. Tibble, 284
Mr. Tibbles, 276
Mrs. Arabella Figg, 357
Mrs. Figg, 284, 368
Mrs. Weasley, 441
muggle, 92, 146, 277
  speak, 293
MULTI option, 299
multicasting, 386
multiplicity, 14
  for attributes, UML, 17
Mundungus Fletcher, 276, 287, 289
MyPlaces, 277, 279

natural language interface, 290
navigability, UML, 14
nested doll, Russian, 161
next(), 195, 324, 328, 330, 345
Nicolas Flamel, 233
Node, 179, 193, 317, 344
NODE_DEFAULT_VOID option, 299
NODE_PREFIX option, 299
notifyObservers(), 389, 394
Number
  12, Grimmauld Place, 277, 287
  4, Privet Drive, 174
Nymphadora Tonks, 287

Object, 11, 77
object, 10, 11
  adapter pattern, 111
  construction
    by copying, 74
    by factory, 21

Object
  Management Group, 12
Obliviator, 146, 154, 458, 466
Observable, 387, 389, 393
Observer, 251, 387, 389, 391
OMG, 12
onion, a metaphor, 161
OO
  Patterns Book, 2
operation
  modifier, UML, 18
  query, UML, 18
  UML, 12, 17
Order of Phoenix, 277, 280, 287
Originator, 372
outputStreamToBeUsedByObservable(),
    393
overriding a method, 40
Owl, 23
OwlEmporium, 24, 34

package, 8, 11
pan-style pizza, 213
parameter-list, UML, 17
parameters
  extrinsic, 214
  intrinsic, 214
ParseException, 317
Parser, 308, 317
parser, 296, 457
  LL, 298
  LL(1), 298
  LL(k), 298
  LR, 298
  LR(k), 298
parser
  generator, 292
parser/lexer generator, 292, 293
PARSER_BEGIN – PARSER_END
    directive, 299
ParserConstants, 317
ParserTokenManager, 317
ParserTreeConstants, 318
parsing, 290
Pascal, 298
Path, 179, 194
PathIterathor, 195
patterns
  behavioral, 3, 249
  creational, 3, 19
  structural, 3, 99

peek(), 276
peppermint, 43, 50
personal assistant, 290
Peter Pettigrew, 376
Petrificus Totalus Curse, 106
Philosopher's Stone, 233, 235
Phineas Nigellus Black, 215
phoenixTailFeather, 63
PHP, 164
pipe, 393
PipedInputStream, 238
PipedOutputStream, 238, 393
PissOffTheReferee, 257
pizza, 213
  Chicago style, 213
  pan style, 213
  take-n-bake, 213
  thin crust, 213
Place, an enum, 279
Platform Nine and Three-Fourth, 441
Player, 263, 264
Pluggable Adapter Pattern, 111
plugin, 126
point-to-point communications, 386
polymorphism, 10, 11, 40, 440
Pomona Sprout, 233
Portkey, 277
portrait maker, 216
PortraitBorderChoices, 216
PortraitMakerAssignment, 216
Potion, 43
potion, 42
  Draught of Peace, 42
  Drink of Despair, 237
  Love, 42
  Riddle of the, 234
  Rudimentary Body, 237
  Wit Sharpening, 42
PotionMaker, 42, 45, 46
PotionMakingFeasibilityViolation, 43, 55
precedence constraints, 38
previous(), 324
PrintStream, 164
Prisoner of Azkaban, 374
private, 8, 11
  constructor, 78, 81, 93
  for access control, 17
Privet Drive, 174, 280
processForInterpretation(), 307, 308
production, as a grammar rule, 290
Professor Everard, 215
profiler, 42

Programming with Objects, 22, 40, 231, 404, 420
property-string, UML, 17, 18
protected, 8, 12
    a declaration, 96
    for access control, 17
ProtectHarryPotter, 277, 280
Prototype, 20
    vs. Singleton, 91
prototype, 75
PrototypeManagerAndDuplicator, 79, 84
proxy, 230
    anonymizing, 233
    as security gateway, 231
    remote, 233
    server, 231
        caching, 231
    Squid, 233
    voting, 230
public, 8, 12
    for access control, 17
pushdown
    automata, 298
    stack, 298

Qt, 440
QuafflePocking, 257
query
    escalation, 253
quicksort, 437
quidditch, 234, 235, 256
Quirinus Quirrell, 233, 408

Range, 349
Ravenclaw, 325
readLine(), 239
reassignDepartment(), 155
receiver, 274, 280
recipe customization, 437
recursive embellishments, 167
Referee, 265
reflection, Java, 331
reflexive association, UML, 15
register(), 135
registeredHumanoids, 135
registerWithObservable(), 390, 393, 394
regular expressions, 457
relation, loop-back, 143
remembrall, 62, 67
RemembrallMaker, 70
remote proxy, 233
Remote Method Invocation, 233

remove(), 344, 345
Remus Lupin, 287, 408, 412
replenishBroomstickStock(), 32
replenishMagicWandStock(), 33
resolveViolation(), 262, 263, 265
responsibility, UML, 14
restoreStateFromMemento(), 377, 379, 380
retireInstanceOfMinisterForMagic(), 93, 94
return-type, UML, 18
Riddle of the Potions, 234
RMI, 233
robot controller, 103
robust iterator, 352
role, UML, 14
Ron Weasley, 234, 235, 431, 441
rootkit, 453
rose thorns, 43, 50
Rudimentary Body Potion, 237
run(), 393, 396
Runnable, 393
Russian nested doll, 161

S-API, 126
saveStateToMemento(), 377, 378, 380
sayHello(), 124
Scabbers, 376
scanner, 296
scarab beetles, 43, 48
School of Magic
    Beauxbatons Academy of Magic, 424
    Durmstrang Institute, 424
    Hogwarts, 92, 104, 106
SchoolOfMagic, 105, 110, 118
Scripting with Objects, 231, 303, 386, 404
Second Wizarding War, 152
SecondTaskManager, 434
secret chamber, 233
Sectumsempra Curse, 106
sendMessageToDarkLord(), 239
serial port, 92
serialization, 232, 239
Service
    API, 126
    Oriented Architecture, 232
setCanCastUnforgivableCurses(), 237
setChanged(), 389
setNeighborhoodsAndDisplayNetwork
        Created(), 200
setNetworkLink(), 200
setter method, 18
Severus Snape, 234, 408, 415
shallow copying, 77

Shield Charm, 106
shopping cart, 23
shortest path algorithm, 182
ShowSyntaxTree, 315
Shrieking Shack, 376
signature, 10, 132
SimpleCharStream, 299
SimpleNode, 317
Singleton, 20
  vs. Prototype, 91
Siri, 290
Sirius Black, 215, 374
slideshow(), 220, 221
Slytherin, 235, 325
sneakascope, 106
SOA, 232
sortAndRank(), 336
sorting algorithms, 437
Sorting Hat, 325
SortingHat, 337
spam, 453
specification perspective, UML, 13
speech synthesis, 154
Squib, 277, 280, 284
Squid proxy, 233
St. Mungo's Hospital, 215, 408
stack, 298
State, 251
state, lexical, 302
static, 11, 12, 17
  method, 11, 12
STATIC option, 299
Stooging, 257
Strategy, 251
StrategyAbstractRoot, 427, 429
Structural Patterns, 3, 99, 249
stub, 232, 317
  class, 299
subclass, 9, 12
super, 10
superclass, 9, 12
surrogate, 230
synchronization, 239, 387
syntax tree 290, 296

take-n-bake pizza, 213
TalkToDarkLord, 235, 238, 239
TalkToDarkWizard, 235, 242
targeted advertisement, 42
taxonomy, 142
TCP/IP, 101
teachDefenseAgainstDarkArts(), 118

Teacher, 266
TeacherForDADA, 105, 107, 109
TeachingDADA, 104, 408, 417
Template Method, 251
templatization, 442
TerminalIO, 177
Test, 148, 158, 268
TestSingleton, 93
TestStoryGenerator, 442, 449
The Burrow, 180, 204, 279
thin crust pizza, 213
Thread, 393, 396
thread synchronization, 239
Thread.sleep(), 239
three-headed dog, 233
time travel, 375
Time-Turner, 374
timer, 221
Token, 317
token, 296
Token Ring, 101
TokenMgrError, 317
Transfiguration, 425
TransfigurationStrategy, 431
travelByBuiltinFlooNetwork(), 182
travelToHogwarts(), 442, 444
Trial, 357, 367
TrialElements, 357, 360
TrialState, 359, 360
tripToKingsCrossStation(), 444
Triwizard Tournament, 294, 424
trojan, 453

UML, 12
UnableToProtectHarryPotterException, 279,
  286
UnauthorizedAccessException, 147–149,
  464, 469
UnauthorizedInstanceException, 95
UnderageWizardFacade, 198, 204
unforgivable curses, 106, 237
unicornTailHair, 63
Unified Modeling Language, 12
UnknownDragonException, 88
unRegister(), 135
unRegisterWithObservable(), 390, 393, 394
update_available_ingredients(), 52
usage views, 176

veela hairs, 66
veelaHair, 63
Viktor Krum, 424

Violations interface, 258, 260
visibility, 17
  private, 17
  protected, 17
  public, 17
visit(), 315, 462
Visitor, 251, 456, 460
  hierarchy, 456
  hook, 454
VisitorForPrintingHouseNames, 462
VisitorForPrintingWizardNames, 462
visual programming
  environments, 276
  languages, 276
Vlissides, 2
Voldemort, 104, 152, 233, 408

wait-notify, 239
Walden Macnair, 375
WandCores, 63
warlock, 178, 199
WarlockFacade, 180

wars, Wizarding, 152
Weasleys, 279
welcomeCeremonyAtHogwarts(), 442, 444
Whomping Willow Tree, 376
Wit Sharpening Potion, 42, 48
Witness, 366
WitSharpeningPotionMaker, 42
Wizard, 147, 235, 237, 277, 280, 282, 464
Wizard Chess, 234
WizardFacade, 180
Wizarding Wars, 152
WizardTraits, 147, 148
Wizengamot, 146, 357
wrapper library, 453
writeChars(), 239
WriteIntToFile.java, 177
writeOneInt(), 177
wxWindows, 440

Zend platform, 164
Zend_Form, 164
zombie, 237

www.ingramcontent.com/pod-product-compliance
Lightning Source LLC
Chambersburg PA
CBHW080939260125
20788CB00015BA/151